Lecture Notes in Computer Science

Lecture Notes in Artificial Intelligence   **16015**

Founding Editor

Jörg Siekmann

Series Editors

Randy Goebel, *University of Alberta, Edmonton, Canada*
Wolfgang Wahlster, *DFKI, Berlin, Germany*
Zhi-Hua Zhou, *Nanjing University, Nanjing, China*

The series Lecture Notes in Artificial Intelligence (LNAI) was established in 1988 as a topical subseries of LNCS devoted to artificial intelligence.

The series publishes state-of-the-art research results at a high level. As with the LNCS mother series, the mission of the series is to serve the international R & D community by providing an invaluable service, mainly focused on the publication of conference and workshop proceedings and postproceedings.

Rita P. Ribeiro · Bernhard Pfahringer ·
Nathalie Japkowicz · Pedro Larrañaga ·
Alípio M. Jorge · Carlos Soares ·
Pedro H. Abreu · João Gama
Editors

Machine Learning and Knowledge Discovery in Databases

Research Track

European Conference, ECML PKDD 2025
Porto, Portugal, September 15–19, 2025
Proceedings, Part III

Springer

Editors
Rita P. Ribeiro
Departamento de Ciencia de Computadores
University of Porto
Porto, Portugal

Nathalie Japkowicz
American University
Washington, D.C., WA, USA

Alípio M. Jorge
Departamento de Ciência de Computadores
University of Porto
Porto, Portugal

Pedro H. Abreu
University of Coimbra
Coimbra, Portugal

Bernhard Pfahringer
University of Waikato
Hamilton, Waikato, New Zealand

Pedro Larrañaga
Technical University of Madrid
Boadilla del Monte, Madrid, Spain

Carlos Soares
Faculdade de Engenharia
University of Porto
Porto, Portugal

João Gama
University of Porto
Porto, Portugal

ISSN 0302-9743   ISSN 1611-3349 (electronic)
Lecture Notes in Artificial Intelligence
ISBN 978-3-032-06065-5   ISBN 978-3-032-06066-2 (eBook)
https://doi.org/10.1007/978-3-032-06066-2

LNCS Sublibrary: SL7 – Artificial Intelligence

© The Editor(s) (if applicable) and The Author(s), under exclusive license
to Springer Nature Switzerland AG 2026

This work is subject to copyright. All rights are solely and exclusively licensed by the Publisher, whether the whole or part of the material is concerned, specifically the rights of translation, reprinting, reuse of illustrations, recitation, broadcasting, reproduction on microfilms or in any other physical way, and transmission or information storage and retrieval, electronic adaptation, computer software, or by similar or dissimilar methodology now known or hereafter developed.
The use of general descriptive names, registered names, trademarks, service marks, etc. in this publication does not imply, even in the absence of a specific statement, that such names are exempt from the relevant protective laws and regulations and therefore free for general use.
The publisher, the authors and the editors are safe to assume that the advice and information in this book are believed to be true and accurate at the date of publication. Neither the publisher nor the authors or the editors give a warranty, expressed or implied, with respect to the material contained herein or for any errors or omissions that may have been made. The publisher remains neutral with regard to jurisdictional claims in published maps and institutional affiliations.

This Springer imprint is published by the registered company Springer Nature Switzerland AG
The registered company address is: Gewerbestrasse 11, 6330 Cham, Switzerland

If disposing of this product, please recycle the paper.

Preface

The 2025 edition of the European Conference on Machine Learning and Principles and Practice of Knowledge Discovery in Databases (ECML PKDD 2025) was held in the vibrant city of Porto, Portugal on September 15–19, 2025. This marks a significant return of the conference to Porto, following successful editions in 2005 and 2015, underscoring the city's enduring appeal as a hub for scientific exchange.

The annual ECML PKDD conference stands as a premier worldwide platform dedicated to showcasing the latest advancements and fostering insightful discussions in the fields of machine learning and knowledge discovery in databases. Held jointly since 2001, ECML PKDD has firmly established its reputation as the leading European conference in these disciplines. It provides researchers and practitioners with an unparalleled opportunity to exchange knowledge, share innovative ideas, and explore the latest technical advancements. Furthermore, the conference deeply values the synergy between foundational theoretical advances and groundbreaking practical data science applications, actively encouraging contributions that demonstrate how Machine Learning and Data Mining are being effectively employed to address complex real-world challenges.

A Hub for Responsible AI and Cutting-Edge Research

As the technological landscape continues to evolve and societal needs shift, the conference remains committed to adapting to and reflecting these dynamic changes. This year's event saw a robust engagement from the global research community with a substantial increase in the number of submissions.

The three main conference days were organised into five distinct tracks:

- The Research Track received an impressive number of 924 submissions, with 226 papers ultimately accepted, reflecting a highly competitive acceptance rate of 24.5%.
- The Applied Data Science Track received a total of 299 submissions, accepting 74 papers, resulting in an acceptance rate of 24.7%.
- The Journal Track continued to bridge the gap between conference and journal publications, accepting 43 papers (27 for the Machine Learning journal and 16 for the Data Mining and Knowledge Discovery journal) out of 297 submissions.
- The Nectar Track, focusing on recent scientific advances at the frontier of machine learning and data mining, received 30 submissions.
- The Demo Track showcased practical applications and prototypes, accepting 15 papers from a total of 30 submissions.

These proceedings cover the papers accepted in the Research and Applied Data Science tracks.

The high quality and diversity of the accepted papers across all tracks underscore the continued vitality and intellectual breadth of the machine learning and data mining communities. We extend our sincere gratitude to all authors for their valuable contributions, to the program committee members and reviewers for their diligent efforts in ensuring the rigorous double-blind review process, and to the organising committee for their tireless work in making ECML PKDD 2025 a resounding success. We believe these proceedings will serve as a valuable resource, inspiring future research and innovation in these rapidly advancing fields.

This year's conference featured seven insightful keynote talks that focused on crucial and emerging areas within Responsible AI, including trustworthy AI, interpretability, and explainability. The keynotes also explored fundamental theoretical issues, covering causality, neural-symbolic systems, large language models (LLMs), and AI for science. We were honoured to host leading experts who shared their valuable perspectives:

- Cynthia Rudin (Duke University) presented on "Many Good Models Lead to …";
- Elias Bareinboim (Columbia University) discussed "Towards Causal Artificial Intelligence";
- Francisco Herrera (University of Granada) addressed "Not Just a Trend: Institutionalizing XAI for Responsible and Compliant AI Systems";
- Mirella Lapata (University of Edinburgh) explored "Compositional Intelligence: Coordinating Multiple LLMs for Complex Tasks";
- Nuria Oliver (ELLIS Alicante Foundation, Spain) spoke on "Towards a Fairer World: Uncovering and Addressing Human and Algorithmic Biases";
- Pedro Domingos (University of Washington) shared insights on "A Simple Unification of Neural and Symbolic AI"; and
- Sašo Džeroski (Jožef Stefan Institute, Slovenia) presented on "Artificial Intelligence for Science".

Fostering Diversity and Inclusion

Our Diversity and Inclusion initiative proudly awarded 10 scholarship grants of €500 to early-career researchers. These grants enabled individuals from developing countries and communities underrepresented in science and technology to attend the conference, present their work, and become integral members of the ECML PKDD community.

Acknowledging Our Contributors and Supporters

We extend our sincere gratitude to everyone who contributed to making ECML PKDD 2025 such a success. Our heartfelt thanks go to the authors, workshop and tutorial organisers, and all participants for their valuable scientific contributions.

An outstanding conference program would not be possible without the immense dedication and substantial time investment from our area chairs, program committee, and organising committee. The smooth execution of the event was also largely due to the hard work of our many volunteers and session chairs. A special acknowledgement goes to the local organisers for meticulously handling every detail, making the conference a truly memorable experience.

Finally, we are incredibly grateful for the generous financial support from our wonderful sponsors. We also appreciate Springer's ongoing support and Microsoft's provision of their CMT software for conference management, as well as their continued assistance. Our sincere thanks also go to the ECML PKDD Steering Committee for their invaluable advice and guidance over the past two years.

September 2025

João Gama
Pedro H. Abreu
Alípio M. Jorge
Carlos Soares
Rita P. Ribeiro
Pedro Larrañaga
Nathalie Japkowicz
Bernhard Pfahringer
Inês Dutra
Mykola Pechenizkiy
Sepideh Pashami
Paulo Cortez

Organization

Honorary Chair

Pavel Brazdil   University of Porto, Portugal

General Chairs

João Gama	University of Porto, Portugal
Pedro H. Abreu	University of Coimbra, Portugal
Alípio M. Jorge	University of Porto, Portugal
Carlos Soares	University of Porto, Portugal

Research Track Program Chairs

Bernhard Pfahringer	University of Waikato, New Zealand
Nathalie Japkowicz	American University, USA
Pedro Larrañaga	Technical University of Madrid, Spain
Rita P. Ribeiro	University of Porto, Portugal

Applied Data Science Track Program Chairs

Inês Dutra	University of Porto, Portugal
Mykola Pechenisky	TU Eindhoven, The Netherlands
Paulo Cortez	University of Minho, Portugal
Sepideh Pashami	Halmstad University, Sweden

Journal Track Chairs

Ana Carolina Lorena	Instituto Tecnológico de Aeronáutica, Brazil
Arlindo Oliveira	Instituto Superior Técnico, Portugal
Concha Bielza	Technical University of Madrid, Spain
Longbing Cao	Macquarie University, Australia
Tiago Almeida	Federal University of São Carlos, Brazil

Nectar Track Chairs

Ricard Gavaldà   Amalfi Analytics, Spain
Riccardo Guidotti   University of Pisa, Italy

Demo Track Chairs

Arian Pasquali   Faktion, Belgium
Nuno Moniz   University of Notre Dame, USA

Local Chairs

Bruno Veloso   University of Porto, Portugal
Rita Nogueira   INESC TEC, Portugal
Shazia Tabassum   INESC TEC, Portugal

Workshop Chairs

Irena Koprinska   University of Sydney, Australia
João Mendes Moreira   University of Porto, Portugal
Paula Branco   University of Ottawa, Canada

Tutorial Chairs

Alicia Troncoso   Universidad Pablo de Olavide, Spain
Nikolaj Tatti   University of Helsinki, Finland

PhD Forum Chairs

Raquel Sebastião   Polytechnic Institute of Viseu, Portugal
Yun Sing Koh   University of Auckland, New Zealand

Awards Committee Chairs

André Carvalho — University of São Paulo, Brazil
Amparo Alonso-Betanzos — University of A Coruña, Spain
Katharina Morik — TU Dortmund, Germany
Vítor Santos Costa — University of Porto, Portugal

Proceedings Chairs

João Vinagre — European Commission (JRC), Spain
Miriam Santos — University of Porto, Portugal
Shazia Tabassum — INESC TEC, Portugal

Diversity and Inclusion Chairs

Inês Sousa — Fraunhofer, Portugal
Zahraa Abdallah — University of Bristol, UK

Discovery Challenge Chairs

Carlos Ferreira — Polytechnic Institute of Porto, Portugal
Peter van der Putten — Leiden University, The Netherlands
Rui Camacho — University of Porto, Portugal

Panel Chairs

Pedro H. Abreu — University of Coimbra, Portugal
Paula Brito — University of Porto, Portugal

Publicity Chair

Carlos Ferreira — Polytechnic Institute of Porto, Portugal

Sponsorship Chairs

Mariam Berry   BNP Paribas, France
Nuno Moutinho   University of Porto, Portugal
Rui Teles   Accenture, Portugal

Social Media Chairs

Luis Roque   ZAAI.ai, Portugal
Ricardo Pereira   University of Coimbra, Portugal
Dalila Teixeira   Creative Matter, USA

Web Chair

Thiago Andrade   University of Porto, Portugal

Senior Program Committee – Research Track

Adam Jatowt   University of Innsbruck, Austria
Andrea Passerini   University of Trento, Italy
Anthony Bagnall   University of Southampton, UK
Arno Knobbe   Leiden University, Netherlands
Arno Siebes   Universiteit Utrecht, Netherlands
Arto Klami   University of Helsinki, Finland
Bernhard Pfahringer   University of Waikato, New Zealand
Bettina Berendt   TU Berlin, Germany
Celine Robardet   INSA Lyon, France
Celine Vens   KU Leuven, Belgium
Cesar Ferri   Universitat Politècnica Valencia, Spain
Charalampos Tsourakakis   Boston University, USA
Chedy Raissi   Inria, France
Chen Gong   Nanjing University of Science and Technology, China
Danai Koutra   University of Michigan, USA
Dimitrios Gunopulos   University of Athens, Greece
Donato Malerba   Università degli Studi di Bari Aldo Moro, Italy
Dragi Kocev   Jožef Stefan Institute, Slovenia
Dunja Mladenic   Jožef Stefan Institute, Slovenia
Eirini Ntoutsi   Universität der Bundeswehr München, Germany

Emmanuel Müller	TU Dortmund, Germany
Ernestina Menasalvas	Universidad Politécnica de Madrid, Spain
Esther Galbrun	University of Eastern Finland, Finland
Evaggelia Pitoura	University of Ioannina, Greece
Evangelos Papalexakis	University of California, Riverside, USA
Fabio A. Stella	University of Milano-Bicocca, Italy
Fabrizio Costa	Exeter University, UK
Fragkiskos Malliaros	CentraleSupélec, France
Georg Krempl	Utrecht University, Netherlands
Georgiana Ifrim	University College Dublin, Ireland
Gustavo Batista	University of New South Wales, Australia
Heikki Mannila	Aalto University, Finland
Hendrik Blockeel	KU Leuven, Belgium
Henrik Bostrom	KTH Royal Institute of Technology, Sweden
Henry Gouk	University of Edinburgh, UK
Ioannis Katakis	University of Nicosia, Cyprus
Jan N. Van Rijn	LIACS, Leiden University, Netherlands
Jefrey Lijffijt	Ghent University, Belgium
Jerzy Stefanowski	Poznań University of Technology, Poland
Jesse Davis	KU Leuven, Belgium
Jesse Read	Ecole Polytechnique, France
Jessica Lin	George Mason University, USA
Jesus Cerquides	IIIA-CSIC, Spain
Jilles Vreeken	CISPA Helmholtz Center for Information Security, Germany
João Gama	INESC TEC - LIAAD, Portugal
Jörg Wicker	University of Auckland, New Zealand
José Hernández-Orallo	Universitat Politècnica de Valencia, Spain
Junming Shao	University of Electronic Science and Technology of China, China
Kai Puolamaki	University of Helsinki, Finland
Manfred Jaeger	Aalborg University, Denmark
Marius Kloft	TU Kaiserslautern, Germany
Marius Lindauer	Leibniz University Hannover, Germany
Mark Last	Ben-Gurion University of the Negev, Israel
Matthias Renz	University of Kiel, Germany
Matthias Schubert	Ludwig-Maximilians-Universität München, Germany
Michele Lombardi	University of Bologna, Italy
Michèle Sebag	LISN CNRS, France
Nathalie Japkowicz	American University, USA
Paolo Frasconi	Università degli Studi di Firenze, Italy

Parisa Kordjamshidi	Michigan State University, USA
Pasquale Minervini	University of Edinburgh, UK
Pauli Miettinen	University of Eastern Finland, Finland
Pedro Larrañaga	Technical University of Madrid, Spain
Peer Kroger	Christian-Albrechts-Universität Kiel, Germany
Peter Flach	University of Bristol, UK
Ricardo B. Prudencio	Universidade Federal de Pernambuco, Brazil
Rita P. Ribeiro	University of Porto and INESC TEC, Portugal
Salvatore Ruggieri	University of Pisa, Italy
Sebastijan Dumancic	TU Delft, Netherlands
Sibylle Hess	TU Eindhoven, Netherlands
Sicco Verwer	Delft University of Technology, Netherlands
Siegfried Nijssen	Université catholique de Louvain, Belgium
Sophie Fellenz	RPTU Kaiserslautern-Landau, Germany
Stefano Ferilli	University of Bari, Italy
Stratis Ioannidis	Northeastern University, USA
Szymon Jaroszewicz	Polish Academy of Sciences, Poland
Tijl De Bie	Ghent University, Belgium
Ulf Brefeld	Leuphana University of Lüneburg, Germany
Varvara Vetrova	University of Canterbury, New Zealand
Wannes Meert	KU Leuven, Belgium
Wei Ye	Tongji University, China
Wenbin Zhang	Florida International University, USA
Willem Waegeman	Universiteit Gent, Belgium
Wouter Duivesteijn	Technische Universiteit Eindhoven, Netherlands
Xiao Luo	University of California, Los Angeles, USA
Yun Sing Koh	University of Auckland, New Zealand
Zied Bouraoui	CRIL CNRS and Université d'Artois, France

Senior Program Committee – Applied Data Science Track

Albrecht Zimmermann	Université de Caen Normandie, France
Andreas Hotho	University of Würzburg, Germany
Anirban Dasgupta	IIT Gandhinagar, India
Anna Monreale	University of Pisa, Italy
Annalisa Appice	University of Bari Aldo Moro, Italy
Bruno Cremilleux	Université de Caen Normandie, France
Carlotta Domeniconi	George Mason University, USA
Dejing Dou	BCG, USA
Fabio Pinelli	IMT Lucca, Italy
Fuzhen Zhuang	Beihang University, China

Gabor Melli	PredictionWorks, USA
Giuseppe Manco	ICAR-CNR, Italy
Glenn Fung	Independent Researcher, USA
Grzegorz Nalepa	Jagiellonian University, Poland
Hui Xiong	Hong Kong University of Science and Technology (Guangzhou), China
Inês Dutra	University of Porto, Portugal
Ioanna Miliou	Stockholm University, Sweden
Ira Assent	Aarhus University, Denmark
Jiayu Zhou	Michigan State University, USA
Jiliang Tang	Michigan State University, USA
Jingrui He	University of Illinois at Urbana-Champaign, USA
João Gama	INESC TEC - LIAAD, Portugal
Jose A. Gamez	Universidad de Castilla-La Mancha, Spain
Ke Liang	National University of Defense Technology, China
Kurt Driessens	Maastricht University, Netherlands
Lars Kotthoff	University of Wyoming, USA
Liang Sun	Alibaba Group, China
Martin Atzmueller	Osnabrück University and DFKI, Germany
Michael R. Berthold	KNIME, Germany
Michelangelo Ceci	University of Bari, Italy
Min-Ling Zhang	Southeast University, China
Mykola Pechenizkiy	TU Eindhoven, Netherlands
Myra Spiliopoulou	Otto-von-Guericke-Universität Magdeburg, Germany
Niklas Lavesson	Blekinge Institute of Technology, Sweden
Nikolaj Tatti	Helsinki University, Finland
Panagiotis Papapetrou	Stockholm University, Sweden
Paolo Frasconi	Università degli Studi di Firenze, Italy
Paulo Cortez	University of Minho, Portugal
Peggy Cellier	INSA Rennes, IRISA, France
Rayid Ghani	Carnegie Mellon University, USA
Sahar Asadi	King (Microsoft), UK
Sandeep Tata	Google, USA
Sepideh Pashami	Halmstad University, Sweden
Slawomir Nowaczyk	Halmstad University, Sweden
Sriparna Saha	IIT Patna, India
Thomas Liebig	TU Dortmund, Germany
Thomas Seidl	LMU Munich, Germany
Tom Diethe	AstraZeneca, UK
Tony Lindgren	Stockholm University, Sweden

Vincent S. Tseng National Yang Ming Chiao Tung University, Taiwan
Vítor Santos Costa Universidade do Porto, Portugal
Xingquan Zhu Florida Atlantic University, USA
Yi Chang Jilin University, China
Yinglong Xia Meta, USA
Yongxin Tong Beihang University, China
Yun Sing Koh University of Auckland, New Zealand
Zhaochun Ren Shandong University, China
Zheng Wang Alibaba DAMO Academy, China
Zhiwei (Tony) Qin Lyft, USA

Program Committee – Research Track

Christoph Bergmeir Monash University, Australia
A. K. M. Mahbubur Rahman Independent University, Bangladesh
Abdulhakim Qahtan Utrecht University, Netherlands
Abhishek A. Fujitsu Research, India
Acar Tamersoy Microsoft, USA
Ad Feelders Universiteit Utrecht, Netherlands
Adam Goodge I2R, A*STAR, Singapore
Adele Jia China Agricultural University, China
Adem Kikaj KU Leuven, Belgium
Aditya Mohan Leibniz Universität Hannover, Germany
Ajay A. Mahimkar AT&T, USA
Akka Zemmari Université de Bordeaux, France
Akshay Sethi MasterCard, USA
Alborz Geramifard Meta, USA
Alessandro Antonucci IDSIA, Switzerland
Alessandro Melchiorre Johannes Kepler University Linz, Austria
Alexander Dockhorn Leibniz University Hannover, Germany
Alexander Schiendorfer Technische Hochschule Ingolstadt, Germany
Alexander Schulz CITEC, Bielefeld University, Germany
Alexandre Termier Université de Rennes 1, France
Alexandre Verine Ecole Normale Supérieure - PSL, France
Alexandru C. Mara Ghent University, Belgium
Ali Ayadi University of Strasbourg, France
Ali Ismail-Fawaz IRIMAS, Université de Haute-Alsace, France
Alicja Wieczorkowska Polish-Japanese Academy of Information Technology, Poland
Alipio M. G. Jorge INESC TEC/University of Porto, Portugal

Alireza Gharahighehi	KU Leuven, Belgium
Alistair Shilton	Deakin University, Australia
Alneu A. Lopes	University of São Paulo, Brazil
Alper Demir	Izmir University of Economics, Turkey
Alvaro Figueira	CRACS and Universidade do Porto, Portugal
Amal Saadallah	TU Dortmund, Germany
Aman Chadha	Stanford University and Amazon, USA
Amer Krivosija	TU Dortmund, Germany
Amir H. Payberah	KTH Royal Institute of Technology, Sweden
Ammar Shaker	NEC Laboratories Europe, Europe
Ana Rita Nogueira	INESC TEC, Portugal
Anand Paul	Louisiana State University HSC, USA
Anastasios Gounaris	Aristotle University of Thessaloniki, Greece
Andre V. Carreiro	Fraunhofer Portugal AICOS, Portugal
André C. P. L. F. de Carvalho	University of São Paulo, Brazil
Andrea Cossu	University of Pisa, Italy
Andrea Mastropietro	University of Bonn, Germany
Andrea Pugnana	University of Trento, Italy
Andrea Tagarelli	DIMES - UNICAL, Italy
Andreas Bender	LMU Munich, Germany
Andreas Nürnberger	Otto-von-Guericke-Universität Magdeburg, Germany
Andreas Schwung	Fachhochschule Südwestfalen, Germany
Andrei Paleyes	University of Cambridge, UK
Andrzej Skowron	University of Warsaw, Poland
Andy Song	RMIT University, Australia
Angelica Liguori	ICAR-CNR, Italy
Anirban Dasgupta	IIT Gandhinagar, India
Anke Meyer-Baese	Florida State University, USA
Anna Beer	University of Vienna, Austria
Anna Krause	Universität Wurzburg and Chair X Data Science, Germany
Anna Monreale	University of Pisa, Italy
Annelot W. Bosman	Universiteit Leiden, Netherlands
Antoine Caradot	Hubert Curien Laboratory, France
Antonio Bahamonde	University of Oviedo, Spain
Antonio Mastropietro	Università di Pisa, Italy
Antonio Pellicani	Università degli Studi di Bari, Aldo Moro, Italy
Antonis Matakos	Aalto University, Finland
Antti Laaksonen	University of Helsinki, Finland
Aomar Osmani	LIPN-UMR CNRS, France
Aonghus Lawlor	University College Dublin, Ireland

Aparna S. Varde	Montclair State University, USA
Apostolos N. Papadopoulos	Aristotle University of Thessaloniki, Greece
Aritra Konar	KU Leuven, Belgium
Arjun Roy	Freie Universität Berlin, Germany
Arthur Charpentier	UQAM, Canada
Arunas Lipnickas	Kaunas University of Technology, Lithuania
Atsuhiro Takasu	National Institute of Informatics, Japan
Aurora Esteban	University of Cordoba, Spain
Baosheng Zhang	Tsinghua University, China
Barbara Toniella Corradini	University of Florence and University of Siena, Italy
Bardh Prenkaj	Technical University of Munich, Germany
Barry O'Sullivan	University College Cork, Ireland
Beilun Wang	Southeast University, China
Benjamin Halstead	University of Auckland, New Zealand
Benjamin Paassen	Bielefeld University, Germany
Benjamin Quost	Université de Technologie de Compiègne, France
Benoit Frenay	University of Namur, Belgium
Bernardo Moreno Sanchez	University of Helsinki, Finland
Bernhard Pfahringer	University of Waikato, New Zealand
Bertrand Cuissart	University of Caen, France
Bin Liu	Chongqing University of Posts and Telecommunications, China
Bin Shi	Xi'an Jiaotong University, China
Bin Wu	Zhengzhou University, China
Bin Zhou	National University of Defense Technology, China
Bitao Peng	Guangdong University of Foreign Studies, China
Bo Kang	Ghent University, Belgium
Bogdan Cautis	Université Paris-Saclay, France
Bojan Evkoski	Central European University, Hungary
Boshen Shi	Institute of Computing Technology, Chinese Academy of Sciences, China
Boualem Benatallah	Dublin City University, Ireland
Brandon Gower-Winter	Utrecht University, Netherlands
Bunil K Balabantaray	NIT Meghalaya, India
Carlos Ferreira	INESC TEC, Portugal
Carlos Monserrat-Aranda	Universitat Politècnica de Valencia, Spain
Carson K. Leung	University of Manitoba, Canada
Catarina Silva	University of Coimbra, Portugal
Cecile Capponi	Aix-Marseille University, France
Celine Rouveirol	LIPN Université de Sorbonne Paris Nord, France

Cesar H. G. Andrade	Porto University, Portugal
Chandrajit Bajaj	University of Texas, Austin, USA
Chang Rajani	University of Helsinki, Finland
Charlotte Laclau	Polytechnique Institute, Télécom Paris, France
Charlotte Pelletier	Université de Bretagne du Sud, France
Chen Wang	DATA61, CSIRO, Australia
Cheng Cheng	Carnegie Mellon University, USA
Cheng Xie	Yunnan University, China
Chenglin Wang	East China Normal University, China
Chenwang Wu	University of Science and Technology of China, China
Chiara Pugliese	IIT Institute of National Research Council, Italy
Chien-Liang Liu	National Chiao Tung University, Taiwan
Chihiro Maru	Chuo University, Japan
Chongsheng Zhang	Henan University, China
Christian Beecks	FernUniversität in Hagen, Germany
Christian M. M. Frey	University of Technology Nuremberg, Germany
Christian Hakert	TU Dortmund, Germany
Christine Largeron	LabHC Lyon University, France
Christophe Rigotti	INSA Lyon, France
Christophe Rodrigues	DVRC Pôle universitaire Léonard de Vinci, France
Christos Anagnostopoulos	University of Glasgow, UK
Christos Diou Harokopio	University of Athens, Greece
Chuan Qin	Chinese Academy of Sciences, China
Chunchun Chen	Tongji University, China
Chunyao Song	Nankai University, China
Claire Nedellec	INRAE, MaIAGE, France
Claudio Borile	CENTAI Institute, Italy
Claudio Gallicchio	University of Pisa, Italy
Claudius Zelenka	Kiel University, Germany
Colin Bellinger	NRC and Dalhousie University, Canada
Collin Leiber	Aalto University, Finland
Cong Qi	New Jersey Institute of Technology, USA
Congfeng Cao	University of Amsterdam, Netherlands
Corrado Loglisci	Università degli Studi di Bari, Aldo Moro, Italy
Cuicui Luo	University of Chinese Academy of Sciences, China
Cuneyt G. Akcora	University of Central Florida, USA
Cynthia C. S. Liem	Delft University of Technology, Netherlands
Dalius Matuzevicius	Vilnius Gediminas Technical University, Lithuania

Dan Li	Sun Yat-sen University, China
Danai Koutra	University of Michigan, USA
Dang Nguyen	Deakin University, Australia
Daniel Neider	TU Dortmund, Germany
Daniel Schlor	Universität Würzburg, Germany
Danil Provodin	TU Eindhoven, Netherlands
Danyang Xiao	Sun Yat-sen University, China
Dario Garcia-Gasulla	Barcelona Supercomputing Center (BSC), Spain
Dario Garigliotti	University of Bergen, Norway
Darius Plonis	Vilnius Gediminas Technical University, Lithuania
Dariusz Brzezinski	Poznań University of Technology, Poland
David Gomez	Universidad Politecnica de Madrid, Spain
David Holzmüller	University of Stuttgart, Germany
David Q. Sun	Apple, USA
Davide Evangelista	University of Bologna, Italy
Debo Cheng	University of South Australia, Australia
Deepayan Chakrabarti	University of Texas at Austin, USA
Deng-Bao Wang	Southeast University, China
Denilson Barbosa	University of Alberta, Canada
Denis Huseljic	University of Kassel, Germany
Denis Lukovnikov	Ruhr-Universität Bochum, Germany
Destercke Sebastien	UTC, France
Di Jin	TikTok, USA
Di Wu	Chongqing Institute of Green and Intelligent Technology, Chinese Academy of Sciences, China
Diana Benavides Prado	University of Auckland, New Zealand
Dianhui Wang	Independent Researcher, Australia
Diego Carrera	STMicroelectronics, Switzerland
Diletta Chiaro	Università degli Studi di Napoli Federico II, Italy
Dimitri Staufer	TU Berlin, Germany
Dimitrios Katsaros	University of Thessaly, Greece
Dimitrios Rafailidis	University of Thessaly, France
Dino Ienco	INRAE, France
Dmitry Kobak	University of Tübingen, Germany
Domenico Redavid	University of Bari, Italy
Dominik M. Endres	Philipps-Universität Marburg, Germany
Dominique Gay	Université de La Réunion, France
Dong Li	Baylor University, USA
Duarte Folgado	Fraunhofer Portugal AICOS, Portugal
Duo Xu	Georgia Institute of Technology, USA

Edoardo Serra	Boise State University, USA
Edouard Fouche	Karlsruhe Institute of Technology (KIT), Germany
Eduardo F. Montesuma	Université Paris-Saclay, France
Edward Apeh	Bournemouth University, UK
Edwin Simpson	University of Bristol, UK
Ehsan Aminian	INESC TEC, Portugal
Ekaterina Antonenko	Mines Paris - PSL, France
Eliana Pastor	Politecnico di Torino, Italy
Emanuela Marasco	George Mason University, USA
Emilio Dorigatti	LMU Munich, Germany
Emilio Parrado-Hernandez	Universidad Carlos III de Madrid, Spain
Emmanouil Krasanakis	CERTH, Greece
Emmanouil Panagiotou	Freie Universität Berlin, Germany
Emre Gursoy	Koc University, Turkey
Engelbert Mephu Nguifo	Université Clermont Auvergne, CNRS, LIMOS, France
Eran Treister	Ben-Gurion University of the Negev, Israel
Erasmo Purificato	Otto-von-Guericke Universität Magdeburg, Germany
Erik Novak	Jožef Stefan Institute, Slovenia
Erwan Le Merrer	Inria, France
Esra Akbas	Georgia State University, USA
Esther-Lydia Silva-Ramirez	Universidad de Cadiz, Spain
Evaldas Vaičiukynas	Kaunas University of Technology, Lithuania
Evangelos Kanoulas	University of Amsterdam, Netherlands
Evelin Amorim	INESC TEC, Portugal
Fabian C. Spaeh	Boston University, USA
Fabio Fassetti	Università della Calabria, Italy
Fabio Fumarola	Prometeia, Italy
Fabio Mercorio	University of Milan-Bicocca, Italy
Fabio Vandin	University of Padova, Italy
Fandel Lin	University of Southern California, USA
Federica Granese	Inria, Université Côte d'Azur, France
Federico Baldo	University of Bologna, Italy
Federico Sabbatini	National Institute for Nuclear Physics (INFN), Italy
Feifan Zhang	China Agricultural University, China
Felipe Kenji Nakano	KU Leuven, Belgium
Fernando Martinez-Plumed	Universitat Politècnica de Valencia, Spain
Filipe Rodrigues	Technical University of Denmark (DTU), Denmark

Flavio Giobergia	Politecnico di Torino, Italy
Florent Masseglia	Inria, France
Florian Beck	JKU Linz, Austria
Florian Lemmerich	University of Passau, Germany
Francesca Naretto	University of Pisa, Italy
Francesco Piccialli	University of Naples Federico II, Italy
Francesco Renna	Universidade do Porto, Portugal
Francisco Pereira	DTU, Denmark
Franco Raimondi	Gran Sasso Science Institute, Italy
Frederic Koriche	Université d'Artois, CRIL CNRS, France
Frederic Pennerath	CentraleSupélec - LORIA, France
Furong Peng	Shanxi University, China
Gabriel Marques Tavares	LMU Munich, Germany
Gabriele Sartor	University of Turin, Italy
Gabriele Venturato	KU Leuven, Belgium
Gaetan De Waele	Ghent University, Belgium
Gaia Saveri	University of Trieste, Italy
Gang Li	Deakin University, Australia
Gaoyuan Du	Amazon, USA
Gavin Smith	University of Nottingham, UK
Geming Xia	National University of Defense Technology, China
Geng Zhao	Heidelberg University, Germany
Gennaro Vessio	University of Bari Aldo Moro, Italy
Geoffrey I. Webb	Monash, Australia
Georgia Baltsou	Centre for Research & Technology, Greece
Geraldin Nanfack	Concordia University, Canada
Germain Forestier	University of Haute Alsace, France
Gerrit Grossmann	DFKI, Germany
Gerrit J. J. van den Burg	Alan Turing Institute, UK
Gherardo Varando	Universitat de Valencia, Spain
Giacomo Medda	University of Cagliari, Italy
Gilberto Bernardes	INESC TEC and University of Porto, Portugal
Giorgio Venturin	University of Padova, Italy
Giovanna Castellano	University of Bari Aldo Moro, Italy
Giovanni Ponti	ENEA, Italy
Giovanni Stilo	Università degli Studi dell'Aquila, Italy
Gisele Pappa	UFMG, Brazil
Giuseppe Manco	ICAR-CNR, IT, Italy
Gizem Gezici	Scuola Normale Superiore, Italy
Gjergji Kasneci	TU Munich, Germany
Goreti Marreiros	ISEP/GECAD, Portugal

Graziella De Martino	University of Bari, Aldo Moro, Italy
Grazina Korvel	Vilnius University, Lithuania
Grigorios Tsoumakas	Aristotle University of Thessaloniki, Greece
Guangyin Jin	National University of Defense Technology, China
Guangzhong Sun	University of Science and Technology of China, China
Guanjin Wang	Murdoch University, Australia
Guilherme Weigert	Cassales University of Waikato, New Zealand
Guillaume Derval	UC Louvain - ICTEAM, Belgium
Guorui Quan	University of Manchester, UK
Guoxi Zhang	Beijing Institute of General Artificial Intelligence, China
Gustau Camps-Valls	Universitat de Valencia, Spain
Gustav Sir	Czech Technical University, Czech Republic
Gustavo Batista	University of New South Wales, Australia
Hachem Kadri	Aix-Marseille University, France
Hadi Asghari	Humboldt Institute for Internet and Society, Germany
Haifeng Sun	University of Science and Technology of China, China
Haihui Fan	Institute of Information Engineering, Chinese Academy of Sciences, China
Haizhou Du	Shanghai University of Electric Power, China
Hajer Salem	AUDENSIEL, France
Hakim Hacid	TII, United Arab Emirates
Hamid Bouchachia	Bournemouth University, UK
Han Wang	Xidian University, China
Hang Yu	Shanghai University, China
Hanna Sumita	Institute of Science Tokyo, Japan
Hao Niu	KDDI Research, Japan
Hao Xue	University of New South Wales, Australia
Hao Yan	Carleton University, Canada
Haowen Zhang	Zhejiang Sci-Tech University, China
Harsh Borse	IIT Kharagpur, India
Heitor M. Gomes	Victoria University of Wellington, New Zealand
Helder Oliveira	FCUP and INESC TEC, Portugal
Helge Langseth	Norwegian University of Science and Technology, Norway
Hendrik Blockeel	KU Leuven, Belgium
Henrique O. Marques	University of Southern Denmark, Denmark
Henryk Maciejewski	Wroclaw University of Science and Technology, Poland

Hideaki Ishibashi	Kyushu Institute of Technology, Japan
Hilde J. P. Weerts	Eindhoven University of Technology, Netherlands
Holger Froening	University of Heidelberg, Germany
Holger Karl	HPI, Germany
Hongbo Bo	University of Bristol, UK
Hongyang Chen	Zhejiang Lab, China
Hua Chu	Xidian University, China
Huaiyu Wan	Beijing Jiaotong University, China
Huaming Chen	University of Sydney, Australia
Huandong Wang	Tsinghua University, China
Huanlai Xing	Southwest Jiaotong University, China
Hui Ji	University of Pittsburgh, USA
Hui (Wendy) Wang	Stevens Institute of Technology, USA
Huiping Chen	University of Birmingham, UK
Humberto Bustince	Universidad Publica de Navarra, Spain
Huong Ha	RMIT University, Australia
Idir Benouaret	Epita Research Laboratory, France
Ines Sousa	Fraunhofer AICOS, Portugal
Ingo Thon	Siemens AG, Germany
Inigo Jauregi Unanue	University of Technology Sydney, Australia
Ioannis Sarridis	Centre for Research & Technology, Greece
Issam Falih	Université Clermont Auvergne, CNRS, LIMOS, France
Ivan Vankov	iris.ai, Norway
Ivor Cribben	University of Alberta, Canada
Jaemin Yoo	KAIST, South Korea
Jakir Hossain	University at Buffalo, USA
Jakub Klikowski	Wroclaw University of Science and Technology, Poland
Jalaj Bhandari	Columbia University, USA
Jaleed Khan	University of Oxford, UK
James Goulding	University of Nottingham, UK
Jan Kalina	Czech Academy of Sciences, Czech Republic
Jan P. Mielniczuk	Polish Academy of Sciences, Poland
Jan Ramon	Inria, France
Jan Verwaeren	Ghent University, Belgium
Jannis Brugger	TU Darmstadt, Germany
Jean-Marc Andreoli	Naverlabs Europe, Netherlands
Jedrzej Potoniec	Poznań University of Technology, Poland
Jeronimo Arenas-Garcia	Universidad Carlos III de Madrid, Spain
Jhony H. Giraldo	Télécom Paris, Institut Polytechnique de Paris, France

Jia Cai	Guangdong University of Finance and Economics, China
Jiahui Jin	Southeast University, China
Jiang Zhong	Independent Researcher, China
Jianwu Wang	University of Maryland, Baltimore County, USA
Jiawei Chen	Tianjin University, China
Jiaxin Ding	Shanghai Jiao Tong University, China
Jidong Yuan	Beijing Jiaotong University, China
Jie Song	Zhejiang University, China
Jie Wu	Fudan University, China
Jie Yang	University of Wollongong, China
Jimeng Shi	Florida International University, USA
Jin Chen	Hong Kong University of Science and Technology, China
Jin Liang	South China Normal University, China
Jing Ren	NUDT, China
Jing Wang	Amazon, USA
Jinghui Zhong	South China University of Technology, China
Jingtao Ding	Tsinghua University, China
Jinli Zhang	Beijing University of Technology, China
Jiri Sima	Czech Academy of Sciences, Czech Republic
João Gama	University of Porto, Portugal
Joao Mendes-Moreira	University of Porto, Portugal
Joao Vinagre	European Commission (JRC), Spain
Joaquim Silva	NOVA LINCS, Universidade Nova de Lisboa, Portugal
Jochen De Weerdt	KU Leuven, Belgium
Joe Mellor	University of Edinburgh, UK
Johanne Cohen	LISN-CNRS, France
Johannes Jakubik	IBM Research, USA
John W. Sheppard	Montana State University, USA
Jonata Tyska Carvalho	Federal University of Santa Catarina, Brazil
Jordi Guitart	Barcelona Supercomputing Center (BSC), Spain
Joris Mattheijssens	Ghent University, Belgium
Jose M. Costa Pereira	University of Porto, Portugal
Jose Oramas	University of Antwerp, sqIRL/IDLab, imec, Belgium
Jose Tomas Palma	University of Murcia, Spain
Joydeep Chandra	Indian Institute of Technology, Patna, India
Juan A. Botia	University of Murcia, Spain
Juan Rodriguez	Universidad de Burgos, Spain
Jukka Heikkonen	University of Turku, Finland

Julien Delaunay	Inria, France
Julien Ferry	Polytechnique Montreal, Canada
Julien Perez	EPITA, France
Jun Zhuang	Boise State University, USA
Jun Yu Hou	Nanjing University, China
Junbo Zhang	JD Intelligent Cities Research, USA
Junze Liu	University of California, Irvine, USA
Jurgita Kapočiūtė-Dzikienė	Tilde SIA, University of Latvia and Tilde IT, Vytautas Magnus University, Lithuania
Justina Mandravickaitė	Vytautas Magnus University, Lithuania
Kamil Adamczewski	Max Planck Institute for Intelligent Systems, Germany
Kamil Michal Ksiazek	Jagiellonian University, Poland
Karim Radouane	Université Sorbonne Paris Nord, France
Kary Framing	Umeå University, Sweden
Katerina Taskova	University of Auckland, New Zealand
Katharina Dost	Jožef Stefan Institute, Slovenia
Kaushik Roy	University of South Carolina, USA
Kejia Chen	Nanjing University of Posts and Telecommunications, China
Ken Kobayashi	Tokyo Institute of Technology, Japan
Khaled Mohammed Saifuddin	Northeastern University, USA
Khalid Benabdeslem	Université de Lyon 1, France
Kim Thang Nguyen	LIG, University Grenoble-Alpes, France
Kira Maag	Heinrich-Heine-Universität Düsseldorf, Germany
Koji Maruhashi	Fujitsu Research, Japan
Koyel Mukherjee	Adobe Research, USA
Kristen M. Scott	KU Leuven, Belgium
Krzysztof Ruda	Polish Academy of Sciences, Poland
Krzysztof Slot	Lodz University of Technology, Poland
Kuldeep Singh	Cerence, Germany
Kushankur Ghosh	University of Alberta, Canada
Lamine Diop	EPITA, France
Latifa Oukhellou	IFSTTAR, France
Laurence Park	Western Sydney University, Australia
Laurens Devos	KU Leuven, Belgium
Len Feremans	Universiteit Antwerpen, Belgium
Lena Wiese	Goethe University Frankfurt, Germany
Lenaig Cornanguer	CISPA Helmholtz Center for Information Security, Germany
Lennert De Smet	KU Leuven, Belgium
Lev Reyzin	University of Illinois at Chicago, USA

Li Wang	National University of Defense Technology, China
Liang Du	Shanxi University, China
Lianyong Qi	China University of Petroleum (East China), China
Lijie Hu	King Abdullah University of Science and Technology, Saudi Arabia
Lijing Zhu	Bowling Green State University, USA
Lingling Zhang	Capital Normal University, China
Lingyue Fu	Shanghai Jiao Tong University, China
Linh Le Pham Van	Deakin University, Australia
Livio Bioglio	University of Turin, Italy
Lixing Yu	Yunnan University, China
Liyan Song	Harbin Institute of Technology, China
Longlong Sun	Chang'an University, China
Luca Corbucci	University of Pisa, Italy
Luca Ferragina	University of Calabria, Italy
Luca Romeo	University of Macerata, Italy
Lucas Pereira	LARSyS, Tecnico Lisboa, Portugal
Luciano Caroprese	ICAR-CNR, Italy
Ludovico Boratto	University of Cagliari, Italy
Luis Rei	Jožef Stefan Institute, Slovenia
Mahardhika Pratama	University of South Australia, Australia
Maiju Karjalainen	University of Eastern Finland, Finland
Makoto Onizuka	Osaka University, Japan
Manali Sharma	Samsung, South Korea
Maneet Singh	MasterCard, India
Manuel M. Garcia-Piqueras	Universidad de Castilla La Mancha, Spain
Manuele Bicego	University of Verona, Italy
Mao A. Cheng	University of California, Berkeley, USA
Marc Plantevit	EPITA, France
Marc Tommasi	Lille University, France
Marcel Wever	Leibniz University Hannover, Germany
Marcilio de Souto	LIFO/Université d'Orleans, France
Marco Lippi	University of Florence, Italy
Marco Loog	Radboud University, Netherlands
Marco Mellia	Politecnico di Torino, Italy
Marco Podda	University of Pisa, Italy
Marco Polignano	Università di Bari, Italy
Marco Viviani	Università degli Studi di Milano Bicocca, Italy
Maria Vasconcelos	Fraunhofer Portugal AICOS, Portugal
Maria Sofia Bucarelli	Sapienza University of Rome, Italy

Mariana Oliveira	Universidade do Porto, Portugal
Mariana Vargas Vieyra	MostlyAI, Austria
Marielle Malfante	CEA, France
Marina Litvak	Shamoon College of Engineering, Israel
Mario Antunes	Universidade de Aveiro, Portugal
Mario Andres Munoz	University of Melbourne, Australia
Marius Koppel	Johannes Gutenberg University Mainz, Germany
Mark Junjie Li	Shenzhen University, China
Marko Robnik-Sikonja	University of Ljubljana, Slovenia
Marta Soare	Université d'Orleans, France
Martin Holena	Czech Academy of Sciences, Czech Republic
Martin Pilat	Charles University, Czech Republic
Martino Ciaperoni	Aalto University, Finland
Marwan Hassani	TU Eindhoven, Netherlands
Masahiro Suzuki	University of Tokyo, Japan
Massimo Guarascio	ICAR-CNR, Italy
Matej Mihelcic	University of Zagreb, Croatia
Mathias Verbeke	KU Leuven, Belgium
Mathieu Lefort	Université de Lyon, France
Matteo Francobaldi	University of Bologna, Italy
Matteo Riondato	Amherst College, USA
Matteo Salis	University of Turin, Italy
Matthew B. Middlehurst	University of Southampton, UK
Matthia Sabatelli	University of Groningen, Netherlands
Mattia Cerrato	JGU Mainz, Germany
Mattia Setzu	University of Pisa, Italy
Mattis Hartwig	German Research Center for Artificial Intelligence, Germany
Matyas Bohacek	Stanford University, USA
Maximilian T. Fischer	University of Konstanz, Germany
Maximilian Münch	University of Applied Sciences, Würzburg-Schweinfurt, Germany
Maximilian Stubbemann	University of Hildesheim, Germany
Maximilian Thiessen	TU Wien, Austria
Maximilian von Zastrow	Southern Denmark University, Denmark
Megha Khosla	TU Delft, Netherlands
Meiyun Zuo	Renmin University of China, China
Meng Liu	National University of Defense Technology, China
Mengying Zhu	Zhejiang University, China
Michael Granitzer	University of Passau, Germany
Michael B. Ito	University of Michigan, USA

Michael G. Madden	National University of Ireland, Galway, Ireland
Michal Wozniak	Wroclaw University of Science and Technology, Poland
Michele Fontana	Università di Pisa, Italy
Michiel Stock	Ghent University, Belgium
Miguel Rocha	University of Minho, Portugal
Miguel Silva	INESC TEC, Portugal
Mike Holenderski	Eindhoven University of Technology, Netherlands
Milos Savic	University of Novi Sad, Serbia
Mina Rezaei	LMU Munich, Germany
Minh P. Nguyen	University of Texas, Austin, USA
Minyoung Choe	Korea Advanced Institute of Science and Technology, South Korea
Minyu Chen	Shanghai Jiaotong University, China
Miquel Perello-Nieto	University of Bristol, UK
Mira Kristin Jurgens	Ghent University, Belgium
Miriam Santos	University of Porto, Portugal
Mirko Bunse	TU Dortmund, Germany
Mirko Polato	University of Turin, Italy
Mitra Baratchi	LIACS, University of Leiden, Netherlands
Mohammed Elbamby	Telefonica Scientific Research, Spain
Moises Rocha dos Santos	University of Porto, Portugal
Monowar Bhuyan	Umeå University, Sweden
Morteza Rakhshaninejad	Ghent University, Belgium
Mounim A. El Yacoubi	Télécom SudParis, France
Muhammad Rajabinasab	University of Southern Denmark, Denmark
Muhao Guo	Arizona State University, USA
Mustapha Lebbah	Paris Saclay University-Versailles, France
Nabeel Hussain Syed	Rheinland-Pfälzische Technische Universität, Kaiserslautern-Landau, Germany
Nandyala Hemachandra	Indian Institute of Technology Bombay, India
Nannan Wu	Tianjin University, China
Nanqing Dong	Shanghai Artificial Intelligence Laboratory, China
Naresh Manwani	International Institute of Information Technology, Hyderabad, India
Natan Tourne	Ghent University, Belgium
Nate Veldt	Texas A&M, USA
Nathalie Japkowicz	American University, USA
Natthawut Kertkeidkachorn	Japan Advanced Institute of Science and Technology (JAIST), Japan
Ngoc-Son Vu	ENSEA, France
Nhat-Tan Bui	University of Arkansas, USA

Nian Li	Tsinghua University, China
Nick Lim	University of Waikato, New Zealand
Nico Piatkowski	Fraunhofer IAIS, Germany
Nicolas Roque dos Santos	University of São Paulo, Brazil
Niklas A. Strauss	LMU Munich, Germany
Nikolaj Tatti	Helsinki University, Finland
Nikolaos Nikolaou	University College London, UK
Nikolaos Stylianou	Information Technologies Institute, Greece
Nikos Kanakaris	University of Southern California, USA
Ning Xu	Southeast University, China
Nripsuta Saxena	University of Southern California, USA
Nuwan Gunasekara	Halmstad University, Sweden
Olga Kurasova	Vilnius University, Lithuania
Olga Slizovskaia	AstraZeneca, UK
Olivier Teste	IRIT, University of Toulouse, France
Oswald C	NIT Trichy, India
Oswaldo Solarte-Pabon	Universidad del Valle, Colombia
Ozge Alacam	University of Bielefeld, Germany
P. S. Sastry	Indian Institute of Science, India
Pablo Olmos	Universidad Carlos III de Madrid, Spain
Panagiotis Karras	University of Copenhagen, Denmark
Panagiotis Symeonidis	University of the Aegean, Greece
Pance Panov	Jožef Stefan Institute, Slovenia
Paolo Bonetti	Politecnico di Milano, Italy
Paolo Merialdo	Università degli Studi Roma Tre, Italy
Paolo Mignone	University of Bari Aldo Moro, Italy
Pascal Welke	TU Wien, Austria
Patrick Y. Wu	American University, USA
Paul Caillon	LAMSADE Université Paris Dauphine - PSL, France
Paul Davidsson	Malmo University, Sweden
Paul Prasse	University of Potsdam, Germany
Paulo J. Azevedo	Universidade do Minho, Portugal
Pawel Teisseyre	Warsaw University of Technology, Poland
Pawel Zyblewski	Wroclaw University of Science and Technology, Poland
Pedro G. Ferreira	University of Porto, Portugal
Pedro Larrañaga	Technical University of Madrid, Spain
Pedro Ribeiro	University of Porto, Portugal
Pedro H. Abreu	CISUC, Portugal
Peijie Sun	Tsinghua University, China
Peng Wu	Shanghai Jiao Tong University, China

Pengpeng Qiao	Institute of Science Tokyo, Japan
Peter Karsmakers	KU Leuven, Belgium
Peter Schneider-Kamp	SDU, Denmark
Peter van der Putten	Leiden University, Netherlands
Petia Georgieva	University of Aveiro, Portugal
Philipp Vaeth	Technical University of Applied Sciences Würzburg-Schweinfurt and Universität Bielefeld, Germany
Philippe Preux	Inria, France
Phung Lai	SUNY-Albany, USA
Pierre Geurts	Montefiore Institute, University of Liège, Belgium
Pierre Monnin	Université Côte d'Azur, Inria, CNRS, I3S, France
Pierre Schaus	UC Louvain, Belgium
Pierre Wolinski	Paris Dauphine University - PSL, France
Pieter Robberechts	KU Leuven, Belgium
Pietro Sabatino	ICAR-CNR, Italy
Pingchuan Ma	HKUST, China
Piotr Habas	Amazon, USA
Piotr Lipinski	University of Wroclaw, Poland
Piotr Porwik	University of Silesia, Katowice, Poland
Prithwish Chakraborty	IBM Corporation, USA
Lucie Flek	Marburg University, Germany
Przemyslaw Biecek	Warsaw University of Technology, Poland
Qiang Sheng	Institute of Computing Technology, Chinese Academy of Sciences, China
Qiang Zhou	Nanjing University of Aeronautics and Astronautics, China
Rafet Sifa	Fraunhofer IAIS, Germany
Raha Moraffah	Arizona State University, USA
Raivydas Simanas	Vilnius University, Lithuania
Rajeev Rastogi	Amazon, USA
Ranya Almohsen	Baylor College of Medicine, USA
Raphael Romero	Ghent University, Belgium
Raquel Sebastiao	ESTGV-IPV & IEETA-UA, Portugal
Ravi Kolla	Sony Research India, India
Raza Ul Mustafa	Loyola University, USA
Remy Cazabet	Université de Lyon 1, France
Renhe Jiang	University of Tokyo, Japan
Reza Akbarinia	Inria, France
Ricardo P. M. Cruz	University of Porto (FEUP), Portugal
Ricardo B. Prudencio	Universidade Federal de Pernambuco, Brazil
Ricardo Rios	Federal University of Bahia, Brazil

Ricardo Santos	Fraunhofer Portugal AICOS, Portugal
Riccardo Guidotti	University of Pisa, Italy
Robertas Damasevicius	Vytautas Magnus University, Lithuania
Roberto Corizzo	American University, USA
Roberto Interdonato	CIRAD, France
Rocio Chongtay	University of Southern Denmark, Denmark
Rohit Babbar	University of Bath, UK and Aalto University, Finland
Romain Tavenard	Université de Rennes, LETG/IRISA, France
Rosana Veroneze	LBiC, Italy
Ruggero G. Pensa	University of Turin, Italy
Rui Meng	BNU-HKBU United International College, USA
Rui Yu	University of Louisville, USA
Ruixuan Liu	Emory University, USA
Runqun Xiong	Southeast University, China
Runxue Bao	University of Pittsburgh, USA
Ruochun Jin	National University of Defense Technology, China
Ruta Juozaitiene	Vytautas Magnus University, Lithuania
Rytis Maskeliunas	PolsI, Poland
Salvatore Ruggieri	University of Pisa, Italy
Sam Verboven	Vrije Universiteit Brussel, Belgium
Sangkyun Lee	Korea University, South Korea
Sara Abdali	University of California, Riverside, USA
Sarah Masud	LCS2, IIIT-D, India
Sarwan Ali	Georgia State University, USA
Satoru Koda	Fujitsu Limited, Japan
Sebastian Buschjager	Lamarr Institute for ML and AI, Germany
Sebastian Jimenez	Ghent University, Belgium
Sebastian Meznar	Jožef Stefan Institute, Ljubljana, Slovenia
Sebastian Ventura Soto	University of Cordoba, Spain
Sebastien Razakarivony	Safran, France
Selpi Selpi	Chalmers University of Technology, Sweden
Sergio Greco	University of Calabria, Italy
Sergio Jesus	Feedzai, Portugal
Sha Lu	University of South Australia, Australia
Shalini Priya	Indian Institute of Technology Patna, India
Shanqing Guo	Shandong University, China
Shaofu Yang	Southeast University, China
Shazia Tabassum	INESCTEC, Portugal
Shengxiang Gao	Kunming University of Science and Technology, China

Shichao Pei	University of Massachusetts, Boston, USA
Shin Matsushima	University of Tokyo, Japan
Shin-ichi Maeda	Preferred Networks, Japan
Shiwen Ni	Chinese Academy of Sciences, China
Shiyou Qian	Shanghai Jiao Tong University, China
Shu Zhao	Anhui University, China
Shuai Li	University of Cambridge, UK and University of Tokyo, Japan, Tsinghua University, China
Shuang Cheng	Institute of Computing Technology, Chinese Academy of Sciences, China
Shubhranshu Shekhar	Brandeis University, USA
Shurui Cao	Carnegie Mellon University, USA
Shuteng Niu	Mayo Clinic, USA
Siamak Ghodsi	Leibniz University of Hannover, Germany
Sihai Zhang	University of Science and Technology of China, China
Silvia Chiusano	Politecnico di Torino, Italy
Silviu Maniu	Université de Grenoble Alpes, France
Simon Gottschalk	L3S Research Center, Leibniz Universität Hannover, Germany
Simona Nistico	University of Calabria, Italy
Simone Angarano	Politecnico di Torino, Italy
Sinong Zhao	Nankai University, China
Siwei Wang	Intelligent Game and Decision Lab, China
Sofoklis Kitharidis	LIACS, Netherlands
Songlin Du	University of Melbourne, Australia
Songlin Du	Southeast University, China
Soumyajit Chatterjee	Nokia Bell Labs, USA
Sourav Dutta	Huawei Research Centre, China
Stefan Duffner	University of Lyon, France
Stefan Heindorf	Paderborn University, Germany
Stefan Kesselheim	Forschungszentrum Jülich, Germany
Stefano Bortoli	Huawei Research Center, China
Stefanos Vrochidis	Information Technologies Institute, CERTH, Greece
Steffen Thoma	FZI Research Center for Information Technology, Germany
Stephan Doerfel	Kiel University of Applied Sciences, Germany
Steven D. Prestwich	University College Cork, Ireland
Suman Banerjee	IIT Jammu, India
Sunil Aryal	Deakin University, Australia
Surabhi Adhikari	Columbia University, USA

Susan McKeever	TU Dublin, Ireland
Swati Swati	Universität der Bundeswehr München, Germany
Szymon Wojciechowski	Wroclaw University of Science and Technology, Poland
Talip Ucar	AstraZeneca, UK
Taro Tezuka	University of Tsukuba, Japan
Tatiana Passali	Aristotle University of Thessaloniki, Greece
Tatiane Nogueira Rios	UFBA, Brazil
Telmo M. Silva Filho	University of Bristol, UK
Teng Lin	Hong Kong University of Technology (Guangzhou), China
Teng Zhang	Huazhong University of Science and Technology, China
Thach Le Nguyen	Insight Centre, Ireland
Thang Duy Dang	Fujitsu Limited, Japan
Thanh-Son Nguyen	A*STAR, Singapore
Theresa Eimer	Leibniz University Hannover, Germany
Thiago Andrade	INESC TEC & University of Porto, Portugal
Thomas Bonald	Telecom Paris, France
Thomas Guyet	Inria, Centre de Lyon, France
Thomas Lampert	University of Strasbourg, France
Thomas L. Lee	University of Edinburgh, UK
Thomas Mortier	Ghent University, Belgium
Tianyi Chen	Boston University, USA
Tie Luo	University of Kentucky, USA
Tiehang Duan	Mayo Clinic, USA
Tijl De Bie	Ghent University, Belgium
Timilehin B. Aderinola	University College Dublin, Ireland
Timo Bertram	Johannes-Kepler Universität, Germany
Timo Ropinski	Ulm University, Germany
Tobias A. Hille	University of Kassel, Germany
Tom Hanika	University of Hildesheim, Germany
Tomas Kliegr	University of Economics, Prague, Czech Republic
Tomasz Michalak	University of Warsaw and Ideas NCBiR, Poland
Tomasz Walkowiak	Wroclaw University of Science and Technology, Poland
Tommaso Zoppi	University of Florence, Italy
Tong Li	Hong Kong University of Technology, China
Tong Mo	Peking University, China
Tongya Zheng	Hangzhou City University, China
Tonio Weidler	Maastricht University, Netherlands
Tony Lindgren	Stockholm University, Sweden

Tsunenori Mine	Kyushu University, Japan
Tuan Le	New Mexico State University, USA
Tuwe Lofstrom	Jönköping University, Sweden
Ulf Johansson	Jönköping University, Sweden
Vadim Ermolayev	Ukrainian Catholic University, Ukraine
Vahan Martirosyan	CentraleSupélec, Belgium
Vana Kalogeraki	Athens University of Economics and Business, Greece
Vanessa Gomez-Verdejo	Universidad Carlos III de Madrid, Spain
Vasileios Iosifidis	SCHUFA Holding, Germany
Vasilis Gkolemis	ATHENA RC, Greece
Victor Charpenay	Mines Saint-Etienne, France
Vincent Derkinderen	KU Leuven, Belgium
Vincent Lemaire	Orange Research, France
Vincenzo Pasquadibisceglie	University of Bari, Aldo Moro, Italy
Virginijus Marcinkevicius	Vilnius University, Lithuania
Vitor Cerqueira	University of Porto, Portugal
Vivek Kumar	Universität der Bundeswehr München, Germany
Vivek Srikumar	University of Utah, USA
Wagner Meira Jr.	UFMG, Brazil
Wei Wu	Ben Gurion University of the Negev, Israel
Weichen Li	RPTU Kaiserslautern-Landau, Germany
Weifeng Xu	Independent Researcher, China
Weike Pan	Shenzhen University, China
Weiwei Jiang	Beijing University of Posts and Telecommunications, China
Weiwei Sun	Carnegie Mellon University, USA
Weiwei Yuan	Nanjing University of Aeronautics and Astronautics, China
Weixiong Rao	Tongji University, China
Wen-Bo Xie	Southwest Petroleum University, China
Wenhao Li	Tongji University, China
Wenhao Zheng	Shopee, Singapore
Wenjie Feng	National University of Singapore, Singapore
Wenjie Xi	George Mason University, USA
Wenshui Luo	Nanjing University of Science and Technology, China
Wentao Yu	Nanjing University of Science and Technology, China
Wenzhe Yi	Wuhan University, China
Wenzhong Li	Nanjing University, China
Wojciech Rejchel	Nicolaus Copernicus University, Torun, Poland

Xi Jiang	Southern University of Science and Technology, China
Xiang Li	East China Normal University, China
Xiang Lian	Kent State University, USA
Xiao Ma	Beijing University of Posts and Telecommunications, China
Xiao Zhang	Shandong University, China
Xiaobing Zhou	Yunnan University, China
Xiaofeng Cao	University of Technology Sydney, Australia
Xiaofeng Gao	Shanghai Jiaotong University, China
Xiaojun Chen	Institute of Information Engineering, Chinese Academy of Sciences, China
Xiao-Jun Zeng	University of Manchester, UK
Xiaoming Zhang	Beihang University, China
Xiaoting Zhao	Etsy, USA
Xiaowei Mao	Beijing Jiaotong University, China
Xiaoyu Shi	Chinese Academy of Sciences, China
Xin Du	University of Edinburgh, UK
Xin Qin	California State University, Long Beach, USA
Xing Tang	Tencent, China
Xing Xing	Tongji University, China
Xinning Zhu	Beijing University of Posts and Telecommunications, China
Xinpeng Lv	National University of Defense Technology, China
Xintao Wu	University of Arkansas, USA
Xinyang Zhang	University of Illinois at Urbana-Champaign, USA
Xinyu Guan	Xi'an Jiaotong University, China
Xixun Lin	Chinese Academy of Sciences, China
Xiyue Zhang	University of Bristol, UK
Xuan-Hong Dang	IBM T.J. Watson Research Center, USA
Xue Li	University of Queensland, Australia
Xue Yan	Institute of Automation, Chinese Academy of Sciences, China
Xuefeng Chen	Chongqing University, China
Xuemin Wang	Guilin University of Electronic Technology, China
Yachuan Zhang	East China University of Science and Technology, China
Yan Zhang	Peking University, China
Yang Li	University of North Carolina at Chapel Hill, USA
Yang Shu	East China Normal University, China
Yang Wei	Nanjing University of Science and Technology, China

Yanhao Wang	East China Normal University, China
Yanmin Zhu	Shanghai Jiao Tong University, China
Yansong Y. L. Li	University of Ottawa, Canada
Yao-Xiang Ding	Nanjing University, China
Yaqi Xie	Carnegie Mellon University, USA
Yasutoshi Ida	NTT, Japan
Yaying Zhang	Tongji University, China
Ye Zhu	Deakin University, Australia
Yeon-Chang Lee	Ulsan National Institute of Science and Technology, South Korea
Yexiang Xue	Purdue University, USA
Yi Wang	Xinjiang Technical Institute of Physics and Chemistry, Chinese Academy of Sciences, China
Yifeng Gao	University of Texas, Rio Grande Valley, USA
Yilun Jin	Hong Kong University of Science and Technology, China
Yin Zhang	University of Electronic Science and Technology of China, China
Ying Chen	RMIT University, Australia
Yinsheng Li	Fudan University, China
Yong Li	Huawei European Research Center, China
Yongyu Wang	JD Logistics, China
Youhei Akimoto	University of Tsukuba/RIKEN AIP, Japan
You-Wei Luo	Sun Yat-sen University and Jiaying University, China
Yuchen Li	Baidu, China
Yuchen Yang	Harbin Institute of Technology, China
Yudi Zhang	Eindhoven University of Technology, Netherlands
Yuhao Li	University of Melbourne, Australia
Yuheng Jia	Southeast University, China
Yujia Zheng	CMU, USA
Yulong Pei	TU Eindhoven, Netherlands
Yuncheng Jiang	South China Normal University, China
Yuntao Shou	Xi'an Jiaotong University, China
Yunyun Wang	Nanjing University of Posts and Telecommunications, China
Yutong Ye	East China Normal University, China
Yuzhou Chen	University of California, Riverside, USA
Zahraa Abdallah	University of Bristol, UK
Zaineb Chelly Dagdia	UVSQ, Paris-Saclay, France
Zehua Cheng	University of Oxford, UK
Zeyu Chen	University of Auckland, New Zealand

Zhaocheng Ge	Huazhong University of Science and Technology, China
Zhe Yang	Soochow University, China
Zhen Liu	Guangdong University of Foreign Studies, China
Zheng Chen	Osaka University, Japan
Zhenghao Liu	Northeastern University, China
Zhenyu Yang	Macquarie University, Australia
Zhi Li	Tsinghua University, China
Zhichao Han	ETHZ, Switzerland
Zhihui Wang	Fudan University, China
Zhilong Shan	South China Normal University, China
Zhipeng Yin	Florida International University, USA
Zhipeng Zou	Nanjing University of Science and Technology, China
Zhiwen Xiao	Southwest Jiaotong University, China
Zhiwen Zhang	LocationMind, Japan
Zhixin Li	Guangxi Normal University, China
Zhiyong Cheng	Shandong Academy of Sciences, China
Zhong Chen	Southern Illinois University, USA
Zhong Li	Leiden University, Netherlands
Zhong Zhang	Tsinghua University, China
Zhongjing Yu	Peking University, China
Zhuang Liu	Dongbei University of Finance and Economics, China
Zhuo Cao	Forschungszentrum Jülich, Germany
Zhuoming Xie	Guangdong University of Technology, China
Zhuoqun Li	Louisiana State University, USA
Zicheng Zhao	Nanjing University of Science and Technology, China
Zichong Wang	Florida International University, USA
Zifeng Ding	University of Cambridge, UK
Ziheng Chen	Walmart, USA
Zijie J. Wang	Georgia Tech, USA
Zirui Zhuang	Beijing University of Posts and Telecommunications, China
Zixing Song	Chinese University of Hong Kong, China
Ziyu Wang	University of Tokyo, Japan
Ziyue Li	University of Cologne, Germany
Zongxia Xie	Tianjin University, China
Zongyue Li	LMU Munich, Germany
Zuojin Tang	Zhejiang University, China

List of Editors

Bernhard Pfahringer	University of Waikato, New Zealand
Nathalie Japkowicz	American University, USA
Pedro Larrañaga	Technical University of Madrid, Spain
Rita P. Ribeiro	University of Porto, Portugal
Alípio M. Jorge	University of Porto, Portugal
Carlos Soares	University of Porto, Portugal
João Gama	University of Porto, Portugal
Pedro H. Abreu	University of Coimbra, Portugal

Program Committee – Applied Data Science Track

Nasrullah Sheikh	IBM Research, USA
Aakarsh Malhotra	MasterCard, USA
Aakash Goel	Amazon, USA
Abdoulaye Sakho	Artefact, France
Abhijeet Pendyala	Ruhr-Universität Bochum, Germany
Abu Shad Ahammed	University of Siegen, Germany
Adi Lin	Didi, China
Aditya Gautam	Meta, USA
Ahmed K. Mohamed	Meta, USA
Akihiro Yoshida	Kyushu University, Japan
Akshay Sethi	MasterCard, USA
Alejandro Kuratomi	Stockholm University, Sweden
Alessandro Gambetti	Nova School of Business and Economics, Portugal
Alessandro Leite	INSA Rouen, Inria, France
Alessio Russo	Politecnico di Milano, Italy
Alex Beeson	University of Warwick, UK
Alexander Galozy	Halmstad University, Sweden
Alexander Karlsson	University of Skovde, Sweden
Alexander Kovalenko	Czech Technical University in Prague, Czech Republic
Alexey Zaytsev	Skoltech, Russia
Alina Bazarova	Forschungszentrum Jülich, Germany
Alix Lheritier	Amadeus SAS, France
Allan Tucker	Brunel University London, UK
Alvaro Figueira	CRACS and Universidade do Porto, Portugal
Aman Gulati	Amazon, USA
Amira Soliman	Halmstad University, Sweden

Ana Gjorgjevikj	Jožef Stefan Institute, Slovenia
Anders Holst	RISE SICS, Sweden
André C. P. L. F. de Carvalho	University of São Paulo, Brazil
Andrea Seveso	University of Milan-Bicocca, Italy
Andreas Bender	LMU Munich, Germany
Andreas Henelius	Independent Researcher, Finland
Andreas Holzinger	University of Natural Resources and Life Sciences, Vienna, Austria
Andrei Shelopugin	Independent Researcher, Brazil
Angelo Impedovo	Niuma, Italy
Aniket Chakrabarti	Amazon, USA
Animesh Prasad	Roku, USA
Anisio Lacerda	UFMG, Brazil
Anli Ji	Georgia State University, USA
Antoine Doucet	La Rochelle Université, France
Anton Borg	Blekinge Institute of Technology, Sweden
Antonio Bevilacqua	Meetecho, Italy
Antonis Klironomos	University of Mannheim, Germany
Aron Henriksson	Stockholm University, Sweden
Artur Chudzik	Polish-Japanese Academy of Information Technology, Poland
Arun Venkitaraman	EPFL, Switzerland
Arunabha Choudhury	ASML, Netherlands
Asem Omari	Higher Colleges of Technology, UAE
Ashman Mehra	Birla Institute of Technology and Science, India
Ashwani Rao	Amazon, USA
Asier Rodriguez	BBVA, Spain
Asma Atamna	Ruhr-Universität Bochum, Germany
Atiye Sadat Hashemi	Halmstad University, Sweden
Atul Anand Gopalakrishnan	SUNY Buffalo, USA
Avani Wildani	Emory University, USA
Aviv Rovshitz	Ben-Gurion University of the Negev, Israel
Axel Brando	Barcelona Supercomputing Center (BSC) and Universitat de Barcelona (UB), Spain
Azadeh Alavi	RMIT University, Australia
Beihong Jin	Institute of Software, China
Benoit Frenay	University of Namur, Belgium
Berkay Aydin	Georgia State University, USA
Bijaya Adhikari	University of Iowa, USA
Bin Li	Alibaba Group, China
Bo Pang	University of Auckland, New Zealand
Bogdan Ruszczak	Opole University of Technology, Poland

Bohao Qu	Agency for Science, China
Bruno Veloso	INESC TEC, FEP-UP, Portugal
Buyue Qian	Xi'an Jiaotong University, China
Camille Kurtz	Université Paris Cité, France
Cangbai Li	Guangdong University of Technology, China
Carlo Metta	ISTI CNR, Italy
Carlos N. Silla	Pontifical Catholic University of Paraná (PUCPR), Brazil
Cecile Bothorel	IMT Atlantique, France
Cesar Ferri	Universitat Politècnica Valencia, Spain
Chang Li	Apple, USA
Chang-Dong Wang	Sun Yat-sen University, China
Chaofan Li	Karlsruhe Institute of Technology, Germany
Chaoyuan Zuo	Nankai University, China
Chen Gao	Tsinghua University, China
Chen Li	Computer Network Information Center, China
Chen Zhao	Baylor University, USA
Chen-Wei Chang	Virginia Tech, USA
Chenxi Xue	Nanjing Normal University, China
Chongke Bi	Tianjin University, China
Christian M. Adriano	Hasso-Plattner Institute, Germany
Christophe Rodrigues	DVRC Pôle universitaire Léonard de Vinci, France
Chuan Li	Sorbonne University, LIPADE, France
Chunhui Zhang	Dartmouth College, USA
Cristina Soguero Ruiz	Rey Juan Carlos University, Spain
Daheng Wang	Amazon, USA
Daifeng Li	Sun Yat-sen University, China
Damien Fay	HPE Labs, Ireland
Dania Herzalla	Technology Innovation Institute, UAE
Daniel Lemire	University of Quebec (TELUQ), Canada
Daniel Trejo Banos	SDSC, USA
Daochen Zha	Rice University, USA
Dawei Cheng	Tongji University, China
Dayne Freitag	SRI International, USA
Di Yao	Institute of Computing Technology, China
Dimitris Nick Dimitriadis	Aristotle University of Thessaloniki, Greece
Diogo F. Soares	Universidade de Lisboa, Portugal
Dirk Pflueger	University of Stuttgart, Germany
Doheon Han	University of Notre Dame, USA
Dongxiang Zhang	Zhejiang University, China
Dongxiao Yu	Shandong University, China

Dugang Liu	Guangdong Laboratory of Artificial Intelligence and Digital Economy (Shenzen), China
Ece Calikus	Uppsala University, Sweden
Edwyn Brient	Thales LAS/Mines Paris PSL, France
Efstathios Stamatatos	University of the Aegean, Greece
Elaine Faria	UFU, Brazil
Elio Masciari	University of Naples, Italy
Emilie Devijver	Université Grenoble Alpes, Inria, CNRS, Grenoble INP, LIG, France
Emmanuelle Claeys	IRIT, France
Enayat Rajabi	Halmstad University, Sweden
Enda Barrett	University of Galway, Ireland
Enyan Dai	Hong Kong University of Science and Technology (Guangzhou), China
Eric Peukert	ScaDS.AI, Germany
Eric Sanjuan	Avignon University, France
Erik Frisk	Linköping University, Sweden
Eui-Hong (Sam) Han	The Washington Post, USA
Eunil Park	Sungkyunkwan University, South Korea
Fabio Carrara	CNR-ISTI, Italy
Fabiola Pereira	Federal University of Uberlandia, Brazil
Fan Yang	Rice University, USA
Fangzhao Wu	MSRA, China
Fangzhou Shi	Didi Chuxing, China
Fathima Nuzla Ismail	State University of New York, USA
Flavio Bertini	University of Parma, Italy
Francesco Dente	EURECOM, France
Francesco Guerra	University of Modena e Reggio Emilia, Italy
Francesco Scala	CNR-ICAR, Italy
Francesco Spinnato	University of Pisa, Italy
Francesco Paolo Nerini	Sapienza University of Rome, Italy
Francisco P. Romero	UCLM, Spain
Franco Maria Nardini	ISTI-CNR, Italy
Francois Schwarzentruber	ENS Lyon, France
Fudong Lin	University of Delaware, USA
Gabriel Augusto Pinheiro	UNIFESP, Brazil
Gan Sun	South China University of Technology, China
Gargi Srivastava	Rajiv Gandhi Institute of Petroleum Technology Jais, India
Giacomo Boracchi	Politecnico di Milano, Italy
Giuseppe Garofalo	DistriNet, KU Leuven, Belgium
Giuseppina Andresini	University of Bari Aldo Moro, Italy

Goran Falkman	University of Skovde, Sweden
Grzegorz Nalepa	Jagiellonian University, Poland
Guanggang Geng	Jinan University, China
Guojun Liang	Halmstad University, Sweden
Haifang Li	Baidu, China
Haina Tang	University of Chinese Academy of Sciences, China
Hancheng Ge	Amazon, USA
Hao Li	National University of Defense Technology, China
Haohui Chen	CSIRO, Australia
Haomin Yu	Aalborg University, Denmark
Haoyi Xiong	Baidu, China
Hiba Najjar	DFKI, Germany
Hillol Kargupta	Agnik, USA
Hong Zhou	Meta, USA
Hongbin Pei	Xi'an Jiao Tong University, China
Hou-Wan Long	Chinese University of Hong Kong, China
Hua Wei	Arizona State University, USA
Huaiyuan Yao	Xi'an Jiaotong University, China
Huan Song	Amazon, USA
Hubert Baniecki	University of Warsaw, Poland
Hyunsung Kim	KAIST, Fitogether, South Korea
Ibtihal El Mimouni	Inria, France
Ildar Baimuratov	L3S Research Center, Germany
Ilir Jusufi	Blekinge Institute of Technology, Sweden
Inaam Ashraf	Bielefeld University, Germany
Ines Sousa	Fraunhofer AICOS, Portugal
Iris Heerlien	Saxion, Netherlands
Isak Samsten	Stockholm University, Sweden
Ishan Verma	TCS Research, India
Ismail Hakki Toroslu	METU, Turkey
Ivan Carrera	EPN, Ecuador
Jaakko Hollmen	Stockholm University, Sweden
Jairo Cugliari	Laboratoire ERIC, France
Jakub Nalepa	Silesian University of Technology, Poland
Jelica Vasiljević	Hoffmann-La Roche, Switzerland
Jens Lundstrom	Halmstad University, Sweden
Jesse Davis	KU Leuven, Belgium
Jiahui Bai	Meta, USA
Jiajun Gu	Carnegie Mellon University, USA
Jiali Pan	Department of Information Management, USA

Jian Yu	Auckland University of Technology, New Zealand
Jiangbin Zheng	Westlake University, China
Jianhua Yin	Shandong University, China
Jingbo Zhou	Baidu, China
Jingjing Liu	MD Anderson Cancer Center, USA
Jingwen Shi	Michigan State University, USA
Jingxuan Wei	University of Chinese Academy of Sciences, China
Jinyoung Han	Sungkyunkwan University, South Korea
Jiue-An Yang	City of Hope Beckman Research Institute, USA
Joao R. Campos	University of Coimbra, Portugal
Jochen De Weerdt	KU Leuven, Belgium
Joe Tekli	Lebanese American University, Lebanon
Joel Ky	University of Lorraine, CNRS, Inria, France
John McCall	Robert Gordon University, UK
John Mitros	University College Dublin, Ireland
Jonas Fischer	Ruhr-Universität Bochum, Germany
Jonas Nordqvist	Linnaeus University, Sweden
Joydeep Chandra	Indian Institute of Technology Patna, India
Julian Martin Rodemann	LMU Munich, Germany
Jun Shen	University of Wollongong, Australia
Junichi Tatemura	Google, USA
Junxuan Li	Microsoft, USA
Jyun-Yu Jiang	Amazon Science, USA
Kai Wang	Shanghai Jiao Tong University, China
Kaiping Zheng	National University of Singapore, Singapore
Kaiwen Dong	University of Notre Dame, USA
Katarzyna Bozek	University of Cologne, Germany
Katerina Schindlerova	UniVie, Austria
Katharina Dost	Jožef Stefan Institute, Slovenia
Katsiaryna Mirylenka	Zalando SE, Germany
Keith Burghardt	ISI, Germany
Klaus Brinker	Hamm-Lippstadt University of Applied Sciences, Germany
Koki Kawabata	Osaka University, Japan
Korbinian Randl	Stockholm University, Sweden
Krzysztof Krawiec	Poznań University of Technology, Poland
Krzysztof Kutt	Jagiellonian University, Poland
Kwan Hui Lim	Singapore University of Technology and Design, Singapore
Lamija Lemes	University of Zenica, Bosnia & Herzegovina
Le Nguyen	University of Oulu, Finland

Lei Li	Hong Kong University of Science and Technology (Guangzhou), China
Lei Liu	York University, Canada
Li Liu	Chongqing University, China
Li Zhang	University College London, UK
Liang Tang	Google, USA
Liang Tong	NEC Labs America, USA
Liang Wang	Alibaba Group, China
Lina Yao	University of New South Wales, Australia
Lingxiao Li	Michigan State University, USA
Lingyang Chu	McMaster University, Canada
Lixin Zou	Wuhan University, China
Lluis Garcia-Pueyo	Meta, USA
Lou Salaun	Nokia Bell Labs, USA
Luca Corbucci	University of Pisa, Italy
Luca Pappalardo	ISTI, Italy
Luca Romeo	University of Macerata, Italy
Luis Ferreira	Olympus Medical Products Portugal, Portugal
Luis Miguel Matos	ALGORITMI Centre, Portugal
Lukas Grasmann	TU Wien, Austria
Lukas Pensel	Johannes Gutenberg University Mainz, Germany
Maciej Grzenda	Warsaw University of Technology, Poland
Maciej Piernik	Poznań University of Technology, Poland
Madiraju Srilakshmi	Dream Sports, India
Mads C. Hansen	A.P. Moller-Maersk, Denmark
Mahardhika Pratama	University of South Australia, Australia
Mahmoud Rahat	Halmstad University, Sweden
Man Tianxing	Jilin University, China
Manish Gupta	Microsoft, USA
Manos Papagelis	York University, Canada
Manuel Lopes	Instituto Tecnico Superior, Portugal
Manuel Portela	Universitat Pompeu Fabra, Spain
Marc Tommasi	Lille University, France
Marco Fisichella	Leibniz Universität, Hannover, Germany
Maria Riveiro	Jonkoping University, Sweden
Maria Ulan	RISE Research Institutes of Sweden, Sweden
Marian Scuturici	LIRIS, France
Marianne Clausel	IECL, France
Mario Doller	University of Applied Sciences, Kufstein, Austria
Marius Schwammle	DLR/BT, Germany
Markus Gotz	Karlsruhe Institute of Technology (KIT), Germany

Markus Leyser	Technische Universität Dresden, Germany
Martin Boldt	Blekinge Institute of Technology, Sweden
Martin Mladenov	Google, USA
Martin Vita	Institute of Physics, Czech Academy of Sciences, Czech Republic
Matthias Demant	Fraunhofer ISE, Germany
Matthias Galipaud	SDSC, Switzerland
Matthias Petri	Amazon, USA
Matthieu Latapy	CNRS, France
Maurice Van Keulen	University of Twente, Netherlands
Maxime Cordy	University of Luxembourg, Luxembourg
Maxwell J. Jacobson	Purdue University, USA
Md Nahid Hasan	Miami University, USA
Md Zia Ullah	Edinburgh Napier University, UK
Mehtab Alam Syed	CIRAD, France
Melanie Neubauer	University of Leoben, Austria
Meng Chen	Shandong University, China
Mengxuan Zhang	Australian National University, Australia
Miao Fan	NavInfo, China
Michael Bain	University of New South Wales, Australia
Michele Bernardini	Uni eCampus.It, Italy
Michiel Dhont	EluciDATA Lab of Sirris, Belgium
Mickael Coustaty	L3i Laboratory, France
Miguel Couceiro	LORIA, France
Mihaela Mitici	Utrecht University, Netherlands
Min Lee	Singapore Management University, Singapore
Min Hun Lee	Singapore Management University, Singapore
Mina Rezaei	LMU Munich, Germany
Ming Ma	Inner Mongolia University, China
Minghao Chen	Tencent, China
Mirco Nanni	CNR-ISTI Pisa, Italy
Mirjam Wattenhofer	Google, USA
Mirko Marras	University of Cagliari, Italy
Mitra Heidari	University of Melbourne, Australia
Modesto Castrillon-Santana	Universidad de Las Palmas de Gran Canaria, Spain
Mohammadmehdi Saberioon	German Research Centre for Geosciences, Germany
Mohammed Amer	Fujitsu Research of Europe, Germany
Mohammed Ghaith Altarabichi	Halmstad University, Sweden
Mojgan Kouhounestani	University of Melbourne, Australia
Moonki Hong	Sogang University, South Korea

Munira Syed	Procter & Gamble, USA
Nan Li	Microsoft, USA
Narendhar Gugulothu	TCS Research, India
Nedra Mellouli	LIASD, Portugal
Ngoc Son Le	University of Hildesheim, Germany
Niklas Lavesson	Blekinge Institute of Technology, Sweden
Niraj Kumar	Fujitsu, Japan
Nitish Kumar	MasterCard, USA
Nuno Cruz Garcia	FCUL, Portugal
Nuno R. P. S. Guimaraes	INESC TEC, University of Porto, Portugal
Nuwan Gunasekara	Halmstad University, Sweden
Pablo Picazo-Sanchez	Halmstad University, Sweden
Pablo Torrijos Arenas	Universidad de Castilla-La Mancha, Spain
Pablo Jose Del Moral Pastor	Ekkono.ai, Finland
Pan He	Auburn University, USA
Panagiotis Kanellopoulos	University of Essex, UK
Panagiotis Papadakos	FORTH-ICS, Greece
Pandey Shourya Prasad	International Institute of Information Technology, Bangalore, India
Panpan Xu	Amazon AWS, USA
Paola Velardi	Sapienza University of Rome, Italy
Paolo Cintia	Kode, Italy
Pascal Plettenberg	Intelligent Embedded Systems, Italy
Paul Boniol	Inria, France
Pavel Blinov	Sber AI Lab, Russia
Pawel Parczyk	Wroclaw University of Science and Technology, Poland
Pedro M. Ferreira	University of Lisbon, Portugal
Pedro Seber	MIT, USA
Peng Qiao	NUDT, China
Pengyuan Wang	University of Georgia, USA
Petr Olegovich Sokerin	Skoltech, Russia
Philipp Bach	University of Hamburg, Germany
Philipp Froehlich	TU Darmstadt, Germany
Philipp Schmidt	Amazon Research, USA
Philipp Zech	University of Innsbruck, Austria
Pinar Karagoz	Middle East Technical University (METU), Turkey
Ping Luo	Chinese Academy of Sciences, China
Po Yang	University of Sheffield, UK
Pop Petrica	Technical University of Cluj-Napoca, Romania
Prathap Manohar Joshi R	Zoho Corporation, India

Praveen Borra	Florida Atlantic University, USA
Praveen Paruchuri	IIIT Hyderabad, India
Qian Li	Curtin University, Australia
Qihang Yao	Georgia Institute of Technology, USA
Qiwei Han	Nova School of Business and Economics, Portugal
Quentin Duchemin	Université Gustave Eiffel, France
Radu Tudor Ionescu	University of Bucharest, Romania
Rafal Kucharski	Jagiellonian University, Poland
Rafet Sifa	Fraunhofer IAIS & University of Bonn, Germany
Ramasamy Savitha	I2R A*STAR, Singapore
Ran Yu	DSIS Research Group, Singapore
Ranga Raju Vatsavai	North Carolina State University, USA
Raphael Couturier	University of Bourgogne Franche-Comte (UBFC), France
Renato M. Assuncao	ESRI, USA
Renaud Lambiotte	University of Oxford, UK
Reuben Kshitiz Borrison	ABB, Switzerland
Reza Shirvany	Zalando SE, Germany
Ricardo R. Pereira	Feedzai, Portugal
Riccardo Rosati	Università Politecnica delle Marche, Ancona, Italy
Richard Allmendinger	University of Manchester, UK
Richard Nordsieck	XITASO GmbH IT and Software Solutions, Germany
Richi Nayak	Queensland University of Technology, Australia
Roberto Trasarti	CNR, Italy
Rogerio Luis de C. Costa	Polytechnic of Leiria, Portugal
Romain Ilbert	Huawei Paris Research Center, France
Roy Ka-Wei Lee	Singapore University of Technology and Design, Singapore
Ruilin Wang	University of Aberdeen, UK
Sabrina Gaito	Università degli Studi di Milano, Italy
Sai Karthikeya Vemuri	Computer Vision Group Jena, Italy
Saisubramaniam Gopalakrishnan	Quantiphi, USA
Sajjad Shumaly	Max-Planck-Institut for Polymer Research, Germany
Salvatore Rinzivillo	KDD Lab, ISTI, CNR, Italy
Samaneh Shafee	LASIGE, Portugal
Sandra Wissing	Fachhochschule Münster, Germany
Sarwan Ali	Georgia State University, USA
Sebastian Becker	Fraunhofer ISST, Germany

Sebastian Honel	Linnaeus University, Sweden
Selin Colakhasanoglu	Saxion University of Applied Sciences, Netherlands
Senzhang Wang	Central South University, China
Sepideh Nahali	York University, Canada
Shahrooz Abghari	Blekinge Institute of Technology, Sweden
Shahroz Tariq	CSIRO, Australia
Shang Yanlei	BUPT, China
Shen Liang	Paris Cité University, France
Shengheng Liu	Southeast University, China
Shereen Elsayed	University of Hildesheim, Germany
Shi-ting Wen	NingboTech University, China
Shiv Krishna Jaiswal	Walmart Global Tech, USA
Shoujin Wang	Macquarie University, Australia
Shuai Li	University of Cambridge, UK and University of Tokyo, UK
Shuchu Han	Capital One Financial Group, Japan
Simon F. Weinberger	EssilorLuxottica, France
Siyuan Chen	Guangzhou University, China
Snehanshu Saha	BITS Pilani Goa Campus, India
Souhaib Ben Taieb	University of Mons, Abu Dhabi
Sriparna Saha	IIT Patna, India
Stefan Rueping	Fraunhofer IAIS, Germany
Stephane Chretien	Université Lyon 2, France
Sunil Aryal	Deakin University, Australia
Susana Ladra	University of A Coruña, Spain
Szymon Bobek	Jagiellonian University, Poland
Szymon Jaroszewicz	Institute of Computer Science, Poland
Szymon Wilk	Poznań University of Technology, Poland
Tanel Tammet	Tallinn University of Technology, Estonia
Thanh Thi Nguyen	Monash University, Australia
Thiago Zangato	Université Sorbonne Paris Nord, France
Theodora Tsikrika	Information Technologies Institute, Greece
Thibault Girardin	Université Jean Monnet, France
Thomas Czernichow	Darwinlabs, Portugal
Thorsteinn Rognvaldsson	Halmstad University, Sweden
Tiago Mendes-Neves	FEUP/INESC TEC, Portugal
Tianshu Yu	Chinese University of Hong Kong (Shenzhen), China
Ting Su	Imperial College London, UK
Tingrui Qiao	University of Auckland, New Zealand
Tobias Glasmachers	Ruhr-Universität Bochum, Germany

Tomas Olsson	RISE SICS, Sweden
Tome Eftimov	Jožef Stefan Institute, Slovenia
Topon Paul	Toshiba Corporation, Japan
Tsuyoshi Okita	Kyushu Institute of Technology, Japan
Unmesh Padalkar	Dream Sports, India
Vahid Shahrivari Joghan	Utrecht University, Netherlands
Valerio Bonsignori	Unipisa, Italy
Vanessa Borst	University of Würzburg, Germany
Venkata Sai Prakash Mukkamala	Quantiphi Analytics, USA
Veselka Boeva	Blekinge Institute of Technology, Sweden
Viacheslav Komisarenko	University of Tartu, Estonia
Vikas Gupta	HPCL, India
Vinayak Gupta	University of Washington, Seattle, USA
Vincent Auriau	Artefact Research Center, France
Vincenzo Pasquadibisceglie	University of Bari, Aldo Moro, Italy
Vincenzo Scotti	KASTEL, Germany
Vinothkumar Kolluru	Stevens Institute of Technology, USA
Vladimir Mic	Aarhus University, Denmark
Wang-Zhou Dai	Nanjing University, China
Wee Siong Ng	Institute for Infocomm Research, Singapore
Wei Cheng	NEC Laboratories America, USA
Wei Li	Harbin Engineering University, China
Wei Wang	Tsinghua University, China
Wei-Peng Chen	Fujitsu Research of America, USA
Wentao Wang	Michigan State University, USA
Wentao Wu	Microsoft Research, USA
Wray Buntine	VinUniversity, Vietnam
Xianchao Wu	Nvidia, USA
Xiang Lian	Kent State University, USA
Xianli Zhang	Xi'an Jiaotong University, China
Xiaobo Jin	Xi'an Jiaotong-Liverpool University, China
Xiaofei Zhou	University of Chinese Academy of Sciences, China
Xiaofeng Gao	Shanghai Jiaotong University, China
Xiaolin Han	Northwestern Polytechnical University, China
Xin Huang	Hong Kong Baptist University, China
Xin Liu	East China Normal University, China
Xing Tang	Tencent, China
Xiuqiang He	Tencent, China
Xiuyuan Hu	Tsinghua University, China
Xueping Peng	University of Technology Sydney, Australia
Yanchang Zhao	CSIRO, Australia

Yang Guo	Xidian University Hangzhou Institute of Technology, China
Yang Song	Apple, USA
Yijun Zhao	Fordham University, USA
Yinghui Wu	Case Western Reserve University, USA
Yingzhen Lin	Harbin Institute of Technology (Shenzhen), China
Yintao Yu	University of Illinois at Urbana-Champaign, USA
Yixiang Fang	Chinese University of Hong Kong, China
Yixuan Cao	Institute of Computing Technology, China
Yizheng Huang	York University, Canada
Yongchao Liu	Ant Group, China
Yu Huang	Indiana University, USA
Yu Wang	University of Oregon, USA
Yuantao Fan	Halmstad University, Sweden
Yucheng Zhou	University of Macau, China
Yue Shi	Meta, USA
Yueyuan Zheng	Beihang University, China
Yunchuan Shi	University of Sydney, Australia
Yunjun Gao	Zhejiang University, China
Yuting Ding	Southeast University, China
Yuzhuo Li	University of Auckland, New Zealand
Zahra Kharazian	Stockholm University, Sweden
Zahra Taghiyarrenani	Halmstad University, Sweden
Zahraa Abdallah	University of Bristol, UK
Zeyi Wen	Hong Kong University of Science and Technology (Guangzhou), China
Zeyu Zhu	National University of Defense Technology, China
Zhanyu Liu	Shanghai Jiao Tong University, China
Zhaogeng Liu	Jilin University, China
Zhaohui Liang	National Library of Medicine, USA
Zhen Zhang	Shandong University, China
Zhendong Chu	Squirrel Ai Learning, China
Zheng Zhang	University of California, USA
Zhengze Li	University of Göttingen, Germany
Zhibin Gu	Hebei Normal University, China
Zhuang Liu	Dongbei University of Finance and Economics, China
Ziyu Guan	Xidian University, China
Zoltan Miklos	Université de Rennes, France
Zunlei Feng	Zhejiang University, China

Program Committee – Demo Track

Andrzej Wójtowicz	Adam Mickiewicz University, Poznań, Poland
Anna Sokol	University of Notre Dame, USA
Arian Pasquali	Faktion AI, Belgium
Bruno Veloso	INESC TEC - FEP-UP, Portugal
Chongsheng Zhang	Henan University, China
Christos Doulkeridis	University of Piraeus, Greece
Danqing Zhang	PathOnAI.org, USA
Fátima Rodrigues	INESC TEC, Portugal
Grigorii Khvatskii	University of Notre Dame, USA
Joe Germino	University of Notre Dame, USA
Jungwon Seo	University of Stavanger, Norway
Ke Li	University of Exeter, England
Manfred Jaeger	Aalborg University, Denmark
Marcin Luckner	Warsaw University of Technology, Poland
Mehwish Alam	Institut Polytechnique de Paris, France
Nuno Moniz	University of Notre Dame, USA
Tânia Carvalho	FCUP, Portugal
Vitor Cerqueira	FEUP, Portugal
Wei-Wei Du	National Yang Ming Chiao Tung University, Taiwan

Additional Reviewers

Andrea D'Angelo
Patrick Altmeyer
Guiseppina Adresini
Vedangi Bengali
Michele Bernardini
Zhi Cao
Louis Carpentier
Alessio Cascione
Lilia Chebbah
Meng Ding
Roberto Esposito
Alina Fastowski
Roger Ferrod
Michele Fontana
Chang Gong
Michal Grzejdziak-Zdziarski
Paul Hahn

Antonia Hain
Md Athikul Islam
Michael Ito
Philipp Jahn
Rahul Kumar
Bishal Lakha
Yuwen Liu
Jerry Lonlac
Shijie Luo
Francesca Naretto
Navid Nobani
Diego Coello de Portugal
Joana Santos
Francesco Scala
Richard Serrano
Nuno Silva
Francesco Spinnato

Pedro C. Vieira
Xiao Wang
Yunyun Wang
Qi Wen
Jianye Xie

Huaiyuan Yao
Yutong Ye
Obaidullah Zaland
Efstratios Zaradoukas
Nan Zhang

Sponsors

Diamond

Platinum

Organization

Gold

Silver

Bronze

Other Sponsors

Partners

Keynotes

Many Good Models Leads to ...

Cynthia Rudin

Duke University, USA

Abstract. As it turns out, many good models leads to amazing things! The Rashomon Effect, coined by Leo Breiman, describes the phenomenon that there exist many equally good predictive models for the same dataset.

This phenomenon happens for many real datasets, and when it does it sparks both magic and consternation, but mostly magic. In light of the Rashomon Effect, my collaborators and I propose to reshape the way we think about machine learning, particularly for tabular data problems in the nondeterministic (noisy) setting. I'll address how the Rashomon Effect impacts (1) the existence of simple-yet-accurate models, (2) flexibility to address user preferences, such as fairness and monotonicity, without losing performance, (3) uncertainty in predictions, fairness, and explanations, (4) reliable variable importance, (5) algorithm choice, specifically, providing advanced knowledge of which algorithms might be suitable for a given problem, and (6) public policy. I'll also discuss a theory of when the Rashomon Effect occurs and why: interestingly, noise in data leads to a large Rashomon Effect. My goal is to illustrate how the Rashomon Effect can have a massive impact on the use of machine learning for complex problems in society.

Towards Causal Artificial Intelligence

Elias Bareinboim

Columbia University, USA

Abstract. While a significant portion of AI scientists and engineers believe we are on the verge of achieving highly general forms of AI, I offer a critical appraisal of this view through a causal lens. In particular, building on foundational developments in the field, I will present my perspective on the relationship between intelligence and causality – and the central role of the latter in building intelligent systems and advancing credible data science.

I frame this discussion in terms of five core capabilities that we should expect from an intelligent AI system: performing causal reasoning and articulating explanations; making precise, surgical, and sample-efficient decisions; generalizing across changing conditions and environments; generating and simulating in a causally consistent manner; and learning causal structures and variables.

In this talk, I will elaborate on this perspective and share current progress toward building causally intelligent AI systems. A more detailed discussion of this thesis is provided in my forthcoming textbook, a draft of which is available here: https://causalai-book.net/.

Not Just a Trend: Institutionalizing XAI for Responsible and Compliant AI Systems

Francisco Herrera

Granada University, Spain

Abstract. As artificial intelligence (AI) systems increasingly mediate decisions in high-stakes domains – from healthcare and finance to public policy – the demand for explainable AI (XAI) has grown rapidly. Yet many current XAI approaches remain disconnected from the practical needs of stakeholders and the requirements of emerging regulatory frameworks. This talk argues that XAI must not be treated as a passing trend or optional technical add-on, but as a foundational principle in the design and deployment of AI systems. We critically examine the state of the field, exposing the gap between model-centric explainability and stakeholder-centric accountability. In response, we propose a framework that aligns explainability with legal, ethical, and social responsibilities, emphasizing co-design with affected users, sensitivity to institutional contexts, and governance over opacity. Our goal is to advance XAI from superficial compliance toward deeply integrated transparency that fosters trust, accountability, and responsible innovation.

Compositional Intelligence: Coordinating Multiple LLMs for Complex Tasks

Mirella Lapata

University of Edinburgh, UK

Abstract. Recent years have witnessed the rise of increasingly larger and more sophisticated language models (LMs) capable of performing every task imaginable, sometimes at (super)human level. In this talk, I will argue that in many realistic scenarios, solely relying on a single general-purpose LLM is suboptimal. A single LLM is likely to underrepresent real-world data distributions, heterogeneous skills, and task-specific requirements. Instead, I will discuss multi-LLM collaboration as an alternative to monolithic generative modeling. By orchestrating multiple LLMs, each with distinct roles, perspectives, or competencies, we can achieve more effective problem-solving while being more inclusive and explainable. I will illustrate this approach through two case studies: narrative story generation and visual question answering, showing how a society of agents can collectively tackle complex tasks while pursuing complementary subgoals. Additionally, I will explore how these agent societies leverage reasoning to improve performance.

Towards a Fairer World: Uncovering and Addressing Human and Algorithmic Biases

Nuria Oliver

ELLIS Alicante Foundation, Spain

Abstract. In my talk, I will first briefly present ELLIS Alicante1, the only ELLIS unit that has been created from scratch as a non-profit research foundation devoted to responsible AI for Social Good. Next, I will provide an overview of AI with a focus on the ethical implications and limitations of today's AI systems, including algorithmic discrimination and bias. On this topic, I will present a few examples of our work on uncovering and mitigating both human and algorithmic biases with AI.

On the human front, I will present the body of work that we have carried out in the context of AI-based beauty filters that are so popular on social media. On the algorithmic front, I will explain the main approaches to address algorithmic discrimination and I will present three novel methods to achieve fairer decisions.

Tensor Logic: A Simple Unification of Neural and Symbolic AI

Pedro Domingos

University of Washington, USA

Abstract. Deep learning has achieved remarkable successes in language generation and other tasks, but is extremely opaque and notoriously unreliable. Both of these problems can be overcome by combining it with the sound reasoning and transparent knowledge representation capabilities of symbolic AI. Tensor logic accomplishes this by unifying tensor algebra and logic programming, the formal languages underlying respectively deep learning and symbolic AI. Tensor logic is based on the observation that predicates are compactly represented Boolean tensors, and can be straightforwardly extended to compactly represent numeric ones. The two key constructs in tensor logic are tensor join and project, numeric operations that generalize database join and project. A tensor logic program is a set of tensor equations, each expressing a tensor as a series of tensor joins, a tensor project, and a univariate nonlinearity applied elementwise. Tensor logic programs can succinctly encode most deep architectures and symbolic AI systems, and many new combinations.

In this talk I will describe the foundations and main features of tensor logic, and present efficient inference and learning algorithms for it. A system based on tensor logic achieves state-of-the-art results on a suite of language and reasoning tasks. How tensor logic will fare on trillion-token corpora and associated tasks remains an open question.

Artificial Intelligence for Science

Sašo Džeroski

Jožef Stefan Institute, Slovenia

Abstract. Artificial intelligence is already transforming science, with its future impact expected to be even greater. Realizing this potential requires addressing key scientific challenges, such as ensuring explainability (of models and their predictions), learning effectively from limited data, and integrating data with prior domain knowledge. It also requires the provision of support for open and reproducible science through formalizing and sharing scientific knowledge.

I will present an overview of my research on the development of AI methods suitable for use in science. These include methods for explainable machine learning – including multi-target prediction and relational learning – that deliver accurate yet interpretable models suitable for complex scientific domains. These methods have been applied in environmental science, life science and materials science. Learning from limited data is critical in science. I will discuss two complementary approaches: semi-supervised learning, which leverages unlabeled data directly, together with labeled data, and foundation models, which use representations learned from vast unlabeled data to support downstream tasks with minimal supervision, i.e., limited amounts of labeled data. Both paradigms expand AI's reach into data-scarce scientific problems.

I will then present our work on automated scientific modeling, where we learn interpretable models of dynamical systems – such as process-based models and differential equations – from time series data and domain knowledge. Finally, I will highlight the role of ontologies and semantic technologies in experimental computer science, including machine learning and optimization. In these areas, we have developed ontologies for the representation and annotation of both data and other artefacts produced by science, such as algorithms, models, and results of experiments.

Contents – Part III

Graph Neural Networks

MPG: An Efficient Multi-scale Point-Based GNN for Non-uniform Meshes 3
    Qinxin Wu, Pengwei Liu, Xingyu Ren, and Dong Ni

Unveiling the Hidden: Movie Genre and User Bias in Spoiler Detection 19
    Haokai Zhang, Shengtao Zhang, Zijian Cai, Heng Wang, Ruixuan Zhu, Zinan Zeng, and Minnan Luo

GraphJCL: A Dual-Perspective Graph-Based Framework for Urban Region Representation via Joint Contrastive Learning 37
    Yaya Zhao, Kaiqi Zhao, Zixuan Tang, Xiaoling Lu, Yuanyuan Zhang, and Yalei Du

Graphs and Networks

DiNgHy: Null Models for Non-degenerate Directed Hypergraphs 57
    Maryam Abuissa, Matteo Riondato, and Eli Upfal

The Densest SWAMP Problem: Subhypergraphs with Arbitrary Monotonic Partial Edge Rewards 75
    Vedangi Bengali, Nikolaj Tatti, Iiro Kumpulainen, Florian Adriaens, and Nate Veldt

How Useful Is Graph Pooling for Node-Level Tasks? 92
    Yijun Duan, Xin Liu, Steven Lynden, Akiyoshi Matono, and Qiang Ma

Community-Aware Graph Transformer: Preserving Community Semantics for Effective Global Aggregation 108
    Yutai Duan, Jie Liu, Jianhua Wu, and Jialin Liu

AB-STE: Adaptive Blended Gradient Estimation for Efficient Binarized Networks 125
    Siddharth Gupta and Akash Kumar

Memory-Enhanced Invariant Prompt Learning for Urban Flow Prediction Under Distribution Shifts 141
    Haiyang Jiang, Tong Chen, Wentao Zhang, Quoc Viet Hung Nguyen, Yuan Yuan, Yong Li, and Hongzhi Yin

EDN: A Novel Edge-Dependent Noise Model for Graph Data 160
   Pintu Kumar and Nandyala Hemachandra

DRNCS: Dual-Level Route Generation Model Based on Node Contraction
and Shortcuts 177
   Zhuoran Li, Yucen Gao, Yu Yin, Xinle Li, Hui Gao, Xiaofeng Gao, and Guihai Chen

GraphWeave : Interpretable and Robust Graph Generation via Random
Walk Trajectories 193
   Rahul Nandakumar and Deepayan Chakrabarti

Towards Deeper GCNs: Alleviating Over-Smoothing via Iterative Training
and Fine-Tuning 211
   Furong Peng, Jinzhen Gao, Xuan Lu, Kang Liu, Yifan Huo, and Sheng Wang

BotTrans: A Multi-source Graph Domain Adaptation Approach for Social
Bot Detection 228
   Boshen Shi, Yongqing Wang, Fangda Guo, Jiangli Shao, Huawei Shen, and Xueqi Cheng

Efficient Approximate Temporal Triangle Counting in Streaming
with Predictions 244
   Giorgio Venturin, Ilie Sarpe, and Fabio Vandin

Backdoor Attacks on Graph Classification via Data Augmentation
and Dynamic Poisoning 263
   Yadong Wang, Zhiwei Zhang, Pengpeng Qiao, Ye Yuan, and Guoren Wang

Healthcare and Bioinformatics

A CNN-Based Local-Global Self-attention via Averaged Window
Embeddings for Hierarchical ECG Analysis 283
   Arthur Buzelin, Pedro Dutenhefner, Turi Rezende, Luisa G. Porfirio, Pedro Bento, Yan Aquino, Jose Fernandes, Caio Santana, Gabriela Miana, Gisele L. Pappa, Antonio Ribeiro, and Wagner Meira Jr.

Uncertainty-Aware Metabolic Stability Prediction with Dual-View
Contrastive Learning 300
   Peijin Guo, Minghui Li, Hewen Pan, Bowen Chen, Yang Wu, Zikang Guo, Leo Yu Zhang, Shengshan Hu, and Shengqing Hu

Stable Vision Concept Transformers for Medical Diagnosis 317
  Lijie Hu, Songning Lai, Yuan Hua, Shu Yang, Jingfeng Zhang, and Di Wang

Gx2Mol: De Novo Generation of Hit-Like Molecules from Gene
Expression Profiles 333
  Chen Li and Yoshihiro Yamanishi

Alternate Geometric and Semantic Denoising Diffusion for Protein Inverse
Folding 350
  Chenglin Wang, Yucheng Zhou, Zhe Wang, Zijie Zhai, Jianbing Shen, and Kai Zhang

Images and Computer Vision

Self-generated Cross-Modal Prompt Tuning 369
  Guiming Cao, Zonghan Wu, Huan Huo, Yuming Ou, and Guandong Xu

Quality-Preserving Extreme Image Compression: Using Interpretable
Conditioning Inputs with Diffusion Models 387
  Shayan Ali Hassan, Danish Humair, Ihsan Ayyub Qazi, and Zafar Ayyub Qazi

Beyond General Edge Utilization: Edge Attention Mean Teacher
for Semi-Supervised Medical Image Segmentation 405
  Kaiwei Sun, Luhan Wang, and Jin Wang

Interpretability and Explainability

Queryable and Interpretable PU Learning Through Probabilistic Circuits 425
  Sieben Bocklandt, Vincent Derkinderen, Koen Vanderstraeten, Wouter Pijpops, Kurt Jaspers, Luc De Raedt, and Wannes Meert

Interpretable Hybrid-Rule Temporal Point Processes 443
  Yunyang Cao, Juekai Lin, Hongye Wang, Wenhao Li, and Bo Jin

SVEBI: Towards the Interpretation and Explanation of Spiking Neural
Networks 460
  Jasper De Laet, Hamed Behzadi-Khormouji, Lucas Deckers, and Jose Oramas

Towards Better Generalization and Interpretability in Unsupervised Concept-Based Models 478
    Francesco De Santis, Philippe Bich, Gabriele Ciravegna, Pietro Barbiero, Tania Cerquitelli, and Danilo Giordano

Tree-Based OWL Class Expression Learner over Large Graphs 495
    Caglar Demir, Moshood Yekini, Michael Röder, Yasir Mahmood, and Axel-Cyrille Ngonga Ngomo

Smooth InfoMax - Towards Easier Post-Hoc Interpretability 512
    Fabian Denoodt, Bart de Boer, and José Oramas

Conformalized Exceptional Model Mining: Telling Where Your Model Performs (Not) Well 528
    Xin Du, Sikun Yang, Wouter Duivesteijn, and Mykola Pechenizkiy

Author Index 545

Graph Neural Networks

MPG: An Efficient Multi-scale Point-Based GNN for Non-uniform Meshes

Qinxin Wu, Pengwei Liu, Xingyu Ren, and Dong Ni(✉)

Zhejiang University, Hangzhou, Zhejiang 310027, China
{22360247,liupw,12332063,dni}@zju.edu.cn

Abstract. Graph Neural Networks (GNNs) have become a powerful tool for modeling complex physical simulations, leveraging their ability to learn from irregular data representations. However, non-uniform meshes introduce significant challenges, particularly in adaptive multi-scale sampling, topological reconstruction, and efficient feature aggregation, often leading to high computational costs. Existing methods struggle to balance efficiency and accuracy due to their inability to dynamically adapt to irregular mesh structures. To address these limitations, we introduce Multi-Scale Point-Based Graph Neural Networks (MPG), a framework that combines point-cloud downsampling with topology-constrained strategies. MPG employs density-aware hierarchical sampling to adaptively retain critical nodes while leveraging a learnable neighborhood aggregation mechanism to enhance local structural sensitivity. Additionally, we introduce adaptive Constrained Delaunay reconstruction, which preserves global topology by eliminating invalid edges and maintaining boundary constraints during coarsening. To further improve efficiency, our model integrates lightweight residual MLPs, enabling scalable dimensions on multi-scale features. MPG's architecture supports dynamic multi-scale compression across diverse physical domains. Evaluations on fluid dynamics, thermochemical reactions, and cavity flow demonstrate that MPG reduces parameter count by at least 84.5% and accelerates training by 17.7% $\sim$ 86.1% per epoch compared to baseline models, while maintaining high single-step rollout accuracy (RMSE$< 10^{-2}$). These results establish MPG as a new benchmark for efficient and accurate simulations on non-uniform meshes, offering a versatile solution for complex physical systems.

Keywords: Non-uniform meshes · Multi-scale · Graph Neural Networks · Physical simulation · Surrogate model

1 Introduction

Non-uniform meshes are widely used in computational fluid dynamics (CFD) and other physics-based simulations, as they enhance accuracy in high-gradient regions and complex geometries. However, their irregular structure poses significant challenges for feature extraction and efficient computation. Traditional numerical solvers, such as finite difference methods [1] and finite element methods [2], provide accurate solutions but suffer from high computational costs, particularly in large-scale or real-time applications. To improve efficiency, data-driven methods have been explored for mesh-based simulations [3–5]. For example, convolutional neural networks (CNNs) leverage local receptive fields and weight sharing, making them effective for structured data [6–8]. However, their reliance on uniform grids necessitates resampling non-uniform meshes, leading to information loss and artificial smoothing. Moreover, CNNs struggle to capture the topological relationships inherent in non-uniform meshes, limiting their ability to model connectivity-dependent physical interactions.

Graph-based neural networks (GNNs) offer a more flexible framework for modeling complex physical systems [9]. By employing edge-node message passing (MP), GNNs can effectively capture local node interactions without the constraints of grid-based representations. As a result, they have been successfully applied to fluid dynamics [10], solid mechanics [11], and multi-physics coupling [12]. Among these, MeshGraphNets [10] stands out as a foundational end-to-end framework, demonstrating the potential of GNNs in mesh-based simulations. However, GNNs face notable challenges in large-scale simulations, including quadratic complexity in message passing [13] and feature oversmoothing [14], which hinder their scalability and accuracy.

To overcome the limitations of standard GNNs, multi-scale GNNs have been introduced to improve computational efficiency and enable hierarchical feature extraction [12, 15–18]. These models construct coarse sub-level graphs to enable longer-range interactions and reduce MP iterations. However, existing methods face challenges in preserving graph connectivity during coarsening. Current methods primarily rely on spatial proximity [17–19], learnable sampling [15], manual mesh partitioning [13, 16], algebraic multigrid algorithms [20], and automated bi-stride sampling [12], each with inherent limitations. Specifically, learnable or random sampling can introduce artificial partitions, hindering information exchange. Spatial proximity-based coarsening often generates incorrect edges, while algebraic multigrid algorithms suffer from cubic complexity. Bi-stride sampling preserves topology but lacks adaptability in feature dimension and sampling scale. Crucially, all these methods rely on deep MP stacks for information propagation, leading to high computational costs.

To overcome these limitations, we propose **MPG**, an efficient multi-scale GNN that integrates point-based feature extraction and graph-based topology preservation. MPG is designed to construct topology-preserving multi-scale graphs, enhance adaptive neighborhood aggregation, and achieve computational efficiency without deep MP stacking.

As illustrated in Fig. 1, MPG effectively coarsens non-uniform meshes while preserving key structural features. By combining hierarchical density-based sampling, topology-constrained Delaunay reconstruction, and residual MLP-based feature extraction, MPG sets a new benchmark for scalable, high-fidelity sim-

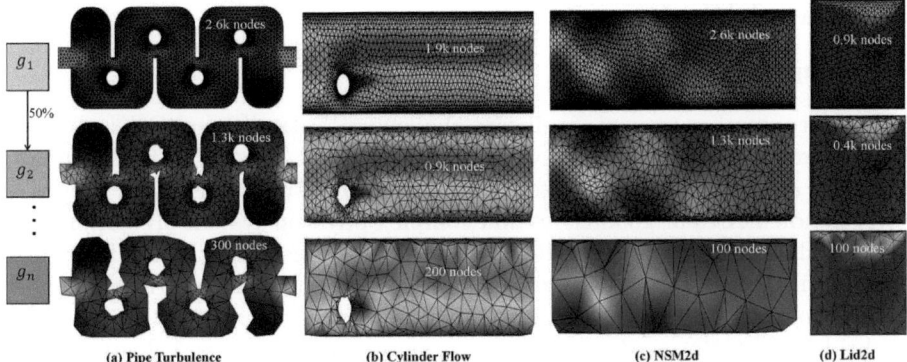

Fig. 1. Example multi-level graphs produced by our proposed method. The coarsening process is particularly challenging for non-uniform meshes with irregular structures, large holes, and non-convex regions. Our Multi-Scale Graph Construction strategy effectively maintains key features and ensures robust connectivity across arbitrary geometries.

ulations of complex physical systems. The contributions of the proposed MPG are summarized as follows:

- **Multi-scale Graph Construction Strategy**: MPG employs a hierarchical density-aware sampling strategy, inspired by point cloud geometric sampling. It applies random sampling in dense regions and farthest point sampling (FPS) in sparse regions to ensure balanced node distributions. To preserve global topology, we incorporate Constrained Delaunay Reconstruction, which prevents incorrect topological connections and ensures accurate edge reconstruction during coarsening. This strategy significantly improves graph connectivity and leads to higher predictive accuracy, achieving RMSE$< 10^{-2}$ across various physical simulation tasks.
- **Robust Neighborhood Aggregation**: Instead of relying on a fixed adjacency matrix, MPG leverages random multi-hop neighborhoods inspired by GraphSAGE [21] to improve local feature propagation. We introduce a learnable aggregation mechanism, dynamically adjusting neighbor importance to enhance adaptability across different resolutions. This approach reduces redundant computations while maintaining accuracy, leading to nearly 85% reduction in model parameters compared to conventional message-passing GNNs.
- **Computational Efficiency and Scalability**: Unlike conventional multi-scale GNNs that rely on deep MP stacking, MPG employs a hierarchical residual MLP-based feature extraction framework, inspired by point cloud feature extraction modules [22]. This design allows MPG to scale independently of mesh size, reducing redundant feature transformations while maintaining accuracy. Experimental results show that MPG accelerates training by 17.7% ∼ 86.1% per epoch compared to baseline models, while achieving competitive accuracy with significantly fewer parameters.

2 Related Work

2.1 Graph-Based Method

Non-uniform meshes present significant challenges for traditional CNNs, because of their irregular structures and varying connectivity. This limitation has motivated the adoption of graph-based methods, which treat meshes as graphs to better handle irregular geometries and complex physical system predictions [20]. Pfaff et al. introduced MeshGraphNets [10], demonstrating the effectiveness of GNNs in capturing both the geometric and topological information inherent in non-uniform meshes. Building on these insights, Zhao et al. proposed a hybrid CNN-GNN model to better capture connectivity and flow pathways within porous media [23]. Expanding the scope of GNN-driven modeling, Han et al. combined GNNs with transformers architectures to predict latent states in physics simulations [24]. Meanwhile, TIE [25] departs from traditional graph edges, simplifying the model and enhancing its capacity to capture spatial relationships through self-attention mechanisms. These works demonstrate the growing potential of hybrid Graph-based models, enhancing their ability to model complex physical systems with non-uniform meshes.

2.2 Multi-scale GNNs

While GNNs offer an effective means of handling non-uniform meshes, large-scale graphs can incur high computational costs. To address these challenges, multi-scale GNN frameworks have been proposed. Graph U-Net [15] first adapts the U-Net architecture to the graph domain by introducing learnable sampling and upsampling opeartions, whereas MS-GNN-Grid [17] relies on voxelization-based sampling, that leverages spatial coordinates for coarsening. However, depending solely on spatial positions and raw node features may be inadequate for accurately capturing the inherent complexity of non-uniform mesh distributions. To further refine multi-scale representations, Yang et al. introduced AMGNET [20], integrating multiple geometric algebra thchniques for mesh coarsening across different scales. Cao et al. proposed BSMS-GNN [12], which employs a two-step breadth-first search (BFS) sampling strategy to preserve vital local information.

2.3 Point Cloud-Based Method

Non-uniform meshes and point clouds share structural similarities, such as unstructured node distribution and geometric irregularity, making point cloud processing techniques relevant for mesh analysis. The primary challenge lies in developing effective feature aggregation operators, which can be categorized into local and global approaches [26]. Pioneering works like PointNet [27] introduced global feature aggregation using symmetric functions, while PointNet++ [28] extended this with hierarchical local feature learning. Subsequent methods, such as KPConv [29] and PointConv [30], further advanced local feature extraction through convolutions and density-adaptive techniques. A notable paradigm shift was demonstrated by Ma et al. [22] in their PointMLP framework, which achieved excellent performance using lightweight geometric affine modules within a residual structure, emphasizing that complex architectures are not always necessary for effective geometric reasoning. Inspired by these advancements, we propose leveraging multi-scale fusion and local feature learning techniques from point cloud processing to enhance mesh node downsampling and improve local information capture.

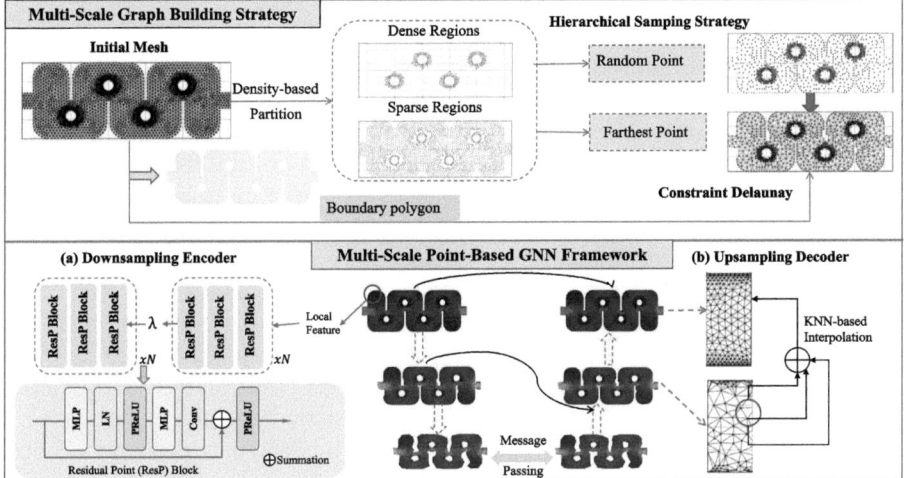

Fig. 2. A model overview of the Multi-Scale Point-Based GNN(MPG) framework. The top panel illustrates the initial mesh partitioning into dense and sparse regions, followed by constrained Delaunay reconstruction for topology preservation. The bottom panel depicts the hierarchical feature extraction and reconstruction process, utilizing lightweight residual MLPs and KNN-based interpolation for efficient multi-scale processing.

3 Multi-scale Graph Constructing

In this section, we will introduce the hierarchical density-based sampling strategy, constrained Delaunay reconstruction, and the corresponding neighborhood definition for local feature aggregation in Sect. 4. All algorithms and preprocessing steps here are completed in one pass, and we can flexibly adjust the sampling ratio of each layer, the proportion between different density regions, and the fixed sizes of neighbor nodes for different physical simulations scenarios.

3.1 Problem Formulation

Multi-scale graph construction aims to generate hierarchical representations of complex systems while preserving essential distribution characteristics and topological structure. For non-uniform meshes, this process involves node selection, feature aggregation, and edge reconstruction, all of which must balance computational efficiency and physical accuracy. An ideal multi-scale graph representation should meet three key requirements: 1) Selected nodes should retain both local geometric details and global distribution characteristics, preserving key high-gradient regions. 2) Neighborhood aggregation: The model should efficiently extract and propagate local features, minimizing computational cost while adapting to variable mesh structures. 3) Edge reconstruction: Connectivity between coarse and fine graph layers must be structurally consistent, preventing incorrect edges that distort the underlying topology.

However, existing multi-scale GNN methods exhibit several limitations. Spatial proximity-based methods often generate incorrect edges across boundaries, distorting topological structures. Learnable sampling methods focus on locally important nodes, failing to capture global mesh distribution. Automated strategies, such as algebraic multigrid and bi-stride sampling, suffer from high computational complexity and limited adaptability in adjusting multi-scale resolutions.

To address these challenges, we propose a Multi-Scale Graph Construction strategy that integrates hierarchical density-based sampling, topology-aware edge reconstruction, and efficient neighborhood aggregation. As illustrated in Fig. 2(top panel), our approach first partitions the input mesh into dense and sparse regions based on local geometric and topological properties. It then applies adaptive sampling techniques to preserve both local details and global structure described in Sect. 3.2. To prevent incorrect topology, we incorporate a Constrained Delaunay edge reconstruction strategy in Sect. 3.4, ensuring smooth transitions between scales. The overall process is formalized in Algorithm 1, which outlines the hierarchical mesh coarsening procedure with Delaunay triangulation.

3.2 Hierarchical Density-Based Sampling Strategy

To simplify non-uniform meshes while preserving geometric and topological fidelity, we introduce a density-based hierarchical sampling strategy. This method classifies mesh regions into dense and sparse regions based on local node degree and average edge length metrics. Nodes in dense regions, characterized by high geometric complexity or sharp gradients, require fine-grained sampling to preserve local features, while sparse regions are coarsened to maintain global structure with reduced computational costs. Given a non-uniform mesh $\mathcal{M} = (\mathcal{V}, \mathcal{E})$, we first compute the global average edge length:

$$\bar{l} = \frac{1}{|\mathcal{E}|} \sum_{e=(u,v)\in\mathcal{E}} \|x_u - x_v\|, \tag{1}$$

where $\|x_u - x_v\|$ denotes the Euclidean distance between nodes u and v. Edges longer than $\bar{l}$ are removed to filter out incorrect long-range connections, creating a refined edge set $\mathcal{E}' = \{e \mid l(e) \leq \bar{l}\}$. On the updated graph $\mathcal{M}' = (\mathcal{V}, \mathcal{E}')$, we recalculate node degrees to determine local density:

$$\bar{d} = \frac{1}{n} \sum_{v \in \mathcal{V}} |\mathcal{N}'(v)|, \qquad (2)$$

Algorithm 1. Hierarchical Mesh Coarsening with Constrained Delaunay Triangulation

---
Require: Mesh $\mathcal{M}$, Positions $\mathbf{P}$, Levels L, Coarsening Ratios $\mathbf{U}$, Neighbor Counts $\mathbf{K}$
Ensure: Coarsened Meshes $\{\mathcal{M}_l\}_{l=1}^L$, Positions $\{\mathbf{P}_l\}_{l=1}^L$, Sampling Indices $\{\mathbf{I}_l\}_{l=1}^L$, Neighbor Indices $\{\mathbf{N}_l\}_{l=1}^L$ Initialize coarse mesh parameters;
1: **while** not converged **do**
2:     Sample nodes from mesh $\mathcal{M}$ based on ratio $\mathbf{U}$;
3:     **for** each level $l = 1, \ldots, L$ **do**
4:        Generate sampling indices $\mathbf{I}_l$;
5:        Update positions $\mathbf{P}_l$;
6:        Construct coarse mesh $\mathcal{M}_l$ via Constrained Delaunay triangulation;
7:        Compute neighbor indices $\mathbf{N}_l$ using fixed-size $\mathbf{K}$;
8:     **end for**
9:     Update coarse mesh and parameters;
10: **end while**

---

where $n = |\mathcal{V}|$ denote the number of nodes in the mesh and $\mathcal{N}'(v)$ denote the set of neighbors of node v. Nodes are classified as $\mathcal{V}_d$ if $d'(v) > \bar{d}$, and $\mathcal{V}_s$ otherwise.

Given a coarsening ratio U (e.g., $U = 0.5$ for 50% downsampling) and a sampling proportion m for dense regions, we define the number of sampled nodes in dense and sparse regions as:

$$k_d = \lfloor U \cdot m \cdot n \rfloor, \quad k_s = \lfloor U \cdot (1-m) \cdot n \rfloor, \qquad (3)$$

where k_d and k_s represent the number of nodes sampled from dense and sparse regions, respectively. The combined sampled node set is then defined as:

$$\begin{cases} V_d = \{v_i \mid v_i \sim \mathcal{U}(\mathcal{V}_d)\}, & |V_d| = k_d, \\ V_s = \{v_i \mid v_i = \text{FPS}(\mathcal{V}_s)\}, & |V_s| = k_s, \end{cases} \qquad (3)$$

Here, $\mathcal{U}(\mathcal{V}_d)$ denotes random sampling from dense regions, and $\text{FPS}(\mathcal{V}_s)$ denotes farthest point sampling based on Euclidean distance. Finally, the full sampling set is $S_i = V_d \cup V_s$. As illustrated in Fig. 3, our hierarchical sampling strategy effectively distinguishes regions requiring detailed local representation from those reflecting global mesh structure, preserving critical geometric details and avoiding errors during coarsening.

3.3 Neighborhood Definition

To reduce computational overhead and enhance local feature aggregation, we define fixed-size neighborhood structures. In traditional GNNs such as GCN [31],

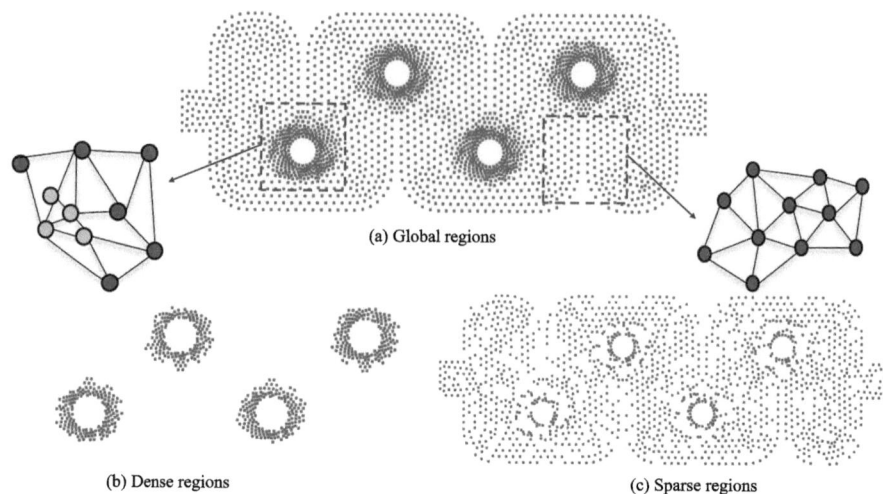

Fig. 3. Illustration of the hierarchical density-based sampling strategy applied to Pipe Turbulence.

stacking K message-passing layers causes each node to aggregate information from an increasingly large receptive field, potentially involving $O(d^K)$ nodes, where d is the node degree. While the per-layer complexity is linear in the number of edges, this cumulative growth increases per-node cost and can lead to over-smoothing.

Inspired by GraphSAGE [21], we instead sample a fixed number of neighbors S per node within 1-hop or 2-hop distance. This constrains the per-node cost to $O(K \cdot S)$ and the total model complexity to $O(K \cdot S \cdot n)$, where n is the number of nodes. Fixed-size neighborhoods improve scalability and ensure consistent computation across varying graph densities.

3.4 Constrained Delaunay Reconstruction

In graph-based mesh processing, accurate edge reconstruction at coarser scales is crucial for preserving geometric and topological integrity. Traditional methods rely on spatial proximity [17–19] or retain edges from sampled nodes [12], but often generate incorrect edges across boundaries, disrupting connectivity.

To address these issues, we propose an adaptive Constrained Delaunay Reconstruction method tailored for multi-scale edge reconstruction, inspired by classical computational geometry techniques that robustly handle non-convex domains and regions with holes [32]. Specifically, we leverage prior mesh information to define a polygonal boundary $\mathcal{B}$, encoding the original mesh's geometry and topology. Given a sampled node set (V'), we construct edges using standard Delaunay triangulation $T(V')$ and validate each candidate edge $e = (u, v)$ against the constraints:

$$E' = \{e \mid e \subseteq \mathcal{B}, e \in T(V')\}. \tag{4}$$

Only edges completely contained within the constrained polygonal region are retained. This ensures robust edge reconstruction, preventing invalid connections and preserving mesh quality.

4 Multi-scale Point-Based GNN(MPG)

In this section, we will introduce MPGNN, a hierarchical GNN where the multi-level structure has been determined by the input mesh and the preprocessing in Sect. 3.

4.1 Problem

Conventional GNNs and multi-scale GNNs rely heavily on stacked message passing (MP) layers to aggregate node and edge features:

$$h_v^{(k)} = \text{AGGREGATE}\left(\{h_u^{(k-1)}, e_{uv}^{(k-1)} \mid u \in \mathcal{N}(v)\}\right), \tag{5}$$

where $h_v^{(k)}$ is the embedding of node v at layer k, and $e_{uv}^{(k-1)}$ is the edge embedding between nodes u and v. However, stacking MP layers significantly increases computational complexity and redundancy, especially for large-scale non-uniform meshes. Additionally, the fixed high-dimensional embeddings (e.g., 128 dimensions) further exacerbate computational overhead.

Inspired by PointMLP [22], which achieves efficient feature extraction on point clouds without complex local operations, we revisit mesh feature learning. Non-uniform meshes structurally resemble point clouds; thus, heavy reliance on MP layers may be unnecessary. We aim to replace stacked MP layers with lightweight residual MLP modules, efficiently extracting node features and improving scalability.

4.2 Encoder

The input is multi-level mesh structure $\{\mathcal{M}_l = (\mathcal{V}_l, \mathcal{E}_l)\}_{l=1}^{L}$. For each mesh level, the encoding operation can be formulated as:

$$g_i = \Phi_{\text{pos}}\left(\mathcal{A}\left(\Phi_{\text{pre}}\left(\mathcal{V}_i, \mathcal{V}_{ij}\right)\right)\right), \tag{6}$$

where $\Phi_{\text{pre}}(\cdot)$ and $\Phi_{\text{pos}}(\cdot)$ represent residual MLP blocks adapted from PointMLP [22]. Specifically, $\Phi_{\text{pre}}(\cdot)$ learns initial node embeddings within local receptive fields, capturing preliminary geometric patterns. For neighborhood aggregation $\mathcal{A}$, we adopt a learnable weighting mechanism inspired by CNN receptive fields:

$$\mathcal{A}(f_i) = \sum_{j \in \mathcal{N}(i)} (W_{i,j} \cdot w_{ij}) \cdot f_j, \quad w_{ij} = \frac{\exp(-\|\mathbf{x}_i - \mathbf{x}_j\|_2)}{\sum_{k \in \mathcal{N}(i)} \exp(-\|\mathbf{x}_i - \mathbf{x}_k\|_2)}. \tag{7}$$

where f_j denotes neighbor features, W denotes learnable parameters, and w_{ij} dynamically adjusts neighbor importance based on spatial relationships.

Finally, the aggregated features are refined by another residual MLP block $\Phi_{\text{pos}}(\cdot)$. Formally, the residual MLP block can be expressed as:

$$\Phi(x) = act(W_2 \cdot act((W_1 \cdot x)))) + x, \tag{8}$$

where W_1 and W_2 are learnable parameters, act denotes nonlinear activation (e.g., PReLU).

By explicitly employing lightweight residual MLP-based feature extraction, the encoder effectively reduces computational overhead and improves dimension scalability. This design avoids deep message passing stacks, significantly enhancing efficiency and generalization on various non-uniform meshes.

4.3 Decoder

For decoder module, we adopt a k-nearest neighbor (KNN) interpolation to efficiently recover fine-level node features [27,28]. For each node x_i in the fine-layer X_f, we identify its k closest nodes from the coarse layer X_c based on Euclidean distance. The interpolated feature x_i is computed by distance-weighted averaging:

$$x_i = \sum_{j \in \mathcal{N}_k(i)} \frac{w_{ij} h_j}{\sum_{j \in \mathcal{N}_k(i)} w_{ij}}, \quad w_{ij} = \frac{1}{d(P_f^i, P_c^j)}, \tag{9}$$

where h_j denotes the coarse-layer feature of neighbor node j, and $d(P_f^i, P_c^j)$ denotes the Euclidean distance between fine-layer node i and coarse-layer node j.

Additionally, we incorporate skip-connections between corresponding encoder and decoder layers, facilitating efficient spatial information transfer. A residual MLP $\Phi(x)$ is further employed to refine interpolated features, enhancing reconstruction accuracy and ensuring structural consistency across mesh resolutions. This encoder-decoder architecture is specifically designed for static multi-scale feature reconstruction, providing a efficient foundation for temporal dynamics prediction in physical simulations.

5 Experiments

5.1 Experimental Setup

Datasets. We evaluate our MPG model on five datasets covering various physical domains: *Cylinder Flow* [14] simulates incompressible fluid flow around a cylinder. *Pipe Turbulence* [33] represents turbulent flow dynamicly within a complex pipe. *Thermochemical Reaction* [34] involves multi-physics complex model to simulate the flow, including fluid flow, heat transfer, mass transfer, and chemical reaction within a thermochemical heat-storage reactor. *Lid2d* [35] focus on incompressible lid-driven cavity flow with varying viscosity and boundary conditions. *NSM2d* [35] deals with incompressible fluid dynamics with complex boundary conditions and initial states.

Baselines. We benchmark MPG against five baselines. *MeshGraphNets* [10] is a foundational graph-based model for mesh representation, evaluated with noise injection(NI). *Graph U-Net* [15] employs learnable graph sampling within a U-Net architecture, specifically tailored to graph structure. *PointMLP* [22] is a purely point-based method for feature extraction without topology structure. *AMGNET* [20] integrates algebraic multigrid algorithms within GNNs graph coarsening. *BSMS-GNN* [12] introduces a novel bi-stride sampling strategy for multi-scale mesh representation. And to our knowledge, it's the current state-of-the-art (SOTA) model.

Evaluation Protocol. We evaluate MPG through two experiments: *1) Feature Reconstruction Evaluation:* We compare MPG with PointMLP, BSMS - GNN, and AMGNET on Cylinder Flow, Pipe Turbulence, and Thermochemical Reaction datasets. Based on multi-scale meshes $\{\mathcal{M}_l^t = (V_l^t, \mathcal{E}_l^t)\}_{l \in (1,L)}^{t \in (1,T)}$ (L multi-scale layers, T time steps), MPG encodes features via the Encoder and reconstructs via the Decoder. *2) Rollout Evaluation:* To assess MPG's generalization in non-uniform mesh simulations, we conduct rollout experiments on long-trajectory Cylinder Flow, Lid2d, and NSM2d datasets with MeshGraphNets, AMGNET, and BSMS-GNN. As MPG focuses on feature reconstruction without explicit temporal modeling, we use BSMS-GNN's Message Passing layer for prediction from $\mathcal{M}_l^t$ to $\mathcal{M}_l^{t+1}$. Both MPG and BSMS-GNN use two multi-scale layers with a fixed 50% downsampling ratio per layer.

In training process, we use both the L2 loss (Eq. (10)) for model optimization. In feature reconstruction, y is from the original $\mathcal{M}_0^t$ and $\hat{y}$ from the reconstructed one. In rollout, y is the ground truth of $\mathcal{M}_l^{t+1}$ and $\hat{y}$ its prediction. For evaluation, RMSE is the primary metric.

$$L_{l2} = \frac{1}{D}\sum_{k=1}^{D}\frac{1}{T}\sum_{t=1}^{T}\frac{1}{m}\sum_{i=1}^{m}\frac{\|y_{k,i}^t - \hat{y}_{k,i}^t\|_2}{\|y_{k,i}^t\|_2} \qquad (10)$$

5.2 Results and Discussion

According to the description of Sect. 5.1, we evaluate in two distinct tasks: feature reconstruction and rollout prediction. The key observations from these evaluations are summarized as follows:

Feature Reconstruction Accuracy. Table 1 summarizes the RMSE results for the feature reconstruction task conducted on Cylinder Flow, Pipe Turbulence, and Thermochemical Reaction datasets. All models demonstrate good reconstruction performance (RMSE< 10^{-3}), while MPG achieves comparable or better accuracy. This highlights that our proposed multi-scale encoding strategy effectively captures essential geometric and physical features, despite using significantly fewer parameters.

Table 1. Feature Reconstruction RMSE ($\times 10^{-4}$) comparison on three datasets. Lower is better. Best result highlighted in bold.

Model	Cylinder Flow	Pipe Turbulence	Thermochemical Reaction
PointMLP	52.50	60.52	109.45
AMGNET	15.76	17.63	22.17
BSMS-GNN	3.23	3.32	3.96
MPG (ours)	**2.72**	**1.74**	3.94

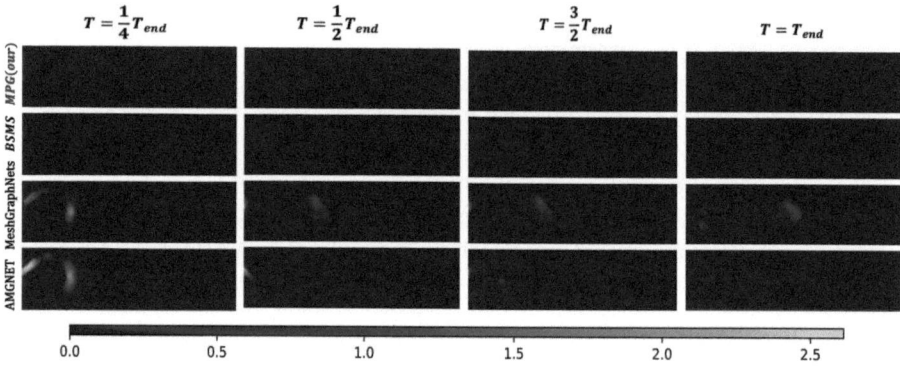

Fig. 4. Rollout Error Snapshots of MeshGraphNets, AMGNET, BSMS, and Our Proposed Model (MPG) on the NSM2d Dataset.

Rollout Prediction and Error Accumulation. For the rollout prediction task (Table 2), conducted on Cylinder Flow, Lid2d, and NSM2d datasets, our MPG model exhibits notably lower error accumulation over the trajectory compared to baselines, particularly on complex mesh structures. Even though single-step prediction errors for Cylinder Flow and NSM2d are similar to BSMS-GNN, MPG achieves these results with approximately only 15% of its parameter count. Figure 4 illustrates the error accumulation over the trajectory for different models, emphasizing the superior performance of MPG in maintaining lower error rates over time.

Computational Efficiency. Notably, the statistics for training and inference time exclude the multi-scale construction, which acts as an independent preprocessing module. As summarized in Table 2, MPG achieves significant improvements in computational efficiency. Specifically, our method reduces training time per epoch by 63.1–86.1% compared to BSMS-GNN, 17.7%–65.3% compared to MeshGraphNets, and 45.0%–73.8% compared to AMGNET across different datasets. Additionally, MPG exhibits a substantial reduction in inference time in the Cylinder Flow and Lid2d datasets. Regarding memory usage, MPG requires less memory than MeshGraphNets and BSMS-GNN. MPG also maintains a lightweight model size, reducing the parameter count by **87.3%** compared to MeshGraphNets and **84.5%** compared to BSMS-GNN. Even compared to the most parameter-efficient AMGNET model, MPG strikes a better balance between model size and predictive accuracy, as AMGNET's extreme parameter reduction leads to higher rollout errors. These gains are enabled by MPG's hierarchical multi-scale construct strategy, adaptive neighborhood aggregation, and lightweight residual MLP framework, establishing it as a new benchmark for scalable and efficient simulations on non-uniform meshes. In summary, the proposed MPG framework demonstrates superior efficiency and accuracy, effectively balancing model compactness, training speed, and predictive performance, setting a new standard for efficient multi-scale GNN simulations.

Table 2. Performance comparison on Rollout Task. Best results are in **bold**, second-best results are underlined.

Measurements	Case	MPG (Ours)	MeshGraphNets	BSMS	AMGNET
RMSE-1 ($\times 10^{-3}$)	Cylinder Flow	4.98	7.98	**4.09**	9.71
	Lid2d	**0.26**	1.22	0.35	0.95
	NSM2d	5.75	23.50	**5.46**	45.9
RMSE-50 ($\times 10^{-2}$)	Cylinder Flow	**3.71**	5.05	4.56	7.34
	Lid2d	**0.95**	4.66	1.13	1.76
	NSM2d	**15.81**	21.19	20.29	18.24
RMSE-all ($\times 10^{-2}$)	Cylinder Flow	**53.16**	63.95	57.27	62.82
	Lid2d	**7.15**	12.04	8.76	9.61
	NSM2d	**30.07**	35.33	33.34	32.49
Training time (s/epoch)	Cylinder Flow	**160.83**	209.26	435.49	440.08
	Lid2d	**140.13**	403.52	647.49	254.96
	NSM2d	**148.71**	180.61	1071.72	568.16
Inference time (ms/step)	Cylinder Flow	**14.13**	16.74	67.45	56.76
	Lid2d	**9.54**	12.42	72.76	10.42
	NSM2d	17.99	**17.88**	136.59	59.14
Training RAM (MiB)	Mean	8964	22583	12572	**6882**
Params (#)	All	296,755	2,331,778	1,917,442	**7,168**

5.3 Ablation Study

Network Details Study. We investigate how network depth and sampling ratios influence reconstruction performance, as illustrated in Fig. 5(a). Specifically, we analyze two key aspects: 1) varying the number of coarse-graining layers while keeping the overall sampling ratio fixed, 2) adjusting the sampling ratios within a fixed two-layer structure. Results demonstrate that a two-layer structure consistently yields better reconstruction accuracy compared to deeper

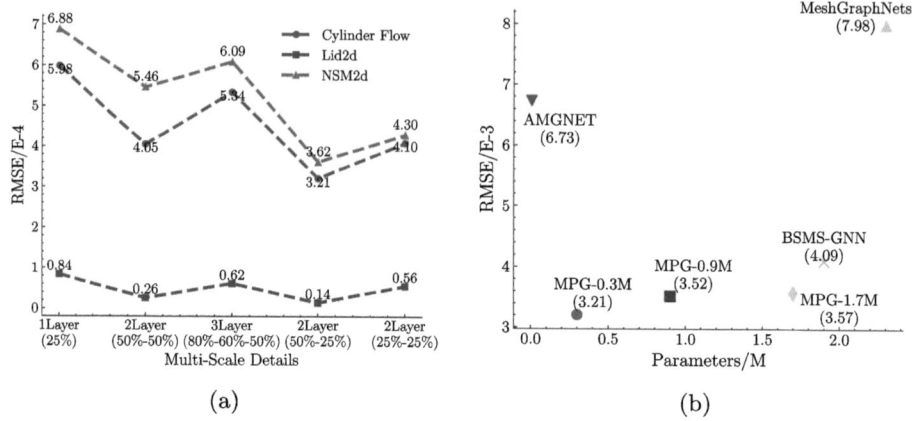

Fig. 5. (a) RMSE across different datasets under varying multi-scale settings. (b) RMSE across different hidden state dimensions with various parameters.

hierarchical designs. Furthermore, within the two-layer setting, a 50%-25% sampling ratio slightly outperforms the standard 50%-50% ratio, which used for fair and direct comparisons with some fix-size baselines in main experiments.

Parameter Study. We further evaluate how parameters influence MPG's reconstruction accuracy. Figure 5(b) demonstrates that MPG achieves better accuracy and computational efficiency without relying on deep MP stacks. Notably, MPG consistently outperforms baseline models across all parameter scales, highlighting the effectiveness of our design even at smaller model sizes.

6 Conclusion

In this work, we introduced MPG, a novel multi-scale point-based GNN designed for efficient and accurate simulation on non-uniform meshes. MPG integrates hierarchical density-based sampling, constrained Delaunay reconstruction, and lightweight feature aggregation to balance computational efficiency and predictive accuracy. By drawing inspiration from point cloud processing and constrained Delaunay triangulation, MPG constructs robust multi-scale representations while preserving essential geometric and topological structures. Experimental results demonstrate that MPG significantly reduces computational overhead, achieving up to 86.1% faster training, lower inference time, and reduced memory consumption, while maintaining high single-step rollout accuracy across each tasks. These results highlight MPG as an efficient and scalable solution for non-uniform mesh simulations, enabling high-fidelity modeling of complex physical systems. Future work could focus on optimizing memory-efficient architectures to support training on even larger-scale meshes with higher resolution.

References

1. Wang, H., et al. Recent advances on machine learning for computational fluid dynamics: a survey. arXiv preprint arXiv:2408.12171 (2024)
2. Zienkiewicz, O.C., Taylor, R.L.: The Finite Element Method Set. Elsevier, Amsterdam (2005)
3. Obiols-Sales, O., Vishnu, A., Malaya, N., Chandramowliswharan, A.: Cfdnet: a deep learning-based accelerator for fluid simulations. In: Proceedings of the 34th ACM International Conference on Supercomputing, pp. 1–12 (2020)
4. Raissi, M., Perdikaris, P., Karniadakis, G.E.: Physics-informed neural networks: a deep learning framework for solving forward and inverse problems involving nonlinear partial differential equations. J. Comput. Phys. **378**, 686–707 (2019)
5. Sun, L., Gao, H., Pan, S., Wang, J.-X.: Surrogate modeling for fluid flows based on physics-constrained deep learning without simulation data. Comput. Methods Appl. Mech. Eng. **361**, 112732 (2020)
6. Tompson, J., Schlachter, K., Sprechmann, P., Perlin, K.: Accelerating eulerian fluid simulation with convolutional networks. In: International Conference on Machine Learning, pp. 3424–3433. PMLR (2017)
7. Kim, B., Azevedo, V.C., Thuerey, N., Kim, T., Gross, M., Solenthaler, B.: Deep fluids: a generative network for parameterized fluid simulations. In: Computer Graphics Forum, vol. 38, pp. 59–70. Wiley Online Library (2019)
8. Fotiadis, S., Pignatelli, E., Valencia, M.L., Cantwell, C., Storkey, A., Bharath, A.A.: Comparing recurrent and convolutional neural networks for predicting wave propagation. arXiv preprint arXiv:2002.08981 (2020)
9. Battaglia, P.W., et al.: Relational inductive biases, deep learning, and graph networks. arXiv preprint arXiv:1806.01261 (2018)
10. Pfaff, T., Fortunato, M., Sanchez-Gonzalez, A., Battaglia, P.W.: Learning mesh-based simulation with graph networks. arXiv preprint arXiv:2010.03409 (2020)
11. Sanchez-Gonzalez, A., Godwin, J., Pfaff, T., Ying, R., Leskovec, J., Battaglia, P.: Learning to simulate complex physics with graph networks. In: International Conference on Machine Learning, pp. 8459–8468. PMLR (2020)
12. Cao, Y., Chai, M., Li, M., Jiang, C.: Efficient learning of mesh-based physical simulation with bi-stride multi-scale graph neural network. In: International Conference on Machine Learning, pp. 3541–3558. PMLR (2023)
13. Fortunato, M., Pfaff, T., Wirnsberger, P., Pritzel, A., Battaglia, P.: Multiscale meshgraphnets. arXiv preprint arXiv:2210.00612 (2022)
14. Chen, F., Wang, Y.C., Wang, B., Kuo, C.C.J.: Graph representation learning: a survey. APSIPA Trans. Signal Inf. Process. **9**, e15 (2020)
15. Gao, H., Ji, S.: Graph u-nets. In: International Conference on Machine Learning, pp. 2083–2092. PMLR (2019)
16. Liu, W., Yagoubi, M., Schoenauer, M.: Multi-resolution graph neural networks for PDE approximation. In: Farkaš, I., Masulli, P., Otte, S., Wermter, S. (eds.) ICANN 2021. LNCS, vol. 12893, pp. 151–163. Springer, Cham (2021). https://doi.org/10.1007/978-3-030-86365-4_13

17. Lino, M., Fotiadis, S., Bharath, A.A., Cantwell, C.D.: Multi-scale rotation-equivariant graph neural networks for unsteady Eulerian fluid dynamics. Phys. Fluids **34**(8), 087110 (2022)
18. Lino, M., Cantwell, C., Bharath, A.A., Fotiadis, S.: Simulating continuum mechanics with multi-scale graph neural networks. arXiv preprint arXiv:2106.04900 (2021)
19. Lino, M., Fotiadis, S., Bharath, A.A., Cantwell, C.: Towards fast simulation of environmental fluid mechanics with multi-scale graph neural networks. arXiv preprint arXiv:2205.02637 (2022)
20. Yang, Z., Dong, Y., Deng, X., Zhang, L.: Amgnet: multi-scale graph neural networks for flow field prediction. Connect. Sci. **34**(1), 2500–2519 (2022)
21. Hamilton, W., Ying, Z., Leskovec, J.: Inductive representation learning on large graphs. Adv. Neural Inf. Process. Syst. **30**, 1–11 (2017)
22. Ma, X., Qin, C., You, H., Ran, H., Fu, Y.: Rethinking network design and local geometry in point cloud: a simple residual mlp framework. arXiv preprint arXiv:2202.07123 (2022)
23. Zhao, Q., Han, X., Guo, R., Chen, C.: A computationally efficient hybrid neural network architecture for porous media: integrating convolutional and graph neural networks for improved property predictions (2023)
24. Han, X., Gao, H., Pfaff, T., Wang, J.X., Liu, L.P.: Predicting physics in mesh-reduced space with temporal attention. arXiv preprint arXiv:2201.09113 (2022)
25. Shao, Y., Loy, X.X., Dai, B.: Transformer with implicit edges for particle-based physics simulation. In: European Conference on Computer Vision, pp. 549–564. Springer, Heidelberg (2022)
26. Zhang, H., et al.: Deep learning-based 3d point cloud classification: a systematic survey and outlook. Displays **79**, 102456 (2023)
27. Qi, C.R., Su, H., Mo, K., Guibas, L.J.: Pointnet: deep learning on point sets for 3d classification and segmentation. In: Proceedings of the IEEE Conference on Computer Vision and Pattern Recognition, pp. 652–660 (2017)
28. Qi, C.R., Yi, L., Su, H., Guibas, L.J.: Pointnet++: deep hierarchical feature learning on point sets in a metric space. Adv. Neural Inf. Process. Syst. **30**, 1–10 (2017)
29. Thomas, H., et al.: Kpconv: flexible and deformable convolution for point clouds. In: Proceedings of the IEEE/CVF International Conference on Computer Vision, pp. 6411–6420 (2019)
30. Wu, W., Qi, Z., Fuxin, L.: Pointconv: deep convolutional networks on 3d point clouds. In: Proceedings of the IEEE/CVF Conference on Computer Vision and Pattern Recognition, pp. 9621–9630 (2019)
31. Yao, L., Mao, C., Luo, Y.: Graph convolutional networks for text classification. In: Proceedings of the AAAI Conference on Artificial Intelligence, vol. 33, pp. 7370–7377 (2019)
32. Chew, L.P.: Constrained delaunay triangulations. In: Proceedings of the Third Annual Symposium on Computational Geometry, pp. 215–222 (1987)
33. Chen, G., Liu, X., Meng, Q., Chen, L., Liu, C., Li, Y.: Learning neural operators on riemannian manifolds. arXiv preprint arXiv:2302.08166 (2023)
34. Xiao, G., Wang, Z., Ni, D., Zhu, P.: Kinetics and structural optimization of cobalt-oxide honeycomb structures based on thermochemical heat storage. Energies **16**(7), 3237 (2023)
35. Liu, P., Hao, Z., Ren, X., Yuan, H., Ren, J., Ni, D.: Papm: a physics-aware proxy model for process systems. arXiv preprint arXiv:2407.05232 (2024)

Unveiling the Hidden: Movie Genre and User Bias in Spoiler Detection

Haokai Zhang[1], Shengtao Zhang[1], Zijian Cai[2], Heng Wang[3], Ruixuan Zhu[1], Zinan Zeng[1], and Minnan Luo[3,4](✉)

[1] Institute of Artificial Intelligence and Robotics, Xi'an Jiaotong University, Xi'an 710049, China
{zhanghaokai,zhangst,1760865856,2194214554}@stu.xjtu.edu.cn
[2] Institute of Automation, Chinese Academy of Sciences, Beijing 100190, China
caizijian2024@ia.ac.cn
[3] School of Computer Science and Technology, Xi'an Jiaotong University, Xi'an 710049, China
wh2213210554@stu.xjtu.edu.cn, minnluo@xjtu.edu.cn
[4] Shaanxi Province Key Laboratory of Big Data Knowledge Engineering, Xi'an Jiaotong University, Xi'an 710049, China

Abstract. Spoilers in movie reviews are important on platforms like IMDb and Rotten Tomatoes, offering benefits and drawbacks. They can guide some viewers' choices but also affect those who prefer no plot details in advance, making effective spoiler detection essential. Existing spoiler detection methods mainly analyze review text, often overlooking the impact of movie genres and user bias, limiting their effectiveness. To address this, we analyze movie review data, finding genre-specific variations in spoiler rates and identifying that certain users are more likely to post spoilers. Based on these findings, we introduce a new spoiler detection framework called GUSD (**G**enre-aware and **U**ser-specific **S**poiler **D**etection), which incorporates genre-specific data and user behavior bias. User bias is calculated through dynamic graph modeling of review history. Additionally, the R2GFormer module combines RetGAT (Retentive Graph Attention Network) for graph information and GenreFormer for genre-specific aggregation. The GMoE (Genre-Aware Mixture of Experts) model further assigns reviews to specialized experts based on genre. Extensive testing on benchmark datasets shows that GUSD achieves state-of-the-art results. This approach advances spoiler detection by addressing genre and user-specific patterns, enhancing user experience on movie review platforms. Our source code is available at https://github.com/AI-explorer-123/GUSD.

Keywords: Spoiler Detection · Movie Genre · User Bias · Mixture-of-Experts

H. Zhang and S. Zhang—Contributed equally to this work.

Supplementary Information The online version contains supplementary material available at https://doi.org/10.1007/978-3-032-06066-2_2.

1 Introduction

Spoilers in movie reviews have become an important component of the movie-viewing experience on popular platforms like IMDb and Rotten Tomatoes [5]. For those who hope to learn the plot of the movie in advance to judge whether they like it or not, the spoilers are helping, while for those who prefer to experience a movie without prior knowledge, the spoilers can severely diminish the enjoyment by revealing crucial plot points, undermining suspense, and eliciting negative emotions among viewers [21]. Thus, effective spoiler detection methods are crucial for maintaining a positive user experience (Fig. 1).

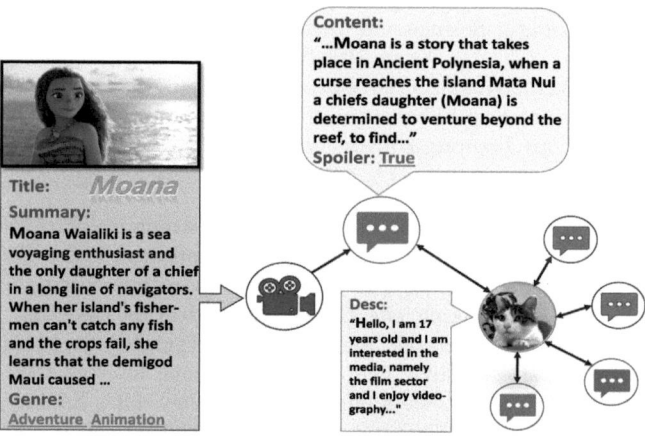

Fig. 1. An illustrative example of the data used in our spoiler detection study. The image shows a review of the movie *Moana*, including the movie's genres (Adventure, Animation), summary, the review's content, and user-specific details. All reviews from the user are color-coded: blue indicates non-spoiler content, while red indicates spoiler content.

Existing spoiler detection methods primarily focus on the textual content of reviews. For example, DNSD [6] integrates review sentences and movie genres, while SpoilerNet [36] utilizes a Hierarchical Attention Network and incorporates the item-specificity information. More recent approaches, such as MVSD [38], incorporate advanced techniques like syntax-aware graph neural networks and external movie knowledge to improve detection performance. Nevertheless, these methods still exhibit notable limitations. Solely relying on textual content proves insufficient for robust spoiler detection [38]. Moreover, spoilers are often genre-specific, with varying characteristics depending on the movie's genre—for instance, suspense films focus on plot details, whereas action films emphasize fight scenes. As a result, two significant challenges in spoiler detection remain unaddressed:

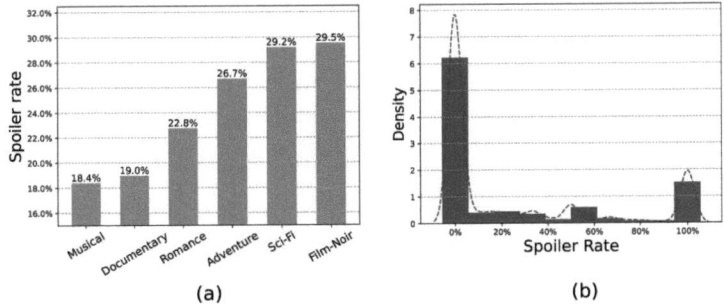

Fig. 2. (a) Spoiler rate across different movie genres (partial) in LCS dataset. (b) Kernel density estimation plot and distribution histogram of spoiler across different users.

- **Diverse Genres.** Previous works have largely ignored the impact of movie genres on the spoiler rate. Our analysis of the dataset indicates substantial differences in spoiler rate across genres, with specific categories defined according to IMDb standards. As shown in Fig. 2(a), movies that heavily rely on plot twists and suspense, such as Film-Noir and Adventure, are more prone to having spoilers in reviews compared to genres like Musical or Documentary. This is understandable since plot-driven movies tend to have more critical plot points that can be spoiled. This variation in spoiler rate demonstrates the importance of considering genre-specific characteristics when developing spoiler detection models. By incorporating genre information, we could better capture these differences and improve the performance of spoiler detection.
- **User-specific Behavior Bias.** User behavior varies significantly, with some users being more prone to posting spoilers than others. Our statistical analysis shows a clear trend where certain users tend to post spoiler reviews more frequently. As illustrated in Fig. 2(b), the graph of user spoiler rate distribution shows that a large proportion of users post very few spoilers, while a smaller, yet significant, group of users frequently post spoilers. This distribution indicates a noticeable user bias, highlighting that certain users are more likely to post spoilers than others. Leveraging these user-specific behavior bias can improve the detection performance by allowing models to adapt to user behavior bias.

To address the challenges of genre-specific spoiler tendencies and user bias in spoiler detection, we propose a comprehensive framework named GUSD (**G**enre-aware and **U**ser-specific **S**poiler **D**etection). This framework integrates genre information, user behavior bias, and global perception GNN. Our method begins with preprocessing movie, user, and review data. Then user bias is captured from review history through dynamic graph modeling. After that, the core component, R2GFormer (RetGAT and GenreFormer), which consists of RetGAT (Retentive Graph Attention Network) and GenreFormer, processes the graph information. RetGAT aggregates all the features globally, and GenreFormer enhances representation by integrating genre features, allowing for comprehensive genre-specific and cross-genre interactions. And an Aggregator combines these features, and then the GMoE (Genre-Aware Mixture of Experts) model assigns reviews to different experts based on their corresponding movie genres, improving traditional MoE model performance. Finally, a classifier performs spoiler detection using the aggregated features.

Extensive experiments show that GUSD achieves state-of-the-art performance. We also conduct robustness studies, ablation studies, and specific experiments on GMoE and user bias to validate our proposed modules' effectiveness.

Our main contributions are summarized as follows:

- We are the first to model the complex interactions between genre-specific information and long-term user review behaviors for spoiler detection, providing a nuanced approach by understanding genre-specific spoiler characteristics and leveraging user behavior bias.
- We propose the GUSD framework, a novel spoiler detection system that integrates several key components: the GenreFormer to capture genre-specific spoiler tendencies, the GMoE model to dynamically assign reviews based on genres, and dynamic graph modeling to capture user bias. This cohesive integration enhances overall accuracy and robustness.
- Our method GUSD achieves state-of-the-art performance in spoiler detection. Extensive experiments on two benchmark datasets demonstrate its robustness and effectiveness, showing superior performance across various conditions.

2 Related Work

2.1 Spoiler Detection

The goal of automatic spoiler detection is to identify spoilers in reviews from domains like television [3], books [36], and movies [3]. Existing approaches to spoiler detection can be broadly classified into three categories: keyword matching methods, machine learning techniques, and deep learning models.

Keyword Matching Methods. These approaches rely on a set of predefined keywords to identify spoilers. Examples include keywords related to sports teams or events [25], or actors' names [12]. Although useful in specific scenarios, this method requires manual keyword definition and lacks generalizability across different application contexts.

Machine Learning Techniques. These methods often involve topic modeling or support vector machines using handcrafted features. For example, Guo et al. [13] applied a bag-of-words representation combined with an LDA-based model for spoiler detection. Jeon et al. [16] developed an SVM classifier incorporating four extracted features, while Boyd et al. [3] utilized lexical features and meta-data of review subjects (e.g., movies and books) in an SVM model.

Deep Learning Models. These models mainly leverage NLP techniques, employing RNNs, LSTMs, Transformer, and language models to process review texts and movie information through end-to-end training. Bao et al. [2] utilized LSTMs, BERT, and RoBERTa for sentence-level spoiler detection. DNSD [6] focused on incorporating external genre information using GRU and CNN. SpoilerNet [36] introduced item-specificity and bias with bi-RNN enhanced by GRU. SDGNN [7] leveraged dependency relations between context words in sentences with graph neural networks to capture semantics.

While some existing methods incorporate genre information and user bias [6,40], they often rely on quite simple techniques such as concatenating or adding these additional features to the initial review features. Such approaches lack the sophistication needed for more effective and intricate modeling of genre features and user biases.

2.2 Mixture of Experts

The Mixture of Experts (MoE) approach, grounded in the Divide-and-Conquer principle, segments an input sample into sub-tasks and trains specialized experts for each sub-task. This method is extensively utilized in NLP to boost model capacity [33] and enhance reasoning capabilities [23]. Shazeer et al. [33] introduced a sparsely-gated Mixture-of-Experts layer, enabling conditional computing in large language models. Fedus et al. [10] developed simplified routing algorithms for MoE to enhance training stability and reduce computational costs. Furthermore, Soft-MoE [29] was introduced to mitigate issues like training instability and token dropping inherent in traditional MoE approaches.

Despite these advancements, traditional MoE methods assign tokens dynamically, which can cause incorrect token assignment, particularly when the dataset contains explicit category information such as movie genres and their associated reviews.

3 Methodology

Figure 3 shows the architecture of our proposed GUSD framework. This framework integrates genre-specific information, user behavior bias, and global receptive RetGAT for spoiler detection. Specifically, movie, user, and review data are first to be preprocessed, while user bias is extracted from review history using dynamic graph modeling. The R2GFormer component, consisting of RetGAT and GenreFormer, then processes graph features. RetGAT aggregates graph data, while GenreFormer handles genre-specific data. An Aggregator aggregates these features. The GMoE model assigns reviews to experts based on their related movie genres. Finally, a classifier utilizes the aggregated features to detect spoilers.

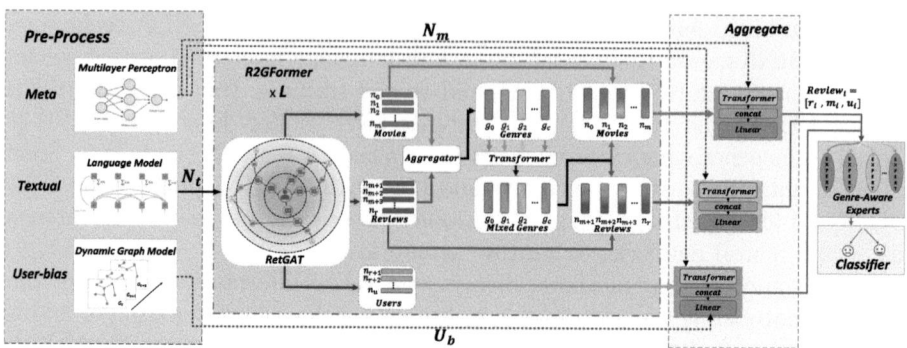

Fig. 3. Overview of our proposed GUSD framework, which integrates genre-specific information, user behavior bias, and global perceptive RetGAT for spoiler detection. It preprocesses movie, user, and review data with MLP and language models, and captures user bias via dynamic graph modeling. Then the data is processed by the R2GFormer component. An Aggregator merges these features, and then GMoE assigns reviews to experts based on genres. Finally, a classifier detects spoilers using the aggregated features.

3.1 Data Preprocessing

Meta Information. For review nodes, user nodes, and movie nodes, each type possesses metadata (details can be found in the supplementary material). After collecting the metadata for all three types of nodes, we pad them to the same length. A two-layer MLP is then employed as the meta encoder, producing the meta embeddings N_m.

Textual Information. The textual content is fundamental for effective spoiler detection. To generate high-quality embeddings, we leverage an LM as our text encoder. Specifically, we augment the initial textual content with the textual descriptions of the node's metadata. This augmentation enriches the embeddings by providing additional contextual information about the node. Subsequently, we employ the LM to encode the nodes' textual information. The encoded embeddings are then transformed using a single-layer MLP, producing refined embeddings N_t.

User Bias Acquisition Using Dynamic-Graph Pre-training. To better capture the dynamic information attributes of users, we adopt the dynamic graph to handle users' review history flexibly. Thus, we need to convert the static dataset into a dynamic format. We utilize the given connections between different nodes and the time information of the reviews to form the dynamic event stream. The details about the formation of the graph will be displayed in Sect. 3.2. Considering the absence of additional information about the dynamic edges, we simply initialize the edge features as zero vectors. Then, we employ the robust DyGFormer [42] as our dynamic graph encoder to capture the interactions among various nodes and utilize Link Prediction as the downstream task. We specifically obtain the features of user nodes as user bias U_b from the dynamic graph encoder.

3.2 R2GFormer

After acquiring the initial meta and textual features of the nodes, we use the textual features N_t, which include rich information about the nodes, as the initial embeddings $N_g^{(0)}$ for **R2GFormer**. This graph encoder not only models the complex relations and interactions between users, reviews, and movies but also handles features from different genres of the entire graph and captures remote dependencies. First, we will introduce how we construct the whole graph. Then, we decompose an R2GFormer layer into two parts: RetGAT and Genreformer, which will be introduced respectively.

Graph Construction. We first construct a directed graph consisting of three types of nodes: { *User, Review, Movie* } and the following three types of edges:

E1 : *Movie − Review* We connect a review node to a movie node if the review is about the movie, but not vice versa. This setup allows movie information to influence the review while ensuring that the review information does not affect the movie.

E2 : *Review − User* We connect a review node to a user node if the review is posted by the user.

E3 : *User − Review* We connect a user node to a review node if the user posts the review.

RetGAT. Inspired by the work of [9,26,34], we propose RetGAT, which extends the RetNet framework by integrating a global perception into GAT, incorporating explicit exponential decay for nodes within k hops and truncation for nodes beyond k hops. This method ensures a broad receptive field while balancing performance and computational complexity by dynamically adjusting the influence of nodes based on their distance, with closer nodes having a higher impact on the final node features.

To achieve this global receptive field, we utilize k parallel GAT layers to separately aggregate information from k-hop neighbors. For each layer, node features are aggregated from different k-hop neighborhoods, applying decay factors to control the influence of information from various hops. Beyond k hops, the influence of nodes is truncated to maintain computational efficiency and focus on relevant information within the k-hop range. Note that we correct the algorithm that previous work [1,37] used to compute k-hop neighbors, and the details are available in the supplementary material.

The decay factor δ_h for hop h ($h \leq k$) is defined as:

$$\delta_h = \exp(-\alpha \cdot h), \tag{1}$$

where α is a hyperparameter controlling the intensity of exponential decay. For the l-th layer, the contribution of the h-th hop neighbors is computed as:

$$N_{g,h}^{(l)} = \delta_h \cdot \text{GAT}_h^{(l)}(\mathcal{A}_h, N_g^{(l-1)}), \tag{2}$$

where $\mathcal{A}_h$ represents the adjacency matrix at the h-th hop, and $N_g^{(l-1)}$ denotes the input node features of the $(l-1)$-th layer.

The final node features $N_g^{(l)}$ for layer l are aggregated from all the k-hop contributions using an Aggregator function:

$$N_g^{(l)} = \text{AGGREGATOR}_r^{(l)}(N_{g,1}^{(l)}, N_{g,2}^{(l)}, \ldots, N_{g,h}^{(l)}, \ldots, N_{g,k}^{(l)}). \tag{3}$$

where $\text{AGGREGATOR}_r^{(l)}$ is the aggregator for RetGAT at the l-th layer, which can be summation, concatenation, or a TransformerEncoder (TRM).

Genreformer. After message passing among different k-hop neighbors, Genreformer aims to pay attention to the entire graph to extract more comprehensive features of different genres. First, the global genre-specific representation is obtained by aggregating the features of all the review and movie nodes belonging to the same genre in the l-th layer, which is as follows:

$$g_j^{(l)} = \text{AGGREGATOR}_g^{(l)}(\{n_{g,i}^{(l)} \mid i \in \mathcal{N}_j\}), \tag{4}$$

where $n_{g,i}^{(l)}$ is the feature of node i in the l-th layer, $\mathcal{N}_j$ denotes the set of nodes (both review and movie nodes) belonging to the j-th genre, and $\text{AGGREGATOR}_g^{(l)}$ is the aggregator of Genreformer in the l-th layer, which can be summation, concatenation, or a TRM.

Next, we use a TRM to facilitate inter-genre information interaction, allowing each genre to acquire information from similar genres to further enrich its features:

$$[g_1^{(l)} g_2^{(l)} \cdots g_j^{(l)} \cdots g_c^{(l)}] = \text{TRM}([g_1^{(l)} g_2^{(l)} \cdots g_j^{(l)} \cdots g_c^{(l)}]), \tag{5}$$

where c is the number of genres.

After interaction among genres, the genre features are fused with the movies and reviews nodes features. Then we incorporate the nodes with their genre features. Since some movies and reviews cover more than one genre, we take the average of the genre features a node covers. Subsequently, we concatenate the review or movie feature and its genre feature, then use an MLP to project it into the desired feature space, i.e.,

$$z_i^{(l)} = \text{MEAN}(\{g_j^{(l)} \mid j \in G_i\}), \tag{6}$$

$$n_{g,i}^{(l)} = \text{MLP}([n_{g,i}^{(l)} \parallel z_i^{(l)}]). \tag{7}$$

where G_i denotes the set of genres to which node i belongs, $n_{g,i}^{(l)}$ denotes the feature of node i in the l-th layer, $z_i^{(l)}$ is the aggregated genre feature for node i in the l-th layer, and $\|$ means concatenation. The MLP projects the concatenated feature into the desired feature space.

Overall Interaction. One layer of our proposed R2GFormer layer, however, cannot enable the information interaction between all information sources. In order to further facilitate the interaction among the nodes, we employ $L\times$ R2GFormer layers for node representation learning. The representation of the nodes is updated after each layer, incorporating information from different sources. This process can be formulated as follows:

$$N_g^{(l)} = \text{R2GFormer}(N_g^{(l-1)}, \mathcal{E}, G). \tag{8}$$

where $\mathcal{E}$ denotes all the edges of the sampling graph, G denotes the genres of every movie and review node. After $L\times$ R2GFormer layers, we obtain the final graph representation $N_g^{(L)}$ of all nodes.

3.3 Multimodal Fusion

Through the data above processed by the R2GFormer, we have obtained the graph structural information and meta information for all nodes, including user, review and movie nodes. The next step is to fuse the multimodal information.

For each type of node, we utilize a type-wise TRM to facilitate inter-modal information interaction, then concatenate features of different modals followed by an MLP to get the final representation for each node, *i.e.*,

$$U_g, U_m, U_b = \text{TRM}([U_g\ U_m\ U_b]), U = \text{MLP}([U_g \| U_m \| U_b])), \tag{9}$$
$$R_g, R_m = \text{TRM}([R_g\ R_m]), R = \text{MLP}([R_g \| R_m])), \tag{10}$$
$$M_g, M_m = \text{TRM}([M_g\ M_m]), M = \text{MLP}([M_g \| M_m]), \tag{11}$$

where U_g, R_g and M_g are derived from N_g, U_m, R_m and M_m are dervied from N_m.

After obtaining the comprehensive representation of each type of node, we then concatenate each review feature r_i with its corresponding movie feature m_i and user feature u_i:

$$r_i = [\ r_i \| m_i \| u_i\ ]. \tag{12}$$

3.4 GMoE

Inspired by the successful applications of Mixture-of-Experts in NLP and bot detection, and its capability to handle the small subsets of the whole dataset, we adopt MoE to handle different genres of reviews. However, distinct from the latent subsets of the dataset in the classic MoE application scenario, our datasets already have the genre information of movies, as well as their related reviews. So we improve MoE to the proposed GMoE.

Specifically, instead of using the gating mechanism in the traditional MoE structure, we assign tokens to experts simply according to their genres: which genre it belongs to, which expert will deal with it; how many genres it belongs to, how many experts will deal with it.

$$r_i = \text{AGGREGATOR}_m(\{\text{Expert}_j(r_i) \mid \forall j \in G_i\}). \tag{13}$$

where G_i denotes the set of genres to which node i belongs; AGGRE-GATOR$_m$ can be summation, concatenation, or a TRM; each Expert is a MLP for simplicity.

3.5 Learning and Optimization

After using GMoE to process genre-specific information, we acquire the final representation r_i for the i-th review. Then we apply a linear transformation to r_i to obtain spoiler detection result $\hat{y}_i$. To train GUSD, We optimize the network by cross-entropy loss with L_2 regularization. The total loss function is as follows:

$$Loss = -\sum_{i \in \mathcal{R}} y_i \log \hat{y}_i + \lambda \sum_{\theta \in \Theta} \theta^2. \tag{14}$$

where $\hat{y}_i$ and y_i are the prediction for the i-th review and its corresponding ground truth, respectively. $\mathcal{R}$ encompasses all the reviews in the training set, while Θ denotes all trainable model parameters in GUSD, and λ is a hyperparameter that maintains the balance between the two parts.

4 Experiment

4.1 Experiment Settings

Dataset. To evaluate our GUSD framework along with 14 other representative baselines on two widely recognized datasets: **LCS** [38] and **Kaggle** [24]:

- **LCS** is a comprehensive dataset for automatic spoiler detection, comprising 1,860,715 reviews, 259,705 users, and 147,191 movies. And about 24.59% (457,500) of the reviews are spoilers.
- **Kaggle**, introduced in 2019, consists of 573,913 valid reviews, 263,407 users, and 1,572 movies. And about 25.87% (150,924) of the reviews are spoilers.

Note that both datasets include the genre information of all movies, with specific categories defined according to IMDb standards, which facilitates the operation of our GUSD framework. Following MVSD [38], we randomly split the reviews into training, validation, and test sets with a ratio of 7:2:1.

Baselines. To achieve a comprehensive evaluation, we compare GUSD with pre-trained language models, GNN-based models, and task-specific baselines. For the pre-trained language models, the procedure involves feeding the review text into the model, averaging all token embeddings, and then applying two fully connected layers to perform spoiler detection. Regarding the GNN-based models, the graph neural network takes the output of RoBERTa [19] as the initial node features. Below, we provide a concise overview of each baseline method.

- **BERT** [8] is a language model pre-trained on extensive natural language data, using masked language modeling and next sentence prediction tasks.
- **RoBERTa** [19] improves upon BERT by eliminating the next sentence prediction task and enhancing masking techniques.
- **BART** [18] is a pre-trained language model that advances traditional autoregressive models through bidirectional encoding and denoising objectives.
- **DeBERTa** [14] refines BERT by implementing disentangled attention and an improved mask decoder, making it a more advanced language model.
- **Bge-Large** [41] is trained on a comprehensive training dataset C-MTP, combining vast unlabeled data and diverse labeled data.
- **GCN** [17] is a foundational graph neural network that performs convolutions on graph nodes and their neighbors, effectively propagating information.
- **R-GCN** [32] extends GCN to handle multi-relational graphs by incorporating relation-specific weights.
- **GAT** [35] is a graph neural network that applies attention mechanisms to dynamically assign importance to neighboring nodes.
- **SimpleHGN** [22] is tailored for heterogeneous graphs, integrating multiple types of nodes and edges with a shared embedding space and adaptive aggregation strategies.
- **GPS** [30] propose a recipe to build a general, powerful, scalable graph Transformer with linear complexity.
- **HGT** [15] design node- and edge-type dependent parameters to characterize the heterogeneous attention over each edge for modeling Web-scale heterogeneous graphs.
- **DNSD** [6] is a spoiler detection method that employs a CNN-based genre-aware attention mechanism.
- **SpoilerNet** [36] uses a hierarchical attention network and GRU alongside item and user bias terms for spoiler detection.
- **MVSD** [38] leverages external movie knowledge and user networks to detect spoilers.

4.2 Main Results

We evaluated our GUSD framework and 14 other baselines on two datasets. The results presented in Table 1 demonstrate the following:

- **GUSD consistently outperforms all baselines across both datasets.** Specifically, compared with the previous state-of-the-art method MVSD [38],

Table 1. Accuracy, AUC, and binary F1-score of GUSD and three types of baseline methods on two spoiler detection datasets. We run all experiments **five times** to ensure a consistent evaluation and report the average performance as well as standard deviation in parentheses. Bold indicates the best performance, underline the second best. GUSD consistently outperforms the three types of methods on both benchmarks.

Model	Kaggle			LCS		
	F1	AUC	Acc	F1	AUC	Acc
BERT	44.02 ±1.09	63.46 ±0.46	77.78 ±0.09	46.14 ±2.84	64.82 ±1.36	79.96 ±0.38
RoBERTa	50.93 ±0.76	66.94 ±0.40	79.12 ±0.10	47.72 ±0.44	65.55 ±0.22	80.16 ±0.03
BART	46.89 ±1.55	64.88 ±0.71	78.47 ±0.09	48.18 ±1.22	65.79 ±0.62	80.14 ±0.07
DeBERTa	49.94 ±1.13	66.42 ±0.59	79.08 ±0.09	47.38 ±2.22	65.42 ±1.08	80.13 ±0.08
Bge-Large	52.51 ±0.58	67.74 ±0.37	77.44 ±0.21	52.68 ±0.36	68.46 ±0.23	79.24 ±0.11
GCN	59.22 ±1.18	71.61 ±0.74	82.08 ±0.26	62.12 ±1.18	73.72 ±0.89	83.92 ±0.23
R-GCN	63.07 ±0.81	74.09 ±0.60	82.96 ±0.16	62.99 ±0.89	76.18 ±0.72	85.19 ±0.21
GAT	60.98 ±0.09	72.72 ±0.60	82.43 ±0.01	65.73 ±0.12	75.92 ±0.13	85.18 ±0.02
SimpleHGN	60.12 ±1.04	71.60 ±0.88	82.08 ±0.26	63.79 ±0.88	74.64 ±0.64	84.66 ±1.61
HGT	63.99 ±0.25	75.61 ±0.25	81.66 ±0.23	60.89 ±0.46	73.96 ±0.53	81.86 ±0.16
GPS	61.04 ±0.84	73.50 ±0.53	81.25 ±0.55	64.21 ±0.30	75.60 ±0.92	82.40 ±0.91
DNSD	46.33 ±2.37	64.50 ±1.11	78.44 ±0.14	44.69 ±1.64	64.10 ±0.74	79.76 ±0.08
SpoilerNet	57.19 ±0.69	70.64 ±0.44	79.85 ±0.10	62.86 ±0.38	74.62 ±0.69	83.23 ±0.23
MVSD	<u>65.08</u> ±0.69	<u>75.42</u> ±0.56	<u>83.59</u> ±0.11	<u>69.22</u> ±0.61	<u>78.26</u> ±0.63	<u>86.37</u> ±0.08
Ours	**80.24** ±0.73	**87.00** ±0.37	**89.65** ±0.36	**75.37** ±0.10	**83.71** ±0.27	**88.32** ±0.08

GUSD achieves **6.1%** higher Binary-F1, **5.5%** higher AUC, and **2.0%** higher accuracy on the LCS dataset, as well as **15.2%** higher Binary-F1, **11.6%** higher AUC, and **6.1%** higher accuracy on the Kaggle dataset. These improvements are statistically significant.
- In both datasets, **graph-based models generally outperform other types of baselines**, reaffirming the importance of analyzing the graph structure of reviews and their corresponding users and movies.
- Compared with DNSD [6], which also focuses on genre features of the reviews, GUSD surpasses DNSD across all three metrics in both datasets, further proving the effectiveness and robustness of our global-aware genreformer and GMoE methods.
- Both SpoilerNet [36] and GUSD utilize user bias, but GUSD outperforms SpoilerNet in all three metrics across both datasets. This demonstrates that our dynamic graph pretraining can better identify the latent behavior pattern of whether a user is likely to post spoilers.

4.3 Ablation Study

As GUSD outperforms all the baselines and has reached state-of-the-art (SOTA) performance across the two datasets, we conducted ablation study to further

Table 2. Ablation study of GUSD on Kaggle Dataset. Bold indicates the best performance, <u>underline</u> the second best.

Category	Ablation Settings	F1	AUC	Acc
User bias	-w/o U_b	78.85	85.78	88.58
RetGAT	approximate way	78.40	85.39	88.39
	normal GAT	78.08	85.22	88.29
GMoE	MLP	78.52	86.09	88.25
	MoE [33]	78.75	86.36	88.54
	Soft MoE [29]	79.10	86.10	88.78
Genreformer	-w/o genreformer	77.73	84.68	88.13
	sum pooling	<u>79.84</u>	<u>86.56</u>	<u>89.28</u>
	max pooling	78.77	85.52	89.13
Ours	GUSD	**80.24**	**87.00**	**89.65**

explore the impact of each part of GUSD on the final performance with the Kaggle Dataset. The results are shown in Table 2.

- To assess the importance of user bias information, we removed the user bias component U_b. The results in Table 2 show an obvious decrease in performance, confirming that user bias information is critical for effective spoiler detection.
- For the RetGAT component, we evaluated two variations: using an approximate method to compute k-hop neighbors [1,37] and replacing our RetGAT with a standard GAT. Both variations lead to a drop in performance, indicating the necessity of our RetGAT design for capturing appropriate graph structures.
- To investigate the impact of GMoE, we replace it with a simple MLP, a traditional MoE [33], and a Soft-MoE [29]. Note that we set the number of experts of the traditional MoE and Soft-MoE to be the same as in GMoE, *i.e.*, the number of genres. From the results shown in Table 2, the full model with GMoE achieves the best performance, highlighting the effectiveness of our GMoE design in handling explicit genre information. Moreover, replacing the GMoE with an MLP performs the worst, proving the rationality of using genre information.
- We also evaluate the Genreformer component by removing it and replacing the mean AGGREGATOR with sum pooling and max pooling. The results in Table 2 show that the full Genreformer with sum AGGREGATOR outperforms these ablated versions, validating the necessity of the Genreformer.

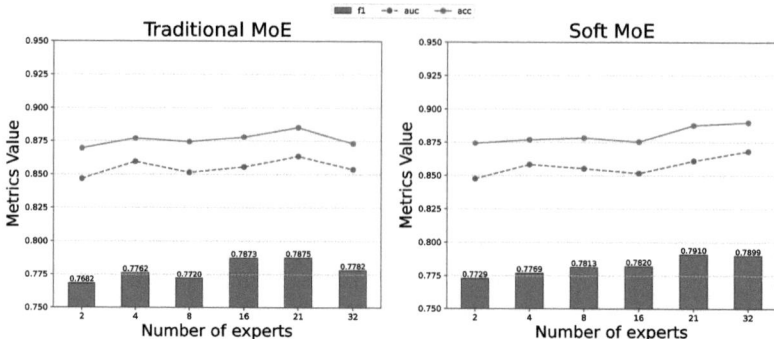

Fig. 4. Performance comparison of different numbers of experts in traditional MoE and Soft-MoE. Note that 21 is the number of genres. The results indicate that GMoE outperforms other variants irrespective of the number of experts.

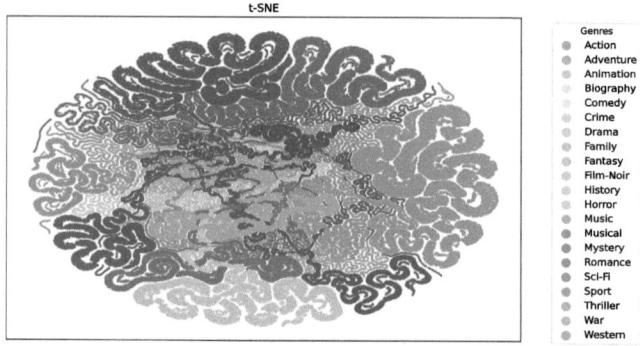

Fig. 5. T-SNE visualization of the features processed by GMoE. Different colors represent different genres, indicating distinct clustering of features according to genres. (Color figure online)

4.4 GMoE Study

In this section, we conduct further experiments on the GMoE to better understand its effectiveness compared to other previous MoE methods such as traditional MoE [33] and Soft-MoE [29].

Different Numbers of Experts. We conduct multiple experiments by varying the number of experts in traditional MoE and Soft-MoE, recording the Binary-F1, AUC, and Accuracy for each configuration. The results are summarized in Fig. 4.

From the results shown in Fig. 4, it is evident that the GMoE consistently outperforms both traditional MoE and Soft-MoE regardless of the number of experts used. Specifically, Soft-MoE performs better than traditional MoE. That is because GMoE uses explicit genre information, eliminating inaccurate dispatch that can occur in traditional MoE and Soft-MoE.

T-SNE Visualization of Features. To further validate the effectiveness of the GMoE, we perform dimensionality reduction on the features of all reviews processed by the GMoE layer. Specifically, we first reduce the dimensionality of the features to 50 dimensions using PCA, and then further reduce them to 2 dimensions using T-SNE. The result plot, shown in Fig. 5, demonstrates that reviews of different genres exhibit distinct features after being processed by the GMoE.

The T-SNE visualization in Fig. 5 indicates that reviews are clustered according to their genres, providing compelling evidence of the effectiveness of our GMoE design. These distinct clusters suggest that GMoE successfully captures and utilizes genre-specific features to enhance its performance. In the visualization, each distinct color represents a different genre. For instance, genres like 'Action' (red), 'Drama' (green), and 'Sci-Fi' (purple) form well-defined clusters, indicating that the features of reviews from these genres are significantly different from each other. The presence of these distinct clusters reaffirms the model's capability to differentiate and leverage genre-specific information effectively.

5 Conclusion

In this paper, we introduce GUSD, a novel spoiler detection framework that integrates Genreformer and GMoE to effectively model diverse genre features. Additionally, GUSD incorporates dynamic graph pretraining to capture user bias related to spoiler posting. Extensive experiments reveal that GUSD significantly outperforms the state-of-the-art models on two major spoiler detection benchmarks. Further analysis validates the effectiveness of our proposed techniques, demonstrating GUSD's superior capability in capturing intricate genre features and modeling user bias for spoiler detection.

Acknowledgments. This work was supported by the National Nature Science Foundation of China (No. 62272374, No. 62192781), the Natural Science Foundation of Shaanxi Province (2024JC-JCQN-62), the National Nature Science Foundation of China (No. 62202367, No. 62250009), the Key Research and Development Project in Shaanxi Province No. 2023GXLH-024, Project of China Knowledge Center for Engineering Science and Technology, and Project of Chinese academy of engineering "The Online and Offline Mixed Educational Service System for 'The Belt and Road' Training in MOOC China", and the K. C. Wong Education Foundation. Lastly, we would like to thank all LUD lab members for fostering a collaborative research environment.

References

1. Atwood, J., Towsley, D.: Diffusion-convolutional neural networks. Adv. Neural Inf. Process. Syst. **29** (2016)
2. Bao, A., Ho, M., Sangamnerkar, S.: Spoiler alert: using natural language processing to detect spoilers in book reviews. arXiv preprint arXiv:2102.03882 (2021)
3. Boyd-Graber, J., Glasgow, K., Zajac, J.S.: Spoiler alert: machine learning approaches to detect social media posts with revelatory information. Proc. Am. Soc. Inf. Sci. Technol. **50**(1), 1–9 (2013)
4. Cai, Z., et al.: Lmbot: distilling graph knowledge into language model for graph-less deployment in twitter bot detection. In: Proceedings of the 17th ACM International Conference on Web Search and Data Mining, pp. 57–66 (2024)
5. Cao, Y., Wang, X., He, X., Hu, Z., Chua, T.S.: Unifying knowledge graph learning and recommendation: towards a better understanding of user preferences. In: The World Wide Web Conference, pp. 151–161 (2019)
6. Chang, B., Kim, H., Kim, R., Kim, D., Kang, J.: A deep neural spoiler detection model using a genre-aware attention mechanism. In: Phung, D., Tseng, V.S., Webb, G.I., Ho, B., Ganji, M., Rashidi, L. (eds.) PAKDD 2018. LNCS (LNAI), vol. 10937, pp. 183–195. Springer, Cham (2018). https://doi.org/10.1007/978-3-319-93034-3_15
7. Chang, B., Lee, I., Kim, H., Kang, J.: "killing me" is not a spoiler: spoiler detection model using graph neural networks with dependency relation-aware attention mechanism. arXiv preprint arXiv:2101.05972 (2021)
8. Devlin, J.: Bert: Pre-training of deep bidirectional transformers for language understanding. arXiv preprint arXiv:1810.04805 (2018)
9. Fan, Q., Huang, H., Chen, M., Liu, H., He, R.: Rmt: retentive networks meet vision transformers. In: Proceedings of the IEEE/CVF Conference on Computer Vision and Pattern Recognition, pp. 5641–5651 (2024)
10. Fedus, W., Zoph, B., Shazeer, N.: Switch transformers: scaling to trillion parameter models with simple and efficient sparsity. J. Mach. Learn. Res. **23**(120), 1–39 (2022)
11. Fey, M., Lenssen, J.E.: Fast graph representation learning with pytorch geometric. arXiv preprint arXiv:1903.02428 (2019)
12. Golbeck, J.: The twitter mute button: a web filtering challenge. In: Proceedings of the SIGCHI Conference on Human Factors in Computing Systems, pp. 2755–2758 (2012)
13. Guo, S., Ramakrishnan, N.: Finding the storyteller: automatic spoiler tagging using linguistic cues. In: Proceedings of the 23rd International Conference on Computational Linguistics (Coling 2010), pp. 412–420 (2010)
14. He, P., Gao, J., Chen, W.: Debertav3: improving deberta using electra-style pre-training with gradient-disentangled embedding sharing. arXiv preprint arXiv:2111.09543 (2021)
15. Hu, Z., Dong, Y., Wang, K., Sun, Y.: Heterogeneous graph transformer. In: Proceedings of the Web Conference 2020, pp. 2704–2710 (2020)
16. Jeon, S., Kim, S., Yu, H.: Don't be spoiled by your friends: spoiler detection in tv program tweets. In: Proceedings of the International AAAI Conference on Web and Social Media, vol. 7, pp. 681–684 (2013)
17. Kipf, T.N., Welling, M.: Semi-supervised classification with graph convolutional networks. arXiv preprint arXiv:1609.02907 (2016)
18. Lewis, M.: Bart: Denoising sequence-to-sequence pre-training for natural language generation, translation, and comprehension. arXiv preprint arXiv:1910.13461 (2019)

19. Liu, Y.: Roberta: a robustly optimized bert pretraining approach, vol. 364 (2019). arXiv preprint arXiv:1907.11692
20. Liu, Y., Tan, Z., Wang, H., Feng, S., Zheng, Q., Luo, M.: Botmoe: twitter bot detection with community-aware mixtures of modal-specific experts. In: Proceedings of the 46th International ACM SIGIR Conference on Research and Development in Information Retrieval, pp. 485–495 (2023)
21. Loewenstein, G.: The psychology of curiosity: a review and reinterpretation. Psychol. Bull. **116**(1), 75 (1994)
22. Lv, Q., et al.: Are we really making much progress? revisiting, benchmarking and refining heterogeneous graph neural networks. In: Proceedings of the 27th ACM SIGKDD Conference on Knowledge Discovery & Data Mining, pp. 1150–1160 (2021)
23. Madaan, A., et al.: Think about it! improving defeasible reasoning by first modeling the question scenario. arXiv preprint arXiv:2110.12349 (2021)
24. Misra, R.: IMDB Spoiler Dataset (2019). https://www.kaggle.com/datasets/rmisra/imdb-spoiler-dataset
25. Nakamura, S., Tanaka, K.: Temporal filtering system to reduce the risk of spoiling a user's enjoyment. In: Proceedings of the 12th International Conference on Intelligent User Interfaces, pp. 345–348 (2007)
26. Nikolentzos, G., Dasoulas, G., Vazirgiannis, M.: K-hop graph neural networks. Neural Netw. **130**, 195–205 (2020)
27. Paszke, A., et al.: Pytorch: an imperative style, high-performance deep learning library. Adv. Neural Inf. Process. Syst. **32** (2019)
28. Pedregosa, F., et al.: Scikit-learn: machine learning in python. J. Mach. Learn. Res. **12**, 2825–2830 (2011)
29. Puigcerver, J., Riquelme, C., Mustafa, B., Houlsby, N.: From sparse to soft mixtures of experts. arXiv preprint arXiv:2308.00951 (2023)
30. Rampášek, L., Galkin, M., Dwivedi, V.P., Luu, A.T., Wolf, G., Beaini, D.: Recipe for a general, powerful, scalable graph transformer. Adv. Neural. Inf. Process. Syst. **35**, 14501–14515 (2022)
31. Rau, D.: Sparsely-gated mixture-of-experts pytorch implementation (2019)
32. Schlichtkrull, M., Kipf, T.N., Bloem, P., van den Berg, R., Titov, I., Welling, M.: Modeling relational data with graph convolutional networks. In: Gangemi, A., et al. (eds.) ESWC 2018. LNCS, vol. 10843, pp. 593–607. Springer, Cham (2018). https://doi.org/10.1007/978-3-319-93417-4_38
33. Shazeer, N., et al.: Outrageously large neural networks: the sparsely-gated mixture-of-experts layer. arXiv preprint arXiv:1701.06538 (2017)
34. Sun, Y., et al.: Retentive network: a successor to transformer for large language models. arXiv preprint arXiv:2307.08621 (2023)
35. Veličković, P., Cucurull, G., Casanova, A., Romero, A., Lio, P., Bengio, Y.: Graph attention networks. arXiv preprint arXiv:1710.10903 (2017)
36. Wan, M., Misra, R., Nakashole, N., McAuley, J.: Fine-grained spoiler detection from large-scale review corpora. arXiv preprint arXiv:1905.13416 (2019)
37. Wang, G., Ying, R., Huang, J., Leskovec, J.: Multi-hop attention graph neural network. arXiv preprint arXiv:2009.14332 (2020)
38. Wang, H., et al.: Detecting spoilers in movie reviews with external movie knowledge and user networks. In: Proceedings of the 2023 Conference on Empirical Methods in Natural Language Processing, pp. 16035–16050 (2023)
39. Wolf, T., et al.: Transformers: State-of-the-art natural language processing. In: Proceedings of the 2020 Conference on Empirical Methods in Natural Language Processing: System Demonstrations, pp. 38–45 (2020)

40. Wróblewska, A., Rzepiński, P., Sysko-Romańczuk, S.: Spoiler in a textstack: how much can transformers help? arXiv preprint arXiv:2112.12913 (2021)
41. Xiao, S., Liu, Z., Zhang, P., Muennighof, N.: C-pack: packaged resources to advance general chinese embedding. 2023. arXiv preprint arXiv:2309.07597 (2023)
42. Yu, L., Sun, L., Du, B., Lv, W.: Towards better dynamic graph learning: new architecture and unified library. Adv. Neural. Inf. Process. Syst. **36**, 67686–67700 (2023)

GraphJCL: A Dual-Perspective Graph-Based Framework for Urban Region Representation via Joint Contrastive Learning

Yaya Zhao[1], Kaiqi Zhao[2], Zixuan Tang[1], Xiaoling Lu[1(✉)], Yuanyuan Zhang[3], and Yalei Du[3]

[1] Center for Applied Statistics, School of Statistics, Renmin University of China, Beijing, China
{zhaoyaya,2021201741,xiaolinglu}@ruc.edu.cn
[2] The University of Auckland, Auckland, New Zealand
kaiqi.zhao@auckland.ac.nz
[3] Beijing Baixingkefu Network Technology Co., Ltd., Beijing, China

Abstract. Graph learning for urban region modeling has gained significant attention for leveraging multi-modal data to generate region representations for downstream task prediction. However, existing models face two key limitations: (1) they primarily adopt a global perspective, overlooking the joint modeling of both local and global aspects, and (2) they rely on redundant, low-information nodes, leading to suboptimal region representations. To address these challenges, we propose GraphJCL, a dual-perspective framework that models both local and global perspectives. Specifically, GraphJCL first constructs local graphs for individual regions and a global graph encompassing all regions, integrating POI, taxi flow, remote sensing, street view, and road network data. Additionally, GraphJCL employs specialized message-passing mechanisms to efficiently capture both local and global graph node representations. Furthermore, GraphJCL incorporates entropy-optimized graph node pruning, retaining only the most informative nodes to enhance final region representations. To ensure the effectiveness of the designed dual-perspective graph framework, GraphJCL introduces a joint contrastive learning approach, optimizing region representations through geography-driven, entropy-optimized, and mutual information-based optimization techniques. Extensive experiments on two real-world datasets across five modalities demonstrate that GraphJCL consistently outperforms state-of-the-art methods on three tasks, validating its flexibility and effectiveness.

Keywords: Urban region representation · Graph neural networks · Joint contrastive learning

1 Introduction

Graph learning [7,18,32] for urban region representation leverages multi-modal data, including Points of Interest (POI), taxi flow, remote sensing imagery, street view imagery, road network data, and socioeconomic indicators, to generate embeddings that effectively capture cross-modal relationships and semantic structures. These embeddings facilitate various downstream tasks, such as check-in prediction [9], crime forecasting [19], and traffic crash prediction [5], thereby supporting smart urban optimiza-

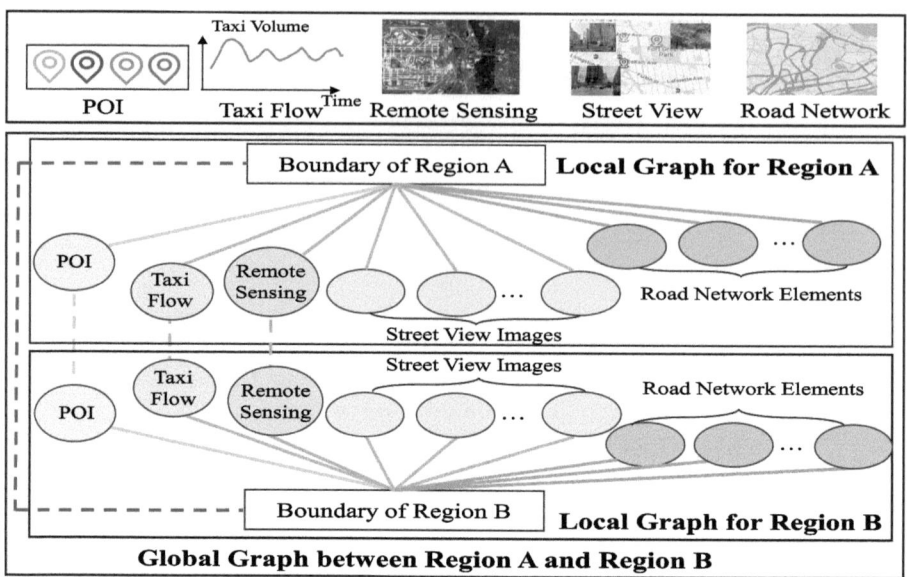

Fig. 1. An illustration of local and global graph construction using two regions. The local graph for each region is modeled independently, containing only nodes and intra-region edges within itself. In contrast, the global graph spans both regions, incorporating nodes from both, intra-region edges (solid lines), and inter-region coarse-grained modality connections edges (dashed lines).

tion [11]. Despite the effectiveness of existing graph learning methods, two key limitations persist. First, **neglecting joint region modeling of local and global aspects.** Local region modeling integrates multi-modal data within a specific region to capture localized information. However, global modeling simultaneously incorporates both intra-region information and inter-region interactions but does not explicitly model individual regions in isolation. Ideally, local and global modeling should work in tandem to produce a comprehensive urban region representation. However, existing methods predominantly focus on global modeling while often neglecting the independent local modeling of individual regions. For instance, methods such as [2,29,30,32] construct a global heterogeneous graph where region representations are optimized jointly, without an independent process for learning region-specific embeddings. Second, **reliance on redundant, low-information nodes.** Many existing methods rely on excessively redundant, low-information nodes to generate final region representations, which negatively impacts representation quality. For example, [28] directly averages the representations of all modality nodes to obtain the final region representation, while [7] averages the representations of all modality nodes and modality-type nodes to produce the final representation. These methods fail to prune low-information nodes, resulting in graphs that include numerous redundant nodes. This lack of refinement leads to inefficient representation learning and ultimately hampers the overall performance of final representations. To address these limitations, we propose GraphJCL, a dual-perspective graph-based framework that models both local and global perspectives. It integrates five modalities:

POI, taxi flow, remote sensing imagery, street view imagery, and road network data, categorized into coarse-grained and fine-grained types based on their characteristics. (1) Coarse-grained modalities capture region-level urban functions by aggregating raw data into representative vectors. POI data is clustered by category to reflect commercial activity, taxi flow is aggregated over time to represent mobility patterns, and remote sensing imagery provides a macro-level view of land use and urban structure. (2) Fine-grained modalities capture spatial topology and local environmental structures. Street view imagery consists of diverse location-specific images, while road network data represents individual road segments with distinct positions and attributes.

Based on this modality classification, GraphJCL constructs both local graphs for individual regions and a global graph encompassing all regions, as illustrated in Fig. 1. Specifically: (1) Local graphs connect each region node to its aggregated POI, taxi flow, and remote sensing imagery vector nodes, along with multiple street view images nodes and road network elements nodes, capturing both functional and spatial characteristics. (2) The global graph establishes inter-region edges only between coarse-grained region nodes (POI, taxi flow, remote sensing) and region boundary nodes, while fine-grained nodes remain unconnected to prevent edge explosion and unnecessary computational overhead. This structure ensures effective inter-region interactions while keeping the graph compact and efficient. Additionally, GraphJCL introduces specialized message-passing mechanisms to capture local and global graph node representations effectively. Furthermore, GraphJCL incorporates entropy-optimized graph node pruning to retain high-information nodes while eliminating redundant ones, ensuring the generation of effective region representations. Finally, to ensure that our designed dual-perspective graph framework functions effectively and draws inspiration from contrastive learning [14,25], GraphJCL employs a joint contrastive learning approach to optimize local region representations from three views, ultimately generating the final region representation. Specifically, it refines region representations using geography-driven and entropy-optimized techniques and integrates global region representations through mutual information-based optimization. These three aspects work together to collectively enhance region representations. In summary, our key contributions are as follows:

- We propose GraphJCL, a dual-perspective graph-based framework, as the first to jointly model both local and global perspectives for urban region representation.
- GraphJCL constructs local graphs for individual regions and a global graph encompassing all regions. It employs tailored message-passing mechanisms to effectively capture both local and global node representations, enabling joint modeling of regional structures. Additionally, it integrates graph node pruning and attention mechanisms to derive more efficient and informative region representations.
- GraphJCL introduces a joint contrastive learning approach, incorporating geography-driven and entropy-optimized contrastive learning techniques, as well as mutual information-based optimization, to refine and enhance region representations.
- Extensive experiments on two real-world datasets spanning five modalities demonstrate that GraphJCL outperforms state-of-the-art methods across three downstream tasks, highlighting its flexibility and effectiveness.

2 Related Work

Graph Representation for Multi-modal Data. Graph embedding for multi-modal data aims to learn low-dimensional vector representations of graph nodes from diverse data sources. Recent advances in graph neural networks (GNNs) have significantly improved these representations. For instance, HetCAN [31] enhances heterogeneous graph representation by incorporating both type-aware and dimension-aware encoders. These GNN-based approaches have gained substantial attention for their effectiveness in multi-modal data representation learning [10,21]. Early methods employed taxi flow patterns to define graph edges [18,23], whereas more recent studies integrate spatial and socio-environmental attributes into heterogeneous graphs for comprehensive urban modeling [7,32,33]. Additionally, graph contrastive learning has shown great potential in urban representation tasks [29]. These approaches highlight the effectiveness of graph-based multi-modal learning for urban region modeling.

Urban Region Representation Learning. Urban region representation learning models can be categorized based on the number of modalities they utilize. Some approaches focus on single-modal data. For instance, [18] leverages taxi data to model urban region embeddings, capturing vehicle movement patterns to reflect the semantic characteristics of urban areas. Similarly, [6] primarily utilizes Points of Interest (POI) features for region representation learning, while [22] employs satellite imagery, leveraging large-scale models to enhance final region representations. Other studies adopt multi-modal data to construct richer and more comprehensive urban region representations [9,24,26,27,30]. For example, [27] introduces a multi-view joint learning framework that integrates taxi data, POI data, and check-in records, effectively capturing cross-modal correlations to model urban regions from multiple perspectives. From a methodological perspective, some studies employ attention mechanisms for modality fusion [8,15,20], while others utilize graph-based approaches for urban region representation learning [7,32]. Our framework utilizes five modalities in a graph-based structure with contrastive learning, effectively capturing effective urban region representations.

3 Preliminaries and Problem Statement

Definition 1 (Urban Regions ($\mathcal{U}$)). *An urban area is partitioned into N non-overlapping regions, denoted as $\mathcal{U} = \{U_1, U_2, \ldots, U_N\}$. Each U_i has a geographical boundary.*

Definition 2 (Coarse-Grained Modalities ($\mathcal{CM}$)). *A modality is considered coarse-grained if it captures region-level urban functional attributes, allowing its data within a region to be aggregated into a single vector representing overall urban functionality. The coarse-grained modalities $\mathcal{CM}$ used are as follows:*

- **Point-of-Interest (POI) ($\mathcal{P}$):** *POI data reflects the commercial activity of a region. Each region U_i is associated with a vector $P_i = \{P_{i1}, P_{i2}, \ldots, P_{iK}\}$, where P_{ij} denotes the count of POIs in category j within region U_i. The K represents the top K POI categories with the highest occurrence frequency across all regions.*

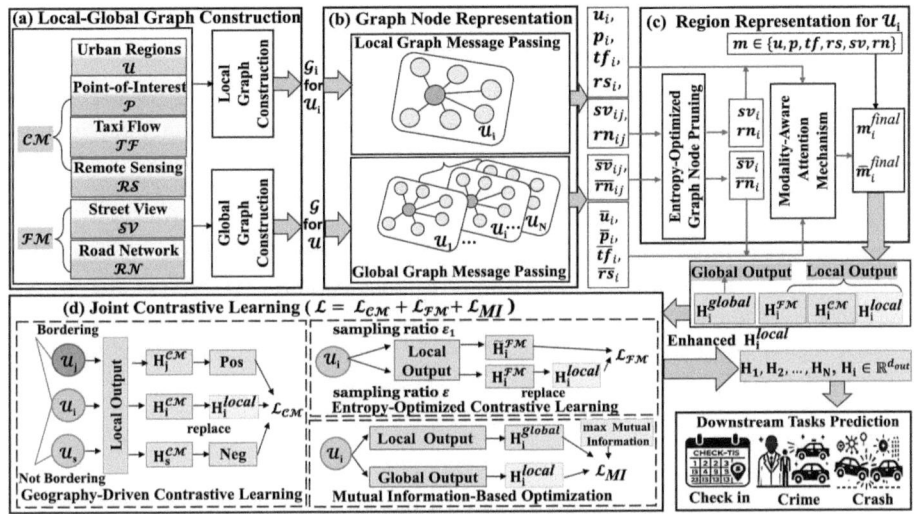

Fig. 2. The framework: (a) GraphJCL constructs local graphs for individual regions and a global graph for all regions. (b) GraphJCL introduces tailored message-passing mechanisms to capture local and global graph node representations. (c) GraphJCL employs entropy-optimized graph node pruning and modality-aware attention mechanisms to derive effective region representations. (d) Geography-driven, entropy-optimized, and mutual information-based contrastive techniques jointly enhance local region representations to generate the final region representations.

- **Taxi Flow ($\mathcal{TF}$):** Taxi flow captures mobility patterns within a region. Each region U_i is associated with a vector $TF_i = \{TF_{i1}, TF_{i2}, \ldots, TF_{iT}\}$, where TF_{ij} represents the taxi flow count in region U_i during the j-th time period. The T represents the total number of periods (e.g., hours in a month), depending on the dataset.
- **Remote Sensing Imagery ($\mathcal{RS}$):** Remote sensing imagery provides a macro-level view of land use and urban structure within a region. Each region U_i is associated with a remote sensing image RS_i.

Definition 3 (Fine-Grained Modalities ($\mathcal{FM}$)). *A modality is considered fine-grained if it captures spatial topology and local environmental structures within a region, meaning that its data points exhibit significant variability and cannot be effectively aggregated into a single vector representation.*

The fine-grained modalities $\mathcal{FM}$ used are as follows:

- **Street View Imagery ($\mathcal{SV}$):** Street view imagery captures local visual characteristics of urban regions through numerous spatially distributed images. Each region U_i contains a collection of street view images, denoted as $\{SV_{i1}, SV_{i2}, \ldots, SV_{i|\mathcal{SV}_i|}\}$, where SV_{ij} represents the street view image with index j within region U_i.
- **Road Network ($\mathcal{RN}$):** The road network captures the topological structure of urban regions. Each region U_i contains a collection of road network elements, denoted as $\{RN_{i1}, RN_{i2}, \ldots, RN_{i|\mathcal{RN}_i|}\}$, where RN_{ij} represents a road segment

or junction with index j within region U_i. The category index RNS_{ij} specifies the type of road element (e.g., trunk road or motorway).

Definition 4 (Downstream Tasks (Y)). *Downstream tasks refer to socio-economic and environmental indicators in urban contexts. For urban area $\mathcal{U}$ with N regions, the L task targets are represented as $Y \in \mathbb{R}^{N \times L}$. This paper focuses on three downstream tasks, check-in counts, crime incidents, and traffic crash counts, where $L = 3$.*

Definition 5 (Problem Statement: Urban Region Representation). *Given urban regions $\mathcal{U}$ along with their associated coarse-grained modalities $\mathcal{CM}$ and fine-grained modalities $\mathcal{FM}$, the objective is to learn a low-dimensional representation $H_i \in \mathbb{R}^{d_{out}}$ for each region U_i. These embeddings $\mathcal{H} = \{H_1, H_2, \ldots, H_N\}$ are used to predict downstream tasks Y.*

4 Methodology

In this section, we introduce GraphJCL, a dual-perspective graph-based framework for urban region representation. Its key components are illustrated in Fig. 2.

4.1 Local-Global Graph Construction

In this subsection, to achieve joint region modeling of local and global aspects, we construct a local graph for each individual region and a global graph for all regions.

Local Graph Construction. For each region U_i, we construct a local heterogeneous graph $\mathcal{G}_i = (\mathcal{V}_i, \mathcal{E}_i)$ to capture its intrinsic features without influence from other regions. Specifically, the node set $\mathcal{V}_i$ consists of six types of nodes:
- **Region**: A node U_i representing the geographic boundary of the region.
- **POI**: A node P_i representing aggregated POI data.
- **Taxi Flow**: A node TF_i representing aggregated taxi mobility patterns.
- **Remote Sensing**: A node RS_i capturing macro-level land use and urban structure.
- **Street View Imagery**: A set of nodes $\{SV_{i1}, SV_{i2}, \ldots, SV_{i|\mathcal{SV}_i|}\}$ representing localized street-level visual environmental features.
- **Road Network**: A set of nodes $\{RN_{i1}, RN_{i2}, \ldots, RN_{i|\mathcal{RN}_i|}\}$ representing the topological structure of road segments and junctions.

The edge set $\mathcal{E}_i$ consists of five types of edges, defining relationships between the region node U_i and other modality nodes:
- $\mathcal{U}\_has\_\mathcal{P}$: An edge (U_i, P_i) that connects the region node to the POI node.
- $\mathcal{U}\_has\_\mathcal{TF}$: An edge (U_i, TF_i) that connects the region node to the taxi node.
- $\mathcal{U}\_has\_\mathcal{RS}$: An edge (U_i, RS_i) that connects the region node to the remote sensing imagery node.
- $\mathcal{U}\_has\_\mathcal{SV}$: A set of edges (U_i, SV_{ij}), where $j = 1, 2, \ldots, |\mathcal{SV}_i|$, that connect the region node to all street view images nodes.
- $\mathcal{U}\_has\_\mathcal{RN}$: A set of edges (U_i, RN_{ij}), where $j = 1, 2, \ldots, |\mathcal{RN}_i|$, that connect the region node to all road network elements nodes.

Based on the local graph construction method above, N local graphs $\mathcal{G}_i$, where $i = 1, 2, \ldots, N$, can be constructed for urban regions $U_1, U_2, \ldots, U_N$, respectively.

Global Graph Construction. For all regions $U_i \in \mathcal{U}, i = 1, 2, \ldots, N$, we construct a global graph $\mathcal{G} = (\mathcal{V}, \mathcal{E})$, which includes all nodes and edges from the local graphs $\mathcal{G}_1, \ldots, \mathcal{G}_N$. Additionally, it introduces four extra types of edges that capture inter-region relationships, based on region nodes $\mathcal{U}$ and coarse-grained modalities: POI ($\mathcal{P}$), Taxi Flow ($\mathcal{TF}$), and Remote Sensing ($\mathcal{RS}$). Fine-grained modalities Street View ($\mathcal{SV}$) and Road Network ($\mathcal{RN}$), do not establish inter-region edges, as they primarily capture local environmental and topological features within a region. The four types are:

- $\mathcal{U}\_sim\_\mathcal{U}$: A set of edges (U_i, U_j) connecting region nodes whose geographical boundaries are adjacent, where $i, j = 1, 2, \ldots, N$ and $i \neq j$.
- $\mathcal{P}\_sim\_\mathcal{P}$: A set of edges (P_i, P_j) connecting POI nodes based on cosine semantic similarity across regions, where $i, j = 1, 2, \ldots, N$ and $i \neq j$.
- $\mathcal{TF}\_sim\_\mathcal{TF}$: A set of edges (TF_i, TF_j) connecting taxi flow nodes based on cosine mobility similarity across regions, where $i, j = 1, 2, \ldots, N$ and $i \neq j$.
- $\mathcal{RS}\_sim\_\mathcal{RS}$: A set of edges (RS_i, RS_j) connecting remote sensing nodes based on cosine satellite similarity across regions, where $i, j = 1, 2, \ldots, N$ and $i \neq j$.

4.2 Graph Node Representation

This subsection introduces the initialization of node representations for different modalities, followed by our designed message passing mechanisms for iterative updates.

Node Initialization for Each Modality

- **Region** ($\mathcal{U}$): An undirected graph is constructed with all region geographic boundary U_i, i = 1,2,...N and edges connecting adjacent regions. The initialization vector $u_i^{(0)} \in \mathbb{R}^{d_{in}}$ for U_i is derived using the Node2Vec algorithm [3].
- **Remote Sensing Imagery** ($\mathcal{RS}$): The initialization vector $rs_i^{(0)} \in \mathbb{R}^{d_{in}}$ for each RS_i is obtained by applying the EfficientNet-B4 model [16].
- **Point-of-Interest (POI)** ($\mathcal{P}$): The initialization vector $p_i^{(0)} \in \mathbb{R}^{d_{in}}$ for each P_i is generated by setting $K = d_{in}$.
- **Taxi Flow** ($\mathcal{TF}$): The initialization vector $tf_i^{(0)} \in \mathbb{R}^{d_{in}}$ for each TF_i is computed by setting $T = d_{in}$.
- **Street View Imagery** ($\mathcal{SV}$): The initialization vector $sv_{i,j}^{(0)} \in \mathbb{R}^{d_{in}}$ is obtained for each street view image $SV_{i,j}$, where $j = 1, 2, \ldots, |\mathcal{SV}_i|$, by leveraging the CLIP-ViT-B/32 model [13].
- **Road Network** ($\mathcal{RN}$): The initialization vector $rn_{i,j}^{(0)} \in \mathbb{R}^{d_{in}}$ is generated for each road network element $RN_{i,j}$, where $j = 1, 2, \ldots, |\mathcal{RN}_i|$, by employing an embedding technique [12].

Local Graph Message Passing Mechanism. For each local graph $\mathcal{G}_i$ in region U_i, the nodes include the region node U_i, POI node P_i, taxi flow node TF_i, remote sensing node RS_i, street view node SV_{ij}, and road network node RN_{ij}. Their node representations at the l-th layer are denoted as $\boldsymbol{u}_i^{(l)}, \boldsymbol{p}_i^{(l)}, \boldsymbol{tf}_i^{(l)}, \boldsymbol{rs}_i^{(l)}, \boldsymbol{sv}_{ij}^{(l)}$, and $\boldsymbol{rn}_{ij}^{(l)}$, respectively, with initial embeddings defined as previously described. To capture region-specific features without interference from other regions, message passing in the local graph occurs only between nodes within the same region. Specifically, the node representations are updated at the l-th layer according to the following GNN update rule:

$$\boldsymbol{u}_i^{(l)} = \sigma \left(\sum_{m \in \{p,tf,rs\}} W_m \boldsymbol{m}_i^{(l-1)} + \sum_{m \in \{sv,rn\}} \sum_{j=1}^{|\mathcal{M}_i|} W_m \boldsymbol{m}_{ij}^{(l-1)} \right),$$
$$\boldsymbol{m}_i^{(l)} = \sigma \left(W_u \boldsymbol{u}_i^{(l-1)} \right), \quad m \in \{p,tf,rs\},$$
$$\boldsymbol{m}_{ij}^{(l)} = \sigma \left(W_u \boldsymbol{u}_i^{(l-1)} \right), \quad m \in \{sv,rn\}, \quad j=1,2,\ldots,|\mathcal{M}_i|,$$
(1)

where σ is the activation function, and W_m and W_u are learnable. The final layer outputs are denoted as $\boldsymbol{u}_i, \boldsymbol{p}_i, \boldsymbol{tf}_i, \boldsymbol{rs}_i, \boldsymbol{sv}_{ij}$, and $\boldsymbol{rn}_{ij}$, all of which belong to $\mathbb{R}^{d_{in}}$.

Global Graph Message Passing Mechanism. For the global graph $\mathcal{G} = (\mathcal{V}, \mathcal{E})$, the nodes in region U_i include the region node U_i, POI node P_i, taxi flow node TF_i, remote sensing node RS_i, street view node SV_{ij}, and road network node RN_{ij}. The node representations at the l-th layer are $\overline{\boldsymbol{u}}_i^{(l)}, \overline{\boldsymbol{p}}_i^{(l)}, \overline{\boldsymbol{tf}}_i^{(l)}, \overline{\boldsymbol{rs}}_i^{(l)}, \overline{\boldsymbol{sv}}_{ij}^{(l)}$, and $\overline{\boldsymbol{rn}}_{ij}^{(l)}$. Each vector lies in $\mathbb{R}^{d_{in}}$ and is initialized as previously described. The global graph captures region representations through interactions across regions. Message passing between regions occurs only for coarse-grained modalities, while fine-grained modalities focusing on local topology do not exchange information across regions. The sets $\mathcal{N}_i^U$ and $\mathcal{N}_i^m$ denote neighboring region nodes and same-modality neighboring nodes across regions, respectively, and σ is the activation function. Specifically, the node representations are updated at the l-th layer according to the following GNN update rule:

$$\overline{\boldsymbol{u}}_i^{(l)} = \sigma \left(\sum_{m \in \{p,tf,rs\}} \overline{W}_m \overline{\boldsymbol{m}}_i^{(l-1)} + \sum_{m \in \{sv,rn\}} \sum_{j=1}^{|\mathcal{M}_i|} \overline{W}_m \overline{\boldsymbol{m}}_{ij}^{(l-1)} + \sum_{j \in \mathcal{N}_i^U} \overline{W}_{uu} \overline{\boldsymbol{u}}_j^{(l-1)} \right),$$
$$\overline{\boldsymbol{m}}_i^{(l)} = \sigma \left(\overline{W}_u \overline{\boldsymbol{u}}_i^{(l-1)} + \sum_{j \in \mathcal{N}_i^m} \overline{W}_{mm} \overline{\boldsymbol{m}}_j^{(l-1)} \right), \quad m \in \{p,tf,rs\},$$
$$\overline{\boldsymbol{m}}_{ij}^{(l)} = \sigma \left(\overline{W}_u \overline{\boldsymbol{u}}_i^{(l-1)} \right), \quad m \in \{sv,rn\}, \quad j=1,2,\ldots,|\mathcal{M}_i|,$$
(2)

where $\overline{W}_m, \overline{W}_{uu}, \overline{W}_u$, and $\overline{W}_{mm}$ are learnable weight matrices. The final layer outputs are denoted as $\overline{\boldsymbol{u}}_i, \overline{\boldsymbol{p}}_i, \overline{\boldsymbol{tf}}_i, \overline{\boldsymbol{rs}}_i, \overline{\boldsymbol{sv}}_{ij}$, and $\overline{\boldsymbol{rn}}_{ij}$, all of which belong to $\mathbb{R}^{d_{in}}$.

4.3 Entropy-Optimized and Multi-modal Region Representation

To eliminate redundant low-information nodes, we propose an entropy-optimized graph node pruning mechanism. Specifically, we compute each node's entropy based on its graph node representation. High-entropy nodes, which carry more informative content, are preserved, while low-entropy redundant nodes are discarded. To obtain region representations, we design a modality-aware attention mechanism to dynamically adjust each modality's contribution, ensuring an effective multi-modal region representation.

Entropy-Optimized Graph Node Pruning Mechanism. To enhance efficiency and reduce redundancy, we perform entropy-optimized graph node pruning on both the local and global graphs. **(1)** In the local graph, $\mathcal{G}_i$, a large number of street view images nodes SV_{ij} are present, with each node represented as $sv_{ij} \in \mathbb{R}^{d_{in}}$. Here, $j = 1, 2, \ldots, |\mathcal{M}_i|$. To assess the informativeness of each node SV_{ij}, we first normalize its feature vector as $sv_{ij,f}^{\text{norm}} = \frac{|sv_{ij,f}|}{\sum_{f=1}^{d_{in}} |sv_{ij,f}|}$ to ensure proportional scaling. We then compute its entropy $H(SV_{ij})$ and sampling probability $P(SV_{ij})$ as:

$$H(SV_{ij}) = -\sum_{f=1}^{d_{in}} sv_{ij,f}^{\text{norm}} \log(sv_{ij,f}^{\text{norm}}), \quad P(SV_{ij}) = H(SV_{ij}) / \sum_{j=1}^{|SV_i|} H(SV_{ij}). \quad (3)$$

Then existence of node SV_{ij} follows a Bernoulli distribution, $SV_{ij} \sim \text{Bern}(P(SV_{ij}))$. Nodes with higher entropy values, and consequently higher $P(SV_{ij})$, are more likely to be retained, while low-entropy nodes are pruned. The retained nodes are selected based on the *sampling ratio* ε. The sampled street view node representations, where each is $sv_{ij} \in \mathbb{R}^{d_{in}}$, are averaged to derive an embedding $sv_i \in \mathbb{R}^{d_{in}}$ for region U_i. Similarly, an embedding for the road network is obtained as $rn_i \in \mathbb{R}^{d_{in}}$.

(2) In the global graph, $\mathcal{G}$, a large number of fine-grained street view images nodes and road network elements nodes are present in the region U_i. Applying the same pruning strategy as in the local graph, we retain high-entropy nodes and average their representations to obtain the final embeddings $\overline{sv}_i, \overline{rn}_i \in \mathbb{R}^{d_{in}}$ for region U_i.

Modality-Aware Attention Mechanism. To effectively capture the varying contributions of different modalities, we apply a modality-aware attention mechanism in both the local and global graphs. **(1)** In the local graph, $\mathcal{G}_i$ of region U_i, modality representations are denoted as $m_i \in \mathbb{R}^{d_{in}}$, where $m \in \{u, p, tf, rs, sv, rn\}$. Since different modalities contribute unequally to the final region representation, an attention weight vector $w_m \in \mathbb{R}^{d_{in}}$ is learned for each modality to capture its importance. The modality-specific representation is computed as $m_i^{attn} = \sigma(w_m \odot m_i)$, where $\odot$ denotes element-wise multiplication and σ is an activation function. To refine the information, a linear transformation [17] is applied, followed by an autoencoder [1] with a *hidden dimension* of d_{hid}, producing the final local modality representation $m_i^{final} \in \mathbb{R}^{d_{out}}$.

(2) In the global graph $\mathcal{G}$, modality representations in region $\mathcal{U}_i$ are given by $\overline{m_i} \in \mathbb{R}^{d_{in}}$, where $m \in \{u, p, tf, rs, sv, rn\}$. Applying the same modality-aware attention mechanism, we derive the final global modality representation as $\overline{m}_i^{final} \in \mathbb{R}^{d_{out}}$.

Local-Global Region Representation. We compute coarse-grained, fine-grained, and overall local region representations $H_i^{\mathcal{CM}}, H_i^{\mathcal{FM}}, H_i^{local} \in \mathbb{R}^{d_{out}}$ and global representation $H_i^{global} \in \mathbb{R}^{d_{out}}$ as described below:

$$H_i^{\mathcal{X}} = \text{Mean}\left(\{m_i^{final} \mid m \in \mathcal{X}\}\right), \quad \mathcal{X} \in \{\mathcal{CM}, \mathcal{FM}, local\},$$
$$\mathcal{CM} = \{p, tf, rs\}, \quad \mathcal{FM} = \{sv, rn\}, \quad local = \{u, p, tf, rs, sv, rn\}, \quad (4)$$
$$H_i^{global} = \text{Mean}\left(\{\overline{m}_i^{final} \mid m \in \{u, p, tf, rs, sv, rn\}\}\right).$$

4.4 Joint Contrastive Learning

To effectively learn multi-modal region representations within our dual-perspective local and global graph framework, we introduce a joint contrastive learning approach that optimizes H_i^{local} from three views.

Geography-Driven Contrastive Learning with $H_i^{\mathcal{CM}}$. The coarse-grained local region representation $H_i^{\mathcal{CM}}$ captures functional attributes with strong geographical continuity. Since neighboring regions exhibit similar coarse-grained representations, we apply contrastive learning by treating geographically adjacent regions, such as U_j, as positive samples and non-adjacent regions, such as U_s, as negative samples. To refine the final region representation, we replace $H_i^{\mathcal{CM}}$ with H_i^{local}, γ is a margin hyperparameter and $\|\cdot\|_2$ represents the L2 norm, the contrastive loss is defined as follows:

$$\mathcal{L}_{\mathcal{CM}} = \max\left(\|H_i^{local} - H_j^{\mathcal{CM}}\|_2 - \|H_i^{local} - H_s^{\mathcal{CM}}\|_2 + \gamma, 0\right). \tag{5}$$

Entropy-Optimized Contrastive Learning with $H_i^{\mathcal{FM}}$. The fine-grained local region representation $H_i^{\mathcal{FM}}$ captures spatial topology and local environmental structures. Due to high variability across regions, all regions except the target are treated as negative samples, with positive samples drawn from the region's own fine-grained data. During graph node pruning, a different *sampling ratio* ε_1. is used to obtain $\tilde{H}_i^{\mathcal{FM}}$, which serves as a positive sample. To refine the final representation, H_i^{local} replaces $H_i^{\mathcal{FM}}$. τ is the temperature hyperparameter. The entropy-optimized contrastive loss is:

$$\mathcal{L}_{\mathcal{FM}} = \sum_{i=1}^{N}\left[-\log\exp\left(\frac{H_i^{local} \cdot \tilde{H}_i^{\mathcal{FM}}}{\tau}\right) \right. \\ \left. + \log\left(\exp\left(\frac{H_i^{local} \cdot \tilde{H}_i^{\mathcal{FM}}}{\tau}\right) + \sum_{j \neq i}\exp\left(\frac{H_i^{local} \cdot H_j^{local}}{\tau}\right)\right)\right], \tag{6}$$

Mutual Information-Based Optimization with H_i^{global}. The global region representation H_i^{global} and the local region representation H_i^{local} capture complementary perspectives from the same regional data. To integrate global information into H_i^{local}, we maximize the mutual information $\mathcal{I}(H_i^{local}, H_i^{global}) = \mathbb{E}\left[\log\frac{p_i^{l,g}}{p_i^l p_i^g}\right]$, where $p_i^{l,g}$, p_i^l, and p_i^g represent the joint and marginal distributions of the local and global representations, respectively. The mutual information is optimized by minimizing the following contrastive loss, with λ as a hyperparameter:

$$\mathcal{L}_{MI} = -\sum_i p_i^{l,g}\left[\log p_i^{l,g} - \lambda\left(\log p_i^l + \log p_i^g\right)\right]. \tag{7}$$

Training. The final objective function is defined as:

$$\mathcal{L} = \mathcal{L}_{\mathcal{CM}} + \mathcal{L}_{\mathcal{FM}} + \mathcal{L}_{MI}. \tag{8}$$

The enhanced local region representation, H_i^{local}, learned jointly through $\mathcal{L}$, serve as the final region embeddings $H_i \in \mathbb{R}^{dout}$. $\mathcal{H} = H_1, H_2, \ldots, H_N$ corresponds to the urban regions $\mathcal{U} = U_1, U_2, \ldots, U_N$ and is used for predicting downstream tasks Y.

Table 1. Dataset statistics. * denotes model training data, and # denotes downstream task data.

	$\mathcal{U}^*$	$\mathcal{P}^*$	$\mathcal{TF}^*$	$\mathcal{RS}^*$	$\mathcal{SV}^*$	$\mathcal{RN}^*$	Crime#	Crash#	Check-in#
NYC	180	20872	848006	180	20698	13200	77701	14564	329153
CHI	77	36963	922746	77	36179	56005	91252	109645	167222

5 Evaluation

5.1 Experimental Setup

Datasets and Metrics. We conduct experiments on two real-world urban datasets from New York City (NYC) and Chicago (CHI) [7,24,28], which provide region-level information $\mathcal{U}$ along with five heterogeneous modalities: Points of Interest (POI) $\mathcal{P}$, taxi flow $\mathcal{TF}$, remote sensing imagery $\mathcal{RS}$, street view data $\mathcal{SV}$, and road network topology $\mathcal{RN}$. These multimodal datasets support three representative downstream tasks: check-in prediction, crime forecasting, and traffic crash prediction. The detailed dataset statistics are summarized in Table 1. To comprehensively evaluate prediction performance, we adopt three widely used metrics: Mean Absolute Error (MAE), Root Mean Squared Error (RMSE), and the Coefficient of Determination (R^2). These metrics jointly assess both the accuracy and robustness of the model across different predictive tasks.

Baselines. To evaluate the performance of GraphJCL, we compare it with seven baseline models: **i)** GraphST [29], a spatiotemporal graph learning model designed for self-supervised learning; **ii)** ReCP [9], a pipeline for consistent representation learning across diverse views; **iii)** HREP [32], a framework leveraging heterogeneous region embedding with prompt learning; **iv)** HAFusion [15], which applies a dual-feature attentive fusion module to capture higher-order correlations within and across region features; **v)** UrbanVLP [4], integrating multi-granularity macro (satellite) and micro (street-view) information; **vi)** MuseCL [24], a multi-semantic contrastive learning framework for fine-grained urban region profiling; and **vii)** GURPP [7], a graph-based urban region pretraining and prompting framework for improved representation learning.

Parameter Settings. For experiments in NYC and CHI, the input and output dimensionality (d_{in} and d_{out}) of all modalities is consistently set to 168. Models for both cities are optimized using Adam optimizer with a learning rate of 0.001 and weight decay of 0.01, and trained for a maximum of 50 epochs. The batch size is configured as 180 for NYC and 77 for CHI. The hyperparameters for contrastive learning are as follows: the margin hyperparameter γ and the temperature hyperparameter τ are both set to 2 and 0.1, respectively, for both cities. The parameter λ is set to 8 for NYC and 7 for CHI.

5.2 Overall Performance

Table 2 presents a performance comparison of baseline models across three tasks in two cities. Since different region representation models utilize different modality sets $\mathcal{UM}$,

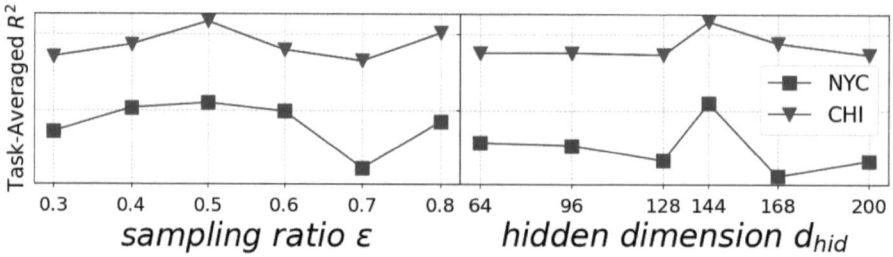

Fig. 3. Hyperparameter study of GraphJCL.

a total of ten modality sets are employed in the regional representation models reviewed in this paper, as detailed in the header of Table 2. Among these, $\mathcal{UM}_1, \mathcal{UM}_2, \mathcal{UM}_3$, and $\mathcal{UM}_4$ correspond to modality sets used by existing models, while the remaining six are novel modality sets introduced by our model. **(1) High Flexibility and Effectiveness:** On existing modality sets, GraphJCL outperforms baseline models across all tasks and cities, highlighting its effectiveness in capturing regional representations from both local and global perspectives. Moreover, its support for ten modality sets demonstrates superior flexibility. **(2) Adaptability to Novel Modality Sets:** GraphJCL consistently performs well across all ten modality sets, proving its adaptability to diverse data distributions and robustness with novel modality sets. **(3) Effective Modality Information Utilization:** The modality sets ($\mathcal{UM}_i$, $i = 3, 4, 5, 6, 7$) are derived by sequentially removing $\mathcal{RN}, \mathcal{SV}, \mathcal{P}, \mathcal{TF}$, or $\mathcal{RS}$ from the full set ($\mathcal{P}, \mathcal{TF}, \mathcal{RS}, \mathcal{SV}, \mathcal{RN}$). The performance decline of GraphJCL when excluding any modality underscores its capability to effectively leverage each modality and integrate their distinct information features.

5.3 Ablation Study

To assess the contributions of different modules in our model, we evaluate five variants of **GraphJCL**: i) **w/o NP**: Removes entropy-optimized graph node pruning. ii) **w/o MA**: Removes the modality-aware attention mechanism. iii) **w/o** $\mathcal{L}_{CM}$: Removes geography-driven contrastive learning. iv) **w/o** $\mathcal{L}_{FM}$: Removes entropy-optimized contrastive learning. v) **w/o** $\mathcal{L}_{MI}$: Removes mutual information-based optimization. Experimental results are shown in Table 3. The results show that **GraphJCL** outperforms all variants, highlighting the importance of its key modules. Notably, removing entropy-optimized local graph node pruning (**w/o NP**) causes the largest performance drop, emphasizing the importance of selecting high mutual-information nodes. Omitting the modality-aware attention mechanism (**w/o MA**) also reduces performance, underlining the need for modality weighting in final region representations. Finally, removing any of the contrastive learning components (**w/o** $\mathcal{L}_{CM}$, **w/o** $\mathcal{L}_{FM}$, or **w/o** $\mathcal{L}_{MI}$) leads to performance degradation, highlighting the significance of joint contrastive learning.

Table 2. Performance comparison of baseline models across three tasks in two cities. $\mathcal{UM}$ represents the corresponding modality set used by each model. A total of 10 modality sets are utilized across all models, as listed below: $\mathcal{TM} = (\mathcal{P}, \mathcal{TF}, \mathcal{RS}, \mathcal{SV}, \mathcal{RN})$, $\mathcal{UM}_1 = (\mathcal{P}, \mathcal{TF})$, $\mathcal{UM}_2 = (\mathcal{RS}, \mathcal{SV})$, $\mathcal{UM}_3 = \mathcal{TM} \setminus \mathcal{RN}$ (i.e., $\mathcal{TM}$ excluding $\mathcal{RN}$), $\mathcal{UM}_4 = \mathcal{TM} \setminus \mathcal{SV}$ (i.e., $\mathcal{TM}$ excluding $\mathcal{SV}$), $\mathcal{UM}_5 = \mathcal{TM} \setminus \mathcal{P}$ (i.e., $\mathcal{TM}$ excluding $\mathcal{P}$), $\mathcal{UM}_6 = \mathcal{TM} \setminus \mathcal{TF}$ (i.e., $\mathcal{TM}$ excluding $\mathcal{TF}$), $\mathcal{UM}_7 = \mathcal{TM} \setminus \mathcal{RS}$ (i.e., $\mathcal{TM}$ excluding $\mathcal{RS}$), $\mathcal{UM}_8 = (\mathcal{P}, \mathcal{TF}, \mathcal{RN})$, $\mathcal{UM}_9 = (\mathcal{RS}, \mathcal{SV}, \mathcal{RN})$.

Model	$\mathcal{UM}$	NYC								
		Check-in			Crime			Crash		
		MAE↓	RMSE↓	R2↑	MAE↓	RMSE↓	R2↑	MAE↓	RMSE↓	R2↑
GraphST [29]	$\mathcal{UM}_1$	1501.3	2838.2	0.284	316.04	496.41	0.103	30.855	42.633	0.162
ReCP [9]	$\mathcal{UM}_1$	823.4	1404.6	0.719	183.74	280.56	0.498	33.518	43.110	0.226
HREP [32]	$\mathcal{UM}_1$	1122.6	1745.4	0.566	201.69	308.86	0.391	26.859	34.483	0.505
HAFusion [15]	$\mathcal{UM}_1$	1051.7	1709.0	0.584	188.15	299.60	0.427	25.177	32.566	0.558
UrbanVLP [4]	$\mathcal{UM}_2$	1508.5	2652.6	0.286	195.30	404.53	0.395	38.421	50.695	0.183
MuseCL [24]	$\mathcal{UM}_3$	1479.3	2781.6	0.313	278.28	394.83	0.433	33.977	44.077	0.104
GURPP [7]	$\mathcal{UM}_4$	900.3	1356.0	0.738	194.64	280.50	0.498	30.194	41.764	0.274
GraphJCL	$\mathcal{UM}_1$	747.5	1269.6	0.771	165.33	251.80	0.595	26.987	34.771	0.497
	$\mathcal{UM}_2$	**610.1**	1072.8	0.836	167.19	270.28	0.534	27.672	35.732	0.468
	$\mathcal{UM}_3$	613.0	1117.1	0.822	162.73	257.18	0.578	26.106	34.869	0.495
	$\mathcal{UM}_4$	691.5	1248.9	0.778	158.35	246.95	0.611	26.861	36.399	0.448
	$\mathcal{UM}_5$	684.4	1142.5	0.814	164.67	258.01	0.575	23.199	30.542	0.612
	$\mathcal{UM}_6$	683.8	1135.7	0.816	170.37	275.84	0.514	22.498	29.430	0.639
	$\mathcal{UM}_7$	683.7	1103.7	0.827	176.39	276.10	0.513	22.891	29.979	**0.651**
	$\mathcal{UM}_8$	770.5	1320.5	0.752	172.18	266.48	0.546	23.027	29.908	0.628
	$\mathcal{UM}_9$	676.7	1142.9	0.814	177.99	264.27	0.554	24.481	31.482	0.587
	$\mathcal{TM}$	676.2	**1027.0**	**0.850**	**158.20**	**235.26**	**0.647**	**22.829**	**29.733**	0.632

Model	$\mathcal{UM}$	CHI								
		Check-in			Crime			Crash		
		MAE↓	RMSE↓	R2↑	MAE↓	RMSE↓	R2↑	MAE↓	RMSE↓	R2↑
GraphST [29]	$\mathcal{UM}_1$	2066.7	5281.3	0.545	566.79	721.12	0.381	548.625	761.611	0.464
ReCP [9]	$\mathcal{UM}_1$	1508.2	3448.3	0.581	322.41	445.39	0.763	384.472	555.310	0.701
HREP [32]	$\mathcal{UM}_1$	2139.5	4174.6	0.385	518.71	679.53	0.448	623.910	811.459	0.362
HAFusion [15]	$\mathcal{UM}_1$	1280.7	3424.5	0.586	578.57	758.15	0.312	655.469	899.352	0.217
UrbanVLP [4]	$\mathcal{UM}_2$	2524.5	5786.6	0.388	570.67	859.28	0.388	613.180	883.680	0.510
MuseCL [24]	$\mathcal{UM}_3$	2264.2	5944.2	0.424	624.35	858.21	0.123	473.063	596.230	0.672
GURPP [7]	$\mathcal{UM}_4$	1251.5	2850.9	0.713	346.84	455.69	0.752	386.788	586.449	0.667
GraphJCL	$\mathcal{UM}_1$	1145.9	2783.3	0.727	302.54	400.827	0.797	367.110	529.178	0.729
	$\mathcal{UM}_2$	1555.0	3526.5	0.561	381.56	498.66	0.703	330.951	469.629	0.786
	$\mathcal{UM}_3$	1154.8	2812.7	0.721	300.32	427.16	0.782	342.628	505.661	0.752
	$\mathcal{UM}_4$	1194.2	2695.4	0.744	317.21	464.22	0.742	335.786	466.867	0.789
	$\mathcal{UM}_5$	1267.7	2860.0	0.712	436.94	592.05	0.581	319.905	469.139	0.789
	$\mathcal{UM}_6$	1139.5	2692.2	0.744	349.06	529.48	0.665	**306.288**	496.011	0.762
	$\mathcal{UM}_7$	1217.8	3011.6	0.680	338.89	463.84	0.743	326.074	479.446	0.777
	$\mathcal{UM}_8$	1001.0	2326.3	0.809	305.38	417.81	0.791	322.057	528.207	0.730
	$\mathcal{UM}_9$	1361.3	2985.7	0.685	437.97	575.19	0.604	313.112	469.137	0.787
	$\mathcal{TM}$	**894.9**	**2115.2**	**0.842**	**293.24**	**391.67**	**0.817**	316.244	**465.734**	**0.790**

Table 3. Performance evaluation of ablation experiments across three tasks in two cities.

Method	NYC								
	Check-in			Crime			Crash		
	MAE↓	RMSE↓	R2↑	MAE↓	RMSE↓	R2↑	MAE↓	RMSE↓	R2↑
w/o NP	730.8	1364.7	0.735	165.68	238.62	0.637	23.968	30.809	0.605
w/o MA	681.4	1035.5	0.847	160.06	247.06	0.610	23.626	31.183	0.595
w/o $\mathcal{L}_{CM}$	687.3	1135.8	0.816	170.02	277.19	0.510	24.555	32.049	0.572
w/o $\mathcal{L}_{FM}$	758.2	1238.7	0.782	174.63	283.53	0.487	23.945	31.593	0.584
w/o $\mathcal{L}_{MI}$	701.4	1053.0	0.842	160.50	241.36	0.628	23.760	31.177	0.595
GraphJCL	**676.2**	**1027.0**	**0.850**	**158.20**	**235.26**	**0.647**	**22.829**	**29.733**	**0.632**

Method	CHI								
	Check-in			Crime			Crash		
	MAE↓	RMSE↓	R2↑	MAE↓	RMSE↓	R2↑	MAE↓	RMSE↓	R2↑
w/o NP	1080.3	2446.7	0.789	366.08	497.45	0.704	333.024	468.868	0.787
w/o MA	928.0	2297.8	0.813	311.24	435.34	0.773	317.946	484.319	0.772
w/o $\mathcal{L}_{CM}$	1098.7	2412.6	0.795	315.98	438.36	0.770	351.831	545.538	0.712
w/o $\mathcal{L}_{FM}$	1103.8	2516.8	0.777	317.49	426.89	0.782	314.124	456.12	0.783
w/o $\mathcal{L}_{MI}$	895.9	2232.3	0.824	294.44	393.11	0.809	323.476	488.833	0.769
GraphJCL	**894.9**	**2115.2**	**0.842**	**293.24**	**391.67**	**0.817**	**288.56**	**434.242**	**0.812**

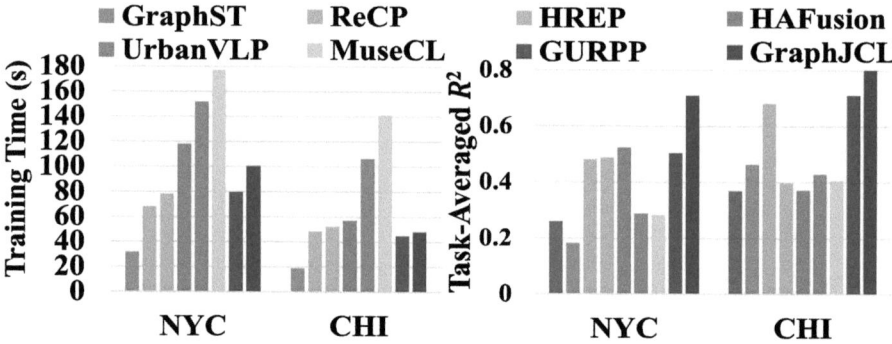

Fig. 4. Efficiency study: The time required for each model to load all data and train for one epoch.

5.4 Hyper-parameter Study

We conduct a detailed analysis of two key hyper-parameters that significantly influence the model's performance: the *sampling ratio* ε used in the entropy-optimized graph node pruning module, and the *hidden dimension* d_{hid} employed in the modality-aware attention mechanism, both introduced in Subsect. 4.3. The effects of these hyper-parameters are illustrated in Fig. 3, where model performance is evaluated using the average coefficient of determination (R^2) across three representative urban prediction tasks: check-in prediction, crime forecasting, and traffic crash prediction. For the NYC dataset, setting the sampling ratio ε to 0.5 and hidden dimension d_{hid} to 144 consistently yields the highest average R^2 across tasks. Similar trends are observed for the CHI dataset, where we also set $\varepsilon = 0.5$ and $d_{hid} = 144$ as optimal. Consequently, we adopt $\varepsilon = 0.5$ and $d_{hid} = 144$ as the default settings for both cities.

5.5 Model Efficiency Study

We evaluate the efficiency of GraphJCL in comparison with state-of-the-art region representation models using the complete modality set $(\mathcal{P}, \mathcal{TF}, \mathcal{RS}, \mathcal{SV}, \mathcal{RN})$. The evaluation procedure involves loading the same raw datasets, applying model-specific preprocessing pipelines, and training each model for one epoch, as illustrated in Fig. 4. All experiments were conducted on an Intel® Xeon® Gold 6148 CPU (80 cores, 2.40 GHz) and a 24 GB NVIDIA RTX 4090 GPU to ensure consistent and fair comparisons. GraphJCL demonstrates superior efficiency by achieving higher predictive accuracy while maintaining competitive processing time when compared to HAFusion, UrbanVLP, and MuseCL. Although GraphST, ReCP, HREP, and GURPP exhibit faster training speeds, their overall performance is limited due to reduced modality usage and oversimplified modeling strategies. By integrating dual-perspective global and local modeling with five different modalities, GraphJCL slightly increases training time but significantly enhances predictive performance, making the additional computational cost a highly worthwhile trade-off for practical applications.

6 Discussion and Conclusion

In this paper, we propose **GraphJCL**, a novel dual-perspective graph framework for urban region representation that models both local and global perspectives. It employs joint contrastive learning to enhance region representations. Experimental results demonstrate the model's flexibility and effectiveness. Future research will explore alternative strategies for integrating local and global learning beyond contrastive optimization, as well as extending the framework to incorporate dynamic data, temporal variations, and contextual information to enhance real-time prediction accuracy and robustness.

Acknowledgments. This work is supported by the MOE Project of Key Research Institute of Humanities and Social Sciences (No.22JJD110001), the National Natural Science Foundation of China (No.72171229) and the Outstanding Innovative Talents Cultivation Funded Programs 2023 of Renmin University of China.

References

1. Berahmand, K., Daneshfar, F., Salehi, E.S., Li, Y., Xu, Y.: Autoencoders and their applications in machine learning: a survey. Artif. Intell. Rev. **57**(2), 28 (2024)
2. Chan, W., Ren, Q., Li, J.: Enhanced urban region profiling with adversarial self-supervised learning. arXiv preprint arXiv:2402.01163 (2024)

3. Grover, A., Leskovec, J.: node2vec: scalable feature learning for networks. In: Proceedings of the 22nd ACM SIGKDD International Conference on Knowledge Discovery and Data Mining, pp. 855–864 (2016)
4. Hao, X., et al.: Urbanvlp: multi-granularity vision-language pretraining for urban region profiling. arXiv preprint arXiv:2403.16831 (2024)
5. Hu, J., Bai, J., Yang, J., Lee, J.J.: Crash risk prediction using sparse collision data: granger causal inference and graph convolutional network approaches. Expert Syst. Appl. **259**, 125315 (2025)
6. Huang, W., Zhang, D., Mai, G., Guo, X., Cui, L.: Learning urban region representations with pois and hierarchical graph infomax. ISPRS J. Photogramm. Remote. Sens. **196**, 134–145 (2023)
7. Jin, J., et al.: Urban region pre-training and prompting: a graph-based approach. arXiv preprint arXiv:2408.05920 (2024)
8. Li, Y., Huang, W., Cong, G., Wang, H., Wang, Z.: Urban region representation learning with openstreetmap building footprints. In: Proceedings of the 29th ACM SIGKDD Conference on Knowledge Discovery and Data Mining, pp. 1363–1373 (2023)
9. Li, Z., Huang, W., Zhao, K., Yang, M., Gong, Y., Chen, M.: Urban region embedding via multi-view contrastive prediction. In: Proceedings of the AAAI Conference on Artificial Intelligence, vol. 38, pp. 8724–8732 (2024)
10. Luo, Y., Chung, F.l., Chen, K.: Urban region profiling via multi-graph representation learning. In: Proceedings of the 31st ACM International Conference on Information & Knowledge Management, pp. 4294–4298 (2022)
11. Mandal, S., O'Connor, N.E.: Llmasmmkg: Llm assisted synthetic multi-modal knowledge graph creation for smart city cognitive digital twins. In: Proceedings of the AAAI Symposium Series, vol. 4, pp. 210–221 (2024)
12. Mikolov, T., Le, Q.V., Sutskever, I., Chen, K., Corrado, G., Dean, J.: Efficient estimation of word representations in vector space. In: International Conference on Learning Representations (ICLR) (2013)
13. Radford, A., et al.: Learning transferable visual models from natural language supervision. In: International Conference on Machine Learning, pp. 8748–8763. PMLR (2021)
14. Shui, C., Li, X., Qi, J., Jiang, G., Yu, Y.: Hierarchical graph contrastive learning for review-enhanced recommendation. In: Bifet, A., Davis, J., Krilavičius, T., Kull, M., Ntoutsi, E., Žliobaitė, I. (eds.) Machine Learning and Knowledge Discovery in Databases. Research Track, pp. 423–440. Springer, Cham (2024). https://doi.org/10.1007/978-3-031-70365-2_25
15. Sun, F., Qi, J., Chang, Y., Fan, X., Karunasekera, S., Tanin, E.: Urban region representation learning with attentive fusion. In: 2024 IEEE 40th International Conference on Data Engineering (ICDE), pp. 4409–4421. IEEE (2024)
16. Tan, M., Le, Q.: Efficientnet: rethinking model scaling for convolutional neural networks. In: International Conference on Machine Learning, pp. 6105–6114. PMLR (2019)
17. Vaswani, A., et al.: Attention is all you need. Adv. Neural Inf. Process. Syst. **30** (2017)
18. Wu, S., et al.: Multi-graph fusion networks for urban region embedding. In: Proceedings of the Thirty-First International Joint Conference on Artificial Intelligence, IJCAI-22, pp. 2312–2318 (2022)
19. Xia, L., et al.: Spatial-temporal sequential hypergraph network for crime prediction with dynamic multiplex relation learning. In: Proceedings of the Thirtieth International Joint Conference on Artificial Intelligence, IJCAI-21, pp. 1631–1637 (2021)
20. Xiao, C., Zhou, J., Xiao, Y., Huang, J., Xiong, H.: Refound: crafting a foundation model for urban region understanding upon language and visual foundations. In: Proceedings of the 30th ACM SIGKDD Conference on Knowledge Discovery and Data Mining (2024)

21. Xu, Z., Zhou, X.: Cgap: urban region representation learning with coarsened graph attention pooling. In: Larson, K. (ed.) Proceedings of the Thirty-Third International Joint Conference on Artificial Intelligence, IJCAI-24, pp. 7518–7526 (2024)
22. Yan, Y., et al.: Urbanclip: learning text-enhanced urban region profiling with contrastive language-image pretraining from the web. In: Proceedings of the ACM Web Conference 2024, WWW '24, pp. 4006–4017 (2024)
23. Yao, Z., Fu, Y., Liu, B., Hu, W., Xiong, H.: Representing urban functions through zone embedding with human mobility patterns. In: Proceedings of the Twenty-Seventh International Joint Conference on Artificial Intelligence (IJCAI-18) (2018)
24. Yong, X., Zhou, X.: Musecl: predicting urban socioeconomic indicators via multi-semantic contrastive learning. In: Larson, K. (ed.) Proceedings of the Thirty-Third International Joint Conference on Artificial Intelligence, IJCAI-24, pp. 7536–7544 (2024)
25. You, Y., Chen, T., Wang, Z., Shen, Y.: Bringing your own view: graph contrastive learning without prefabricated data augmentations. In: Proceedings of the Fifteenth ACM International Conference on Web Search and Data Mining, WSDM '22, pp. 1300–1309 (2022)
26. Zhang, L., Long, C., Cong, G.: Region embedding with intra and inter-view contrastive learning. IEEE Trans. Knowl. Data Eng. **35**(9), 9031–9036 (2022)
27. Zhang, M., Li, T., Li, Y., Hui, P.: Multi-view joint graph representation learning for urban region embedding. In: Proceedings of the Twenty-Ninth International Conference on International Joint Conferences on Artificial Intelligence, pp. 4431–4437 (2021)
28. Zhang, Q., Huang, C., Xia, L., Wang, Z., Li, Z., Yiu, S.: Automated spatio-temporal graph contrastive learning. In: Proceedings of the ACM Web Conference 2023, pp. 295–305 (2023)
29. Zhang, Q., Huang, C., Xia, L., Wang, Z., Yiu, S.M., Han, R.: Spatial-temporal graph learning with adversarial contrastive adaptation. In: International Conference on Machine Learning, pp. 41151–41163. PMLR (2023)
30. Zhang, Y., Fu, Y., Wang, P., Li, X., Zheng, Y.: Unifying inter-region autocorrelation and intra-region structures for spatial embedding via collective adversarial learning. In: Proceedings of the 25th ACM SIGKDD International Conference on Knowledge Discovery & Data Mining, pp. 1700–1708 (2019)
31. Zhao, Z., Ge, Q., Cheng, A., Liu, Y., Li, X., Wang, S.: HetCAN: a heterogeneous graph cascade attention network with dual-level awareness. In: Bifet, A., Davis, J., Krilavičius, T., Kull, M., Ntoutsi, E., Žliobaitė, I. (eds.) Machine Learning and Knowledge Discovery in Databases. Research Track, pp. 57–73. Springer, Cham (2024). https://doi.org/10.1007/978-3-031-70365-2_4
32. Zhou, S., He, D., Chen, L., Shang, S., Han, P.: Heterogeneous region embedding with prompt learning. In: Proceedings of the AAAI Conference on Artificial Intelligence, vol. 37, pp. 4981–4989 (2023)
33. Zou, X., et al.: Learning geospatial region embedding with heterogeneous graph. arXiv preprint arXiv:2405.14135 (2024)

Graphs and Networks

DiNGHy: Null Models for Non-degenerate Directed Hypergraphs

Maryam Abuissa[1]($\boxtimes$)[iD], Matteo Riondato[2][iD], and Eli Upfal[1][iD]

[1] Brown University, Providence, RI 02912, USA
{maryam_abuissa,eliezer_upfal}@brown.edu
[2] Amherst College, Amherst, MA 01002, USA
mriondato@amherst.edu

Abstract. Non-degenerate directed hypergraphs, i.e., directed hypergraphs where a node cannot be both in the tail and the head of a hyperedge, model important scenarios, from contact networks for analyzing the spread of information or diseases, to bill cosponsoring graphs for studying the bipartisanship of elected representatives. Existing null models for dihypergraphs allow degeneracy, and most samples drawn from them are degenerate, even when the starting network is not, making these models unrealistic in many cases. An inappropriate null model may lead to wrongly accepting/rejecting a hypothesis when performing statistical hypothesis testing. We introduce the first null models for non-degenerate dihypergraphs, and present DiNGHy, a suite of Markov-Chain-Monte-Carlo algorithms to sample from them. The Markov chain underlying our algorithm is not irreducible in general, so we give mild sufficient conditions for irreducibility. We show that existing methods cannot be used to sample from our null models, and evaluate our algorithms on real and artificial dihypergraphs, comparing the results of hypothesis tests when using our null models versus existing ones that allow degeneracy, and measuring their empirical mixing time.

Keywords: Graph Analysis · Hypothesis Testing · Markov Chain Monte Carlo · Network Science

1 Introduction

Hypergraphs overcome the limitations of dyadic (i.e., "classic") graphs to model "more-than-binary" relationships between entities [2,3]. Such relationships are omnipresent in real scenarios, from co-authorship networks [16], to protein interactions [9], to contact networks [4]. There are many data analysis tasks and corresponding algorithms whose input is one or more hypergraphs [14].

The goal of knowledge discovery from data is to use results obtained from data to *identify new facts about the Data Generating Process (DGP)*, of which the available data is only a limited, noisy, random sample [21]. In the framework of statistical hypothesis testing [15], one first formulates a hypothesis, usually expressed

---

Supplementary Information The online version contains supplementary material available at https://doi.org/10.1007/978-3-032-06066-2_4.

© The Author(s), under exclusive license to Springer Nature Switzerland AG 2026
R. P. Ribeiro et al. (Eds.): ECML PKDD 2025, LNAI 16015, pp. 57–74, 2026.
https://doi.org/10.1007/978-3-032-06066-2_4

as whether known properties of the DGP can sufficiently explain a result obtained from the available data. The hypothesis is then tested by comparing the observed result to the distribution of results over the datasets the DGP may produce. When there is a low probability that the DGP produces datasets with as or more extreme values than the observed value, it is seen as evidence against the hypothesis, i.e., that the known properties of the DGP cannot sufficiently explain the observed result. The DGP is formally captured by a *null model* (see Sect. 3.2 for definitions), a collection of datasets and a distribution over these datasets. The key *algorithmic* challenge is to develop efficient methods to draw samples from the collection according to the distribution. The samples create a distribution over the value of interest, to which the observed value can be compared. The *modeling* challenge is even more important for hypothesis testing: the null model must be *realistic*, i.e., it must capture as many known properties as possible about the DGP. In particular, it should not include any dataset that the DGP cannot produce. Failure to do so may lead to an inaccurate distribution of possible results, changing the outcome of hypothesis testing.

Null models for *undirected* hypergraphs are available (see Sect. 2), but limited attention has been devoted to null models for directed ones (dihypergraphs);

Contributions. We introduce novel realistic null models for dihypergraphs, and give algorithms to sample from them.[1]

- Our null models are defined over non-degenerate dihypergraphs, i.e., dihypergraphs where a node cannot be present in both the head and the tail of the same hyperedge. This restriction is representative of many real scenarios, from U.S. Congress bill sponsorship, to contagion by contact, and is not captured by existing null models [20]. Thus, our null models are more realistic. They exactly preserve the in-/out-degree and the head-/tail-hyperedge-dimension sequences of an observed hypergraph, extending the popular microcanonical configuration model. We give null models for both edge-ordered and edge-unordered dihypergraphs, defined in Sect. 5.
- We describe and analyze Markov-Chain-Monte-Carlo (MCMC) algorithms, DiNgHy (edge-ordered) and DiNgHy-U (edge-unordered) (for DIrected Non-deGenerate HYpergraphs), to sample from the hypergraph ensembles of our null models according to any user-specified probability distribution, which is a necessary step in statistical hypothesis testing. Our Markov chains use simple transitions; the crux of our analysis is proving an easy-to-check mild condition on the degree and hyperedge-dimension sequences of the observed network that guarantees the irreducibility of the Markov chain.
- The results of our evaluation on real and artificial datasets highlights how the outcome of hypothesis tests may greatly differ between our null model and that of Preti et al. [20], We also give evidence that their algorithm cannot be used with rejection sampling to sample non-degenerate dihypergraphs. Finally, we show faster empirical mixing time of our algorithm compared to a baseline derived from the algorithm by Preti et al. [20].

---

[1] Theoretical proofs and additional experimental results are in the supplementary materials.

2 Related Work

Hypergraph mining has many applications in different settings. Lee et al. [14] survey the area in depth, so here we focus on the works most related to ours.

Many null models are available for dyadic (i.e., non-hyper) graphs, preserving different properties of the observed network, either exactly (microcanonical models) or in expectation (canonical models), together with algorithms, usually MCMC, to sample from these graph ensembles [7, 10, and references therein]. The null model over bipartite graphs with fixed degree sequences (a.k.a. the configuration model) has been deeply studied [10, 11]. We use pairs of bipartite graphs to define an equivalent representation of dihypergraphs, and build on a result by Kannan et al. [11] about the irreducibility of a Markov chain on bipartite graphs to show the irreducibility of our Markov chain on dihypergraphs.

Proving irreducibility is usually the key theoretical challenge in developing MCMC algorithms. For directed graphs, irreducibility is not guaranteed, because edge swaps cannot directly flip a directed triangle. Lamar [13] gives tight conditions on the degree sequence that imply irreducibility for digraphs. Similar issues arise on dihypergraphs, but a novel approach, and conditions on the observed degree and edge-dimension sequences, are required to prove irreducibility.

(Di-)hypergraphs have received relatively little attention, despite their practical importance [2, 3]. Many contributions study the configuration model for undirected hypergraphs [5, 6, 8, 24], or define maximum entropy models [23] or models that preserve higher order constraints [18, 19]. These approaches cannot be adapted to dihypergraphs.

Kim et al. [12] extend the preferential attachment model on hypergraphs [8] to dihypergraphs, preserving, *in expectation*, the node degrees and the hyperedge head- and tail- dimension sequences. As observed by Preti et al. [20], the generated networks do not resemble real ones, despite the adopted mechanism.

Preti et al. [20] introduce two microcanonical null models for (possibly degenerate) dihypergraphs, and MCMC methods to sample from them. Both null models allow degeneracy; the first null model maintains the same properties as ours otherwise, and the other preserves additional constraints based on the joint degree distribution. Many DGPs would not create degenerate dihypergraphs (see Sect. 3.1), thus these null models would be unrealistic for such scenarios (see Sect. 6.2), potentially leading to invalid conclusions from statistical hypothesis tests (see Sect. 6.1).

We distinguish between edge-ordered dihypergraphs and edge-unordered dihypergraphs (see Sect. 3.1 for formal definitions). These concepts are not the same as those of vertex- and stub-labeled hypergraphs [5], which relate to the labeling of nodes. Rather, our distinction is related to the concepts of row-order-agnostic and row-order-aware null models introduced by Abuissa et al. [1] for transactional datasets (i.e., for binary matrices), but not immediately extendable to dihypergraphs (see Sect. 5).

3 Preliminaries

3.1 Directed Hypergraphs

A directed hypergraph (dihypergraph) $G \doteq (N, E)$ has a set $N = \{n_1, \ldots, n_{|N|}\}$ of nodes, and a multiset (a.k.a., a bag) $E = \{\{e_1, \ldots, e_{|E|}\}\}$ of directed hyperedges [20], where each hyperedge $e_i = (\mathsf{t}(e_i), \mathsf{h}(e_i))$ has a *tail* $\mathsf{t}(e_i) \subseteq N$ and a *head* $\mathsf{h}(e_i) \subseteq N$ (i.e., $e_i \in 2^N \times 2^N$). A hyperedge represents a relation from the nodes in the tail to those in the head, matching the graphical representation of directed edges as arrows, with the source being on the tail of the arrow, and the destination being on the arrowhead.[2] The head and tail of a hyperedge are both sets, not multisets, and they are assumed to be non-empty. Although the set constraint may be relaxed, to the best of our knowledge, it is not required or even reasonable to do so in most situations modeled by dihypergraphs. We denote the union of the head and the tail of a hyperedge e as $\mathsf{n}(e)$.

For each $n \in N$, the *out-degree* $\mathsf{odeg}_G(n)$ (resp. the *in-degree* $\mathsf{ideg}_G(n)$) *of n in G* is the number of hyperedges in E whose tails (resp. heads) contain n, i.e.,

$$\mathsf{odeg}_G(n) \doteq |\{e \in E : n \in \mathsf{t}(e)\}| \ .$$

(resp. $\mathsf{ideg}_G(n) \doteq |\{e \in E : n \in \mathsf{h}(e)\}|$). The *degree* $\mathsf{deg}_G(n)$ of n in G is the sum of its out- and in-degrees, $\mathsf{deg}_G(n) \doteq \mathsf{odeg}_G(n) + \mathsf{ideg}_G(n)$.

For each hyperedge $e \in E$, the *tail-dimension* $\mathsf{tdim}_G(e)$ (resp. *head-dimension* $\mathsf{hdim}_G(e)$) *of e in G* is the number of nodes in its tail, i.e., $\mathsf{tdim}_G(e) \doteq |\mathsf{t}(e)|$ (resp. in is head, i.e., $\mathsf{hdim}_G(e) \doteq |\mathsf{h}(e)|$). The *dimension or size* $\mathsf{dim}_G(e)$ *of e in G* is the sum of its tail and head dimensions, $\mathsf{dim}_G(e) \doteq \mathsf{tdim}_G(e) + \mathsf{hdim}_G(e)$.

(Non-)Degenerate Dihypergraphs. We say that a dihypergraph $G = (N, E)$ is *degenerate* if there exist a node $n \in N$ and a hyperedge $e \in E$ s.t. n belongs to both the tail and the head of e.[3] Many natural settings impose the requirement that dihypergraphs are not degenerate. For example, dihypergraphs can model U.S. Congress bill sponsorships, where the sponsor is in the tail of a hyperedge, and the cosponsor(s) are in the head [20]. The resulting dihypergraph is non-degenerate, since a representative cannot both sponsor and cosponsor the same bill. Similarly, when modeling contact networks in disease diffusion [20], the same entity cannot be in both the infecting and infected groups of one interaction. On the other hand, in a dihypergraph where hyperedges represent citations between groups of authors, degeneracy will arise whenever there are self-citations. In this example, whether self-citation should be included depends on the analysis to be performed. Preti et al. [20] define a null model that includes degenerate dihypergraphs, while ours only includes non-degenerate dihypergraphs.

---

[2] Preti et al. [20] call "head" what we call "tail" and vice versa. We follow the convention for directed diadic graphs, due to the representation of directed edges as arrows.

[3] In *undirected* hypergraphs, the term "degenerate" denotes that a node appears multiple times in a hyperedge [5]. Our use is related: if we transform a degenerate dihypergraph into an undirected hypergraph by merging the head and tail of each hyperedge, the resulting undirected hypergraph will be degenerate.

Edge-Ordered and Edge-Unordered Dihypergraphs. It is always assumed that each node of N has a unique identifier, or label, and w.l.o.g., we can assume N has a fixed, arbitrary total order. On the other hand, it may or may not be desirable to distinguish between identical hyperedges (recall that E is a multiset), resulting in dihypergraphs that are effectively different mathematical objects. Assigning a unique identifier to hyperedges is equivalent to imposing that the set of hyperedges E has a *fixed, arbitrary total order*, i.e., it is a sequence $E = \langle e_1, \ldots, e_{|E|} \rangle$. In this case, different orderings of E lead to different dihypergraphs. This fact naturally leads to referring to dihypergraphs whose hyperedges have unique identifiers as *Edge-Ordered Dihypergraphs (EODs)*, and therefore to dihypergraphs whose hyperedges do not have unique identifiers as *Edge-Unordered Dihypergraphs (EUDs)*. The choice of whether to represent a network as an EOD or as an EUD must be deliberate, as they are different objects, which may lead to different outcomes for hypothesis tests performed on the different models, as discussed by Abuissa et al. [1] for binary matrices.

For any EOD H, we denote with $\mathsf{ideg}(H)$ (resp. $\mathsf{odeg}(H)$) the sequence of the in-degrees (resp. out-degrees) of its nodes, and with $\mathsf{tdim}(H)$ (resp. $\mathsf{hdim}(H)$) the sequence of the tail dimensions (resp. head dimensions) of its hyperedges.

3.2 Null Models and Hypothesis Testing

A *null model* $M = (\mathcal{D}, \pi)$ of dihypergraphs is a representation of the DGP: $\mathcal{D}$ is the collection of dihypergraphs that the DGP may generate, and π is a probability distribution over $\mathcal{D}$. The DGP generates $G \in \mathcal{D}$ with probability $\pi(G)$. $\mathcal{D}$ is defined starting from an *observed dihypergraph* $\mathring{G}$ and a set $\mathcal{P}$ of functions over the set of all dihypergraphs. $\mathcal{P}$ represents structural properties of the datasets that the DGP may generate, e.g., the set of nodes, the number of hyperedges, and/or the number of (hypergraph) triangles. $\mathcal{D}$ contains all and only the dihypergraphs with the same values as $\mathring{G}$ for all properties in $\mathcal{P}$, including $\mathring{G}$.[4] M is used to test whether the value $q(\mathring{G})$ of a property $q \notin \mathcal{P}$ can be explained by the properties in $\mathcal{P}$, by measuring the likelihood of observing a value as or more extreme than $q(\mathring{G})$ among the dihypergraphs in $\mathcal{D}$. Formally, we are interested in computing p-value of $q(\mathring{G})$, i.e., the probability that $q(G)$ is as or more extreme than $q(\mathring{G})$ when G is sampled from $\mathcal{D}$ according to π. When the p-value is smaller than a critical value α chosen by the user, it allows the user to reject, with a confidence $1 - \alpha$, the hypothesis that $q(\mathring{G})$ is explained only by $\mathcal{P}$.

The p-value is hard to compute exactly except in the most simple cases [15], but an empirical p-value can be obtained through a Monte Carlo approach by drawing samples from $\mathcal{D}$ according to π, and using the empirical distribution of $q(\cdot)$ across the samples to approximate its true distribution. From a computational point of view, the key ingredient needed to obtain this approximation is an efficient algorithm that can sample from $\mathcal{D}$ according to π.

Our goal in this work is to develop such an algorithm for a specific choice of $\mathcal{P}$, where $\mathcal{D}$ is a collection of *non-degenerate* EODs or EUDs.

---

[4] $\mathcal{D}$, and therefore M, depends on $\mathring{G}$ but the notation does not, to keep it light.

4 A Null Model for Non-degenerate EODs

We now introduce a null model for non-degenerate EODs, and present a Markov Chain Monte Carlo (MCMC) algorithm to sample from this model. In Sect. 5 we do the same for EUDs.

Given an observed *non-degenerate* EOD $\mathring{G} = (\mathring{N}, \mathring{E})$, we define the null model $M = (\mathcal{D}, \pi)$ where $\mathcal{D}$ contains all and only the EODs $G = (N, E)$ such that:

- $N = \mathring{N}$; and
- $\mathsf{ideg}(G) = \mathsf{ideg}(\mathring{G})$ and $\mathsf{odeg}(G) = \mathsf{odeg}(\mathring{G})$, i.e., the set of vertices and the in/out degree sequences are preserved; and
- $\mathsf{tdim}(G) = \mathsf{tdim}(\mathring{G})$ and $\mathsf{hdim}(G) = \mathsf{hdim}(\mathring{G})$, i.e., the head/tail dimension sequences are preserved; and
- G is non-degenerate.

Although π can be any distribution over $\mathcal{D}$, we focus on the *uniform* distribution in this paper, and present DINGHY, an MCMC algorithm to sample uniformly from $\mathcal{D}$. This algorithm can be used to sample from $\mathcal{D}$ according to any distribution by using the Metropolis-Hastings approach [17, Ex.10.12].

Preti et al. [20] introduce a null model, along with a sampling algorithm, NUDHY, that preserves the first three properties but not the last one. Thus, even if $\mathring{G}$ is non-degenerate, the null model by Preti et al. [20] may contain both degenerate and non-degenerate dihypergraphs, which is often undesirable. A null model should capture everything known about the DGP as closely as possible. If it is known or assumed that the DGP would never produce a degenerate dihypergraph, then such dihypergraphs should not be included in $\mathcal{D}$, to avoid leading to incorrect outcomes when testing hypotheses. For example, consider the congress cosponsoring case described in Sect. 3.1, whose DGP would never produce degenerate dihypergraphs. Assume that we are interested in studying the likelihood that a U.S. Senator is a cosponsor of a bill whose first sponsor is the other Senator from the same state (each state as exactly two Senators). If we assume the null model by Preti et al. [20], the expectation over $\mathcal{D}$ of this likelihood is roughly doubled, i.e., the distribution of this quantity is completely different depending on the choice of whether to allow degeneracy in the null model. Since the distribution is different, the results of testing the hypothesis may also be different. In Sect. 6 we give experimental evidence of such issues.

One may be tempted to use the algorithm NUDHY by Preti et al. [20] as a subroutine in a rejection sampling scheme to draw samples uniformly from the space of non-degenerate dihypergraphs. This approach would not be successful, since non-degenerate dihypergraphs are extremely sparse within the space including degenerate dihypergraphs, as we show in Sect. 6. In fact, every sample drawn by NUDHY is degenerate, even when $\mathring{G}$ is not. We therefore introduce, in the next section, a new algorithm to sample directly from the space of non-degenerate dihypergraphs.

4.1 Sampling Uniformly from the Null Model

Our MCMC algorithm DiNgHy draws uniform samples from $\mathcal{D}$ by running a Markov Chain (MC) whose set of states is $\mathcal{D}$ and whose stationary distribution is uniform. We start by describing the directed graph $\mathcal{G}$ of the states, i.e., for which ordered pairs $(G, G') \in \mathcal{D} \times \mathcal{D}$ the transition probability from G to G' is strictly positive, and we show that this graph is strongly connected (Theorem 1). We then present an algorithm to draw the next state of the MC from the current state, and we prove that the resulting transition probabilities lead to a uniform stationary distribution for the MC. Before these steps, we introduce an equivalent representation of EODs that we use throughout this section.

EODs as Ordered Pairs of Bipartite Graphs. Any EOD $G = (N, E)$ can be represented as an ordered pair $(\mathsf{B}_t(G), \mathsf{B}_h(G))$ of bipartite graphs $\mathsf{B}_t(G) = (N, E, \mathsf{E}_t(G))$ and $\mathsf{B}_h(G) = (N, E, \mathsf{E}_h(G))$, where N and E are the two sets of *vertices* of these bipartite graphs,[5]. There is an edge $(n, e) \in \mathsf{E}_t(G)$ in the bipartite graph $\mathsf{B}_t(G)$ iff n is in the *tail* of e, for $n \in N$ and $e \in E$, and similarly for $\mathsf{E}_h(G)$ and the head. Formally, $\mathsf{E}_t(G) \doteq \{(n, e) \in N \times E : n \in \mathsf{t}(e)\}$ and $\mathsf{E}_h(G) \doteq \{(n, e) \in N \times E : n \in \mathsf{h}(e)\}$.

Fact 1. *An EOD G has a unique representation as an ordered pair $(\mathsf{B}_t(G), \mathsf{B}_h(G))$ of bipartite graphs.*

On the other hand, not every pair of bipartite graphs (T, H) with the same sets of vertices is a representation of a *non-degenerate* EOD: the edge sets of T and H must be disjoint for the corresponding EOD to be non-degenerate.

We can transform the set of properties $\mathcal{P}$ that define $\mathcal{D}$ into a set of properties $\mathcal{P}'$ over pairs (T, H) of bipartite graphs which have $\mathring{N}$ and $\mathring{E}$ as their sets of left and right vertices:

- for every $n \in \mathring{N}$, the degree of n in T (resp. in H) is $\mathsf{odeg}_{\mathring{G}}(n)$ (resp. $\mathsf{ideg}_{\mathring{G}}(n)$); and
- for every $e \in \mathring{E}$, the degree of e in T (resp. in H) is $\mathsf{hdim}_{\mathring{G}}(n)$ (resp. $\mathsf{tdim}_{\mathring{G}}(n)$); and
- the EOD corresponding to (T, H) must be non-degenerate, meaning there are no $n \in \mathring{N}, e \in \mathring{E}$ such that (n, e) is an edge of both T and H.

We can then define the set $\mathcal{D}_\mathsf{B}$ of pairs of bipartite graphs as

$$\mathcal{D}_\mathsf{B} \doteq \{(\mathsf{B}_t(G), \mathsf{B}_h(G)) : G \in \mathcal{D}\} \ .$$

There is a bijection between $\mathcal{D}_\mathsf{B}$ and $\mathcal{D}$. In the rest of this section we define an MC on $\mathcal{D}_\mathsf{B}$ whose stationary distribution is uniform, since a uniform sample from $\mathcal{D}_\mathsf{B}$ corresponds to a uniform sample from $\mathcal{D}$.

---

[5] To avoid confusion, we use *nodes* for dihypergraphs, and *vertices* for bipartite graphs. Conceptually, the vertices in the bipartite graphs are the nodes in G and the *identifiers* of the hyperedges of G.

The Directed Graph of the States. To describe the directed graph $\mathcal{G} = (\mathcal{D}_\mathsf{B}, \mathcal{E})$ of states, we first define the *swap* (a.k.a. switch [11]), an operation that transforms a bipartite graph B into another bipartite graph B' with the same degree sequences as B. We then restrict swaps to define an operation on $\mathcal{D}_\mathsf{B}$ that transforms a pair $(T, H) \in \mathcal{D}_\mathsf{B}$ into another pair $(T', H') \in \mathcal{D}_\mathsf{B}$.

Definition 1. *Given a bipartite graph $T = (V, U, W)$, let $v_1, v_2 \in V$, $v_1 \neq v_2$, and $u_1, u_2 \in U$, $u_1 \neq u_2$ such that $e_1 \doteq (v_1, u_1), e_2 \doteq (v_2, u_2) \in W$ and $e'_1 \doteq (v_1, u_2), e'_2 \doteq (v_2, u_1) \notin W$. The swap $\mathsf{s}_T(e_1, e_2)$ is the operation that transforms T into the bipartite graph $T' = (V, U, W')$ where $W' = (W \setminus \{e_1, e_2\}) \cup \{e'_1, e'_2\}$. We refer to $\mathsf{s}_T(e_1, e_2)$ as a swap from T to T'.*

We now define the *Non-Degenerating Swap (NDS)* operation from $\mathcal{D}_\mathsf{B}$ to itself. There are two kinds of NDSs, the the *Tail-Non-Degenerating Swap (TNDS)* and the *Head-Non-Degenerating Swap (HNDS)*.

Definition 2. *Let $(T, H) \in \mathcal{D}_\mathsf{B}$, with $T = (\mathring{N}, E, Q)$ and $H = (\mathring{N}, E, Z)$. Let $\ell_1 = (n_1, e_1)$, $\ell_2 = (n_2, e_2) \in Q$ be two edges in T such that $\mathsf{s}_T(\ell_1, \ell_2)$ is a swap from T to some T', and such that $(n_1, e_2), (n_2, e_1) \notin Z$. The Tail-Non-Degenerating Swap (TNDS) $\mathsf{ts}_{T,H}(\ell_1, \ell_2)$ is the operation that transforms (T, H) into $(T', H) \in \mathcal{D}_\mathsf{B}$ by applying $\mathsf{s}_T(\ell_1, \ell_2)$ to T.*

Definition 3. *Let $(T, H) \in \mathcal{D}_\mathsf{B}$, with $T = (\mathring{N}, E, Q)$ and $H = (\mathring{N}, E, Z)$. Let $r_1 = (n_1, e_1)$, $r_2 = (n_2, e_2) \in Z$ be two edges in H such that $\mathsf{s}_H(r_1, r_2)$ is a swap from H to some H', and such that $(n_1, e_2), (n_2, e_1) \notin Q$. The Head-Non-Degenerating Swap (HNDS) $\mathsf{hs}_{T,H}(r_1, r_2)$ is the operation that transforms (T, H) into $(T, H') \in \mathcal{D}_\mathsf{B}$ by applying $\mathsf{s}_H(r_1, r_2)$ to H.*

In the directed graph $\mathcal{G} = (\mathcal{D}_\mathsf{B}, \mathcal{E})$, there is an edge from $(T, H) \in \mathcal{D}_\mathsf{B}$ to $(T', H') \in \mathcal{D}_\mathsf{B}$ (it must hold either $T = T'$ or $H = H'$) if there is a NDS from (T, H) to (T', H'). It is evident there can be at most one NDS between any two states. Any NDS is reversible, i.e., if there is a NDS q from (T, H) to (T', H'), then there is a NDS $\mathsf{rev}(q)$ (the *reversal* of q) of the same type (i.e., head- or tail-) from (T', H') to (T, H). Thus we say that (T, H) and (T', H') are neighbors.

There exist dihypergraphs, like digraphs, where $\mathcal{G}$ is not strongly connected under NDSs (consider flipping a directed triangle). Irreducibility under the edge swap on digraphs requires complex conditions [13]. Dihypergraphs face a similar issue, but the proof for digraphs does not extend to dihypergraphs. We use a novel approach to show that under mild conditions, $\mathcal{G}$ is strongly connected, which is necessary for the MC to have a unique stationary distribution. We first need some technical definitions.

Let $(T, H) \in \mathcal{D}_\mathsf{B}$, with $T = (\mathring{N}, E, W)$ and $H = (\mathring{N}, E, Z)$. For an edge $w \in W$ (resp. $z \in Z$), let $\mathsf{tse}_{T,H}(w)$ (resp. $\mathsf{hse}_{T,H}(z)$) be the set of edges $w' \in W$ (resp. $z' \in Z$) such that $\mathsf{ts}_{T,H}(w, w')$ is a TNDS (resp. $\mathsf{hs}_{T,H}(z, z')$ is a HNDS.)

Now let $(T, H') \in \mathcal{D}_\mathsf{B}$ be distinct from (T, H) (i.e., $H \neq H'$). For $w \in W$, let $\mathsf{ttse}_{T,H,H'}(w)$ be the set of edges w' in W such that $\mathsf{ts}_{T,H}(w, w')$ is a TNDS on (T, H) and a TNDS on (T, H'). Let $(T', H) \in \mathcal{D}_\mathsf{B}$ be distinct from (T, H) (i.e.,

$T \neq T'$). Similarly, for $z \in Z$, let $\mathsf{hhse}_{H,T,T'}(h)$ be the set of edges z' in Z such that $\mathsf{hs}_{T,H}(z, z')$ is a HNDS on (T, H) and a HNDS on (T', H).

Theorem 1. *Assume that at least one of the two following pairs of conditions hold for every $(T, H) \in \mathcal{D}_\mathsf{B}$:*

Pair 1 (1) *for every edge z in H, $|\mathsf{hse}_{T,H}(z)| \geq 1$; and* (2) *for every edge z in H and for every $(T, H') \in \mathcal{D}_\mathsf{B}$, $|\mathsf{ttse}_{T,H,H'}(z)| \geq 1$.*
Pair 2 (1) *for every edge w in T, $|\mathsf{tse}_{T,H}(w)| \geq 1$; and* (2) *for every edge w in T and for every $(T', H) \in \mathcal{D}_\mathsf{B}$, $|\mathsf{hhse}_{H,T,T'}(w)| \geq 1$.*

Then the directed state graph is strongly connected.

The intuition behind the proof is that for any $(T, H), (T', H') \in \mathcal{D}_\mathsf{B}$, we first construct a sequence of NDSs, possibly a mix of TNDSs and HDNSs, from (T, H) to some (T', H''). If $H'' \neq H'$, we then build another sequence of NDSs from (T', H'') to some (T''', H'). If $T''' \neq T'$, the final step is a sequence of TNDSs from (T''', H') to (T', H') that "undo" the TNDSs from the second phase, i.e., they are the reversals of TNDSs from the second phase applied in reverse order.

Proof. Let us first assume that at least the first pair of conditions hold. We later adapt the proof to the case when only the second pair of conditions hold.

Our proof works in three phases. Given any two $(T, H), (T', H') \in \mathcal{D}_\mathsf{B}$, we first construct a sequence of NDSs, possibly a mix of TNDSs and HDNSs, from (T, H) to some (T', H''). We are done iff $H'' = H'$. Otherwise, in the second phase, we build another sequence of NDSs, again possibly a mix of HNDSs and TNDSs, from (T', H'') to some (T''', H'). It holds $T''' = T'$ iff only HNDSs appear in this second sequence, in which case we are done. Otherwise, the third phase involves a sequence of TNDSs from (T''', H') to (T', H'). The TNDSs in this third sequence are the reversals of TNDSs from the second sequence, applied in reverse order, i.e., the reversals of TNDSs that were applied later in the second sequence are applied earlier in the third sequence.

We use a result by Kannan et al. [11] as a blackbox in the following way. Given any two bipartite graphs $B = (L, R, E)$ and $B' = (L, R, E')$ with the same degree sequences, Kannan et al. [11, Lemma 3.1] show how to obtain a sequence of swaps that transforms B into B' by moving closer to B' at every step, in the sense that the next swap in the sequence transforms the current graph $B'' = (L, R, E'')$ into $B''' = (L, R, E''')$ such that $|E' \cap E''| < |E' \cap E'''|$.

If $T \neq T'$, we start our first phase, and obtain, using the method by Kannan et al. [11], a sequence of swaps that would transform T into T'. Let (T^c, H^c) be the current pair (at the beginning $(T^c, H^c) = (T, H)$). As long as the next proposed swap in the sequence is a TNDS on (T^c, H^c), we apply it. If the proposed swap $\mathsf{s}_T((n_1, e_1), (n_2, e_2))$ is not a TNDS on (T^c, H^c), then it must be that at least one of (n_1, e_2) and (n_2, e_1), possibly both, is an edge in H^c. By appropriately transforming H^c through one or two HNDSs, the proposed swap will become a TNDS on (T^c, H^c). Indeed, if (n_1, e_2) is an edge in H^c, we can take any $(n, e) \in \mathsf{hse}_{T^c, H^c}((n_1, e_2))$, which exists by the first condition in the hypothesis, and apply the swap $\mathsf{s}_{H^c}((n_1,e_2),(n,e))$ to H^c. This swap is a HNDS by definition of $\mathsf{hse}_{T^c,H^c}((n_1,e_2))$. We proceed similarly if (n_2,e_1) is an edge of H^c. The current pair (T^c, H^c) is now such that the swap $\mathsf{s}_T((n_1,e_1),(n_2,e_2))$ is a TNDS on (T^c, H^c), so we can apply it. By repeating the process with the next swap proposed in the sequence, we arrive at a pair $(T', H'') \in \mathcal{D}_\mathsf{B}$. If all the proposed swaps were TNDSs, then it must be that $H'' = H'$, otherwise it is possible that $H'' \neq H'$.

If $H'' \neq H'$, we enter the second phase. We obtain, using the method by Kannan et al. [11], a sequence of swaps that would transform H'' into H'. Let (T^c, H^c) be the current pair, initialized as $(T^c, H^c) = (T', H'') \in \mathcal{D}_\mathsf{B}$. As long as the next proposed swap in the sequence is a HNDS on (T^c, H^c), we apply it. Consider now the case when the proposed swap $\mathsf{s}_H((n_1,e_1),(n_2,e_2))$ is not a HNDS on (T^c, H^c). It is a swap proposed by the method by Kannan et al. [11], so at least one of (n_1,e_2) and (n_2,e_1) is an edge in H'. Assume, w.l.o.g., that (n_1,e_2) is an edge in H'. Thus, it must be that $(n_1,e_2) \notin T^c$, because $(T^c, H') \in \mathcal{D}_\mathsf{B}$ by construction, and if (n_1,e_2) were in T^c, the dihypergraph G such that $\mathsf{B}_\mathsf{t}(G) = T^c$ and $\mathsf{B}_\mathsf{h}(G) = H'$ would be degenerate, i.e., it would be $(T^c, H') \notin \mathcal{D}_\mathsf{B}$, which would be a contradiction. For the swap $\mathsf{s}_H((n_1,e_1),(n_2,e_2))$ not to be a HNDS on (T^c, H^c), it must be that (n_2,e_1) is an edge in T^c. Let then $(n,e) \in \mathsf{ttse}_{T^c,H^c,H'}((n_2,e_1))$, which exists by the second condition in the hypothesis, and apply the swap $\mathsf{s}_{T^c}((n_2,e_1),(n,e))$ to T^c. This swap is guaranteed to be a TNDS from the definition of $\mathsf{ttse}_{T^c,H^c,H'}((n_2,e_1))$. The current pair (T^c, H^c) is now such that the swap $\mathsf{s}_H((n_1,e_1),(n_2,e_2))$ is a HNDS on (T^c, H^c), so we can apply it. By repeating the process with the next swap proposed in the sequence, we arrive at a pair $(T'', H') \in \mathcal{D}_\mathsf{B}$. If all the proposed swaps were HNDSs, then it must be that $T'' = T'$, otherwise it is possible that $T'' \neq T'$.

If $T'' \neq T'$, we enter the third phase. In this phase, we apply, in reverse order, the reversals of the TNDSs performed in the second phase, so we end up at (T', H'). Consider the ordered sequence $\mathsf{s} = \langle q_1, \ldots, q_\ell \rangle$ of the TNDSs performed in the second phase (if we are in the third phase, this sequence must be nonempty), and now consider the sequence rs of TNDSs obtained by flipping the order of the sequence, and replacing each TNDSs with its reversal, i.e., $\mathsf{rs} = \langle \mathsf{rev}(q_\ell), \ldots, \mathsf{rev}(q_1) \rangle$. When we applied the TNDS q_ℓ during the second phase, we moved from some $(\tilde{T}, \tilde{H})$ to $(T'', \tilde{H})$. The TNDS $q_\ell = \mathsf{ts}_{\tilde{T},\tilde{H}}(z,y)$ belong to $\mathsf{ttse}_{\tilde{T},\tilde{H},H'}(z)$, by construction. This TNDS q_ℓ is therefore a TNDS on $(\tilde{T}, \tilde{H})$ and on $(\tilde{T}, H')$, by definition of $\mathsf{ttse}_{\tilde{T},\tilde{H},H'}(z)$. In particular, if we applied it to $(\tilde{T}, H')$, we would move to (T''', H'). Thus, by applying $\mathsf{rev}(q_\ell)$ to (T''', H'), we move to $(\tilde{T}, H')$, and $\mathsf{rev}(q_\ell)$ is a TNDS on (T'', H') because q_ℓ is a TNDS, and every NDS is reversible. We can repeat this reasoning for $q_{\ell-1}$ and $\mathsf{rev}(q_{\ell-1})$: when we apply the TNDS $\mathsf{rev}(q_{\ell-1})$ to $(\tilde{T}, H')$ we obtain $(\hat{T}, H')$, where $\hat{T}$ is such that during the second phase we applied $q_{\ell-1}$ to $(\hat{T}, \hat{H})$ to obtain $(\tilde{T}, \hat{H})$. Continuing this way, when we applied q_1 during the second phase we moved from $(T', \check{H})$ to $(\check{T}, \check{H})$, hence when we apply $\mathsf{rev}(q_1)$ to $(\check{T}, H')$ we move to (T', H'). Thus, there is a sequence of NDSs from any $(T, H) \in \mathcal{D}_\mathsf{B}$

to any other $(T', H') \in \mathcal{D}_\mathsf{B}$ if the first pair of conditions in the hypothesis holds, i.e., in this case the graph is strongly connected.

When only the second pair of conditions holds, we can adapt the proof by first "fixing" H to go to (T'', H'), then move to (T', H'') in the second phase, and finally to (T', H') in the third phase. □

The following result gives an easy-to-compute condition on the degree and hyperedge dimension sequences of the observed non-degenerate EOD $\mathring{G}$ for the hypothesis of Theorem 1 to hold. It is a corollary of the four technical lemmas that are stated and proved in the supplementary materials. The quantities $\mathsf{odeg}(\cdot)$ and $\mathsf{ideg}(\cdot)$ can be switched to obtain another sufficient condition.

Corollary 1. *Let n^* be the node with maximum degree in $\mathring{G}$, and e^* be the hyperedge with maximum dimension in $\mathring{G}$. If the following condition holds:*
$(\mathsf{dim}_{\mathring{G}}(e^*) - 1)(2\mathsf{deg}_{\mathring{G}}(n^*) - 1) + 1 < \|\mathsf{ideg}(\mathring{G})\|_1;$ *and*
$2(\mathsf{dim}_{\mathring{G}}(e^*) - 1)(2\mathsf{deg}_{\mathring{G}}(n^*) - 1) + 1 < \|\mathsf{odeg}(\mathring{G})\|_1;$
then the condition from Theorem 1 holds.

Our analysis is constrained by the path proposed by Kannan et al. [11]. As a result, we conjecture that the conditions of both Theorem 1 and Corollary 1 could be tightened using a more carefully tailored sequence of switches.

Drawing the Next State of the Markov Chain. We now present an algorithm that, given a pair $(T, H) \in \mathcal{D}_\mathsf{B}$ representing the current state of the MC, draws a neighbor $(T', H') \in \mathcal{D}_\mathsf{B}$ of (T, H). We then show that the transition probabilities resulting from this algorithm lead to a uniform stationary distribution over $\mathcal{D}_\mathsf{B}$.

The pseudocode of the algorithm is presented in Algorithm 1. We start by drawing an unordered pair of *distinct* hyperedges $(e_1, e_2) \in \mathrm{E} \times \mathrm{E}$ uniformly at random (u.a.r.) from the set of such pairs (line 1). We then decide whether to perform a HNDS or a TNDS involving these hyperedges, by flipping a biased coin with a probability of heads b, a user-specified parameter (line 2).[6] If the outcome is *heads*, and there is at least one HNDS involving e_1 and e_2 on (T, H), we select one by first drawing a node n_1 u.a.r. from $\mathsf{h}(e_1)\setminus\mathsf{n}(e_2)$ (line 5), and then similarly drawing n_2 u.a.r. from $\mathsf{h}(e_2)\setminus\mathsf{n}(e_1)$ (line 6). The sets we draw from ensure that the resulting swap is a HNDS. We then perform the HNDS $\mathsf{hs}_{T,H}((n_1, e_1), (n_2, e_2))$ on (T, H) to obtain (T', H'), which is returned (lines 7 and 8). If there is no HNDS involving e_1 and e_2, we take a self-loop from the state (T, H) to itself (line 9). If the outcome of the biased coin was tails, we proceed in a similar fashion with a TNDS (lines 10–16). Any neighbor of (T, H) can be returned in output by Algorithm 1.

---

[6] In our experiments we use $b = \|\mathsf{odeg}(\mathring{G})\|_1/(\|\mathsf{odeg}(\mathring{G})\|_1 + \|\mathsf{ideg}(\mathring{G})\|_1)$, which is a heuristic value to roughly balance the number of HNDSs and TNDSs performed.

Algorithm 1: Drawing the next state of the MC

Input: the current state $(T, H) \in \mathcal{D}_B$, with $T = (\mathring{N}, E, W)$, and $H = (\mathring{N}, E, Z)$, the coin heads probability b
Output: the next state $(T', H') \in \mathcal{D}_B$

1. $(e_1, e_2) \leftarrow$ unordered pair of distinct hyperedges in E chosen u.a.r.
2. flip $\leftarrow$ outcome of a flip a biased coin with heads probability b
3. **if** *flip is* heads **then**
4.   **if** $h(e_1) \setminus n(e_2) \neq \emptyset$ **and** $h(e_2) \setminus n(e_1) \neq \emptyset$ **then**
5. $n_1 \leftarrow$ node drawn u.a.r. from $h(e_1) \setminus n(e_2)$
6. $n_2 \leftarrow$ node drawn u.a.r. from $h(e_2) \setminus n(e_1)$
7. $(T, H') \leftarrow$ result of applying $\text{hs}_{T,H}((n_1, e_1), (n_2, e_2))$ on (T, H)
8.   **return** (T, H')
9.   **else return** (T, H)
10. **else**
11.   **if** $t(e_1) \setminus (h(e_2) \cup t(e_2)) \neq \emptyset$ **and** $t(e_2) \setminus (h(e_1) \cup t(e_1)) \neq \emptyset$ **then**
12. $n_1 \leftarrow$ node drawn u.a.r. from $t(e_1) \setminus n(e_2)$
13. $n_2 \leftarrow$ node drawn u.a.r. from $t(e_2) \setminus n(e_1)$
14. $(T', H) \leftarrow$ result of applying $\text{ts}_{T,H}((n_1, e_1), (n_2, e_2))$ on (T, H)
15.   **return** (T', H)
16.   **else return** (T, H)

Stationary Distribution. This result shows that the transition probabilities arising from Algorithm 1 allow us to sample uniformly from $\mathcal{D}_B$. It relies on the transition matrix being doubly-stochastic.

Theorem 2. *The unique stationary distribution of the MC is uniform over $\mathcal{D}_B$.*

We can then use the MC as part of our MCMC algorithm DiNGHy to sample uniformly from $\mathcal{D}$, by running the MC starting from $\mathring{G}$ until it mixes, and taking the state of the MC at that point as the sample from $\mathcal{D}$.

5 A Null Model for Non-degenerate Edge-Unordered Hypergraphs

We extend the null model introduced in Sect. 4 to non-degenerate EUDs, to obtain a null model $(\mathcal{D}_U, \pi)$, where $\mathcal{D}_U$ is the set of all the non-degenerate EUDs with the same in-/out-degree and head-/tail-hyperedge dimension sequence as the observed non-degenerate EUD $\mathring{G}$. The algorithm DiNGHy presented in Sect. 4.1 is easily modified as follows, to obtain an algorithm DiNGHy-U for sampling uniformly from $\mathcal{D}_U$.

There is a surjective function $\text{o2u}(\cdot)$ from $\mathcal{D}$ to $\mathcal{D}_U$, mapping any EOD $G \in \mathcal{D}$ to the EUD $\text{o2u}(G) \in \mathcal{D}_U$ obtained by removing the hyperedge identifiers from G. For any EUD G', we denote with $\text{o2u}^{-1}(G')$ the inverse image of G' through $\text{o2u}()$, i.e., $\text{o2u}^{-1}(G') = \{\text{EOD } G : \text{o2u}(G) = G'\}$. The following result gives an expression for $|\text{o2u}^{-1}(G')|$.

Lemma 1. *Let $G = (N, E)$ be a EUD. Let $t^* \doteq \max_{e \in E} \mathsf{tdim}_G(e)$ and $h^* \doteq \max_{e \in E} \mathsf{hdim}_G(e)$. For $1 \leq i \leq t^*$ and $1 \leq j \leq h^*$, let $E_{i,j} \doteq \{\!\{e \in E : \mathsf{tdim}_G(e) = i \wedge \mathsf{hdim}_G(e) = j\}\!\}$ be the multiset of hyperedges with tail dimension i and head dimension j. Let $\bar{E}_{i,j} \doteq \{e_{i,j,1}, \ldots, e_{i,j,u_{i,j}}\}$ be the set of such hyperedges, and $\bar{E}$ be the set version of E. For $1 \leq k \leq u_{i,j}$, let $w_{i,j,k} \doteq \mathsf{m}_E(e_{i,j,k})$ be the multiplicity of $e_{i,j,k}$ in E. Then, the number $|\mathsf{o2u}^{-1}(G)|$ of edge-labeled hypergraphs mapped to G by $\mathsf{o2u}(\cdot)$ is*

$$|\mathsf{o2u}^{-1}(G)| = \prod_{i=1}^{t^*}\prod_{j=1}^{h^*} \binom{|E_{i,j}|}{w_{i,j,1}, \ldots, w_{i,j,u_{i,j}}} = \frac{\prod_{i=1}^{t^*}\prod_{j=1}^{h^*} |E_{i,j}|!}{\prod_{e \in \bar{E}} \mathsf{m}_G(e)!} \ . \tag{1}$$

We can use Lemma 1 and the Metropolis-Hastings (MH) approach to modify the stationary distribution π of the MC over EODS from Sect. 4.1, so that, for every EOD $G \in \mathcal{D}$, it holds

$$\pi(G) = \frac{1}{|\mathcal{D}_\mathsf{U}||\mathsf{o2u}^{-1}(\mathsf{o2u}(G))|} \ . \tag{2}$$

The MC is modified as follows to achieve the above. At every step, an EOD B is *proposed* as the next state of the MC by drawing it from the neighbors of the current state A wrt the original transition probabilities of the MC. B is accepted as the next state of the MC with probability

$$\min\{1, \frac{\pi(B)p_{B,A}}{\pi(A)p_{A,B}}\} = \min\{1, \frac{|\mathsf{o2u}^{-1}(\mathsf{o2u}(A))|}{|\mathsf{o2u}^{-1}(\mathsf{o2u}(B))|}\},$$

as, per Theorem 2, the transition probabilities are symmetric in our original MC (i.e., $p_{B,A} = p_{A,B}$). The correctness of the MH approach guarantees that the stationary distribution of this modified MC is as in Eq. (2). Thus we can sample an EOD $G \in \mathcal{D}$ using this modified MC, and consider the EUD $\mathsf{o2u}(G)$ as a uniform sample from $\mathcal{D}_\mathsf{U}$, because for every EUD $G' \in \mathcal{D}_\mathsf{U}$ the probability that it is sampled is

$$\sum_{G \in \mathsf{o2u}^{-1}(G')} \pi(G) = \frac{1}{|\mathcal{D}_\mathsf{U}|} \ .$$

6 Experimental Evaluation

The goal of our experimental evaluation is threefold:

- assess the structural differences between the space of non-degenerate EODS we introduce and the space where degeneracy is allowed, proposed by Preti et al. [20]. In particular, we aim to understand the presence and amount of degeneracy in samples from the latter, and whether the outcome of hypothesis tests differ depending on which null model is used (results in Sect. 6.1);
- study the behavior of NuDHy [20] when the observed EOD is non-degenerate, to evaluate the possibility of using this algorithm as a subroutine in a rejection sampling scheme to sample non-degenerate EOD (results in Sect. 6.1);
- evaluate the empirical mixing time of our algorithm DiNgHy, compared to NuDHy and a baseline DiNgHy-B (results in Sect. 6.2).

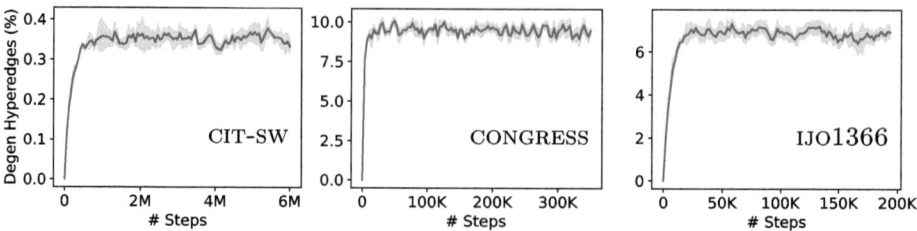

Fig. 1. Mean percentage (over 33 samples, 95% confidence interval shaded) of degenerate hyperedges as function of the number of steps of the Markov chain.

Implementation and Datasets. We use Preti et al.s publicly available implementation of NuDHy [20] (specifically, the NuDHy-Degs variant), which is a standard swap chain on the bipartite representation of a dihypergraph. Off of this codebase, we implement our algorithm DiNgHy, and a baseline DiNgHy-B used to evaluate the mixing time.[7] DiNgHy-B uses the same approach as NuDHy with the additional constraint that swaps do not cause degeneracy (i.e., they are NDSs). DiNgHy takes a novel approach to select NDSs (see Sect. 4.1).

We use datasets used by Preti et al. [20] and synthetic datasets.[8]

6.1 Difference Between the Null Models

For all datasets, we measured the percentage of samples with at least one degenerate edge on 500 samples from the space that allows degeneracy, drawn using NuDHy. For every dataset, *all* 500 samples included degeneracy, even when the dataset was non-degenerate.

Figure 1 shows the percentage of hyperedges that are degenerate as a function of the number of steps taken by the Markov chain when starting from the observed network. This quantity increases sharply by the first measurement, and stabilizes soon after, without ever disappearing, i.e., at *every* measurement, the current state of the Markov chain was a degenerate EOD.

For each sample, we also count the degenerate hyperedges, and the nodes that participate in any degenerate hyperedge. Results are in Table 1. Samples where $\mathring{G}$ was a real dataset have up to 10% degenerate hyperedges, and up to 99% of nodes participating in degenerate edges. The synthetic datasets demonstrate that high density networks exhibit higher degeneracy.

All these results indicate that the two sample spaces, thus the null models, are very different, which was the first goal of our experimental evaluation (more evidence is given below). In particular, non-degenerate EODs are extremely sparse in the sample space that includes degenerate ones. Thus, one cannot use NuDHy as a rejection sampling subroutine to produce non-degenerate samples, which was

---

[7] Implementation available from https://github.com/acdmammoths/dinghy-code.
[8] Details in the supplementary materials.

Table 1. Median amount of degeneracy in 33 samples per observed network, obtained by NuDHy.

Dataset	Degenerate edges		Nodes in degenerate edges	
	Count	Normalized	Count	Normalized
CONGRESS	178	9.55%	100	99.01%
IAF1260B	129	6.19%	247	14.81%
IJO1366	152	6.75%	294	16.29%
ECOLI (ND)	29	3.17%	60	8.55%
CIT-SW	179	0.34%	806	4.87%
DBLP-9 (ND)	272	0.29%	1023	4.87%
ENRON	379	0.25%	1859	3.28%
MATH (ND)	58	0.06%	228	0.66%
ORD (ND)	378	0.08%	722	0.11%
SYNTHETIC 160	1274	99.53%	1280	100%
SYNTHETIC 80	927	72.42%	1280	100%
SYNTHETIC 40	351	27.42%	1280	100%
SYNTHETIC 20	96	7.5%	1000	78.12%
SYNTHETIC 10	27	2.11%	227	17.73%

our second goal, and justifies the need to develop our new algorithm DiNgHy to sample directly from the space of non-degenerate EODs.

To further evaluate the importance of using the right null model when performing statistical hypothesis testing, we compare the distributions of the numbers of directed cycles of sizes 2 and 3 in the digraph projections of samples obtained with NuDHy and with DiNgHy.[9] Figure 2 shows the distributions of the number of directed 3-cycles for some of the datasets. Results for other datasets are in the supplementary materials, and are qualitatively similar. For all datasets, the distributions are clearly different. For IAF1260B and IJO1366, this difference leads to opposite outcomes of hypothesis tests. We compute the *empirical* p-value of a quantity $q(\mathring{G})$ as the ratio of sampled dihypergraphs G where $|q(G) - \mu| \geq |q(\mathring{G}) - \mu|$, where μ is the mean value of q over the samples. The number of directed 3-cycles in IAF1260B and IJO1366 is marked as non-signicant under the degeneracy-allowed null model (NuDHy), with p-values of 0.97 and 0.73 respectively. Under our more appropriate null model, the p-values are 0 and 0.33 respectively, indicating that existing knowledge about the DGP *does not* explain the observed number of directed 3-cycles. The p-values for other real datasets is zero under both null models, since the observed value is outside both distributions, but the distributions are still distinct.

---

[9] For this experiment, we exclude ENRON, ORD (ND), MATH (ND), and DBLP-9 (ND) due to a prohibitive runtime of more than 22 h per dataset. Corollary 1 does not hold on some of the dihypergraphs we consider, because it is not tight. We conjecture that the MCs for these cases are still irreducible. If not, the distribution would be uniform over the strongly connected component that includes the observed network.

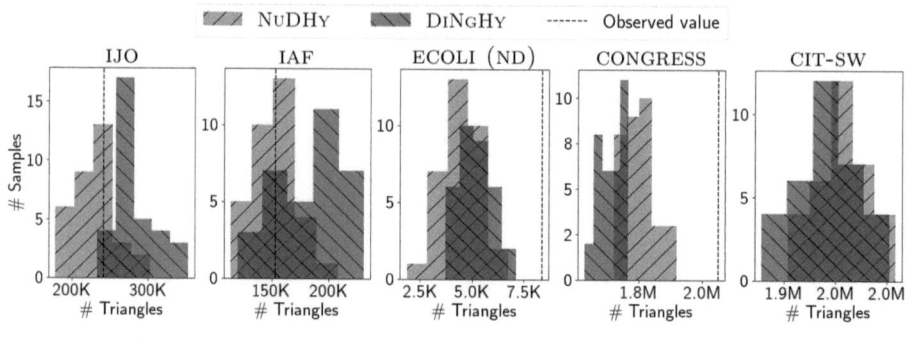

(a) Results on a subset of datasets used for experiments in [20].

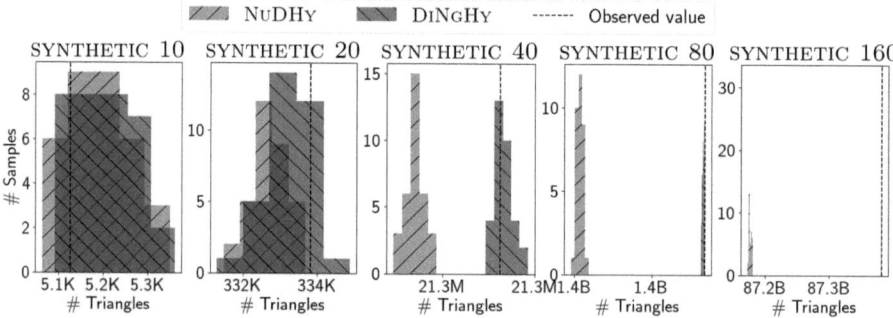

(b) Results on synthetic datasets, identified by their edge size.

Fig. 2. Empirical distributions of the number of 3-cycles in 33 samples. The observed value is omitted when far from both empirical distributions.

On synthetic datasets with higher density, and therefore degeneracy, the distributions are more distinct. On all but the least dense synthetic dataset, the observed number of 3-cycles is found to be significant under the degeneracy-allowed null model, and non-significant under our null model. Results for directed 2-cycles are similar (see the supplementary materials).

In all cases the distributions over the two null models are different, so there exist critical thresholds for which a hypothesis would be rejected under one null model but not under the other. This fact stresses the profound difference between our null models and that of Preti et al. [20], emphasizing the importance of choosing the appropriate null model when testing hypotheses.

6.2 Convergence

The perturbation score [22] is a popular measure for the empirical mixing time of MCMC algorithms that sample from null models over dyadic graphs and binary matrices. Given two binary matrices, it is defined as the fraction of entries with value 1 in one matrix that have value 0 in the other. We extend the perturbation score between two dihypergraphs $\mathring{G}$ and G as the average of the perturbation score between the incidence matrices of $B_t(\mathring{G})$ and $B_t(G)$, and the perturbation score between the incidence matrices of $B_h(\mathring{G})$ and $B_h(G)$.

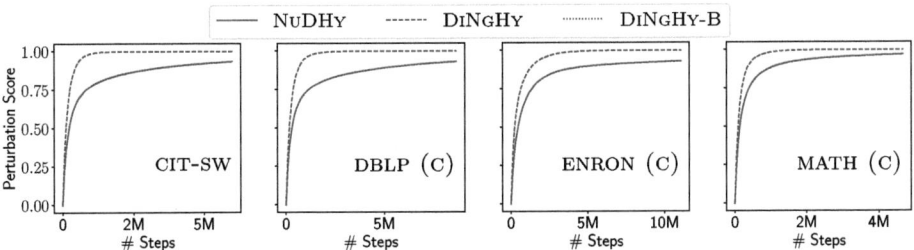

Fig. 3. Perturbation score as function of the steps on the Markov chain. In each case, the curves for NuDHy and DiNgHy-B perfectly overlap.

On the datasets satisfying Corollary 1, we use the same number of steps s as Preti et al. [20] to take a single sample for each dataset (details in the supplementary materials), and we measure the perturbation score between $\mathring{G}$ and the current state of the Markov Chain every $\frac{s}{100}$ steps, for a total of 100 measurements.

Figure 3 shows the perturbation score as function of the number of steps. DiNgHy converges faster than DiNgHy-B and NuDHy, with the latter two showing identical behavior (overlapping curves). Thus, the different approach to choosing NDSs taken by DiNgHy is to be preferred, as it leads to faster mixing.

7 Conclusion

We introduce the first null models for edge-ordered and edge-unordered non-degenerate dihypergraphs, capturing important properties of the observed network. By preserving non-degeneracy, our models are more realistic than existing ones in many scenarios, and thus should be preferred for statistical hypothesis testing. Our MCMC algorithms sample from the null models according to any user-specified distribution, and converge quickly. Directions for future work include strengthening the sufficient conditions for irreducibility (Theorem 1 and Corollary 1), and developing more descriptive null models for dihypergraphs, and efficient algorithms to sample from them.

Acknowledgments. This work is supported in part by the National Science Foundation awards CAREER-2238693 and AF-2312241, and by the National Science Foundation Graduate Research Fellowship Program under Grant No. 2439559. Any opinions, findings, and conclusions or recommendations expressed in this material are those of the Authors and do not necessarily reflect the views of the National Science Foundation.

Disclosure of Interests. The authors have no competing interests to declare that are relevant to the content of this article.

References

1. Abuissa, M., Lee, A., Riondato, M.: ROhAN: row-order agnostic null models for statistically-sound knowledge discovery. DMKD **37**(4) (2023)
2. Battiston, F., et al.: Networks beyond pairwise interactions: structure and dynamics. Phys. Rep. **874**, 1–92 (2020)
3. Bick, C. et al: What are higher-order networks? SIAM Rev. **65**(3) (2023)
4. Billings, J.C.W., et al.: Simplex2Vec embeddings for community detection in simplicial complexes. arXiv:1906.09068 (2019)
5. Chodrow, P.S.: Configuration models of random hypergraphs. J. Compl. Netw. **8**(3) (2020)
6. Choe, M., et al.: Representative and back-in-time sampling from real-world hypergraphs. ACM TKDD **18**(6) (2024)
7. Cimini, G., et al.: The statistical physics of real-world networks. Nat. Rev. Phys. **1**(1) (2019)
8. Do, M., et al.: Structural patterns and generative models of real-world hypergraphs. In: KDD 2020 (2020)
9. Feng, S., et al.: Hypergraph models of biological networks to identify genes critical to pathogenic viral response. BMC Bioinf. **22**(1) (2021)
10. Fosdick, B.K., et al.: Configuring random graph models with fixed degree sequences. SIAM Rev. **60**(2) (2018)
11. Kannan, R., et al.: Simple Markov-chain algorithms for generating bipartite graphs and tournaments. Rand. Struct. Alg. **14**(4) (1999)
12. Kim, S., et al.: Reciprocity in directed hypergraphs: measures, findings, and generators. arXiv:2210.05328 (2023)
13. Lamar, M.D.: On uniform sampling simple directed graph realizations of degree sequences. arXiv:9123834 (2018)
14. Lee, G., et al.: A survey on hypergraph mining: patterns, tools, and generators. ACM Comp. Surv. (2025)
15. Lehmann, E.L., Romano, J.P.: Testing Statistical Hypotheses. 4 edn. (2022)
16. Luo, Q., et al.: Sampling hypergraphs via joint unbiased random walk. World Wide Web **27**(2) (2024)
17. Mitzenmacher, M., Upfal, E.: Probability and Computing (2005)
18. Miyashita, R., et al.: Random hypergraph model preserving two-mode clustering coefficient. In: Wrembel, R., Gamper, J., Kotsis, G., Tjoa, A.M., Khalil, I. (eds.) DaWaK 2023. LNCS, vol. 14148, pp. 191–196. Springer, Cham (2023). https://doi.org/10.1007/978-3-031-39831-5_18
19. Nakajima, K., Shudo, K., Masuda, N.: Randomizing hypergraphs preserving degree correlation and local clustering. IEEE TNSE **9**(3) (2021)
20. Preti, G., et al.: Higher-order null models as a lens for social systems. Phys. Rev. X **14**(3) (2024)
21. Riondato, M.: Statistically-sound knowledge discovery from data. In: SDM 2023 (2023)
22. Strona, G., et al.: A fast and unbiased procedure to randomize ecological binary matrices with fixed row and column totals. Nat. Comm. **5**(1) (2014)
23. Sun, H., Bianconi, G.: Higher-order percolation processes on multiplex hypergraphs. Phys. Rev. E **104**(3) (2021)
24. Zeng, Y., et al.: Hyper-null models and their applications. Entropy **25** (2023)

The Densest SWAMP Problem: Subhypergraphs with Arbitrary Monotonic Partial Edge Rewards

Vedangi Bengali[1(✉)], Nikolaj Tatti[2], Iiro Kumpulainen[2], Florian Adriaens[2], and Nate Veldt[1]

[1] Texas A&M University, College Station, TX, USA
{vedangibengali,nveldt}@tamu.edu
[2] University of Helsinki, HIIT, Helsinki, Finland
{nikolaj.tatti,iiro.kumpulainen,florian.adriaens}@helsinki.fi

Abstract. We consider a generalization of the densest subhypergraph problem where nonnegative rewards are given for including partial hyperedges in a dense subhypergraph. Prior work addressed this problem only in cases where reward functions are convex, in which case the problem is poly-time solvable. We consider a broader setting where rewards are monotonic but otherwise arbitrary. We first prove hardness results for a wide class of non-convex rewards, then design a $1/k$-approximation by projecting to the nearest set of convex rewards, where k is the maximum hyperedge size. We also design another $1/k$-approximation using a faster peeling algorithm, which (somewhat surprisingly) differs from the standard greedy peeling algorithm used to approximate other variants of the densest subgraph problem. Our results include an empirical analysis of our algorithm across several real-world hypergraphs.

Keywords: Densest subhypergraphs · Approximation algorithms

1 Introduction

Dense subgraph discovery is a widely studied primitive in graph mining, with applications including team formation [12,22], motif discovery [11], and fraud detection [9]. One of the most common problems in dense subgraph discovery is the densest subgraph problem (DSG). For a graph $G = (V, E)$, DSG seeks a node set $S \subseteq V$ that maximizes the ratio between (induced) edges and nodes, i.e.,

$$\underset{S \subseteq V}{\text{maximize}} \quad \frac{|E(S)|}{|S|}, \qquad (1)$$

Supplementary Information The online version contains supplementary material available at https://doi.org/10.1007/978-3-032-06066-2_5.

where $E(S) = \{(u,v) \in E \colon u, v \in S\}$. There are known polynomial-time algorithms for exactly solving DSG using flow-based methods [13] and linear programming [6]. There is also a simple greedy 1/2-approximation based on *peeling* (iteratively removing a minimum degree node) [4,6]. Many results for variants of DSG focus on extending one or more of these basic techniques (flow, linear programming, and peeling) to more general settings [8, 15, 16, 18, 19, 24–26].

This paper focuses on generalizations of DSG to hypergraphs, which group nodes into (hyper)edges involving an arbitrary number of nodes (rather than just two). As a motivating application that we will consider throughout the manuscript, finding dense regions of a hypergraph provides a particularly natural approach for team formation. There are already a number of methods for team formation based on dense subgraph discovery [12, 21, 22]. These operate under the assumption that a dense region of a social network represents a good team for a future task, since it encodes a group of people who have already collaborated extensively in the past. Using a hypergraph rather than a graph for this application is arguably more natural, since it directly captures entire previous *team* interactions as hyperedges, rather than only previous pairwise relationships.

The simplest generalization of DSG to hypergraphs is to find a node set S that maximizes the ratio between the number of edges *completely contained in S* and $|S|$. This was first considered 30 years ago in the context of circuit decomposition [15] and has been considered by many others since [5,14]. While this is a natural extension of the standard DSG problem in graphs, there are many applications in which *partially* including a hyperedge also intuitively contributes to notions of density. Consider again the example of team formation. When forming a new team, adding even a *subset* of people from a previous collaboration intuitively matches the belief that previous collaborations help contribute to good future team interactions. However, the standard densest subhypergraph objective only gives a reward for including an entire hyperedge (i.e., all members of some previous team) to the new team.

In this paper, we focus on new algorithms for a generalized densest subhypergraph objective introduced by Zhou et al.[26], which incorporates positive rewards for partially included edges. In more detail, each edge has a nonnegative monotonic reward function r, and the overall objective is to maximize a sum of partial rewards divided by the size of the output set (Sect. 2 includes a formal definition). Zhou et al. [26] proved that there exist reward functions for which this general problem becomes **NP**-hard. However, they then focused on convex reward functions, in which case the problem is a special case of the poly-time solvable densest supermodular subset problem [7]. They designed an exact algorithm for this convex case based on solving maximum s-t flow problems, and showed that a standard greedy peeling algorithm yields a $1/k$-approximation where k is the maximum hyperedge size.

Our Contributions. We focus on the problem of finding a densest Subhypergraph With Arbitrary Partial edge rewards (SWAMP). By arbitrary, we mean that rewards are not required to be convex, as was the focus for Zhou et al. [26]. Our contributions include the following:

- We completely settle the complexity of SWAMP for all reward functions, significantly strengthening prior hardness results. Concretely, when applying the same reward function r to every edge, SWAMP is either poly-time solvable because r is convex, trivially optimized by a single node if r is non-convex but satisfies a certain extremal condition, or is otherwise **NP**-hard.
- We design peeling algorithms for the non-convex case that come with a $1/k$-approximation. Somewhat surprisingly, this approximation is not obtained by the standard greedy peeling method (which gives a $1/k$ approximation for the convex case), but rather with a peeling method that makes locally suboptimal choices about which node to remove in each step.
- We design approximation algorithms based on projecting non-convex rewards to convex rewards and then solving the latter problem. In the worst case, these come with a $1/k$-approximation.
- We introduce a new integer linear programming formulation for finding optimal solutions to SWAMP, that works even for (small-scale) **NP**-hard cases.
- We implement these algorithms and demonstrate their performance on real-world datasets, showing they exceed their theoretical guarantees in practice.
- We show that as a consequence of having approximation guarantees for SWAMP, we obtain approximations for constrained variants of our objective.

Other Related Work. We refer to Lanciano et al. [19] for an extensive recent survey on variants of the densest subgraph problem. We briefly cover several results that are particularly relevant to our paper. Several variants of DSG include constraints on the number of nodes in the output set S, including two variants introduced by Andersen and Chellapilla [2] called the densest at-most-k ($|S| \leq k$), and the densest at-least-k ($|S| \geq k$) problems. In other problem variants, the goal is to find a dense subgraph that ensures nodes with different node labels are included in the output. In some cases, node labels represent "skills" and the goal is to form a (dense) team of individuals to cover certain skill sets [12,22]. In other cases, node labels represent disjoint protected classes and the goal is to form a dense subgraph that is "diverse" or "fair" [1,17,21]. Approximation algorithms for several of these variants build upon earlier approximation algorithms for the densest at-least-k variant [12,21].

Recently, Chekuri et al. [8] introduced the densest supermodular subset problem (DSS) where the goal is to maximize $F(S)/|S|$ where $F: 2^V \to \mathbb{R}^+$ is a non-negative monotone supermodular function defined over a ground set V. Their results for this objective include a fast flow-based approximation algorithm, faster greedy peeling methods, and extensions to cardinality-constrained variants (e.g., the constraint $|S| \geq k$). The greedy peeling method starts with the entire node set V, finds a node $v = \arg\min F(V) - F(V - v)$, and then removes it. At the next step, the same strategy is applied to the remaining node set. At the end, the method chooses the subset of nodes considered along the way with the best objective. This strategy is greedy in the sense that it removes the node that leads to the smallest decrease in the numerator of the objective at each step. This peeling method directly generalizes existing peeling methods for several special cases [6, 25, 26], including the $1/k$-approximation for the generalized densest subhypergraph objective of Zhou et al. [26].

2 The Densest SWAMP Problem

We consider a generalized maximum density problem with a hypergraph input $H = (V, E, w, \{r_e : e \in E\})$. Each $e \in E$ comes with a non-negative scalar weight $w(e) \geq 0$ and an *edge-reward function* $r_e \colon \{0, 1, \ldots, |e|\} \to \mathbb{R}_{\geq 0}$. The latter assigns a non-negative reward based on the *number* of nodes in the hyperedge included in a node set S, even if e is not entirely contained in S. We assume the reward function is monotonic and gives no reward for including no nodes from the edge:

$$0 = r_e(0) \leq r_e(1) \leq r_e(2) \leq \cdots \leq r_e(|e|).$$

This encodes the belief that including more of a hyperedge within a set should contribute more to the measure of density.

Problem 1. For input $H = (V, E, w, \{r_e : e \in E\})$, the Densest Subhypergraph With Arbitrary Monotonic Partial edge rewards problem (SWAMP) seeks to solve

$$\max_{S \subseteq V} \Gamma(S) = \frac{f(S)}{|S|}, \quad \text{where } f(S) = \sum_{e \in \mathcal{E}} w(e) \cdot r_e(|e \cap S|). \tag{2}$$

If the rewards satisfy $r_e(i) = 0$ for $i < |e|$ and $r_e(|e|) = 1$, then this corresponds to the standard densest subhypergraph objective. Zhou et al. [26] were the first to study Problem 1, though focused almost exclusively on the convex case. A discrete monotonic edge-reward function $r_e \colon \{0, 1, \ldots, |e|\} \to \mathbb{R}_{\geq 0}$ is said to be convex if:

$$r_e(i+1) - r_e(i) \geq r_e(i) - r_e(i-1) \quad \text{for } i \in \{1, 2, \ldots, |e| - 1\}. \tag{3}$$

We instead focus on the case where rewards are monotonic but otherwise arbitrary, i.e., not restricted to be convex.

In our study of hardness results, we consider a special case of SWAMP where the input is a hypergraph with maximum edge size k and we use the same reward function r for every edge. We refer to this as SWAMP(r). In this case, r represents a parameter defining the *problem* rather than a reward function that is inherently part of the input. Our goal is to characterize the complexity of SWAMP(r) under different choices for r.

We also consider two-sized constrained variants. The first is to maximize $\Gamma(S)$ subject to a cardinality constraint $|S| \geq \ell$ (where ℓ is an input to the problem), which we refer to as CARD-SWAMP. We also consider a fair variant.

Problem 2. Assume nodes of $H = (V, E, w, \{r_e\})$ are partitioned into node classes $\{C_1, C_2, \ldots, C_m\}$, and let a parameter ℓ_i be given for C_i for $i = 1, 2, \ldots, m$. The Densest Fair SWAMP problem (FAIR-SWAMP) is defined by

$$\underset{S \subseteq V}{\text{maximize}} \quad \Gamma(S) \quad \text{subject to} |S \cap C_i| \geq \ell_i, \text{for } i = 1, 2, \ldots, m. \tag{4}$$

If we think of nodes as individuals, the classes in Problem 2 can represent *skills* that must be present when forming a team of individuals based on their past collaborations. As another example, classes could represent categories that must be fairly represented in the output set (e.g., selecting faculty members from all faculty ranks to represent an academic department on some internal committee).

3 Computational Complexity of SWAMP(r)

The complexity of SWAMP(r) is known in the convex case.

Theorem 1 ([26]). *If r is convex, SWAMP(r) is polynomial-time solvable.*

In addition, Zhou et al. [26] showed that for *some* choice of reward functions (where some rewards are convex but others are not), Problem 1 is **NP**-hard. We strengthen this result by showing that for *every* non-convex r (minus a corner case, described below), SWAMP(r) is **NP**-hard. This provides us with a full picture of the computational complexity of SWAMP(r).

Let us first describe a corner case when the optimal solution is a single node. This generalizes a result of Zhou et al. [26] which says that if r is concave, a single node defines the optimal solution.

Theorem 2. *Assume r such that for every $i \in \{1, 2, \ldots, k\}$, it holds that $r(1) \geq r(i)/i$. Then there is an optimal solution for SWAMP(r) consisting of a single node.*

Proof. For instance $H = (V, E, w)$, let O be the solution for SWAMP(r). Let $o \in O$ be the node maximizing $f(\{o\})$. Then

$$\Gamma(O) = \frac{f(O)}{|O|} = \frac{1}{|O|} \sum_{e \in E} w(e) \cdot r(|e \cap O|)$$

$$\leq \frac{1}{|O|} \sum_{e \in E} w(e) \cdot r(1) \cdot |e \cap O| = \frac{1}{|O|} \sum_{x \in O} f(\{x\}) \leq f(\{o\}) = \Gamma(\{o\}),$$

proving the claim. □

The main result of this section now states that if the conditions in Theorems 1–2 are not satisfied, then SWAMP(r) is **NP**-hard, see Appendix for proof.

Theorem 3. *Assume r such that for some positive integers i and j we have $r(i)/i > r(1)$ and $2r(j) > r(j-1) + r(j+1)$. Then SWAMP(r) is **NP**-hard.*

4 Solving SWAMP with an Integer Linear Program

We introduce a new ILP formulation for solving the decision version of the problem, which asks whether there exists some set S with density greater than α for some pre-specified α. More formally, finding S with $\Gamma(S) > \alpha$ is equivalent to finding S for which $f(S) - \alpha|S| > 0$. We will solve the latter using an ILP, and once we have the solution, we can solve SWAMP by performing a binary search on α. This construction is similar to the approach by Goldberg [13] for finding the densest subgraph.

We consider the following integer linear program.

$$\text{maximize} \quad \left(\sum_{e \in E} w(e) \sum_{i=1}^{|e|} \delta_{e,i} \cdot y_{e,i} \right) - \alpha \sum_{v \in V} x_v$$

$$\text{s.t.} \quad y_{e,i} \leq \frac{1}{i} \sum_{v \in e} x_v \qquad \text{for } e \in E, \ i = 1, 2, \ldots, |e|, \quad (5)$$

$$y_{e,i} \in \{0, 1\} \qquad \text{for } e \in E, \ i = 1, 2, \ldots, |e|,$$

$$x_v \in \{0, 1\} \qquad \text{for } v \in V.$$

In the above, we have defined

$$\delta_{e,i} = r_e(i) - r_e(i-1) \geq 0$$

so that if we include k nodes from edge e in the set S, we know that this gives a reward of

$$r_e(k) = \sum_{i=1}^{k} \delta_{e,i}.$$

This ILP includes a variable $x_v \in \{0, 1\}$ that indicates whether node v is contained in the optimal density set S ($x_v = 1$) or not ($x_v = 0$). The variable $y_{e,i}$ is designed to satisfy

$$y_{e,i} = \begin{cases} 1 & \text{if } |e \cap S| \geq i \\ 0 & \text{otherwise.} \end{cases} \quad (6)$$

Observe that if this is the case, then the first part of the objective function of the ILP is exactly the edge reward

$$\sum_{e \in E} w(e) \sum_{i=1}^{|e|} \delta_{e,i} \cdot y_{e,i} = \sum_{e \in E} w(e) \sum_{i=1}^{|e \cap S|} \delta_{e,i} = \sum_{e \in E} w(e) \cdot r_e(|e \cap S|).$$

We just need to confirm that for the optimal solution, the $y_{e,i}$ variables will indeed satisfy Eq. (6). Observe first of all that maximizing the objective, plus the fact that the $\delta_{e,i}$ are all positive, will ensure that the $y_{e,i}$ variables will be set to 1 whenever possible. Now, note that the constraint

$$y_{e,i} \leq \frac{1}{i} \sum_{v \in e} x_v$$

is equivalent to a bound $y_{e,i} < 1$ if $|e \cap S| < i$, and otherwise it amounts to a bound $y_{e,i} \leq c$ for some $c \geq 1$ if $|e \cap S| \geq i$.

5 Approximating SWAMP

Our most significant algorithmic contributions are peeling-based approximation algorithms for the **NP**-hard regime of SWAMP. Our findings are surprising for two reasons. First of all, our peeling approach for the **NP**-hard non-convex case has a $1/k$-approximation, which is just as good as the peeling approximation guarantee for the (poly-time solvable) convex case. The second surprise is that our approximation guarantees *do not* come from using the standard existing greedy peeling algorithm, which peels away a node in a way that leads to the best objective in the subsequent step. Rather, our guarantees work only for certain peeling strategies that may make locally suboptimal choices for which node to remove at each step. In addition to our peeling algorithms, we design another $1/k$-approximation based on projecting non-convex reward functions to convex rewards and then exactly solving the resulting convex problem.

Algorithm 1. Approximates the densest subgraph problem, SWAMP

Require: Hypergraph $\mathcal{H} = (V, E, r_e)$, and a bound function $s_e(\cdot)$.
1: $X \leftarrow V$ and $Y \leftarrow V$
2: **while** $X \neq \emptyset$ **do**
3: $\quad v \leftarrow \arg\min_{u \in X} \sum_{e:u \in e} r_e(|e \cap X|) - s_e(|e \cap X| - 1)$.
4: $\quad X \leftarrow X \setminus \{v\}$.
5: $\quad$ **if** $\Gamma(X) \geq \Gamma(Y)$, **then** $Y \leftarrow X$.
Ensure: Y.

5.1 Peeling algorithm

Here we describe a peeling algorithm, which will result in a $1/k$ approximation for SWAMP. For notational simplicity, we will assume that $w(e) = 1$. Note that we can make this assumption without the loss of generality since we can incorporate the weights directly to the rewards r_e.

The greedy peeling algorithm by Zhou et al. [26] operates by iteratively deleting a vertex v with the smallest decrease in f, that is,

$$f(S) - f(S \setminus \{v\}) = \sum_{e:v \in e} r_e(|e \cap S|) - r_e(|e \cap S| - 1), \tag{7}$$

and then returning the best tested subgraph.

Unfortunately, this approach yields a guarantee only when r_e is convex and can fail for non-convex rewards. We extend the approach by replacing the second r_e in Eq. 7 with a different function s_e, which needs to be specified separately.

The pseudo-code for the algorithm is given in Algorithm 1. We will show that certain choices for s_e lead to a guarantee.

The following result shows the conditions required for s_e so that Algorithm 1 yields an approximation guarantee.

Theorem 4. *Assume a hypergraph $H = (V, E, \{r_e\})$ and a function s_e for each $e \in E$ satisfying $0 \le s_e(i) \le r_e(i)$ and $r_e(i) - s_e(i-1) \le r_e(i+1) - s_e(i)$ Then Algorithm 1 yields a $1/k$ approximation for SWAMP.*

To prove the claim, we need the following standard lemma.

Lemma 1. *Let $O \subseteq V$ be an optimal solution. Then for any $o \in O$,*

$$\Gamma(O) \le \sum_{e:o \in e} r_e(|e \cap O|) - r_e(|e \cap O| - 1).$$

Proof. By optimality of O, it holds

$$\Gamma(O) \ge \frac{f(O \setminus \{o\})}{|O| - 1} = \frac{f(O) - (f(O) - f(O \setminus \{o\}))}{|O| - 1}.$$

Rewriting this inequality and using $\Gamma(O) = \frac{f(O)}{|O|}$ shows that $\Gamma(O) \le f(O) - f(O \setminus \{o\})$. See also [26, Theorem 4]. Thus,

$$\Gamma(O) \le f(O) - f(O \setminus \{o\})$$
$$= \sum_{e \in E}(r_e(|e \cap O|) - r_e(|e \cap (O \setminus \{o\})|))$$
$$= \sum_{e:o \in e}(r_e(|e \cap O|) - r_e(|e \cap (O \setminus \{o\})|)),$$

proving the lemma. □

Proof (Proof of Theorem 4). Let $O \subseteq V$ be an optimal solution. Let X' be the subgraph X defined by the while loop in Algorithm 1 when the first vertex from O is deleted. Call that vertex x. Note that since each edge e contains at most k vertices, it holds that

$$k\Gamma(X') \ge \frac{1}{|X'|} \sum_{u \in X'} \sum_{e:u \in e} r_e(|e \cap X'|)$$
$$\ge \sum_{e:x \in e} r_e(|e \cap X'|)$$
$$\ge \sum_{e:x \in e} r_e(|e \cap X'|) - s_e(|e \cap X'| - 1),$$

where the second inequality follows from our choice of x in Algorithm 1. Furthermore, as $O \subseteq X'$ by the imposed conditions on s_e it holds that

$$\sum_{e:x \in e} r_e(|e \cap X'|) - s_e(|e \cap X'| - 1) \ge \sum_{e:x \in e} r_e(|e \cap O|) - s_e(|e \cap O| - 1)$$
$$\ge \sum_{e:x \in e} r_e(|e \cap O|) - r_e(|e \cap O| - 1).$$

Since $x \in O$, we can use Lemma 1, and the theorem follows. □

Next, we show two options for s, both satisfying the conditions in Theorem 4.

Theorem 5. *Assume a hypergraph $H = (V, E, \{r_e\})$. Let $b_e(i) = 0$ and $u_e(i) = r_e(i+1) - \max_{0 \leq j \leq i} (r_e(j+1) - r_e(j))$. Then b_e and u_e satisfy the conditions for s_e in Theorem 4. Moreover, any s_e that satisfies the conditions in Theorem 4 will have $b_e(i) \leq s_e(i) \leq u_e(i)$. If r_e is convex, then $u_e = r_e$.*

Proof. The function b_e satisfies the constraints since r_e is monotonic.
Let us write $M_e(i) = \max_{0 \leq j \leq i}(r_e(j+1) - r_e(j))$. Then

$$u_e(i) = r_e(i+1) - M_e(i) \leq r_e(i+1) - (r_e(i+1) - r_e(i)) = r_e(i)$$

and

$$u_e(i) - u_e(i-1) = r_e(i+1) - r_e(i) - (M_e(i) - M_e(i-1)) \leq r_e(i+1) - r_e(i),$$

showing that u_e satisfies the constraints.

To prove the second claim, assume that s_e satisfies the constraints and assume inductively that $s_e(i-1) \leq u_e(i-1)$. If $M_e(i-1) < M_e(i)$, then $M_e(i) = r_e(i+1) - r_e(i)$, and immediately $s_e(i) \leq r_e(i) = u_e(i)$, proving the claim. Otherwise, assume $M_e(i-1) = M_e(i)$. Then

$$\begin{aligned}
s_e(i) &\leq s_e(i-1) + r_e(i+1) - r_e(i) \\
&\leq u_e(i-1) + r_e(i+1) - r_e(i) \\
&= r_e(i+1) - M_e(i-1) = r_e(i+1) - M_e(i) = u_e(i),
\end{aligned}$$

proving the claim.

If r_e is convex, then $M_e(i) = r_e(i+1) - r_e(i)$ and $u_e(i) = r_e(i)$, proving the last claim. □

Runtime Analysis. Finding the node v in Algorithm 1 can be done with a priority queue. Maintaining such structure requires $\mathcal{O}(k \cdot \deg(v))$ updates when removing a single vertex v, each taking $\mathcal{O}(\log n)$ time for a total running time of $\mathcal{O}(pk \log n)$, where $p = \sum_{e \in E} |e| = \sum_{v \in V} \deg(v)$.

5.2 Approximations based on projecting to convexity

Given a set of reward functions $\{r_e \colon e \in E\}$ and a corresponding objective $\max_{S \subseteq V} \Gamma(S)$, another approach to approximating SWAMP is to replace each r_e with a nearby convex function $\hat{r}_e$, and maximize a related objective $\hat{\Gamma}(S) = \frac{1}{|S|}\sum_{e \in E} w(e) \hat{r}_e(|S \cap e|)$. As an initial observation, these objectives differ by at most the maximum ratio between original (r_e) and projected ($\hat{r}_e$) rewards.

Proposition 1. *If $r_e(i) \geq \hat{r}_e(i)$ for every $e \in E$ and every $i \in [|e|] = \{1, \ldots, |e|\}$, then for every $S \subseteq V$ we have $\hat{\Gamma}(S) \leq \Gamma(S) \leq \rho \cdot \hat{\Gamma}(S)$, where*

$$\rho = \max_{e \in E} \max_{i \in [|e|]} \frac{r_e(i)}{\hat{r}_e(i)}.$$

Proof. The first inequality follows from the assumption that $r_e(i) \geq \hat{r}_e(i)$. The definition of ρ implies that for every $e \in E$ and $i \in [|e|]$, we have $r_e(i) \leq \rho \cdot \hat{r}_e(i)$, which yields the second inequality $\Gamma(S) \leq \rho \cdot \hat{\Gamma}(S)$.

This approximation is tight in the sense that we can always construct a hypergraph H with a node set S for which $\Gamma(S) = \rho \cdot \hat{\Gamma}(S)$. In more detail, consider a pair of rewards functions r and $\hat{r}$ and let $t = \operatorname{argmax}_i \frac{r(i)}{\hat{r}(i)}$. Then construct a k-uniform hypergraph $H = (V, E)$ with a node set S satisfying $|e \cap S| \in \{0, t\}$ for every $e \in E$. Use the same reward function r for every edge when defining Γ, and the reward function $\hat{r}$ for every edge when defining r. Then

$$\Gamma(S) = \frac{\sum_{e \in E} r(|e \cap S|)}{|S|} = \frac{\sum_{e \in E} \rho \cdot \hat{r}(t)}{|S|} = \rho \cdot \hat{\Gamma}(S).$$

Given a non-convex nonnegative monotonic reward function $r \colon [0, k] \to \mathbb{R}^+$, our goal is then to find a *convex* nonnegative monotonic function $\hat{r} \leq r$ such that $\max_i r(i)/\hat{r}(i)$ is small. This can be cast as a small linear program.

$$\begin{aligned}
\underset{\hat{r}}{\text{maximize}} \quad & \kappa \\
\text{such that} \quad & r(i)\kappa \leq \hat{r}(i) \leq r(i) & & i = 0, 1, 2, \ldots, k \\
& 2\hat{r}(i) \leq \hat{r}(i-1) + \hat{r}(i+1) & & i = 2, 3, \ldots, k-1 \\
& \hat{r}(i+1) \geq \hat{r}(i) & & i = 1, 2, \ldots, k-1
\end{aligned}$$

The resulting approximation factor is given by $\rho = 1/\kappa$. We have dropped the e from the subscript of r_e and $\hat{r}_e$ above since we must solve this generic optimization problem for each edge reward function individually. This problem is equivalent to finding the lower convex hull of the points $\{(0,0), (1, r(1)), \ldots, (k, r(k))\}$, which can be done in $O(k)$ time [3]. Using the monotonicity of r, we can bound the worst-case approximation factor. See Appendix for a proof.

Proposition 2. *Let $r \colon [0, k] \to \mathbb{R}^+$ be a monotonic reward function satisfying $r(0) = 0$. There exists a nonnegative monotonic convex function $\hat{r}$ satisfying $\hat{r}(i) \leq r(i) \leq k \cdot \hat{r}(i)$ for every $i \in \{1, 2, \ldots, k\}$.*

Observe that this approximation is tight. If r is defined by $r(0) = 0$ and $r(x) = 1$ for $x \in (0, k]$, then $\hat{r}(x) = x/k$ and $r(1)/\hat{r}(1) = k$. Propositions 1 and 2 tell us that after performing optimal projections, Γ and $\hat{\Gamma}$ differ by at most a factor $1/k$, which leads to the following result.

Theorem 6. *A β-approximate solution to $\max_{S \subseteq V} \hat{\Gamma}(S)$ yields a $\frac{\beta}{k}$-approximate solution for $\max_{S \subseteq V} \Gamma(S)$.*

Since $\hat{\Gamma}$ includes only convex edge rewards, we can optimally solve it using flow-based methods, yielding a $1/k$-approximation for the original objective Γ. To provide a runtime analysis, we assume all original rewards $r_e(i)$ are integers. After projecting, the new rewards $\hat{r}_e$ are not necessarily integers. However, new rewards can be expressed as rational numbers with denominators that range between 1 and k. For a simple runtime analysis, we can scale all new rewards by $k!$ to obtain new convex integer reward functions $r'_e = k! \cdot \hat{r}_e \leq k^k \cdot r_e$. The flow-based approach of Zhou et al. [26] for this integer convex rewards case relies on performing a binary search over the interval $[0, W]$ where $W = \sum_{e \in E} r'_e(|e|) \leq k^k \sum_{e \in E} r_e(|e|)$. This has a runtime of $\mathcal{O}(\text{mincut}(p, p \cdot k) \log W)$ time where $p = \sum_{e \in E} |e|$ is the size of the hypergraph and $\text{mincut}(N, M)$ is the complexity of solving a minimum s-t cut problem in a graph with N nodes and M edges. To put this expression into a form that only involves the original rewards $\{r_e : e \in E\}$, observe that $\log W \leq k \log k + \log(\sum_{e \in E} r_e(|e|))$.

Algorithm 2. Approximates the CARD-SWAMP problem

Require: Hypergraph H, the cardinality constraint ℓ.
1: $S \leftarrow \emptyset$, $H_1 \leftarrow H$, $i \leftarrow 1$
2: **while** $|S| < \ell$ **do**
3:    $S_i \leftarrow$ (approximate) densest SWAMP in H_i
4:    $H_{i+1} \leftarrow \text{CONTRACT}(H_i, S_i)$
5:    $S \leftarrow S \cup S_i$
6:    $i \leftarrow i + 1$
7: $S' \leftarrow S_1 \cup \cdots \cup S_{i-2}$ padded with arbitrary nodes so that S' has ℓ nodes
Ensure: either S or S', whichever has the higher density.

Note finally that if we project the non-convex rewards and apply the existing $1/k$-approximation greedy peeling algorithm for $\hat{\Gamma}$ [26], this is only guaranteed to produce a $1/k^2$-approximate solution using this analysis. This again highlights utility of our peeling algorithms that work directly on the non-convex objective and yield a $1/k$-approximate solution.

6 Approximation Algorithms for Constrained Variants

The approximability of SWAMP has immediate implications for the approximability of CARD-SWAMP and FAIR-SWAMP. We will now explore these results.

Let us first consider the CARD-SWAMP problem, where the solution must have at least ℓ nodes. Here we will adopt the algorithm by Khuller and Saha [18] which was used to solve the constrained variant in regular graphs, and further extended to work with supermodular rewards by Chekuri et al. [8].

The algorithm, given in Algorithm 2, iteratively finds an approximate densest SWAMP, say S_i from the current hypergraph, say H_i, removes S_i from H_i (while keeping the edges), and adds S_i to the solution S, until S is large enough. Then the returned value is either S, or S', a set corresponding to S during the previous round, plus padded arbitrary nodes to satisfy the constraint.

Algorithm 2 requires a subroutine for contracting the discovered set from the current hypergraph. Given a hypergraph $H = (V, E, w, \{r_e\})$ and a set of nodes U we define a contracted hypergraph $H' = (V', E', w', \{r'_e\}) = \text{CONTRACT}(H, U)$ as follows. The nodes are $V' = V \setminus U$, the hyperedges E' consist of the hyperedges in E with nodes in U removed, and the weights w' correspond to the weights w. To define the rewards, let $e \in E$ be a hyperedge and $a = e \setminus U$ be the contracted hyperedge. Let $j = |e \cap U|$. We define the contracted reward as $r'_a(i) = r_e(i+j) - r_e(j)$.

We have the following approximation result, which we prove in Appendix.

Theorem 7. *Assume that we can α-approximate SWAMP, then Algorithm 2 yields $\frac{\alpha}{\alpha+1}$ approximation for CARD-SWAMP. Consequently, using Algorithm 1 together with Algorithm 2 yields $\frac{1}{k+1}$ approximation.*

We can now use Theorem 7 and the algorithm proposed by Miyauchi et al. [21] to obtain an approximation result for FAIR-SWAMP.

Theorem 8. *Assume an instance FAIR-SWAMP with $\{\ell_i\}$ constraints. Let S be the α-approximation for CARD-SWAMP with $\ell = \sum_i \ell_i$. Let c_i be the number of nodes with color i in S. Let S' be S padded with any $\ell_i - c_i$ nodes of color i, for every color i. Then S' yields $\alpha/2$-approximation for FAIR-SWAMP. Consequently, using Algorithms 1 and 2 yields $1/(2k+2)$ approximation.*

Note that originally this algorithm was designed for standard graphs (i.e., hypergraphs with $k = 2$). However, the proof for Theorem 8 is identical to the proof by Miyauchi et al. [21], and therefore omitted. We conjecture that a better approximation is possible using an approach for normal graphs by Gajewar and Das Sarma [12]. We leave exploring this direction as a future work.

7 Experiments and Analysis

We now analyze the performance of algorithms over a variety of hypergraphs using several different convex and non-convex reward functions. We implement all the algorithms in Julia and use publicly available hypergraph datasets. All experiments were conducted on a research server with 1TB of RAM.[1]

Datasets. The *contact-high-school* (CHS) [10,20] and *contact-primary-school* (CPS) [10,23] datasets represent student interactions at a high school and primary school, respectively, with students as nodes and group interactions as hyperedges. *Senate-committees* (SC) and *House-committees* (HC) contain labeled nodes representing US Senate and House members with political party affiliations [10]. Here hyperedges denote the committee memberships. In the *Trivago* hypergraph (Triv), nodes are vacation rentals and hyperedges are rentals clicked during the same user browsing session on `Trivago.com`. We specifically use a subset of a larger hypergraph [10], defined by considering only vacation rentals in Fukuoka, Japan. We preprocess each hypergraph by eliminating self-loops and dangling nodes, and extracting their largest connected component while preserving multi-edges. Hypergraph statistics are shown in Table 2. We choose hypergraphs that are small enough so that we can find optimal solutions using the ILP, as a point of comparison for our approximation algorithms.

---

[1] The code and Appendix are available at repository: The Densest SWAMP Problem.

Table 1. Edge-reward functions and their definitions

Function r_e		Function r_e	
1. atleast-two	$r_e(i) = \mathbf{1}[\, i \geq 2\,]$	4. standard	$r_e(i) = \mathbf{1}[\, i = |e|\,]$
2. atleast-half	$r_e(i) = \mathbf{1}\big[\, i \geq \lceil |e|/2 \rceil \,\big]$	5. quadratic	$r_e(i) = i^2/|e|$
3. all-but-one	$r_e(i) = \mathbf{1}[\, i \geq |e|-1 \,]$	6. square-root	$r_e(i) = \sqrt{i}$

Reward Functions. We use a range of edge-reward functions from non-convex to convex. For simplicity, we assume that in a given hypergraph, all edges use the same function to compute r_e and that each edge has weight 1. The function definitions are presented in Table 1. To avoid trivial solutions (as noted in Theorem 2), we set $r_e(1) = 0$ for functions 1, 2, 3, and 6. This is especially important for 2-node hyperedges while using reward functions 1, 2, and 3.

Algorithms. For finding the optimal solution, we implement the Exact method that iteratively solves the ILP (using Gurobi optimization software) as described in Sect. 4. Instead of using a binary search, we begin with the entire hypergraph and iteratively search for a denser and denser subset until no more improvement is possible, as this tends to converge in 4-5 iterations. We compare Exact against several approximation algorithms. Algorithm 1 is referred to as as PeelMax when we set $s_e = u_e$ as specified in Theorem 5, as Greedy when $s_e(i) = r_e(i)$, and as PeelZero when $s_e(i) = 0$. DegPeel is the greedy peeling algorithm for the standard densest subhypergraph objective: peeling based solely on the degree (number of incident hyperedges) in the induced hypergraph. For the projection-based approximations, we first project each non-convex r_e onto its nearest convex $\hat{r}_e$. We then run a flow-based method and Greedy methods using projected rewards. The projection-plus-flow approach solves the projected problem exactly using a maxflow solver, as described in [26]. It comes with a $1/k$-approximation guarantee, while the latter is a $1/k^2$ approximation.

Performance Analysis. Table 2 shows runtimes and objective values for our methods. As a first observation, we see that our projection-based flow method is exceptionally fast. Even the peeling methods, although not optimized for runtime, are still orders of magnitude faster than exactly solving the objective using the ILP solver. For instance, in the CPS hypergraph with the objective using *atleast-two* reward function for every edge, the ILP approach requires approximately 29 minutes, whereas Greedy and ProjFlow find the densest solution in under a second. Furthermore, our approximation algorithms all produce approximation ratios in practice that are close to 1, showing that these methods far exceed their theoretical guarantees and produce nearly optimal solutions. This illustrates that even for cases where SWAMP is **NP**-hard, peeling methods can provide a fast and accurate approach in practice, comparable to the success of peeling methods for poly-time solvable variants. We note also that for these hypergraphs and reward functions, applying direct peeling methods tends to give a slightly better approximation than projecting to nearby convex rewards. As another interesting observation, the standard greedy peeling method (setting

Table 2. Objective and runtime values of ILP, peeling and projection based strategies. Dashes indicate that Exact did not complete within the allotted time.

$|V|,|E|,k$	CHS 327, 7818, 5		CPS 242, 12704, 5		SC 282, 315, 31		HC 1290, 340, 81		Triv 262, 910, 16	
	Obj.	Run	Obj.	Run	Obj.	Run	Obj.	Run	Obj.	Run
atleast-two										
Exact	27.078	416	60.549	1760	–	–	–	–	11.53	2.4
PeelMax	26.871	0.15	60.02	0.42	21.0	0.89	14.0	24.01	11.09	0.06
Greedy	27.065	0.2	60.549	0.59	15.90	1.14	11.88	32.77	11.41	0.02
PeelZero	26.871	0.16	60.022	0.45	21.0	1.11	14.0	23.98	11.09	0.02
DegPeel	26.725	0.06	58.714	0.06	11.5	0.01	7.625	3.20	10.5	0.008
ProjFlow	26.451	0.16	58.34	0.21	12.22	0.07	7.7	0.43	10.76	0.02
ProjGreedy	26.451	0.2	58.34	0.58	12.22	0.86	7.625	25.57	10.76	0.02
atleast-half										
Exact	27.078	515	60.549	1711	–	–	–	–	9.625	2.33
PeelMax	26.871	0.16	60.02	0.43	3.0	0.89	1.571	23.81	9.179	0.02
Greedy	27.065	0.2	60.549	0.6	2.775	1.02	2.0	29.07	9.56	0.02
PeelZero	26.871	0.16	60.022	0.43	3.0	1.10	2.38	23.76	9.51	0.02
DegPeel	26.725	0.05	58.714	0.07	2.66	0.01	1.321	3.2	9.02	0.008
ProjFlow	26.451	0.18	58.34	0.21	2.32	0.07	2.28	0.39	9.378	0.03
ProjGreedy	26.451	0.19	58.344	0.59	2.32	0.86	2.23	25.36	9.378	0.02
all-but-one										
Exact	26.926	249.9	60.16	1716	1.83	6794	1.22	100.97	7.769	1.39
PeelMax	26.784	0.16	59.66	0.44	1.66	0.91	1.07	24.32	7.725	0.02
Greedy	26.867	0.2	60.16	0.6	1.8	0.95	1.105	25.62	7.763	0.02
PeelZero	26.784	0.16	59.66	0.44	1.66	1.12	1.07	24.29	7.725	0.02
DegPeel	26.593	0.05	58.47	0.08	1.66	0.01	0.936	3.23	7.375	0.008
ProjFlow	26.424	0.28	58.26	0.32	1.233	0.05	0.976	0.32	7.34	0.02
ProjGreedy	26.424	0.19	55.266	0.6	1.233	0.88	1.0	24.31	7.36	0.02
standard										
ExactFlow	25.597	0.24	54.475	0.33	1.176	0.13	0.823	0.5	5.52	0.10
Greedy	25.575	0.15	54.475	0.4	1.176	0.88	0.77	24.87	5.52	0.02
PeelZero	25.575	0.15	54.475	0.43	1.176	1.13	0.77	24.82	5.52	0.02
DegPeel	25.581	0.15	54.475	0.14	1.176	0.04	0.794	3.22	5.52	0.04
quadratic										
ExactFlow	71.45	0.44	145.47	0.68	26.91	0.25	12.52	1.33	31.10	0.08
Greedy	71.34	0.15	145.377	0.42	26.91	0.84	12.52	23.50	31.10	0.02
PeelZero	70.874	0.16	145.06	0.41	26.78	1.09	12.25	23.14	31.10	0.02
DegPeel	69.85	0.06	143.70	0.07	25.24	0.01	11.59	3.20	29.50	0.008
square-root										
Exact	41.34	495	91.7	4469	–	–	–	–	17.15	17.22
PeelMax	41.06	0.16	91.21	0.42	29.69	0.89	20.48	24.02	16.86	0.02
Greedy	41.14	0.2	91.72	0.58	29.26	0.87	18.38	24.99	17.14	0.02
PeelZero	41.05	0.15	90.83	0.42	29.69	1.58	17.67	23.23	16.27	0.02
DegPeel	41.06	0.06	89.92	0.06	19.64	0.01	11.94	3.28	16.16	0.008
ProjFlow	40.86	0.29	89.76	0.35	21.88	0.2	13.6	0.97	16.35	0.11
ProjGreedy	40.61	0.2	89.76	0.58	21.88	0.86	12.80	24.76	16.35	0.02

Table 3. Evaluating edge composition of optimal densest SWAMP solutions using five reward functions on two hypergraphs: CHS and CPS.

	atleast-two		atleast-half		all-but-one		$\|E(S)\|$		$\|S\|$	
	CHS	CPS	CHS	CPS	CHS	CPS	CHS	CPS	CHS	CPS
atleast-two	3791	7932	3791	7932	3762	7956	3053	6052	140	131
atleast-half	3791	7932	3791	7932	3762	7956	3053	6052	140	131
all-but-one	4055	8349	4055	8349	4039	8303	3404	6574	150	138
standard	6182	11341	6182	11341	6175	11337	6041	10895	236	200
quadratic	757	4206	757	4206	755	4152	651	3040	29	75

$s_e = r_e$) usually produces the best approximation results among peeling methods, despite the fact that our approximation guarantees do not apply to this approach.

Qualitative Comparison. As a final point of comparison, Table 3 reports qualitative aspects of the dense subsets produced by exactly solving SWAMP (using Exact) with different reward functions on two hypergraphs (CFS and CPS). The columns atleast-two, atleast-half, and all-but-one list the number of hyperedges (fully or partially contained in S) that intersect S in at least two nodes, at least $\lceil|e|/2\rceil$ nodes, or at least $|e| - 1$ nodes, respectively. We also report the number of edges completely contained ($|E(S)|$) and the subset size ($|S|$). Each reward function leads to a dense subset with distinct characteristics: for instance, the standard objective tends to produce larger subgraphs whereas the quadratic objective tends to produce smaller subgraphs. This provides a simple check that finding the densest SWAMP using different reward functions does indeed allow us to capture meaningfully different types of density patterns in practice.

8 Conclusions and Discussion

We have presented comprehensive hardness results and new approximation algorithms for a dense subhypergraph objective where rewards are given for partially included edges. Our most significant finding is that peeling algorithms can achieve the same approximation guarantee for **NP**-hard variants of the problem as they do for poly-time variants that are special cases of the densest supermodular subset problem. This is somewhat surprising given that previous approximations for peeling seem to inherently rely on the supermodularity property. As one interesting observation, our theory does not apply to the standard greedy peeling strategy ($s_e = r_e$), but this strategy still seems to work well in practice. One open direction is to explore whether there are cases where the standard greedy strategy performs poorly, or whether we can prove an approximation for this approach using a different technique. Another direction for future work is to explore hardness of approximation results for **NP**-hard variants of SWAMP.

Acknowledgments. This research is supported by the Academy of Finland project MALSOME (343045) and by the Helsinki Institute for Information Technology (HIIT). The research is also supported by the Army Research Office (ARO) under Award Number W911NF-24-1-0156. The views and conclusions contained in this document are those of the authors and should not be interpreted as representing the official policies, either expressed or implied, of the Army Research Office or the U.S. Government.

Disclosure of Interests. The authors have no competing interests to declare that are relevant to the content of this article.

References

1. Anagnostopoulos, A., Becchetti, L., Fazzone, A., Menghini, C., Schwiegelshohn, C.: Spectral relaxations and fair densest subgraphs. In: CIKM, pp. 35–44 (2020)
2. Andersen, R., Chellapilla, K.: Finding dense subgraphs with size bounds. In: WAW, pp. 25–37 (2009)
3. Andrew, A.M.: Another efficient algorithm for convex hulls in two dimensions. Inf. Process. Lett. **9**(5), 216–219 (1979)
4. Asahiro, Y., Iwama, K., Tamaki, H., Tokuyama, T.: Greedily finding a dense subgraph. J. Algorithms **34**(2), 203–221 (2000)
5. Bera, S.K., Bhattacharya, S., Choudhari, J., Ghosh, P.: A new dynamic algorithm for densest subhypergraphs. In: TheWebConf, pp. 1093–1103 (2022)
6. Charikar, M.: Greedy approximation algorithms for finding dense components in a graph. In: International Workshop on Approximation Algorithms for Combinatorial Optimization, pp. 84–95. Springer (2000)
7. Chekuri, C., Quanrud, K.: $(1 - \epsilon)$-approximate fully dynamic densest subgraph: linear space and faster update time. arXiv preprint arXiv:2210.02611 (2022)
8. Chekuri, C., Quanrud, K., Torres, M.R.: Densest subgraph: supermodularity, iterative peeling, and flow. In: SODA, pp. 1531–1555 (2022)
9. Chen, T., Tsourakakis, C.: Antibenford subgraphs: unsupervised anomaly detection in financial networks. In: KDD, pp. 2762–2770 (2022)
10. Chodrow, P.S., Veldt, N., Benson, A.R.: Hypergraph clustering: from blockmodels to modularity. Sci. Adv. (2021)
11. Fratkin, E., Naughton, B.T., Brutlag, D.L., Batzoglou, S.: MotifCut: regulatory motifs finding with maximum density subgraphs. Bioinformatics **22**(14), e150–e157 (2006)
12. Gajewar, A., Das Sarma, A.: Multi-skill collaborative teams based on densest subgraphs. In: SDM, pp. 165–176 (2012)
13. Goldberg, A.V.: Finding a maximum density subgraph, Technical report, UC Berkeley (1984)
14. Hu, S., Wu, X., Chan, T.H.: Maintaining densest subsets efficiently in evolving hypergraphs. In: CIKM, pp. 929–938 (2017)
15. Huang, D.H., Kahng, A.B.: When clusters meet partitions: new density-based methods for circuit decomposition. In: ED&TC, pp. 60–64 (1995)
16. Huang, Y., Gleich, D.F., Veldt, N.: Densest subhypergraph: negative supermodular functions and strongly localized methods. In: TheWebConf, pp. 881–892 (2024)
17. Kariotakis, E., Sidiropoulos, N.D., Konar, A.: Fairness-aware dense subgraph discovery. TMLR (2025)
18. Khuller, S., Saha, B.: On finding dense subgraphs. In: ICALP, pp. 597–608 (2009)

19. Lanciano, T., Miyauchi, A., Fazzone, A., Bonchi, F.: A survey on the densest subgraph problem and its variants. ACM Comput. Surv. **56**(8), 1–40 (2024)
20. Mastrandrea, R., Fournet, J., Barrat, A.: Contact patterns in a high school: a comparison between data collected using wearable sensors, contact diaries and friendship surveys. PLoS ONE **10**(9), e0136497 (2015)
21. Miyauchi, A., Chen, T., Sotiropoulos, K., Tsourakakis, C.E.: Densest diverse subgraphs: how to plan a successful cocktail party with diversity. In: KDD, pp. 1710–1721 (2023)
22. Rangapuram, S.S., Bühler, T., Hein, M.: Towards realistic team formation in social networks based on densest subgraphs. In: WWW, pp. 1077–1088 (2013)
23. Stehlé, J., et al.: High-resolution measurements of face-to-face contact patterns in a primary school. PLoS ONE **6**(8), e23176 (2011)
24. Tsourakakis, C.: The k-clique densest subgraph problem. In: Proceedings of the 24th International Conference on World Wide Web, pp. 1122–1132 (2015)
25. Veldt, N., Benson, A.R., Kleinberg, J.: The generalized mean densest subgraph problem. In: KDD, pp. 1604–1614 (2021)
26. Zhou, Y., Hu, S., Sheng, Z.: Extracting densest sub-hypergraph with convex edge-weight functions. In: International Conference on Theory and Applications of Models of Computation, pp. 305–321. Springer (2022)

How Useful Is Graph Pooling for Node-Level Tasks?

Yijun Duan[1(✉)], Xin Liu[2], Steven Lynden[2], Akiyoshi Matono[2], and Qiang Ma[1]

[1] Kyoto Institute of Technology, Kyoto, Japan
{yijun,qiang}@kit.ac.jp
[2] AIST, Tokyo, Japan
{xin.liu,steven.lynden,a.matono}@aist.go.jp

Abstract. As an essential component of graph neural networks, graph pooling is indispensable for graph-level tasks such as graph classification and generation. However, certain node-level tasks inherently require graph pooling, particularly *multiple instance learning (MIL) on graphs*, a weakly supervised learning paradigm where only set-level labels are available for training node-level predictors. Existing *embedding-based pooling* aggregates node embeddings to obtain a holistic graph-level representation, neglecting direct inference of node labels. To address this limitation, we propose *instance-based pooling*, which maps node embeddings to node probabilities before generating graph representations. We prove that embedding-based pooling methods can be seamlessly transformed into instance-based ones without losing permutation invariance or expressiveness, while the latter offers better interpretability. Extensive experiments on diverse benchmark datasets validate the effectiveness of our proposed method, providing key insights into the selection of pooling methods for different machine learning tasks on graphs.

Keywords: Graph Pooling · Graph Multiple Instance Learning · Instance-level Learning · Weakly supervised learning

1 Introduction

Graph representation learning (GRL) is one of the most effective solutions for machine learning tasks on graphs [21]. It consists of two fundamental components: the *message passing* module, which learns node embeddings, and the *pooling* module, which aggregates node information into subgraph representations. Node-level tasks typically rely solely on message passing, while graph-level tasks require both components.

However, *certain node-level tasks inherently rely on graph pooling*. A key reason is the difficulty of obtaining sufficient node labels due to data annotation constraints. Consider the task of *multiple instance learning (MIL) on graphs*. MIL is a weakly supervised learning paradigm where instances are grouped into sets, called bags, and only bag-level labels are available for training instance-level predictors. Traditional MIL assumes that instances are i.i.d., while given the versatility of graphs in modeling complex relationships in real-world scenarios, extending MIL to graph data can facilitate various practical tasks and attract significant interest. For example, in drug discovery, the goal is to identify pharmacophore molecules (instance/node labels) that contribute to the properties of complex molecular compounds (bag/graph labels). In such a scenario, obtaining bag labels is often significantly more cost-effective and feasible than acquiring instance labels. Figure 1 illustrates the distinction between semi-supervised learning and multiple instance learning on graphs.

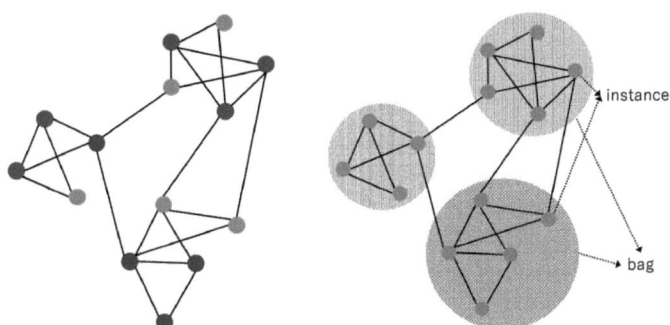

Fig. 1. An illustration of semi-supervised learning and multiple instance learning (our task) on graphs. The colors represent node labels, with gray nodes indicating unlabeled nodes. In multiple instance learning, nodes (called instances) are arranged in sets (called bags), and bag labels are determined by unknown instance labels based on different assumptions. To predict instance labels based on *bag labels*, both the message passing layer and the graph pooling layer are essential. (Color figure online)

Can existing graph pooling methods effectively address node-level MIL tasks? Mainstream pooling approaches aggregate instance embeddings into a bag embedding, followed by a classifier computing the bag probability [19]. We refer to this as **embedding-based pooling**. This training paradigm does not involve any inference or fitting of instance labels. To address this limitation, inspired by instance-based MIL methods for non-graph data (e.g., [25,27]), we propose a novel graph pooling paradigm in this paper: **instance-based pooling**. Instead of directly aggregating embeddings, it first maps instance embeddings to instance probabilities and then constructs bag probabilities based on these instance probabilities. We demonstrate that, under certain conditions, any embedding-based pooling method can be seamlessly transformed into an instance-based pooling method without any loss of permutation-invariance or expressive power. Furthermore, we show that, due to the linearity of instance-based models, SHAP values [20] provide a more precise characterization of each instance's contribution to the model's decision compared to attention scores.

We analyze the performance of embedding-based pooling and instance-based pooling using synthetic bags on four benchmark datasets. Specifically, we evaluate four commonly used attention modules and two feature aggregators. Two strategies for generating bag labels from instance labels are examined. While our primary focus is instance-level classification, we also conduct additional experiments on bag-level tasks to assess the generality of the pooling models. The main experimental findings are summarized as follows: (1) instance-based pooling is more effective in instance classification tasks under the standard MIL assumption; (2) both pooling strategies exhibit comparable performance for instance classification under the collective MIL assumption; (3) for bag classification under the standard MIL assumption, embedding-based pooling is more effective.

In summary, our contributions are as follows:

- We introduce the instance-level graph multiple instance learning task for the first time, providing a deep exploration of the role of graph pooling in node-level tasks.
- We propose a straightforward and general transformation rule that converts embedding-based pooling models into instance-based models.
- We systematically analyze the key theoretical properties of embedding-based and instance-based models, including their permutation invariance, expressiveness and interpretability.
- We conduct extensive experiments on standard graph datasets across various MIL tasks, which offer valuable insights into the selection of pooling methods when handling graph structures at different levels.

2 Problem Formulation and Notations

Let $\mathcal{G} = (\mathcal{V}, \mathcal{E})$ denote the input graph with node set $\mathcal{V}$ and edge set $\mathcal{E}$. $\mathcal{V} = \{v_1, v_2, ..., v_n\}$, where n is the number of nodes. k denotes the number of classes. Nodes (called instances) are arranged in sets (called bags). Only bag labels are available during model training.

Let $\mathcal{X}$ denote a bag consisting of m instances $\{v_1, v_2, ..., v_m\}$. In MIL, bag label $\mathcal{Y}$ is determined by unknown instance labels $\{y_1, y_2, ..., y_m\}$ based on different assumptions. In this paper, the standard assumption [8] is mainly focused. Given a trigger class $t \in \{1, 2, ..., k\}$, we refer to the nodes that belong to t as positive instances, and the other nodes as negative instances. The standard MIL assumption states that positive bags contain at least one positive instance, and negative bags contain only negative instances. Formally, $\mathcal{Y}$ is determined by:

$$\mathcal{Y} = \begin{cases} +1 & if \quad \exists y \in \{y_1, y_2, ..., y_m\}, y = t \\ -1 & if \quad \forall y \in \{y_1, y_2, ..., y_m\}, y \neq t \end{cases} \quad (1)$$

Our target is then to learn an instance-level binary classifier to predict the label of nodes within the bags. Our work is useful in many real-world scenarios where it is desirable to detect key instances that trigger the bag label, such as automating cancer diagnosis and grading.

3 Preliminary: Embedding-Based Pooling

When dealing with set-level representation learning on graphs, a widely used solution is **embedding-based pooling** [19]. In our problem, it computes the bag probability $\theta(\mathcal{X}) \in [0,1]$ in the following way:

$$\theta(\mathcal{X}) = \text{CLS}(\text{AGGR}(\{\alpha_i \cdot \text{MP}(v_i), v_i \in \mathcal{X}\})) \tag{2}$$

$$\alpha_i = \text{ATT}(v_i) \tag{3}$$

Here, $\theta(\mathcal{X})$ consists of 4 functions: MP, CLS, ATT, and AGGR. MP consists of message-passing layer(s), and works as a node feature extractor. Attention module ATT computes the attention weight α_i for node v_i, which can be used to measure the instance contribution in the bag representation and interpret model predictions. The aggregator AGGR aggregates the attended instance embeddings to obtain a bag representation. The most common practice is sum, with alternative choices including max [23]. Finally, the bag embedding is processed by the classifier CLS, and a bag label is predicted. The selection of MP, CLS, ATT and AGGR jointly determines the implementation of a pooling method and its effectiveness and complexity.

4 Proposed Method: Instance-Based Pooling

One inherent limitation of embedding-based pooling is its inability to train instances in the label space. For node-level MIL tasks, a natural assumption is that an effective pooling method should be capable of estimating instance probabilities during training. To achieve this, we do not require complex designs—simply swapping CLS and AGGR in embedding-based models suffices. We refer to the new model as **instance-based pooling**, which is formulated as follows:

$$\theta(\mathcal{X}) = \text{AGGR}(\{\text{CLS}(\alpha_i \cdot \text{MP}(v_i)), v_i \in \mathcal{X}\}) \tag{4}$$

$$\alpha_i = \text{ATT}(v_i) \tag{5}$$

Different from embedding-based pooling, CLS learns the instance probability $\theta(v_i)$ during training, which is then combined by AGGR to form the bag probability $\theta(\mathcal{X})$. This allows the learning model to effectively accommodate both bag-level training and instance-level inference[1]. Similarly, the implementations of MP, ATT, CLS and AGGR are task-specific. Finally, an illustration of aforementioned two types of pooling paradigms is shown below in Fig. 2.

---

[1] Another alternative design of instance-based pooling follows the formulation $\theta(\mathcal{X}) = \text{AGGR}(\alpha_i \cdot \{\text{CLS}(\text{MP}(v_i)), v_i \in \mathcal{X}\}), \alpha_i = \text{ATT}(v_i)$.

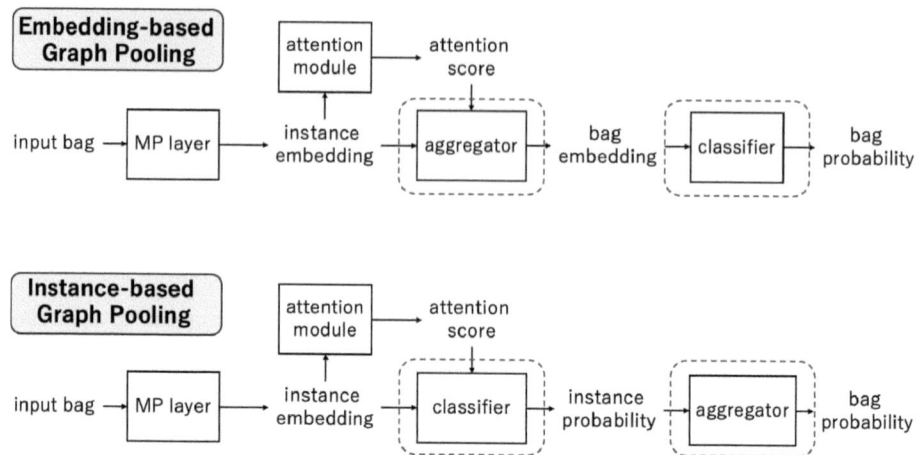

Fig. 2. A comparison between **embedding-based pooling** (existing) and **instance-based pooling** (proposed). Embedding-based pooling: *instance embedding -¿ bag embedding -¿ bag probability*; instance-based pooling: *instance embedding -¿ instance probability -¿ bag probability*.

5 Key Theoretical Properties of Pooling Models

In this section, we first prove that the transformation from embedding-based pooling to instance-based pooling does not compromise the original model's permutation invariance (Sect. 5.1) or expressive power (Sect. 5.2), which are key properties of MIL models and graph neural networks, respectively. Finally, by investigating the relationship between instance probability and SHAP values (Sect. 5.3), we demonstrate that instance-based models offer superior interpretability.

5.1 Permutation-Invariance

The standard MIL assumption (please refer to Eq. (1)) suggests that neither the ordering nor the dependency of instances within a bag exists. Therefore, when computing the bag probability $\theta(\mathcal{X})$, for any permutation π, we should have $\theta(\{v_1, v_2, ..., v_m\}) = \theta(\{v_{\pi(1)}, v_{\pi(2)}, ..., v_{\pi(m)}\})$. Such property is referred to as *permutation-invariance*. To verify whether the pooling models possess this property, we first introduce the following Fundamental Theorem of Symmetric Functions with monomials [11,30]:

Theorem 1. *A function $F(\mathcal{X})$ operating on a countable set $\mathcal{X}$ is invariant to the permutation of instances in $\mathcal{X}$ if and only if it can be decomposed in the form $\rho(\sum_{v_i \in \mathcal{X}} \psi(v_i))$, where ρ and ψ are suitable transformations.*

Theorem 1 introduces a general form of functions that satisfy the property of permutation invariance. Based on it, we make the following corollary:

Corollary 1. *When AGGR is the summation operater, both embedding-based pooling and instance-based pooling are invariant to permutation.*

Proof. The set function $F(\mathcal{X})$ in Theorem 1 is the bag probability $\theta(\mathcal{X})$. For embedding-based pooling, when sum is the aggregator, transformation ψ and ρ corresponds to $\alpha_i \cdot \text{MP}(v_i)$ and CLS, respectively. For instance-based pooling, ψ is the instance probability $\text{CLS}(\alpha_i \cdot \text{MP}(v_i))$, and ρ is the identity function.

5.2 Expressiveness

The expressive power of a GNN refer to its ability to encode and process feature information on the graph as well as graph structure information, e.g., the ability to distinguish non-isomorphic graphs [31]. In graph theory, the Weisfeiler-Leman test (WL test) is a classic heuristic method to judge whether two graphs are isomorphic [16]. We prove below that when certain conditions are satisfied, both embedding-based pooling and instance-based pooling are capable of retaining distinct information in the graph. To begin, we first state the following theorem concerning the expressive power of graph pooling operators [1]:

Theorem 2. *For WL-distinguishable graphs, a graph pooler satisfying the following conditions will produce coarsened graphs that remain WL-distinguishable: (1) the message-passing layers compute different sums of node features; (2) the cluster assignment matrix is right-stochastic up to a constant λ; (3) the features of supernodes are convex combinations of the input node features.*

We assume that the pooling models discussed in Sect. 3 and Sect. 4 satisfy the above properties. Note that in this case, MP is implied to be powerful, and AGGR is implied to be the summation operator. We prove below that, under additional constraints on CLS, both instance-based pooling and embedding-based pooling preserve the expressive power of MP:

Corollary 2. *Let $\mathcal{X}^1$ and $\mathcal{X}^2$ denote two WL-distinguishable bags, the pooled bags $\hat{\mathcal{X}}^1$ and $\hat{\mathcal{X}}^2$ generated by an instance-based model remain WL-distinguishable if the following additional conditions hold: (4) CLS is an additive function; (5) CLS is an injective function.*

Proof. Suppose that $\mathcal{X}^1/\mathcal{X}^2$ contains m nodes, while $\hat{\mathcal{X}}^1/\hat{\mathcal{X}}^2$ contains l supernodes ($l < m$). Let $\mathcal{U}^1$, $\mathcal{U}^2$, $\hat{\mathcal{U}}^1$ and $\hat{\mathcal{U}}^2$ denote the corresponding node embedding/probability matrix of $\mathcal{X}^1$, $\mathcal{X}^2$, $\hat{\mathcal{X}}^1$ and $\hat{\mathcal{X}}^2$, respectively. Here, $\mathcal{U}^1$ and $\mathcal{U}^2$ are computed by MP. Given condition 1, we have:

$$\sum_{i=1}^{m} \mathcal{U}_i^1 \neq \sum_{i=1}^{m} \mathcal{U}_i^2 \tag{6}$$

Here, $\mathcal{U}_i^1$ and $\mathcal{U}_i^2$ denote the i-th row of $\mathcal{U}^1$ and $\mathcal{U}^2$ respectively, which correspond to the vector of the i-th instance in the bag. Suppose that $\hat{\mathcal{X}}^1$ and $\hat{\mathcal{X}}^2$ are not WL-distinguishable. Then, there exists a one-to-one mapping ω from $\{1, 2, ..., l\}$ to $\{1, 2, ..., l\}$ such that:

$$\hat{\mathcal{U}}_j^1 = \hat{\mathcal{U}}_{\omega(j)}^2, \forall j = 1, 2, ..., l \tag{7}$$

Let $\mathcal{M} \in \mathbb{R}^{m \times l}$ denote the assignment matrix, where $\mathcal{M}_{ij}$ represents the weight that assigns a node i to a supernode j. Given condition 3, we have:

$$\sum_{i=1}^m \text{CLS}(\mathcal{U}_i^1 \cdot \mathcal{M}_{ij}^1) = \sum_{i=1}^m \text{CLS}(\mathcal{U}_i^2 \cdot \mathcal{M}_{i\omega(j)}^2), \forall j = 1, 2, ..., l \tag{8}$$

Give condition 4, we can swap CLS with the summation operator as:

$$\text{CLS}(\sum_{i=1}^m \mathcal{U}_i^1 \cdot \mathcal{M}_{ij}^1) = \text{CLS}(\sum_{i=1}^m \mathcal{U}_i^2 \cdot \mathcal{M}_{i\omega(j)}^2), \forall j = 1, 2, ..., l \tag{9}$$

Given condition 5, we have:

$$\sum_{i=1}^m \mathcal{U}_i^1 \cdot \mathcal{M}_{ij}^1 = \sum_{i=1}^m \mathcal{U}_i^2 \cdot \mathcal{M}_{i\omega(j)}^2, \forall j = 1, 2, ..., l \tag{10}$$

We sum the vectors of all supernodes:

$$\sum_{j=1}^l \sum_{i=1}^m \mathcal{U}_i^1 \cdot \mathcal{M}_{ij}^1 = \sum_{j=1}^l \sum_{i=1}^m \mathcal{U}_i^2 \cdot \mathcal{M}_{i\omega(j)}^2 \tag{11}$$

which can be rewritten as:

$$\sum_{i=1}^m \mathcal{U}_i^1 \cdot \sum_{j=1}^l \mathcal{M}_{ij}^1 = \sum_{i=1}^m \mathcal{U}_i^2 \cdot \sum_{j=1}^l \mathcal{M}_{i\omega(j)}^2 \tag{12}$$

Since $\sum_{j=1}^l \mathcal{M}_{ij}^1 = \sum_{j=1}^l \mathcal{M}_{i\omega(j)}^2 = \lambda$, $\forall i = 1, 2, ..., m$ (Cond. 2). We have:

$$\sum_{i=1}^m \mathcal{U}_i^1 = \sum_{i=1}^m \mathcal{U}_i^2 \tag{13}$$

Notice that the above equation contradicts Eq. (6). Therefore, $\hat{\mathcal{X}}^1$ and $\hat{\mathcal{X}}^2$ remain WL-distinguishable.

For embedding-based models, note that Eq. (9) can be directly derived from Eq. (7). That means, it is not necessary to assume the additivity of CLS function to generate WL-distinguishable coarsened bags, while the remaining four conditions are required to hold.

5.3 Interpretability

In this study, we adopt the SHAP framework [20] to analyze the interpretability of MIL methods motivated by [12], where SHAP values provide insights into how each input instance contributes to a bag-level prediction. A key distinction from [12] is that our analysis targets at input instances which are not mutually independent, which is a fundamental characteristic of graph-structured data.

Clearly, instance-based pooling is a linear model. Regarding the independence of instances, we consider the following two cases: (1) the interdependence among instances will be sufficiently captured by MP, and thus instances can be assumed independent during the pooling phase for computational simplicity; (2) instances remain dependent during pooling. We discuss both cases separately below. In what follows, we denote the SHAP value of $\theta(v_i)$ as $\phi(v_i)$.

Independent Instances. For linear models with independent features, the computation of SHAP values relies on the following theorem [20]:

Theorem 3. *Give a linear regression model $f(x) = \sum_{i=1}^{m} w_i x_i + b$, where all features $x_1, x_2, ..., x_m$ are independent, we have:*

$$\phi(x_i) = w_i(x_i - E[x_i]) \tag{14}$$

which immediately inspires our computation as follows:

Corollary 3. *For instance-based pooling models, $\phi(v_i)$ takes the following simple form, where instance probabilities $\theta(v_1), \theta(v_2), ..., \theta(v_m)$ are independent:*

$$\phi(v_i) = \theta(v_i) - E[\theta(v_i)] \tag{15}$$

Proof. In Eq. (14), x_i, w_i, and b correspond to $\theta(v_i)$, 1, and 0 in Eq. (4), respectively. Note that AGGR is required to be the summation operator.

Dependent Instances. For linear models with dependent features, the computation of SHAP values becomes more complex. First, we state the following theorem regarding the contribution function $\tau(\cdot)$ defined on an instance subset $\mathcal{X}_\mathcal{S}$, where $\mathcal{X}_\mathcal{S}^*$ denote a subset of input instances:

Theorem 4. *For instance-based pooling models, $\tau(\mathcal{X}_\mathcal{S})$ takes the following form, where instance probabilities $\theta(v_1), \theta(v_2), ..., \theta(v_m)$ are dependent:*

$$\tau(\mathcal{X}_\mathcal{S}) = \sum_{v_i \in \mathcal{X}_{\overline{\mathcal{S}}}} E[\theta(v_i) | \mathcal{X}_\mathcal{S} = \mathcal{X}_\mathcal{S}^*] + \sum_{v_i \in \mathcal{X}_\mathcal{S}} \theta(v_i) \tag{16}$$

Proof. We make the following derivations:

$$\tau(\mathcal{X}_\mathcal{S}) = E[\theta(\mathcal{X}) | \mathcal{X}_\mathcal{S} = \mathcal{X}_\mathcal{S}^*] \tag{17}$$

$$= E[\sum_{v_i \in \mathcal{X}_{\overline{\mathcal{S}}}} \theta(v_i) + \sum_{v_i \in \mathcal{X}_{\mathcal{S}}} \theta(v_i) | \mathcal{X}_{\mathcal{S}} = \mathcal{X}_{\mathcal{S}}^*] \qquad (18)$$

$$= \sum_{v_i \in \mathcal{X}_{\overline{\mathcal{S}}}} E[\theta(v_i) | \mathcal{X}_{\mathcal{S}} = \mathcal{X}_{\mathcal{S}}^*] + \sum_{v_i \in \mathcal{X}_{\mathcal{S}}} E[\theta(v_i) | \mathcal{X}_{\mathcal{S}} = \mathcal{X}_{\mathcal{S}}^*] \qquad (19)$$

$$= \sum_{v_i \in \mathcal{X}_{\overline{\mathcal{S}}}} E[\theta(v_i) | \mathcal{X}_{\mathcal{S}} = \mathcal{X}_{\mathcal{S}}^*] + \sum_{v_i \in \mathcal{X}_{\mathcal{S}}} \theta(v_i) \qquad (20)$$

Notice that a key distinction from independent instances is that, when $v_i \in \mathcal{X}_{\overline{\mathcal{S}}}$, we have $p(\theta(v_i)|\mathcal{X}_{\mathcal{S}} = \mathcal{X}_{\mathcal{S}}^*) \neq p(\theta(v_i))$, which leads to $E[\theta(v_i)|\mathcal{X}_{\mathcal{S}} = \mathcal{X}_{\mathcal{S}}^*] \neq E[\theta(v_i)]$. In this case, solving for $\tau(\mathcal{X}_{\mathcal{S}})$ depends on a proper and efficient estimation of $E[\theta(v_i)|\mathcal{X}_{\mathcal{S}} = \mathcal{X}_{\mathcal{S}}^*]$, which is typically more difficult than estimating $E[\theta(v_i)]$. Given $\tau(\mathcal{X}_{\mathcal{S}})$, $\phi(v_i)$ can be then computed based on the definition of the Shapley value [20].

6 Experimental Settings

6.1 Datasets

We use four widely-used benchmark datasets consisting of diverse types of networks, including CORA-ML [2], CITESEER [28], AMAZON [24] and ACTOR [22]. All of the above datasets are available at PyTorch Geometric Library [7]. Below is a brief description of each dataset above.

- CORA-ML is a citation network consisting of 2,995 scientific publications classified into one of 7 classes. Each publication in the dataset is described by a 2879-dim 0/1-valued word vector indicating the absence/presence of the corresponding word from the dictionary. The network contains 16,316 citation links in total.
- CITESEER is another classical citation network containing of 3,327 scientific publications from 6 research areas, such as AI, DB, and HCI. Similarly, each paper is described by a 3703-dim 0/1-valued word vector. This citation network consists of 9,104 links.
- AMAZON denotes a Amazon product network, where nodes represent goods and edges represent that two goods are frequently bought together. Given product reviews as 745-dim bag-of-words node features, the classification task is to map goods to their respective product category. This network contains 7,650 nodes, 238,162 edges and 8 classes.
- ACTOR refers to an actor network, where each node corresponds to an actor, and the edge between two nodes denotes co-occurrence on the same Wikipedia page. The 932-dim node features correspond to some keywords in the Wikipedia pages. The task is to classify the nodes into categories in term of words of actor's Wikipedia. This network contains 7,600 nodes, 30, 019 edges and 5 classes.

6.2 Analyzed Methods and Metrics

We implement and test four representative embedding-based pooling models with their instance-based version. They include: (1) two most straightforward and commonly used methods, sum-pool and mean-pool; (2) two attention models, GlobalAttention [18] and Set2Set [26]. To enhance the reproducibility of the experimental results, we rely on the open source implementation of all models provided by PyTorch Geometric Library [7]. For a fair comparison, all models use GraphSAGE [10] as the node feature extractor MP, and a 1-layer MLP as the classifier CLS. For sum-pool, ATT is equivalent to the identity function. All the analyzed methods are evaluated by the classification accuracy and AUC.

6.3 Bag Label Generation

We design the following process to synthesize bags and their label, which is consistent with the standard MIL assumption (please refer to Eq. (1)). Let bag $\mathcal{X} = \{v_1, v_2, ..., v_m\}$ with label $\mathcal{Y}$ as defined in Sect. 2, the following steps are conducted: (1) a trigger class t is randomly selected based on the uniform distribution; (2) m nodes are randomly sampled to form a bag $\mathcal{X}$. Then, $\mathcal{Y} = 1$ if $\mathcal{X}$ contains an instance belonging to t, and $\mathcal{Y} = -1$ otherwise. Step 2 is repeated until the number of bags reaches the set value. Note that when t represents a minority class, the classification task becomes more challenging due to the imbalanced class distribution, which is common in real-world scenarios [5].

6.4 Key Experimental Configurations

We set the number and size of bags to 500 and 2, respectively. Then, we randomly split the bags into a 60%/20%/20% split for training, validation, and testing. Note that bag labels are used during training, while node labels are used for hyperparameter tuning and testing. Hyperparameters of MP (learning rate, weight decay, number of hidden units, and dropout rate) are tuned on the validation set. All models are trained using the Adam optimizer [14] until convergence, with the maximum training epoch being 500. A server equipped with an NVIDIA RTX 6000 Ada GPU is used to conduct the experiments in this study.

7 Experimental Results

7.1 Performance of Analyzed Methods in Node Prediction

Table 1 shows the comparison between representative embedding-based methods and their instance-based version in instance prediction. It can be observed that, out of a total of 32 comparisons, instance-based models outperform in 19 cases, underperform in 10 cases, and perform equally with embedding-based models in 3 cases. Thus, instance-based models exhibit a clear advantage. The experiments indeed suggest that when training node classifiers with set labels, adopting the instance-based pooling is more likely to be a better practice.

Table 1. Performance of all analyzed methods in terms of instance-level MIL on graphs. "-emb" and "-ins" represent embedding-based and instance-based models, respectively. In the comparison, results where instance-based models perform better are underlined in blue (positive results), those where embedding-based models perform better are underlined in red (negative results), and equivalent results are underlined in gray.

Datasets	CORA-ML		CITESEER		AMAZON		ACTOR	
Metrics	Accuracy	AUC	Accuracy	AUC	Accuracy	AUC	Accuracy	AUC
sum-emb	0.963	0.953	0.874	0.877	0.888	0.520	0.602	0.690
sum-ins	0.947	0.961	0.901	0.908	0.888	0.693	0.689	0.683
mean-emb	0.926	0.765	0.927	0.742	0.909	0.510	0.675	0.536
mean-ins	0.942	0.843	0.875	0.828	0.909	0.634	0.634	0.532
GlobalAttention-emb	0.935	0.881	0.891	0.882	0.948	0.968	0.684	0.610
GlobalAttention-ins	0.871	0.938	0.896	0.835	0.948	0.885	0.652	0.613
Set2Set-emb	0.828	0.501	0.868	0.951	0.751	0.515	0.878	0.526
Set2Set-ins	0.930	0.746	0.873	0.936	0.838	0.739	0.913	0.589

7.2 Pooling with max as the Aggregator

While most MIL models use sum as the aggregator, max that takes the feature-wise maximum across all instances is still regarded as an effective alternative in certain scenarios [11,23]. With max as the aggregator, the embedding-based pooling takes the following form:

$$\theta(\mathcal{X}) = \text{CLS}(\max(\{\alpha_i \cdot \text{MP}(v_i), v_i \in \mathcal{X}\})) \tag{21}$$

Similarly, the instance-based pooling is re-formulated as:

$$\theta(\mathcal{X}) = \max(\{\text{CLS}(\alpha_i \cdot \text{MP}(v_i)), v_i \in \mathcal{X}\}) \tag{22}$$

We additionally conduct a comparative analysis of embedding-based pooling and instance-based pooling when max is used. Consistent with sum-pool, GraphSAGE and a 1-layer MLP are selected as MP and CLS, respectively. ATT is implemented as an identity function. The results are summarized in Table 2.

Table 2. Performance of pooling methods with max as the aggregator. Positive, negative and equivalent results are underlined in blue, red and gray, respectively.

Datasets	CORA-ML		CITESEER		AMAZON		ACTOR	
Metrics	Accuracy	AUC	Accuracy	AUC	Accuracy	AUC	Accuracy	AUC
max-emb	0.909	0.860	0.874	0.775	0.985	0.788	0.582	0.546
max-ins	0.936	0.842	0.905	0.899	0.738	0.905	0.663	0.546

It is encouraging to see from Table 2 that with max as the aggregator, instance-based pooling still exhibits as a better practice in most test scenarios (5/8). Embedding-based models outperform in only 25% of the comparisons.

It is worth noting that although instance-based pooling using max can still be proved to be permutation-invariant as long as it can be arbitrarily approximated by a Hausdorff continuous symmetric function [23], its WL-test-equivalence as well as superior interpretability over embedding-based models no longer hold.

7.3 Pooling Under the Collective MIL Assumption

Our previous discussion focuses on the *standard* MIL assumption, which can be relaxed to the *collective* MIL assumption, where bags are not triggered by a single instance, but by an accumulation of multiple instances. More concretely, under the collective assumption, a bag $\mathcal{X} = \{v_1, v_2, ..., v_m\}$ is positive if and only if it contains more than $\gamma \cdot m$ positive instances. The label generation rule is formally presented as follows, where $\gamma \in [0, 1]$, $y_i \in \{0, 1\}$:

$$\mathcal{Y} = \begin{cases} +1 & if \ \sum_{i=1}^{m} y_i \geq \gamma \cdot m \\ -1 & if \ \sum_{i=1}^{m} y_i < \gamma \cdot m \end{cases} \quad (23)$$

To synthesize bags, we conduct the following sampling process: (1) a trigger class t is randomly selected as the positive label; (2) m nodes are arbitrarily sampled to form a bag $\mathcal{X}$. Then, $\mathcal{Y} = 1$ if $\mathcal{X}$ contains no less than $\gamma \cdot m$ instance belonging to t, and $\mathcal{Y} = -1$ otherwise. Step 3 is repeated until the number of bags reaches the predefined value. In our experiments, we set $m = 3$ and $\gamma = 0.5$. This means that a bag is labeled as positive only if it contains at least two trigger instances. To prevent the number of positive bags from being too small, we ensure that 20% of the bags include two trigger instances and one non-trigger instance. In this way, at least 20% of the bags are positive. The experimental results show that, under the collective MIL assumption, instance-based and embedding-based models perform comparably: each leads in 13 comparisons, while they tie in 6 cases. Taken together with the results in Tables 1, 2, and 3, we consider the performance of instance-based models on node-level tasks to be reliable.

Table 3. Model performance under the *collective MIL assumption*. Positive, negative and equivalent results are underlined in blue, red and gray, respectively.

Datasets	CORA-ML		CITESEER		AMAZON		ACTOR	
Metrics	Accuracy	AUC	Accuracy	AUC	Accuracy	AUC	Accuracy	AUC
sum-emb	0.959	0.584	0.830	0.624	0.941	0.553	0.645	0.500
sum-ins	0.948	0.621	0.961	0.622	0.781	0.576	0.645	0.516
mean-emb	0.970	0.583	0.882	0.600	0.862	0.523	0.671	0.546
mean-ins	0.867	0.616	0.857	0.616	0.862	0.512	0.671	0.553
GlobalAttention-emb	0.910	0.606	0.844	0.588	0.828	0.515	0.675	0.565
GlobalAttention-ins	0.847	0.592	0.873	0.616	0.828	0.507	0.699	0.548
Set2Set-emb	0.885	0.592	0.816	0.621	0.803	0.511	0.745	0.503
Set2Set-ins	0.874	0.594	0.882	0.609	0.803	0.503	0.755	0.503

7.4 Performance of Analyzed Methods in Bag Prediction

A pooling model that generalizes across different graph structures would bring significant benefits to graph learning tasks. In this section, we examine whether instance-based models can retain their performance advantage in bag-level tasks. To achieve this, we test the performance of all methods on bag-level MIL tasks (see Table 4). Following the synthetic method described in Sect. 6.3, we construct 1,500 bags, with 300, 200, and 1,000 bags used for training, validation, and testing, respectively. Following [6], the bag size is increased to be 10.

For bag-level classification tasks, embedding-based models deliver superior performance in the majority of comparisons (18 out of 32). Specifically, their advantage is more pronounced in terms of accuracy. This observation contrasts with the results presented in the preceding sections, and implies that instance-based pooling and embedding-based pooling excel at capturing local and global features, respectively. Therefore, for tasks such as graph classification, our experiments suggest continuing to use classical embedding-based models, unless there are additional requirements for model interpretability. Developing a pooling model that is applicable to both graph-level and node-level learning tasks would be an interesting and challenging direction for future work.

Table 4. Performance of all analyzed methods on the bag prediction task. Positive, negative and equivalent results are underlined in blue, red and gray, respectively.

Datasets	CORA-ML		CITESEER		AMAZON		ACTOR	
Metrics	Accuracy	AUC	Accuracy	AUC	Accuracy	AUC	Accuracy	AUC
sum-emb	0.736	0.772	0.878	0.702	0.961	0.924	0.676	0.501
sum-ins	0.682	0.669	0.878	0.635	0.681	0.893	0.676	0.535
mean-emb	0.809	0.717	0.901	0.670	0.896	0.819	0.851	0.499
mean-ins	0.806	0.677	0.895	0.681	0.623	0.860	0.851	0.514
GlobalAttention-emb	0.834	0.818	0.787	0.860	0.644	0.500	0.917	0.499
GlobalAttention-ins	0.788	0.763	0.737	0.783	0.644	0.500	0.917	0.501
Set2Set-emb	0.859	0.895	0.845	0.782	0.642	0.502	0.945	0.488
Set2Set-ins	0.791	0.850	0.837	0.689	0.642	0.500	0.945	0.496

8 Discussions

In this section, we provide additional discussions as follows:

- For node-level tasks, if training with bag labels can achieve expected performance, it would substantially reduce the effort for node label annotations. Moreover, since the number of bag labels is typically much smaller than that of node labels, this also leads to more efficient model training.
- This study has certain experimental limitations. For example, we have not evaluated the models on a wider range of benchmark datasets or with more

embedding-based models. In addition, we did not examine how model performance varies with bag size. For MIL tasks based on the standard assumption, classification typically becomes more difficult as the bag size increases, especially in the case of synthetic data. Finally, compared to other paradigms for describing the graph pooling process (e.g., the SRC model [9]), the generalizability of embedding-based models is limited.
- Large Language Models (LLMs) can assist MIL on graphs in several key ways. First, LLMs can generate high-quality synthetic labels or bag-level descriptions to augment training data under weak supervision. Second, LLMs may facilitate the interpretation of MIL decisions by generating natural language explanations for instance-level contributions. Finally, their ability to generalize across modalities allows for flexible integration of multimodal metadata, aiding cross-domain graph representation learning.

9 Related Works

This work explores a novel task in Multiple Instance Learning (MIL), a type of weakly supervised learning problem that originated in the 1990s [4,13]. Instead of receiving a set of instances that are individually labeled, the learning model receives a set of labeled bags, each containing many instances. Due to the diverse characteristics of tasks, MIL can be classified into four categories based on the following attributes: the composition of bags, the types of data distribution, the ambiguity of instance labels, and the task to be performed, each presenting different challenges [3]. MIL typically involves two levels of tasks: bag-level and instance-level, and we tackle the latter. MIL algorithms are often only effective for one of them [3,11]. Given the prevalence of weakly supervised inexact data in real-world scenarios, MIL finds numerous applications in diverse domains (e.g., [17]). Since MIL is a long-established field that covers a diverse range of topics, we refer the readers to surveys (e.g., [3]) for more information.

On the other hand, this work is closely related to graph pooling from the methodological perspective. Graph pooling models condense a graph into a smaller-sized graph or a single vector, thus working as an essential component for graph-level tasks that require holistic graph-level representations, such as graph classification and graph generation. Generally, designs of graph pooling could be roughly divided into flat pooling (e.g., [18,26]) and hierarchical pooling, while the latter can be further categorized into node cluster pooling (e.g., [29]) and node drop pooling (e.g., [15]). Existing pooling methods have been demonstrated to be successful in capturing high-order information on a wide range of applications; however, designing effective pooling operators for node-level tasks are still key challenges [19]. Furthermore, graph pooling faces critical challenges including interpretability, robustness, efficiency, expressiveness and so on. Similarly, we refer the readers to [9,19] for a more complete and detailed introduction on graph pooling techniques. Our work addresses the lack of designs of effective pooling model for node-level tasks, and provides a comprehensive discussion of the key properties of different pooling paradigms.

10 Conclusions

In this work, we introduce the node-level MIL task for the first time and investigate the role of graph pooling in this context. We propose a general approach to transform classical embedding-based pooling into an instance-based style, which is intrinsically more suitable for node-level tasks. Furthermore, we analyze key theoretical properties of both frameworks, including permutation invariance, expressiveness, and interpretability. Experimental evaluations on benchmark datasets, simulating various application scenarios, demonstrate the effectiveness of instance-based models. This work pioneers the extension of graph pooling beyond graph-level tasks to node-level tasks, providing both theoretical and empirical insights. As future work, we will explore the design of pooling mechanisms with stronger generalization capabilities and higher efficiency.

Acknowledgments. This paper is based on results obtained from the project, "Research and Development Project of the Enhanced infrastructures for Post-5G Information and Communication Systems" (JPNP20017), commissioned by the New Energy and Industrial Technology Development Organization (NEDO), and was supported by JSPS KAKENHI Grant Numbers JP25K21275, JP25K03231, JP23H03451.

References

1. Bianchi, F.M., Lachi, V.: The expressive power of pooling in graph neural networks. Adv. Neural. Inf. Process. Syst. **36**, 71603–71618 (2023)
2. Bojchevski, A., Günnemann, S.: Deep Gaussian embedding of graphs: unsupervised inductive learning via ranking. arXiv preprint arXiv:1707.03815 (2017)
3. Carbonneau, M.A., Cheplygina, V., Granger, E., Gagnon, G.: Multiple instance learning: a survey of problem characteristics and applications. Pattern Recogn. **77**, 329–353 (2018)
4. Dietterich, T.G., Lathrop, R.H., Lozano-Pérez, T.: Solving the multiple instance problem with axis-parallel rectangles. Artif. Intell. **89**(1–2), 31–71 (1997)
5. Duan, Y., et al.: Dual cost-sensitive graph convolutional network. In: 2022 International Joint Conference on Neural Networks (IJCNN), pp. 1–8. IEEE (2022)
6. Duan, Y., Liu, X., Jatowt, A., Yu, H.T., Lynden, S.J., Matono, A.: Inexact graph representation learning. In: IJCNN (2024)
7. Fey, M., Lenssen, J.E.: Fast graph representation learning with PyTorch geometric. arXiv preprint arXiv:1903.02428 (2019)
8. Foulds, J., Frank, E.: A review of multi-instance learning assumptions. Knowl. Eng. Rev. **25**(1), 1–25 (2010)
9. Grattarola, D., Zambon, D., Bianchi, F.M., Alippi, C.: Understanding pooling in graph neural networks. IEEE Trans. Neural Netw. Learn. Syst. **35**(2), 2708–2718 (2022)
10. Hamilton, W., Ying, Z., Leskovec, J.: Inductive representation learning on large graphs. Adv. Neural Inf. Process. Syst. **30** (2017)
11. Ilse, M., Tomczak, J., Welling, M.: Attention-based deep multiple instance learning. In: International Conference on Machine Learning, pp. 2127–2136. PMLR (2018)

12. Javed, S.A., Juyal, D., Padigela, H., Taylor-Weiner, A., Yu, L., Prakash, A.: Additive MIL: intrinsically interpretable multiple instance learning for pathology. Adv. Neural. Inf. Process. Syst. **35**, 20689–20702 (2022)
13. Keeler, J., Rumelhart, D., Leow, W.: Integrated segmentation and recognition of hand-printed numerals. Adv. Neural Inf. Process. Syst. **3** (1990)
14. Kingma, D.P., Ba, J.: Adam: a method for stochastic optimization. arXiv preprint arXiv:1412.6980 (2014)
15. Lee, J., Lee, I., Kang, J.: Self-attention graph pooling. In: International Conference on Machine Learning, pp. 3734–3743. PMLR (2019)
16. Leman, A., Weisfeiler, B.: A reduction of a graph to a canonical form and an algebra arising during this reduction. Nauchno-Technicheskaya Informatsiya **2**(9), 12–16 (1968)
17. Li, W., Duan, L., Xu, D., Tsang, I.W.H.: Text-based image retrieval using progressive multi-instance learning. In: 2011 International Conference on Computer Vision, pp. 2049–2055. IEEE (2011)
18. Li, Y., Tarlow, D., Brockschmidt, M., Zemel, R.: Gated graph sequence neural networks. arXiv preprint arXiv:1511.05493 (2015)
19. Liu, C., et al.: Graph pooling for graph neural networks: progress, challenges, and opportunities. arXiv preprint arXiv:2204.07321 (2022)
20. Lundberg, S.: A unified approach to interpreting model predictions. arXiv preprint arXiv:1705.07874 (2017)
21. Ma, Y.T.: Deep Learning on Graphs. Cambridge University Press (2021)
22. Pei, H., Wei, B., Chang, K.C.C., Lei, Y., Yang, B.: Geom-GCN: geometric graph convolutional networks. arXiv preprint arXiv:2002.05287 (2020)
23. Qi, C.R., Su, H., Mo, K., Guibas, L.J.: PointNet: deep learning on point sets for 3D classification and segmentation. In: Proceedings of the IEEE Conference on Computer Vision and Pattern Recognition, pp. 652–660 (2017)
24. Shchur, O., Mumme, M., Bojchevski, A., Günnemann, S.: Pitfalls of graph neural network evaluation. arXiv preprint arXiv:1811.05868 (2018)
25. Sirinukunwattana, K., Raza, S.E.A., Tsang, Y.W., Snead, D.R., Cree, I.A., Rajpoot, N.M.: Locality sensitive deep learning for detection and classification of nuclei in routine colon cancer histology images. IEEE Trans. Med. Imag. **35**(5), 1196–1206 (2016)
26. Vinyals, O., Bengio, S., Kudlur, M.: Order matters: sequence to sequence for sets. arXiv preprint arXiv:1511.06391 (2015)
27. Wang, X., Yan, Y., Tang, P., Bai, X., Liu, W.: Revisiting multiple instance neural networks. Pattern Recogn. **74**, 15–24 (2018)
28. Yang, Z., Cohen, W., Salakhudinov, R.: Revisiting semi-supervised learning with graph embeddings. In: International Conference on Machine Learning, pp. 40–48. PMLR (2016)
29. Ying, Z., You, J., Morris, C., Ren, X., Hamilton, W., Leskovec, J.: Hierarchical graph representation learning with differentiable pooling. NeurIPS **31** (2018)
30. Zaheer, M., Kottur, S., Ravanbakhsh, S., Poczos, B., Salakhutdinov, R.R., Smola, A.J.: Deep sets. Adv. Neural Inf. Process. Syst. **30** (2017)
31. Zhang, B., et al.: The expressive power of graph neural networks: a survey. IEEE Trans. Knowl. Data Eng. (2024)

Community-Aware Graph Transformer: Preserving Community Semantics for Effective Global Aggregation

Yutai Duan, Jie Liu(✉), Jianhua Wu, and Jialin Liu

College of Artificial Intelligence, Nankai University, 300350 Tianjin, China
{ytduan,wujianhua,2120220573}@mail.nankai.edu.cn, jliu@nankai.edu.cn

Abstract. Graph Transformers (GTs) address the locality limitation of traditional GNNs, which aggregate only local neighbor information, by leveraging global attention. However, they suffer from two significant issues: neglecting community structures and information over-squeezing. In this paper, we first identify these two problems and propose a Community-Aware Graph Transformer (CoGT) to solve them. CoGT introduces a novel node-community-global hierarchical aggregation framework. This design preserves community-level semantics while reducing the volume of aggregated information, alleviating the over-squeezing problem. CoGT first employs a two-stage positional encoding to identify latent communities and enhance semantic consistency. Then, a hierarchical and parallel transformer computation method based on community representations facilitates global information interaction. Furthermore, we enable community-wise parallel attention computation, improving computational efficiency. Experimental results demonstrate that CoGT outperforms existing methods across multiple real-world datasets.

Keywords: Graph transformer · Graph representation learning

1 Introduction

The core objective of Graph Representation Learning (GRL) [27] is to capture both topological structure and semantic information by modeling node interactions. Traditional Graph Neural Networks (GNNs) [24], limited by local neighborhood aggregation, struggle to uncover long-range dependencies [3,23]. Graph Transformers (GTs) [22,26], using global attention mechanisms [16], enable interactions across all nodes, significantly enhancing node representations. This global aggregation can overcome local neighborhood limitations and identify distant nodes with potential benefits [25]. However, many studies have focused on improving the efficiency of GTs while ignoring the problems of global aggregation in GRL: the loss of community structure semantics and information over-squeezing.

Loss of Community Structure Semantics (Sect. 2.1): Graph data often exhibit a hierarchical community structure [14], an inherent property of graph data. Therefore, to describe a graph from a global rather than a local perspective, community-based semantics best capture its nature [7]. GTs introduce global perspectives into node representations via global information exchange. However, existing GTs use homogeneous global attention that overlooks hierarchical community semantics, undermining the graph's global structure. This leads to semantic inconsistencies across hierarchical levels, where core and peripheral nodes are treated uniformly, failing to capture their distinct roles. Moreover, this indiscriminate aggregation of large volumes of node features introduces an additional challenge: information over-squeezing, which diminishes the quality of node representations by blending informative signals with excessive noise.

Information Over-Squeezing (Sect. 2.2): Global attention aggregates information from all nodes simultaneously. This may lead to over-squeezing, where high-weight noise mixes with low-weight signals, resulting in the loss of important information. This disrupts the hierarchical structure of the central node, flattening the influence of all nodes on it. This is similar to over-squashing in GNN [18], which is essentially the problem of weakening or losing important signals caused by receiving too much information. From a structural entropy perspective [13], this is equivalent to using a global structure to represent each node, which increases the structural entropy of node representations. As a result, node features learned in a high-entropy space are suboptimal. While global aggregation uncovers latent information, a balance must be struck between global aggregation and information over-squeezing.

To this end, we propose a Community-Aware Graph Transformer (CoGT), which features two key designs: Learnable Two-stage Positional Encoding (TiCoding) and Hierarchical and Parallel Transformer Computation (HPTC). CoGT achieves hierarchical, semantics-aware global aggregation by identifying latent communities in graphs. Specifically, TiCoding first injects global positional information into nodes via a local structure encoder and leverages the result to detect potential communities. Each identified community is assigned a unique encoding to model community semantics explicitly. HPTC extracts community representations and computes the hybrid attention that integrates information from central nodes, intra-community nodes, and inter-community representations to update node embeddings. We also crafted a parallelized attention computation process to improve efficiency. This design not only explicitly models community semantics but also replaces large-scale node features with community representations for aggregating, alleviating the over-squeezing issue.

The contributions of this paper can be summarized as follows:

- We propose CoGT that mitigates community semantics loss and information over-squeezing via latent community discovery and hierarchical aggregation with parallel and efficient attention computation.
- We design TiCoding for effective multi-semantic positional encoding and introduce HPTC for efficient hierarchical aggregation, enabling community-aware modeling while alleviating over-squeezing.

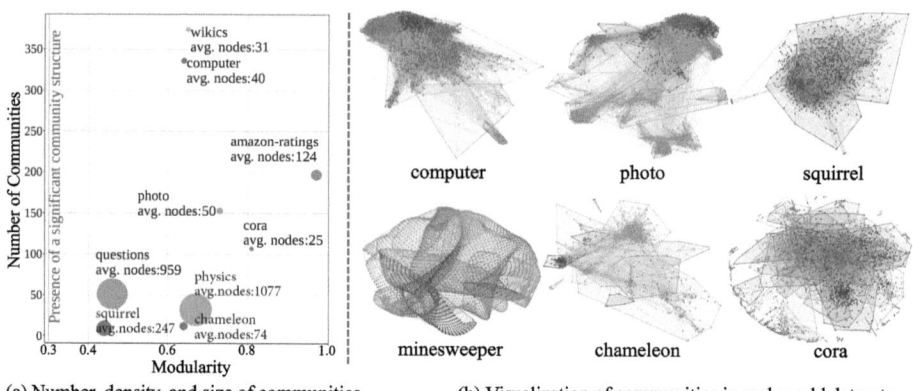

Fig. 1. The community structure is prominently present in graphs. (a) Statistics of community-related metrics. Modularity reflects the density of communities within a graph to some extent, while the size of each point represents the average community size. (b) Visualization for different communities in datasets by coloring the nodes according to their respective communities.

- We conduct an empirical study revealing community semantics loss and oversqueezing as limitations in existing GTs.
- Extensive experiments show that CoGT achieves superior performance and by explicitly modeling community-level semantics.

2 Empirical Investigation

2.1 Community Structures Prevalent in Graphs

To highlight the importance of explicitly modeling community-level semantics, we analyzed key community-related metrics from common graph datasets, including the number of communities N_C, the average number of nodes in communities N_{avg}, and modularity [14] $Q = \frac{1}{2e} \sum_{i,j} \left(A_{ij} - \frac{d_i d_j}{2e} \right) \delta(c_i, c_j)$, where e is the edge numbers, A_{ij} is the adjacency matrix, d_i is the degree of node v_i, and $\delta(c_i, c_j)$ equals 1 if v_i and v_j are in the same community and 0 otherwise. The results are shown in Fig. 1(a). We use the Louvain algorithm [14] for community detection on common graph datasets and count the number of communities. We set the community granularity to 1.2, ensuring that the algorithm identifies larger communities, rather than smaller, loosely connected ones. Based on the community partitioning results, we calculated modularity Q to quantify the extent of the community structure. We also visualized the communities in datasets by coloring the nodes according to their respective communities in Fig. 1(b).

The results in Fig. 1(a) show that: (1) Common graph datasets typically exhibit dense community structures, with each graph containing tens to hundreds of communities. (2) Generally, when the modularity $Q > 0.3$, the community structure can be considered significant. All datasets exceed this threshold,

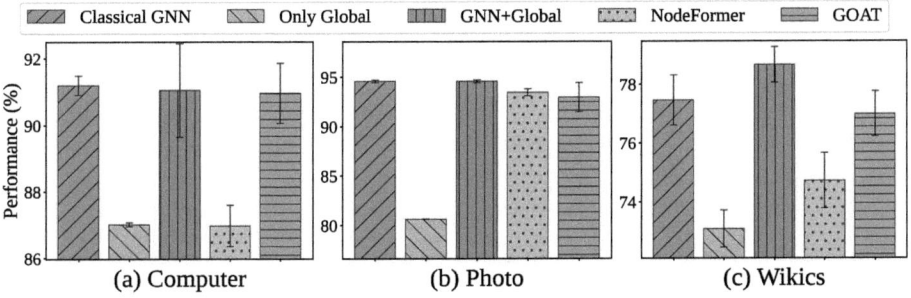

Fig. 2. A set of comparative experiments to demonstrate the issue of information over-squeezing in GTs. Global node aggregation alone performs significantly worse than GNNs, emphasizing important neighbors, indicating that global aggregation suffers from the information over-squeezing problem.

with most having Q values greater than 0.6, indicating that these graphs feature significant community structures. (3) The calculation shows that $N_C \times N_{avg} \geq$ total number of nodes N, with some datasets approaching $2N$. This indicates that the community structure covers nearly all nodes in the graph, with some nodes playing roles in multiple communities, which supports the discovery of latent information through global aggregation. (4) From the visualizations, we can easily observe significant community structures, with dense connections generally present within the communities.

In summary, we conclude that community-level semantics are a crucial and often overlooked level of semantic granularity. However, existing methods often overlook modeling the community structure, resulting in the loss of community-level semantics during the global aggregation process.

2.2 Information Over-Squeezing in GTs

We conducted empirical studies to validate that the use of simple global aggregation leads to the issue of information over-squeezing. We selected the best-performing model from GCN, GAT, and GraphSAGE as the baseline performance of classical GNNs. We compared it with models using only transformer-based global aggregation, classical GNNs with global aggregation, and two prominent GTs. The results are shown in Fig. 2.

Our findings are as follows: (1) Information Over-Squeezing Issue: Using only GNNs significantly outperforms global aggregation alone. Compared to GNNs, purely global aggregation injects excessive information into each node, making their structural representations overly similar. This leads to a low signal-to-noise ratio, making node differentiation challenging. (2) In contrast, GNNs emphasize crucial information through local aggregation while inherently preserving some community structures, resulting in more effective representations. (3) When naively combining GNNs with global aggregation, performance degradation is observed in two out of three datasets, indicating that global aggregation exacerbates the over-squeezing issue. This phenomenon is also evident in the performance of state-of-the-art GT models, such as NodeFormer and GOAT in the figure, suggesting that directly integrating global aggregation suffers from severe information compression. (4) However, the performance improvement on the enhanced WikiCS dataset suggests that global aggregation can be beneficial by identifying latent yet useful node relationships.

Based on these observations, we need to find a balance between global aggregation and information over-squeezing, ensuring that the benefits of global aggregation are leveraged while avoiding issues like over-squeezing.

3 Related Work

3.1 Graph Representation Learning

The goal of GRL is to integrate node or graph-level features with supervision signals through an end-to-end training process [27], generating discriminative low-dimensional representations. Traditional approaches primarily include matrix factorization, e.g., Laplacian Eigenmaps [1], and random walk-based shallow models, e.g., DeepWalk [15], Node2Vec [8]. While these methods effectively capture the statistical properties of graph structures, they suffer from a strong dependence on feature engineering and lack adaptive parameters, making it difficult to jointly optimize representations for downstream tasks.

The emergence of GNNs [24] marked a significant shift toward deep learning-based approaches in GRL. Message-passing GNNs [9], e.g., GCN [11] and GAT [19], aggregate neighborhood features iteratively to capture local structural patterns. Specifically, GCNs [3] employ spectral convolution operations to establish a paradigm for information propagation, whereas GATs [20] introduce attention mechanisms to enhance the interpretability of the aggregation process. However, classical GNNs are fundamentally constrained by their local aggregation assumption, limiting their ability to model long-range and latent dependencies [6]. This limitation is particularly pronounced in domains with complex topological structures, such as social networks and molecular graphs. To overcome the bottleneck of local neighborhood aggregation, Transformer architectures have been introduced into GRL, leading to the development of GTs [16,22]. GTs leverage global attention mechanisms to compute attention between any pair of nodes [2,26], effectively capturing long-range and latent dependencies in graph structures.

3.2 Transformer Models

Transformer models [5] were proposed for natural language processing, where its key innovation lies in eliminating the sequential dependencies inherent in traditional recurrent neural networks. Instead, it leveraged self-attention mechanisms to model global interactions between sequence elements. The success of ViT [10] in computer vision, surpassing the performance of Convolutional Neural Networks, highlighted the generalizability of attention mechanisms across different modalities. This realization has driven the extension of Transformers to GRL.

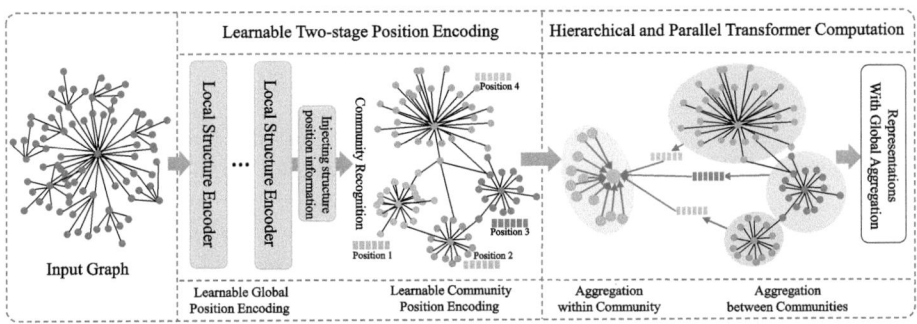

Fig. 3. The CoGT framework.

GTs treat all nodes in the graph as interactive attention units [21], allowing direct computation of attention weights between any pair of nodes [4]. Current research efforts focus on enhancing the scalability of Transformer models for large-scale graphs [12,17,22]. However, existing approaches often overlook two critical challenges associated with global attention aggregation in GRL: (1) excessive reliance on node-level interactions may weaken the semantic representation at the community level; (2) global attention can lead to an "Information Over-Squeezing" effect, increasing noise interference and diminishing the effectiveness of crucial information.

4 Methodology

4.1 Overview

The goal of CoGT is to explicitly model community-level semantics during the global aggregation step through hierarchical aggregation. By using community-level features instead of a large number of node features in attention-based aggregation, CoGT effectively mitigates the issue of information over-squeezing.

The CoGT framework is shown in Fig. 3. To model a community-level semantic in the global aggregation process, we first apply a two-stage positional encoding to all nodes in the graph. In the first stage, a local structure encoder is used to encode the position of each node. Based on this encoding, nodes are then communityed, and each community is assigned a community-level positional encoding to distinguish different communities. Next, the communityed feature matrix is passed to the HPTC layer for attention-based computation. This layer not only enables global aggregation but also mitigates excessive information squeezing. Furthermore, its design inherently supports parallel computation at the community level, significantly enhancing computational efficiency.

4.2 Two-Stage Positional Encoding

For a graph $\mathcal{G}(E, X)$ with edge set E and node features X, where the total number of nodes is N, we first apply a local structure encoder to inject positional information into each node's representation:

$$\mathbf{X} = \text{LocalStructureEncoder}(\mathcal{G}(E, X)), \quad (1)$$

where $\mathbf{X} \in \mathbb{R}^{N \times F}$ denotes the encoded feature matrix, and F is the hidden dimension. We adopt graph convolutional networks as the local structure encoder.

To ensure a differentiable community assignment process and prevent excessive community sizes that may cause memory overflow and semantic imbalance, we design a classification-based assignment strategy with a constraint on the "average community size $N_m = \lceil \frac{N}{M} \rceil$", where M is the number of communities. We formulate node assignment as a classification problem and apply the softmax function to normalize the probability $Z'_{i,j}$ of assigning node i to community j:

$$\mathbf{Z} = \mathbf{X}\mathbf{W}_C, \quad Z'_{i,j} = \frac{\exp(\mathbf{Z}_{i,j})}{\sum_{k=1}^{M} \exp(\mathbf{Z}_{i,k})}, \quad (2)$$

where $\mathbf{W}_C \in \mathbb{R}^{F \times M}$ is a learnable matrix, and $\mathbf{Z}$ is the assignment score matrix. We enforce a fixed number of nodes, N_m, per community by sorting nodes based on assignment probabilities and selecting the top N_m nodes. Then, we assign a learnable community position embedding $\mathbf{E}_m \in \mathbb{R}^F$ to each community C_m to distinguish its semantics and enhance intra-community node consistency:

$$\mathbf{X}'_i = \mathbf{X}_i + \mathbf{E}_m (i \in C_m), \quad (3)$$

Based on node-community affiliations, we obtain the reorganized feature matrix $\mathbf{X}' \in \mathbb{R}^{M \times N_m \times F}$, which incorporates twofold positional semantics. Here, $\mathbf{X}'[m, :, :]$ represents the features of all nodes in C_m.

4.3 Hierarchical and Parallel Transformer Computation

We employ hierarchical aggregation to achieve global feature interaction while mitigating the information over-squeezing problem. First, we compute the query, key, and value matrices for each community C_m. We directly feed $\mathbf{X}'$ into linear layers to compute the $\mathbf{Q}$, $\mathbf{K}$, and $\mathbf{V}$ in parallel, which reduces memory peak usage because the tensor size of each community is much smaller than the original $\mathbf{X}$:

$$\mathbf{Q}_m = \mathbf{W}_Q \mathbf{X}'_m, \quad \mathbf{K}_m = \mathbf{W}_K \mathbf{X}'_m, \quad \mathbf{V}_m = \mathbf{W}_V \mathbf{X}'_m, \quad (4)$$

where $\mathbf{W}_{(\cdot)}$ are learnable weights, F is the hidden dimension, $\mathbf{X}'_m$ is $\mathbf{X}'[m, :, :]$.

To mitigate the information over-squeezing issue caused by the $O(N^2)$ level of feature interactions among all nodes globally, we introduce community-level features to replace node-level interactions outside the community. Nodes within the same community interact via node features, while nodes from different communities engage through a set of community-level features. Since community features have higher semantic consistency and are much fewer in number compared to node features, they effectively prevent information over-squeezing and high noise within node features, thereby improving the efficiency of feature interactions.

We compute the community-level query ($\mathbf{C}^Q$), key ($\mathbf{C}^K$), and value ($\mathbf{C}^V$) matrices, which are obtained by applying an aggregation function to the features of each community, followed by concatenation:

$$\mathbf{c}_m^Q = \text{Agg}(\mathbf{Q}_m), \quad \mathbf{c}_m^K = \text{Agg}(\mathbf{K}_m), \quad \mathbf{c}_m^V = \text{Agg}(\mathbf{V}_m), \tag{5}$$

$$\mathbf{C}^Q = \|_{m=1}^{M}(\mathbf{c}_m^Q), \quad \mathbf{C}^K = \|_{m=1}^{M}(\mathbf{c}_m^K), \quad \mathbf{C}^V = \|_{m=1}^{M}(\mathbf{c}_m^V), \tag{6}$$

where $\mathbf{c}_m^Q, \mathbf{c}_m^K, \mathbf{c}_m^V$ is the query, key, and value for community m. $\text{Agg}(\cdot)$ denotes to the aggregation operation, and $\|_{m=1}^{M}$ denotes concatenation. To improve computational efficiency, we employ simple aggregation methods such as mean pooling.

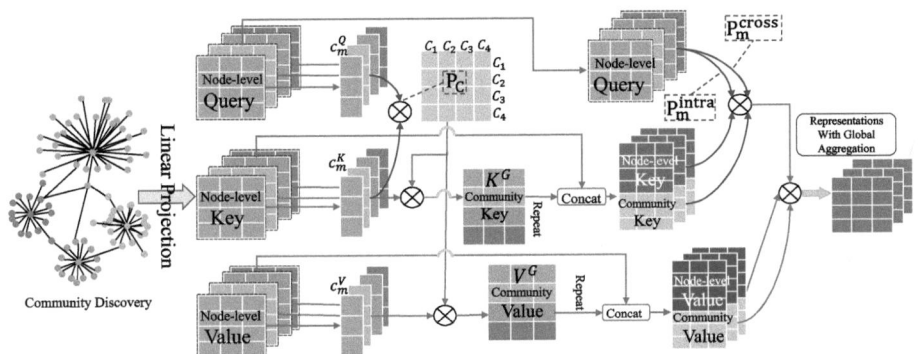

Fig. 4. HPTC leverages community features to enable parallel attention computation at the community level. This design not only incorporates community semantics but also enhances computational efficiency.

Next, we refine the community-level key and value representations using community-level attention, allowing the community features to be optimized and enriched in semantic information. The community-level attention matrix $\mathbf{P}_C \in \mathbb{R}^{M \times M}$ is computed as:

$$\mathbf{P}_C = \sigma\left(\frac{\mathbf{C}^Q \mathbf{C}^{K\top}}{\sqrt{F}}\right), \quad \mathbf{K}^G = \mathbf{P}_C \mathbf{C}^K, \quad \mathbf{V}^G = \mathbf{P}_C \mathbf{C}^V. \tag{7}$$

Here, σ denotes the activation function, and we use tanh as the activation function in this work. The use of `tanh` for activation is to maintain computational efficiency at the $O(N)$ level, rather than the common N-level of `softmax`. Furthermore, positive or negative attentional values can also be considered to aggregate or depress the features of corresponding communities.

To establish global semantic dependencies for each node, we compute intra-community and cross-community attention as follows:

$$\mathbf{P}_m^{\text{intra}} = \sigma\left(\frac{\mathbf{Q}_m \mathbf{K}_m^\top}{\sqrt{F}}\right), \quad \mathbf{P}_m^{\text{cross}} = \sigma\left(\frac{\mathbf{Q}_m \mathbf{K}^{G\top}}{\sqrt{F}}\right), \tag{8}$$

where $\mathbf{P}_m^{\text{intra}} \in \mathbb{R}^{N_m \times N_m}$ captures interactions between nodes within the same community, and $\mathbf{P}_m^{\text{cross}} \in \mathbb{R}^{N_m \times M}$ models interactions between nodes in community m and all communities globally. Notably, both $\mathbf{P}_m^{\text{intra}}$ and $\mathbf{P}_m^{\text{cross}}$ can be efficiently computed in a single step by concatenating $\mathbf{K}_m$ and $\mathbf{K}^G$. Moreover, since we reshape the feature matrix into 3 dimensions, $\mathbf{P}_m^{\text{intra}}$ and $\mathbf{P}_m^{\text{cross}}$ computation for M communities can be performed in parallel simultaneously.

Finally, we apply the attention scores to both node-level and community-level value matrices to generate the final node representations for C_m:

$$\mathbf{H}_m = [\mathbf{P}_m^{\text{cross}} \| \mathbf{P}_m^{\text{cross}}] \cdot [\mathbf{V}_m \| \mathbf{V}^G], \tag{9}$$

where $[\cdot \| \cdot]$ denotes a concatenation operation along columns, and each row of $\mathbf{H}_m \in \mathbb{R}^{N_m \times F}$ corresponds to the representation of a node in community m. These representations incorporate information from other nodes within the same community as well as global information from all M communities. Finally, we restore the original order of the feature matrix through the node indexes generated by the community assignment. It is worth noting that the computation of all M community representation matrices is performed in parallel, significantly reducing both computational time and peak memory usage.

5 Theoretical Justification

5.1 Global Feature Interaction via Cross-Community Attention

Although the model avoids explicit attention computation for all node pairs through community partitioning, the hierarchical aggregation mechanism still enables information interaction between any two nodes in the input graph. For any two nodes $v_i \in C_m$ and $v_j \in C_n$:

If v_i and v_j are in the same community (i.e., $m = n$), their interaction is directly modeled by node-level attention. The weight of v_i on v_j is defined as:

$$\mathbf{P}_m^{\text{intra}}(i,j) = \sigma\left(\frac{\mathbf{Q}_m[i,:]\mathbf{K}_m[j,:]^\top}{\sqrt{F}}\right), \tag{10}$$

where $\mathbf{P}_m^{\text{intra}}(i,j)$ directly encode the semantic similarity between v_i and v_j. The local aggregation result for node v_i is $\mathbf{h}_i^{\text{local}} = \sum_{j \in C_m} \mathbf{P}_m^{\text{intra}}(i,j)\mathbf{V}_m[j,:]$, explicitly capturing fine-grained associations within the community.

If the nodes belong to different communities (i.e., $m \neq n$), their interaction is indirectly achieved through community-level features. The node features of community C_m are aggregated into a community feature $\mathbf{c}_m^V$, which is further weighted by the inter-community attention matrix $\mathbf{P}_C \in \mathbb{R}^{M \times M}$ to form the updated global feature $\mathbf{V}^G$. The elements of $\mathbf{P}_C$ are computed as:

$$\mathbf{P}_C(m,n) = \sigma\left(\frac{\mathbf{c}_m^Q \mathbf{c}_n^{K\top}}{\sqrt{F}}\right), \tag{11}$$

where $\mathbf{P}_C(m,n)$ represents the attention weight of community C_m on C_k. Each row $\mathbf{v}_n^G \in \mathbb{R}^F$ of $\mathbf{V}^G$ denotes the higher-order representation of community C_n in the global semantic space. The interaction between cross-community nodes v_i and v_j is achieved through the cross-community attention matrix $\mathbf{P}_m^{\text{cross}} \in \mathbb{R}^{N_m \times M}$, whose elements are defined as:

$$\mathbf{P}_m^{\text{cross}}(i,n) = \sigma\left(\frac{\mathbf{Q}_m[i,:]\mathbf{K}^G[n,:]^\top}{\sqrt{F}}\right), \tag{12}$$

where $\mathbf{P}_m^{\text{cross}}(i,k)$ represents the weight of $v_i \in C_m$ on community C_k. The global aggregation result for v_i is $\mathbf{h}_i^{\text{global}} \propto \sum_{k=1}^M \mathbf{P}_m^{\text{cross}}(i,k)\mathbf{V}^G[k,:]$. Notably, the information of node $v_j \in C_n$ is transmitted to v_i through its community's $\mathbf{V}^G[k,:]$, i.e., $\mathbf{h}_i^{\text{global}} \propto \mathbf{P}_m^{\text{cross}}(i,n)\mathbf{V}^G[n,:]$. Since $\mathbf{V}^G[n,:]$ is the updated $\mathbf{c}_n^V$, this process indirectly establishes cross-community dependencies.

From the perspective of gradient propagation, regardless of whether nodes belong to the same community, their gradients can be backpropagated through local or global paths. For $v_j \in C_n$, its gradient contribution to $v_i \in C_m$ is:

$$\frac{\partial \mathcal{L}}{\partial \mathbf{X}_j} = \begin{cases} \frac{\partial \mathcal{L}}{\partial \mathbf{h}_i^{\text{local}}} \cdot \frac{\partial \mathbf{P}_m^{\text{intra}}(i,j)}{\partial \mathbf{X}_j} & m = n \\ \frac{\partial \mathcal{L}}{\partial \mathbf{h}_i^{\text{global}}} \cdot \frac{\partial \mathbf{P}_m^{\text{cross}}(i,n)}{\partial \mathbf{K}^G[n,:]} \cdot \frac{\partial \mathbf{K}^G[n,:]}{\partial \mathbf{c}_n^K} \cdot \frac{\partial \mathbf{c}_n^K}{\partial \mathbf{X}_j} & m \neq n \end{cases}. \tag{13}$$

This indicates that the hierarchical aggregation mechanism still enables information interaction between any two nodes in the input graph.

5.2 Reducing Structural Entropy via Community Segmentation

This study introduces structural entropy to quantify the structural information encoded in node representations. Traditional graph transformers employ global attention to enable full-node interactions, effectively leveraging graph structures but leading to high structural entropy. The fully connected interaction mechanism makes nodes highly susceptible to noise, particularly in large-scale graphs, where irrelevant interactions dilute critical semantic information.

To address this issue, we propose a hierarchical propagation strategy based on community partitioning. First, fine-grained intra-community attention is performed to capture local dependencies while avoiding inter-community noise. Then, global information exchange is achieved through the aggregation of community representations, which filters noise while preserving essential semantics. This strategy optimizes the information propagation path from $N-1$ to $N_m - 1 + N$, ensuring $N_m - 1 + M \ll N - 1$, significantly reducing structural entropy. In conventional methods, structural entropy is determined by interactions between all node pairs, formulated as:

$$\mathcal{H}_{\text{global}} \propto - \sum_{\text{all nodes } N} p \log p, \tag{14}$$

where p represents the dependency strength between any two nodes, resulting in a high entropy value. In contrast, our method decomposes entropy into

Table 1. Statistics of the datasets used in this paper.

Dataset	Type	# Nodes	# Edges	# Features	Classes	Metric
Amazon-Computer	Homophily	13,752	245,861	767	10	Accuracy
Amazon-Photo	Homophily	7,650	119,081	745	8	Accuracy
Coauthor-CS	Homophily	18,333	81,894	6,805	15	Accuracy
Cora	Homophily	2,708	5,278	1,433	7	Accuracy
WikiCS	Homophily	11,701	216,123	300	10	Accuracy
ogbn-proteins (large)	Homophily	132,534	39,561,252	8	2	ROC-AUC
Squirrel	Heterophily	2,223	46,998	2,089	5	Accuracy
Chameleon	Heterophily	2,277	31,421	2,325	5	Accuracy
Amazon-Ratings	Heterophily	24,492	183,831	300	5	ROC-AUC
Minesweeper	Heterophily	10,000	39,402	6	2	ROC-AUC
Questions	Heterophily	48,921	118,540	301	2	ROC-AUC
pokec (large)	Heterophily	1,632,803	30,622,564	65	2	Accuracy

local interaction entropy (within communities) and global propagation entropy (between condensed community representations):

$$\mathcal{H}_{\text{new}} \propto - \sum_{\text{intra-community } N_m} p \log p - \sum_{\text{inter-community } M} q \log q, \quad (15)$$

where p represents the dependency strength between two nodes in one community, analogous to $\mathbf{P}^{\text{intra}}$, and q represents the dependency strength between community features, analogous to $\mathbf{P}^{\text{cross}}$. Consequently, CoGT updates node representations using only intra-community node information and the coarse-grained, sparse linkage structure between communities. This approach results in significantly lower structural entropy compared to methods that perform interactions at the global node level, mitigating the issue of information over-squeezing.

6 Experiments

6.1 Experimental Setup

For the datasets, we selected several commonly used homophilic and heterophilic graphs, including large graphs. The specific data set statistics are shown in Table 1. The training, validation, and test splits for each dataset follow the official partitioning method provided for that dataset. Except for the ogbn-proteins, Amazon-Ratings, Questions, and Minesweeper datasets, which are evaluated using the ROC-AUC metric, all other datasets are evaluated using accuracy. This setting follows the evaluation protocol used in previous works. ROC-AUC (Area Under the Receiver Operating Characteristic Curve) measures a model's ability to distinguish between positive and negative classes and is particularly

Table 2. Node classification results on homophilic datasets. The top first, blue second, and darkgreen third results are highlighted.

Model	Computer	Photo	CS	Cora	WikiCS	ogbn-proteins
GCN	89.65 ± 0.52	92.70 ± 0.20	92.92 ± 0.12	81.60 ± 0.40	77.47 ± 0.85	72.51 ± 0.35
GraphSAGE	91.20 ± 0.29	94.59 ± 0.14	93.91 ± 0.13	82.68 ± 0.47	74.77 ± 0.95	77.68 ± 0.20
GAT	90.78 ± 0.13	93.87 ± 0.11	93.61 ± 0.14	83.00 ± 0.70	76.91 ± 0.82	72.02 ± 0.44
GraphGPS	91.19 ± 0.54	95.06 ± 0.13	93.93 ± 0.12	82.84 ± 1.03	78.66 ± 0.49	76.83 ± 0.26
NAGphormer	91.22 ± 0.14	**95.49 ± 0.11**	**95.75 ± 0.09**	82.12 ± 1.18	77.16 ± 0.72	73.61 ± 0.33
Exphormer	**91.47 ± 0.17**	95.35 ± 0.22	94.93 ± 0.01	82.77 ± 1.38	78.54 ± 0.49	74.58 ± 0.26
NodeFormer	86.98 ± 0.62	93.46 ± 0.35	**95.64 ± 0.22**	82.20 ± 0.90	74.73 ± 0.94	**77.45 ± 1.15**
GOAT	90.96 ± 0.90	92.96 ± 1.48	94.21 ± 0.38	**83.18 ± 1.27**	77.00 ± 0.77	74.18 ± 0.37
Polynormer	**93.68 ± 0.21**	**96.46 ± 0.26**	95.53 ± 0.16	**83.25 ± 0.93**	**80.10 ± 0.67**	**78.97 ± 0.47**
CoGT	94.01 ± 0.28	96.56 ± 0.31	95.93 ± 0.20	83.98 ± 0.76	81.23 ± 0.24	81.33 ± 0.37

Table 3. Node classification results on heterophilic datasets. The top first, blue second, and darkgreen third results are highlighted.

Model	amazon-ratings	minesweeper	squirrel	chameleon	questions	pokec
GCN	48.70 ± 0.63	89.75 ± 0.52	38.67 ± 1.84	41.31 ± 3.05	76.09 ± 1.27	75.45 ± 0.17
GraphSAGE	53.63 ± 0.39	93.51 ± 0.57	36.09 ± 1.99	37.77 ± 4.14	76.44 ± 0.62	75.63 ± 0.38
GAT	52.70 ± 0.62	**93.91 ± 0.35**	35.62 ± 2.06	39.21 ± 3.08	**76.79 ± 0.71**	72.23 ± 0.18
GraphGPS	53.10 ± 0.42	90.63 ± 0.67	39.67 ± 2.84	40.79 ± 4.03	71.73 ± 1.47	OOM
NAGphormer	51.26 ± 0.72	84.19 ± 0.66	39.99 ± 3.90	**44.39 ± 3.93**	68.17 ± 1.53	**76.59 ± 0.25**
Exphormer	**53.51 ± 0.46**	90.74 ± 0.53	**40.41 ± 2.42**	**42.06 ± 2.44**	73.94 ± 1.06	OOM
NodeFormer	43.86 ± 0.35	86.71 ± 0.88	38.52 ± 1.57	34.73 ± 4.14	74.27 ± 1.46	71.00 ± 1.30
Polynormer	**54.81 ± 0.49**	**97.46 ± 0.36**	**41.97 ± 2.14**	41.97 ± 3.14	78.92 ± 0.89	**86.10 ± 0.05**
CoGT	55.31 ± 0.54	97.52 ± 0.37	45.10 ± 1.28	45.38 ± 3.39	77.98 ± 1.03	86.14 ± 0.05

useful in imbalanced classification scenarios. In the preprocessing stage, we first convert the graph into an undirected graph and then add self-loops.

We compare CoGT with both classic GNNs and recent GTs. The GNN baselines include GCN [11], GraphSAGE [9], and GAT [19], which rely on local message passing. The GTs include GraphGPS [16], NAGphormer [2], Exphormer [17], NodeFormer [21], GOAT [12], and Polynormer [4].

We ran each experiment ten times with different random seeds and reported the average results. Regarding hyperparameter settings, the type for the local structure encoder is selected from {GCN, GAT, GraphSAGE}, with the number of layers ranging from [2, 12]. The learning rate is chosen from {0.01, 0.005, 0.001, 0.0005}, and weight decay is selected from {0, 5e-4, 5e-5}. For the number of communities, we select values from [0, 70] for medium-sized graphs. For large graphs, to ensure a fair comparison, we use a batch size of 10,000 for ogbn-proteins and a batch size of 550,000 for pokec, setting the number of communities to 15 and 425, respectively. Finally, the number of layers for CoGT is chosen from {1, 2}.

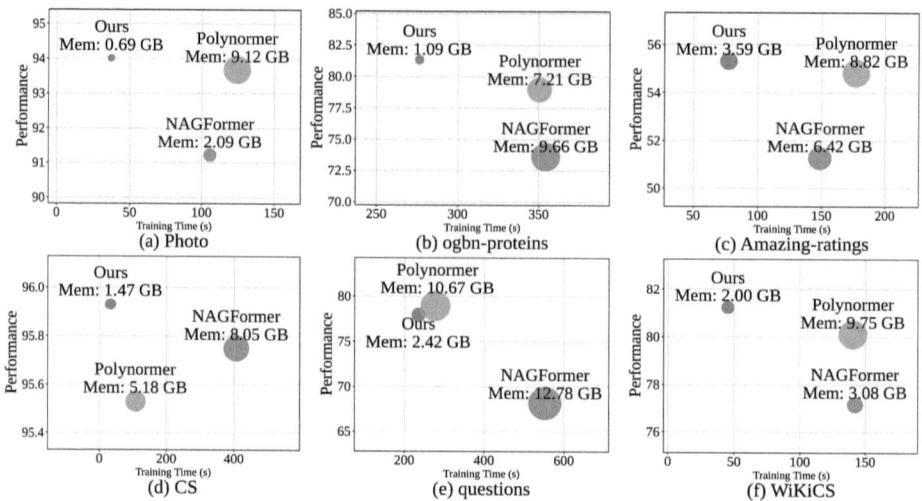

Fig. 5. Comparison of CoGT and SOTA GTs in terms of performance, efficiency, and memory consumption. The size of each point represents memory consumption.

6.2 Experimental Results

Tables 2 and 3 present the comprehensive performance of CoGT across a wide range of datasets. The selected datasets include diverse types, such as homophilic and heterophilic graphs, as well as large graphs containing a single component.

CoGT achieves outstanding performance in various scenarios and achieves the best results on multiple datasets. The key difference between CoGT and previous GTs is that it explicitly models community-level semantics during the global aggregation process. Our design provides the transformer layer with features that incorporate structural semantics, which are crucial characteristics of graph data. We believe that the performance gains of CoGT primarily stem from this step. By utilizing community-level features in the attention calculation, CoGT avoids the problem of excessive feature noise that arises from introducing node features of $O(N)$ complexity. Moreover, community-level features are derived from a community process with positional encodings, where the node semantics within each community are more consistent, allowing the central nodes to effectively aggregate valuable information while filtering out noise.

Notably, CoGT also achieves the best performance on two large-scale datasets, indicating that global aggregation using community features remains effective even for large graphs. This also confirms the existence of the information over-squeezing problem in the global aggregation process.

6.3 Efficiency Analysis

In the design of CoGT, we employ several strategies to enhance the overall model efficiency. These include utilizing a community-structured parallel atten-

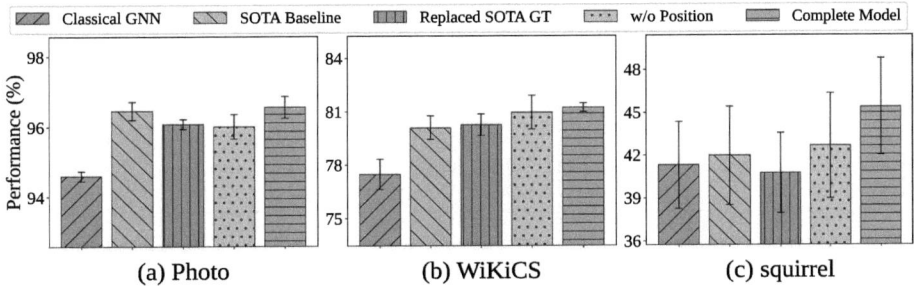

Fig. 6. The results of ablation studies. The results show that removing the proposed components leads to varying degrees of performance degradation.

tion mechanism within the transformer layer, replacing the quadratic-complexity Softmax function with the linearly-complex ReLU function, and incorporating efficient average pooling aggregation.

In terms of complexity, to prevent any community from growing too large during the aggregation process and further increasing memory consumption, we adopted a strategy where each community contains an average number of nodes. As a result, the number of nodes in a community scales with the size of the graph, leading to quadratic complexity. To address this issue, we merge the community features during computation, aggregating the features of M communities into K through block averaging, thereby achieving linear complexity.

The comparison between CoGT and SOTA baseline methods in terms of efficiency is shown in Fig. 5. From the figure, it is evident that CoGT not only achieves superior performance but also demonstrates advantages in terms of peak memory usage and training time. This is attributed to the parallel attention computation, which significantly boosts model efficiency. By decomposing the multiplication of large feature matrices into parallel multiplications of smaller matrices, the required peak memory usage is greatly reduced.

6.4 Ablation Study

Figure 6 presents the results of experiments validating the effectiveness of various components of CoGT. We replaced the HPTC layer with the SOTA method, Polynormer, to assess the effectiveness of the proposed HPTC layer. We also removed the community positional encoding to verify the importance of this step. The results show that replacing CoGT with other GT layers led to a performance decline, indicating that explicitly modeling community semantics is effective. Furthermore, removing the positional encoding also resulted in a performance drop, demonstrating that community positional encoding is beneficial. We believe this encoding highlights the semantic distinctions between communities, which is important for attention modeling.

Additionally, we conducted experiments to explore the impact of community count on model performance, with the results shown in Fig. 7. It can be observed

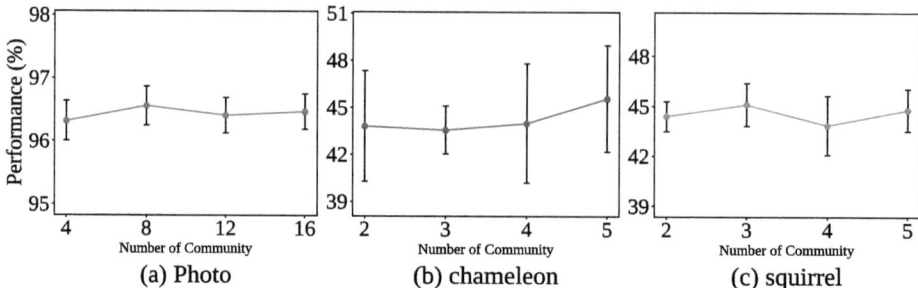

Fig. 7. The results of proposed CoGT under different community numbers. The results indicate that the optimal number of communities varies across datasets, suggesting that different datasets require different levels of semantic granularity in community representation.

that the optimal number of communities varies across different datasets. We interpret this result as indicating that the communities with clear semantic distinctions differ across datasets, similar to how universities have varying numbers and types of academic departments. From an empirical perspective, we hypothesize that the hyperparameter for community count is proportional to the number of nodes and the number of label categories.

7 Conclusion

In this paper, we first identify two key challenges that may limit the expressiveness of global attention mechanisms in GRL: (1) the absence of community-level semantics and (2) the issue of information over-squeezing. To address these issues, we propose CoGT, a novel GT variant that explicitly models community-level semantics by identifying latent communities within the graph. This design not only enhances higher-order semantic representation but also reduces the volume of aggregated information, alleviating the over-squeezing effect. Furthermore, we provide theoretical justifications to support the effectiveness of CoGT's design. Extensive experiments demonstrate that CoGT outperforms existing methods in performance while maintaining efficiency.

Currently, CoGT is not yet capable of automatically adapting the number of communities to different datasets; this value still needs to be set empirically. Therefore, a direction for future work is to develop a version of CoGT that supports adaptive community number selection. In addition, the current design of CoGT primarily targets node-level tasks, and it could be further extended to support edge-level and graph-level tasks in the future.

Acknowledgments. This research is supported by the National Natural Science Foundation of China under the grant No. 62376129, National Key Research and Development Program of China under the grant No. 2023YFF0725003, Tianjin Science and Technology Major Project under the grant No. 24ZXZSSS00420, Tianjin Natural Science Foundation under the grant No. 24JCYBJC01950, and Tiankai Higher Education

Science and Technology Park Enterprise R&D Special Project under the grant No. 23YFZXYC00029.

References

1. Belkin, M., Niyogi, P.: Laplacian eigenmaps for dimensionality reduction and data representation. Neural Comput. **15**(6), 1373–1396 (2003)
2. Chen, J., Gao, K., Li, G., He, K.: NAGphormer: a tokenized graph transformer for node classification in large graphs. In: The Eleventh International Conference on Learning Representations (2022)
3. Chen, M., Wei, Z., Huang, Z., Ding, B., Li, Y.: Simple and deep graph convolutional networks. In: International Conference on Machine Learning, pp. 1725–1735. PMLR (2020)
4. Deng, C., Yue, Z., Zhang, Z.: Polynormer: polynomial-expressive graph transformer in linear time. In: The Twelfth International Conference on Learning Representations (2024)
5. Devlin, J., Chang, M.W., Lee, K., Toutanova, K.: Bert: pre-training of deep bidirectional transformers for language understanding. In: Proceedings of the 2019 Conference of the North American Chapter of the Association for Computational Linguistics: Human Language Technologies, Volume 1 (Long and Short Papers), pp. 4171–4186 (2019)
6. Dwivedi, V.P.: Long range graph benchmark. Adv. Neural. Inf. Process. Syst. **35**, 22326–22340 (2022)
7. Girvan, M., Newman, M.E.: Community structure in social and biological networks. Proc. Natl. Acad. Sci. **99**(12), 7821–7826 (2002)
8. Grover, A., Leskovec, J.: node2vec: scalable feature learning for networks. In: Proceedings of the 22nd ACM SIGKDD International Conference on Knowledge Discovery and Data Mining, pp. 855–864 (2016)
9. Hamilton, W., Ying, Z., Leskovec, J.: Inductive representation learning on large graphs. Adv. Neural Inf. Process. Syst. **30** (2017)
10. Han, K., et al.: A survey on vision transformer. IEEE Trans. Pattern Anal. Mach. Intell. **45**(1), 87–110 (2022)
11. Kipf, T.N., Welling, M.: Semi-supervised classification with graph convolutional networks. In: International Conference on Learning Representations (2017)
12. Kong, K., Chen, J., Kirchenbauer, J., Ni, R., Bruss, C.B., Goldstein, T.: GOAT: a global transformer on large-scale graphs. In: International Conference on Machine Learning, pp. 17375–17390. PMLR (2023)
13. Li, A., Pan, Y.: Structural information and dynamical complexity of networks. IEEE Trans. Inf. Theory **62**(6), 3290–3339 (2016)
14. Newman, M.E., Girvan, M.: Finding and evaluating community structure in networks. Phys. Rev. E **69**(2), 026113 (2004)
15. Perozzi, B., Al-Rfou, R., Skiena, S.: Deepwalk: online learning of social representations. In: Proceedings of the 20th ACM SIGKDD International Conference on Knowledge Discovery and Data Mining, pp. 701–710 (2014)
16. Rampášek, L., Galkin, M., Dwivedi, V.P., Luu, A.T., Wolf, G., Beaini, D.: Recipe for a general, powerful, scalable graph transformer. Adv. Neural. Inf. Process. Syst. **35**, 14501–14515 (2022)

17. Shirzad, H., Velingker, A., Venkatachalam, B., Sutherland, D.J., Sinop, A.K.: Exphormer: sparse transformers for graphs. In: International Conference on Machine Learning, pp. 31613–31632. PMLR (2023)
18. Topping, J., Di Giovanni, F., Chamberlain, B.P., Dong, X., Bronstein, M.M.: Understanding over-squashing and bottlenecks on graphs via curvature. In: International Conference on Learning Representations
19. Veličković, P., Cucurull, G., Casanova, A., Romero, A., Liò, P., Bengio, Y.: Graph attention networks. In: International Conference on Learning Representations (2018)
20. Wang, X., et al.: Heterogeneous graph attention network. In: The World Wide Web Conference, pp. 2022–2032 (2019)
21. Wu, Q., Zhao, W., Li, Z., Wipf, D., Yan, J.: Nodeformer: a scalable graph structure learning transformer for node classification. In: Advances in Neural Information Processing Systems (2022)
22. Wu, Q., et al.: SGFormer: simplifying and empowering transformers for large-graph representations. Adv. Neural. Inf. Process. Syst. **36**, 64753–64773 (2023)
23. Wu, Z., Jain, P., Wright, M., Mirhoseini, A., Gonzalez, J.E., Stoica, I.: Representing long-range context for graph neural networks with global attention. Adv. Neural. Inf. Process. Syst. **34**, 13266–13279 (2021)
24. Wu, Z., Pan, S., Chen, F., Long, G., Zhang, C., Philip, S.Y.: A comprehensive survey on graph neural networks. IEEE Trans. Neural Netw. Learn. Syst. **32**(1), 4–24 (2020)
25. Ying, C., et al.: Do transformers really perform badly for graph representation? Adv. Neural. Inf. Process. Syst. **34**, 28877–28888 (2021)
26. Yun, S., Jeong, M., Kim, R., Kang, J., Kim, H.J.: Graph transformer networks. Adv. Neural Inf. Process. Syst. **32** (2019)
27. Zhang, Z., Cui, P., Zhu, W.: Deep learning on graphs: a survey. IEEE Trans. Knowl. Data Eng. **34**(1), 249–270 (2020)

AB-STE: Adaptive Blended Gradient Estimation for Efficient Binarized Networks

Siddharth Gupta[✉] and Akash Kumar

Ruhr-Universität Bochum, Bochum, Germany
{siddharth.gupta,akash.kumar}@rub.de

Abstract. Binary Neural Networks (BNNs) offer a highly efficient alternative to traditional deep learning models by drastically reducing memory and computational demands, making them well-suited for deployment in resource-constrained environments like edge devices. Despite their efficiency, BNNs are often limited by inaccurate and unstable gradient estimation using traditional Straight Through Estimator (STE) methods, which disrupt gradient flow and impede convergence. BinaryConnect introduced STE to approximate the gradients of the sign function; however, this approximation causes significant inconsistencies, ultimately compromising training stability. While various methods have been proposed to address these issues, many fail to consider that minimizing estimation error can inadvertently reduce gradient stability. Such highly divergent gradients can increase the risk of vanishing or exploding gradients, thereby hindering effective training. In this paper, we propose two novel Adaptive Blended Straight Through Estimators (*AB-STE*): *AB-ArcTan-STE* and *AB-Tanh-STE*. Unlike previous methods, AB-STE blends a linear component with a non-linear function to provide both stability and expressiveness during training, addressing key challenges faced by BNNs. By combining the simplicity of linearity with the representational power of non-linearity, AB-STE maintains a balanced gradient flow throughout training, ensuring both stability and effective learning. Extensive experiments on CIFAR-10 and ImageNet demonstrate that AB-STE achieves superior performance, surpassing existing state-of-the-art methods. Specifically, our *AB-Tanh-STE* achieved an accuracy of 94.60% on ResNet-18 for CIFAR-10, and a Top-1 accuracy of 67.96% on ImageNet, demonstrating the effectiveness of our adaptive blending strategy in enhancing training stability and accuracy. Notably, the parameters were binarized to achieve efficiency while maintaining stable gradient flow.

Keywords: Binary Neural Networks (BNNs) · Straight Through Estimator (STE) · Gradient Estimation · Quantization · Deep Learning

1 Introduction

Deep neural networks (DNNs), particularly convolutional neural networks (CNNs), have achieved remarkable success across a wide range of computer

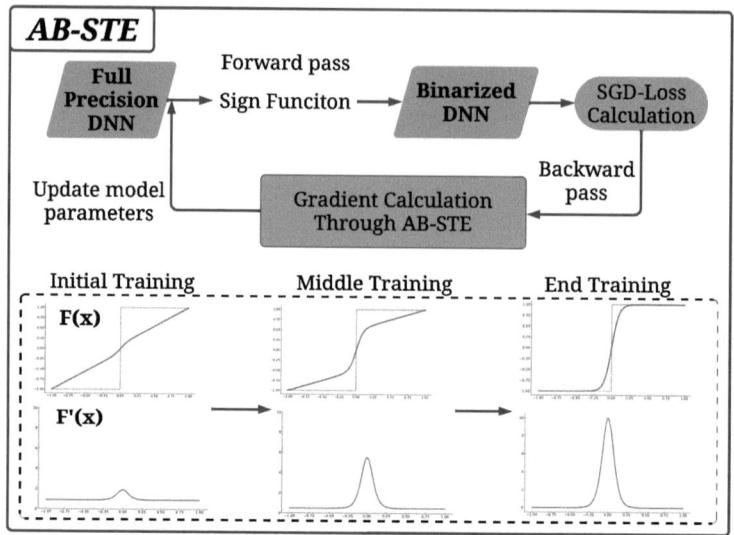

Fig. 1. Proposed framework for *AB-STE*

vision tasks, such as image classification [2,3], object detection [4,5], and semantic segmentation [6]. Despite their success, the deployment of these models on resource-constrained edge devices, like mobile phones, smartwatches, and cameras, is challenging due to their large number of parameters and high computational demands. To address these challenges, binarizing DNNs has emerged as a promising approach, providing a significant reduction in memory footprint and computational costs [7]. Binarizing the parameters of DNNs makes them easier to deploy on hardware since convolution operations can be implemented as efficient bitwise operations [9]. However, a major challenge in binarization is the inability to propagate gradients effectively through binary activations, which leads to poor model accuracy and hinders the training of deep architectures [10,11].

BinaryConnect [7] and BinaryNet [8] were among the first approaches to binarize both weights and activations. These methods employed the straight-through estimator (STE) to approximate the gradients of the sign function during backpropagation, which led to significant improvements in training binarized networks. However, the inconsistency between the forward pass (binarizing weights and activations) and the backward pass (approximating gradients) introduces a critical problem, leading to poor gradient flow and reduced accuracy in deeper networks. To mitigate the issues caused by traditional STE, ReSTE [1] proposed a balanced approach to stabilize gradients similar to STE, while incorporating flexibility through a power function. However, ReSTE's effectiveness is limited near zero values, resulting in gradients that are not sufficiently smooth. Although previous methods attempted to narrow the estimation error, they often led to divergent gradients. This motivated our design of *AB-STE*, which introduces an adaptive approach to ensure both stability and effective gradient flow.

The proposed *Adaptive Blended Straight Through Estimator (AB-STE)* employs a blend of two components: a linear component for stability and a non-linear component for expressiveness, which approximates the sign function. This adaptive blend evolves throughout training to maintain gradient stability while enhancing the model's representational capacity. In the initial phase, the forward function, $F(x)$, behaves similarly to a linear function ($y = x$), providing stability with low gradient magnitudes for the backward function, $F'(x)$. As training progresses, $F(x)$ evolves to approximate the non-linear characteristics of the sign function, resulting in higher gradient magnitudes through $F'(x)$. This progression enhances the model's ability to learn more complex representations while maintaining a stable gradient flow. Figure 1 illustrates the training framework of *AB-STE*, highlighting how the adaptive evolution of $F(x)$ and $F'(x)$ helps improve both stability and learning during different training stages. Our function moves from a simple linear approximation to a more step-like behavior, while maintaining smooth gradients throughout backpropagation to support effective training. We further illustrate the forward and backward passes of the proposed estimator in Fig. 2. The plots demonstrate how our function transitions from an initial STE-like behavior to a more refined step-function approximation over the course of training while maintaining smooth gradients throughout. This ensures both effective approximation and stable gradient flow, facilitating robust and efficient model training.

The main contributions of this paper are as follows:

Adaptive Blended Straight-Through Estimators (AB-STE): We propose two novel adaptive blended estimators, *AB-Tanh-STE* and *AB-ArcTan-STE*, which combine linear and non-linear components to stabilize and improve gradient flow during BNN training.

Enhanced Gradient Stability and Smoothness Our approach addresses the inconsistency problem in traditional STE methods by balancing gradient smoothness and stability, reducing the risk of vanishing or exploding gradients.

Blended Function for Forward and Backward Passes The proposed blended function incorporates a linear component for stability and a non-linear component for expressiveness, enabling the transition from STE-like behavior to step-function approximation during training.

Extensive Experimental Validation Experiments conducted on CIFAR-10 and ImageNet datasets demonstrate the superior performance of *AB-STE* compared to existing state-of-the-art estimators for BNNs.

Open-Source Implementation We provide an open-source implementation of *AB-STE* (https://github.com/sid-3dev/AB_STE) to encourage reproducible research and further development in efficient neural network training.

The remainder of this paper is organized as follows: Section 2 reviews the state-of-the-art techniques for DNN binarization. Section 3 introduces our proposed methods and their theoretical analysis, followed by the results and analysis in Sect. 4. Finally, Sect. 5 provides concluding remarks and insights.

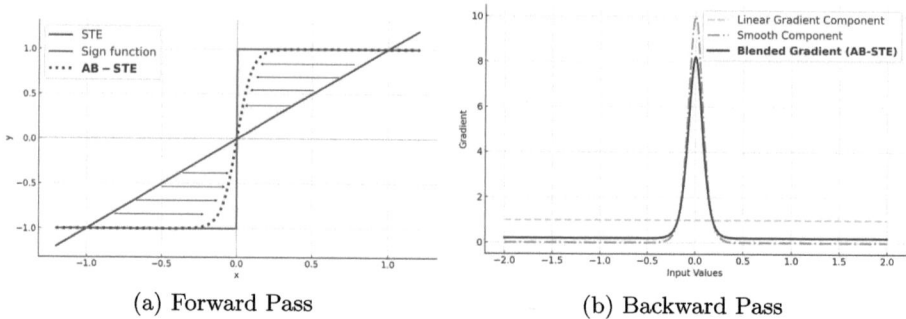

(a) Forward Pass (b) Backward Pass

Fig. 2. An intuitive illustration of adaptive blending of linear smooth components to show how our function moves from STE to Sign function approximation while keeping the gradient smooth during backpropagation for improved BNN training.

2 Related Work

Network binarization seeks to enhance the speed of neural network inference while significantly reducing memory requirements, all with minimal accuracy loss. One effective strategy to achieve this is by employing bitwise operations in low-precision networks. By converting 32-bit parameters such as weights and activations into binary form, computational efficiency is considerably boosted, and memory consumption is greatly decreased. BinaryConnect [7] and BinaryNet [8] were pioneering approaches that focused on binarizing network weights and both weights and activations, respectively, for use during both training and inference. These works utilized straight-through estimators to enable training of deep neural networks with binarized parameters, particularly addressing the non-differentiability issue that arises during the binarization process. In binarized neural networks, weights and activations are often represented using a sign function, which complicates gradient computation through standard backpropagation due to its discontinuous nature. To circumvent this problem, STE approximates the backward gradient, allowing effective network training. During the forward pass, a binarization function such as the sign function is used:

$$x_b = \text{sign}(x) = \begin{cases} +1 & \text{if } x \geq 0 \\ -1 & \text{if } x < 0 \end{cases} \quad (1)$$

However, the gradient of this function is zero almost everywhere, making it unsuitable for backpropagation. In STE, the gradient is approximated in a simpler form, treating the forward binarization as an identity function during the backward pass. This can be mathematically represented as:

$$\frac{\partial L}{\partial x} \approx \frac{\partial L}{\partial x_b} \cdot \mathbf{1}_{|x| \leq 1} \quad (2)$$

where L is the loss function, x_b is the binarized version of x, and $\mathbf{1}_{|x| \leq 1}$ is an indicator function that constrains the gradient to pass through values of x in the range $[-1, 1]$. This simple approximation effectively allows gradients to flow through the network, enabling the model to learn and adapt weights despite the non-differentiable nature of the binarization step. Using STE, the model can be trained to achieve comparable accuracy to its full-precision counterpart, while greatly benefiting from reduced complexity and memory footprint.

Despite the use of STE, the accuracy of binary networks remains significantly lower compared to their full-precision counterparts. Various strategies have been proposed to address this issue. [12] introduced architectural changes to enhance the expressiveness of binary networks, though these improvements depend heavily on modifying network architecture. Other methods, such as knowledge distillation and additional regularizations [13,14], aim to improve training but often result in increased computational costs during training.

Many studies have focused on improving gradient estimation in binary neural networks (BNNs). For instance, Bi-Real-Net [12] employs a piece-wise polynomial, DSQ [15] introduces a tanh-based function, IR-Net uses an error decay estimator function, and FDA [16] applies Fourier series to improve gradient computation. While these methods have demonstrated good performance, they often overlook the importance of gradient stability. Reducing estimation error too aggressively can lead to highly divergent gradients, increasing the risk of gradient vanishing or exploding, which ultimately impairs effective training.

The authors of ReSTE [1] proposed a method for stable gradient calculation; however, the resulting gradient space is not smooth, which limits training capability during binarization. To address these challenges, we propose an **Adaptive Blended Straight-Through Estimator (AB-STE)**. Compared to other estimators, our approach provides stable training with smooth gradients, resulting in better overall performance. Extensive experiments show that our method surpasses existing state-of-the-art methods, effectively addressing both the gradient stability and smoothness challenges in binarized networks.

3 Proposed Techniques

3.1 Adaptive Blended Straight Through Estimator (AB-STE)

The authors of ReSTE [1] demonstrate that the sign function and STE represent two extremes in terms of gradient stability. The sign function has zero gradients almost everywhere and an infinite gradient at the origin, leading to either vanishing or exploding gradients, resulting in high gradient instability. In contrast, STE approximates the gradients of the sign function using a linear function, which does not alter the backward gradient during estimation.

Considering these characteristics, we designed an estimator for gradients that balances stability and expressiveness. Therefore, we introduce a blend of linearity and non-linearity in the estimator that aims to reduce the discrepancy between forward and backward computations. Equation (3) represents the forward pass for the proposed AB-STE. By incorporating a blending factor f and a tunable

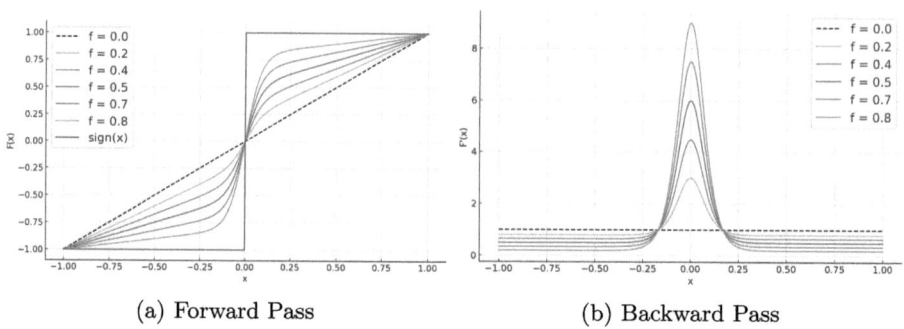

(a) Forward Pass (b) Backward Pass

Fig. 3. Showing the behaviour of Advaptive Blended Tanh based Straight Through Estimator (AB-Tan-STE) with different factor (f) values

scaling parameter k, the model can adaptively adjust the ratio between the linear and tanh components based on the training dynamics, allowing a more flexible and accurate representation of the gradients.

$$F(x) = (1 - f) \cdot x + f \cdot \tanh(kx) \qquad (3)$$

where f controls the blend between the linear and non-linear parts, and k is a scaling factor for x. When $f = 0$, this blending function behaves as a standard STE, and when $f = 1$, it functions similarly to the tanh function (as an approximation of the sign function). During training, we start with low values of f and gradually increase it as the number of epochs progresses. This approach allows us to initially leverage the stability of STE and gradually incorporate the expressiveness of the tanh function. In Fig. 3, we illustrate the changes in the function as f changes. It can be observed that $F(x)$ behaves more like an STE when f is small and more like a sign function as f increases.

backward pass function $F'(x)$ is given by:

$$F'(x) = (1 - f) + f \cdot k \cdot \text{sech}^2(kx) \qquad (4)$$

Figure 3 also shows the derivative $F'(x)$. As f increases, $F'(x)$ provides a high and smooth peak near zero, indicating the function's ability to effectively calculate gradients throughout training, thereby ensuring gradient stability and reducing the risk of gradient vanishing or exploding. Furthermore, we introduce another adaptive blended function for straight-through estimation called **AB-ArcTan-STE**. This estimator blends a linear function with an arctan function, as defined in Eq. (5). The use of the arctan function in this blend aims to extend the range of the resulting function, which allows the model to retain gradient information over a broader spectrum of input values. This makes the estimator more effective, particularly when handling larger values of x. The arctan function also provides a more gradual gradient decay, contributing to increased stability and smoother gradient flow during training. The backward pass of AB-ArcTan-STE is presented in Eq. (6).

Algorithm 1. Adaptive Blended Straight-Through Estimator (AB-STE)

Input: Training dataset: X, epochs: N, learning rate: η, initial blending factor: f_0, scaling parameter: k
Initialize model parameters θ
for $epoch = 1 \ldots N$
for $batch\ B \subset X$
Forward Pass: Compute activations using the sign function:

$$y \leftarrow \text{sign}(x)$$

Calculate loss $L(\theta)$ using output y
Backward Pass: Compute gradient of the loss with respect to parameters using the blended gradient function:

$$F'(x) \leftarrow (1-f) + f \cdot k \cdot \text{sech}^2(kx) \quad \text{(for AB-Tanh-STE)}$$

$$F'(x) \leftarrow \frac{1-f}{2} + \frac{f \cdot k}{\arctan(2k) \cdot (1 + (k \cdot x)^2)} \quad \text{(for AB-ArcTan-STE)}$$

Use $F'(x)$ to compute parameter gradients (not applied to activations)
Update model parameters using stochastic gradient descent:

$$\theta \leftarrow \theta - \eta \cdot \nabla_\theta L(\theta)$$

Update blending factor f (e.g., linearly or exponentially increase f with epochs)

$$F(x) = \frac{1-f}{2} \cdot x + \frac{f}{\arctan(2k)} \cdot \arctan(k \cdot x) \qquad (5)$$

$$F'(x) = \frac{1-f}{2} + \frac{f \cdot k}{\arctan(2k) \cdot (1 + (k \cdot x)^2)} \qquad (6)$$

$\arctan(x)$ is the angle between $-\frac{\pi}{2}$ and $\frac{\pi}{2}$ radians whose tangent is x.

Further, we present an Algorithm 1 that utilizes the Adaptive Blended Straight-Through Estimator (AB-STE) for training binarized models. In the forward pass, activations are computed using the sign function to maintain binarized representation. During the backward pass, a blended gradient function $F'(x)$, combining linear and non-linear components, is used to compute parameter gradients, enabling smooth and adaptive gradient updates. The blending factor f is gradually increased throughout training to transition from stable linear gradients to more expressive non-linear gradients, effectively balancing stability and learning capacity. This approach helps mitigate gradient instability, ensuring efficient training of binarized models.

3.2 Theoretical Analysis of Adaptive Blended Straight-Through Estimator (AB-STE)

We provide a theoretical analysis of the proposed Adaptive Blended Straight Through Estimator, focusing on stability, convergence, and gradient properties.

Specifically, we analyze the impact of the blending factor f and scaling parameter k on gradient flow, stability, and convergence.

Gradient Stability and Variance Lemma 1 (Gradient Stability): The variance of the gradient $F'(x)$ decreases as the blending factor f increases from 0 to 1, resulting in a smoother gradient update.
   Proof:

1. Consider the derivative function $F'(x)$. The variance $\text{Var}(F'(x))$ depends on the value of f and the distribution of the input x.
2. When $f = 0$, $F'(x) = 1$, which results in no variance in gradient values.
3. When $f > 0$, the variance of $F'(x)$ depends on the contribution of the term $f \cdot k \cdot \text{sech}^2(kx)$.
4. Since $\text{sech}^2(kx)$ is bounded between 0 and 1, the variance of the gradient is limited and depends on f and k. As f increases, the contribution of the nonlinear term becomes more prominent, resulting in a more stable and smoothed gradient.

Implication: This analysis indicates that increasing the blending factor f results in a more stable gradient update, which is crucial for reducing the risk of sudden changes in gradient values, thus improving overall training stability.

Smoothness of Gradient Flow. The smoothness of the gradient is crucial to avoid vanishing or exploding gradients during training. The smoothness property of the proposed estimator is analyzed using the second-order derivative of $F(x)$.

Lemma 2 (Smoothness of Gradient Flow): The gradient $F'(x)$ of AB-STE is Lipschitz continuous with a Lipschitz constant that depends on the blending factor f and the scaling parameter k.
   Proof:

1. The second derivative of $F(x)$ is given by:

$$F''(x) = f \cdot k^2 \cdot \text{sech}^2(kx) \cdot \tanh(kx)$$

2. The Lipschitz constant L for $F'(x)$ can be bounded by the maximum value of $|F''(x)|$:

$$L \leq f \cdot k^2$$

3. Since $f \in [0, 1]$ and $\text{sech}^2(kx) \leq 1$, the Lipschitz constant depends linearly on f and quadratically on k. This implies that the smoothness of the gradient increases with smaller values of k, while larger values of k can result in sharper changes in gradient, potentially causing instability.

Implication: Ensuring that the Lipschitz constant is appropriately controlled helps maintain smooth gradient flow, thereby reducing the risk of gradient explosion or vanishing, particularly in deep networks.

Gradient Flow Improvement. Furthermore, when $f \to 1$, the gradient $F'(x)$ has a peak near zero that helps maintain sufficient gradient flow through the layers, especially during backpropagation. This prevents gradients from vanishing in deeper layers and improves convergence.

In summary, the theoretical analysis shows that AB-STE effectively maintains gradient stability and smoothness through careful control of the blending factor f and the scaling parameter k. The variance of the gradient $F'(x)$ is reduced as f increases, ensuring stable updates, while the Lipschitz continuity of $F'(x)$ guarantees smooth gradient flow, reducing the risk of vanishing or exploding gradients. By gradually increasing f, AB-STE ensures effective gradient flow throughout the network, leading to improved convergence during training, particularly for deep binarized models.

4 Experimental Setup and Results

4.1 Datasets and Training Setup

This study uses two popular datasets commonly employed in the binary neural network literature: **CIFAR-10** [18] and **ImageNet ILSVRC-2012** [17].

The CIFAR-10 dataset consists of 50,000 training images and 10,000 testing images across 10 categories, with each image having a resolution of 32×32 and three RGB color channels. The ImageNet ILSVRC-2012 dataset is a large-scale dataset with over 1.2 million training images and 50,000 validation images, each at a resolution of 224×224, covering 1,000 categories.

To ensure a fair comparison with existing methods, we adopted similar training settings as other binary methods [1,19,20]. We used pre-processing techniques such as RandomCrop, RandomHorizontalFlip, and Normalize for both CIFAR-10 and ImageNet. The models were trained using Stochastic Gradient Descent (SGD) with an initial learning rate of 0.1, and a cosine learning rate decay schedule was employed to gradually reduce the learning rate during training.

For CIFAR-10, the models were trained for 1,000 epochs, while for ImageNet, training was conducted for 250 epochs. The hyperparameter k, which controls the iterative nature of the adaptive blending, was fixed at 10 throughout the experiments. We varied the blending factor f between 0.2 and 0.8 to study its impact on training performance and gradient stability. Importantly, parameter quantization was employed during training, whereas activations were kept at full precision to maintain expressive feature representations and ensure stable gradient flow.

4.2 Results and Analysis

The proposed Adaptive Blended Straight-Through Estimators (AB-STE) were evaluated using the CIFAR-10 and ImageNet datasets, focusing on both accuracy and training stability compared to the existing state-of-the-art methods.

In these experiments, we applied parameter binarization while retaining full-precision activations, which allowed us to effectively maintain gradient stability and minimize the impact of quantization on the training dynamics.

Results on CIFAR-10. Table 1 summarizes the results of the CIFAR-10 experiments across different architectures, including VGG-small, ResNet-18, and ResNet-20. We compare our proposed AB-Tanh-STE and AB-ArcTan-STE with other established methods like DoReFa-Net [20], IR-Net [19], and ReSTE [1]. Our AB-Tanh-STE and AB-ArcTan-STE consistently demonstrated performance that was comparable to or better than the current state-of-the-art methods.

The AB-Tanh-STE method, in particular, achieved the highest accuracy across all three architectures, with an accuracy of **93.16%** on VGG-small and **94.60%** on ResNet-18, which were very close to their floating-point counterparts. This highlights the effectiveness of our adaptive blending strategy in maintaining stability while achieving high accuracy, despite parameter binarization.

Table 1. Accuracy Comparison on CIFAR-10 Across Different Architectures. The proposed AB-Tanh-STE and AB-ArcTan-STE methods consistently achieve competitive accuracy compared to floating-point and state-of-the-art binary methods, using parameter quantization while keeping activations at full precision.

Architecture	Method	Accuracy (%)
VGG-small	Floating Point	93.30
	DoReFa-Net [20]	92.13
	IR-Net [19]	90.92
	ReSTE [1]	92.53
	AB-Tanh-STE (ours)	**93.16**
	AB-ArcTan-STE (ours)	93.00
ResNet-18	Floating Point	94.86
	DoReFa-Net [20]	94.13
	IR-Net [19]	94.33
	ReSTE [1]	93.68
	AB-Tanh-STE (ours)	**94.60**
	AB-ArcTan-STE (ours)	94.18
ResNet-20	Floating Point	91.74
	DoReFa-Net [20]	90.79
	IR-Net [19]	91.03
	ReSTE [1]	91.32
	AB-Tanh-STE (ours)	**91.54**
	AB-ArcTan-STE (ours)	91.12

Results on ImageNet The results on the ImageNet dataset are presented in Table 2. For ResNet-18, our methods show clear improvements in Top-1 and Top-5 accuracy compared to previous estimators. Specifically, AB-Tanh-STE achieved a **Top-1 accuracy of 67.96%** and AB-ArcTan-STE achieved a **Top-5 accuracy of 87.66%**, surpassing the ReSTE baseline. For ResNet-34, AB-Tanh-STE achieved a **Top-1 accuracy of 71.31%** and a **Top-5 accuracy of 89.98%**, which outperformed ReSTE and demonstrated the effectiveness of our proposed method on larger architectures.

The adaptive blending strategy enables our models to maintain a stable training process, even on a challenging dataset such as ImageNet, where the vast number of categories and high resolution of images pose significant challenges for binary neural networks. By using parameter quantization with full-precision activations, our methods demonstrate that adaptive blending not only stabilizes training but also provides an effective means to achieve high accuracy.

Table 2. Accuracy Comparison on ImageNet ILSVRC-2012 Across Different Architectures. The proposed AB-Tanh-STE and AB-ArcTan-STE methods show improvements in Top-1 and Top-5 accuracy while using parameter quantization and full-precision activations, highlighting their effectiveness on large-scale datasets.

Architecture	Method	Top-1 Acc (%)	Top-5 Acc (%)
ResNet-18	Floating Point	69.58	89.19
	ReSTE [1]	67.66	87.48
	AB-Tanh-STE (ours)	**67.96**	87.64
	AB-ArcTan-STE (ours)	67.68	**87.66**
ResNet-34	Floating Point	73.32	91.27
	ReSTE [1]	70.66	89.43
	AB-Tanh-STE (ours)	**71.31**	**89.98**
	AB-ArcTan-STE (ours)	71.18	89.71

4.3 Effect of Blending Factor

During training, the blending factor f was linearly increased from **0.2** to **0.8**. This approach allowed the model to benefit from stable training in the initial epochs while gradually introducing non-linearity to enhance representational capacity. Our results indicate that such adaptive blending, combined with parameter quantization and full-precision activations, is crucial for achieving an optimal balance between gradient smoothness and model expressiveness, leading to consistent improvements in both CIFAR-10 and ImageNet benchmarks.

The experiments on CIFAR-10 and ImageNet demonstrate that the proposed **AB-STE** methods outperform traditional binary neural network training techniques by effectively balancing gradient stability and expressiveness. The use of a blended function allows us to avoid the gradient vanishing and exploding issues that often hinder STE-based training methods.

4.4 Computational Resources Analysis

Table 3. Comparison of FLOPs and Training Time Across Methods

Method	FLOPs per Input	CIFAR-10 Time (s/epoch)	ImageNet Time (mm:ss/epoch)	CIFAR-10 Acc. (%)	ImageNet Acc. (%)
ReSTE	10 (5 for power, 4 for comparisons, 1 for sign)	16	10:56	93.68	67.66
AB-Tanh-STE	6 (2 for tanh, 4 for blending)	14	10:33	94.60	67.96
AB-ArcTan-STE	7 (3 for arctan, 4 for blending)	12	10:22	94.18	67.68

To evaluate computational efficiency, we conducted a FLOP (floating point operations) analysis for backpropagation and measured the training time per epoch for each method. These analyses help assess the computational cost of the proposed approaches in comparison to ReSTE. Table 3 summarizes the FLOP requirements per input element during backpropagation, alongside training time per epoch on CIFAR-10 and ImageNet using the ResNet-18 architecture. As observed, AB-Tanh-STE and AB-ArcTan-STE require fewer FLOPs per input compared to ReSTE, resulting in notable speedups in training time. The reduction in FLOPs is achieved by eliminating power operations and reducing conditional checks, thereby improving computational efficiency.

ReSTE's backpropagation operation includes multiple conditional checks and power operations, leading to higher computational cost and longer training times. In contrast, AB-Tanh-STE and AB-ArcTan-STE leverage simpler mathematical functions such as tanh and arctan, which require fewer computations. Optimized gradient flow reduces unnecessary computations while preserving accuracy. Efficient FLOP reduction enables 14% and 25% speedups on CIFAR-10 and 4% and 6% speedups on ImageNet, respectively. These results highlight that AB-Tanh-STE and AB-ArcTan-STE not only improve accuracy but also significantly reduce computational costs, making them more efficient for large-scale BNN training. To balance hardware efficiency and accuracy, we chose to binarize only weights during training while keeping activations in full precision. Binarized weights are well-suited for accumulation-based hardware accelerators such as YodaNN [21] and FINN [22], which replace multiplications with bitwise operations (XNOR + popcount), reducing computation and memory requirements. Previous studies, such as XNOR-Net [23], have shown that binarizing both weights and activations during training severely impacts accuracy, particularly on complex datasets like ImageNet. Keeping activations full-precision during training preserves gradient information and improves accuracy. Activations can still be binarized during inference, ensuring computational efficiency without retraining.

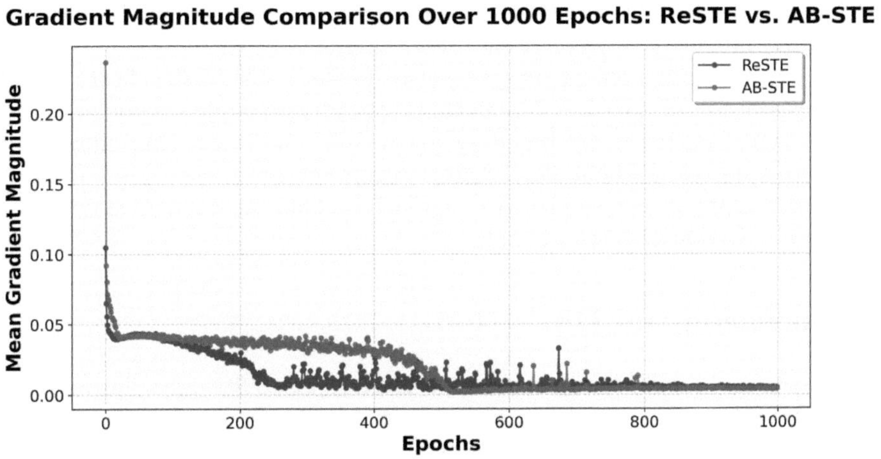

Gradient Magnitude Comparison Over 1000 Epochs: ReSTE vs. AB-STE

Fig. 4. Training of ResNet-18 with CIFAR-10 dataset

These results demonstrate that AB-Tanh-STE and AB-ArcTan-STE improve the accuracy of BNNs while significantly reducing training time and computational overhead, making them well-suited for efficient hardware deployment without sacrificing model performance.

4.5 Gradient Analysis

In Fig. 4, we present a comparison of the mean gradient magnitude across training epochs for ReSTE (blue) and the proposed AB-Tanh-STE (red). The results demonstrate that AB-STE maintains higher gradient magnitudes in the early training phase, ensuring a stronger learning signal and preventing premature convergence. In contrast, ReSTE exhibits a faster decay in gradient magnitudes, potentially limiting the network's ability to explore the optimization landscape effectively during initial training.

As training progresses, AB-STE stabilizes the gradient magnitudes at a consistently higher level compared to ReSTE, facilitating smoother and more structured training dynamics. The gradual decay of gradients in AB-STE ensures that weight updates remain effective, preventing the issue of vanishing gradients commonly observed in deep networks. In contrast, ReSTE experiences notable fluctuations and sharp drops in gradient magnitude, particularly after epoch 200, suggesting less stable weight updates, which could impact model robustness and convergence stability. Beyond epoch 400, AB-STE exhibits lower gradient variance, indicating that it allows for more controlled and adaptive optimization steps. The consistent gradient flow observed in AB-STE contributes to improved training efficiency, ensuring that the network retains sufficient gradient magnitudes for meaningful updates while avoiding instability. On the other hand,

ReSTE continues to show irregular oscillations throughout training, making the optimization process less predictable.

The observed improvements in gradient behavior highlight the effectiveness of the proposed AB-STE method in maintaining gradient stability while preserving representational capacity. By blending linear and non-linear components, AB-STE ensures better gradient flow, reduced gradient saturation, and improved robustness, making it a more effective approach for training binarized deep neural networks in adversarial settings.

5 Conclusion and Discussion

In this work, we introduced two novel Adaptive Blended Straight-Through Estimators (AB-STE): **AB-Tanh-STE** and **AB-ArcTan-STE**, aimed at improving the training of Binary Neural Networks (BNNs). Our approach addresses the critical challenges of gradient instability and inaccurate gradient flow in traditional STE-based methods. By blending linearity and non-linearity, AB-STE maintains both gradient stability and expressiveness, significantly enhancing the overall convergence and training efficiency of BNNs. The extensive experimental evaluation on CIFAR-10 and ImageNet demonstrates that our proposed estimators outperform existing state-of-the-art methods, achieving superior accuracy while preserving training stability. The adaptive nature of our blended estimator provides a flexible mechanism to navigate the challenges of gradient estimation, balancing simplicity and complexity in a manner that improves training outcomes for BNNs. By progressively increasing the non-linearity throughout training, AB-STE effectively mitigates the risks associated with gradient vanishing and exploding, leading to smoother and more stable training dynamics.

Our work also highlights potential directions for future research in **multi-bit quantization-aware training**. The adaptive blending strategy introduced in AB-STE could be extended beyond binary networks to more general quantization schemes, offering a promising pathway to address gradient estimation challenges in multi-bit quantization settings. Moreover, the success of AB-STE in stabilizing gradient flow may provide insights into mitigating the effects of activation quantization during network training, further enhancing the applicability of quantized neural networks to resource-constrained environments. In summary, the proposed AB-STE offers an effective solution to the gradient-related challenges faced by BNNs, and its adaptive blended approach lays a foundation for future advances in quantization-aware training for both binary and multi-bit networks. We believe that this work paves the way for more robust and efficient training methods for neural networks deployed on edge devices, potentially broadening the scope of practical deep learning applications.

Acknowledgment. This research is supported by the German Research Foundation (DFG) under project X-ReAp (380524764) 'X-ReAp: Cross(X)-Layer Runtime Reconfigurable Approximate Architecture.'

References

1. Wu, X.M., Zheng, D., Liu, Z., Zheng, W.S.: Estimator meets equilibrium perspective: a rectified straight through estimator for binary neural networks training. In: Proceedings of the IEEE/CVF International Conference on Computer Vision, pp. 17055–17064 (2023)
2. Krizhevsky, A., Sutskever, I., Hinton, G.E.: ImageNet classification with deep convolutional neural networks. Commun. ACM **60**(6), 84–90 (2017)
3. Szegedy, C., et al.: Going deeper with convolutions. In: Proceedings of the IEEE Conference on Computer Vision and Pattern Recognition, pp. 1–9 (2015)
4. Girshick, R., Donahue, J., Darrell, T., Malik, J.: Rich feature hierarchies for accurate object detection and semantic segmentation. In: Proceedings of the IEEE Conference on Computer Vision and Pattern Recognition, pp. 580–587 (2014)
5. Li, R., Wang, Y., Liang, F., Qin, H., Yan, J., Fan, R.: Fully quantized network for object detection. In: Proceedings of the IEEE/CVF Conference on Computer Vision and Pattern Recognition, pp. 2810–2819 (2019)
6. Everingham, M., Eslami, S.A., Gool, L., Williams, C.K., Winn, J., Zisserman, A.: The pascal visual object classes challenge: a retrospective. Int. J. Comput. Vis. **111**, 98–136 (2015)
7. Courbariaux, M., Bengio, Y., David, J.P.: BinaryConnect: training deep neural networks with binary weights during propagations. Adv. Neural Inf. Process. Syst. **28** (2015)
8. Courbariaux, M., Bengio, Y.: BinaryNet: Training deep neural networks with weights and activations constrained to +1 or −1. arXiv (2016). arXiv preprint arXiv:1602.02830
9. Wang, Z., Lu, J., Tao, C., Zhou, J., Tian, Q.: Learning channel-wise interactions for binary convolutional neural networks. In: Proceedings of the IEEE/CVF Conference on Computer Vision and Pattern Recognition, pp. 568–577 (2019)
10. Jung, S., et al.: Learning to quantize deep networks by optimizing quantization intervals with task loss. In: Proceedings of the IEEE/CVF Conference on Computer Vision and Pattern Recognition, pp. 4350–4359 (2019)
11. Qin, H., Gong, R., Liu, X., Bai, X., Song, J., Sebe, N.: Binary neural networks: a survey. Pattern Recogn. **105**, 107281 (2020)
12. Liu, Z., Wu, B., Luo, W., Yang, X., Liu, W., Cheng, K.T.: BI-real net: enhancing the performance of 1-bit CNNs with improved representational capability and advanced training algorithm. In: Proceedings of the European Conference on Computer Vision (ECCV), pp. 722–737 (2018)
13. Tian, Y., Krishnan, D., Isola, P.: Contrastive representation distillation. arXiv preprint arXiv:1910.10699 (2019)
14. Bai, Y., Wang, Y.X. and Liberty, E.: PROXQUANT: Quantized neural networks via proximal operators. arXiv preprint arXiv:1810.00861 (2018)
15. Gong, R., et al.: Differentiable soft quantization: bridging full-precision and low-bit neural networks. In: Proceedings of the IEEE/CVF International Conference on Computer Vision, pp. 4852–4861 (2019)
16. Xu, Y., Han, K., Xu, C., Tang, Y., Xu, C., Wang, Y.: Learning frequency domain approximation for binary neural networks. Adv. Neural. Inf. Process. Syst. **34**, 25553–25565 (2021)
17. Deng, J., Dong, W., Socher, R., Li, L.J., Li, K., Fei-Fei, L.: ImageNet: a large-scale hierarchical image database. In: 2009 IEEE Conference on Computer Vision and Pattern Recognition, pp. 248–255. IEEE (2009)

18. Krizhevsky, A., Hinton, G.: Learning multiple layers of features from tiny images (2009) [online]
19. Qin, H., et al.: Forward and backward information retention for accurate binary neural networks. In: Proceedings of the IEEE/CVF Conference on Computer Vision and Pattern Recognition, pp. 2250–2259 (2020)
20. Zhou, S., Wu, Y., Ni, Z., Zhou, X., Wen, H., Zou, Y.: DoReFa-Net: Training low bitwidth convolutional neural networks with low bitwidth gradients. arXiv preprint arXiv:1606.06160 (2016)
21. Andri, R., Cavigelli, L., Rossi, D., Benini, L.: YodaNN: an architecture for ultralow power binary-weight CNN acceleration. IEEE Trans. Comput. Aided Des. Integr. Circuits Syst. **37**(1), 48–60 (2017)
22. Umuroglu, Y., et al.: FINN: a framework for fast, scalable binarized neural network inference. In: Proceedings of the 2017 ACM/SIGDA International Symposium on Field-Programmable Gate Arrays, pp. 65–74 (2017)
23. Rastegari, M., Ordonez, V., Redmon, J., Farhadi, A.: XNOR-Net: ImageNet classification using binary convolutional neural networks. In: European Conference on Computer Vision, pp. 525–542. Cham: Springer International Publishing (2016)

Memory-Enhanced Invariant Prompt Learning for Urban Flow Prediction Under Distribution Shifts

Haiyang Jiang[1], Tong Chen[1(✉)], Wentao Zhang[2], Quoc Viet Hung Nguyen[3], Yuan Yuan[4], Yong Li[4], and Hongzhi Yin[1]

[1] The University of Queensland, Brisbane, QLD, Australia
{haiyang.jiang,tong.chen}@uq.edu.au
[2] Peking University, Beijing, China
wentao.zhang@pku.edu.cn
[3] Griffith University, Gold Coast, Australia
[4] Tsinghua University, Beijing, China
y-yuan20@mails.tsinghua.edu.cn, liyong07@tsinghua.edu.cn

Abstract. While Spatial-Temporal Graph Neural Networks (STGNNs) excel at urban flow prediction, they struggle with distribution shifts caused by dynamic spatial-temporal environments. To improve generalizability to out-of-distribution (OOD) data, a typical solution is to disentangle invariant patterns that carry stable causal effects from variant ones that are environment-dependent. Existing OOD-robust methods attempt to model these environments but face challenges in quantifying dynamic changes and suffer from high computational costs. As a solution, we propose Memory-enhanced Invariant Prompt Learning (MIP), which enables environmental interventions directly within the latent space by learning a memory bank from the spatial-temporal urban flow graphs. Then, by performing spatial-temporal interventions on the variant prompts, diverse environments are constructed in the latent space to facilitate invariant learning. The invariant prompts, together with a memory-enhanced causal graph, are fed into an STGNN backbone to produce accurate predictions. Extensive experiments on two public urban flow datasets confirm MIP's effectiveness in improving robustness against OOD data.

Keywords: Spatial-temporal Graph Neural Networks · Out-of-distribution Generalization · Invariant Learning

1 Introduction

Urban flow prediction, which forecasts traffic, pedestrian, and public transportation dynamics, is crucial for smart cities [18], public transit management [7,33],

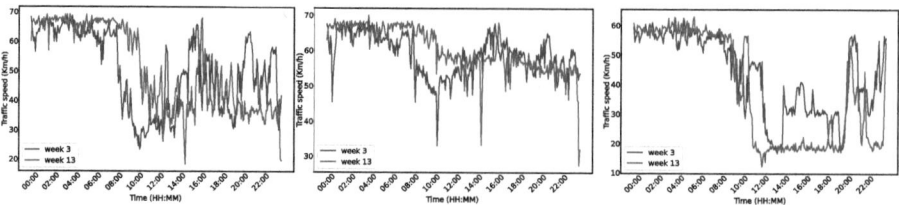

(a) Traffic speed at node A. (b) Traffic speed at node B. (c) Traffic speed at node C.

Fig. 1. The sampled traffic speed recorded by three sensors in the METR-LA dataset, where nodes B and C are two closest sensors of Node A. The records correspond to two Wednesdays in the 3rd and 13th weeks of the dataset.

and ride-sharing services [4,37]. Typically modeled as a spatial-temporal graph, nodes (e.g., traffic sensors or geographical grids [29]) in urban flow are connected based on proximity, with the goal of predicting future traffic flow at each node. To effectively model these spatial-temporal dependencies, recent solutions are built upon deep learning-based approaches, particularly Spatial-Temporal Graph Neural Networks (STGNNs) [17,33,36]. These models leverage Graph Neural Networks (GNNs) [17,33] to capture spatial correlations and sequential models like Recurrent Neural Networks (RNNs) [17,20] and Temporal Convolution Networks (TCNs) [33,36] for learning temporal dependencies. Some STGNNs further enhance predictions by incorporating dynamic graph structures based on temporal feature similarities [3,26,34] or modeling complex spatial-temporal interactions [6,12].

Most STGNNs operate under the assumption that urban flow data adheres to the independent and identically distributed (I.I.D.) nature, which rarely holds true in real-world scenarios. In reality, once deployed, a trained model may need to perform inference on unseen data with patterns that are distinct significantly from the training data, a phenomenon referred to as distribution shift or out-of-distribution (OOD) during the test phase. Figure 1 provides a real example from the METR-LA traffic dataset (see Sect. 5 for details), which demonstrates the traffic of three locations on two Wednesdays. Firstly, urban flow exhibits *continuous distribution shifts*. For each of the three geographic nodes, the two traffic records demonstrate entirely different patterns. Such continuous distribution shifts at each location disrupt long-term spatial-temporal patterns and hinder the generalizability of STGNNs. Secondly, there are *heterogeneous shifts across locations*. Although both nodes B and C are adjacent to node A, their patterns shift in distinct manners. This discrepancy complicates spatial correlations, as GNNs propagate noise from affected nodes. In urban flow prediction, spatial-temporal regularities can be easily disrupted by unexpected events such as traffic accidents or extreme weather. Moreover, during inference, it is generally impractical to assume prior knowledge about the occurrence of such perturbations that result in OOD data, thereby compromising prediction accuracy and diminishing the effectiveness of existing STGNNs. While frequent retraining can alleviate this issue, it is computationally prohibitive in such high-throughput applications. Thus, before entering the update cycle, an ideal STGNN should stay accurate for a reasonable period of time by generalizing to changed data distributions.

With the presence of distribution shifts in urban flow prediction, a key to enhancing the generalizability of STGNNs is to discover and leverage the invariant (i.e., causal) patterns within spatial-temporal data. Many studies on OOD generalization [1,25] point out that distribution shifts are driven by the dynamics of underlying environments, where invariant risk minimization [2,22,31] can be leveraged to optimize the model with augmented data drawn from diverse environments. As such, some methods [23,24] decouple invariant patterns from variant ones learned from the data. For example, when handling graph-structured data, [5,32,38] learn two disentangled graph structures that contain either invariant or variant connections between nodes. Unfortunately, these models are misaligned with urban flow prediction tasks as they only focus on a static graph topology that does not assume the temporal evolution of node features.

To this end, we aim to build an OOD-robust STGNN that can distinguish invariant spatial-temporal patterns from urban flow data. Specifically, we propose Memory-enhanced Invariant Prompt learning (MIP), a novel solution to urban flow prediction. In MIP, we attach a memory bank to the STGNN architecture, which learns and memorizes the causal patterns from the dynamic node features. Based on the information stored in the memory bank, a new graph structure reflecting the semantic causality between different locations is built, providing a complementary graph view to the default, distance-based graph structure for node representation learning. Then, the prompt vectors carrying invariant or variant patterns are extracted respectively by attentively querying the memory bank with each node's features. Furthermore, to facilitate end-to-end optimization via invariant risk minimization and ensure disentanglement between invariant and variant patterns, we put forward an innovative intervention pipeline that directly operates on the extracted variant prompts. Different from existing invariant learning methods [35,40], MIP bypasses the need for learning additional representations of different environments, and the designed intervention is a simple-yet-effective approach for implicitly mimicking the effect from data distribution shifts to node representations. The disentangled invariant patterns, along with both the geographical and causal graphs, are eventually fed into a spatial-temporal backbone model to make accurate urban flow predictions. To be concise, our contributions are summarized below:

- **New Challenge.** We highlight a largely overlooked challenge in urban flow prediction: the pervasive presence of OOD data that hinders model generalizability. To address this, we propose a new framework, namely MIP to mitigate distribution shifts in urban flow prediction.
- **New Method.** We extract invariant and variant features from a trainable memory bank and generate a supplementary graph structure. By implementing interventions on variant patterns and leveraging an invariant learning

scheme, the invariant patterns are disentangled from the noisy data to facilitate accurate predictions.
– **State-of-the-art Performance.** Extensive experiments on two real-world benchmark datasets have demonstrated the superiority of our method over state-of-the-art baselines when faced with OOD urban flow data.

2 Related Work

2.1 Deep Learning for Urban Flow Prediction

Recently, spatial-temporal neural networks (STGNNs) have established themselves as state-of-the-art choices for urban flow prediction. STGNNs consist of GNN-based modules and sequential models that are alternately stacked, where typical variants include DCRNN [17], GWNet [33], STGCN [36] and ST-MGCN [9]. Furthermore, attention mechanisms, including multi-head attention, are additionally used in fusing spatial and temporal information, such as GMAN [39], ASTGCN [10], and PDFormer [13]. Moreover, introducing some trainable features can also improve the performance of STGNNs, even with naive backbone models, such as STID [27], STAEformer [21], and MegaCRN [14]. Besides, some physical theories can also guide spatial-temporal prediction, such as PGML [15] and STDEN [11]. However, these methods are designed based on the I.I.D assumption, making the extracted patterns solely dependent on the observed samples. Thus, these methods are prone to incorrect predictions when facing unobserved data with distribution shifts.

2.2 Handling Out-of-Distribution (OOD) Data in Prediction

There are some models [23,35,40] dedicated to overcoming distribution shifts in spatial-temporal data. For example, CaST [35] disentangles the environmental feature and the entity feature based on causal treatments [23], and it replaces the environment feature with the vector closest to it in the environment codebook, which contains vectors representing environments. CauSTG [40] designs a hierarchical invariance explorer, which merges the models trained across various environments. STONE [28] learns both spatial and temporal similarity matrices as adjacency matrices for STGNN to make predictions and implements intervention by masking these two adjacency matrices. By differentiating raw data from distinct environments, the aforementioned methods can capture data exhibiting distribution shifts, enabling STGNNs to learn features across diverse distributions. Consequently, STGNNs can achieve accurate predictions on OOD data. However, these methods are heavily dependent on specifically designed model mechanisms and exhibit high sensitivity to the number of virtual environments.

3 Preliminaries

3.1 Problem Formulation

In urban flow data, a geolocation graph can be defined as: $\mathcal{G} = \{\mathcal{V}, \mathcal{E}\}$, where $\mathcal{V}$ is the set of N nodes and $\mathcal{E}$ is the set of edges. Correspondingly, $\mathbf{A} \in \{0,1\}^{N \times N}$ is the derived adjacency matrix. In $\mathcal{G}$, a node is a spatial object like a traffic sensor, where the edges between nodes are commonly established by thresholding their physical distances [33,36], thus $\mathbf{A}$ is constant in this task. At each time step $1 \leq t \leq T$, all nodes' dynamic features are represented via a matrix $\mathbf{X}^t \in \mathbb{R}^{N \times k}$, with k representing the dimensionality of time-varying features. Following the commonly adopted setting [33], given the observed T historical observations $\{\mathbf{X}^t\}_{t=1}^T$ and the geolocation graph $\mathcal{G}$, the task objective is to train a model that predicts the next T urban flow signals $\{\mathbf{X}^{t'}\}_{t'=T+1}^{2T}$:

$$\mathbf{Y} \simeq f_\theta(\mathbf{X}, \mathcal{G}), \tag{1}$$

where $\mathbf{X}, \mathbf{Y} \in \mathbb{R}^{T \times N \times k}$ are respectively the tensorized versions of input $\{\mathbf{X}^t\}_{t=1}^T$ and output $\{\mathbf{X}^{t'}\}_{t'=T+1}^{2T}$, and $f_\theta(\cdot)$ is the prediction model parameterized by θ.

Usually, the optimization of θ is based on the I.I.D assumption, which means the training and test samples are drawn from the same distribution. In urban flow prediction, this assumption can hardly be guaranteed as the training and test data points are drawn from different environments, respectively denoted by E_{train} and E_{test}. Thus, the optimal model parameter θ^* should achieve minimal generalization error on an OOD test set, described as follows:

$$\min \mathbb{E}_{(\mathbf{X}',\mathbf{Y}') \sim p(\mathbf{X}',\mathbf{Y}'|E_{test})} \mathcal{L}(f_\theta(\mathbf{X}', \mathcal{G}), \mathbf{Y}'),$$
$$s.t.\ \theta^* = \arg\min_\theta \mathbb{E}_{(\mathbf{X},\mathbf{Y}) \sim p(\mathbf{X},\mathbf{Y}|E_{train})} \mathcal{L}(f_\theta(\mathbf{X}, \mathcal{G}), \mathbf{Y}),\ E_{train} \neq E_{test}, \tag{2}$$

where $\mathcal{L}(\cdot)$ quantifies the prediction error.

3.2 Invariant Learning Under Distribution Shifts

Let $\mathbf{H}_I, \mathbf{H}_V \in \mathbb{R}^{T \times N \times d}$ respectively denote all $T \times N$ variant and invariant patterns with dimensionality d extracted from input $\mathbf{X}$. Drawing on causality theory [23,24], there exists a prediction function $\mathrm{pred}(\cdot)$, for which the invariant feature $\mathbf{H}_I$ is sufficiently predictive for $\mathbf{Y}$ and the variant feature $\mathbf{H}_V$ does not hold causation to $\mathbf{Y}$ [32,38]. Given that, we can rewrite our objective below:

$$\arg\min_{\theta,\psi} \mathbb{E}_{(\mathbf{X},\mathbf{Y}) \sim p(\mathbf{X},\mathbf{Y}|E_{train})} \mathcal{L}(f_\theta(\mathbf{H}_I, \mathcal{G}), \mathbf{Y}),$$
$$s.t.\ \mathbf{H}_I, \mathbf{H}_V = f_\psi(\mathbf{X}),\ \mathbf{Y} \perp \mathbf{H}_V | \mathbf{H}_I, \tag{3}$$

where we use $\mathbf{H}_I, \mathbf{H}_V \in \mathbb{R}^{T \times N \times d}$ to respectively denote all $T \times N$ variant and invariant patterns with dimensionality d extracted from input $\mathbf{X}$. Here, $f_\psi(\cdot)$ is the invariant learning backbone model parameterized by ψ that disentangles invariant patterns with the variant ones from the dynamic node features. In this setup, the prediction model f_θ is only fed with the invariant patterns to derive final predictions. Based on the formulation, a key step is to train $f_\psi(\cdot)$ towards distinguishing invariant and variant patterns. To achieve this, based on the interventional distribution in causality theory [32], a common objective can be described following invariant learning loss:

$$\min_\psi \mathbb{E}_{(\hat{\mathbf{X}},\mathbf{Y}) \sim p(\hat{\mathbf{X}},\mathbf{Y}|\hat{E})} \mathcal{L}(\mathrm{pred}(f_\psi(\hat{\mathbf{X}}), \mathcal{G}), \mathbf{Y})$$
$$+ \lambda Var_{(\hat{\mathbf{X}},\mathbf{Y}) \sim p(\hat{\mathbf{X}},\mathbf{Y}|\hat{E})} \mathcal{L}(\mathrm{pred}(f_\psi(\hat{\mathbf{X}}), \mathcal{G}), \mathbf{Y}), \tag{4}$$

where $\hat{E} \neq E_{train}$ denotes an intervention sampled from an intervention set, which imposes changes on the original environment and leads to features $\hat{\mathbf{X}} \neq \mathbf{X}$ with shifted distributions. Ideally, $\hat{E}$ only performs intervention on variant patterns, leaving the invariant features unaffected. pred($\cdot$) denotes a predictor that uses both invariant and variant patterns emitted by $f_\psi(\hat{\mathbf{X}})$ to predict the ground truth label. Note that as pred($\cdot$) is not responsible for generating the final predictions, it does not necessarily share the same structure or parameterization with $f_\theta(\cdot)$. The first term minimizes the prediction loss, whereas in the second term, Var denotes the variance and λ is a balancing hyperparameter. As the variant patterns are unrelated to the label $\mathbf{Y}$, the prediction should remain stable regardless of the variant patterns introduced by $\hat{E}$, translating into a lower variance. As such, $f_\psi(\cdot)$ is trained to differentiate invariant patterns $\mathbf{H}_I$ and variant patterns $\mathbf{H}_V$ amid distribution shifts in urban flow.

4 MIP: The Proposed Method

In this section, we introduce a universal framework named Memory-enhanced Invariant Prompt learning (MIP) for urban flow prediction under OOD scenarios, whose main components are depicted in Fig. 2. In what follows, we unfold the design of MIP by introducing the design of the memory bank, as well as the backbones for invariant learning (i.e., $f_\psi(\cdot)$) and spatial-temporal prediction (i.e., $f_\theta(\cdot)$) backbone model.

4.1 Memory-Enhanced Invariant Prompt Learning

A key advantage of MIP is that rather than generating intervened environments $\hat{E}$ and simulating changes in latent patterns, it directly intervenes in the latent space to mimic representation changes after intervention. To do this, we first mine latent patterns correlated with predicted labels from time-varying node features. Therefore, we extract and store these representative causal features with a memory bank [14]. The memory bank can be represented as $\mathbf{\Phi} \in \mathbb{R}^{M \times d}$, where M and d represent the number of virtual nodes and their dimensions, respectively. Essentially, each of the M virtual nodes in the memory bank is assigned a d-dimensional prototype vector $\mathbf{\Phi}[m] \in \mathbb{R}^d$ ($m \leq M$) that summarizes a part of the latent, invariant features within the spatial-temporal node features $\mathbf{X}$. The memory bank $\mathbf{\Phi}$ supports two subsequent computations: generating variant and invariant prompts through a querying process as described below, and providing a causal graph to supplement the geographical graph for node representation learning as described in Sect. 4.3.

Learning Invariant and Variant Prompts. As a core part of OOD generalization, given all nodes' temporal features $\mathbf{X}^t \in \mathbb{R}^{N \times k}$ at time t, MIP extracts both causal and spurious patterns from them – which we term invariant and variant prompts in this work. To do this, we firstly project $\mathbf{X}^t$ into a query matrix $\mathbf{Q}_t \in \mathbb{R}^{N \times d}$:

$$\mathbf{Q}_t = \mathbf{X}_t \mathbf{W}_Q + \mathbf{b}_Q, \tag{5}$$

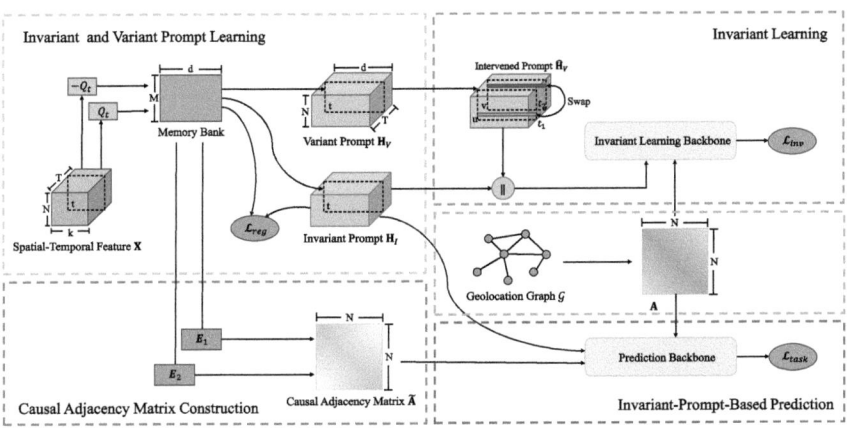

Fig. 2. The main components of MIP.

where $\mathbf{W}_Q \in \mathbb{R}^{k \times d}$ and $\mathbf{b}_Q \in \mathbb{R}^d$ are trainable parameters of the linear layer. As $\mathbf{Q}_t$ contains both invariant and variant patterns, we further disentangle them by querying the invariant memory bank. To obtain invariant prompts, we multiply the query matrix $\mathbf{Q}_t$ with the memory bank $\mathbf{\Phi}$ to obtain an affinity matrix $\mathbf{S}_I^t$, based on which the invariant prompt can be drawn from the memory bank in a self-attentive fashion. This process can be formulated as:

$$\mathbf{H}_I^t = \mathbf{S}_I^t \mathbf{\Phi}, \ \mathbf{S}_I^t = \mathrm{softmax}\left(\mathbf{Q}_t \mathbf{\Phi}^\top\right), \tag{6}$$

where $\mathbf{H}_I^t \in \mathbb{R}^{N \times d}$ is the computed invariant prompt. Similarly, the variant prompt can be extracted in an analogous process, with a minor modification:

$$\mathbf{H}_V^t = \mathbf{S}_V^t \mathbf{\Phi}, \ \mathbf{S}_V^t = \mathrm{softmax}\left(-1 \cdot \mathbf{Q}_t \mathbf{\Phi}^\top\right), \tag{7}$$

where negation is applied before the softmax function, so as to flip the score distribution and assign higher weights to invariant patterns that are less relevant to the memory $\mathbf{\Phi}$. As this is executed for all time steps, we can obtain a sequence of T prompts $\{\mathbf{H}_I^1, \mathbf{H}_I^2, ..., \mathbf{H}_I^T\}$ and $\{\mathbf{H}_V^1, \mathbf{H}_V^2, ..., \mathbf{H}_V^T\}$. By respectively concatenating invariant and variant prompts across time, we can obtain two prompt tensors $\mathbf{H}_I, \mathbf{H}_V \in \mathbf{R}^{T \times N \times d}$ for subsequent computations.

4.2 Invariant Learning with Latent Intervention

As per our discussions earlier, the variant prompt $\mathbf{H}_V$ is environment-dependent but unrelated to the label $\mathbf{Y}$, and the invariant prompt $\mathbf{H}_I$ is causally linked to $\mathbf{Y}$. To distill $\mathbf{H}_I$ from $\mathbf{X}$, a common approach as described in Sect. 3.2 is to perform invariant learning with intervened raw data $\hat{\mathbf{X}}$. However, directly intervening the raw data is a less favorable option for urban flow prediction tasks due to the risk of introducing additional noises, while some workarounds [30,32, 35] need to additionally parameterize and learn the underlying environments

Algorithm 1. INTERVENE($\mathbf{H}_V, r$)

1: **Input**: Variant prompt tensor $\mathbf{H}_V \in \mathbb{R}^{T \times N \times d}$, intervention rate r
2: **Output**: Intervened variant prompt $\hat{\mathbf{H}}_V \in \mathbb{R}^{T \times N \times d}$
3: $\hat{\mathbf{H}}_V \leftarrow \mathbf{H}_V$
4: **for** s=1,2,...,$\lfloor \frac{rN}{2} \rfloor$ **do**
5:    Randomly sample a node pair (w, v) s.t. $w, v \in [1, N]$;
6:    Randomly select a time step pair (i, j) s.t. $i, j \in [1, T]$;
7:    $\hat{\mathbf{H}}_V[i, w] \leftarrow \mathbf{H}_V[j, v], \hat{\mathbf{H}}_V[j, v] \leftarrow \mathbf{H}_V[i, w]$;
8: **end for**
9: **return** $\hat{\mathbf{H}}_V$

---

in order to alter the raw data distribution. Also, when STGNNs are used as the predictor pred($\cdot$), multiple complex forward passes are required to optimize Eq.(4), which is computationally impractical considering the large spatial and temporal spans N and T in urban flow graphs.

Latent Intervention Mechanism. In this paper, we innovatively propose to generate spatial-temporal interventions in the latent space, which more effectively mimics the changes in the learnable patterns after possible distribution shifts within the input data. Specifically, given the extracted variant prompts $\mathbf{H}_V$, we exchange features in $\mathbf{H}_V$ between different nodes and time points with a predefined rate r. The details of the latent intervention mechanism are described in Algorithm 1. To be succinct, we simplify this process into the following:

$$\hat{\mathbf{H}}_V = \text{INTERVENE}(\mathbf{H}_V, r), \tag{8}$$

where $\hat{\mathbf{H}}_V$ denotes the intervened variant prompts after rN feature exchanges between nodes have taken place. Note that, the swap is not constrained to node features at the same time step, so as to account for the spatial-temporal fluctuations within the variant patterns. Also, by producing intervened variant prompts with representations learned from the original input data, the generated $\hat{\mathbf{H}}_V$ remains plausible and challenging for refining the invariant prompts $\hat{\mathbf{H}}_I$.

Invariant Learning. After obtaining the intervened variant prompts $\hat{\mathbf{H}}_V$, we are able to train the prompt extractor described in Sect. 4.1 via invariant learning, so as to distinguish the invariant and variant prompts. To achieve this, the invariant and the intervened variant prompts are concatenated and then input into a supplementary predictor pred($\cdot$) to generate predictions:

$$\tilde{\mathbf{Y}} = \text{pred}(\mathbf{H}_I || \hat{\mathbf{H}}_V, \mathbf{A}), \tag{9}$$

where $||$ denotes tensor concatenation along the last dimension, $\tilde{\mathbf{Y}} \in \mathbb{R}^{T \times N \times k}$ is the predicted urban flow at all locations and time steps. The choice of pred($\cdot$) is flexible with most STGNNs. Since pred($\cdot$) is only responsible for differentiating invariant and variant prompts and will not be used for computing the final predictions, we adopt GWNet [33], a simple yet effective STGNN as pred($\cdot$). For training, we first define the loss for a single node n at one time step t:

$$l(t,n) = \frac{1}{k}\sum_{k'=1}^{k} |\tilde{\mathbf{Y}}[t,n,k'] - \mathbf{Y}[t,n,k']|, \tag{10}$$

based on which the invariant learning loss is defined:

$$\mathcal{L}_{inv} = \mathbb{E}_{(t,n)}l(t,n) + \lambda_1 Var_{(t,n)}l(t,n), \ t \in [1,T], \ n \in [1,N], \tag{11}$$

where the first and second terms respectively reduce the mean and variance of the prediction error across locations and time steps. More specifically, the first term ensures that pred($\cdot$) is optimized towards correctly predicting the urban flow in different environments with $\mathbf{H}_I$, while the second term enforces that when the predictions are conditioned on $\mathbf{H}_I$, there are minimal performance fluctuations despite the presence of noisy signals from intervened variant prompts $\mathbf{H}_V$.

4.3 Urban Flow Prediction with Causal Graph Generation

Once the invariant features $\mathbf{H}_I$ are extracted, a spatial-temporal backbone model is in place for producing the final predictions. In MIP, our backbone model consists of alternately stacked GNN layers and temporal Transformer layers, which take invariant prompts $\mathbf{H}_I$ and adjacency matrix $\mathbf{A}$ as its input. However, $\mathbf{A}$ is normally constructed solely based on the physical distances between nodes. As a result, this can introduce biases during GNN's information propagation, because geographic proximity does not necessarily imply similar temporal patterns, especially in OOD scenarios. In this section, we introduce a memory-based approach for generating a causal graph as a supplement to $\mathbf{A}$, followed by details of the backbone STGNN.

Causal Graph Generation. To address the limitation of the geolocation graph that is purely distance-based, we introduce an auxiliary graph based on the semantic distance between causal node representations, which are constructed from highly invariant features from the memory bank $\mathbf{\Phi}$. This causal graph complements the geolocation-based graph, thus providing additional predictive signals. This memory bank-based causal graph is constructed as the following:

$$\tilde{\mathbf{A}} = \text{softmax}\left(\mathbf{E}_1 \mathbf{E}_2^\top\right), \ \mathbf{E}_1 = \mathbf{W}_A \mathbf{\Phi}, \ \mathbf{E}_2 = \mathbf{W}_B \mathbf{\Phi}, \tag{12}$$

where $\mathbf{W}_A, \mathbf{W}_B \in \mathbb{R}^{N \times M}$ are trainable projection matrices that map the M prototype vectors in the memory bank into N node representations $\mathbf{E}_1$ and $\mathbf{E}_2$. As the memory bank already encapsulates critical information about the urban flow, the newly developed causal adjacency matrix provides additional information propagation channels between nodes.

GNN Layer. The GNN layer is fed with both the geographical and causal adjacency matrices $\mathbf{A}, \tilde{\mathbf{A}}$ and the invariant prompts $\mathbf{H}_I$ to learn node representations with information propagation. Since the geographical adjacency matrix $\mathbf{A}$ is symmetric and hardly captures the directed nature of interactions in urban flow data, we derive forward and backward transition matrices from $\mathbf{A}$ through a bidirectional, degree-weighted random walk [17]:

$$\mathbf{P}_f = \mathbf{D}^{-1}\mathbf{A}, \ \mathbf{P}_b = (\mathbf{D}^\top)^{-1}\mathbf{A}^\top, \tag{13}$$

where $\mathbf{D}$ is the degree matrix of $\mathbf{A}$. It is worth mentioning that, the GNN layer processes each time step t separately. By incorporating the causal adjacency matrix, for each time step t, the propagation process in the GNN from layer l to $l+1$ is summarized as follows:

$$\mathbf{G}_{l+1}^t = \sum_{z=0}^{Z}(\mathbf{P}_f^z \mathbf{G}_l^t \mathbf{W}_1^z + \mathbf{P}_b^z \mathbf{G}_l^t \mathbf{W}_2^z + \tilde{\mathbf{A}}^z \mathbf{G}_l^t \mathbf{W}_3^z), \qquad (14)$$

where $z \leq Z$ controls the order of the information propagation, and $\mathbf{W}^{(k)} \in \mathbb{R}^{d \times d}$ denotes the learnable weights. Note that the initial node embeddings are set to $\mathbf{G}_0^t = \mathbf{H}_I^t$ when $l = 0$.

Temporal Transformer Layer. Once the GNN layer processes all graphs at all time steps, we can collect T feature matrices produced by the final graph propagation layer, denoted by $\mathbf{G}^1, \mathbf{G}^2, ..., \mathbf{G}^T \in \mathbb{R}^{N \times d}$. For a certain node n, we can stack all its d-dimensional, time-sensitive features across T steps into a matrix, denoted by $\mathbf{G}_n \in \mathbb{R}^{T \times d}$. With that, we learn the dependencies across all temporal features of a node through a transformer layer as:

$$\begin{aligned}\mathbf{G}_n' &= \mathrm{softmax}\left(\frac{\mathbf{G}_n \mathbf{W}_Q (\mathbf{G}_n \mathbf{W}_K)^\top}{\sqrt{d}}\right)(\mathbf{G}_n \mathbf{W}_V), \\ \mathbf{Z}_n &= \mathrm{MLP}(\mathbf{G}_n'),\end{aligned} \qquad (15)$$

where $\mathbf{W}_Q, \mathbf{W}_K, \mathbf{W}_V \in \mathbb{R}^{d \times d}$ are trainable query, key and value projection weights, and $\mathrm{MLP}(\cdot)$ denotes a feedforward multilayer perceptron.

Prediction Layer. After obtaining N outputs for all nodes $\mathbf{H}_1', \mathbf{H}_2', ..., \mathbf{H}_N' \in \mathbb{R}^{T \times d}$, we can stack all feature matrices into $\mathbf{Z} \in \mathbb{R}^{T \times N \times d}$. Then, we generate the final predictions with an MLP:

$$\hat{\mathbf{Y}} = \mathrm{MLP}(\mathbf{Z}), \qquad (16)$$

where the MLP projects $\mathbf{Z}$ into $\hat{\mathbf{Y}} \in \mathbb{R}^{T \times N \times k}$ that carries the predicted urban flow per time step per location.

4.4 Model Optimization

Now, we detail the optimization strategy for MIP. Firstly, based on the prediction $\hat{\mathbf{Y}} \in \mathbb{R}^{L \times N \times k}$ generated by the backbone model, the prediction error is as follows:

$$\mathcal{L}_{task} = \frac{1}{TN} \sum_{t,n,k'=1}^{T,N,k} |\hat{\mathbf{Y}}[t, n, k'] - \mathbf{Y}[t, n, k']|. \qquad (17)$$

In addition, as we extract invariant prompts from a memory bank, we use an auxiliary regularization loss to enhance the quality of features stored within the memory bank:

$$\mathcal{L}_{reg} = \sum_{t,n}^{T,N} \max\left\{\|\mathbf{H}_I^t[n]-\mathbf{\Phi}[a]\|^2 - \|\mathbf{H}_I^t[n]-\mathbf{\Phi}[b]\|^2 + \kappa, 0\right\} + \sum_{t,n}^{T,N} \|\mathbf{H}_I^t[n]-\mathbf{\Phi}[a]\|^2, \tag{18}$$

where κ is a distance margin, a, b are the indices of the most and second similar virtual nodes w.r.t. node n based on the affinity score $\mathbf{S}_I^t$ computed in Eq.(6). As such, $\mathcal{L}_{reg}$ encourages diversity within the information encoded by different virtual node prototype vectors in the memory bank. Finally, the optimization objective aims to minimize the following overall loss:

$$\mathcal{L} = \mathcal{L}_{task} + \mathcal{L}_{inv} + \lambda_2 \mathcal{L}_{reg}, \tag{19}$$

with a balancing hyperparameter λ_2. As MIP is being trained towards convergence, the intervention on variant patterns, i.e., $\hat{\mathbf{H}}_V = \text{Intervene}(\mathbf{H}_V, r)$ is re-executed in every training epoch, so as to inject more variations in the supervision signals. It is worth noting that, once MIP is trained, only the spatial-temporal backbone model described in Sect. 4.3 is activated for making predictions in the inference stage.

5 Experiments

5.1 Experimental Settings

We evaluate our model on two well-established benchmarks, namely METR-LA [17] and NYCBike [37]. METR-LA [17] is a traffic speed prediction dataset collected with 207 sensors across Los Angeles, from 1st March 2012 to 30th June 2012, the data points are sampled with 5 5-minute time interval. NYCBike1 [37] is a dataset of bike rental records from 1st April 2014 to 30th September in New York City, where the city is divided into 8 × 16 equally-sized grids, and the data points are sampled with a 1-hour time interval. As NYCBike1 records both in and out flows of bikes, we treat them as two prediction tasks and respectively denote them as NYCBike1 (In) and NYCBike1 (Out).

We split both datasets chronologically: the first 60% is for training, the following 10% for validation, and three test sets are constructed by evenly slicing the remaining data (10% for each). This is to fully mimic real-world application scenarios where a trained model is expected to provide predictions for multiple consecutive time periods with varying distributions. For convenience, we number the tree test sets with 0, 1, and 2. Generally, as test sets 0–2 become farther apart from the training set in time, their distribution shifts tend to become stronger. Based on the number of time steps available, we predict the next 12 time steps based on the past 12 on METR-LA and predict the next 6 time steps based on the past 6 on NYCBike. We compare MIP with the following state-of-the-art baselines: STGCN [36], DCRNN [17],STNorm [8], GMSDR [19],MegaCRN [14], CauSTG [40], TESTAM [16]. Similar to previous studies [19,28,33], we evaluate all methods in terms of Mean Absolute Error (MAE), Root Mean Square Error

(RMSE), and Mean Absolute Percentage Error (MAPE). Hyperparameters and implementation notes are available in our released code: https://github.com/Ocean-Jiang0729/MIP.

Table 1. Performance comparison results. The best results are marked in bold and the second-best results are underlined.

METR-LA	test set 0			test set 1			test set 2			overall results		
	MAE	RMSE	MAPE	MAE	RMSE	MAPE	MAE	RMSE	MAPE	MAE	RMSE	MAPE
STGCN	3.33	7.15	10.14%	3.63	7.47	10.90%	3.63	7.58	10.21%	3.53	7.40	10.42%
DCRNN	3.33	7.28	10.01%	3.58	7.49	10.80%	3.69	7.87	10.41%	3.53	7.55	10.41%
STNorm	3.33	7.17	10.09%	3.65	7.57	11.16%	3.63	7.61	10.23%	3.53	7.45	10.49%
GMSDR	3.27	6.99	9.75%	**3.49**	7.36	10.83%	**3.50**	7.47	10.01%	**3.42**	7.27	10.20%
MegaCRN	**3.22**	7.05	9.69%	3.64	7.65	11.04%	3.79	8.00	10.75%	3.55	7.57	10.49%
CauSTG	3.33	7.08	9.86%	3.64	7.44	10.81%	3.66	7.55	10.10%	3.55	7.36	10.26%
TESTAM	3.36	7.33	9.56%	3.62	7.58	**10.26%**	3.69	7.89	9.98%	3.56	7.60	9.93%
MIP	3.28	**6.87**	**9.52%**	3.55	**7.19**	10.40%	3.57	**7.28**	**9.73%**	3.46	**7.11**	**9.88%**

NYCBike1 (In)	test set 0			test set 1			test set 2			overall results		
	MAE	RMSE	MAPE	MAE	RMSE	MAPE	MAE	RMSE	MAPE	MAE	RMSE	MAPE
STGCN	4.90	8.41	50.38%	4.69	7.55	51.11%	5.33	9.42	63.05%	4.97	8.46	54.84%
DCRNN	6.24	10.04	80.58%	5.90	9.18	77.03%	6.47	10.74	92.59%	6.20	9.99	83.40%
STNorm	4.83	8.52	46.49%	**4.53**	8.29	50.51%	5.28	9.37	56.21%	4.88	8.38	49.35%
GMSDR	5.10	8.96	48.70%	4.86	8.14	49.14%	5.41	9.68	61.02%	5.12	8.92	52.95%
MegaCRN	**4.62**	**7.96**	46.65%	5.15	8.87	55.35%	5.62	9.51	65.81%	5.13	8.78	55.93%
CauSTG	4.95	8.51	49.21%	4.83	**7.91**	49.47%	5.37	9.45	59.73%	5.05	8.63	52.80%
TESTAM	5.06	8.51	47.69%	5.18	8.38	49.23%	5.83	9.93	59.42%	5.04	8.66	51.13%
MIP	4.74	8.13	**45.10%**	4.56	7.27	**43.32%**	**5.26**	**9.18**	**55.27%**	**4.87**	**8.16**	**47.56%**

NYCBike1 (Out)	test set 0			test set 1			test set 2			overall results		
	MAE	RMSE	MAPE	MAE	RMSE	MAPE	MAE	RMSE	MAPE	MAE	RMSE	MAPE
STGCN	5.04	8.84	46.64%	4.78	7.83	47.81%	5.51	9.56	62.02%	5.11	8.74	52.16%
DCRNN	5.38	9.04	54.46%	4.97	7.84	52.51%	5.78	10.15	65.90%	5.38	9.01	57.62%
STNorm	5.19	9.23	44.80%	4.83	7.90	43.63%	5.57	9.70	58.47%	5.20	8.94	48.97%
GMSDR	4.98	8.75	45.79%	4.73	7.74	44.74%	5.55	9.56	60.67%	5.09	8.68	50.40%
MegaCRN	5.53	9.58	49.97%	5.13	8.49	48.76%	5.82	10.48	64.23%	5.49	9.51	54.32%
CauSTG	5.04	8.73	46.13%	4.95	8.04	46.68%	5.60	9.71	**56.65%**	5.20	8.83	49.82%
TESTAM	**4.88**	**8.45**	43.63%	5.08	8.59	46.03%	5.54	9.59	56.81%	5.16	8.88	48.82%
MIP	4.94	8.68	44.72%	**4.66**	**7.56**	**43.22%**	**5.51**	**9.45**	57.60%	**5.03**	**8.56**	**48.51%**

5.2 Performance Comparison with Baselines

We compare MIP with SOTA baselines, recording the final horizon matrices in Table 1. MIP consistently outperforms all baselines across the three test sets, demonstrating strong generalization, versatility, and adaptability in urban flow prediction. On the METR-LA dataset, as test set 0 is the closest to the training set, its

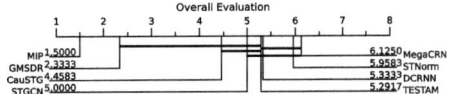

Fig. 3. Critical difference w.r.t. performance on all 9 test sets. Smaller scores indicate better performance.

distribution changes less than the other two test sets. Thus, the models achieve similar performance on test 0, and some baselines get the best result, such as the MAPE of MegaCRN on test set 0. However, the distribution shift happens more on test 1 and test 2, and the performance of all the models becomes worse. Some baseline models, such as MegaCRN, TESTAM, and GMSDR, get similar RMSE on test set 0, while their RMSE scores on test set 1 and test set 2 increase largely. On the NYCBike1 dataset, all the models perform well on test set 1 on both bikes' in and out tasks. A reasonable explanation is that the distribution of this test set is more similar to that of the training set. Although TESTAM achieved the best performance on all three evaluation matrices on test set 0, it performed worse on test sets 1 and 2, even with the biggest RMSE on test set 1. Notably, while some models outperform MIP on test set 0, they struggle with distribution shifts and consequently exhibit performance degradation on test set 2. Moreover, when evaluating these models across all test sets (referred to as overall results), our model consistently delivers superior performance across all evaluation metrics, with the sole exception of achieving second place in terms of MAE on the METR-LA dataset. In Fig. 3, we also calculate the critical difference diagram of all the models on all the datasets and evaluation matrices. By obtaining the highest rank among all 9 test sets, MIP demonstrates the ability to provide stable predictions across test sets that exhibit a variety of distribution shifts.

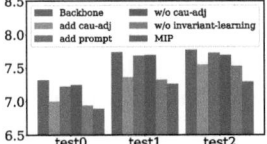
(a) METR-LA dataset.

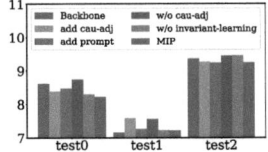
(b) NYCBike1 dataset(In).

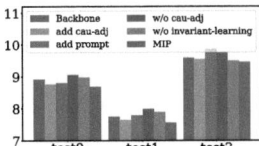
(c) NYCBike1 dataset(Out).

Fig. 4. Ablation study: RMSE of MIP and its variants.

5.3 Ablation Study

To explore the significance of each core component in MIP, we carry out an ablation study with the following variants: **Backbone** is the backbone model alone; **add cau-adj** only adds the causal adjacency matrix based on the backbone model; **add prompt** only feeds the prompt learned from the memory bank into the backbone model and omits the causal adjacency matrix and the invariant learning loss; **w/o cau-adj** removes the causal adjacency matrix; and **w/o invariant learning** removes the invariant loss.

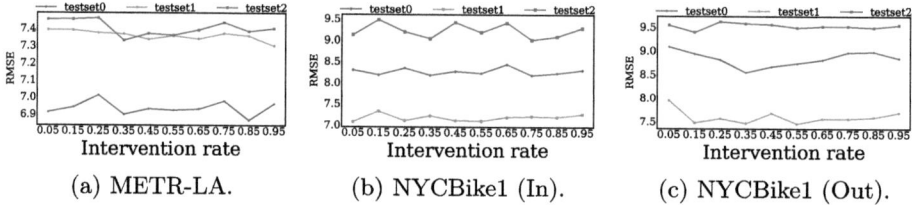

(a) METR-LA.   (b) NYCBike1 (In).   (c) NYCBike1 (Out).

Fig. 5. RMSE of MIP with different intervention rates.

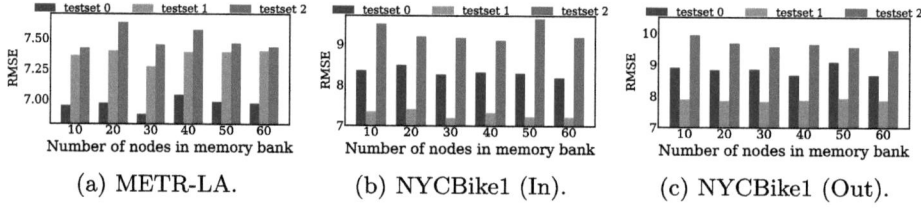

(a) METR-LA.   (b) NYCBike1 (In).   (c) NYCBike1 (Out).

Fig. 6. RMSE of MIP with different virtual node numbers in the memory bank.

The results are presented in Fig. 4. We can see that MIP beats all the variants on both datasets. The backbone model gets the worst results on most of the test sets, as the naive GNNs and temporal Transformer layers cannot capture the distribution shift and the heterophily of the node features. **add cau-adj** performs much better than the backbone model, even better than **add prompt** and **w/o cau-adj** sometimes, as the causal adjacency matrix connects nodes with similar urban flow data, even if they are far away from each other in topology. **add prompt** performs better than the backbone model, as it learns some useful features from the memory bank. The performance of **w/o cau-adj** decreases much more than **MIP**. Even though it distinguishes the invariant and variant prompts with the invariant learning loss, its RMSE is bigger than the **w/o invariant learning**. As the invariant prompts are propagated to their distance-based neighbours rather than their semantic-based neighbours, some nodes receive the opposite features from their own features. **w/o invariant** learning gets worse results than **MIP** as it mixes the invariant and variant prompts together for the absence of invariant learning.

5.4 Parameter Sensitivity Analysis

Intervention Rate : The intervention rate is closely related to the ability to separate the invariant and variant features. We set this parameter from 0.05 to 0.95 with an interval of 0.1, and evaluate our model on both datasets. In Fig. 5, we record the RMSE of the final horizon. The MIP demonstrates insensitivity to varying intervention rates, as evidenced by the small fluctuating RMSE across different levels of intervention. In the spatial-temporal model, the intervened variant prompts will propagate to all the nodes in an urban graph, even a small intervention rate will make all the nodes contain variant patterns before the prediction layer. Thus, the change in intervention rate does not influence the prediction RMSE.

Number of Nodes in Memory Bank: We investigate the sensitivity of the number of nodes in the memory bank and show the results in Fig. 6. The MIP performs well on all the datasets with 30 nodes in the memory bank. With a small number of nodes, MIP cannot extract high-quality invariant features due to the limited diversity. On the contrary, with more nodes in the memory bank, diverse invariant features lead to the increasing training difficulty of both the prediction model and the invariant learning backbone model.

The Weight Coefficients in The Loss Function: In Eq.(19), the loss function consists of task loss, invariant loss, and auxiliary loss. The composition ratio of the last two losses is controlled with hyperparameters λ_1 and λ_2, and we implement an experiment to investigate which one works better. Firstly, we

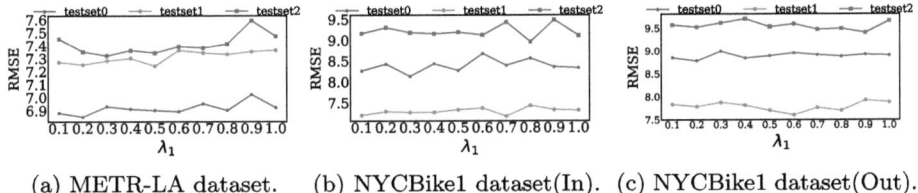

(a) METR-LA dataset.   (b) NYCBike1 dataset(In).   (c) NYCBike1 dataset(Out).

Fig. 7. RMSE of MIP with different settings of λ_1.

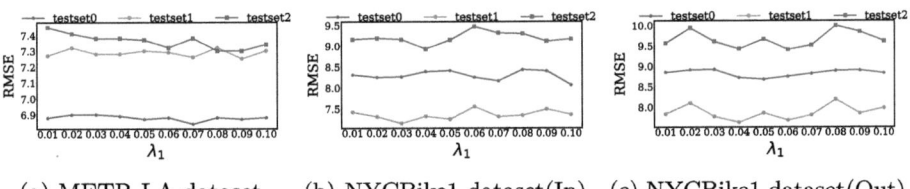

(a) METR-LA dataset.   (b) NYCBike1 dataset(In).   (c) NYCBike1 dataset(Out).

Fig. 8. RMSE of MIP with different settings of λ_2.

set $\lambda_2 = 0.01$, and λ_1 from 0.1 to 1.0, with a step as 0.1, and record the RMSE of the last horizon on both datasets in Fig. 7. On all the datasets, the RMSE of the test set 0 is stable, and it fluctuates on test sets 1 and 2. Concretely, on the METR-LA dataset, the model gets better generalization ability at λ_1 is 0.3, as the RMSE on the test set 2 is the smallest. As for the NYCBike1 dataset, the RMSE also fluctuates on test set 1 and test set 2, which indicates that the MIP is not sensitive to this hyper-parameter on this dataset. Furthermore, we set $\lambda_1 = 0.1$ and λ_2 from 0.01 to 0.1, with the step as 0.01, and the results are shown in Fig. 8. On all the datasets, the RMSE on test sets 0 and 1 fluctuates. On the METR-LA dataset, the RMSE on test set 2 gradually decreases as λ_2 rises, as there are more nodes in this dataset, the proportion of $\mathcal{L}_1$ and $\mathcal{L}_2$ should be larger to make sure the invariant prompt are diversity enough for all the nodes. While on the NYCBike1 dataset, the RMSE on test set 2 reaches the low point at about 0.04 or 0.05, as the number of nodes in this dataset is less than it in METR-LA, a low proportion of $\mathcal{L}_1$ and $\mathcal{L}_2$ can make the invariant prompt to be diversity enough for NYCBike1 dataset. All these experiments are carried out with 30 nodes in the memory bank.

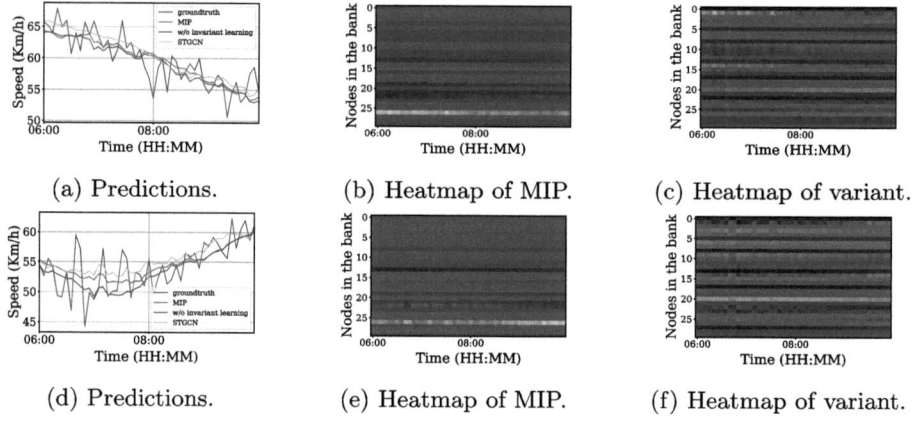

(a) Predictions. (b) Heatmap of MIP. (c) Heatmap of variant.

(d) Predictions. (e) Heatmap of MIP. (f) Heatmap of variant.

Fig. 9. Case study on MIP's prediction performance under distribution shifts.

5.5 Case Study

We further conduct a case study in Fig. 9, where we randomly select a sensor in the METR-LA dataset and visualize its real and predicted traffic speeds in test sets 0 and 2. To ensure a fair comparison, the same time period on Tuesday is used for this sensor. In Fig. 9a and 9d, the tendencies of ground truths are totally different, which means distribution shift happens. Moreover, the prediction of MIP is closest to the ground truth, while the variant model and the baseline make biased predictions. Furthermore, the heatmap of two prompt scores corresponding to each sample(Fig. 9b and 9c, Fig. 9e and 9f) show completely different distributions, the prompt score of MIP tend to select more feature from a certain memory node, while the variant tends to combine features from various memory nodes. This phenomenon demonstrates that invariant learning can help the model extract invariant prompts and overcome the OOD problem.

6 Conclusion

In this paper, we introduce a new framework named MIP to solve the distribution shift problem in urban flow prediction. MIP stores the most important informative signal during the training process in a memory bank. Then, a memory-based causal graph structure is generated based on the memory bank. Furthermore, the invariant and variant prompts are extracted from the memory bank and we design a spatial-temporal intervention mechanism to create diverse distribution and propose an invariance learning regularization to help the prompt extractor separate the invariant and variant prompts. Extensive experiments on two real-world datasets demonstrate that our method can better handle spatial-temporal distribution shifts than state-of-the-art baselines.

Acknowledgments. This work was partially supported by the Australian Research Council, under the streams of Future Fellowship (Grant No. FT210100624), Discovery Early Career Researcher Award (Grants No. DE230101033), Discovery Project (Grant No. DP240101108 and DP240101814), and Linkage Project (Grant No. LP230200892 and LP240200546).

References

1. Ahuja, K., Shanmugam, K., Varshney, K., Dhurandhar, A.: Invariant risk minimization games. In: ICML, pp. 145–155. PMLR (2020)
2. Arjovsky, M., Bottou, L., Gulrajani, I., Lopez-Paz, D.: Invariant risk minimization. arXiv preprint arXiv:1907.02893 (2019)
3. Bai, L., Yao, L., Li, C., Wang, X., Wang, C.: Adaptive graph convolutional recurrent network for traffic forecasting. NeurIPS **33**, 17804–17815 (2020)
4. Chen, C., Yao, F., Mo, D., Zhu, J., Chen, X.M.: Spatial-temporal pricing for ride-sourcing platform with reinforcement learning. Transp. Res. Part C: Emerg. Technol. **130**, 103272 (2021)
5. Chen, G., et al.: Causality and independence enhancement for biased node classification. In: CIKM, pp. 203–212 (2023)
6. Cini, A., Marisca, I., Zambon, D., Alippi, C.: Taming local effects in graph-based spatiotemporal forecasting. NeurIPS **36** (2024)
7. Cui, Y., et al.: Roi-demand traffic prediction: a pre-train, query and fine-tune framework. In: ICDE, pp. 1340–1352 (2023)
8. Deng, J., et al.: St-norm: spatial and temporal normalization for multi-variate time series forecasting. In: SIGKDD, pp. 269–278 (2021)
9. Geng, X., et al.: Spatiotemporal multi-graph convolution network for ride-hailing demand forecasting. In: AAAI, vol. 33, pp. 3656–3663 (2019)

10. Guo, S., Lin, Y., Feng, N., Song, C., Wan, H.: Attention based spatial-temporal graph convolutional networks for traffic flow forecasting. In: AAAI, vol. 33, pp. 922–929 (2019)
11. Ji, J., Wang, J., Jiang, Z., Jiang, J., Zhang, H.: STDEN: towards physics-guided neural networks for traffic flow prediction. In: AAAI, vol. 36, pp. 4048–4056 (2022)
12. Ji, J., et al.: Spatio-temporal self-supervised learning for traffic flow prediction. In: AAAI, vol. 37, pp. 4356–4364 (2023)
13. Jiang, J., et al.: PDFormer: propagation delay-aware dynamic long-range transformer for traffic flow prediction. In: AAAI. AAAI Press (2023)
14. Jiang, R., et al.: Spatio-temporal meta-graph learning for traffic forecasting. In: AAAI, vol. 37, pp. 8078–8086 (2023)
15. Jiang, W., et al.: Physics-guided active sample reweighting for urban flow prediction. arXiv preprint arXiv:2407.13605 (2024)
16. Lee, H., Ko, S.: Testam: a time-enhanced spatio-temporal attention model with mixture of experts. arXiv preprint arXiv:2403.02600 (2024)
17. Li, Y., Yu, R., Shahabi, C., Liu, Y.: Diffusion convolutional recurrent neural network: data-driven traffic forecasting. arXiv preprint arXiv:1707.01926 (2017)
18. Li, Z., Huang, C., Xia, L., Xu, Y., Pei, J.: Spatial-temporal hypergraph self-supervised learning for crime prediction. In: ICDE, pp. 2984–2996 (2022). https://doi.org/10.1109/ICDE53745.2022.00269
19. Liu, D., Wang, J., Shang, S., Han, P.: Msdr: Multi-step dependency relation networks for spatial temporal forecasting. In: SIGKDD, pp. 1042–1050 (2022)
20. Liu, H., Zhu, C., Zhang, D., Li, Q.: Attention-based spatial-temporal graph convolutional recurrent networks for traffic forecasting. In: International Conference on Advanced Data Mining and Applications, pp. 630–645. Springer (2023)
21. Liu, H., et al.: Spatio-temporal adaptive embedding makes vanilla transformer SOTA for traffic forecasting. In: CIKM, pp. 4125–4129 (2023)
22. Liu, Y., et al.: Flood: a flexible invariant learning framework for out-of-distribution generalization on graphs. In: SIGKDD, pp. 1548–1558 (2023)
23. Neuberg, L.G.: Causality: models, reasoning, and inference, by judea pearl, cambridge university press, 2000. Econ. Theory **19**(4), 675–685 (2003)
24. Pearl, J.: Causal inference in statistics: a primer. John Wiley and Sons (2016)
25. Rojas-Carulla, M., Schölkopf, B., Turner, R., Peters, J.: Invariant models for causal transfer learning. J. Mach. Learn. Res. **19**(36), 1–34 (2018)
26. Shang, C., Chen, J., Bi, J.: Discrete graph structure learning for forecasting multiple time series. arXiv preprint arXiv:2101.06861 (2021)
27. Shao, Z., Zhang, Z., Wang, F., Wei, W., Xu, Y.: Spatial-temporal identity: a simple yet effective baseline for multivariate time series forecasting. In: CIKM, pp. 4454–4458 (2022)
28. Wang, B., et al.: Stone: a spatio-temporal OOD learning framework kills both spatial and temporal shifts. In: SIGKDD, pp. 2948–2959 (2024)
29. Wang, Y., et al.: Gallat: a spatiotemporal graph attention network for passenger demand prediction. In: 2021 ICDE, pp. 2129–2134. IEEE (2021)
30. Wu, Q., Nie, F., Yang, C., Bao, T., Yan, J.: Graph out-of-distribution generalization via causal intervention. In: WWW, pp. 850–860 (2024)
31. Wu, Q., Zhang, H., Yan, J., Wipf, D.: Handling distribution shifts on graphs: an invariance perspective. arXiv preprint arXiv:2202.02466 (2022)
32. Wu, Y.X., Wang, X., Zhang, A., He, X., Chua, T.S.: Discovering invariant rationales for graph neural networks. arXiv preprint arXiv:2201.12872 (2022)
33. Wu, Z., Pan, S., Long, G., Jiang, J., Zhang, C.: Graph WaveNet for deep spatial-temporal graph modeling. arXiv preprint arXiv:1906.00121 (2019)

34. Wu, Z., et al.: Connecting the dots: multivariate time series forecasting with graph neural networks. In: SIGKDD, pp. 753–763 (2020)
35. Xia, Y., et al.: Deciphering spatio-temporal graph forecasting: a causal lens and treatment. NeurIPS **36** (2024)
36. Yu, B., Yin, H., Zhu, Z.: Spatio-temporal graph convolutional networks: a deep learning framework for traffic forecasting. IJCAI (2018)
37. Zhang, J., Zheng, Y., Qi, D.: Deep spatio-temporal residual networks for citywide crowd flows prediction. In: AAAI, vol. 31 (2017)
38. Zhang, Z., et al.: Dynamic graph neural networks under spatio-temporal distribution shift. NeurIPS **35**, 6074–6089 (2022)
39. Zheng, C., Fan, X., Wang, C., Qi, J.: GMAN: a graph multi-attention network for traffic prediction. In: AAAI, vol. 34, pp. 1234–1241 (2020)
40. Zhou, Z., et al.: Maintaining the status quo: Capturing invariant relations for OOD spatiotemporal learning. In: SIGKDD, pp. 3603–3614 (2023)

EDN: A Novel Edge-Dependent Noise Model for Graph Data

Pintu Kumar[✉] and Nandyala Hemachandra

Indian Institute of Technology Bombay, Mumbai, India
{pintuk,nh}@iitb.ac.in

Abstract. An important structural feature of a graph is its set of edges, as it captures the relationships among the nodes (the graph's topology). Existing node label noise models like Symmetric Label Noise (SLN) and Class Conditional Noise (CCN) disregard this important node relationship in graph data; and the Edge-Dependent Noise (EDN) model addresses this limitation. EDN posits that in real-world scenarios, label noise may be influenced by the connections between nodes. We explore three variants of EDN. A crucial notion that relates nodes and edges in a graph is the degree of a node; we show that in all three variants, the probability of a node's label corruption is dependent on its degree. Additionally, we compare the dependence of these probabilities on node degree across different variants. We performed experiments on popular graph datasets using 5 different GNN architectures and 8 noise robust algorithms for graph data. The results demonstrate that 2 variants of EDN lead to greater performance degradation in both Graph Neural Networks (GNNs) and existing noise-robust algorithms, as compared to traditional node label noise models. We statistically verify this by posing a suitable hypothesis-testing problem. This emphasizes the importance of incorporating EDN when evaluating noise robust algorithms for graphs, to enhance the reliability of graph-based learning in noisy environments. Link to code: https://github.com/pintu-dot/edn.

Keywords: Graph Learning · New Label Noise Model for Graphs · Noise Robust Node Classification · Structure Aware Noise Model

1 Introduction

Graph Neural Networks (GNNs) have shown good performance on the graph node classification task [1, 2]. GNNs assume that the available labels for training data are clean and noise-free, which may not be the case when working with real-world data [3]. Labels of real-world data are prone to noise, and noise can creep into data for many reasons, like expensive labelling, lack of expertise, human weariness, erroneous devices, adversaries changing labels, insufficient information

---

Supplementary Information The online version contains supplementary material available at https://doi.org/10.1007/978-3-032-06066-2_10.

to provide labels, etc. [3,4]. Hence, effectively learning for graph data in the presence of label noise has gained attention from the community [5–11].

One of the main reasons behind GNN's superior performance compared to traditional multilayer perceptron is that GNNs incorporate structural information during learning. Structural information is an integral part of graph data. However, all current work on noise-robust graph learning uses one of the following: 1. Symmetric Label noise, 2. Pairwise noise/Class-Conditional noise, 3. Instance-Dependent noise. These noise models were originally proposed for i.i.d. data and not for graph data, and hence, they assume that label noise is independent of the structure of the node.

Consider a graph where nodes represent users in an online discussion forum. An edge between two nodes captures the interaction between users on a platform, such as a reply, comment, or question-answer exchange. Every user is assigned one of two labels {*helpful, not helpful*}. In such a graph, label noise can creep in two scenarios: **1.** Two helpful users who interacted with each other disagreed with each other or, due to some misunderstanding, couldn't convey their point of view, and hence, labelled each other as *not helpful*; **2.** Similarly, two unhelpful users might get incorrectly labelled as *helpful* because of a rare good discussion or due to colluding. In such graphs, noise dependent on just one node is not useful; rather, noise should be passed through edges. The labels of nodes on both sides of the edge should be changed together. We refer to this approach of adding noise to node labels as an edge-dependent noise model (EDN). In this work, we study three variants of edge-dependent noise and their impact on learnability.

The main contributions of the paper are as follows: **1.** Propose three variants of EDN, in which noise is passed through edges. **2.** For these noise models, we derive closed-form expressions for the probabilities of label change in terms of node degree. **3.** We analytically compare these probabilities as a function of node degree. **4.** We perform detailed experiments to check the behaviour of existing GNN architectures and noise-robust graph learning algorithms in the presence of EDN, using 5 different GNN architectures and 8 noise-robust graph learning algorithms. **5.** Based on confidence intervals of test accuracies for various noise models on many datasets, we observe that two variants of EDN at many noise levels substantially degrade the performance as compared to the existing noise label models. **6.** We pose this as a suitable hypothesis test problem to statistically verify our observations, and we conclude the same.

2 Related Work Existing Node Label Noise Models

Let $\mathcal{G} = (\mathcal{V}, \mathcal{E})$ be a graph, where $\mathcal{V}$ denotes the set of vertices and $\mathcal{E} \subseteq \mathcal{V} \times \mathcal{V}$ denotes the set of edges. Each node $v_i \in \mathcal{V}$, have an associated label $y_i \in \{1, 2, \cdots, K\}$. In models for label flipping, we can associate a discrete-time Markov chain [12] on the state space of labels $\{1, 2, \cdots, K\}$ in which each flip in the label corresponds to a state transition of the Markov Chain. We give details of the existing methods for adding noise to node labels; in each case, we identify the transition probability matrix of the associated Markov chain.

2.1 Symmetric Label Noise

Symmetric Label Noise (SLN) [4,13] assumes that the label of a node is changed with some fixed probability ρ (and hence retained with probability $1-\rho$). Also, the probability of a label being reassigned to each of the other classes is the same, which is $\rho/(K-1)$. Mathematically, if y and y' denote true and noisy label respectively, then $P(y'=n|y=m) = \frac{\rho}{K-1}$, where $n,m \in \{1,2,\ldots,K\}$ and $m \neq n$. Transition probability matrix for SLN (Q_{sln}) is given by

$$Q_{sln} = \begin{bmatrix} 1-\rho & \frac{\rho}{K-1} & \frac{\rho}{K-1} & \cdots & \frac{\rho}{K-1} \\ \frac{\rho}{K-1} & 1-\rho & \frac{\rho}{K-1} & \cdots & \frac{\rho}{K-1} \\ \vdots & \ddots & \ddots & \ddots & \vdots \\ \frac{\rho}{K-1} & \cdots & \ddots & 1-\rho & \frac{\rho}{K-1} \\ \frac{\rho}{K-1} & \frac{\rho}{K-1} & \cdots & \frac{\rho}{K-1} & 1-\rho \end{bmatrix} \quad (1)$$

2.2 Class Conditional Noise

In Class Conditional Noise (CCN) [4,13], the probability with which the label is changed depends on both y and y'. The probability of a node of class m being reassigned to class n is given by ρ_{mn} ($P(y'=n|y=m) = \rho_{mn}$), where $m \neq n$. So, a node with label m is flipped with probability $\rho_m = \sum_{i=1, i \neq m}^{K} \rho_{mi}$ and the label is retained with the probability $1-\rho_m$. The transition probability matrix (Q_{ccn}) is given by

$$Q_{ccn} = \begin{bmatrix} 1-\rho_1 & \rho_{12} & \rho_{13} & \cdots & \rho_{1K} \\ \rho_{21} & 1-\rho_2 & \rho_{23} & & \rho_{2K} \\ \vdots & & \ddots & \ddots & \vdots \\ \rho_{(K-1)1} & & & 1-\rho_{K-1} & \rho_{(K-1)K} \\ \rho_{K1} & \rho_{K2} & \cdots & \rho_{K(K-1)} & 1-\rho_K \end{bmatrix}$$

Pairwise Noise: Pairwise Noise (PWN) [13] is a special class of CCN. The motivation behind Pairwise Noise is that one is more likely to mislabel two similar classes. For Pairwise Noise $\rho_1 = \rho_2 = \ldots = \rho_K = \rho$, and the label is flipped to the next label (with probability ρ). The transition probability matrix Q_{pwn} is given by

$$Q_{pwn} = \begin{bmatrix} 1-\rho & \rho & 0 & \cdots & 0 \\ 0 & 1-\rho & \rho & & 0 \\ \vdots & & \ddots & \ddots & \vdots \\ 0 & & & 1-\rho & \rho \\ \rho & 0 & \cdots & 0 & 1-\rho \end{bmatrix} \quad (2)$$

Many label noise robust algorithms for graphs have been proposed to tackle existing node label noise. DGNN [6] employs backward loss correction. PIGNN

[7] leverages pairwise interactions (PI) between nodes for noise-resistant learning. RNCGLN [8] uses pseudo-labeling within a self-training framework to correct noisy labels. NRGNN [9] connects unlabeled nodes with high feature similarity to labelled nodes for better pseudo-labelling. RTGNN [10] enhances information flow by bridging labelled and unlabeled nodes while employing dual GNNs for noise mitigation. CRGNN [11] combines contrastive learning and dynamic cross-entropy loss to encourage robust feature learning. CGNN [5] integrates graph contrastive learning and a sample selection strategy based on the homophily assumption to filter noisy labels. DeGLIF [14] uses the influence function to identify and relabel noisy nodes in the graph. In our work, we would check how these algorithms perform in the presence of structure-dependent noise like EDN.

Some works, such as [15,16], introduce structural noise into the graph by dropping edges. In contrast, our work focuses on node label noise propagated through the edges, rather than modifying the graph structure itself. Next, [17] and [18] explore structurally motivated adversarial or noisy label settings on graphs. However, they primarily focus on label flips and structural changes that mislead GNN's training, whereas our EDN model introduces a fundamentally different approach where label noise arises due to edge connectivity, making it structure-dependent and degree-sensitive.

3 A Novel Edge-Dependent Noise Model (EDN)

Assume $\mathcal{G} = (\mathcal{V}, \mathcal{E})$, is an undirected graph, having m nodes. $\mathcal{X} = \{x_1, \ldots, x_m\}$ and $\mathcal{Y} = \{y_1, \ldots, y_m\}$ are the set of feature vectors and the set of true labels associated with corresponding nodes, respectively. We propose a node-label noise model for graphs (called edge-dependent noise model (EDN)) where the noisy labels of connected nodes are correlated as these noisy labels depend on the edge connecting them. Similar to existing noise models, edge-dependent noise models inject noise into the graph in two steps: 1. Selecting nodes whose labels should be changed, 2. Deciding new labels for selected nodes. What differentiates EDN from existing label noise models is that in EDN, the selection of nodes for label change depends on their structural information.

3.1 Selecting Nodes to Change their Labels

In the proposed EDN model, we sample each edge with **fixed probability** ρ; these sampled edges are called noisy edges. These noisy edges suggest that the labels of nodes on both sides of the noisy edge should be changed. For a node with degree 1, the label is changed if the edge incident to that node is noisy. For nodes with a degree $n > 1$, incident edges may have conflicting opinions on changing the label of the node. Based on how these opinions are aggregated, we have three variants:

Majority Vote (MV): The label of a node v is changed if more than or equal to half of the edges incident to v are noisy. If the degree of v is $deg(v)$, the probability of a node getting selected to change its label is hence given by $q(deg(v), \rho)$

$$q(deg(v), \rho) = \sum_{i=\lceil \frac{deg(v)}{2} \rceil}^{deg(v)} \binom{deg(v)}{i} \rho^i (1-\rho)^{deg(v)-i}. \qquad (3)$$

Veto Power (Veto): The label of a node v is changed if at least one of the incident edges to v is noisy. The probability of the label of a node v with degree $deg(v)$ getting changed is hence given by $r(deg(v), \rho)$

$$r(deg(v), \rho) = 1 - \binom{deg(v)}{0}(1-\rho)^{deg(v)} = 1 - (1-\rho)^{deg(v)}. \qquad (4)$$

Sequential Flipping (seq): In this variant, the label of a node sequentially evolves. For a node v, we consider all its *noisy incident edges*. The first noisy incident edge changes the label to a new class. The second noisy edge changes the label from this new class to another (with a possibility of reverting to the original label). This process continues for all noisy edges. The probability with which a node v with degree $deg(v)$ is flipped depends on how new labels are assigned when observing a noisy edge and is discussed in Sect. 3.2.

3.2 Assigning Noisy Labels to Selected Nodes

For Majority vote and Veto power, after selecting nodes whose labels are to be changed, we use SLN and Pairwise noise [4,13] to assign a new label. The difference between the existing and the EDN variants is that existing models have the same probability of selecting every node, whereas, in our noise model, the *probability of selecting a node is dependent on the degree of the node*. This is demonstrated by Eq. 3,4,5 and 6. Existing noise models have the same transition probability matrix for all nodes, whereas EDN has different transition probability matrices for nodes with different degrees. In sequential flipping, the assignment of a new label due to a noisy edge follows SLN and Pairwise Noise. Both these sub-variants lead to different probabilities of flipping a node.

Sequential Flipping + SLN: Each edge incident to node v is noisy with probability ρ. So, due to a single edge, the label of node v is unchanged with probability $1-\rho$, and the label changes to a different class with probability ρ. In the case of sequential flipping + SLN, when a noisy edge alters the label, the new label is selected according to the SLN model. This means that each possible class is equally likely, with a probability of $\frac{\rho}{K-1}$. The transition probability matrix associated with the noise caused by a single edge is given by Q_{SLN} from Eq. 1. If v has degree n, then the transition probability matrix for Sequential flipping + SLN is Q_{SLN}^n (relabelling n times, every time starting with a new label). Q_{SLN}

is a symmetric matrix, using the diagonalization property of symmetric matrix (Spectral theorem) [19], we derive Q_{SLN}^n as follows:

$$Q_{SLN}^n = \frac{1}{K}\begin{bmatrix} 1 \& 1 & 1 & \cdots & 1 \\ 1 & 1 & 1\& & 1 \\ \vdots & & \ddots & & \vdots \\ 1 & & 1 & 1 \\ 1 & 1 & \cdots & 1 & 1 \end{bmatrix} + \left(1 - \frac{K\rho}{K-1}\right)^n \begin{bmatrix} \frac{K-1}{K} & -\frac{1}{K} & -\frac{1}{K} & \cdots & -\frac{1}{K} \\ -\frac{1}{K} & \frac{K-1}{K} & -\frac{1}{K} & & -\frac{1}{K} \\ \vdots & & \ddots & & \vdots \\ -\frac{1}{K} & & & \frac{K-1}{K} & -\frac{1}{K} \\ -\frac{1}{K} & -\frac{1}{K} & \cdots & -\frac{1}{K} & \frac{k-1}{K} \end{bmatrix}$$

Detailed derivation for Q_{SLN}^n is available in Appendix A. Using Q_{SLN}^n, for a node v starting with the true label y, the probability of the label being changed to a specific class is given by:

$$s\_sc(deg(v), \rho) = \frac{1}{K}\left(1 - \left(1 - \frac{K\rho}{K-1}\right)^{deg(v)}\right).$$

For the node v, when using Sequential flipping + SLN model, the probability of its label being flipped is $(K-1) \times s\_sc(n)$ and is hence given by

$$s_{sln}(deg(v), \rho) = \frac{K-1}{K}\left(1 - \left(1 - \frac{K\rho}{K-1}\right)^{deg(v)}\right). \tag{5}$$

Sequential Flipping + PWN: In sequential flipping with PWN, label reassignment due to a single edge follows the pairwise noise model. The corresponding transition probability matrix is given by Q_{pwn} from Eq. 2. If v has degree n, then the transition probability matrix for Sequential flipping with the pairwise noise is Q_{pwn}^n (relabelling n times, every time starting with a new label). Observe that in Q_{pwn}, each row is a rightward cyclic shift of the previous row, which makes it a circulant matrix [19,20]. We use the eigendecomposition of the circulant matrix [19,20] to obtain Q_{pwn}^n. Since Q_{pwn}^n is a product of circulant matrices, it remains circulant [19,20], meaning the entire matrix is characterised by its first row. The first row of Q_{pwn}^n is given by:

$$Q_{pwn}^n[0, j] = \sum_{m=0}^{n} \binom{n}{m}\rho^m(1-\rho)^{n-m}\delta_{m-j} \mod K.$$

Detailed derivation for Q_{pwn}^n is in the Appendix B. For the node v, when using the Sequential flipping + PWN model, the probability of its label being flipped is

$$s_{pwn}(deg(v), \rho) = \sum_{j=1}^{K-1}\sum_{m=1}^{deg(v)} \binom{deg(v)}{m}\rho^m(1-\rho)^{deg(v)-m}\delta_{m-j} \mod K \tag{6}$$

In all three variants, the probability of a node's label changing *depends on its degree*. The relationship between node degree and this probability is illustrated in

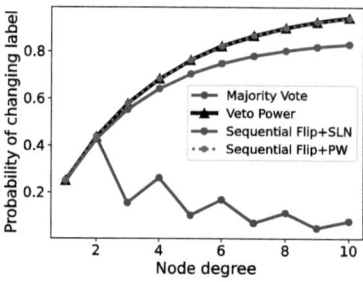 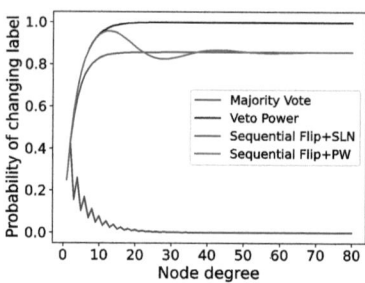

Fig. 1. Node degree vs probability of label change for three variants of EDN. We use $\rho = 0.25$ (the probability of an edge being noisy) and use $K = 7$ for sequential flipping.

Fig. 1. We observe that for a fixed ρ, in the majority vote variant, the probability $q(deg(v), \rho)$ decreases with slight fluctuations as the node degree increases. In the other two variants, both the probabilities $r(deg(v), \rho)$ and $s_{sln}(deg(v), \rho)$ monotonically increase and saturate at 1 and $\frac{K-1}{K}$ respectively. We summarize this as Theorem 1, with its proof provided in Appendix C:

Theorem 1. *Three variants of EDN satisfy the following properties:*

1. *For a fixed ρ, $r(deg(v), \rho)$ is an increasing function of $deg(v)$. Also, $s(deg(v), \rho)$ is an increasing function of $deg(v)$ for $\rho < \frac{K-1}{K}$.*
2. *$r(deg(v), \rho) \geq q(deg(v), \rho) \; \forall \; deg(v)$ and fixed ρ.*
3. *If $\rho < \frac{K-1}{K}$, then $s_{sln}(deg(v), \rho) < \frac{K-1}{K}$ and $s_{sln}(n) = \frac{K-1}{K}$ iff $\rho = \frac{K-1}{K}$.*

The curve for s_{pwn} initially follows veto power and then oscillates to converge to seq+SLN. For $deg(v) \leq K - 1$, we have $s_{pwn}(deg(v), \rho) = r(deg(v), \rho)$. In Fig. 1, we observe that s_{pwn} forms a cycle of alternating increasing and decreasing phases. For a node v_i, without loss of generality, assume that its label $y_i = 1$. If $deg(v) = 1$, its label gets changed to class 2 with some probability, but never to any other class. If $deg(v) = 2$, v, moving from Q_{pwn} to Q_{pwn}^2, if the node has been already assigned label 2, it can not return to the original label and can either remain in 2 or get reassigned to class 3. If v_i was not assigned label 2, it now has the probability ρ of getting assigned to class 2. This implies $s_{pwn}(2, \rho) > s_{pwn}(1, \rho)$; meaning, s_{pwn} starts with an increasing phase. If $deg(v) = K - 1$, then it can be reassigned to any class, and s_{pwn} is an increasing function of node degree up to this point. At $deg(v) = K$, if v_i was reassigned to class K by its first $K - 1$ edges, then there is a small probability it gets reassigned to label 1. When this probability exceeds that of class 1 reassigned to class 2 (which occurs at $n = 13$ for $K = 7$), then it starts to decrease. and the decreasing phase will continue until another cycle is completed again, explaining the alternating pattern.

Recall Q_{pwn} is the transition probability matrix of a discrete-time Markov chain. This Markov chain is aperiodic and has only one communicating class, and $\pi = [1/K, 1/K, \ldots, 1/K]$ is the unique stationary distribution for Q_{pwn}.

Hence, Q_{pwn}^n converges to a matrix Q^*, where every row of Q^* equals π [12]. So, $s_{pwn}(deg(v), \rho)$ converges to $(K-1) \times \frac{1}{K}$, this value is same as the upper bound for s_{sln}. We summarize this discussion about s_{pwn} as:

Theorem 2. $s_{pwn}(deg(v), \rho)$, the probability with which the label of node v is changed in presence of Sequential flipping+PWN model, satisfies the following:

1. s_{pwn} forms a cycle of alternating increasing and decreasing phases. It initially increases, followed by a period of decrease, and this pattern continues.
2. For any fixed ρ we have $s_{pwn}(deg(v), \rho) = r(deg(v), \rho)$, for $deg(v) \leq K-1$.
3. $s_{pwn}(deg(v), \rho)$ converges to $\frac{K-1}{K}$ as $deg(v) \to \infty$.

4 Experiments and Results

4.1 Datasets and their Splits

We test the impact of EDN on existing GNNs and Noise-robust algorithms. using Citeseer [21], Cora [21], and Amazon photo [22], with splits similar to DeGLIF [14]. Details about dataset statistics are in Table 1. These datasets were selected as they vary in node count, feature dimensions, and average degree.

Table 1. Dataset Statistics

Dataset	# Nodes	# Edges	Feature dim	# Classes
CiteSeer	3,327	9,104	3,703	6
Cora	2,708	10,556	1,433	7
Amazon Photo	7,650	238,162	745	8

Datasets Split Details: We use split similar to [14]. For the Cora dataset, we use 172 nodes per class for training, 500 nodes for validation, and 1000 nodes for testing. For the Citeseer dataset, we use 250 randomly sampled nodes per class for training, 500 nodes for validation, and 1000 nodes for testing. For the Amazon Photo dataset, we use 54 nodes per class for training, 500 nodes in total for validation, and the rest of the nodes for testing. All datasets have been fetched from the PyTorch Geometric library, with feature normalisation being true.

4.2 Injecting EDN Noise

The same value of ρ can lead to different levels of noise using different variants of EDN noise models. Also, as variants of EDN are degree-dependent, graphs with different degree distributions can have different noise levels for the same ρ. Let $d(n)$ represent the degree distribution of a graph, then the expected noise level in the graph is given by $\sum_{i=1}^{maxdegree} l(i)d(i)$ where l is q, r or s. To make a fair comparison with the existing noise model and among different variants of EDN, we choose different ρ for each variant and each dataset so that the expected noise level in the graph is the same. A ready-to-refer value of ρ for different datasets, corresponding to overall noise levels in the graph ranging from 5% to 50% in increments of 5%, is available in Table 6 of the supplementary material.

4.3 Experimental Setup

We add different types of noise to data, where the noise level is between 5% and 50% in increments of 5%. GCN, GraphSAGE, GAT and Graph Transformer have been implemented using Pytorch Geometric using GCNConv, SAGEConv, GAT-Conv and Graph Transformer respectively. For GCN and GraphSAGE we use 1 hidden layer of size 16 and relu activation. For GAT and Graph Transformer, we use 1 hidden layer with 8 heads of size 8. For GIN we use implementation by [13]. It is worth mentioning that the comparison is not between GNNs but between different noise models, so using slightly different architectures for different GNNs strengthens our experiments. We use implementation by [13] for all noise-robust algorithms except for DeGLIF for, which we use implementation by [14]. Each experiment is repeated 10 times, with mean ± standard deviation reported. Models are trained on a 24 GB Nvidia RTX 4090 GPU.

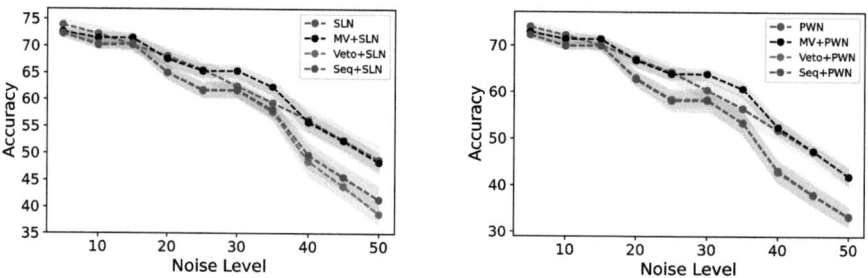

Fig. 2. GCN accuracy at same noise level but different noise models on Citeseer dataset.

4.4 Computational Results

In this section, we attempt to empirically understand the impact of EDN on existing graph learning algorithms. To do so we try to answer following questions:

Q1. How does GCN Architecture Perform in the Presence of EDN?
GCN [23] is one of the widely used GNN architecture, it is also used as a backbone for many noise robust algorithms for graph [9,10,14]. We test GCN under different noise variants of EDN, as well as SLN and PWN. Results for the Citesser dataset are reported in Fig. 2. Results for all datasets at 5%, 25%, and 45% noise level is presented in Table 2. Due to the large size of tables and lack of space, results for all datasets at all noise levels are provided in Tables 7,8,9 in the supplementary material. GCN performance in the presence of the Majority vote variant is comparable to existing noise models, SLN and PWN. GCN shows more degradation in performance when injected with Veto Power and Sequential flipping variants of EDN as compared to the existing node label noise model. At low noise levels (less than 15%) the gap is low. However, at higher noise levels, veto power and sequential flipping gap widen, and they degrade GCN performance the most.

EDN: A Novel Edge-Dependent Noise Model for Graph Data

Table 2. Comparison of noise model variants across GNN architecture. Reported values are accuracy±std of 10 repetitions.

	GNN Architecture	Noise Level	SLN	MV + SLN	Veto + SLN	Seq + SLN	PWN	MV + PWN	Veto + PWN	Seq + PWN
	GCN	5%	73.92±1.1	72.64±0.5	72.27±0.7	72.34±0.6	73.99±1	72.91±0.6	72.24±0.6	72.23±0.58
		25%	65.55±1.74	65.34±1.20	61.64±1.43	61.79±1.42	64.29±1.91	63.93±1.22	58.42±1.76	58.17±2.43
		45%	52.47±2.39	52.33±1.55	43.86±2.21	45.57±2.21	47.30±2.34	47.36±1.25	37.93±2.02	38.05±2.56
C	GIN	5%	71.92±4.50	69.52±1.93	68.59±2.76	67.76±3.35	67.99±3.27	68.56±3.01	68.78±2.22	68.58±1.95
I		25%	60.12±5.71	63.39±3.58	54.51±4.01	55.42±6.26	54.22±9.29	61.47±3.51	49.34±7.72	49.98±4.16
T		45%	42.29±8.80	47.87±7.42	37.98±5.40	39.28±5.53	39.19±3.55	46.07±6.53	34.25±5.86	33.50±1.65
E	GraphSAGE	5%	75.95±0.96	74.96±0.51	74.69±0.49	74.61±0.62	75.97±0.88	75.07±0.56	74.00±0.53	75.69±1.30
S		25%	70.96±1.49	70.70±1.07	68.42±1.36	68.99±0.91	68.93±1.92	68.33±1.07	63.27±1.43	65.70±2.16
E		45%	59.61±1.99	59.97±1.79	52.89±2.11	54.17±2.08	49.71±2.85	49.19±1.56	41.19±2.29	44.32±4.10
E	GAT	5%	76.46±1.53	74.75±0.67	74.33±0.89	74.36±0.67	76.62±1.49	74.93±0.85	74.39±0.66	76.61±1.39
R		25%	74.59±1.61	73.06±1.04	71.81±1.06	72.16±1.39	73.31±1.84	71.32±1.50	68.13±1.45	71.42±2.64
		45%	70.88±1.64	70.45±1.81	66.60±2.33	67.51±1.87	55.00±3.75	53.93±2.64	43.41±3.18	45.97±6.50
	Graph Transformer	5%	76.28±0.86	75.64±0.52	76.28±0.50	76.54±0.54	76.10±1.40	75.50±0.14	76.16±0.35	75.50±0.95
		25%	70.24±1.63	70.36±0.60	68.84±0.68	68.68±0.86	68.86±1.03	67.48±1.12	64.94±0.68	65.45±2.00
		45%	58.10±1.24	59.22±1.42	52.38±0.60	53.58±0.94	49.04±2.25	48.94±2.43	43.00±1.01	44.09±2.77
	GCN	5%	84.73±0.94	85.00±0.44	85.19±0.74	85.09±0.73	84.27±0.98	85.36±0.48	85.36±0.50	84.58±0.54
		25%	76.46±1.48	77.46±1.99	74.49±2.09	74.65±2.03	71.97±1.77	74.84±2.58	68.85±2.30	76.35±1.44
		45%	62.29±2.29	63.16±2.94	57.12±2.54	58.06±2.54	50.52±2.76	52.86±3.87	44.28±2.62	50.18±3.92
	GIN	5%	80.95±2.01	81.11±0.88	80.45±2.63	82.11±2.60	80.35±2.38	83.34±1.55	80.77±2.21	79.36±1.99
		25%	79.02±2.77	77.87±5.65	74.90±2.73	76.57±2.59	73.66±3.74	73.32±4.28	64.84±3.21	67.62±2.51
C		45%	71.02±4.38	75.17±2.36	66.79±0.6	65.95±11.8	48.40±5.01	53.90±4.37	45.55±10.1	48.36±3.33
O	GraphSAGE	5%	83.10±1.19	83.38±0.68	83.37±1.18	83.41±1.09	82.84±1.31	83.56±0.46	83.22±1.13	84.43±0.81
R		25%	70.72±1.85	72.39±2.37	68.83±1.91	69.02±2.12	67.69±2.50	69.64±2.76	66.53±1.93	71.6±2.48
A		45%	55.27±2.50	53.93±3.23	51.14±2.74	51.35±2.62	47.20±3.15	49.40±3.33	46.21±2.12	47.77±5.17
	GAT	5%	79.50±1.80	80.05±1.02	80.39±1.14	80.45±1.20	79.99±1.24	79.43±1.51	79.45±1.37	79.06±1.5
		25%	70.33±2.16	69.58±2.69	70.77±2.57	70.48±1.44	65.87±3.48	65.64±2.34	64.80±2.47	66.09±2.37
		45%	57.46±3.68	57.14±3.53	55.49±2.94	55.56±3.14	44.76±3.42	46.71±3.98	43.82±3.07	45.25±5.46
	Graph Transformer	5%	84.42±0.84	84.78±0.29	84.70±0.41	84.64±0.67	84.06±0.71	84.70±0.14	84.96±0.54	84.12±0.99
		25%	75.30±0.91	76.56±0.70	77.18±0.67	77.50±0.87	72.12±1.05	72.18±1.08	72.88±0.95	70.33±2.01
		45%	61.16±1.75	62.16±1.86	61.32±1.56	60.62±2.15	50.08±2.15	51.32±0.92	51.28±1.44	48.11±2.4
	GCN	5%	86.78±1.43	83.65±6.28	85.05±4.56	83.55±6.18	86.66±1.46	84.65±5.59	85.35±4.21	84.85±2.89
A		25%	83.96±2.99	78.28±9.38	81.87±4.08	80.58±7.92	77.00±5.47	74.15±9.42	70.81±7.69	66.82±8.03
M		45%	73.45±5.67	75.36±8.82	66.92±11.98	67.85±11.36	44.15±4.85	49.57±7.92	40.74±2.65	40.03±5.61
A	GIN	5%	80.24±4.32	81.32±2.95	67.86±17.91	64.96±15.31	66.24±17.36	78.02±3.71	77.10±5.15	34.24±6.73
Z		25%	50.58±19.81	67.24±16.88	35.04±2.90	33.62±8.99	50.16±10.96	69.38±14.52	41.78±10.62	33.94±7.74
O		45%	34.38±7.71	40.28±4.80	24.74±4.46	27.04±7.18	33.52±17.39	48.84±17.31	25.14±3.94	22.58±7.66
N	GraphSAGE	5%	90.56±0.86	90.41±0.61	90.29±0.82	90.20±0.64	90.39±1.01	90.64±0.50	90.29±0.79	89.93±1.16
		25%	81.73±2.29	84.06±1.34	82.15±1.89	82.15±2.09	77.96±2.87	80.25±2.78	77.73±3.13	74.08±4.06
P		45%	65.88±3.47	68.72±2.34	61.36±4.87	62.66±4.42	50.78±4.01	55.60±4.85	47.78±4.23	43.61±6.1
H	GAT	5%	78.20±1.79	79.07±1.89	77.75±1.95	77.29±1.60	77.36±2.45	78.79±1.52	76.30±1.64	76.81±1.79
O		25%	63.20±3.03	66.08±2.52	63.13±2.32	62.52±2.51	61.67±1.34	63.45±3.42	61.21±1.97	58.14±3.82
T		45%	47.79±3.67	48.55±3.52	46.59±3.19	46.70±3.37	45.01±2.82	47.40±4.53	42.69±3.05	40.29±4.36
O	Graph Transformer	5%	85.57±0.83	80.87±8.55	84.13±1.88	84.25±1.36	85.48±0.95	85.80±0.72	84.32±1.22	84.94±0.61
		25%	74.34±3.35	76.04±2.34	71.73±2.25	72.54±3.45	71.27±4.41	73.05±2.94	72.28±1.72	69.8±1.86
		45%	58.77±2.13	58.33±4.13	57.54±2.01	57.76±1.11	54.38±2.85	49.03±6.71	54.25±3.26	49.8±4.64

Q2. How do Other GNN Architectures Perform in the Presence of EDN? Maybe GCN is not robust enough for EDN, what about other GNN architectures, we test common GNN architectures GIN [24], GraphSage [25], GAT [26], and Graph Transformer [27]. Result for Citeseer with 40% noise is pictorially reported in Fig. 3. For all datasets at 5%, 25%, and 45% noise levels, result is presented in Table 2. Detailed results for all datasets at all noise levels are in Tables 7,8,9. We observe that, similar to GCN, other GNN architectures' performance is also degraded more in the presence of Veto power and the Sequential flipping variant of EDN as compared to the existing noise model and majority vote variant.

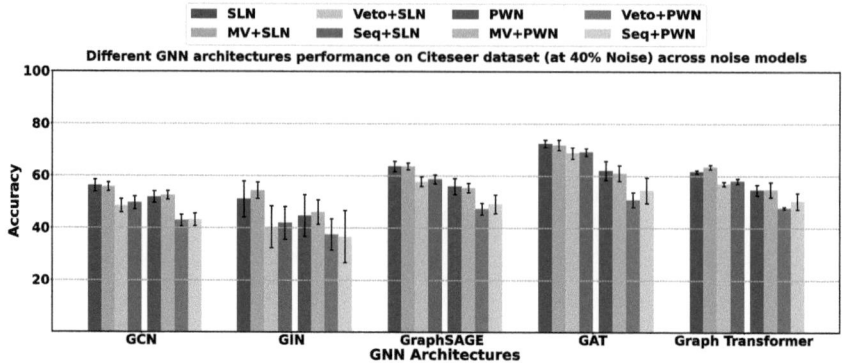

Fig. 3. Comparison of noise model variants across GNN architectures. A cluster is for an architecture, and coloured bars show the accuracy of the corresponding noise type.

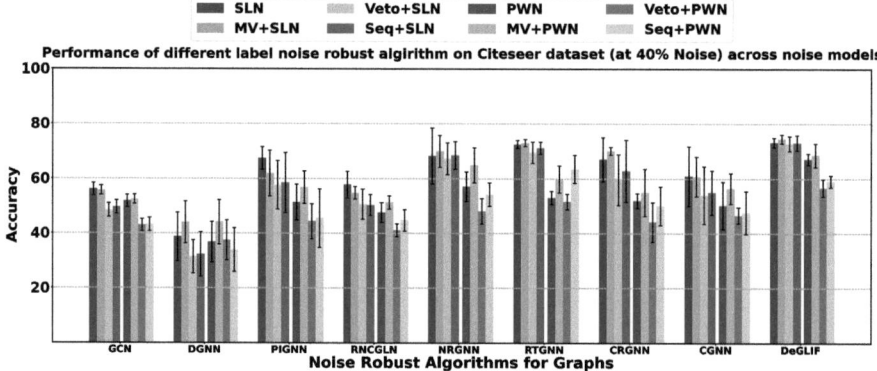

Fig. 4. Comparison of noise model variants across graph label noise-robust algorithms. A cluster is for an algorithm, and coloured bars show the accuracy of a noise type.

Q3. How does the Existing Label Noise Robust Algorithm Perform in the Presence of EDN? Next, we evaluate noise-robust algorithms DGNN [6], PIGNN [7], RNCGLN [8], NRGNN [9], RTGNN [10], CRGNN [11], CGNN [5], and DeGLIF [14] under different noise variants of EDN, as well as SLN and CCN. Graphical representation of the result for the Citeseer dataset with 40% noise is in Fig. 4. For all datasets at 5%, 25%, and 45% noise level, result is presented in Tables 3 and 4. Detailed results for all datasets are in Tables 10,11,12 in the supplementary material. At low noise levels, these algorithms give comparable results across all noise models. At higher noise levels, most algorithms (Fig. 4) show trends similar to GCN. Performance under the majority vote variant is comparable to or better than SLN or CCN. However, under the Veto Power and sequential variants, almost all algorithms struggle to learn as robustly as they do with SLN or CCN.

The Majority Vote (MV) algorithm penalizes low-degree nodes, making its performance decline similar to SLN or PW. On the other hand, Veto power and Sequential flipping have higher noise levels for higher degrees (Fig. 3). Variants of EDN leading to a greater performance drop suggest that the structure of nodes plays a critical role in how noise impacts performance, making such EDN variants valuable for robust evaluations.

Table 3. Comparison of noise model variants across graph label noise robust algorithms for Citeseer and Cora datasets. Reported values are accuracy±std of 10 repetitions.

	Noise Robust Methods	Noise Level	SLN	MV+SLN	Veto+SLN	Seq+SLN	PWN	MV+PWN	Veto+PWN	Seq+PWN
CITESEER	DGNN	5%	66.46±2.84	65.15±2.37	62.17±2.41	60.28±3.58	64.04±2.22	66.06±1.90	61.92±8.79	58.12±13.30
		25%	53.07±4.92	51.18±10.06	45.02±6.99	44.70±6.52	49.78±5.92	53.62±6.91	46.24±6.07	42.28±12.04
		45%	41.89±6.73	43.71±4.72	29.48±6.39	27.27±9.29	32.62±6.84	44.71±5.86	32.83±4.41	34.20±7.13
	PIGNN	5%	76.58±2.04	72.83±3.60	71.34±5.36	71.61±5.36	74.02±2.20	73.60±1.74	71.63±5.38	73.14±2.17
		25%	71.61±3.67	69.62±3.46	66.79±6.75	66.11±8.15	66.19±5.57	68.11±4.49	62.79±4.89	63.62±7.72
		45%	60.79±11.05	56.18±9.03	56.32±3.70	58.49±7.80	44.47±7.21	49.97±7.33	38.14±4.95	44.48±9.20
	RNCGLN	5%	72.15±3.13	69.00±3.88	68.33±1.98	67.54±1.51	69.86±3.23	68.05±2.46	68.87±2.75	72.08±3.06
		25%	65.09±4.12	62.51±2.37	64.76±4.86	62.41±4.41	58.22±2.80	61.01±2.82	56.50±2.01	58.88±3.38
		45%	51.68±5.01	51.01±3.35	44.24±4.52	45.94±4.38	41.87±2.96	46.81±3.73	37.95±3.20	40.72±1.63
	RTGNN	5%	73.98±4.38	74.31±1.04	74.26±1.53	73.95±1.35	74.18±0.80	74.07±1.15	74.12±0.97	75.08±1.32
		25%	72.47±1.78	72.81±1.55	72.82±1.97	71.95±3.23	65.87±2.81	71.07±2.65	66.09±2.46	70.22±3.38
		45%	70.25±1.97	71.09±2.30	64.59±5.95	69.16±2.81	42.61±4.55	53.90±3.99	45.36±3.73	54.05±3.09
	NRGNN	5%	75.76±0.99	74.19±1.47	74.22±1.19	74.14±1.15	71.69±3.75	73.56±2.35	74.53±1.63	76.58±3.30
		25%	73.78±1.02	72.68±2.15	70.86±4.00	70.40±4.18	67.06±2.90	72.08±2.89	66.07±6.16	69.92±1.67
		45%	70.80±2.43	70.73±5.18	65.17±6.89	64.09±8.24	46.98±3.99	55.79±5.34	40.30±5.00	49.60±10.83
	CRGNN	5%	76.34±2.41	74.74±1.86	74.64±1.79	74.24±2.41	75.09±1.07	74.78±2.31	74.30±1.48	74.88±3.26
		25%	73.22±1.63	70.35±6.12	71.21±3.16	72.50±1.97	65.98±4.25	70.15±1.75	58.29±9.09	65.34±3.45
		45%	64.84±4.24	64.16±8.81	57.43±7.86	63.37±5.93	45.19±3.63	52.46±3.34	40.44±3.00	42.56±6.28
	CGNN	5%	77.80±0.83	74.20±1.74	73.69±1.85	73.11±3.40	72.67±4.49	73.51±2.24	74.21±1.59	76.60±4.10
		25%	69.86±4.46	70.54±3.82	69.04±5.15	70.09±4.03	61.63±9.43	67.52±6.32	60.02±7.17	63.08±9.39
		45%	58.62±8.03	55.96±11.66	50.57±11.89	50.62±10.95	44.70±6.39	50.49±6.26	41.45±3.50	46.02±4.30
	DeGLIF	5%	77.58±1.10	77.36±1.24	77.64±1.71	77.50±1.80	77.92±1.24	77.34±1.41	77.64±1.42	77.74±1.2
		25%	76.10±1.21	76.24±1.48	75.86±2.28	76.04±1.96	74.86±2.20	75.94±2.44	73.40±1.72	74.4±2.95
		45%	70.58±1.44	72.38±2.06	71.18±2.99	71.98±2.90	59.48±3.76	62.02±3.25	47±5.34	52.48±8.28
CORA	DGNN	5%	78.32±4.81	82.68±2.81	79.80±1.65	78.08±4.58	74.66±9.15	82.50±0.95	78.38±7.58	79.18±1.75
		25%	74.90±5.87	79.38±2.39	65.20±11.22	65.38±13.62	61.78±9.81	77.36±3.91	53.28±12.29	66.54±7.27
		45%	62.34±12.99	60.08±15.94	40.26±8.56	40.10±8.99	46.64±11.84	45.02±11.65	30.94±6.26	52.36±8.54
	PIGNN	5%	80.19±3.16	81.48±2.16	81.81±2.22	81.71±2.15	80.05±3.50	81.58±1.97	81.79±1.88	81.48±2.84
		25%	79.84±2.30	80.11±2.09	80.66±2.37	78.41±5.17	76.54±3.43	75.71±3.57	72.85±3.54	72.87±8.57
		45%	75.68±2.69	75.74±2.92	74.95±6.39	74.61±5.72	49.64±10.92	46.89±9.64	47.60±7.82	57.05±10.22
	RNCGLN	5%	83.82±5.00	84.06±4.05	85.32±2.00	87.04±2.01	83.78±2.71	82.08±3.42	88.32±2.02	81.38±0.61
		25%	80.26±5.05	80.24±3.99	71.54±6.55	70.50±4.53	71.94±5.37	77.00±9.12	64.98±3.93	70.60±1.39
		45%	56.52±5.79	61.22±6.57	51.68±5.66	55.40±5.21	52.40±8.32	63.90±8.12	42.58±2.93	49.72±0.79
	RTGNN	5%	73.54±2.02	74.42±2.12	74.64±1.78	75.04±1.70	75.29±3.09	73.91±2.63	74.28±1.90	73.95±1.58
		25%	75.67±3.00	72.20±3.70	74.12±3.52	73.16±5.07	70.44±3.29	62.89±6.02	55.39±9.03	68.75±4.56
		45%	66.44±7.61	64.95±8.76	68.27±6.98	71.45±5.01	57.38±6.77	51.81±3.87	40.51±8.34	42.77±7.32
	NRGNN	5%	75.13±3.77	75.47±1.73	75.65±2.62	73.19±2.98	75.40±2.21	74.81±1.82	76.12±2.36	74.99±2.20
		25%	75.03±4.14	73.52±1.88	75.46±2.96	75.05±1.90	69.89±7.82	64.88±7.89	64.97±6.98	65.47±7.14
		45%	71.63±7.77	65.53±9.80	69.96±7.19	70.07±5.05	50.58±13.34	40.34±9.91	40.91±10.40	49.96±6.07
	CRGNN	5%	84.10±1.86	83.99±1.48	84.18±1.72	84.36±1.53	84.26±1.64	84.28±0.92	83.70±1.58	82.16±4.84
		25%	78.25±1.88	76.40±2.57	76.43±5.53	77.58±2.64	75.71±2.56	74.05±2.41	67.48±4.64	69.94±6.77
		45%	65.02±10.42	60.58±12.98	62.98±6.41	60.63±7.09	48.32±9.40	49.27±6.13	46.61±7.83	44.22±7.37
	CGNN	5%	83.70±3.67	82.43±4.47	83.15±3.11	82.81±3.26	83.57±2.19	83.15±2.76	78.94±11.48	83.27±2.92
		25%	79.46±3.45	74.93±5.98	77.06±4.52	76.29±4.45	75.82±3.25	70.34±9.60	70.54±3.38	71.37±10.88
		45%	67.76±6.19	63.57±9.94	65.63±13.02	65.15±13.00	51.20±7.78	47.45±6.24	46.39±8.02	47.56±10.42
	DeGLIF	5%	88.79±2.60	88.77±2.79	87.04±6.67	89.41±1.99	88.20±2.12	88.73±2.32	88.86±2.41	84.46±0.8
		25%	87.33±2.74	85.71±6.37	86.17±3.31	85.68±5.04	86.63±1.84	87.60±2.01	73.27±16.10	80.74±1.15
		45%	84.85±2.21	83.60±2.00	75.33±7.08	78.58±6.30	60.11±3.78	63.50±6.69	44.94±2.33	61.2±6.07

Table 4. Comparison of noise model variants across noise robust algorithms for graphs for the Amazon Photo dataset. Reported values are accuracy ± std of 10 repetitions.

Noise Robust Methods		Noise Level	SLN	MV+ SLN	Veto+ SLN	Seq+ SLN	PWN	MV+ PWN	Veto+ PWN	Seq+ PWN
	DGNN	5%	78.32±4.81	82.68±2.81	79.80±1.65	78.08±4.58	74.66±9.15	82.50±0.95	78.38±7.58	61.44±27.08
		25%	74.90±5.87	79.38±2.39	65.20±11.22	65.38±13.62	61.78±9.81	77.36±3.91	53.28±12.29	55.50±5.54
		45%	62.34±12.99	60.08±15.94	40.26±8.56	40.10±8.99	46.64±11.84	45.02±11.65	30.94±6.26	35.96±4.80
	PIGNN	5%	88.9±0.4	89.56±0.58	90.72±0.31	92.42±0.59	89.74±1.26	88.02±0.96	89.96±0.58	90.06±0.88
		25%	86.8±3.4	88.96±1.72	90.30±0.65	90.52±0.50	85.22±2.21	87.52±2.15	74.56±2.17	82.10±2.06
A		45%	82.2±4.2	87.22±2.37	79.86±7.22	80.64±3.36	60.44±8.51	62.38±9.04	42.86±6.44	63.52±2.81
M	RNCGLN	5%	83.82±5.00	84.06±4.05	85.32±2.00	87.04±2.01	83.78±2.71	82.08±3.42	88.32±2.02	84.48±3.53
A		25%	80.26±5.05	80.24±3.99	71.54±6.55	70.50±4.53	71.94±5.37	77.00±9.12	64.98±3.93	69.96±6.36
Z		45%	56.52±5.79	61.22±6.57	51.68±5.66	55.40±5.21	52.40±8.32	63.90±8.12	42.58±2.93	48.34±1.06
O	RTGNN	5%	80.8±5.3	81.93±2.17	81.46±2.44	84.14±2.19	82.24±0.86	83.45±1.10	81.95±1.42	82.04±1.53
N		25%	82.9±4.9	82.63±3.85	82.93±3.32	81.96±2.17	83.17±3.79	84.88±3.15	69.78±3.62	76.19±6.53
		45%	86±1.3	84.98±1.62	75.71±7.21	74.46±5.80	60.86±8.45	58.03±12.32	47.17±8.88	60.56±3.57
P	NRGNN	5%	69±8	87.52±0.90	87.34±1.68	88.40±2.77	89.74±1.26	87.08±1.67	86.56±1.54	85.90±2.81
H		25%	55.1±5.4	86.92±2.84	85.92±0.64	86.08±0.90	85.22±2.21	85.52±2.32	72.50±4.41	81.24±5.63
O		45%	54.5±6.2	86.70±1.72	73.78±4.98	81.42±2.51	60.44±8.51	66.20±8.31	49.90±3.87	58.78±1.89
T	CRGNN	5%	59.04±12.73	44.60±12.81	54.28±14.68	54.52±14.41	54.80±12.30	52.82±12.77	47.36±15.24	37.54±46.21
O		25%	45.02±10.86	37.82±11.13	35.76±11.64	35.22±14.65	47.68±20.70	31.22±7.03	41.32±7.76	32.74±39.74
		45%	29.48±15.05	31.20±5.21	23.12±5.72	18.82±4.97	33.14±13.04	37.74±8.31	27.42±4.28	19.78±21.92
	CGNN	5%	39.08±28.12	28.70±12.19	23.32±6.22	33.60±21.41	33.82±19.18	25.10±7.71	32.08±11.53	56.84±25.81
		25%	34.08±23.35	22.70±8.20	24.30±5.93	25.88±24.09	31.26±18.21	22.48±3.59	29.08±7.08	47.86±14.05
		45%	16.62±9.35	17.40±9.27	20.84±7.90	22.96±11.08	22.74±12.74	24.44±7.80	25.78±7.39	36.52±9.30
	DeGLIF	5%	88.79±2.60	88.77±2.79	87.04±6.67	89.41±1.99	88.20±2.12	88.73±2.32	88.86±2.41	89.09±2.13
		25%	87.33±2.74	85.71±6.37	86.17±3.31	85.68±5.04	86.63±1.84	87.60±2.01	73.27±16.10	79.08±4.45
		45%	84.85±2.21	83.60±2.00	75.33±7.08	78.58±6.30	60.11±3.78	63.50±6.69	44.94±2.33	52.92±11.73

4.5 Hypothesis Testing

All experiments to check the impact of EDN on GNN architectures and noise robust algorithms for graphs are repeated 10 times. For a particular noise level, Let $\{x_1^s, \ldots x_{10}^s\}$, denote accuracy values obtained by GNN when noise is injected using SLN. Similarly let $\{x_1^v, \ldots, x_1^v\}$ denote accuracy values obtained by GNN when noise is injected using Veto Power + SLN model. We want to use the theory of hypothesis testing to check if some of the variant of EDN really lead to more degradation in performance as compared to existing noise models. To do so, let, $d_i = x_i^s - x_i^v$. Then $\bar{d} = \bar{x}^s - \bar{x}^v$. We assume that d_i are sampled from a normal distribution with an unknown mean μ_d and unknown variance σ_d^2. We define hypothesis test as follows [28,29]:

Null Hypothesis $H_0 : \mu_d \leq 0$
Alternate Hypothesis $H_1 : \mu_d > 0$

We would like to mention that the normal distribution has a domain of $(-\infty, \infty)$, but the possible values of d_i are restricted to $[-100, 100]$. Empirically, almost all observed values of d_i lie within $[-10, 10]$ and exhibit a small standard deviation. As a result, the probability of a well-fitted normal distribution assigning values beyond $[-100, 100]$ is extremely low. Therefore, it is reasonable to assume that d_i are sampled from a normal distribution. The estimate for a mean of d_i is given by $\bar{d}_i$. The pooled estimator S_d^2 for variance of d_i is given by

(assuming that population variance of SLN and Veto+SLN are the same)

$$S_d^2 = \frac{(n-1)S_s^2 + (n-1)S_v^2}{2n-2} = \frac{S_s^2 + S_v^2}{2}$$

where, S_s^2 and S_v^2 are sample variance for SLN and Veto+SLN varaints respectively. Then, the test statistic is given by

$$T = \frac{\bar{d} - 0}{\sqrt{S_d^2 \left(\frac{1}{n} + \frac{1}{n}\right)}} = \frac{\sqrt{n}\bar{d}}{\sqrt{S_s^2 + S_v^2}}$$

The significance level α test is to *reject* H_0 if $T \geq t_{\alpha, 2n-2}$; not reject H_0, otherwise. Here $t_{\alpha, 2n-2}$ denotes t-distribution with degree of freedom $2n - 2$. Significance level α means that the probability of H_0 getting rejected when it is actually true is never greater than α. In our experiment, we expect the data to support the alternative hypothesis H_1, but do not want to make the assertion unless the data really gives convincing support. So, we have set up the test so that the alternate hypothesis is the one that we expect data to support and we hope to prove. Alternate hypothesis in such setup is also called the research hypothesis. By choosing a small α as the significance level, we minimize the risk of incorrectly concluding that the data supports the research hypothesis when it is actually false [29]. Common choices for α are 0.1, 0.05, and 0.005; here, we choose $\alpha = 0.05$.

Illustrative Examples. (A) Let us look at a few examples. For Citeseer data set, GCN architecture in presence of 5% noise, we have $\bar{x}^s = 73.92$, $\bar{x}^v = 72.27$, $S_s = 1.1$, $S_v = 0.7$ (from Table 2), and thus, $T = \frac{\sqrt{10} \times (73.92 - 72.27)}{\sqrt{1.1^2 + 0.7^2}} = 4.00184$. For significance level $\alpha = 0.05$, the value of $t_{\alpha, 18} = 1.734$. As, $T > t_{0.05, 18}$ so we reject H_0. It means for the Citeseer dataset at 5% noise, GCN performs worse in the presence of Veto + SLN as compared to SLN, and the probability of incorrectly concluding this is at most 5%. In fact, in this case, $T > t_{0.0005, 18} = 3.921643$, so the probability of incorrectly concluding rejection of H_0 is at most 0.05%.

(B) For Citeseer data set, GIN architecture in presence of 45% noise, we have $\bar{x}^s = 42.29$, $\bar{x}^v = 37.98$, $S_s = 8.8$, $S_v = 5.4$ (from Table 2), and hence, $T = 1.32$. This means, $T < t_{0.05, 18}$ and we accept H_0.

Analysis of Hypothesis Tests: We perform hypothesis testing for all datasets, for all GNN architectures and all noise robust algorithms and the results are presented in Table 5. We divide noise levels into three subclass, Low (5% − 15% noise levels), Medium (20% − 35% noise levels), and High (40% − 50% noise levels). Overall represents aggregate across all noise levels. We revisit questions asked in Sect. 4.4 through the lens of hypothesis testing. For GCN architectures, we have 10 noise levels × 3 datasets × 2 sub-variants (SLN and PWN) = 60 hypothesis tests. Out of 60, we were able to reject 32 null hypotheses with

$\alpha = 0.05$. As in (B), accepting H_0 at a low significance level does not always mean that the null hypothesis is true, but it means that we are unable to reject it with high confidence. In example (B) clearly $\bar{d} > 0$, but as the variances are high, we are not confident if $\bar{d} > 0$ is due to a change in noise model or due to inherent randomness in the learning process (randomness in training set sampling, stochastic gradient descent, etc.). So, when we are able to reject H_0, we can say with high confidence that the decrease in performance is due to a change in the noise model (for example, a change from SLN to Veto+SLN).

Table 5. Summary of all Hypothesis Tests: The fraction of cases in which we rejected the null hypothesis at significance level $\alpha = 0.05$. Even algorithms designed to handle graph label noise experience greater performance degradation due to EDN compared to the existing noise models. We can say this with high confidence for 34% cases under Veto Power and 22% cases under Sequential Flipping. The same is true for 41% cases for GNN architectures.

Noise Model	Noise Level	GCN	GNN Architectures	Existing Noise Robust Algorithms
Veto Power	Low	$6/18 \approx 0.33$	$24/90 \approx 0.27$	$26/144 \approx 0.18$
	Medium	$10/24 \approx 0.42$	$45/120 \approx 0.38$	$54/192 \approx 0.28$
	High	$16/18 \approx 0.89$	$55/90 \approx 0.61$	$85/144 \approx 0.59$
	Overall	$32/60 \approx 0.53$	$124/300 \approx 0.41$	$165/480 \approx 0.34$
Sequential Flipping	Low	$7/18 \approx 0.38$	$23/90 \approx 0.26$	$26/144 \approx 0.18$
	Medium	$9/24 \approx 0.38$	$41/120 \approx 0.34$	$41/192 \approx 0.21$
	High	$14/18 \approx 0.78$	$59/90 \approx 0.66$	$39/144 \approx 0.27$
	Overall	$30/60 \approx 0.5$	$123/300 \approx 0.41$	$106/480 \approx 0.22$

From Table 5, we observe that Veto Power and Sequential Flipping cause greater performance degradation than traditional noise models across different noise levels. GCN is the most affected by EDN, while other GNN architectures show slightly more robustness. However, none of the GNN architecture performs similarly to the existing noise model and EDN across noise levels. Existing noise robust algorithms also fail to completely tackle two variants of EDN. Overall, at $\alpha = 0.05$ significance level, in 34% cases, Veto power degrades the performance of noise robust algorithm more as compared to existing noise models; sequential flipping degrades more performance in 22% of cases. This number increases to 41% for GNN architectures and increases to 50% for GCN. Also, we observe that the impact of EDN becomes prominent with an increase in noise levels.

5 Conclusion

In this work, we introduce a novel noise model for graph data called Edge-Dependent Noise (EDN). Unlike existing noise models used for graph data that were originally designed for i.i.d. data, EDN captures the impact of connections among nodes, on node label noise. We propose three variants of EDN -

Majority Vote, Veto Power, and Sequential Flipping. In all three variants, the probability of a node's label being flipped is directly determined by its degree, making implementation feasible even for large graphs. This degree-dependency is a distinguishing feature of EDN. We theoretically compare the probabilities of label flipping as a function of the node degree for various EDN variants that we propose. Experiments followed by hypothesis testing on results reveal that EDN, especially the Veto power and Sequential flipping variants, leads to more significant performance degradation compared to existing noise models like SLN and CCN. This highlights the critical role of node in understanding the impact of noise on GNN performance, making EDN a valuable tool for robust evaluations of GNNs. This underscores the need for further research into developing noise-robust algorithms specifically designed to handle the complexities of edge-dependent noise in graph data. As the differences in accuracies that we consider are in the interval $[-100, 100]$, one can pursue the hypothesis testing approach in a more principled way without resorting to normal approximations or assuming equal population variance. Our hypothesis testing framework is Berhens-Fisher problem and currently has no completely satisfactory solution (Sec. 8.4.3 of [28]).

References

1. Xiao, S., Wang, S., Dai, Y., Guo, W.: Graph neural networks in node classification: survey and evaluation. Mach. Vis. Appl. **33**(1), 1–19 (2021). https://doi.org/10.1007/s00138-021-01251-0
2. Zhou, J., et al.: Graph neural networks: a review of methods and applications. AI Open (2020)
3. Ju, W., et al.: A survey of graph neural networks in real world: imbalance, noise, privacy and OOD challenges. ArXiv, abs/2403.04468 (2024)
4. Tripathi, S., Hemachandra, N.: Label noise: problems and solutions. Tutorial at IEEE DSAA (2020)
5. Yuan, J., et al.: Learning on graphs under label noise. ICASSP (2023)
6. NT, H., Jin, C.J., Murata, T.: Learning graph neural networks with noisy labels. arXiv preprintarXiv:1905.01591 (2019)
7. Du, X., et al.: Noise-robust graph learning by estimating and leveraging pairwise interactions. Trans. Mach. Learn. Res. (2021)
8. Zhu, Y., et al.: Robust node classification on graph data with graph and label noise. In: AAAI Conference on Artificial Intelligence (2024)
9. Dai, E., Aggarwal, C., Wang, S., NRGNN: learning a label noise resistant graph neural network on sparsely and noisily labeled graphs. In: Proceedings of the 27th ACM SIGKDD, pp. 227–236 (2021)
10. Qian, S., et al.: Robust training of graph neural networks via noise governance. In: ACM International Conference on Web Search and Data Mining (2023)
11. Li, X., Li, Q., Li, D., Qian, H., Wang, J.: Contrastive learning of graphs under label noise. Neural Netw. (2024)
12. James, R.: Norris. Cambridge University Press, Markov Chains (1997)
13. Wang, Z., et al.: NoisyGL: a comprehensive benchmark for graph neural networks under label noise. NeurIPS Dataset Benchmark (2024)
14. Kumar, P., Hemachandra, N.: DeGLIF for Label Noise Robust Node Classification using GNNs. arXiv, abs/2506.00244 (2025)

15. Chen, Z., et al.: ADEdgeDrop: adversarial edge dropping for robust graph neural networks. ArXiv, abs/2403.09171 (2024)
16. Rong, Y., Huang, W., Xu, T., Huang, J.: DropEdge: towards deep graph convolutional networks on node classification. In: International Conference on Learning Representations (2019)
17. Liu, X., Si, S., Zhu, X., Li, Y., Hsieh, C.: A unified framework for data poisoning attack to graph-based semi-supervised learning. In: Neural Information Processing Systems (2019)
18. Zhang, M., Hu, L., Shi, C., Wang, X.: Adversarial label-flipping attack and defense for graph neural networks. In: 2020 IEEE International Conference on Data Mining (ICDM) (2020)
19. Strang, G.: Linear algebra and its applications (2000)
20. Davis, P.J.: Circulant Matrices. Monographs and textbooks in pure and applied mathematics, Wiley (1979)
21. Yang, Z., Cohen, W.W., Salakhutdinov, R.: Revisiting semi-supervised learning with graph embeddings. ArXiv, abs/1603.08861 (2016)
22. Shchur, O., Mumme, M., Bojchevski, A., Günnemann, S.: Pitfalls of graph neural network evaluation. arXiv preprintarXiv:1811.05868 (2018)
23. Kipf, T.N., Welling, M.: Semi-supervised classification with graph convolutional networks. arXiv preprintarXiv:1609.02907 (2016)
24. Xu, K., Hu, W., Leskovec, J., Jegelka, S.: How powerful are graph neural networks? ArXiv, abs/1810.00826 (2018)
25. Hamilton, W.L., Ying, Z., Leskovec, J.: Inductive representation learning on large graphs. In: NIPS (2017)
26. Velickovic, P., et al.: Graph attention networks. ArXiv, abs/1710.10903 (2017)
27. Shi, Y., et al.: Unified massage passing model for semi-supervised classification. IJCAI, Masked label prediction (2021)
28. Ross, S.M.: Introduction to Probability and Statistics for Engineers and Scientists. Academic Press, 6th edn (2020)
29. Casella, G., Berger, R.L.: Statistical Inference. Taylor and Francis, 2nd edn (2024)

DRNCS: Dual-Level Route Generation Model Based on Node Contraction and Shortcuts

Zhuoran Li[1], Yucen Gao[1], Yu Yin[2], Xinle Li[2], Hui Gao[2], Xiaofeng Gao[1(✉)], and Guihai Chen[1]

[1] School of Computer Science, Shanghai Key Laboratory of Scalable Computing and Systems, Shanghai Jiao Tong University, Shanghai, China
{airplane,guo_ke}@sjtu.edu.cn, {gao-xf,gchen}@cs.sjtu.edu.cn
[2] Didi Global Inc, Beijing, China
{yinyu,lixinle,deangaohui}@didiglobal.com

Abstract. Route prediction is a fundamental task in mapping services, with critical applications in trajectory reconstruction and route recommendation. However, existing algorithms face efficiency challenges, particularly for long routes. The primary challenge is to enhance computational efficiency while maintaining prediction accuracy, especially in large-scale, real-time scenarios. To address this challenge, we propose an accelerated route generation model **DRNCS** based on node contraction and shortcut acceleration, utilizing a dual-level model specifically designed for path prediction. By effectively employing Shortcut-Edge Differential Contraction, we manage to contract nodes in a way that avoids the common problem of out-degree explosion, which is typically encountered in conventional node contraction methods. This approach allows us to transform the original graph into a much sparser representation, preserving the structural integrity while significantly reducing the complexity of the graph. We then compute and store the most likely shortcuts using two methods: merging historical routes and applying a probability-based bidirectional Dijkstra's algorithm on historical paths. Ultimately, the final prediction results are generated by predicting on the sparse graph and invoking the stored shortcut data, which is produced by the model trained on the original graph. Through in-depth experiments on real-world datasets, we establish that our model imparts significant improvement in generation speed while maintaining query accuracy over state-of-the-art approaches and demonstrates advantages in reachability. This provides robust support for the practical application of our algorithm in real-world route generation scenarios.

Keywords: Route Recommendation · Path Optimization

This work was supported by the National Key R&D Program of China [2024YFF0617700], the National Natural Science Foundation of China [U23A20309, 62272302, 62372296], the CCF-DiDi GAIA Collaborative Research Funds for Young Scholars [202404]. Xiaofeng Gao is the corresponding author.

1 Introduction

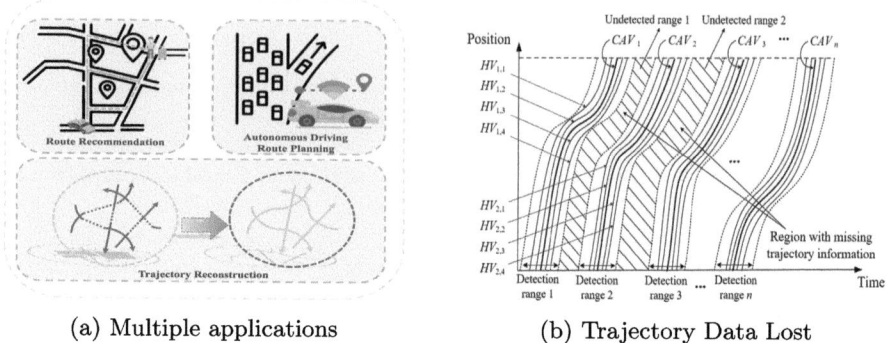

(a) Multiple applications (b) Trajectory Data Lost

Fig. 1. Application Scenarios of route Recommendation

Route generation technology has significant potential in optimizing urban mobility [5], aiding applications such as helping taxi drivers select faster routes for quicker pickups and improving customer satisfaction [9]. It also enables autonomous vehicles to choose less congested paths, reducing travel time during peak hours and alleviating overall traffic congestion. Additionally, as shown in Fig. 1b [14], real-world trajectory data is often incomplete or discontinuous. In such cases, route generation can reconstruct trajectories and forecast potential routes of moving objects, providing valuable insights into future traffic conditions and helping urban planners optimize infrastructure and traffic management [17].

In real-world scenarios, as illustrated in Fig. 2, the straightforward application of shortest path algorithm to infer the most likely route, intuitively assuming that the shortest path is always the best option, can lead to significant errors, particularly as trajectory length increases and the scale of the road network expands. In this context, considerable scholarly attention has been devoted to the optimization of route generation technologies in recent years. Notably, the NEUROMLR [6] framework has reported marked enhancements in both precision and recall rates. Despite these advancements, prevailing algorithms continue to grapple with substantial challenges pertaining to the time required for route generation, especially in the context of longer path problems, where pronounced search delays are frequently observed. This challenge is particularly evident within the NEUROMLR-D variant, wherein the average prediction time for a single path exceeds three seconds when processing extensive road networks and extended routes. Such performance is insufficient to satisfy the requirements of practical applications.

In light of the current state of research, the following pivotal question emerges: **How can we significantly enhance the efficiency of the search**

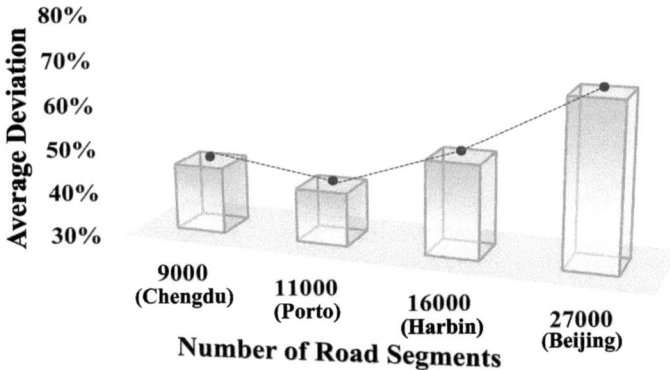

Fig. 2. Loss of Shortest Path

process while preserving the accuracy of route predictions to fulfill practical application requirements?

To address this critical issue, we recognize that the extended time required for predicting long paths primarily stems from the massive number of nodes needing processing. Inspired by the CH algorithm [3] that accelerates shortest path computation through node contraction and shortcut addition, we propose **DRNCS** – a **D**ual-Level **R**oute Generation framework based on **N**ode **C**ontraction and **S**hortcuts. Our dual-level acceleration mechanism operates through two complementary tiers: **Architectural-Level Acceleration:** We design a hierarchical learning system where (1) a *contracted-graph model* predicts key nodes on a simplified topology to establish sparse routing skeletons, while (2) an *original-graph model* generates probabilistic shortcuts between these nodes using transition probabilities learned from historical trajectories. **Inference-Level Enhancement:** During path generation, we implement: (1) dynamic shortcut injection from precomputed high-probability connections to bypass redundant node computations, and (2) accuracy preservation through hybrid verification combining model predictions with bidirectional Dijkstra search on transition-probability-weighted graphs. This hierarchical design achieves acceleration through graph contraction while preserving precision via shortcut verification, effectively balancing efficiency and accuracy.

We have carried out the following work in this paper: We propose a node contraction method, Shortcut-Edge Differential Contraction, which uses a top-down edge difference as the criterion to transform the original graph into a sparse representation, while concurrently processing the original trajectory data to construct sparse graph trajectory datasets. Utilizing the original graph, we conduct model training to generate the necessary data for shortcut creation which involves merging historical trajectory information (i.e., selecting a representative historical route from numerous historical trajectories) and calculating the most likely shortcuts using bidirectional Dijkstra's algorithm on the graph weighted by transition probabilities. Based on the sparse graph trajectory datasets mentioned above, we first trained the model on the sparse graph, then made predictions on it, and finally obtained the final prediction result by combining the predicted paths with the shortcut dataset. Finally, we conduct extensive experiments using real-world city dataset to validate our approach. our contributions within this paper are as follows:

- **Maintained Prediction Accuracy:** We employed appropriate embedding techniques and probabilistic prediction models, enabling us to sustain high levels of prediction accuracy and reachability.
- **Accelerated the Prediction Process:** We proposed Shortcut-Edge Differential Contraction to generate a sparse graph, then applied historical path merging and bidirectional Dijkstra's algorithm on graph weighted by transition probabilities based on model training results to obtain shortcut dataset, accelerating subsequent query processes.
- **Refined Dual-Level Model Design:** Our model is trained on both the original and sparse graphs, allowing for more effective acquisition of shortcut and final prediction data.
- **Experimental Validation:** Extensive experiments conducted on real-world city dataset validate the effectiveness of our model and a substantial enhancement in prediction efficiency.

2 Related Work

2.1 Path Prediction Algorithm

Shortest Path-Based Route Prediction. The shortest path is the simplest approach for route prediction, widely used in existing studies [10,11,16]. [10] proposes the spMM model, leveraging geometric and topological road network features, while [16] incorporates traffic signal delays and left turns into a heuristic cost function. Building on this, [11] constructs a candidate graph favoring straighter paths. However, these methodologies do not adequately account for driver preferences in route selection. In reality, drivers consider various factors beyond the length and straightness of the route. Consequently, the most likely route frequently diverges from the shortest path, as shown in the Fig. 2. This suggests that a singular focus on distance is insufficient for accurately predicting the most likely route.

Route Prediction Based on RNN. To address the challenges associated with route prediction using the shortest path, several existing methods have been proposed that utilize RNNs based on historical trajectories: In the realm of route prediction, several notable models have emerged, each with distinct principles and limitations. **DEEPST** [8] uses variational autoencoders to capture trajectory and traffic relationships but struggles with poor reachability for unseen points. **CSSRNN** [15] leverages RNNs and road network constraints but suffers from long query times, low reachability, and data dependency.

NEUROMLR [6] combines Lipschitz embeddings with GCNs for accuracy, with two variants: NEUROMLR-D (Dijkstra's Algorithm) and NEUROMLR-G (Greedy Algorithm). NEUROMLR-D enhances shortest-path calculations but has high query latency, while NEUROMLR-G improves speed and reachability but remains inefficient for long routes, requiring further optimization.

Route Prediction Based on Transformer. While autoregressive models like RNNs have been the cornerstone of route prediction, recent research has increasingly adopted Transformer architectures for their ability to model complex dependencies. [1] employs a Transformer-based framework to capture spatiotemporal correlations in road networks, while [7] introduces BERT-Trip, a BERT-inspired model which is a self-supervised contrastive learning framework for route recommendation that addresses the challenges of learning effective trip representations without labeled data and eliminating the need for manually designed negative samples. Despite their effectiveness, the substantial parameter size of Transformer-based models presents challenges, particularly in inference speed, which constrains their applicability in real-time scenarios (Table 1).

Table 1. Limitations of Existing Route Prediction Models

Model	Limitations
DEEPST	Inability to predict points not in original data; suboptimal reachability
CSSRNN	Poor reachability; extended query time; reliance on high-quality training data
NEUROMLR-D	Prolonged query time; less suitable for real-time applications
NEUROMLR-G	Significant delays for longer routes; need for further optimization
BERT-Trip	High training costs; Prolonged query time.

In summary, while each method presents unique advantages in predictive capabilities and model design, it is evident that current path prediction methods face significant challenges related to slow query speeds. To mitigate this issue, we investigate various potential approaches aimed at effectively accelerating queries while preserving an acceptable level of accuracy. One particularly promising avenue is inspired by the **Contraction Hierarchies (CH)** algorithm, which enhances the efficiency of shortest path queries through the contraction of nodes and the incorporation of shortcuts.

2.2 Node Contraction Method

Contraction Hierarchies (CH). Contraction Hierarchies (CH) [3] enhance the efficiency of shortest path queries through a preprocessing phase that simplifies the graph structure. This is achieved by contracting less significant nodes while preserving essential connectivity through the introduction of shortcut edges, which maintain the correctness of shortest path distances. Once the preprocessing is complete, shortest path queries are executed using a bidirectional variant of Dijkstra's algorithm [2], which simultaneously explores the search space from both the source and target nodes. This approach effectively reduces the number of processed nodes, thereby significantly improving query performance.

The classical CH algorithm cannot be directly applied to our context of predicting the most likely route. We need to address the following issues:

1. **What criteria should be used for node contraction?** In our application scenario, it is crucial to minimize the increase in out-degree as much as possible, as this will affect the speed at which our model predicts potential nodes. Therefore, We propose Shortcut-Edge Differential Contraction, a top-down approach that uses edge difference as the criterion for node contraction. This approach ensures that we can contract more nodes without causing an explosion in out-degree.
2. **How can we generate shortcuts that are more aligned with the most likely route prediction scenario?** Directly using the shortcuts derived from classical algorithms is not feasible. Consequently, we employ bidirectional Dijkstra's algorithm on a probabilistic graph generated from historical data to create shortcuts that are more representative of the most likely route. This enables acceleration in our predictions.

3 Problem Formulation and Transformation

We begin with the definitions of **Road Network**, **Route** and **Query**. Subsequently, we formally present the research problem and provide its transformation. For the sake of clarity and ease of reference, the notation employed in this paper is presented in Table 2.

Table 2. Notation and Description Table

Notation	Description
$G(V, E)$	A directed graph consisting of vertices V and edges E.
$|V|, |E|$	Number of nodes and edges.
G_{neg_log}	The graph G weighted by the negative logarithm of probabilities.
R, R^*	True routes and Predicted routes.
$SC^{(1)}, SC^{(2)}$	Shortcuts filtered through historical trajectories and Shortcuts generated based on probabilistic graphs.
$|R|, |R^*|$	Number of edges in the true route and in the predicted route, respectively.
$|R^*_{d=d^*}|$	Count of predicted paths matching the original path's endpoint.
$q = (s, d, t)$	A query is represented by a tuple, involving start node s, destination node d, and time t.
$Pr(R|q)$	The probability of selecting route R given a specific query q.
P_S	The set of historical paths within the historical trajectory that share the same start-end pair.
$P(e)$	Probability of selecting edge. e.
UnConf	The unnormalized confidence score for predictions.
$Q((\text{curr}, \text{nbr})|\text{curr}, d; \Theta)$	Transition probability from the current node to a neighboring node, given the destination and parameterized by Θ.
N2V(node)	The embedding of a node using the node2vec algorithm.
W	Weight matrix for a layer in the neural network.
T_{total}	Total time taken to generate all predicted routes.

Definition 1 (Road Network). A road network is represented as a directed graph $G(V, E)$, in which V and E represent the vertices (crossroads) and edges (road segments) respectively.

Definition 2 (Route). A route $r = [e_i]_{i=1}^n$ is a sequence of adjacent road segments, where $e_i \in E$. In practical applications, a route, $R(s,d) = \{v_1, \ldots, v_k\}$ represents a simple path from the source node $s = v_1$ to the destination $d = v_k$ in the road network G, with no cycles. Similarly, it can be expressed as a sequence of edges $R(s,d) = \{e_1, \ldots, e_{k-1}\}$, where $e_i = (v_i, v_{i+1})$.

Definition 3 (Query). A query is represented by a tuple $q = (s,d,t)$, where s and d are the source and destination nodes within the set of nodes V, respectively. The variable t indicates the time when the trajectory takes place.

Problem Statement. Given a road network $G(V,E)$ and a historical trajectory dataset $D = (T(m))_{m=1}^M$, alongside a query $q = (s,d,t)$, the objective is to infer the most likely route $R^*(s,d)$ based on the traffic patterns contained in D. Formally, the most likely route is defined as:

$$R^*(s,d) = \arg\max_{R(s,d) \in G} \Pr(R(s,d) \mid q) \tag{1}$$

Problem Transformation. The problem of predicting the most likely route can be framed as a path search problem on the graph. Mathematically, the probability of a route R can be formulated as the product of the probabilities of its individual edges. Formally, we have:

$$\Pr(R|q) = \prod_{i=1}^{|R|} \Pr(R.e_i | R.e_0 \rightarrow R.e_{i-1}, s, d, t) \tag{2}$$

where $\Pr(R.e_i | R.e_0 \rightarrow R.e_{i-1}, s, d, t)$ denotes the probability that route R traverses edge $R.e_i$ given the path taken thus far and the query parameters $q = (s,d,t)$. Past studies have shown that human mobility patterns conform to the Markovian assumption [13], which states that the future state depends only on the present state and not on the sequence of events that preceded it. Consequently, the above equation reduces to:

$$\Pr(R|q) = \prod_{i=1}^{|R|} \Pr(R.e_i | v_i, d, t) \tag{3}$$

With these simplifications, Eq. (2) reduces to:

$$R^*(s,d) = \arg\max_{\forall R \in G} \prod_{i=1}^{|R|} \Pr(R.e_i | v_i, d, t) = \arg\min_{\forall R \in G} \sum_{i=1}^{|R|} -\log(\Pr(R.e_i | v_i, d, t)) \tag{4}$$

This transformation indicates that the problem of selecting the most probable route has been converted into a problem of searching for the shortest path on a weighted graph, where the weights correspond to the negative logarithm of the probabilities. We denote this weighted graph as G_{neg_log}.

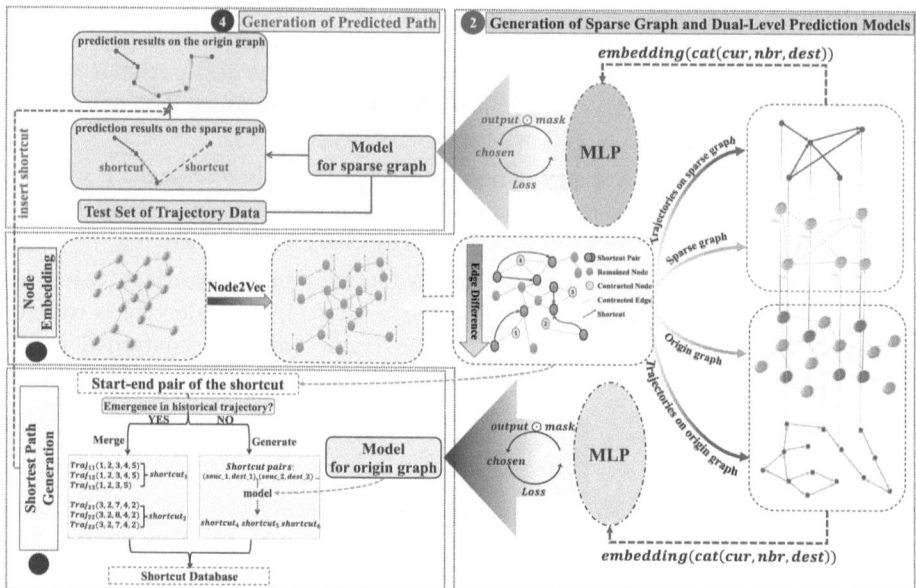

Fig. 3. Framework of DRNCS: **DRNCS** first generates node embeddings using node2vec, then contracts nodes based on edge difference to create a sparse graph and shortcut pairs. The model is trained separately on both the original and sparse graphs, producing a dual-level model. During the shortcut database generation, two approaches are used: merging historical paths and generating shortcuts based on model results from the original graph. Finally, in the inference phase, predictions are made on the sparse graph, conbining the stored shortcut data to derive the final results.

4 Modeling

Our model incorporates several key components: generating node embeddings, creating sparse graph, training models with original path information on the original graph, and training models using sparsified trajectory data on the sparse graph, generating shortcuts with two distinct approaches, executing the inference phase. The framework of our model is illustrated in Fig. 3.

4.1 Node Embedding Generation

The node2vec algorithm [4] effectively captures the structural features of nodes in a graph using a flexible random walk strategy. For our study, which aims to predict the most likely route, we require node embeddings that account for complex factors beyond simple metrics like distance and geographic coordinates. Thus, we selected node2vec as our embedding method.

4.2 Sparse Graph Modeling

To address the query speed issue of route generation, we aim to minimize the increase in the maximum out-degree of nodes during the graph contraction process. So we propose **Shortcut-Edge Differential Contraction**, where we select **edge difference**—defined as the difference between the number of shortcuts added during node contraction and the sum of the node's original in-degree and out-degree—as our criterion for node contraction. Furthermore, we employ a **top-down** approach to control the scale of out-degree increase as much as possible. The node contraction process is presented in Algorithm 1.

Algorithm 1: Shortcut-Edge Differential Contraction

Input: Graph $G = (V, E)$, Contraction ratio r
Output: Shortcut pairs $shortcut\_pair$, Sparse Gragh G^*
1 copy G to G^*
2 **while** *(number of contracted nodes $<$ total nodes $\times r$)* **do**
3   Select the node with the minimum edge difference in G^*;
4   Contract the selected node;
5   **for** *each predecessor p of the contracted node* **do**
6   **for** *each successor s of the contracted node* **do**
7   **if** *not edge (p, s) exists in G^** **then**
8   Add edge (p, s) in G^*;
9   Store (p, s) in $shortcut\_pair$;

10 **return** $shortcut\_pair, G^*$;

The algorithm in Algorithm 1 initializes a new graph G^* as a copy of G (line 2) and iteratively contracts nodes until $r \times |V|$ nodes are removed (line 3). In each iteration, the node with the smallest *edge difference* is selected to minimize connectivity disruption (lines 4-6). Once contracted (lines 7-9), shortcut edges are added between its predecessor p and successor s if no direct edge (p, s) exists, storing them in *shortcut_pair*. The algorithm terminates when the contraction ratio is met, returning G^* and the shortcut pairs for model training (line 10).

4.3 Model Training

After completing the node embedding, we train on the original trajectories from the original graph and the processed sparse trajectories from the sparse graph, obtaining the trained models at **two levels**. The trained model from the sparse graph will be used to infer phase, while the trained model from the original graph will be utilized for shortcut generation. The specific details of the model training are as follows: We obtained our embedding results by concatenating the embeddings generated by node2vec, where the 'neighbors' (nbr) include both the true neighboring nodes of each node and the virtual neighboring nodes, represented by -1, which are added through padding to ensure that each node has the same number of neighbors. After obtaining the final embeddings, we pass these embeddings through a multi-layer perceptron (MLP) to convert the vector into a scalar unnormalized confidence value, defined as follows:

$$embedding = cat(N2V(curr), N2V(nbr)N2V(dest)) \quad (5)$$

$$\text{UnConf} = f(nbr, curr, dest) = \text{MLP}(embedding), \quad nbr \in N(curr) \quad (6)$$

The transition probability $Q((curr, v)|curr, d; \Theta)$ can be computed as follows:

$$Q((curr, nbr)|curr, dest; \Theta) = \frac{\exp(f(nbr, curr, dest))}{\sum_{nbr' \in N(curr)} \exp(f(nbr', curr, dest))} \quad (7)$$

This equation normalizes the unnormalized confidence by the sum of the exponential values of the confidence for all neighbors $nbr' \in N(curr)$.

Next, we generate a mask based on the actual neighbors of the nodes to filter the unnormalized confidence. We apply the mask to set the confidence values to zero for neighbors represented by -1 (indicating the absence of such neighbors):

$$\text{UnConf}^* = \text{UnConf} \odot \text{mask} \quad (8)$$

We then select the candidate with the highest confidence, simplified as:

$$\text{chosen} = \arg\max_i (\text{UnConf}^*_i), \quad \text{for } i \in \{1, 2, \ldots, \max\_nbrs\} \quad (9)$$

Finally, the model parameters Θ are optimized through *cross-entropy loss* over trajectories in **D**, defined as:

$$\text{Loss}(\Theta) = -\frac{1}{|D|} \sum_{R \in D} \sum_{j=1}^{|R|} \log Q(R.e_j | R.nbr_j, R.dest; \Theta) \quad (10)$$

4.4 Shortcut Generation

To generate shortcut data within a short timeframe, we developed our shortcut database based on whether the required start-end shortcut pairs have appeared in historical trajectory data. We employed two approaches for this purpose:

$SC^{(1)}$ generation For the start-end pairs that have been observed in the historical data, we utilized a merging approach. Within the historical trajectories, for paths sharing the same start and end points, we computed the precision of each path relative to the others and calculated the average precision as our selection criterion. The path with the highest average precision was selected as the final shortcut data $SC^{(1)}$ for that specific start-end pair.

$$SC^{(1)} = \arg\max_{R_i \in P_S} \frac{1}{N} \sum_{j=1}^{N} \text{Precision}(R_i, R_j), \quad \text{where } R_i, R_j \in P_S \tag{11}$$

$SC^{(2)}$ **generation** For those start-end pairs of shortcuts that do not appear in the historical trajectory, firstly, for a given shortcut's starting point S and endpoint D, we consider all nodes in the graph as potential source nodes, with D designated as the destination. We then utilize the model trained on the original graph to generate the transition probabilities $P(e)$ for each edge e:

$$P(e) = f(nbr, curr, dest), \quad curr \in G \tag{12}$$

where f represents the function derived from our trained model.

Next, we transform these transition probabilities into negative logarithmic weights for incorporation into the graph:

$$W(e) = -\log(P(e)) \tag{13}$$

Following this, we apply a bidirectional Dijkstra's algorithm to identify the most likely route between S and D:

$$SC^{(2)} = \text{BidirectionalDijkstra}(S, D, W) \tag{14}$$

This route $SC^{(2)}$ is then stored in the shortcut dataset. The time complexity of Dijkstra's [12] is $O((|E|+|V|)\log|V|)$, where $|E|$ and $|V|$ represent the number of edges and vertices, respectively.

While this time complexity may be impractical for real-time route recommendation systems, it is exceptionally well-suited for our scenario for the following reasons: First, Dijkstra's algorithm is only used during the preprocessing phase to compute the shortcuts, which is a low-frequency operation. Second, the shortcuts we generate are relatively short compared to the routes that need to be predicted in real-world applications, which reduces the number of nodes and edges that need to be explored during the search process.

4.5 Inference Phase

For a given query $q = (S, D)$, we employ a greedy search algorithm, which relies exclusively on transition probabilities. The prediction of a transition probability $P(e = (curr, nbr)|curr, dest)$ is achieved through a forward pass within the architectural framework of the model. This search is performed on the sparse graph, where we predict the most probable transitions between nodes based on the learned probabilities. To further refine the predictions, we incorporate previously obtained shortcut datasets—those generated in Sect. 4.4. These shortcuts provide additional context or connections, which are then inserted into the predicted results to enhance the accuracy and robustness of the final prediction.

5 Experiments

5.1 Dataset

The data used in our experiments, presented in Table 3 [1] [2], includes road network and trajectory data from five cities: Chengdu (CD), Porto (PT), Harbin (HRB), Beijing (BJ), and Shenzhen with its surrounding areas (SZ). These datasets, rigorously cleaned and preprocessed, cover diverse road network scales and configurations, closely reflecting real-world urban scenarios. This ensures our model's applicability to large-scale practical settings.

Table 3. Details of datasets

City	CD	PT	HRB	BJ	SZ
Number of nodes	3,973	5,330	6,598	31,199	79,348
Number of edges	9,255	11,491	16,292	72,156	171,313
Number of trajectories	3,600,503	1,426,312	1,133,548	1,382,948	1,007,209
Average number of edges/trip	22.93	51.07	56.81	36.08	37.02

5.2 Metric

Since the actual length of an edge is not considered as a criterion during the route generation process, and in order to comprehensively test the efficiency and accuracy of our model's predictions, the metrics evaluated in this experiment can be simplified as follows:

$$\text{Precision} = \frac{|R^* \cap R|}{|R^*|}, \text{Recall} = \frac{|R^* \cap R|}{|R|}, \text{Reachability} = \frac{|R^*_{d=d^*}|}{|R^*|}$$

$$\text{Query Time} = \frac{T_{\text{total}}}{|R^*|}, \text{Generated Paths Rate} = \frac{|R^*|}{T_{\text{total}}}$$

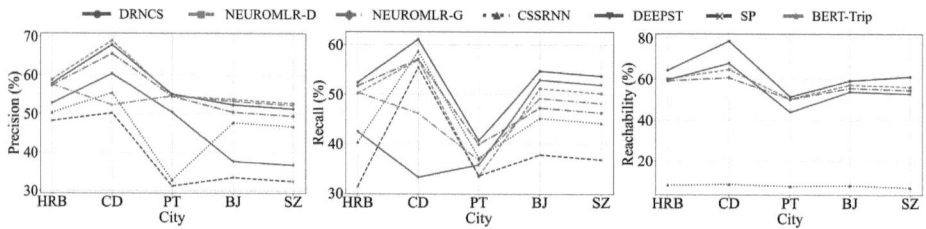

Fig. 4. Model Prediction Accuracy Comparison

---
[1] https://drive.google.com/file/d/1bICE26ndR2C29jkfG2qQqVkmpirK25Eu/view
[2] https://github.com/lehaifeng/T-GCN/tree/master/data

5.3 Baseline Methods

We compare the performance of our model with the following baseline models:

- DEEPST (Deep Spatio-Temporal Model) [8]
- CSSRNN (Convolutional Spatiotemporal Sequence Prediction with RNN) [15]
- NEUROMLR-D (NEUROMLR using Dijkstra's Algorithm) [6]
- NEUROMLR-G (NEUROMLR using Greedy Algorithm) [6]
- SP (Shortest Path) [2]
- BERT-Trip [7]

5.4 Implementation Details

The models in this paper are trained with Python 3.6 and PyTorch 2.4.1 on a machine with a 1.70 GHz Intel(R) Core(TM) i5-1240P processor and 16 GB RAM. For the comparative experiments, we use 200 epochs and a batch size of 512. The code is available at https://github.com/iairplane/DRNCS.git.

5.5 Comparison with Baseline Methods

Precision and Recall. As shown in Fig. 4, the results indicate that, under the same number of training iterations, our model outperforms the NEUROMLR-G, DEEPST, CSSRNN and BERT-Trip methods in terms of accuracy, while maintaining a level of accuracy comparable to NEUROMLR-D. This suggests that our model construction and shortcut generation have achieved desired effect.

Query Time and Generated Paths Rate. Delving deeper into the query time metrics, our model demonstrates exceptional enhancements across different datasets, as shown in Table 4. In the Chengdu dataset, the query speed improved by over 45.5%, by over 40.0% in the Porto dataset, by over 57.1% in Harbin, and by over 47.8% in Shenzhen. Notably, a 57.5% improvement was observed in the Beijing dataset. These results collectively illustrate the substantial optimization of query time realized by our model, aligning perfectly with our initial objective of leveraging shortcuts to expedite the computation of the most likely route.

5.6 Analysis of Ablation Study Results

The core component of our model is the shortcut database, primarily consisting of $SC^{(1)}$ and $SC^{(2)}$. Therefore, in the ablation study, we validate the effectiveness of the overall and partial shortcuts in enhancing efficiency while preserving accuracy. Additionally, as selecting appropriate criteria and ratios for node contraction is crucial in model construction, we conduct multiple ablation studies to determine the optimal parameters for our model. The experiment validating the effectiveness of the shortcut in improving query efficiency was conducted on road network datasets of varying scales, while the other experiments were conducted using the Chengdu dataset.

Table 4. Model Performance Metrics

Model	Query Time (ms/trip)					Generated Paths Rate (trips/s)				
	HRB	CD	PT	BJ	SZ	HRB	CD	PT	BJ	SZ
DRNCS	**0.3**	**0.6**	**0.3**	**0.7**	**0.8**	**3356**	**1678**	**3345**	**1432**	**1249**
NEUROMLR-D	243	201	221	314	378	4.11	4.98	4.52	3.18	2.64
NEUROMLR-G	0.7	1.1	0.6	1.1	1.3	1428	902	1667	909	845
CSSRNN	0.9	1.2	1.1	1.4	1.5	1112	773	972	714	678
BERT-Trip	217	236	219	421	489	4.61	4.23	4.56	2.42	2.04

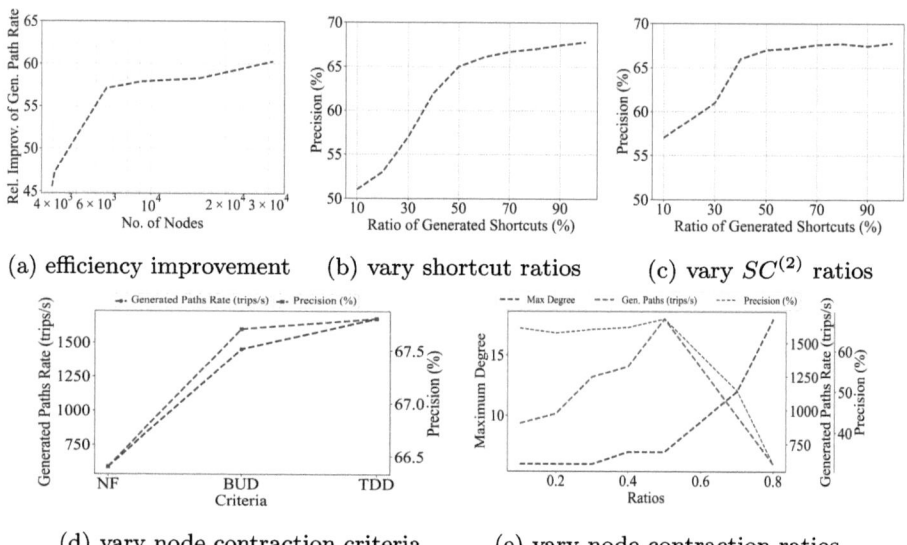

(a) efficiency improvement (b) vary shortcut ratios (c) vary $SC^{(2)}$ ratios

(d) vary node contraction criteria (e) vary node contraction ratios

Fig. 5. Results of the Ablation Study

Effect of Shortcut. As discussed in the previous section, incorporating shortcuts allows us to maintain accuracy while significantly speeding up inference. To further validate our model, we conducted two ablation experiments. First, we tested road networks of varying sizes, comparing the inference speed of DRNCS with and without shortcut insertion, using the Relative Improvement of Generated Paths Rate to show how speed differences increase with network size. The results in Fig. 5a confirm the effectiveness of shortcut insertion. Second, we replaced some shortcuts in our database with Dijkstra-generated shortest paths and compared model prediction accuracy at different proportions. The results, presented in Fig. 5b, validate the effectiveness of the shortcuts.

Effect of $SC^{(2)}$ Component of Shortcut. To further validate the effect of shortcuts generated by bidirectional Dijkstra's algorithm on a graph weighted by transition probabilities, we systematically replaced a subset of these shortcuts with Dijkstra-generated shortest paths at varying proportions, and compared the resulting differences in precision. The results, presented in Fig. 5c, demonstrate the effectiveness of the shortcuts in enhancing model performance.

Criteria for Node Contraction. We employed three criteria for potential node contraction: node occurrence frequency in historical paths (**NF**), bottom-up edge difference (**BUD**), and top-down edge difference (**TDD**). Each criterion was applied to reduce 30% of the nodes across the entire graph, with the comparison results shown in Fig. 5d. The results indicate that selecting the top-down edge difference as the criterion for node contraction effectively maximizes control over the increase in node out-degree, thereby enhancing prediction accuracy and improving search speed. Additionally, the top-down node contraction method demonstrates a notably faster contraction speed.

Ratios for Node Contraction. In order to achieve a balance between accuracy and query speed, we tested the precision and query rate of our model under different contraction ratios. The comparison results are presented in Fig. 5e. Thus, to simultaneously maintain a high prediction accuracy and a faster query rate, we ultimately selected a contraction ratio of 0.5.

6 Conclusion

Route generation plays a critical role in numerous downstream applications. In practical scenarios, when addressing the problem of recommending the most likely route, it is not only imperative to ensure high prediction accuracy, but also to significantly improve the inference speed. This latter aspect remains a key limitation of existing route generation models. To mitigate this issue, we propose **DRNCS**, an accelerated dual-level route generation model based on node contraction and shortcuts. Specifically, we transformed the original graph into a sparse graph through Shortcut-Edge Differential Contraction. By training the model on both the original trajectories from the original graph and the sparse trajectories from the sparse graph, we successfully generated a dual-level trained model. Furthermore, we employed a shortcut generation approach that consists of two distinct methods: first, merging historical paths, and second, generating shortcuts based on the trained model from the original graph. This comprehensive methodology enabled us to create a more accurate shortcut database in a significantly reduced timeframe. Ultimately, the final prediction results are derived by performing predictions on the sparse graph while invoking the stored shortcut data. Additionally, testing on road network datasets of varying scales demonstrated that our approach achieved over 40% improvement in query speed, while effectively maintaining satisfactory accuracy and reachability. Notably, this optimization in query speed becomes even more pronounced as the scale of the road network increases, thereby highlighting the practical applicability and advantages of our model in real-world scenarios.

References

1. Bhumika, Das, D.: Marrs: a framework for multi-objective risk-aware route recommendation using multitask-transformer. In: Proceedings of the 16th ACM Conference on Recommender Systems (2022). https://api.semanticscholar.org/CorpusID: 252216597
2. Dijkstra, E.W.: A note on two problems in connexion with graphs. Numer. Math. **1**, 269–271 (1959)
3. Geisberger, R., Sanders, P., Schultes, D., Delling, D.: Contraction hierarchies: faster and simpler hierarchical routing in road networks. In: McGeoch, C.C. (ed.) Exper. Algorithms, pp. 319–333. Springer, Berlin Heidelberg (2008)
4. Grover, A., Leskovec, J.: node2vec: scalable feature learning for networks. In: Proceedings of the 22nd ACM SIGKDD International Conference on Knowledge Discovery and Data Mining (2016)
5. Hsieh, H.P., Lin, F.: Recommending taxi routes with an advance reservation – a multi-criteria route planner. Int. J. Urban Sci. **26**, 162 – 183 (2021). https://api.semanticscholar.org/CorpusID:233810149
6. Jain, J.L., Bagadia, V., Manchanda, S., Ranu, S.: Neuromlr: Robust & reliable route recommendation on road networks. In: Neural Information Processing Systems (2021)
7. Kuo, A.T., Chen, H., Ku, W.S.: Bert-trip: effective and scalable trip representation using attentive contrast learning. In: 2023 IEEE 39th International Conference on Data Engineering (ICDE), pp. 612–623 (2023). https://api.semanticscholar.org/CorpusID:260171278
8. Li, X., Cong, G., Cheng, Y.: Spatial transition learning on road networks with deep probabilistic models. In: IEEE 36th International Conference on Data Engineering (ICDE), pp. 349–360 (2020)
9. Li, X., Cong, G., Sun, A., Cheng, Y.: Learning travel time distributions with deep generative model. The World Wide Web Conference (2019)
10. Rahmani, M., Koutsopoulos, H.N.: Path inference of low-frequency GPS probes for urban networks. In: International IEEE Conference on Intelligent Transportation Systems, pp. 1698–1701 (2012)
11. Rahmani, M., Koutsopoulos, H.N.: Path inference from sparse floating car data for urban networks. Transport. Res. Part C-emerging Technol. **30**, 41–54 (2013)
12. Tarjan, R.E.: Data structures and network algorithms. In: CBMS-NSF Regional Conference Series in Applied Mathematics (1983)
13. Wang, J., Wu, N., Zhao, W.X., Peng, F., Lin, X.: Empowering a* search algorithms with neural networks for personalized route recommendation. In: Proceedings of the 25th ACM SIGKDD International Conference on Knowledge Discovery & Data Mining (2019)
14. Wang, Y., Wei, L., Chen, P.: Trajectory reconstruction for freeway traffic mixed with human-driven vehicles and connected and automated vehicles. Transport. Res. Part C: Emerg. Technol. **111**, 135–155 (2020)
15. qing Wu, H., Chen, Z., Sun, W., Zheng, B., Wang, W.: Modeling trajectories with recurrent neural networks. In: International Joint Conference on Artificial Intelligence (2017)
16. Zheng, Y., Quddus, M.A.: Weight-based shortest-path aided map-matching algorithm for low-frequency positioning data (2011)
17. Mahmood, M.T., Ali, M.E., Cheema, M.A., Rashid, S.M.M., Sellis, T.: PathOracle: a deep learning based trip planner for daily commuters. In: Machine Learning and Knowledge Discovery in Databases: European Conference (2022)

GraphWeave : Interpretable and Robust Graph Generation via Random Walk Trajectories

Rahul Nandakumar[✉] and Deepayan Chakrabarti

The University of Texas at Austin, Austin, TX 78713, USA
{rahul.nandakumar,deepay}@utexas.edu

Abstract. Given a set of graphs from some unknown family, we want to generate new graphs from that family. Recent methods use diffusion on either graph embeddings or the discrete space of nodes and edges. However, simple changes to embeddings (say, adding noise) can mean uninterpretable changes in the graph. In discrete-space diffusion, each step may add or remove many nodes/edges. It is hard to predict what graph patterns we will observe after many diffusion steps. Our proposed method, called GraphWeave, takes a different approach. We separate pattern generation and graph construction. To find patterns in the training graphs, we see how they transform vectors during random walks. We then generate new graphs in two steps. First, we generate realistic random walk "trajectories" which match the learned patterns. Then, we find the optimal graph that fits these trajectories. The optimization infers all edges jointly, which improves robustness to errors. On four simulated and five real-world benchmark datasets, GraphWeave outperforms existing methods. The most significant differences are on large-scale graph structures such as PageRank, cuts, communities, degree distributions, and flows. GraphWeave is also 10x faster than its closest competitor. Finally, GraphWeave is simple, needing only a transformer and standard optimizers.

Code is available at https://github.com/rahulnanda1999/GraphWeave.

Keywords: Graph Generation · Diffusion · Random Walk · Trajectory

1 Introduction

Suppose that we have a set of molecules with some desirable property. For example, these molecules bind to a target protein to treat a disease. Our goal is to find other molecules that have this property. We can formalize this as a graph generation problem. Each molecule is a graph of atoms connected by bonds. The desirable property corresponds to some unknown patterns common to the given graphs. We want to generate new graphs that possess these patterns automatically. As another example, suppose we want to detect bots in a social network.

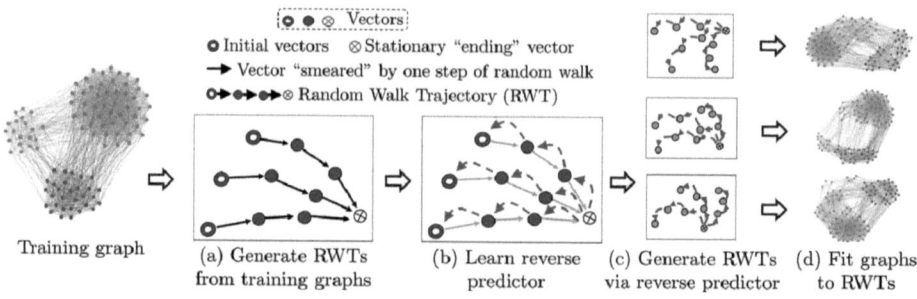

Fig. 1. *Overview of* GraphWeave: (a) Given one or more training graphs, we generate random walk trajectories (RWTs) from various starting vectors. (b) We learn to predict the previous step of a trajectory. (c) To generate a new graph, we first apply the reverse predictor several times on an "ending" vector (shown by ⊗). We show that the ending vectors are simple to generate (Theorem 1). (d) Second, we find the optimal graph that fits the generated RWTs. *The process works even with one training graph.* Indeed, we generated the three graphs on the right from the single graph on the left (colors are added for clarity).

Bots and regular users have different linkage patterns. However, we may have too few examples of bots to train a classifier. To augment the training data, we can generate synthetic graphs whose link patterns match those of the known bots. This can improve classification accuracy without increasing the cost.

In this paper, we tackle the problem of generating new graphs whose structure matches a set of training graphs. We do not consider node or edge features, which we can infer by a post-processing step. For instance, for molecule graphs, we can infer a node's feature (what atom it is) from its degree (number of bonds), and this determines its edge feature (bond strengths). Now, even generating the graph structure is a complex problem. Small-scale patterns (e.g., a benzene ring) might be important for some cases. In other applications, large-scale patterns may matter more (e.g., the ratios of various atoms, i.e., the degree distribution). No method can match all possible patterns. Clarity about the patterns a method tries to match improves its interpretability.

However, existing methods rarely make their choices explicit. One class of methods creates graphs by diffusion on the space of graph embeddings. They start from a random embedding, iteratively change it, and map the final embedding to a graph [5,20]. But even simple changes in embedding space (e.g., adding noise) may mean complex and unintuitive modifications to the graph structure. Hence, the generative process is hard to interpret.

Another class of methods changes the graph structure instead of its embedding. For instance, some methods apply local changes to the graph in each iteration [16,19]. Each step might add or remove a few nodes and edges, so the changes are intuitive. However, these local changes must add up to the desired global patterns. The need for coordinated local changes makes the process sensitive to errors. Other approaches make global changes to the graph structure in each iteration [2,17]. While this approach is very flexible, predicting what patterns will result from a series of complex changes is difficult. This affects the interpretability of such methods.

> How can we generate graphs matching multi-scale patterns in an interpretable way?

We make two design choices to achieve this goal. First, we focus on *patterns that can be learned from random walks* on graphs. Specifically, we construct Random Walk Trajectories (RWTs) that track how vectors evolve over random walks. We show that several standard graph families have unique RWT signatures. Hence, RWTs can intuitively capture helpful patterns. Also, many applications are based on random walks. So, graphs generated with the right RWT signatures can immediately positively impact such applications.

Our second design choice is to generate graphs via *optimization* on RWTs. In other words, we generate RWTs and find the optimal graph that fits these RWTs. Our approach separates the matching of patterns (via RWTs) from the graph construction (by optimization). This "division of labor" offers many benefits. RWTs are easier to generate than graphs since RWTs are naturally in a vector space. Graph construction via optimization increases flexibility. For instance, we can impose constraints (e.g., sparsity) or add regularization for robustness.

Our contributions: Our proposed method, named GRAPHWEAVE, generates Random Walk Trajectories (RWTs) and then optimally weaves them together into a coherent graph. We discuss GRAPHWEAVE's advantages below.

1. **Formulation:** We cast graph generation as a two-step problem: generate realistic patterns and then optimize a graph to fit them. The patterns we track are derived from random walk trajectories (RWTs). The optimized graph is then helpful for any downstream tasks that rely on random walks. GRAPHWEAVE's separation of pattern generation from graph optimization simplifies the generative process. To our knowledge, GRAPHWEAVE *is the first to demonstrate this optimization-based approach.*
2. **Interpretability:** RWTs track how random walks affect vectors. This basic process underlies many graph-theoretic problems. For example, the vector could represent people's opinions in a social network. Then, the RWT would show how opinions evolve dynamically. Hence, RWTs are easily interpretable.
3. **Multi-scale structure:** We show that RWTs can capture large-scale graph structures. These include communities, flows, cut sizes, and degree distributions. By varying the RWT initializations, we can also explore local structures, such as the neighborhoods of high-degree nodes. Hence, the set of RWTs of a graph can capture multi-scale structures.
4. **Robustness:** GRAPHWEAVE jointly optimizes all edges of the generated graph. The optimization's inputs come from multiple RWTs. Hence, the resulting graph is robust to occasional errors in the RWT generation process.

5. **Simplicity:** GRAPHWEAVE needs only a transformer to generate RWTs and a standard optimizer to find the best-fit graph. Both of these are off-the-shelf tools. Hence, GRAPHWEAVE's implementation is simple and reliable.
6. **Strong experimental results:** On four simulated and five real-world datasets, GRAPHWEAVE outperforms state-of-the-art methods. GRAPHWEAVE is particularly strong in matching large-scale graph structures like PageRank, cuts, communities, degree distributions, and flows. Furthermore, GRAPHWEAVE is $10x$ faster than its closest competitor.

2 Proposed Method

We are given a set $\mathcal{G}$ of undirected graphs, possibly of different sizes. We want to generate new graphs that "look like" the graphs in $\mathcal{G}$. For example, if $\mathcal{G}$ contains stochastic block model graphs, the generated graphs should match that family.

To generate such graphs, we must identify patterns from the graphs in $\mathcal{G}$. Now, the space of all possible patterns is too large. So, we must choose a subset of intuitive and widely applicable patterns. We focus on random walk patterns since random walks underpin many graph applications. Specifically, GRAPHWEAVE constructs random walk trajectories, as defined below.

Definition 1 (Smoothed Random Walk Trajectory (RWT)). *An RWT has four parameters: (a) an adjacency matrix $A \in \{0,1\}^{n \times n}$ of an undirected graph on n nodes, (b) a function $f : \mathbb{R}_+ \to \mathbb{R}_+$, (c) a smoothing parameter $\alpha \in (0,1)$, and (d) the number of steps k. Let d_i denote the degree of node i, and $d'_i := (1-\alpha)d_i + \alpha$ the node's smoothed degree. We assume that all nodes have positive degree. Also, define the smoothed normalized adjacency matrix $L \in \mathbb{R}^{n \times n}$ and the "starting vector" $\boldsymbol{v} \in \mathbb{R}^n$ as follows:*

$$L_{ij} := \frac{(1-\alpha)A_{ij} + \alpha \cdot \mathbb{1}_{i=j}}{\sqrt{d'_i \cdot d'_j}} \qquad v_i := n\frac{f(d_i)}{\sum_j f(d_j)}. \tag{1}$$

Then, the k-step Smoothed Random Walk Trajectory $RWT(A, f, \alpha, k)$ is the ordered sequence of vectors $\{\boldsymbol{v}, L\boldsymbol{v}, L^2\boldsymbol{v}, \ldots, L^k\boldsymbol{v}\}$.

Remark 1. We use the normalized adjacency L in Definition 1 instead of the random walk transition matrix $D^{-1}A$ since the symmetry of L simplifies later steps. We note that both matrices have the same eigenvalues and closely related eigenvectors.

We can construct several RWTs for any graph by varying the function $f(\cdot)$. For example, if $f(d_i)$ increases with d_i, the relative weight of high-degree nodes in the starting vector increases. Then, the RWT explores the neighborhood of such nodes in more detail.

The smoothing parameter α in Definition 1 adds "self-loops" to all the nodes. The presence of self-loops slows down the random walk, leading to smoother trajectories. The higher the value of α, the smoother the trajectory. We find that smoother trajectories are easier to predict and, hence, easier to generate. Next, we show several examples of RWTs.

Example 1 (Erdos-Renyi Graphs). Suppose $\mathcal{G}$ contains Erdos-Renyi random graphs with connection probability p. In other words, the jth graph has $n^{(j)}$ nodes, and each node pair is linked with probability p. For simplicity, we ignore smoothing ($\alpha = 0$). Then, all nodes in the jth graph have degree $\approx n^{(j)}p$ if $n(j)$ is large enough. Hence, for smooth $f(\cdot)$, every entry of this graph's starting vector is ≈ 1. In other words, all Erdos-Renyi graphs, irrespective of their sizes, start their RWTs close to the all-ones vector $\mathbf{1}$. Furthermore, we can show that $L^{(j)}\mathbf{1} \approx \mathbf{1}$ for the normalized adjacency matrices $L^{(j)}$ of such graphs. So, the RWTs of random graphs start near $\mathbf{1}$, fluctuate around that point, and eventually converge.

Example 2 (Stochastic Blockmodel (SBM)). Suppose $\mathcal{G}$ contains graphs sampled from an SBM with the following parameters. There are two communities with sizes in the ratio $\beta : 1-\beta$. The probability of an edge between two nodes is p if they are from the same community and q otherwise. Suppose we choose $f(x) = 1$ for all x. Then, the starting vectors $\boldsymbol{v}^{(j)}$ equal $\mathbf{1}$ for all graphs. We can show that for large enough k, the random walk vector $(L^{(j)})^k \boldsymbol{v}^{(j)}$ converges to a vector $\boldsymbol{w}$ with clustered entries. Specifically, let

$$\kappa_1 := \beta p + (1-\beta)q, \quad \kappa_2 := p + q - \kappa_1, \quad \nu := \frac{\beta\sqrt{\kappa_1} + (1-\beta)\sqrt{\kappa_2}}{\beta\kappa_1 + (1-\beta)\kappa_2}.$$

Then, $\boldsymbol{w}_i = \sqrt{\kappa_1}/\nu$ if node i belongs to the first community, and $\sqrt{\kappa_2}/\nu$ otherwise (via Theorem 1 proved later). Thus, the RWT evolves from $\mathbf{1}$ to the vector $\boldsymbol{w}$ with clustered entries, irrespective of the graph's size.

Example 3 (Preferential Attachment). Suppose $\mathcal{G}$ contains graphs created from the Barabasi-Albert model [1]. Then, for any graph, the distribution of node degrees follows a power-law with exponent 3. As in the SBM example, take $f(x) = 1$ for all x, so the starting vectors equal $\mathbf{1}$. The ending vectors of the random walks are proportional to the square roots of the degrees (Theorem 1 later). These follow a power-law distribution with exponent 5.

Example 4 (Expected-degree Random Graphs). Suppose $\mathcal{G}$ contains random graphs whose expected degrees match those of SBMs. Then, the starting and ending vectors will be the same as in Example 2, but the intermediate vectors will be different.

The above examples show that graphs from different families have different RWT signatures. In all cases, the RWTs started from the all-ones vector. But, they traced trajectories with different ending vectors. For other choices of $f(\cdot)$, RWTs can explore (say) high-degree nodes and their neighborhoods. GRAPH-WEAVE automatically exploits such patterns to generate new graphs from the same family.

Main Idea: GRAPHWEAVE has three steps. First, we construct RWTs from the graphs in $\mathcal{G}$. From these, we learn to reverse RWTs. In other words, given a vector from an RWT, GRAPHWEAVE learns to predict the previous vector. Second, we use this reverse predictor to generate new RWTs. To do this, we need an "ending" vector. All the generated RWTs share the same ending vector but trace different trajectories. We show how to construct a realistic ending vector, and why we can think of the generated RWTs as being from the same graph. Third, from the generated RWTs, GRAPHWEAVE infers the underlying graph. Crucially, we infer all edges of this graph jointly. We can generate multiple graphs by repeating the second and third steps from different ending vectors. Next, we provide details for each of the three parts of GRAPHWEAVE.

2.1 Learning to Reverse RWTs

Given a set $\mathcal{G} = \{A_i\}$ of graphs and a set $\mathcal{F} = \{f_\ell(\cdot)\}$ of functions, we construct the set of all RWTs $\mathcal{R} := \{RWT(A, f, \alpha, k)\}_{A \in \mathcal{G}, f \in \mathcal{F}}$. Recall that each RWT is a sequence of vectors $v_1, v_2, \ldots, v_k$, where a pair (v_j, v_{j+1}) represents one step of a random walk on some graph in $\mathcal{G}$.

Next, we learn to reverse the RWTs, that is, to predict v_j given v_{j+1} and $f(\cdot)$. The predictor must know $f(\cdot)$ since two different RWTs may arrive at the same v_{j+1} via different paths. Each path is determined by its starting vector, which depends on $f(\cdot)$. To build the predictive model, we face two challenges.

- *Arbitrary length input/outputs:* The length of the vectors v_j and v_{j+1} is the number of nodes in the graph. Since the graphs in $\mathcal{G}$ can have different sizes, the lengths of vectors in $\mathcal{R}$ can vary.
- *Permutation invariance:* The model must be invariant to permutations of the components of v_j and v_{j+1} since a permutation is just a reordering of the nodes. Such reordering should not affect the model's predictions.

Our solution is simple and elegant: we use a transformer. Transformers can adapt to inputs of arbitrary context length. In our case, the input vector is $v_{j+1} \in \mathbb{R}^n$, where the graph size n varies between the graphs in $\mathcal{G}$. For a transformer, this means a context of length n, where each item in the context is one-dimensional. Given such an input, the transformer's output is also of length n, like the desired output vector v_j. So, the same transformer can work for input/output vector pairs of all sizes. Also, a transformer without position embeddings or causal masking is invariant under permutations. Thus, a vanilla transformer matches our desiderata.

However, we can significantly improve this transformer using embeddings. Formally, we construct a binning function $B : \mathbb{R}_+ \to [K]$ and an embedding $\mathcal{E} : [K] \to \mathbb{R}^m$. For vectors, we apply these functions elementwise. In other words, $B(v)$ is the vector formed by applying $B(\cdot)$ to each element of v; $\mathcal{E}(v)$ is defined similarly. The user chooses the number of bins K and the embedding dimension m. Higher values for K and m lead to more flexibility in the transformer.

Now, we preprocess the data to use these embeddings. Specifically, in the RWTs, we replace each vector v with $v \otimes \mathcal{E}(B(v))$. We further augment each

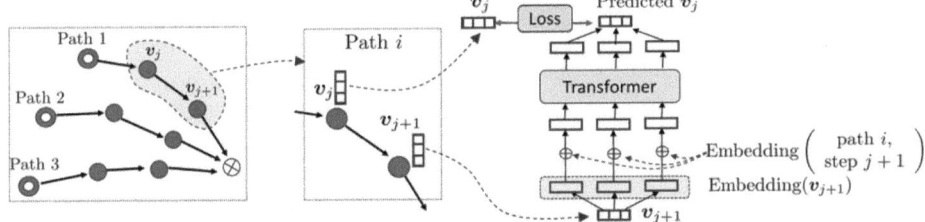

Fig. 2. *Training the reverse predictor:* For every pair of successive vectors $(\boldsymbol{v}_j, \boldsymbol{v}_{j+1})$ from a path i of an RWT, we compare $\boldsymbol{v}_j$ against a predicted vector $\hat{\boldsymbol{v}}_j$ obtained from $\boldsymbol{v}_{j+1}$. To create $\hat{\boldsymbol{v}}_j$, the elements of $\boldsymbol{v}_{j+1}$ are first converted into a sequence of embeddings. Then, we add embeddings reflecting the function f used for the starting vector of path i, and the step $j+1$ within path i. Finally, we transform these embeddings and project them to generate $\hat{\boldsymbol{v}}_j$.

input vector with an embedding that encodes the choice of $f(\cdot)$ and the current step in the RWT. Specifically, we define an embedding $\mathcal{E}'$ such that $\mathcal{E}'(f, j) \in \mathbb{R}^m$, for all functions $f \in \mathcal{F}$ and steps $j \in [k]$. Given an input vector $\boldsymbol{v}_{j+1}$ at step $j+1$ for function $f(\cdot)$, we define

$$T_\Phi(\boldsymbol{v}_{j+1}, f, j+1) := \text{Transformer}_\Phi(\boldsymbol{v}_{j+1} \otimes \mathcal{E}(B(\boldsymbol{v}_{j+1})) \\ + \mathbf{1} \otimes \mathcal{E}'(f, j+1)),$$

where Φ represents the transformer's parameters. The transformer's input is now a length-n sequence of m-dimensional embeddings, as is the output. Finally, we add a linear projection layer to convert the output back to $\mathbb{R}^n$:

$$P_{\Phi,\Psi}(\boldsymbol{v}_{j+1}, f, j+1) := \text{Project}_\Psi\left(T_\Phi(\boldsymbol{v}_{j+1}, f, j+1)\right) \text{ to } \mathbb{R}^n,$$

where Ψ are the projection parameters. Given an input $\boldsymbol{v}_{j+1}$, this projected output is our prediction for $\boldsymbol{v}_j$. We train the transformer to minimize the mean-squared error between the predicted and actual values of $\boldsymbol{v}_j$.

$$\Phi, \Psi, \mathcal{E}, \mathcal{E}' = \arg\min \sum_{(\boldsymbol{v}_j, \boldsymbol{v}_{j+1})} \left(P_{\Phi,\Psi}(\boldsymbol{v}_{j+1}, f, j+1) - \boldsymbol{v}_j\right)^2.$$

Figure 2 illustrates this process. After training, we have a reverse predictor $P_{\Phi,\Psi}$ (henceforth, P) such that

$$P(\boldsymbol{v}_{j+1}, f, j+1) \approx \boldsymbol{v}_j \text{ for all } \boldsymbol{v}_j \to \boldsymbol{v}_{j+1} \text{ in the RWTs of } \mathcal{G}. \qquad (2)$$

2.2 Generating RWTs

Suppose we have learned an accurate reverse predictor. Then, given an "ending" vector $\bar{\boldsymbol{v}}_k$ and a choice of $f(\cdot)$, we can work backward by repeatedly predicting the previous vector: $\bar{v}_k \to \bar{v}_{k-1} \to \ldots \to \bar{v}_1$. Different choices of $f(\cdot)$ yield different sequences for the same $\bar{v}_k$. We call the sequence $\{\bar{v}_1, \ldots, \bar{v}_k\}$ a *generated* RWT.

A generated RWT will only be realistic for special choices of $\bar{v}_k$. In particular, we want $\bar{v}_k$ to be the ending vector for some graph from the same family as the graphs in $\mathcal{G}$. Formally, we want $\bar{v}_k = \bar{L}^k \bar{v}_1$, where $\bar{L}$ is the smoothed normalized adjacency of such a graph. But we do not know $\bar{v}_1$ or $\bar{L}$. The following theorem shows how to select $\bar{v}_k$.

Theorem 1. *Consider an n-node graph with degrees $\{d_i\}$, smoothed degrees $\{d'_i\}$, starting vector $v \in \mathbb{R}^n_+$ built using a function $f(d_i)$, and smoothed normalized adjacency L, as in Definition 1. Let w be a vector with entries*

$$w_i := \gamma \cdot \sqrt{d'_i}$$

$$\text{where } \gamma = \frac{n\left(\sum_j f(d_j) \sqrt{d'_j}\right)}{\left(\sum_j f(d_j)\right)\left(\sum_j d'_j\right)}.$$

Then, we have:

$$\lim_{k \to \infty} \|L^k v - w\| = 0.$$

Proof. From Lemma 1 in the Appendix, the largest eigenvalue of L is 1 with eigenvector u_1 having components $u_{1;i} = \sqrt{d'_i}/(\sum_j d'_j)$. The matrix L is irreducible (since the graph is connected) and aperiodic (since $\alpha > 0$ induces self-loops). Hence, no other eigenvalue has absolute value 1. Next, we observe that $v^T u_1 > 0$, since both v and u_1 are in the positive orthant. Hence, $L^k v$ tends to the vector $(v^T u_1) u_1$, which is seen to be the vector w.

Theorem 1 shows that a realistic ending vector $\bar{v}_k$ must be close to w, and w only depends on the degrees $\{d_i\}$. So, to construct $\bar{v}_k$, we must generate a realistic degree distribution that matches the family $\mathcal{G}$. One approach is to sample a graph $G \in \mathcal{G}$ and perturb its degree distribution. Another option is to fit a model to the degree distributions of the graphs in $\mathcal{G}$. For example, we can fit a power law or a lognormal since they are widely observed in real-world data. Then, we can sample a new degree distribution from this fitted model. Either way, we get a realistic degree distribution $\{d_i\}$.

Now, we generate an RWT as follows. Using $\{d_i\}$ and a choice of $f \in \mathcal{F}$, we construct the ending vector $\bar{v}_k$ (Theorem 1). Next, we use the reverse predictor P from Sect. 2.1 to predict $\bar{v}_{k-1} := P(\bar{v}_k)$, $\bar{v}_{k-2} := P(\bar{v}_{k-1})$, and so on. Proceeding this way, we construct all the vectors $\{\bar{v}_1, \ldots, \bar{v}_k\}$. This sequence of vectors is the *generated RWT*.

By repeating these steps with the same $\bar{v}_k$ but different $f \in \mathcal{F}$, we can generate several RWTs. We must now construct the sparse graph corresponding to the generated RWTs. The following section shows how.

Remark 2 (Differences from traditional diffusion). Like diffusion models, GRAPHWEAVE has forward and reverse processes. However, in diffusion, the forward process adds random noise. In GRAPHWEAVE, the forward process is deterministic. It represents the evolution of a vector during random walks. Now, a forward process is only useful if it converges to an easy-to-sample stationary point. In diffusion models, this point is often the standard Gaussian distribution ("100%-noise"). Theorem 1 shows that GRAPHWEAVE's forward process also converges. But our stationary vector represents the convergence of random walks, not noise. Since random walks are widely used in applications, learning their patterns via RWTs can be more beneficial than learning a noise process on graphs.

Remark 3 (Single ending vector in Fig. 1). Theorem 1 shows that the ending vector is the same for all starting vectors after normalization by the appropriate γ. Figure 1 shows this visually. However, Definition 1 uses unnormalized starting vectors so that we can discuss Examples 2-4 using the same starting vectors.

2.3 Inferring the Graph

Given a set of generated RWTs, we want to find one graph that generates them. Suppose $\bar{v}_j$ and $\bar{v}_{j+1}$ are successive vectors in one of the generated RWTs. Then, the smoothed normalized adjacency matrix L for this graph must satisfy $L\bar{v}_j = \bar{v}_{j+1}$. This relation holds for every pair of successive vectors. Formally, let V_1 be a matrix with rows $\{\bar{v}_j\}$ and V_2 a matrix with rows $\{\bar{v}_{j+1}\}$. Then,

$$V_1 L = V_2. \tag{3}$$

From Definition 1, the matrix L is of the form

$$L = (D')^{-1/2}((1-\alpha)A + \alpha I)(D')^{-1/2}, \tag{4}$$

where A is the adjacency matrix of the desired graph, D' is a diagonal matrix with entries $D'_{ii} = (1-\alpha)d_i + \alpha$ and d_i is the degree of node i. Note that we know the $\{d_i\}$ since we generated the degree distribution as the first step in creating RWTs (Sect. 2.2).

Plugging Eq. 4 into Eq. 3, we find A by solving:

$$\text{minimize}_A \sum_{i,j \in [n]} |X_{ij}| \tag{5}$$

$$\text{where } X = V_1(D')^{-1/2}((1-\alpha)A + \alpha I)(D')^{-1/2} - V_2,$$
$$A_{ij} \in \{0,1\} \text{ for all } i,j \in [n],$$
$$A = A^T, \text{Trace}(A) = 0, A\mathbf{1} = \mathbf{d},$$

where $\mathbf{d}$ is the vector with entries d_i. The constraints ensure that A is an unweighted graph with degrees $\mathbf{d}$. Equation 5 is an Integer Linear Program that can be solved by standard tools such as Gurobi.

Remark 4. An alternative to Eq. 5 is to relax the requirement $A_{ij} \in \{0,1\}$ to $A_{ij} \in [0,1]$. This results in a convex problem:

$$\text{minimize}_{\tilde{A}} \sum_{ij} |X_{ij}| \tag{6}$$

$$\text{where } X = \|V_1(D')^{-1/2}((1-\alpha)\tilde{A} + \alpha I)(D')^{-1/2} - V_2\|_F^2,$$
$$0 \leq \tilde{A} \leq 1, \text{Trace}(A) = 0, \tilde{A} = \tilde{A}^T, \tilde{A}\mathbf{1} = \mathbf{d}.$$

This results in a *weighted* graph $\tilde{A}$. We can construct A by rounding the entries of $\tilde{A}$ as follows:

$$A_{ij} := \mathbb{1}_{\tilde{A}_{ij} > a^\star + b^\star \log d_i}, \tag{7}$$

$$\text{where } a^\star, b^\star = \arg\min_{a,b} \frac{1}{n} \sum_{i=1}^{n} \left| \frac{\sum_j \mathbb{1}_{\tilde{A}_{ij} > a + b \log d_i}}{d_i} - 1 \right|.$$

The choice of $(a^\star, b^\star)$ minimizes the relative error between the node degrees of A and the desired degrees $\{d_i\}$. We can select $(a^\star, b^\star)$ by grid search over a chosen range. While this approach offers no guarantees for the objective of Eq. 5, it often works well in practice.

2.4 Overall Algorithm

Algorithm 1 shows the pseudocode for GRAPHWEAVE. We first build the RWTs for the graphs in $\mathcal{G}$. Then, we train a transformer to reverse each step of the observed RWTs. To generate a graph, we first generate a realistic degree distribution. The degree distribution gives us the ending vector $\bar{v}_k$ (Theorem 1). Starting from $\bar{v}_k$, we generate RWTs in reverse order by repeatedly applying the transformer (Eq. 2). Finally, we infer the graph corresponding to the generated RWTs by solving Eq. 5. We can generate multiple graphs by reusing the transformer with different degree distributions.

Implementation Details: For the binning function, we use $B(\mathbf{v}) := \lfloor c(\mathbf{v} - \mu)/\sigma \rfloor$, where μ and σ are the mean and standard deviation of all vector entries in the training set, c is a parameter that controls the number of bins, and the binning function is applied elementwise to $\mathbf{v}$. In our experiments, we set $c = 3$, $\alpha = 0.9$, and $k = 10$. For the set of functions $\mathcal{F}$, we use power laws: $\mathcal{F} = \{f : \mathbb{R}_+ \to \mathbb{R}_+; f(d) = d^\beta, \beta \in \{\pm 1, \pm 2\}\}$. We also simplify the form of $\mathcal{E}'(f, j)$ by adding an embedding of $f(\cdot)$ and and embedding of j.

Computational Complexity: We first consider the cost of training. We construct $|\mathcal{F}| \times |\mathcal{G}|$ RWTs. For each RWT, the main cost is the k sparse-matrix-vector multiplications $L\mathbf{v}_j$. This takes $O(kE)$ time, where E is the maximum number of edges in any graph in $\mathcal{G}$. Hence, creating RWTs takes $O(|\mathcal{F}||\mathcal{G}|kE)$ time. To train the transformer, we have $k|\mathcal{F}||\mathcal{G}|$ input vectors from the RWTs. For each vector, the attention mechanism considers $O(n^2)$ pairs, where n is the maximum number of nodes. Each pair has a cost proportional to the embedding dimension

Algorithm 1. GRAPHWEAVE

1: **function** GRAPHWEAVE($\mathcal{G}, \mathcal{F}, \alpha, k$)
2:     $\mathcal{R} \leftarrow \cup_{A \in \mathcal{G}} \cup_{f \in \mathcal{F}} RWT(A, f, \alpha, k)$
3:     $\mathcal{D} \leftarrow \{(\boldsymbol{v}_j, \boldsymbol{v}_{j+1}); \boldsymbol{v}_j \to \boldsymbol{v}_{j+1}$ in some RWT in $\mathcal{R}\}$
4:     Define $B : \mathbb{R} \to [K]$ ▷ Binning function with K bins
5:     Define $B(\boldsymbol{v}) := [B(\boldsymbol{v}_1), B(\boldsymbol{v}_2), \ldots, B(\boldsymbol{v}_n)]^T$ for any $\boldsymbol{v} \in \mathbb{R}^n$

    ▷ **Learn to reverse RWTs**
6:     Define $\mathcal{E} : [K] \to \mathbb{R}^m$ ▷ value embedding function
7:     Define $\mathcal{E}' : |\mathcal{F}| \times k \to \mathbb{R}^m$ ▷ setting embedding function
8:     Define $T_\Phi \leftarrow$ Transformer : $\mathbb{R}^{n \times m} \to \mathbb{R}^{n \times m}$ for any n
9:     $P_{\Phi, \Psi}(\boldsymbol{v}, j, f) \leftarrow \text{Project}_\Psi (T_\Phi(\boldsymbol{v} \otimes \mathcal{E}(B(\boldsymbol{v}))) + \mathbf{1} \otimes \mathcal{E}'(f, j)))$
10:     $\Phi, \Psi, \mathcal{E}, \mathcal{E}' \leftarrow \arg\min \sum_{(\boldsymbol{v}_j, \boldsymbol{v}_{j+1}) \in \mathcal{D}} (P_{\Phi, \Psi}(\boldsymbol{v}_{j+1}, f, j+1) - \boldsymbol{v}_j)^2$

    ▷ **Generate degree distribution**
11:     $G \leftarrow$ sample graph from $\mathcal{G}$
12:     $\{d_i\} \leftarrow$ Perturbed degree distribution of G
13:     $d'_i \leftarrow (1 - \alpha) d_i + \alpha$ for all nodes i

    ▷ **Generate RWTs**
14:     $V_1, V_2 \leftarrow \phi$
15:     **for all** $f \in \mathcal{F}$ **do**
16:        $\bar{\boldsymbol{v}}_k \leftarrow \gamma \sqrt{\boldsymbol{d}'}$ ▷ $\boldsymbol{d}'$ has entries d'_i; γ is from Theorem 1
17:        $\bar{\boldsymbol{v}}_{k-j} \leftarrow P_{\Phi, \Psi}(\bar{\boldsymbol{v}}_{k-j+1}, f, k - j + 1)$ for $j = 1, 2, \ldots, k - 1$
18:        $V_1 \leftarrow V_1 \cup \{\bar{\boldsymbol{v}}_j; j = 1, \ldots, k - 1\}$
19:        $V_2 \leftarrow V_2 \cup \{\bar{\boldsymbol{v}}_{j+1}; j = 1, \ldots, k - 1\}$
20:     **end for**

    ▷ **Infer graph**
21:     $A \leftarrow$ solve Equation 5 using V_1 and V_2
22:     **return** unweighted graph with adjacency matrix A
23: **end function**

m. We assume that the transformer's size is fixed (i.e., $O(1)$ layers and heads). So, the cost of training the transformer is $O(|\mathcal{F}||\mathcal{G}|kn^2m)$, and this is also the overall cost of training.

To generate a graph, we create its RWTs via $k|\mathcal{F}|$ passes of the transformer. Each pass takes $O(n^2m)$ time. Since Integer Linear Programs (Eq. 5) can have variable costs, we instead analyze the convex optimization (Eq. 6). To generate a graph of n nodes requires $O(n^2)$ parameters. The main cost is in computing the matrix-matrix product of V_1 (size $k|\mathcal{F}| \times n$ and $(D')^{-1/2} \tilde{A} (D')^{-1/2}$ (size $n \times n$) in the objective. Assuming we run gradient descent for a fixed number of steps, the convex optimization takes $O(\text{MatMult}(k|\mathcal{F}| \times n, n \times n))$ time. The threshold step (Eq. 7) costs $O(n^2)$ for grid search. Hence, the total cost of generation is $O(k|\mathcal{F}|n^2m + \text{MatMult}(k|\mathcal{F}| \times n, n \times n)) = O(k|\mathcal{F}|n^2m)$.

Note that the dominant costs are training a transformer, matrix multiplication, and convex optimization. There are fast off-the-shelf libraries for all three.

3 Experiments

We ran experiments to compare the quality of graph generated by GRAPHWEAVE against state of the art competing methods.

Comparison Metrics: We consider measures of node centrality (degree and Pagerank), local neighborhoods (clustering coefficient and ORBIT scores), quality of random partitions (cut-size, conductance, and modularity), connectivity between random node pairs (max-flow and resistance), and overall connectivity (if the graph is connected or not). Apart from overall connectivity, each measure results in a vector $\phi(G)$ for any graph G (e.g., the vector of node degrees, or the modularities of 100 random partitions). We then compute the relative error

$$\text{error}_\phi(\mathcal{G}_{gen} \mid \mathcal{G}_{test}) := \left| \frac{\sum_{G_i \in \mathcal{G}_{gen}, G_j \in \mathcal{G}_{test}} \text{distance}(\phi(G_i), \phi(G_j))}{\sum_{G_i, G_j \in \mathcal{G}_{test}} \text{distance}(\phi(G_i), \phi(G_j))} \times \frac{|\mathcal{G}_{test}|}{|\mathcal{G}_{gen}|} - 1 \right|, \tag{8}$$

where $\mathcal{G}_{gen}$ is the set of generated graphs, $\mathcal{G}_{test}$ the set of test graphs from the same family as the training data, and the distance function is the Wasserstein metric between any two vectors $\phi(G_i)$ and $\phi(G_j)$. If the generated graphs fit the test distribution, the error is close to 0.

Competing Methods: We compare GRAPHWEAVE against several state of the art methods: DiGress [17], GSDM [11], GRASP [14] GDSS [8], and GraphRNN [19]. Apart from GraphRNN, which is an autoregressive model, all the others use diffusion. These methods are recent, and have been shown to outperform older methods. Hence, we compare GRAPHWEAVE against these methods.

Simulated Datasets: We consider four types of simulated graphs: (a) a *stochastic blockmodel* with 3 communities containing 50%, 30%, and 20% of the nodes, and a connection probability of 0.8 for nodes in the same community and 0.3 otherwise, (b) a *Watts-Strogatz model* with 4 edges per node and a rewiring probability of 0.3, (c) a Barabasi-Albert *preferential attachment model*, and (d) a *expected-degree random graph model*, whose degrees are the same as the Stochastic Blockmodel.

Real-World Datasets: We also tested our method on five real-world benchmark datasets. These include (a) *Cora* (b) *Citeseer*, and (c) *Pubmed*, where the nodes represent documents and edges represent citation relationships from which we extract 3-hop ego networks [15]. We also use (d) *Proteins*, containing molecular graphs with 100 to 500 nodes in each graph [4], and (e) *QM9*, comprising stable organic molecules with up to nine heavy atoms [18].

Experimental Settings: For each dataset and each method, we train on 100 graphs and then generate (at least) 40 graphs. We compute various comparison metrics for each of the generated graphs, and compare them against unseen test graphs from the same dataset using Eq. 8.

Quality of Graph Generation: Table 1 compares all competing methods for the simulated datasets. We find that GRAPHWEAVE *generally outperforms the*

Table 1. *Comparison on simulated datasets:* The quality of the generated graphs is measured via Eq. 8 (lower is better). GRAPHWEAVE outperforms other methods, especially for the large-scale metrics like degree distributions, cut sizes, conductance, and max-flow. Also, GRAPHWEAVE and GDSS are the only methods that always generate connected graphs.

		Degree	Pagerank	Connected Graphs?	Cut sizes	Conductance	Modularity	Clustering Coefficient	ORBIT	Max Flow	Resistance
Stochastic Blockmodel	DiGress	0.10	0.42	✓	3.15	0.14	0.11	**1.16**	2.90	1.50	1.74
	GSDM	18.14	11.77	×	35.78	8.67	24.15	31.13	19.65	19.29	791.98
	GDSS	2.66	0.34	✓	23.79	0.53	4.13	22.14	16.54	11.79	28.65
	GRASP	2.09	12.45	✓	16.01	2.61	1.45	10.69	10.89	12.47	39.99
	GraphRNN	37.15	5.71	×	60.62	8.56	31.88	18.54	31.05	32.63	2170.56
	GraphWeave	**0.02**	**0.02**	✓	**0.02**	**0.03**	**0.10**	4.27	**1.35**	**0.01**	**0.02**
Watts Strogatz	DiGress	0.06	0.47	✓	6.17	0.14	**0.18**	**2.07**	3.99	0.46	1.94
	GSDM	2.72	2.84	✓	2281.93	3.70	8.41	5.41	9537.24	313.18	18.94
	GDSS	2.50	1.33	✓	1347.60	3.33	7.22	2.69	3681.39	176.23	18.26
	GRASP	2.98	2.07	×	3294.84	3.50	9.57	11.85	13067.07	393.88	19.05
	GraphRNN	0.71	5.13	×	138.97	5.41	7.16	2.67	9.78	25.58	53.64
	GraphWeave	**0.02**	**0.18**	✓	**0.22**	**0.11**	0.22	2.90	**3.65**	**0.02**	**1.77**
Preferential Attachment	DiGress	0.09	**0.01**	✓	1.80	**0.08**	0.06	**0.04**	**0.02**	0.30	**0.27**
	GSDM	0.88	4.78	✓	1637.97	3.90	6.60	9.48	549.15	225.39	35.19
	GDSS	0.97	4.29	✓	891.67	3.57	5.27	4.69	192.20	121.26	33.01
	GRASP	2.73	2.32	×	48.04	0.30	0.86	6.37	3.65	5.13	32.46
	GraphRNN	6.91	5.94	×	180.42	5.53	12.39	2.69	5.50	18.81	184.25
	GraphWeave	**0.01**	0.21	✓	**0.01**	0.09	**0.01**	0.85	0.27	**0.00**	1.50
Random Graph with degrees like SBM	DiGress	0.05	**0.01**	✓	**0.01**	0.14	**0.02**	**0.01**	**0.00**	0.03	**0.03**
	GSDM	4.92	1.94	✓	18.59	0.47	3.50	19.43	15.14	8.34	25.31
	GDSS	2.80	0.38	✓	21.13	0.44	3.52	20.12	17.86	10.22	25.20
	GRASP	1.52	10.67	✓	13.39	2.07	1.15	10.23	9.86	10.33	26.09
	GraphRNN	37.85	4.35	×	54.74	8.17	29.26	19.29	32.32	29.14	1980.06
	GraphWeave	**0.02**	0.03	✓	0.03	**0.05**	0.34	10.17	4.54	**0.02**	0.06

competing methods in measures of large-scale graph structures. For example, GRAPHWEAVE excels are predicting node degrees and cut sizes. GRAPHWEAVE is also the best or close to the best for other metrics such as modularity, max-flow, and resistance. The closest competing method is DiGress, but DiGress sometimes generates disconnected graphs. In contrast, GRAPHWEAVE always generates connected graphs. Also, GRAPHWEAVE is significantly faster than DiGress, as we show later.

GRAPHWEAVE does particularly well for the Stochastic Blockmodel family of graphs. This is because such graphs show large-scale community structure, and random walks can pick up such structure.

Table 2 compares the quality of all competing methods on the real-world datasets. The results mirror those for the simulated datasets. For large-scale measures such as the distribution of cut sizes, GRAPHWEAVE is the best on all datasets. Furthermore, it is either the best or close to the best for degree distributions, Pagerank centrality distributions, conductance, and modularity.

Effect of Optimization: We compared our two optimization approaches: the Integer Linear Program of Eq. 5 (*Integer*), and the convex relaxation with rounding of Eqs. 6 and 7 (*Convex*). We also considered a baseline (*Random*) that picks a random graph with the same degrees as *Integer*. The comparison metric is the objective function of Eqs. 5 and 6, which measures how closely the generated graph matches the desired RWTs.

Table 2. *Comparison on real-world datasets (lower is better).* GRAPHWEAVE is best, or close to best, for most measures and datasets.

		Degree	Pagerank	Cut sizes	Conductance	Modularity	Clustering Coefficient	ORBIT	Max Flow	Resistance
Cora	DiGress	1.73	0.10	0.99	0.12	0.09	1.06	0.25	1.63	**0.05**
	GSDM	0.34	0.13	7.53	0.20	0.38	1.40	5.37	41.11	2.13
	GDSS	**0.01**	0.11	32.23	0.35	0.60	1.70	95.62	117.72	2.26
	GRASP	0.03	5.30	0.71	0.85	1.27	1.14	0.47	7.15	0.77
	GraphRNN	13.13	**0.02**	0.20	0.44	**0.07**	1.08	0.30	3.26	7.18
	GraphWeave	**0.01**	**0.02**	**0.18**	**0.11**	**0.07**	**0.67**	**0.16**	**0.18**	0.69
Pubmed	DiGress	10.25	**0.04**	0.36	0.07	0.45	0.43	0.45	1.06	0.18
	GSDM	0.37	0.16	4.04	**0.02**	0.06	1.02	4.07	15.79	1.42
	GDSS	**0.00**	0.28	14.71	0.05	0.20	1.65	80.79	51.05	1.57
	GRASP	0.02	17.31	0.21	2.65	3.45	1.45	0.98	0.67	0.21
	GraphRNN	11.50	0.15	0.26	0.13	**0.04**	0.38	0.20	1.07	6.83
	GraphWeave	0.07	0.07	**0.03**	0.11	0.07	**0.26**	**0.03**	**0.06**	**0.01**
Citeseer	DiGress	8.87	**0.04**	0.60	**0.02**	0.08	1.19	0.24	0.99	0.64
	GSDM	0.21	0.13	3.71	**0.02**	0.10	1.49	8.30	20.45	1.41
	GDSS	0.11	0.13	11.42	0.09	0.27	2.02	90.31	54.23	1.54
	GRASP	**0.08**	0.79	2.45	0.23	0.32	1.87	16.37	13.13	0.75
	GraphRNN	14.09	0.10	0.24	0.17	**0.00**	1.32	**0.05**	1.91	3.95
	GraphWeave	0.17	0.07	**0.03**	0.13	0.08	**0.48**	0.09	**0.23**	**0.23**
QM9	DiGress	0.06	**0.01**	0.11	**0.27**	**0.23**	0.35	0.08	**0.14**	0.04
	GSDM	0.25	0.03	2.60	0.98	0.76	1.76	4.09	3.19	0.91
	GDSS	0.09	0.20	0.85	0.61	0.48	0.94	1.22	1.01	0.30
	GRASP	**0.01**	0.11	0.06	0.54	0.39	**0.03**	0.12	0.19	**0.03**
	GraphRNN	**0.01**	0.09	0.22	0.63	0.38	0.64	0.39	0.29	**0.03**
	GraphWeave	0.03	**0.00**	**0.02**	0.39	0.31	0.47	**0.06**	0.33	0.07
Proteins	DiGress	5.94	0.33	1.03	1.87	3.41	7.19	4.64	4.17	0.61
	GSDM	0.74	**0.00**	10.20	0.10	0.75	3.74	2254.53	35.68	1.63
	GDSS	0.78	0.01	36.58	0.19	1.11	**2.95**	22210.10	96.64	1.69
	GRASP	0.89	31.57	2.51	14.43	8.98	5.40	1010.18	10.48	**0.60**
	GraphRNN	2.30	0.16	0.24	0.19	**0.06**	4.88	**1.51**	4.01	12.04
	GraphWeave	**0.01**	0.03	**0.00**	**0.04**	**0.06**	5.62	2.33	**0.66**	3.25

Table 3 shows that *Integer* is between 20% − 55% better than *Convex*, and both are significantly better than *Random*. The difference between *Integer* and *Convex* is because the latter needs to threshold edges from $[0, 1]$ to $\{0, 1\}$. This thresholding step (Eq. 7) can increase the error in RWT reconstruction.

Wall-Clock Time: Figure 3 compares the wall-clock times for the various methods. We see that GRAPHWEAVE has the fastest training time, and has reasonable generation time. Furthermore, GRAPHWEAVE *is 10x faster than its closest competitor (DiGress)*.

Sensitivity Analysis: We investigate the sensitivity of our measures to variations in the hyperparameters c, α, and k. Recall that c controls the number of bins in the binning function $B(\boldsymbol{v})$, α smoothes the RWTs, and k is the length of an RWT. All the previous experiments used the baseline setting of $(c = 3, k = 10, \alpha = 0.9)$. We ran experiments varying one hyperparameter at a time. We report all metrics normalized relative to their values in the baseline setting. Hence, a normalized value greater than 1 implies worse performance than the baseline, and lower than 1 implies better performance.

Table 3. *Fidelity: of RWT reconstruction:* The graph generated by the Integer Linear Program (Eq. 5) is significantly better than the alternatives.

Improvement of	Stochastic Blockmodel			Preferential Attachment		
Integer over	50 nodes	100 nodes	200 nodes	50 nodes	100 nodes	200 nodes
Convex	31%	57%	18%	58%	47%	21%
Random	80%	91%	82%	79%	67%	55%

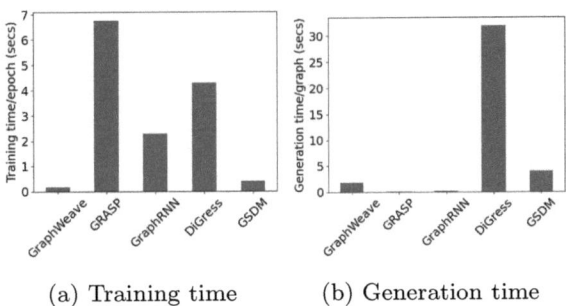

(a) Training time   (b) Generation time

Fig. 3. *Wall-clock times:* GDSS is much slower, and is not shown.

Figure 4 summarizes these results. In each plot, the horizontal red line at 1 indicates the baseline level. Deviations from this line indicate how strongly a given metric is affected by changing the corresponding parameter. Overall, no hyperparameter setting dominates the baseline setting. We also observe that:

- **Varying c** mainly affects *cut sizes* and *resistance*. Higher the value of c, better the performance for *cut sizes*.
- **Varying α** has a more pronounced effect, particularly at $\alpha = 0.99$, where several metrics (e.g., *pagerank, resistance*) exhibit large deviations from baseline. Thus, too much smoothing can negatively affect GRAPHWEAVE's performance.
- **Varying k** impacts *cut sizes* and *resistance* more than other metrics. This is similar to the effect of varying c.

4 Related Work

Graphs can be generated by autoregressive models, normalizing flow-based models, VAEs, GANs, and diffusion-based methods. We discuss these below.

Autoregressive Models: These generate graphs sequentially by adding one node or edge at a time. Each step considers the previously generated structure. The underlying method can be a recurrent neural network like GraphRNN [19]), or attention mechanisms like GRAN [10], or a combination with diffusion like

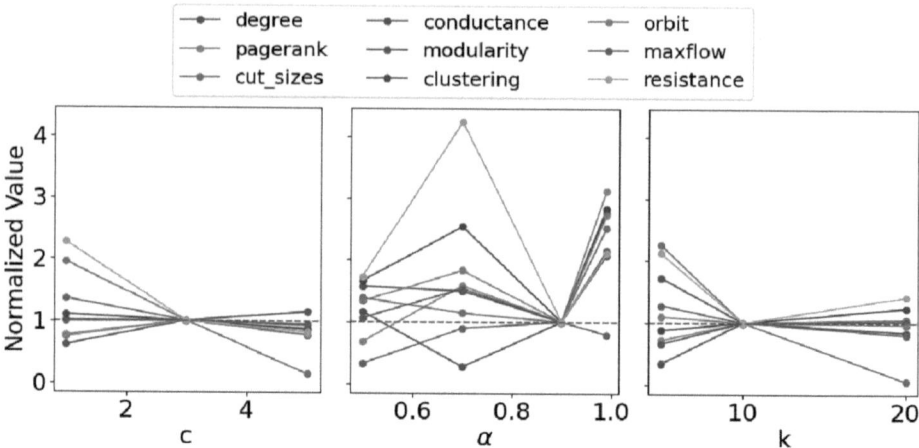

Fig. 4. Sensitivity of normalized graph metrics to hyperparameter variations. Each metric is normalized to 1 at the baseline ($c=3, k=10, \alpha=0.9$), and deviations from 1 indicate sensitivity to the corresponding parameter.

GraphARM [9]. However, autoregressive models are often sensitive to node orderings, and node permutations can lead to divergent generation paths.

Normalizing Flows: These methods provide a reversible transformation between graphs and a latent distribution, enabling easy likelihood computation. GraphNVP [12] uses flows for molecule generation. GraphAF [16] introduces improvements to improve the quality and validity of the generated graphs.

VAEs and GANs: A VAE maps a graph to a latent space, and can reconstructs the graph from a latent embedding via probabilistic decoders [7]. GANs have also been applied to graph generation [2]. SPECTRE [13] integrates spectral features to enhance the GAN's expressivity. MolGAN [3] extends GANs for molecular graph generation by incorporating reinforcement learning. However, many GAN-based models suffer from training instability and mode collapse, making them less reliable for diverse graph distributions. Also, the black-box nature of adversarial training makes them hard to interpret [6].

Diffusion Models: Buoyed by the success of diffusion for image generation, these methods have come to the fore recently. GDSS [8] leverages a system of stochastic differential equations to jointly learn node and edge distributions. DiGress [17] introduces a discrete diffusion model that edits node and edge attributes through Markov transitions. GSDM [11] applies diffusion on the spectrum of the adjacency matrix, while GRASP [14] focuses on the spectrum of the Laplacian. While these methods are the state of the art, we show that GRAPH-WEAVE outperforms them, particularly for large-scale structures like the distribution of cut sizes of random partitions and node Pagerank distributions. Furthermore, GRAPHWEAVE is faster than its closest competitors.

5 Conclusions

To the question *"How can we generate a graph with the right patterns?"*, we give a two-step answer: first generate the patterns, then optimize the graph. We choose to focus on patterns that we can learn from random walks. The reason is that many downstream applications use random walks, so graphs generated this way can have a significant impact. The optimization step makes the graph robust to noise in the generated patterns. It also lets us impose constraints on the graph, such as desired degree distributions.

GRAPHWEAVE puts this idea into practice via a fast, interpretable, and simple algorithm. GRAPHWEAVE learns to predict random walk trajectories, which show how random walks transform a vector of node attributes. Then, using this predictor, we generate new trajectories. Finally, we find the optimal graph that fits these trajectories. The algorithm only requires a transformer and an optimizer. Experiments on several simulated and benchmark datasets show that GRAPHWEAVE outperforms the state of the art, and is among the fastest methods.

A Smoothed Normalized Adjacency Matrix

Lemma 1. *Let A, d'_i, and L be defined as in Definition 1. Let $D' = \mathrm{diag}(d'_i)$. Let $\beta_1 \geq \cdots \geq \beta_n$ be the eigenvalues of L. Then, $\beta_1 = 1$ with the corresponding eigenvector being $(D'^{1/2}\mathbf{1})/\|D'^{1/2}\mathbf{1}\|$, and $\beta_n > -1$.*

Proof. We have $L = D'^{-1/2}\left((1-\alpha)A + \alpha I\right) D'^{-1/2}$. Since $A\mathbf{1} = D\mathbf{1}$, we have $LD'^{1/2}\mathbf{1} = D'^{-1/2}((1-\alpha)A + \alpha I)\mathbf{1} = D'^{-1/2}((1-\alpha)D + \alpha I)\mathbf{1} = D'^{1/2}\mathbf{1}$. So, 1 is an eigenvalue of L with eigenvector $(D'^{1/2}\mathbf{1})/\|D'^{1/2}\mathbf{1}\|$. To show that it is the largest eigenvalue, we show that $I - L$ is positive semidefinite. We have

$$I - L = D'^{-1/2}(D' - (1-\alpha)A - \alpha I)D'^{-1/2} = (1-\alpha)D'^{-1/2}(D-A)D'^{-1/2}$$
$$= (1-\alpha)D'^{-1/2}D^{1/2}(I - D^{-1/2}AD^{-1/2})D^{1/2}D'^{-1/2}.$$

Now, D and D' are positive definite, and so is $I - D^{-1/2}AD^{-1/2}$, since

$$\mathbf{x}^T(I - D^{-1/2}AD^{-1/2})\mathbf{x} = \sum_i x_i^2 - \sum_{(i,j) \in E} \frac{2x(i)x(j)}{\sqrt{d'_i d'_j}} = \sum_{(i,j) \in E}\left(\frac{x(i)}{\sqrt{d'_i}} - \frac{x(j)}{\sqrt{d'_j}}\right)^2 \geq 0,$$

for any $\mathbf{x}$. So $I - L$ is positive semidefinite. Similarly, we show that L's smallest eigenvalue is greater than -1 by showing that $I + L$ is positive definite.

$$I + L = D'^{-1/2}(D' + (1-\alpha)A + \alpha I)D'^{-1/2} = (1-\alpha)D'^{-1/2}(D+A)D'^{-1/2} + 2\alpha D'^{-1}$$
$$= (1-\alpha)D'^{-1/2}D^{1/2}(I + D^{-1/2}AD^{-1/2})D^{1/2}D'^{-1/2} + 2\alpha D'^{-1}.$$

The second term is positive definite. The first term is positive semidefinite since

$$\mathbf{x}^T(I + D^{-1/2}AD^{-1/2})\mathbf{x} = \sum_{(i,j) \in E}\left(\frac{x(i)}{\sqrt{d'_i}} + \frac{x(j)}{\sqrt{d'_j}}\right)^2 \geq 0.$$

References

1. Albert, R., Barabási, A.L.: Statistical mechanics of complex networks. Rev. Mod. Phys. **74**(1), 47 (2002)
2. Bojchevski, A., Shchur, O., Zügner, D., Günnemann, S.: Netgan: Generating graphs via random walks. In: ICML, pp. 610–619 (2018)
3. De Cao, N., Kipf, T.: Molgan: An implicit generative model for small molecular graphs. arXiv:1805.11973 (2018)
4. Dobson, P.D., Doig, A.J.: Distinguishing enzyme structures from non-enzymes without alignments. J. Mol. Biol. **330**(4), 771–783 (2003)
5. Evdaimon, I., et al.: Neural graph generator: feature-conditioned graph generation using latent diffusion models (2024). https://arxiv.org/abs/2403.01535
6. Guo, X., Zhao, L.: A systematic survey on deep generative models for graph generation. IEEE Trans. Pattern Anal. Mach. Intell. **45**(5), 5370–5390 (2022)
7. Jin, W., Barzilay, R., Jaakkola, T.: Junction tree variational autoencoder for molecular graph generation. In: ICML, pp. 2323–2332 (2018)
8. Jo, J., Lee, S., Hwang, S.J.: Score-based generative modeling of graphs via the system of stochastic differential equations. In: ICML (2022)
9. Kong, L., Cui, J., Sun, H., Zhuang, Y., Prakash, B.A., Zhang, C.: Autoregressive diffusion model for graph generation. In: ICML (2023)
10. Liao, R., et al.: Efficient graph generation with graph recurrent attention networks. In: NeurIPS, vol. 32 (2019)
11. Luo, T., Mo, Z., Pan, S.J.: Fast graph generation via spectral diffusion. IEEE Trans. Pattern Anal. Mach. Intell. **46**(05), 3496–3508 (2024)
12. Madhawa, K., Ishiguro, K., Nakago, K., Abe, M.: Graphnvp: An invertible flow model for generating molecular graphs. arXiv:1905.11600 (2019)
13. Martinkus, K., Loukas, A., Perraudin, N., Wattenhofer, R.: Spectre: spectral conditioning helps to overcome the expressivity limits of one-shot graph generators. In: ICML, pp. 15159–15179. PMLR (2022)
14. Minello, G., Bicciato, A., Rossi, L., Torsello, A., Cosmo, L.: Graph generation via spectral diffusion. arXiv:2402.18974 (2024)
15. Sen, P., Namata, G., Bilgic, M., Getoor, L., Galligher, B., Eliassi-Rad, T.: Collective classification in network data. AI Mag. **29**(3), 93–93 (2008)
16. Shi, C., Xu, M., Zhu, Z., Zhang, W., Zhang, M., Tang, J.: GraphAF: a flow-based autoregressive model for molecular graph generation. arXiv:2001.09382 (2020)
17. Vignac, C., Krawczuk, I., Siraudin, A., Wang, B., Cevher, V., Frossard, P.: Digress: discrete denoising diffusion for graph generation. arXiv:2209.14734 (2022)
18. Wu, Z., et al.: Moleculenet: a benchmark for molecular machine learning. Chem. Sci. **9**(2), 513–530 (2018)
19. You, J., Ying, R., Ren, X., Hamilton, W., Leskovec, J.: GraphRNN: generating realistic graphs with deep auto-regressive models. In: ICML, pp. 5708–5717 (2018)
20. Zhou, C., Wang, X., Zhang, M.: Unifying generation and prediction on graphs with latent graph diffusion (2024). https://arxiv.org/abs/2402.02518

Towards Deeper GCNs: Alleviating Over-Smoothing via Iterative Training and Fine-Tuning

Furong Peng[1], Jinzhen Gao[2], Xuan Lu[2(✉)], Kang Liu[2], Yifan Huo[2], and Sheng Wang[3]

[1] Institute of Big Data Science and Industry, Shanxi University/Key Laboratory of Evolutionary Science Intelligence of Shanxi Province, Taiyuan, China
pengfr@sxu.edu.cn
[2] Shanxi University, Taiyuan, China
{202322404011,202222407023,202422409007}@email.sxu.edu.cn,
xuanlu@sxu.edu.cn
[3] Zhengzhou University of Aeronautics, Zhengzhou, China
wangsheng1910@zua.edu.cn

Abstract. Graph Convolutional Networks (GCNs) suffer from severe performance degradation in deep architectures due to over-smoothing. While existing studies primarily attribute the over-smoothing to repeated applications of graph Laplacian operators, our empirical analysis reveals a critical yet overlooked factor: trainable linear transformations in GCNs significantly exacerbate feature collapse, even at moderate depths (e.g., 8 layers). In contrast, Simplified Graph Convolution (SGC), which removes these transformations, maintains stable feature diversity up to 32 layers, highlighting linear transformations' dual role in facilitating expressive power and inducing over-smoothing. However, completely removing linear transformations weakens the model's expressive capacity.

To address this trade-off, we propose **Layer-wise Gradual Training (LGT)**, a novel training strategy that progressively builds deep GCNs while preserving their expressiveness. LGT integrates three complementary components: (1) *layer-wise training* to stabilize optimization from shallow to deep layers, (2) *low-rank adaptation* to fine-tune shallow layers and accelerate training, and (3) *identity initialization* to ensure smooth integration of new layers and accelerate convergence. Extensive experiments on benchmark datasets demonstrate that LGT achieves state-of-the-art performance on vanilla GCN, significantly improving accuracy even in 32-layer settings. Moreover, as a training method, LGT can be seamlessly combined with existing methods such as PairNorm and ContraNorm, further enhancing their performance in deeper networks. LGT offers a general, architecture-agnostic training framework for scalable deep GCNs. The code is available at https://github.com/jfklasdfj/LGT_GCN.

Keywords: GCNs · Over-smoothing · Fine-tune · LoRA

1 Introduction

Graph Neural Networks (GNNs) [4,6,8] have become a powerful paradigm for learning from graph-structured data, achieving notable success across applications such as social network analysis [5,31], molecular property prediction [15], and traffic forecasting [13]. Among them, Graph Convolutional Networks (GCNs) [2,11] are widely adopted for their ability to aggregate neighborhood information through iterative message passing.

Despite their effectiveness, GCNs face severe performance degradation when scaled to deeper architectures due to the over-smoothing problem, where node representations become indistinguishable across layers [1,19]. Although previous studies primarily attribute over-smoothing to repeated applications of the graph Laplacian [14], our empirical analysis (Fig. 1) reveals a critical yet underexplored cause: the linear transformations in GCN layers substantially accelerate feature collapse, even at moderate depths such as 8 layers. Interestingly, as shown in Fig. 1, Simplified Graph Convolution (SGC) [28], which removes both linear transformations and nonlinearities, maintains stable performance and separable node representations even at 32 layers. This contrast highlights a fundamental trade-off: while linear transformations are essential for expressive feature learning, they also intensify over-smoothing in deep GCNs. Existing methods, however, largely overlook this dual role, leaving the challenge of balancing expressiveness and smoothness unresolved.

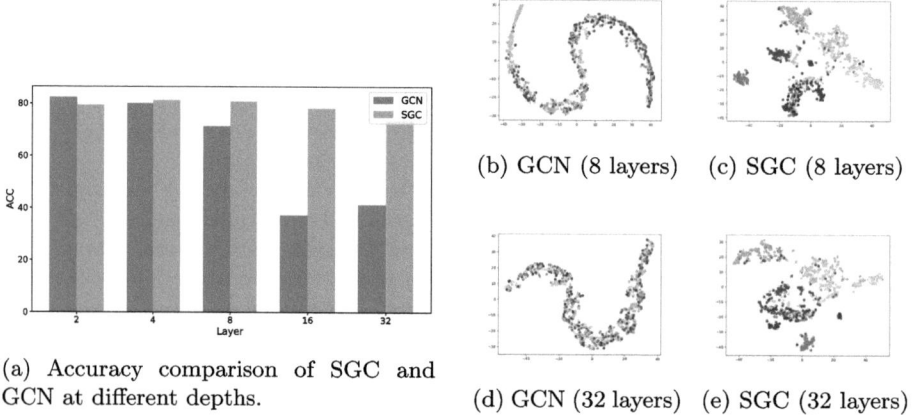

(a) Accuracy comparison of SGC and GCN at different depths.

(b) GCN (8 layers) (c) SGC (8 layers)

(d) GCN (32 layers) (e) SGC (32 layers)

Fig. 1. Comparison of over-smoothing in GCN and SGC on Cora. (a) Accuracy trend with increasing depth, where GCN suffers severe degradation beyond 8 layers, while SGC maintains stable performance. (b-e) Node embedding visualization (via t-SNE [16]) at different depths: GCN's features collapse as depth increases, whereas SGC preserves clear class separability even at 32 layers.

To address the limitations of deep GCNs, we introduce Layer-wise Gradual Training (LGT), a novel training paradigm designed to mitigate over-smoothing while preserving model expressiveness. Instead of training all layers simultaneously, LGT progressively expands the network depth, integrating three key strategies: incremental layer-wise training, low-rank adaptation (LoRA), and identity initialization.

Incremental Layer-wise Training. Traditional GCNs perform well in shallow settings but deteriorate rapidly as depth increases. To leverage this property, LGT adopts a staged training approach, gradually increasing depth while ensuring node embeddings remain discriminative at each step. Unlike prior layer-wise training strategies that require retraining the entire model upon adding new layers, LGT maintains previously learned representations, reducing computational redundancy and improving convergence stability.

Low-Rank Adaptation for Efficient Fine-tuning. While freezing earlier layers prevents over-smoothing, it also limits adaptation to new layers. To address this, LGT integrates Low-Rank Adaptation (LoRA) [10], enabling lightweight fine-tuning of pre-trained layers via a low-rank decomposition of weight updates. This approach significantly accelerates convergence, reducing the need for full retraining while maintaining representational flexibility.

Identity Initialization for Stable Expansion. Random initialization of newly added layers can disrupt learned representations, causing performance fluctuations. Inspired by SGC [28], which maintains performance using a fixed identity matrix as the linear transformation, LGT initializes new layers using identity matrices. This ensures smoother integration, reducing optimization instability and enhancing training efficiency.

By combining these strategies, LGT enables deep GCNs to achieve superior depth scalability, faster convergence, and improved classification accuracy while maintaining a lightweight and architecture-agnostic design. This framework not only provides a novel solution to over-smoothing but also establishes a robust foundation for training deep graph networks efficiently. Extensive experiments on semi-supervised node classification benchmarks demonstrate that LGT significantly alleviates over-smoothing and achieves state-of-the-art (SOTA) performance in deep vanilla GCNs (e.g., 32 layers), outperforming existing anti-oversmoothing methods. Furthermore, LGT is model-agnostic and can be seamlessly integrated with normalization-based techniques (e.g., PairNorm [30] and ContraNorm [9]) to further improve their performance.

In summary, our contributions are as follows:

- We identify trainable linear transformations as a critical cause of oversmoothing in moderate depth and propose a *training-based solution* fundamentally different from prior architectural modifications or regularization approaches.
- We introduce Layer-wise Gradual Training (LGT), a general and efficient strategy that combines incremental training, low-rank adaptation, and identity initialization, substantially improving the performance of deep vanilla GCNs and achieving SOTA results. LGT is also compatible with existing anti-over-smoothing techniques.

The remainder of this paper is organized as follows: Sect. 2 reviews related work, Sect. 3 formalizes the problem to evaluate over-smoothing, Sect. 4 details the proposed LGT method, Sect. 5 presents experimental results, and Sect. 6 concludes the paper.

2 Related Work

Existing approaches to alleviating over-smoothing in GCNs can be broadly categorized into two groups: (1) modifying message-passing mechanisms and (2) constraining node representations. Below, we review models in each category.

2.1 Message-Passing-Based Approaches

Message-passing-based methods aim to adjust the information aggregation process to mitigate over-smoothing [21,27]. Graph Attention Networks (GAT) [26] assign adaptive weights to neighbors, promoting selective aggregation. However, GAT models often face gradient instability and complex optimization in deep architectures. DropEdge [22] randomly removes edges during training, reducing redundant aggregation. OrderedGNN [25] structurally organizes neurons based on hop distances to constrain message passing. ResGCN [12] and JK-Net [29] introduce cross-layer connections to retain information from shallow layers, while PSNR [32] combines residual links with adaptive normalization to capture multi-hop features. Although effective to some extent, these methods rely heavily on graph-dependent heuristics or sensitive hyperparameter tuning, limiting their generalization.

2.2 Representation-Based Approaches

Another line of work focuses on directly constraining node representations to prevent feature homogenization. EGNN [33] introduces Dirichlet energy regularization to preserve informative gradients across layers. ContraNorm [9] and PairNorm [30] maintain feature variance through normalization, while BatchNorm-GCN [3] applies batch normalization to stabilize feature distributions. Although these methods effectively mitigate over-smoothing, they may also suppress useful feature interactions when applied excessively, limiting model expressiveness.

2.3 Our Motivation and Distinction

In contrast to existing methods that focus on modifying message passing or enforcing explicit feature constraints, our proposed LGT addresses over-smoothing from a training strategy perspective. By incrementally training deeper layers and applying low-rank adaptation to earlier layers, LGT implicitly regularizes feature propagation without altering GCN architecture or graph structure. Unlike prior methods, LGT maintains representation diversity and depth scalability through an optimization-centered approach, and is inherently compatible with normalization-based techniques such as PairNorm and ContraNorm for further performance gains.

3 Problem Definition

Referring the methods of evaluating over-smoothing [11,21], we consider the standard semi-supervised node classification task on a graph $\mathcal{G} = (\mathcal{V}, \mathcal{E})$, where $\mathcal{V} = \{v_1, v_2, \ldots, v_n\}$ is the set of nodes and $\mathcal{E}$ is the set of edges. Each node $v_i \in \mathcal{V}$ is associated with a feature vector $x_i \in \mathbb{R}^f$, and all node features form the feature matrix $\mathbf{X} \in \mathbb{R}^{n \times f}$. A subset of nodes $\mathcal{V}_L = \{v_1, \ldots, v_m\}$ with $m \ll n$ are labeled, while the remaining nodes $\mathcal{V}_U = \mathcal{V} \setminus \mathcal{V}_L$ are unlabeled.

The graph structure is encoded via the adjacency matrix $\mathbf{A} \in \{0,1\}^{n \times n}$, where $\mathbf{A}_{ij} = 1$ if an edge exists between nodes v_i and v_j. We adopt the normalized graph Laplacian:

$$\mathbf{L} = \mathbf{D}^{-\frac{1}{2}} (\mathbf{A} + \mathbf{I}) \mathbf{D}^{-\frac{1}{2}}, \tag{1}$$

where $\mathbf{I}$ is the identity matrix and $\mathbf{D}$ is the diagonal degree matrix with $\mathbf{D}_{ii} = \sum_j \mathbf{A}_{ij}$.

The objective of semi-supervised node classification is to train a GCN that minimizes the cross-entropy loss over labeled nodes:

$$\mathcal{L} = - \sum_{v_i \in Y_L} \sum_{c=1}^{C} y_{i,c} \log \hat{y}_{i,c}, \tag{2}$$

where C is the number of classes, $y_{i,c}$ is the one-hot label, and $\hat{y}_{i,c}$ is the predicted class probability for node v_i.

A key challenge arises when scaling GCNs to deep architectures due to the over-smoothing effect, where node representations $H^{(K)}$ progressively converge to a subspace with minimal discriminative information:

$$\lim_{K \to \infty} H^{(K)} \approx \mathbf{C}, \tag{3}$$

where $\mathbf{C}$ is a constant matrix independent of node identity. This phenomenon severely degrades classification accuracy on unlabeled nodes. Therefore, an effective GCN should maintain high classification accuracy even as the network depth K increases. Our goal is to design a training strategy that mitigates over-smoothing while enabling deeper GCNs to preserve discriminative node representations.

4 Layer-Wise Gradual Training

While deep GCNs suffer from over-smoothing, our empirical analysis (Fig. 1) reveals that trainable linear transformations accelerate feature collapse even at moderate depths. However, removing these transformations compromises model expressiveness, highlighting a key trade-off: GCNs require transformation layers for feature learning but must mitigate their role in over-smoothing to remain effective in deep architectures.

To address this, we introduce Layer-wise Gradual Training (LGT)—a progressive training strategy that incrementally deepens GCNs while preserving feature discriminability at each stage, as shown in Fig. 2. Instead of training all layers simultaneously, LGT stabilizes optimization and prevents feature degradation through structured training. LGT consists of three key components: (1) *Incremental Layer-wise Training*, which prevents abrupt optimization difficulties by progressively adding layers, ensuring stable feature learning at each depth; (2) *Low-Rank Adaptation (LoRA)* [10], which lightly fine-tunes frozen layers to retain expressiveness without excessive parameter updates. (3) *Identity Matrix Initialization*, which ensures smooth integration of new layers, reducing parameter shifts and accelerating convergence. Empirical results (Sect. 5) confirm that LGT significantly improves classification accuracy in deep GCNs (e.g., 32 layers) while reducing computational overhead. The following sections detail each component.

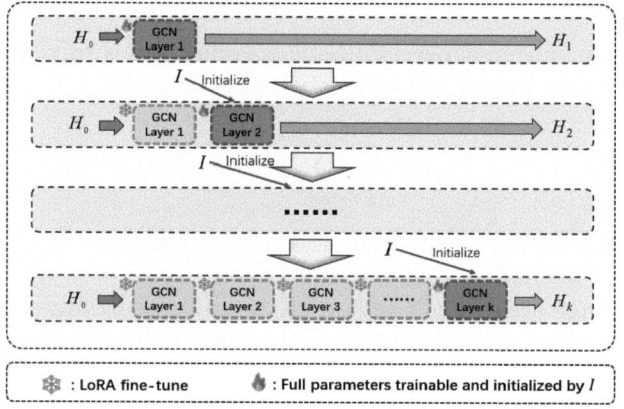

Fig. 2. Illustration of Layer-wise Gradual Training (LGT). At each stage, only the newly added layer is fully trained, while shallow layers are fine-tuned via LoRA. Once stabilized, a new layer is added and initialized with an identity matrix to ensure smooth integration.

4.1 Incremental Layer-Wise Training

To address over-smoothing caused by rapid parameter growth, LGT decomposes GCN training into multiple stages. At each stage, only one new layer is added and trained, while all previously trained layers are fine-tuned (via LoRA). This staged optimization prevents feature collapse between layers and stabilizes feature propagation as depth increases.

First Layer Training. We start by training the first GCN layer to capture local neighborhood structures. Training proceeds until convergence based on validation performance, after which the layer is frozen.

Incremental Layer Addition. New GCN layers are added sequentially. At each step, only the new layer is fully trained, while shallow layers are slightly adapted using LoRA. Early stopping is applied to each stage to prevent overfitting. This procedure ensures that each layer progressively refines representations without causing over-smoothing or collapse.

4.2 Low-Rank Adaptation (LoRA)

While freezing earlier layers stabilizes training, it may restrict representation learning capacity. To balance stability and flexibility, we introduce LoRA [10] to adaptively fine-tune frozen layers using low-rank updates. Instead of fully updating the weight matrix $\mathbf{W}^{(k)} \in \mathbb{R}^{d_{\text{in}} \times d_{\text{out}}}$, we add a learnable low-rank component:

$$\tilde{\mathbf{W}}^{(k)} = \mathbf{W}_0^{(k)} + \mathbf{A}^{(k)} \mathbf{B}^{(k)}, \tag{4}$$

where $\mathbf{W}_0^{(k)}$ is the frozen pretrained weight, and $\mathbf{A}^{(k)} \in \mathbb{R}^{d_{\text{in}} \times r}, \mathbf{B}^{(k)} \in \mathbb{R}^{r \times d_{\text{out}}}$ are low-rank matrices with $r \ll \min(d_{\text{in}}, d_{\text{out}})$. The forward propagation becomes:

$$\mathbf{H}^{(k+1)} = \sigma(\mathbf{L}\mathbf{H}^{(k)}(\mathbf{W}_0^{(k)} + \mathbf{A}^{(k)} \mathbf{B}^{(k)})), \tag{5}$$

and only $\mathbf{A}^{(k)}, \mathbf{B}^{(k)}$ are updated during training. This significantly reduces memory and computational cost while preserving adaptability in deep models.

4.3 Identity Matrix Initialization

Proper initialization of new layers is crucial for stable incremental training. Random initialization may lead to unstable gradients and disrupt previously learned representations, as shown in Fig. 3. We initialize each newly added layer's weights as an identity matrix, ensuring initial outputs align with the prior layer's features:

$$\mathbf{H}^{(k+1)} = \sigma(\mathbf{L}\mathbf{H}^{(k)}\mathbf{W}^{(k)}) \approx \sigma(\mathbf{L}\mathbf{H}^{(k)}), \tag{6}$$

thus providing a smooth transition for training deeper layers. As demonstrated in Fig. 3, identity initialization significantly improves stability and accelerates convergence compared to random initialization.

4.4 Summary

In summary, LGT integrates incremental layer-wise training, low-rank adaptation, and identity initialization into a unified framework that enables deep GCNs

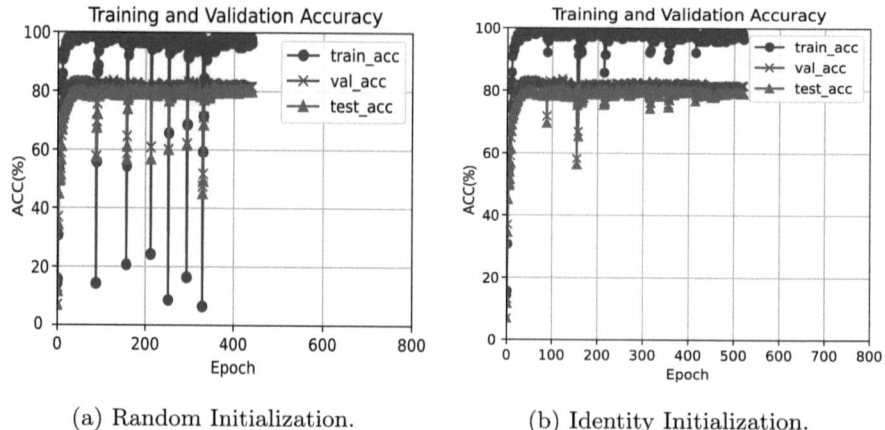

(a) Random Initialization. (b) Identity Initialization.

Fig. 3. Effect of initialization methods. Identity initialization stabilizes the training of newly added layers compared to random initialization.

to avoid over-smoothing while retaining strong representational power. Unlike prior methods that modify GCN architectures or impose explicit constraints on node representations, LGT addresses over-smoothing through an optimization-centric training paradigm, offering a scalable and compatible solution for training deep GCNs. The effectiveness of LGT is validated through extensive experiments in the next section.

5 Experiments

We conduct comprehensive experiments to evaluate the effectiveness of our proposed LGT in alleviating over-smoothing for deep GCNs on *semi-supervised node classification* tasks [11]. All models are evaluated using classification accuracy (ACC) as the primary metric. Our evaluation covers 4 benchmark datasets and 6 state-of-the-art baselines.

5.1 Experimental Setup

Datasets. To evaluate the generalizability of LGT across diverse graph domains, we conduct experiments on 4 widely used citation and co-authorship datasets: Cora [17,23], Citeseer [7,23], Pubmed [18,23], and AmazonPhoto [24]. The statistics of these datasets are summarized in Table 1. For all datasets, we follow the widely adopted semi-supervised learning setting [11], randomly selecting 20 labeled nodes per class for training, and reserving 1,000 nodes each for validation and test sets. The remaining nodes are treated as unlabeled. To ensure robustness, we repeat each experiment with 5 random splits and report the mean performance.

Table 1. The summary of dataset

Datasets	Cls.	Nodes	Edges	Feat.	Train/Valid/Test
Cora	7	2708	5429	1433	140/1000/1000
Citeseer	6	3327	4732	2703	120/1000/1000
Pubmed	3	19717	44338	500	60/1000/1000
AmazonPhoto	8	7650	119043	745	160/1000/1000

Baselines. To thoroughly validate the effectiveness of LGT, we compare several representative and state-of-the-art GCN-based models that address over-smoothing. The baselines include:

- **GCN (ICLR'17)** [11]: A foundational graph convolutional network model that performs neighborhood aggregation with learned linear transformations.
- **SGC (ICML'19)** [28]: A simplified GCN variant that removes nonlinear activations and collapses multiple layers into a single linear transformation to study the role of propagation.
- **PairNorm (ICLR'20)** [30]: A normalization technique that preserves feature variance across layers to prevent feature collapse.
- **ContraNorm (ICLR'23)** [9]: A method introducing implicit feature decorrelation to maintain node diversity and alleviate over-smoothing.
- **IresGCN (ICML'24)** [20]: An inverse residual GCN framework that adjusts message passing directions to preserve personalized node information.
- **PSNR (NeurIPS'24)** [32]: A posterior sampling and adaptive residual method that adaptively retains hierarchical information during propagation.

These baselines cover a wide range of anti-over-smoothing techniques, including normalization, residual connections, and structural adjustments. Thus, they provide a strong basis for assessing the performance and compatibility of LGT.

5.2 Effectiveness on Alleviating Over-Smoothing

To evaluate LGT's effectiveness in mitigating over-smoothing, we measure classification accuracy across different depths (4, 8, 16, and 32 layers) on four benchmark datasets: Cora, Citeseer, Pubmed, and AmazonPhoto. LGT is applied to GCN, ContraNorm, and PairNorm to assess its generalizability. The complete results are shown in Table 2, where the performances of best and second-best are highlighted, and the improvements brought about by LGT are marked with ↑.

Performance Gains in Deep GCNs. Applying LGT to vanilla GCN leads to a significant accuracy boost in deep layers. On Cora, for example, GCN+LGT achieves 82.0% accuracy at 32 layers, doubling the performance of standard GCN (41.3%). Similar trends are observed across datasets, confirming that *LGT effectively prevents over-smoothing and supports stable deep GCN training*. Additionally, GCN+LGT consistently outperforms SGC at 32 layers across all datasets,

Table 2. Classification accuracy (ACC) across different datasets (in percent)

Dataset	Model	Layers			
		4	8	16	32
Cora	SGC	$79.88_{\pm1.00}$	$79.08_{\pm1.42}$	$75.90_{\pm1.91}$	$69.62_{\pm2.57}$
	IresGCN	$79.28_{\pm1.85}$	$78.78_{\pm0.63}$	$79.04_{\pm0.54}$	$78.94_{\pm0.92}$
	PSNR	$79.90_{\pm1.00}$	$79.00_{\pm1.39}$	$79.54_{\pm0.73}$	$79.48_{\pm0.83}$
	GCN	$78.58_{\pm1.29}$	$71.30_{\pm1.54}$	$37.20_{\pm2.22}$	$40.46_{\pm0.78}$
	GCN+LGT	$80.94_{\pm1.03}^{\uparrow}$	$80.76_{\pm1.28}^{\uparrow}$	$80.58_{\pm0.49}^{\uparrow}$	$81.06_{\pm0.97}^{\uparrow}$
	ContraNorm	$79.74_{\pm0.77}$	$78.96_{\pm1.06}$	$79.42_{\pm1.88}$	$80.10_{\pm1.01}$
	ContraNorm+LGT	$80.36_{\pm1.20}^{\uparrow}$	$80.34_{\pm0.94}^{\uparrow}$	$80.66_{\pm1.63}^{\uparrow}$	$80.62_{\pm0.84}^{\uparrow}$
	PairNorm	$78.40_{\pm1.88}$	$78.10_{\pm1.05}$	$77.76_{\pm1.70}$	$77.46_{\pm1.22}$
	PairNorm+LGT	$79.50_{\pm0.56}^{\uparrow}$	$77.50_{\pm1.49}$	$78.88_{\pm0.24}^{\uparrow}$	$79.68_{\pm1.33}^{\uparrow}$
Citeseer	SGC	$69.66_{\pm0.61}$	$69.56_{\pm1.15}$	$69.06_{\pm1.63}$	$67.90_{\pm1.37}$
	IresGCN	$65.20_{\pm2.21}$	$66.30_{\pm1.76}$	$66.38_{\pm1.46}$	$67.26_{\pm2.13}$
	PSNR	$66.60_{\pm2.23}$	$65.00_{\pm2.45}$	$65.64_{\pm1.47}$	$64.38_{\pm2.80}$
	GCN	$65.54_{\pm1.80}$	$50.70_{\pm3.64}$	$25.58_{\pm1.13}$	$25.70_{\pm3.65}$
	GCN+LGT	$69.58_{\pm1.23}^{\uparrow}$	$69.46_{\pm1.35}^{\uparrow}$	$69.74_{\pm1.07}^{\uparrow}$	$69.58_{\pm0.53}^{\uparrow}$
	ContraNorm	$66.52_{\pm1.41}$	$66.42_{\pm1.07}$	$66.34_{\pm1.92}$	$66.28_{\pm1.57}$
	ContraNorm+LGT	$68.18_{\pm2.12}^{\uparrow}$	$68.48_{\pm1.35}^{\uparrow}$	$68.50_{\pm1.28}^{\uparrow}$	$68.52_{\pm1.16}^{\uparrow}$
	PairNorm	$67.66_{\pm2.40}$	$67.64_{\pm2.12}$	$66.66_{\pm2.84}$	$65.40_{\pm2.00}$
	PairNorm+LGT	$69.06_{\pm1.90}^{\uparrow}$	$68.48_{\pm1.44}^{\uparrow}$	$65.12_{\pm2.12}$	$65.80_{\pm2.50}^{\uparrow}$
Pubmed	SGC	$74.30_{\pm1.22}$	$73.74_{\pm2.05}$	$72.44_{\pm0.97}$	$70.08_{\pm0.73}$
	IresGCN	$77.24_{\pm1.13}$	$77.70_{\pm2.03}$	$76.92_{\pm0.43}$	$77.48_{\pm1.79}$
	PSNR	$76.94_{\pm1.65}$	$77.24_{\pm1.33}$	$77.24_{\pm0.71}$	$77.42_{\pm1.07}$
	GCN	$77.04_{\pm2.12}$	$70.48_{\pm3.43}$	$44.24_{\pm3.49}$	$47.70_{\pm4.11}$
	GCN+LGT	$77.94_{\pm2.12}^{\uparrow}$	$77.34_{\pm1.48}^{\uparrow}$	$77.82_{\pm1.43}^{\uparrow}$	$77.70_{\pm1.09}^{\uparrow}$
	ContraNorm	$77.94_{\pm2.04}$	OOM	OOM	OOM
	ContraNorm+LGT	$77.88_{\pm1.22}$	$77.40_{\pm1.81}$	OOM	OOM
	PairNorm	$77.02_{\pm1.37}$	$77.92_{\pm2.33}$	$77.90_{\pm1.41}$	$77.40_{\pm0.65}$
	PairNorm+LGT	$77.08_{\pm0.71}^{\uparrow}$	$76.96_{\pm0.94}$	$77.14_{\pm0.52}$	$77.32_{\pm0.98}$
AmazonPhoto	SGC	$89.18_{\pm0.54}$	$87.50_{\pm1.42}$	$84.84_{\pm2.07}$	$75.80_{\pm4.41}$
	IresGCN	$90.26_{\pm1.40}$	$90.48_{\pm2.05}$	$90.76_{\pm1.50}$	$91.68_{\pm1.18}$
	PSNR	$90.98_{\pm0.61}$	$90.72_{\pm1.02}$	$91.14_{\pm0.31}$	$91.26_{\pm1.25}$
	GCN	$90.22_{\pm0.61}$	$88.40_{\pm0.96}$	$64.24_{\pm3.18}$	$69.94_{\pm5.36}$
	GCN+LGT	$91.10_{\pm0.76}^{\uparrow}$	$91.02_{\pm0.52}^{\uparrow}$	$91.26_{\pm0.72}^{\uparrow}$	$91.34_{\pm0.25}^{\uparrow}$
	ContraNorm	$91.14_{\pm1.25}$	$91.48_{\pm0.88}$	$91.64_{\pm0.45}$	$91.56_{\pm0.75}$
	ContraNorm+LGT	$91.74_{\pm0.89}^{\uparrow}$	$91.52_{\pm0.33}^{\uparrow}$	$91.56_{\pm0.70}^{\uparrow}$	$91.80_{\pm0.91}^{\uparrow}$
	PairNorm	$91.14_{\pm0.59}$	$90.54_{\pm0.28}$	$90.76_{\pm0.53}$	$91.00_{\pm1.00}$
	PairNorm+LGT	$91.40_{\pm0.71}^{\uparrow}$	$90.94_{\pm0.81}^{\uparrow}$	$89.90_{\pm1.46}$	$91.38_{\pm0.40}^{\uparrow}$

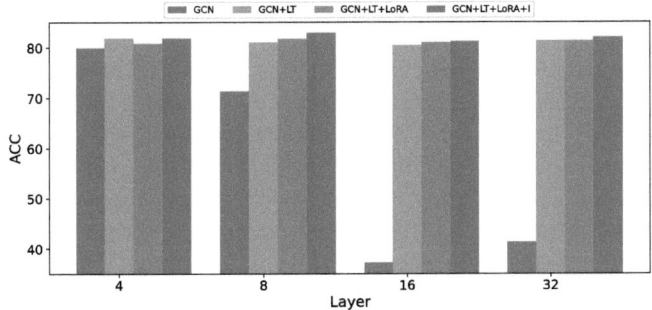

Fig. 4. Results of ablation study (Cora).

with 10–15% gains on Cora and AmazonPhoto. Interestingly, GCN+LGT also surpasses SGC at moderate depths (4 layers) on Cora, Pubmed, and AmazonPhoto, demonstrating that *proper training can balance expressiveness and smoothness*, preserving GCN's advantages.

Compatibility with Existing Anti-over-smoothing Methods. When applied to ContraNorm, LGT enhances its performance on Cora, Citeseer, and AmazonPhoto. On Pubmed, where standard ContraNorm suffers from out-of-memory (OOM) issues at 8 layers, LGT improves efficiency, producing competitive results at 4 layers and valid outputs at 8 layers. For PairNorm, LGT improves performance in 10 out of 16 settings, further confirming its broad applicability to existing anti-over-smoothing techniques.

In summary, LGT (1) effectively mitigates over-smoothing for deep GCNs, (2) improves the deep model performance, and (3) complements existing anti-over-smoothing methods, offering a general and scalable training strategy.

5.3 Ablation Study

To systematically assess the individual contributions of each component in LGT, we perform ablation studies on four GCN-based variants: (1) standard GCN as baseline, (2) GCN with Layer-wise Training (GCN+LT), (3) GCN with LT and Low-Rank Adaptation (GCN+LT+LoRA), and (4) full LGT incorporating LT, LoRA, and Identity Initialization (GCN+LT+LoRA+I). Figure 4 reports the comparison results on the Cora dataset.

As shown in Fig. 4, the introduction of LT significantly improves GCN performance in all depths (4 to 32 layers), with especially notable gains in 16 layers. Furthermore, adding LoRA and identity initialization brings additional improvements for deeper models (8–32 layers), demonstrating their roles in enhancing representation capacity and stabilizing optimization. These results confirm the positive and complementary contributions of all three components in alleviating over-smoothing and improving deep GCN performance.

5.4 Training Efficiency Analysis

We evaluate the training efficiency of LGT on Cora and AmazonPhoto datasets, as shown in Fig. 5. Applying LGT to both GCN and PairNorm, we observe that LGT not only improves GCN's classification accuracy (e.g., from 70% to over 80% on Cora) but also significantly reduces training time by avoiding full-model optimization through progressive layer-wise updates, as shown in Table 3. Although PairNorm already addresses over-smoothing, integrating LGT further reduces its training time without compromising accuracy. These results indicate that LGT complements existing normalization methods by enhancing training efficiency while maintaining or improving model performance.

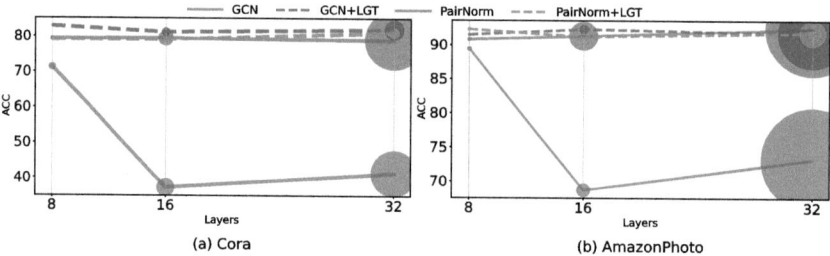

Fig. 5. Training efficiency and accuracy comparison. Line plots show classification accuracy across different network depths, and circle sizes indicate relative training time. LGT significantly improves GCN's accuracy while reducing training time. For PairNorm, LGT enhances training efficiency without sacrificing accuracy, highlighting its complementary effect.

Table 3. Training Time Comparison

Models	Cora			AmazonPhoto		
	Layer 8	Layer 16	Layer 32	Layer 8	Layer 16	Layer 32
GCN	115 s	293 s	784 s	72 s	228 s	1760 s
GCN+LGT	28 s	135 s	326 s	41 s	1452 s	1194 s
PairNorm	46 s	252 s	1006 s	61 s	485 s	1627 s
PairNorm+LGT	42 s	62 s	170 s	55 s	69 s	447 s

5.5 Effect of Rank in LoRA

We analyze the impact of the rank parameter in LoRA on model performance under varying network depths on AmazonPhoto. As shown in Fig. 6, rank influences classification accuracy, particularly in deeper networks.

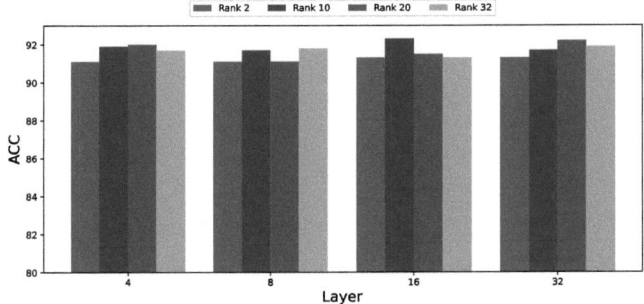

Fig. 6. Results of rank changing over layers (AmazonPhoto).

Overall, **rank=10** achieves the most stable and consistently high performance across 4, 8, and 16 layers, striking a balance between expressiveness and computational efficiency. Conversely, while **rank=32** exhibits comparatively over rank=10 in shallow networks (8 layers), it generally underperforms compared to 4 and 16 layers, likely due to over-parameterization and reduced generalization.

These results highlight the critical role of rank selection: overly small ranks limit model capacity, while excessively large ranks introduce redundancy and unnecessary computational overhead. Thus, **rank=10** is recommended for practical use, offering robust performance across depths with controlled complexity.

5.6 Node Embedding Visualization

We visualize the 32-layer node embeddings on the Cora dataset using t-SNE to assess feature separability under deep architectures. As shown in Fig. 7, vanilla GCN suffers from severe over-smoothing, with highly mixed node features and indistinct class boundaries. In contrast, GCN+LGT produces well-separated and compact clusters, demonstrating improved feature discrimination and effective mitigation of over-smoothing. Moreover, combining LGT with ContraNorm (ContraNorm+LGT) further enhances class separability compared to ContraNorm alone, confirming LGT's compatibility and complementary effect. These results highlight that LGT enables deep GCNs to preserve expressive and discriminative node representations.

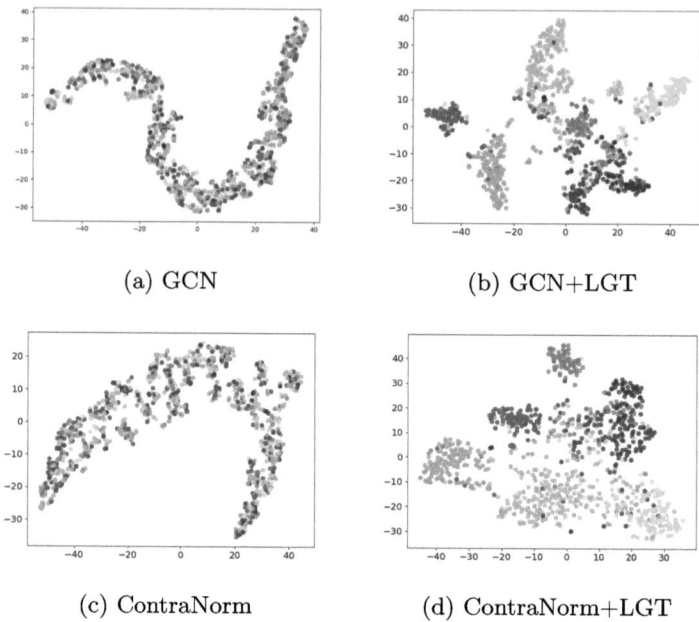

Fig. 7. The node embedding visualization of GCN, ContraNorm, and their respective variants GCN+LGT and ContraNorm+LGT under the 32th layer.

6 Conclusion

This paper revisits the over-smoothing problem in deep GCNs and identifies trainable linear transformations, rather than just the graph Laplacian, as a key factor exacerbating feature collapse. To address this, we propose Layer-wise Gradual Training (LGT), a novel training strategy that progressively deepens GCNs while preserving feature expressiveness. LGT integrates incremental layer-wise training for stabilized optimization, low-rank adaptation for efficient fine-tuning, and identity initialization for smooth layer expansion. Extensive experiments demonstrate that LGT significantly improves deep GCN performance, mitigating over-smoothing while enhancing training efficiency. Moreover, LGT is highly compatible with existing anti-over-smoothing techniques, such as PairNorm and ContraNorm, extending their scalability to deeper architectures. The efficiency analysis highlights faster convergence and improved stability.

Despite these advantages, two key areas warrant further exploration. (1) *Theoretical insights into LGT's optimization benefits.* The over-smoothing can be viewed as a degenerate optimization issue. LGT preserves well-initialized shallow layers and prevents unstable gradient interference from randomly initialized deep layers. A deeper theoretical analysis—possibly through saddle-point theory or local optimization landscapes—could explain how LGT helps GCNs converge toward desirable optimization regions, thereby preventing over-smoothing. (2) *Interaction with existing anti-over-smoothing methods.* While LGT enhances several approaches, its impact varies across datasets (e.g., PairNorm on Pubmed). Future work will explore the relationship between training-based and structure-based regularization to refine deep GCN optimization.

Overall, LGT provides a general, training-centric solution for deep GCNs, shifting the focus from architectural design to optimization strategies and paving the way for more effective and scalable graph learning models.

Acknowledgments. This work was supported by the National Natural Science Foundation of China (Nos. 62276162, 62272286), the Fundamental Research Program of Shanxi Province (Nos. 202203021222016, 202402020101004), the Central guidance for Local scientific and technological development funds (Nos. YDZJSX20231B001, YDZJSX2025D088), and the Key Laboratory of Evolutionary Science Intelligence of Shanxi Province.

References

1. Chen, D., Lin, Y., Li, W., Li, P., Zhou, J., Sun, X.: Measuring and relieving the over-smoothing problem for graph neural networks from the topological view. In: Proceedings of the AAAI Conference on Artificial Intelligence, vol. 34, pp. 3438–3445 (2020)
2. Chen, M., Wei, Z., Huang, Z., Ding, B., Li, Y.: Simple and deep graph convolutional networks. In: III, H.D., Singh, A. (eds.) Proceedings of the 37th International Conference on Machine Learning. Proceedings of Machine Learning Research, vol. 119, pp. 1725–1735. PMLR (13–18 Jul 2020)
3. Chen, Y., Tang, X., Qi, X., Li, C.G., Xiao, R.: Learning graph normalization for graph neural networks. Neurocomputing **493**, 613–625 (2022). https://doi.org/10.1016/j.neucom.2022.01.003
4. Defferrard, M., Bresson, X., Vandergheynst, P.: Convolutional neural networks on graphs with fast localized spectral filtering. In: Advances in Neural Information Processing Systems, vol. 29 (2016)
5. Fan, W., et al.: Graph neural net works for social recommendation. In: The World Wide Web Conference, pp. 417–426. WWW '19, Association for Computing Machinery, New York, NY, USA (2019)
6. Feng, W., et al.: Graph random neural networks for semi-supervised learning on graphs. Adv. Neural. Inf. Process. Syst. **33**, 22092–22103 (2020)
7. Giles, C.L., Bollacker, K.D., Lawrence, S.: Citeseer: an automatic citation indexing system. In: Proceedings of the Third ACM Conference on Digital Libraries, pp. 89–98. DL '98, Association for Computing Machinery, New York, NY, USA (1998). https://doi.org/10.1145/276675.276685
8. Gilmer, J., Schoenholz, S.S., Riley, P.F., Vinyals, O., Dahl, G.E.: Neural message passing for quantum chemistry. In: Proceedings of the 34th International Conference on Machine Learning - Volume 70, pp. 1263–1272. ICML'17, JMLR.org (2017)
9. Guo, X., Wang, Y., Du, T., Wang, Y.: Contranorm: a contrastive learning perspective on oversmoothing and beyond. In: The Eleventh International Conference on Learning Representations (2023)

10. Hu, E.J., et al.: LoRA: Low-rank adaptation of large language models. In: International Conference on Learning Representations (2022)
11. Kipf, T.N., Welling, M.: Semi-supervised classification with graph convolutional networks. In: International Conference on Learning Representations (2017)
12. Li, G., Muller, M., Thabet, A., Ghanem, B.: DeepGCNs: Can GCNs go as deep as CNNs? In: Proceedings of the IEEE/CVF International Conference on Computer Vision, pp. 9267–9276 (2019)
13. Li, H., et al.: A survey on graph neural networks in intelligent transportation systems. arXiv preprint arXiv:2401.00713 (2024)
14. Li, Q., Han, Z., Wu, X.M.: Deeper insights into graph convolutional networks for semi-supervised learning. In: Proceedings of the Thirty-Second AAAI Conference on Artificial Intelligence and Thirtieth Innovative Applications of Artificial Intelligence Conference and Eighth AAAI Symposium on Educational Advances in Artificial Intelligence. AAAI'18/IAAI'18/EAAI'18, AAAI Press (2018)
15. Lin, X., Quan, Z., Wang, Z.J., Ma, T., Zeng, X.: KGNN: Knowledge graph neural network for drug-drug interaction prediction. In: Bessiere, C. (ed.) Proceedings of the Twenty-Ninth International Joint Conference on Artificial Intelligence, IJCAI-20, pp. 2739–2745. International Joint Conferences on Artificial Intelligence Organization (7 2020). https://doi.org/10.24963/ijcai.2020/380,main track
16. Maaten, L., Hinton, G.: Visualizing data using t-SNE. J. Mach. Learn. Res. **9**(86), 2579–2605 (2008)
17. McCallum, A.K., Nigam, K., Rennie, J., Seymore, K.: Automating the construction of internet portals with machine learning. Inf. Retrieval **3**, 127–163 (2000)
18. Namata, G., London, B., Getoor, L., Huang, B., Edu, U.: Query-driven active surveying for collective classification. In: 10th International Workshop on Mining and Learning with Graphs, vol. 8, p. 1 (2012)
19. Oono, K., Suzuki, T.: Graph neural networks exponentially lose expressive power for node classification. In: International Conference on Learning Representations (2020)
20. Park, M., Heo, J., Kim, D.: Mitigating oversmoothing through reverse process of gnns for heterophilic graphs. In: Proceedings of the 41st International Conference on Machine Learning, ICML'24, JMLR.org (2024)
21. Peng, F., Liu, K., Lu, X., Qian, Y., Yan, H., Ma, C.: TSC: A simple two-sided constraint against over-smoothing. In: Proceedings of the 30th ACM SIGKDD Conference on Knowledge Discovery and Data Mining, pp. 2376–2387 (2024)
22. Rong, Y., Huang, W., Xu, T., Huang, J.: Dropedge: Towards deep graph convolutional networks on node classification. arXiv preprint arXiv:1907.10903 (2019)
23. Sen, P., Namata, G., Bilgic, M., Getoor, L., Gallagher, B., Eliassi-Rad, T.: Collective classification in network data. AI Mag. **29**(3), 93–106 (2008). https://doi.org/10.1609/aimag.v29i3.2157
24. Shchur, O., Mumme, M., Bojchevski, A., Günnemann, S.: Pitfalls of graph neural network evaluation. arXiv preprint arXiv:1811.05868 (2018)
25. Song, Y., Zhou, C., Wang, X., Lin, Z.: Ordered GNN: ordering message passing to deal with heterophily and over-smoothing. In: The Eleventh International Conference on Learning Representations (2023)
26. Veličković, P., Cucurull, G., Casanova, A., Romero, A., Liò, P., Bengio, Y.: Graph attention networks. In: International Conference on Learning Representations (2018)
27. Wang, K., et al.: The snowflake hypothesis: training deep GNN with one node one receptive field. arXiv preprint arXiv:2308.10051 (2023)

28. Wu, F., Souza, A., Zhang, T., Fifty, C., Yu, T., Weinberger, K.: Simplifying graph convolutional networks. In: Chaudhuri, K., Salakhutdinov, R. (eds.) Proceedings of the 36th International Conference on Machine Learning. Proceedings of Machine Learning Research, vol. 97, pp. 6861–6871. PMLR (09–15 Jun 2019)
29. Xu, K., Li, C., Tian, Y., Sonobe, T., Kawarabayashi, K.i., Jegelka, S.: Representation learning on graphs with jumping knowledge networks. In: Dy, J., Krause, A. (eds.) Proceedings of the 35th International Conference on Machine Learning. Proceedings of Machine Learning Research, vol. 80, pp. 5453–5462. PMLR (10–15 Jul 2018)
30. Zhao, L., Akoglu, L.: Pairnorm: Tackling oversmoothing in GNNs. In: International Conference on Learning Representations (2020)
31. Zhou, J., et al.: Graph neural networks: a review of methods and applications. AI Open **1**, 57–81 (2020)
32. Zhou, J., et al.: Deep graph neural networks via posteriori-sampling-based node-adaptative residual module. In: Globerson, A., Mackey, L., Belgrave, D., Fan, A., Paquet, U., Tomczak, J., Zhang, C. (eds.) Advances in Neural Information Processing Systems, vol. 37, pp. 68211–68238. Curran Associates, Inc. (2024)
33. Zhou, K., et al.: Dirichlet energy constrained learning for deep graph neural networks. In: Beygelzimer, A., Dauphin, Y., Liang, P., Vaughan, J.W. (eds.) Advances in Neural Information Processing Systems (2021)

BotTrans: A Multi-source Graph Domain Adaptation Approach for Social Bot Detection

Boshen Shi[1,2], Yongqing Wang[1(✉)], Fangda Guo[1], Jiangli Shao[1,2], Huawei Shen[1,2], and Xueqi Cheng[1,2]

[1] State Key Laboratory of AI Safety, Institute of Computing Technology, Chinese Academy of Sciences, Beijing 100190, China
shiboshen15@mails.ucas.ac.cn, wangyongqing@ict.ac.cn
[2] University of Chinese Academy of Sciences, Beijing 100190, China

Abstract. Transferring extensive knowledge from relevant social networks has emerged as a promising solution to overcome label scarcity in detecting social bots and other anomalies with GNN-based models. However, effective transfer faces two critical challenges. Firstly, the network heterophily problem, which is caused by bots hiding malicious behaviors via indiscriminately interacting with human users, hinders the model's ability to learn sufficient and accurate bot-related knowledge from source domains. Secondly, single-source transfer might lead to inferior and unstable results, as the source network may embody weak relevance to the task and provide limited knowledge. To address these challenges, we explore multiple source domains and propose a multi-source graph domain adaptation model named *BotTrans*. We initially leverage the labeling knowledge shared across multiple source networks to establish a cross-source-domain topology with increased network homophily. We then aggregate cross-domain neighbor information to enhance the discriminability of source node embeddings. Subsequently, we integrate the relevance between each source-target pair with model optimization, which facilitates knowledge transfer from source networks that are more relevant to the detection task. Additionally, we propose a refinement strategy to improve detection performance by utilizing semantic knowledge within the target domain. Extensive experiments on real-world datasets demonstrate that *BotTrans* outperforms the existing state-of-the-art methods, revealing its efficacy in leveraging multi-source knowledge when the target detection task is unlabeled.

Keywords: Graph domain adaptation · Social bot detection · Transfer learning

1 Introduction

Social bots are typically defined as automated social media profiles created to perform specific functions, such as data collection, content sharing, promotion, and activities aimed at political influence [2,11]. As artificial intelligence advances, social bots increasingly demonstrate the ability to mimic complex aspects of human social behavior. They can manipulate public discussions by spreading misinformation, fabricating artificial environments, and even influencing the thoughts and convictions of users [36]. As a result, the significance of identifying social bots is progressively growing.

Many attempts at bot detection extract discriminative patterns from user metadata, tweet content and action sequences with shallow and deep methods. Recently, models based on Graph Neural Networks (GNNs) have demonstrated several advantages in social bot detection, especially in capturing and utilizing complex relationships and structures [1,6]. However, due to the evolution of bot strategies and the complex behaviors of bots, they face challenges stemming from the scarcity of annotations [2]. Therefore, to detect bots or other anomalies in the challenging unlabeled scenarios, researchers have proposed GNN-based knowledge transfer methods, in which graph domain adaptation (GDA) appears as an effective paradigm [3–5, 30, 31]. The underlying premise is that **social bots exhibit consistent features and behavioral patterns across social platforms**. With the domain adaptation technique, GDA models can effectively learn bot-related knowledge from task-relevant graphs with abundant bot labels (source domains) and transfer it to task graphs (target domains).

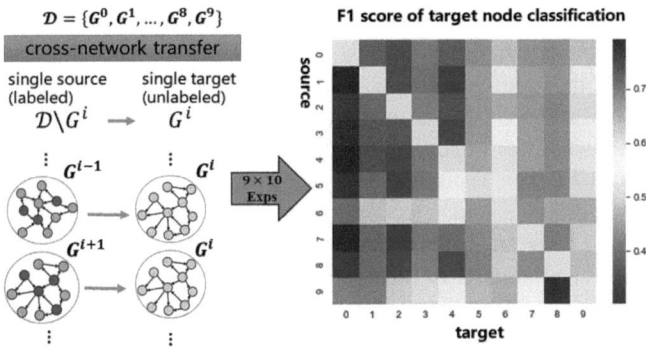

Fig. 1. Network-relevance by conducting 9×10 cross-network transfer tasks between every two networks.

Although promising, transferring knowledge for detecting social bots faces two challenges which previous studies have largely ignored. Firstly, **the social bot-related knowledge learned from source domains could be insufficient and inaccurate**. As bots frequently interact with human users to conceal their malicious activities, network heterophily arises, i.e. nodes with dissimilar features and labels are connected [13, 39]. Aggregating information in a strongly heterophilous neighborhood makes GNNs learn less discriminative node embeddings, especially for social bots. Therefore, ignoring this challenge will raise source training errors and increase classification risk on target domains.

Another key challenge is that **transferring knowledge from a single source domain may lead to inferior and unstable adaptation performance**. Prior works have mainly considered transferring from a single source domain, which may exhibit low relevance to the task and provide limited bot-related knowledge for the model. To facilitate a better understanding, we conducted 9×10 single-source&single-target transfer experiments with a typical GDA model [3] over ten domains, each of which represents a different social network with social bots and human users (see Sect. 5.1 for details). We quantify network relevance based on classification performance. If transferring from source i to target j yields higher accuracy than from source k, we infer that i is more relevant to j than k. Figure 1 reveals that when the target domain is fixed, the transfer results from different source domains are inconsistent. Similarly, the relevance of the same source domain to different target domains also varies, which is hard to predict prior to implementation.

To address the above challenges, we explore multiple source graph domains and propose a novel multi-source graph domain adaptation (MSGDA) model, *BotTrans*, to address the unlabeled detection task. Generally, *BotTrans* develops three key modules to guarantee the effectiveness of multi-source knowledge transfer:

1. **Cross Source Domain Message-Passing (CSD-MP).** It alleviates network heterophily problem and enables the model to learn social-bot knowledge more sufficiently from sources. The key idea is sharing labeling knowledge across multiple sources to create a neighborhood with higher homophily for each source node. Specifically, a cross-source-domain topology is established to connect each source node to similar nodes that may be beneficial (e.g., nodes with the same labels) and originate from other source domains. Such cross-source-domain topology embodies higher homophily, and we utilize the aggregated node information from it to improve the discriminative power of source embeddings.
2. **Selective Multi-Source Transfer (SMST).** It integrates abundant knowledge from multiple source domains and selectively transfers the most task-relevant knowledge. In particular, we leverage domain-level similarity between each source domain and target domain as an indicator of the relevance of that source domain to the task. Such similarity is computed from both semantic and structural domain information. Subsequently, we apply a weighting strategy during optimization to guide the model in transferring more knowledge from source domains that exhibit higher task relevance to the task.
3. **Anomaly Refinement (AR).** It further utilizes the semantic knowledge of the target domain to improve detection performance. A potential risk of knowledge transfer is that models trained on source domains may under-fit on the target domain, which is caused by noisy source labels, i.e., bots are mislabeled as human users. Considering the difficulties in identifying noisy source labels and the missing of target labels, we resort to refining inferior target predictions with the node-level heterophily score.

Overall, these modules follow the stages of knowledge transfer, which include learning on sources, transferring knowledge to the target, and exploring additional target knowledge. To sum up, we summarize the main contributions of this work as follows:

1. To the best of our knowledge, we are among the first to study the problem of applying multi-source graph domain adaptation to social bot detection, with the aim of alleviating the scarcity of social bot labels.
2. We propose a novel MSGDA model *BotTrans*. It significantly improves detection performance by alleviating network heterophily on source domains, transferring extensive and task-relevant knowledge to target domains, and refining target detection results.

3. We conduct extensive experiments based on real-world social bot detection datasets, and the results demonstrate that *BotTrans* achieves state-of-the-art performance in unlabeled detection tasks.

2 Related Works

GNN-Based Social Bot Detection. Recently, researchers have resorted to GNN-based models to detect social bots [1,6,7,20,36,39]. Firstly, as social relationships are more complicated to camouflage, exploring complex social relationships could reveal more discriminative patterns of bots [10,21]. Secondly, bots tend to act in groups to pursue malicious goals and implicitly form bot communities [2]. Many studies focus solely on addressing label scarcity or network heterophily problems within the task graph, ignoring the potential benefits of exploring auxiliary knowledge from related social platforms with richer annotations, which indicates the importance of developing *BotTrans*.

Graph Domain Adaptation. To overcome the label scarcity problem on graphs, researchers have developed graph domain adaptation (GDA) as an effective transfer learning paradigm on graphs [24]. It typically involves integrating GNNs with domain adaptation techniques to learn network-invariant and label-related node embeddings for graph-related tasks [3,23,25,26,31,32,37,38]. GDA has been extended to cross-domain anomaly detection tasks by designing additional topology reconstruction module (Commander [4]) or anomaly-specific objectives for learning social bot-related knowledge on source domains (ACT [30]). However, they may not be optimal solutions for detecting social bots, as they consider neither the network heterophily problem nor knowledge from multiple sources. Currently, very few works have attempted to resolve the challenging multi-source graph domain adaptation tasks. Representative works include NESTL [12], MSDS [16], and GDN [5]. However, they either over-simplifies source-target relevance or relies on target labels. Consequently, we develop *BotTrans* to effectively transfer knowledge from multiple source graphs for detecting social bots in the challenging unlabeled scenario.

3 Problem Formulation

In this work, we formulate the unlabeled social bot detection task as a **cross-graph node classification problem**. Specifically, given source graphs ($G^{S_1}, \cdots, G^{S_m}$) with abundant labels as source domains, the objective is to learn a detection model transferring labeling knowledge from multiple source domains to predict whether the nodes in the target graph G^T is a bot or not. Each source graph includes a node feature matrix, an adjacency matrix, and node-level labels indicating whether a node represents a bot or not. In contrast, G^T is entirely unlabeled. All graphs share the same feature space.

4 Methodology

The framework of *BotTrans* is illustrated in Fig. 2. Initially, the CSD-MP module generates discriminative source node embeddings by integrating in-domain and cross-source-domain information. Subsequently, the SMST module trains a shared classifier across multiple source domains and adapts it to the target domain with a domain-level weighting strategy. Finally, the AR module refines the classification results output by the under-fitted source classifier during the inference stage. We discuss the details of *BotTrans* in the following sections.

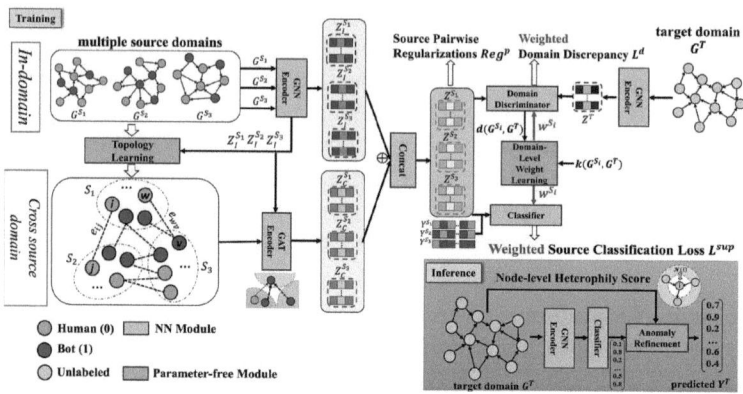

Fig. 2. Overview of *BotTrans* framework.

4.1 Cross Source Domain Message-Passing

Generally, the CSD-MP module generates node embeddings for all source and target domains. It additionally enhances the discriminability of source node embeddings to facilitate the transfer of more bot-related knowledge. Besides, it aligns the latent embedding spaces of multiple source domains, promoting more stable adaptation from multiple sources to the target.

Given m source graphs $(G^{S_1}, \cdots, G^{S_m})$ and a target graph G^T, we first utilize a shared GNN encoder f to generate node embeddings Z_I via message-passing inside each network, which is called in-domain message-passing. Take the lth layer of GCN [18] as an example, the in-domain message-passing for computing the embedding of node i from domain D is:

$$Z_{I,i}^{D,(l)} = \sigma(b^{(l-1)} + \sum_{j \in \mathcal{N}(i) \cup i} \frac{1}{c_{ij}} Z_{I,j}^{D,(l-1)} W^{(l-1)}) \tag{1}$$

where $D \in \{S_1, \cdots, S_m, T\}$, $b^{(l-1)}$ and $W^{(l-1)}$ are parameters; $\mathcal{N}(i)$ represents all one-hop neighbors of node i and $c_{ij} = \sqrt{|\mathcal{N}(i)|}\sqrt{|\mathcal{N}(j)|}$. σ denotes non-linear activation like ReLU.

Following in-domain message-passing, we aim to enhance the discriminability of node embeddings deteriorated by network heterophily. While existing works focus on addressing this problem within the task graph [6,36,39], we instead explore common knowledge about bots and human users shared across multiple source graphs. Particularly, we learn a cross-source-domain topology to connect each source node to more advantageous neighbors. Although they originate from different source domains than the central node, they likely share similar labels and patterns with it and are located nearby in the embedding space. Thus, their information could contribute to recovering the discriminability of central node embeddings via message-passing.

To start with, for any source node i from source domain p, we identify its Top-K similar nodes from all source domains excluding p based on cosine similarity between node embeddings, and we establish cross-domain edges between i and each of these K nodes. Thus, a Top-K sparse topology is created. However, edges may contain sub-optimal cross-domain connections between bots and human users, as the feature-camouflage characteristic of social bots may make their embeddings similar to human users. To score the quality of these edges, we resort to the consistency of local subgraph structures. As social relations are more difficult to camouflage, the local subgraph structure, which reveals account behaviors, could be similar within users in the same class (i.e., bot or human user). However, such subgraph-similarity is challenging for GNNs to capture. Therefore, for amy cross-domain edge $E_{ij}^{p,q}$ connecting node i, j from source domains p and q, we explicitly assign value $e_{ij}^{p,q}$ to it by measuring structural similarity between 3-hop ego-networks $G^p(i)$, $G^q(j)$ centred at i and j, respectively:

$$e_{ij}^{p,q} = k(G^p(i), G^q(j)) \in (0,1) \qquad (2)$$

where k indicates graphlet kernel which maps local subgraphs to fixed-dim vectors and calculates such embedding similarity.

Consequently, we conduct message-passing on these cross-source-domain edges to compute enhanced embeddings Z_C, which is initialized with Z_I. We adopt a 1-layer Graph Attention Network (GAT) encoder f_a for aggregating beneficial information from cross-domain neighbors [28]. Generally, the cross-source-domain message-passing could be represented as:

$$Z_{C,i}^{D,(l)} = \sigma(b^c + \sum_{j \in \mathcal{N}(i) \cup i} \alpha_{ij} Z_{C,j}^{D',(l)} W^c) \qquad (3)$$

where $D, D' \in \{S_1, \cdots, S_m\}$ and $D \neq D'$. $\mathcal{N}(i)$ refers to cross-domain neighbors of node i from the other source domains. Attention coefficient α_{ij} (simple for $\alpha_{ij}^{D,D'}$) is computed by:

$$\alpha_{ij} = \frac{exp(s_{ij})}{\sum_{h \in \mathcal{N}(i)} exp(s_{ih})}$$

$$s_{ij} = \sigma'(a^c[z_{C,i}^{D,(l)} W^c \| z_{C,j}^{D',(l)} W^c \| e_{ij}^{D,D'} W_e^c])$$

where b^c, W^c, a^c and W_e^c are parameters of GAT, σ' represents LeakyReLU activation.

As the aggregated information from cross-domain neighbors might encompass diverse data distributions, and the updated node embeddings may be noisy. To alleviate this problem and further stabilize adaptation, we align the latent embedding spaces of source domains with a pairwise regularization Reg^p:

$$Reg^p = \sum_i \sum_{j, j \neq i} Disc(Z_C^{S_i}, Z_C^{S_j}) \qquad (4)$$

where $Disc$ indicates discrepancy measurement (e.g., Maximum Mean Discrepancy).

Finally, the overall embedding z_i for any source node i is obtained by aggregating embeddings from both in-domain ($Z_{I,i} \in \mathbb{R}^h$, Eq. 1) and cross-domain ($Z_{C,i} \in \mathbb{R}^h$, Eq. 3) channels, which enhances the discriminability of node embeddings while accurately encoding the inherent knowledge within each source domain:

$$z_i = \beta_1 Z_{I,i} + \beta_2 Z_{C,i} \tag{5}$$

where coefficients β_1 and β_2 are computed by applying a linear transformation matrix W^{cat} mapping from $\mathbb{R}^{2h}$ to $\mathbb{R}^2$:

$$\beta_{1(2)} = \frac{exp(W^{cat}[Z_{I,i}\|Z_{C,i}])_{1(2)}}{\sum_{h\in\{1,2\}} exp(W^{cat}[Z_{I,i}\|Z_{C,i}])_h}$$

4.2 Selective Multi-source Transfer

Following the network embedding via Eq. 5, we selectively transfer knowledge from multiple source graphs. The key idea is measuring the relevance between each source and target graph, i.e., (G^{S_k}, G^T). In this section, we first introduce a trivial multi-source adaptation pipeline to learn network-invariant and label-related embeddings with adversarial domain adaptation technique, then we discuss how to improve it in multi-source tasks.

First of all, we use available labels in all source domains to train a shared classifier g, which will let source domain embeddings learn label-related knowledge:

$$L^{sup} = -\sum_k \frac{1}{n^k} \sum_{i=1}^{n^k} y_i^{S_k} log(g(f(z_i^{S_k}))) \tag{6}$$

where i indicates the ith node, S_k is the kth source domain, n^k is the number of training samples from source graph G^{S_k}, $y_i^{S_k}$ is groundtruth label of node i and $g(f(z_i^{S_k}))$ is the predicted logits.

Following the supervised training on source graphs, we eliminate domain discrepancy by modelling it with Wasserstein-1 distance, which has been proven to be effective in previous studies [14,37]. Consequently, we could learn network-invariant embeddings and transfer label-related knowledge from source to target graphs. Generally, the first Wasserstein distance between the source and target distributions of node embedding Z^{S_k} and Z^T is formulated as:

$$W_1(Z^{S_k}, Z^T) = \sup_{\|d\|_L \leq 1} \mathbb{E}_{z \sim Z^{S_k}}[d(z)] - \mathbb{E}_{z' \sim Z^T}[d(z')] \tag{7}$$

where $\|d\|_L \leq 1$ is Lipschitz continuity constraint, and d is domain critic outputting a real number for any input node embedding. In practice, we approximate Eq. 7 by maximizing the following domain critic loss:

$$L^d = \sum_k \frac{1}{n^{S_k}} \sum_i^{n^{S_k}} d(z_i^{S_k}) - \frac{1}{n^T} \sum_j^{n^T} d(z_j^T) \tag{8}$$

Therefore, by regarding the encoder f from network embedding as generator and the domain critic d as discriminator, we solve the following minimax problem:

$$\min_{\Theta_f, \Theta_{oth}} \max_{\Theta_d} L^d$$

where Θ_f, Θ_d denote encoder and classifier parameters, and Θ_{oth} includes all other model parameters including f_a and W^{cat}.

In the above trivial settings, all sources are equally adapted to the target. Given the varying degrees of relevance between each source domain and the task, assigning equal weight to sources during supervised training and adaptation may either introduce noisy and irrelevant information from low-relevant sources or neglect beneficial knowledge from high-relevant sources, potentially impairing adaptation performance. To address this problem, we compute domain-level similarity w^k between each source graph G^{S_k} and target graph G^T. Subsequently, we employ a selective knowledge transfer strategy:

$$L^{sup} = -\sum_k \frac{w^k}{n^k} \sum_{i=1}^{n^k} y_i^{S_k} log(g(f(z_i^{S_k})))$$

$$L^d = \sum_k w^k (\frac{1}{n^k} \sum_i^{n^k} d(z_i^{S_k}) - \frac{1}{n^T} \sum_j^{n^T} d(z_j^T)) \quad (9)$$

Generally, the weighted L^{sup} and L^d encourage the model to learn bot-related patterns and transfer more knowledge from source graphs that are more similar to target graph, respectively.

The domain-level weight w^k simultaneously models semantic and structural similarities between the source and target domains. First of all, as the output by domain discriminator d directly measures similarity between latent embedding spaces, we take it into account and compute semantic similarity score $w^{k,d} \in (0,1)$:

$$w^{k,d} = \exp(-|\frac{1}{n^k} \sum_i^{n^k} d(z_i^{S_k}) - \frac{1}{n^T} \sum_j^{n^T} d(z_j^T)|)$$

Moreover, measuring the consistency of user behaviors from different domains is equally important because users usually exhibit different social behaviors on platforms with varying functionalities. These social behaviors are characterized by social relationships. Therefore, we apply graphlet kernel to compute structural similarity score $w^{k,g} \in (0,1)$ between topologies of each source graph G^{S_k} and target graph G^T: $w^{k,g} = k(G^{S_k}, G^T)$, which is similar with Eq. 2. Consequently, w^k is computed from both semantic and structure channels:

$$w^k = \gamma w^{k,d} + (1-\gamma) w^{k,g} \quad (10)$$

where balancing coefficient γ is set manually.

4.3 Anomaly Refinement

In the inference stage, as source classifier g may under-fit on the target graph due to noisy source labels, we refine the target predictions from g with "free" target domain knowledge. Specifically, we adopt the node-level heterophily score of each target node, which is defined from raw feature space:

$$score_i = 1 - cosine(x_i, \frac{1}{|\mathcal{N}(i)|} \sum_{j \in \mathcal{N}(i)} x_j)$$

where $cosine$ indicates cosine similarity, x_i and x_j are raw node features. A higher value of $score_i$ indicates greater diversification of node i from its neighbors, which suggests a potential bot. Therefore, during the inference stage, prediction logits for the target graph are refined by:

$$y_i^{pred} = \lambda g(f(z_i)) + (1 - \lambda) score_i \tag{11}$$

where $g(f(z_i))$ represents prediction logits output by GNN encoder f and source classifier g. Hyper-parameter λ is set manually.

4.4 Training, Inference, and Complexity

Putting all the ingredients together, i.e., Eq. 4 and 9, the overall loss of the proposed *BotTrans* is as follows:

$$\min_{\Theta_f, \Theta_g, \Theta_{oth}} \{L^{sup} + \eta_1 Reg^p + \max_{\Theta_d} \eta_2 L^d\} \tag{12}$$

where η_1 and η_2 are balancing coefficients.

After training, we employ the encoder f and classifier g to infer the probabilities that target nodes are social bots. These logits are further refined via Eq. 11.

The additional complexity of *BotTrans* mainly stems from the CSD-MP and SMST module. In particular, SMST incurs a relatively low cost as it depends solely on discriminator outputs and pre-processed graph kernel scores (offline). The CSD-MP module introduces additional complexity through an extra GAT layer, f_a. Given m subgraphs from sources, each containing $|v|$ nodes, the cross-source-domain topology then consists of $m|v|$ nodes and $Km|v|$ edges. Consequently, the complexity of f_a is approximately $O(m|v|dd' + Km|v|d)$, where d and d' represent the input and output feature dimensions. Therefore, the subgraph sampling strategy and a small K keep the whole scale acceptable.

5 Experiments

We evaluate *BotTrans* to address the following research questions:

RQ1 How does *BotTrans* perform compared to baselines?
RQ2 How does each module of *BotTrans* contribute to the overall effectiveness?
RQ3 Can *BotTrans* stably excel when the number of source domains grows or source labels are limited?
RQ4 How sensitive is *BotTrans* to hyper-parameters?

5.1 Experimental Settings

Real-World Dataset. As the majority of public social bot datasets originate from Twitter, we mainly adopt three real-world, well-established datasets TwiBot-22, TwiBot-20 and MGTAB [8,9,27]. In particular, we build ten domains based on ten networks from these datasets. In addition to non-overlapping nodes and edges, users in different sub-networks have different social interests and their neighborhoods reflect distinct aspects of the whole Twitter network, leading to obvious feature- and structure- shifts across sub-networks. Thus, it is an effective strategy to test model transferability. *To better focus on the two challenges proposed in this paper, we made a simplified assumption that the proportions of bots and human users are approximately balanced.*

Baselines. *Inductive GNNs:* GCN [18] and GraphSAGE [15] are trained on source domains and applied to the target domain without adaptation. *Graph out-of-distribution (OOD) generalization:* We adopt EERM [33] and ISGIB [35], which are first trained on source domains and subsequently used to make predictions directly on the target domain. *Single-source Graph Domain Adaptation:* We adopt ADAGCN [3], GRADE [31] and UDAGCN [32]. *Single-source Cross-Domain Graph Anomaly Detection:* We adopt ACT [30] and COMMANDER [4]. We use trivial multi-source settings for the above two categories, in which all sources are equally adapted. *Multi-Source Domain Adaptation:* we adopt M^3SDA [22] and replace the encoder with GCN. *Multi-source Graph Transfer Learning:* we adopt MSDS [16] and NESTL [12], both suitable for tasks involving multiple source graphs and an unlabelled target graph. *Unsupervised Graph Anomaly Detection:* we adopt DGI+Local Outlier Factor (LOF), DGI+Isolation Forest (IF), CoLA [19], and CONAD [34]. Specifically, DGI+LOF and DGI+IF indicate we firstly learn node embeddings with deep graph infomax [29] and apply unsupervised outlier detectors to discover social bots.

Evaluation Protocol. To build transfer tasks, we treat any domain as target domain G^T (unlabeled) and select from the remaining domains as source domains (fully labeled). For efficiency, we first fix the number of source domains (m) at 2, 4, and 9, then build transfer tasks like: $\mathbf{G^{S_1}}, \cdots, \mathbf{G^{S_m}} \to \mathbf{G^T}$. Subsequently, when $m=2$ or $m=4$, we fix two transfer tasks for each target domain: the transfer from the m most relevant source domains (High-m) and the m least relevant source domains (Low-m). Such relevance is assessed through preliminary experiments in Fig. 1, where a higher result indicate higher domain relevance. When $m=9$, all the remaining nine domains are used as sources. In total, each model is evaluated over twenty transfer tasks ($m=2$), twenty tasks ($m=4$), and ten tasks ($m=9$), respectively. This strategy efficiently assesses the model's knowledge transfer capability under different settings.

Implement Details. In *BotTrans*, we use 2-layer GCN as in-domain encoder, 2-layer MLP as classifier and 1-layer MLP as domain discriminator, which are kept the same for baseline models. The graphlet kernels are implemented with Orca [17], which could be fast pre-processed before training. γ and λ are set a priori to 0.5, and balancing coefficients η_1, η_2 are both set to 1. We use top-5 neighbors to construct cross-source-domain topology. We train *BotTrans* in a mini-batch manner with batch size equals 64 for all domains. For unsupervised methods, we use a prior contamination rate 0.5. We adopt the Adam optimizer with learning rate of 1e-4 and weight decay of 1e-5. Each experiment is repeated 5 times.

5.2 Detection Effectiveness and Efficiency

To answer **RQ1**, we conducted extensive experiments under various transfer settings and summarize the results in Tables 1 and 2.

Compared to Supervised Methods: Generally, *BotTrans* consistently outperforms and achieves significant performance improvements of around 3% in both F1 and AUC. Remarkably, in the Low-m transfer tasks with less similar source domains, *BotTrans* maintains superior performance, unlike other baselines like AdaGCN or M^3SDA which exhibit a performance drop of up to 8% from High-m to Low-m tasks. This demonstrates *BotTrans*'s robust capability in transferring knowledge even under challenging conditions. Furthermore, key observations from Table 1 include: 1) *BotTrans* significantly surpasses single-source GDA models and multi-source graph transfer learning models, highlighting the effectiveness of our approach in alleviating source network heterophily and embedding over-smoothing, and selective knowledge-transfer strategy when leveraging multiple source domains, 2) Graph OOD models typically underperform in multi-source domain tasks. This limitation is likely attributed to the absence of specific knowledge of target domain, which hinders the model's ability to bridge the distribution gap between source and target domains, and 3) CDAD models underperform in social bot detection, likely due to their inability to adequately transfer bot-related knowledge and limited generalizability to the social bot detection task.

Table 1. Multi-source transfer results (second best underlined). For 2 or 4 sources, we report the averaged F1-score over all 20 tasks and the High/Low-m F1-score over 10 corresponding tasks. For 9 sources, we report the averaged F1-score over all 10 tasks. We also report AUC-ROC scores averaged over all tasks.

	2 sources				4 sources				9 sources	
	F1-avg	High-mF1-avg	Low-mF1-avg	AUC-avg	F1-avg	High-mF1-avg	Low-mF1-avg	AUC-avg	F1-avg	AUC-avg
GCN	0.6463	0.6904	0.6021	0.7047	0.6738	0.6991	0.6485	0.7245	0.7054	0.7544
GraphSAGE	0.6486	0.7116	0.5856	0.7187	0.6989	0.7156	0.6853	0.7552	0.7098	0.7802
EERM	0.6308	0.6686	0.5931	0.6842	0.6464	0.6525	0.6403	0.7164	0.6767	0.7482
ISGIB	0.6521	0.6880	0.6162	0.7265	0.6786	0.6933	0.6640	0.7523	0.688	0.7628
AdaGCN	0.7206	<u>0.7682</u>	0.6821	0.7501	<u>0.7536</u>	<u>0.7644</u>	0.7246	0.7748	<u>0.7768</u>	<u>0.8246</u>
Grade	<u>0.7280</u>	0.7258	<u>0.7202</u>	0.7417	0.7338	0.7460	0.7224	0.7382	0.6544	0.7563
UDAGCN	0.7090	0.7344	0.6836	<u>0.7806</u>	0.7481	0.7579	<u>0.7483</u>	<u>0.7892</u>	0.762	0.824
Commander	0.6501	0.6611	0.6411	0.7060	0.6546	0.6894	0.6411	0.7370	0.6530	0.7543
ACT	0.4148	0.4100	0.4197	0.4794	0.4270	0.4218	0.4313	0.4908	0.3960	0.4761
M^3SDA	0.7014	0.7415	0.6613	0.7519	0.7098	0.7227	0.6993	0.7409	0.7014	0.7309
MSDS	0.6579	0.6606	0.6552	0.6713	0.6572	0.6650	0.6494	0.6793	0.6732	0.7043
NESTL	0.5427	0.6058	0.4796	0.7261	0.5502	0.6188	0.4941	0.7261	0.5283	0.7262
BotTrans	**0.7569**	**0.7819**	**0.7319**	**0.7983**	**0.7851**	**0.7926**	**0.7789**	**0.8260**	**0.8000**	**0.8524**

Compared to Unsupervised Methods: we compare model performance on each domain d with *BotTrans*'s result, which is given by the best result among all multi-source adaptation tasks with d as target domain. The results in Table 2 demonstrate that even the best baseline DGI+IF is significantly inferior to *BotTrans*, with a performance decrease of 18.34% $\sim$ 36.82%. These results prove the necessity of knowledge transfer for detecting social bots.

Table 2. Unsupervised experiment results (F1-score). '↑' indicates the performance gain of *BotTrans* against the best unsupervised model.

	0	1	2	3	4	5	6	7	8	9
DGI+LOF	0.5471	0.5455	0.5392	0.5582	0.6017	0.4808	0.5106	0.4928	0.5190	0.5157
DGI+IF	**0.5797**	**0.6477**	**0.6572**	0.5484	**0.6966**	**0.6215**	**0.5280**	**0.5254**	**0.5510**	**0.5170**
CoLA	0.4824	0.4975	0.5022	0.5118	0.5012	0.4971	0.4835	0.4920	0.4894	0.5005
CONAD	0.4207	0.4419	0.4498	0.4506	0.4383	0.4339	0.4802	0.4128	0.4134	0.3945
BotTrans	36.82%↑	24.60%↑	20.66%↑	33.30%↑	18.48%↑	20.24%↑	18.34%↑	31.93%↑	27.76%↑	32.20%↑

Effectiveness Analysis: Guided by the theory of generalization bounds, we explore the reasons behind our model's effectiveness by experimentally assessing its capability to minimize the supervised loss within the sources and to reduce discrepancies between source and target domains. Thus, we plot the training process in three representative transfer tasks for *BotTrans* with another strong baseline AdaGCN in Fig. 3. Key findings include: 1) *BotTrans* achieves lower source training error L^{sup}, indicating the CSD-MP module mitigates the network heterophily and over-smoothing problem in source domains, and 2) *BotTrans* achieves lower domain divergence L^d, indicating the SMST module proposes better adaptation strategy in multi-source tasks.

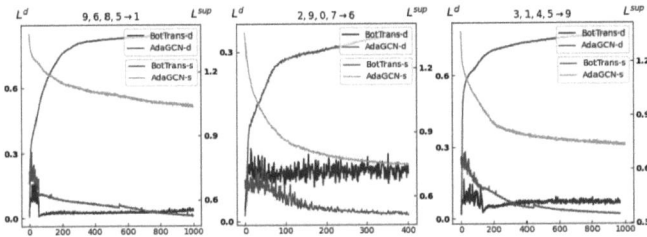

Fig. 3. Training with L^d and L^{sup}. X-axis: training epoch. Y-axis: L^d (left, maximized) and L^{sup} (right, minimized). d and s are short for L^d and L^{sup}.

Efficiency Analysis: We compare with strong baselines in Table 1. *Time Complexity*: *BotTrans*'s running time matches AdaGCN but is 2×M³SDA's, 3×Commander's, and 4×Grade's. However, it offers up to 19% performance boost. *Spatial Complexity*: *BotTrans* only requires an additional few hundred megabytes in memory and GPU usage, which is mainly introduced by CSD-MP. Overall, *BotTrans* achieves a balance between effectiveness and efficiency.

5.3 Ablation Study

To address RQ2, we perform ablation studies by incrementally adding key model components, with results summarized in Table 3. We begin with a variant, Base, which uses a simple GCN encoder (Eq. 1) and single-source adaptation components (Eq. 6 and 8). Next, we implement CSD-MP (w/o. edge feature), based on Base, but with cross-source-domain topology excluding edge features. We then sequentially introduce three additional variants. The results demonstrate that progressively adding components improves performance. Specifically, the full CSD-MP module yields a performance increase of 1.6%~2.9% across various transfer tasks, which we attribute to its effective mitigation of the network heterophily issue. Additionally, SMST enhances performance by 1.1%~2.7%, highlighting the importance of selective knowledge adaptation. Finally, the AR module contributes an improvement of 0.8%~1.4%, addressing potential issues with noisy source labels.

Table 3. Ablation study results (F1). When there are 2 or 4 sources, we report the results averaged over 20 tasks. When there are 9 sources we report the results averaged over 10 tasks.

	2 sources	4 sources	9 sources
Base	0.7179	0.7239	0.7418
+CSD-MP (w/o. edge feature)	0.7253	0.7341	0.7466
+CSD-MP	0.7346	0.7521	0.7573
+CSD-MP+SMST	0.7456	0.7747	0.7846
+CSD-MP+SMST+AR	0.7536	0.7846	0.7980

5.4 Stability

To address **RQ3**, we evaluate model stability under varying numbers of source domains and label utilization rates. This is important since, in practice, it can be difficult to obtain a large number of source domains with sufficient bot-related labels. A robust model should therefore perform consistently well regardless of these factors. We select strong baselines along with *BotTrans*, fix two target domains(e.g., G^1 and G^2), and measure performance as the number of source domains increases from 2 to 9. As shown in Fig. 4, *BotTrans* consistently outperforms baselines and benefits from more source domains. Next, we fix two representative tasks and vary the labeled source node ratio from 10% to 100%. As illustrated in the figure, *BotTrans* achieves strong results across all labeling rates, demonstrating robustness and adaptability even with limited supervision.

5.5 Sensitivity

We perform sensitivity analysis of *BotTrans* on important hyper-parameters to answer **RQ4**, including cross-source-domain neighboring number K, balancing coefficients λ from Eq. 11 and η_1 from Eq. 12, and batch size. As Fig. 5 reveals, the default settings are adequate for most adaptation tasks, eliminating the need for extensive tuning. Besides, when K is added up to 5 that enables stable model performance, further increasing K tends to incorporate more noisy information from other source domains and deteriorate performance. Moreover, given that model performs better when values of γ and λ lie between 0 and 1 compared to when they are set to 0 or 1, we can also validate the effectiveness of domain-level similarity score computing (Eq. 10) and consistency-score refinement (Eq. 11).

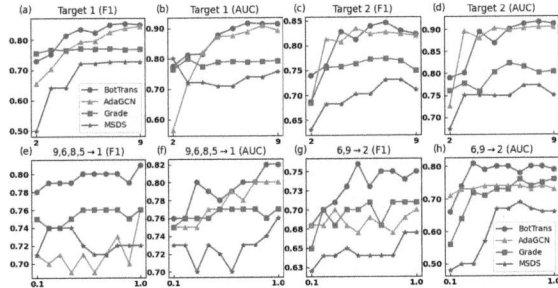

Fig. 4. Increasing the number of source domains (a-d) and increasing the percentage of labeled source nodes (e-h).

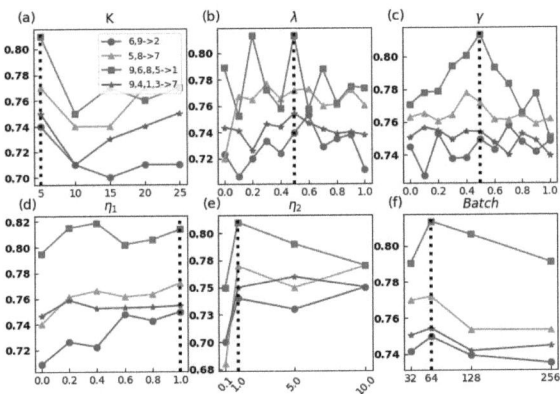

Fig. 5. Hyper-parameters tuning, where default settings are marked with vertical dotted lines.

6 Conclusion

To alleviate the label scarcity issue in detecting social bots with GNN-based methods, we introduce *BotTrans*, a novel MSGDA model designed to transfer extensive bot-related knowledge from multiple social networks. It comprises three key modules focused on mitigating network heterophily in source domains, selectively transferring relevant knowledge from source domains relevant to the target domain, and refining target detection results. Experimental studies prove that *BotTrans* outperforms all SOTA baselines in unlabeled detection tasks. In the future, we will explore more approaches, including pre-trained graph models and large language models.

Acknowledgments. This work was supported by the National Key Research and Development Program of China under Grant No. 2022YFB3103704, the National Natural Science Foundation of China under Grant Nos. 62372434, U21B2046, and 62302485, CAS Special Research Assistant Program and the Key Research Project of Chinese Academy of Sciences (No. RCJJ-145-24-21).

References

1. Breuer, A., Eilat, R., Weinsberg, U.: Friend or faux: graph-based early detection of fake accounts on social networks. In: Proceedings of The Web Conference 2020, pp. 1287–1297 (2020)
2. Cresci, S.: A decade of social bot detection. Commun. ACM **63**(10), 72–83 (2020)
3. Dai, Q., Wu, X.M., Xiao, J., Shen, X., Wang, D.: Graph transfer learning via adversarial domain adaptation with graph convolution. IEEE Transactions on Knowledge and Data Engineering (2022)
4. Ding, K., Shu, K., Shan, X., Li, J., Liu, H.: Cross-domain graph anomaly detection. IEEE Trans. Neural Netw. Learn. Syst. **33**(6), 2406–2415 (2021)
5. Ding, K., Zhou, Q., Tong, H., Liu, H.: Few-shot network anomaly detection via cross-network meta-learning. In: Proceedings of the Web Conference 2021, pp. 2448–2456 (2021)
6. Dou, Y., Liu, Z., Sun, L., Deng, Y., Peng, H., Yu, P.S.: Enhancing graph neural network-based fraud detectors against camouflaged fraudsters. In: Proceedings of the 29th ACM International Conference on Information & Knowledge Management, pp. 315–324 (2020)
7. Feng, S., Tan, Z., Li, R., Luo, M.: Heterogeneity-aware twitter bot detection with relational graph transformers. In: AAAI (2022)
8. Feng, S., et al.: TwiBot-22: towards graph-based twitter bot detection. Adv. Neural. Inf. Process. Syst. **35**, 35254–35269 (2022)
9. Feng, S., Wan, H., Wang, N., Li, J., Luo, M.: TwiBot-20: a comprehensive twitter bot detection benchmark. In: Proceedings of the 30th ACM International Conference on Information & Knowledge Management (2021)
10. Feng, S., Wan, H., Wang, N., Luo, M.: BotRGCN: twitter bot detection with relational graph convolutional networks. In: Proceedings of the 2021 IEEE/ACM International Conference on Advances in Social Networks Analysis and Mining, pp. 236–239 (2021)
11. Ferrara, E., Varol, O., Davis, C., Menczer, F., Flammini, A.: The rise of social bots. Commun. ACM **59**(7), 96–104 (2016)
12. Fu, C., Zheng, Y., Liu, Y., Xuan, Q., Chen, G.: NES-TL: network embedding similarity-based transfer learning. IEEE Trans. Netw. Sci. Eng. **7**(3), 1607–1618 (2019)
13. Gong, Z., et al.: Beyond homophily: robust graph anomaly detection via neural sparsification. In: Proceedings of International Joint Conference on Artificial Intelligence, pp. 2104–2113 (2023)
14. Gulrajani, I., Ahmed, F., Arjovsky, M., Dumoulin, V., Courville, A.C.: Improved training of Wasserstein GANs. Adv. Neural Inf. Processing Syst. **30** (2017)
15. Hamilton, W., Ying, Z., Leskovec, J.: Inductive representation learning on large graphs. Adv. Neural Inf. Process. Syst. **30** (2017)
16. He, H., Yang, H., Zhang, W., Wang, Y., Zou, Z., Li, T.: MSDS: a novel framework for multi-source data selection based cross-network node classification. IEEE Transactions on Knowledge and Data Engineering (2023)
17. Hočevar, T., Demšar, J.: A combinatorial approach to graphlet counting. Bioinformatics **30**(4), 559–565 (2014)
18. Kipf, T.N., Welling, M.: Semi-supervised classification with graph convolutional networks. In: 5th International Conference on Learning Representations, ICLR 2017, Toulon, France, April 24-26, 2017, Conference Track Proceedings (2017)
19. Liu, Y., Li, Z., Pan, S., Gong, C., Zhou, C., Karypis, G.: Anomaly detection on attributed networks via contrastive self-supervised learning. IEEE Transactions on Neural Networks and Learning Systems (2021)
20. Magelinski, T., Beskow, D., Carley, K.M.: Graph-Hist: graph classification from latent feature histograms with application to bot detection. In: AAAI (2020)

21. Moghaddam, S.H., Abbaspour, M.: Friendship preference: scalable and robust category of features for social bot detection. IEEE Trans. Dependable Secure Comput. **20**(2), 1516–1528 (2022)
22. Peng, X., Bai, Q., Xia, X., Huang, Z., Saenko, K., Wang, B.: Moment matching for multi-source domain adaptation. In: Proceedings of the IEEE/CVF International Conference on Computer Vision, pp. 1406–1415 (2019)
23. Shen, X., Pan, S., Choi, K.S., Zhou, X.: Domain-adaptive message passing graph neural network. Neural Netw. **164**, 439–454 (2023)
24. Shi, B.S., Wang, Y.Q., Guo, F.D., Xu, B.B., Shen, H.W., Cheng, X.Q.: Domain adaptation for graph representation learning: Challenges, progress, and prospects. J. Comput. Sci. Technol. 1–18 (2025)
25. Shi, B., Wang, Y., Guo, F., Shao, J., Shen, H., Cheng, X.: Improving graph domain adaptation with network hierarchy. In: Proceedings of the 32nd ACM International Conference on Information and Knowledge Management, pp. 2249–2258 (2023)
26. Shi, B., Wang, Y., Shao, J., Shen, H., Li, Y., Cheng, X.: Node classification across networks via category-level domain adaptive network embedding. Knowl. Inf. Syst. **65**(12), 5479–5502 (2023)
27. Shi, S., et al.: MGTAB: A multi-relational graph-based twitter account detection benchmark (2023)
28. Veličković, P., Cucurull, G., Casanova, A., Romero, A., Lio, P., Bengio, Y.: Graph attention networks. arXiv preprint arXiv:1710.10903 (2017)
29. Veličković, P., Fedus, W., Hamilton, W.L., Liò, P., Bengio, Y., Hjelm, R.D.: Deep graph infomax. arXiv preprint arXiv:1809.10341 (2018)
30. Wang, Q., Pang, G., Salehi, M., Buntine, W., Leckie, C.: Cross-domain graph anomaly detection via anomaly-aware contrastive alignment. In: AAAI (2023)
31. Wu, J., He, J., Ainsworth, E.: Non-IID transfer learning on graphs. In: AAAI (2023)
32. Wu, M., Pan, S., Zhou, C., Chang, X., Zhu, X.: Unsupervised domain adaptive graph convolutional networks. In: Proceedings of The Web Conference 2020, pp. 1457–1467 (2020)
33. Wu, Q., Zhang, H., Yan, J., Wipf, D.: Towards distribution shift of node-level prediction on graphs: an invariance perspective. In: International Conference on Learning Representations (2022)
34. Xu, Z., Huang, X., Zhao, Y., Dong, Y., Li, J.: Contrastive attributed network anomaly detection with data augmentation. In: Pacific-Asia Conference on Knowledge Discovery and Data Mining (2022)
35. Yang, L., et al.: Individual and structural graph information bottlenecks for out-of-distribution generalization. IEEE Transactions on Knowledge and Data Engineering (2023)
36. Yang, Y., et al.: RoSGAS: adaptive social bot detection with reinforced self-supervised GNN architecture search. ACM Trans. Web **17**(3), 1–31 (2023)
37. You, Y., Chen, T., Wang, Z., Shen, Y.: Graph domain adaptation via theory-grounded spectral regularization. In: The Eleventh International Conference on Learning Representations (2023)
38. Zhang, X., Du, Y., Xie, R., Wang, C.: Adversarial separation network for cross-network node classification. In: Proceedings of the 30th ACM International Conference on Information & Knowledge Management, pp. 2618–2626 (2021)
39. Zhou, M., Feng, W., Zhu, Y., Zhang, D., Dong, Y., Tang, J.: Semi-supervised social bot detection with initial residual relation attention networks. In: Joint European Conference on Machine Learning and Knowledge Discovery in Databases, pp. 207–224. Springer (2023)

Efficient Approximate Temporal Triangle Counting in Streaming with Predictions

Giorgio Venturin[1], Ilie Sarpe[2], and Fabio Vandin[1](✉)

[1] University of Padova, Padova, Italy
giorgio.venturin@phd.unipd.it, fabio.vandin@unipd.it
[2] KTH Royal Institute of Technology, Stockholm, Sweden
ilsarpe@kth.se

Abstract. Triangle counting is a fundamental and widely studied problem on static graphs, and recently on *temporal graphs*, where edges carry information on the timings of the associated events. *Streaming* processing and resource *efficiency* are crucial requirements for counting triangles in modern massive temporal graphs, with millions of nodes and up to billions of temporal edges. However, current exact and approximate algorithms are unable to handle large-scale temporal graphs. To fill such a gap, we introduce **STEP**, a scalable and efficient algorithm to approximate temporal triangle counts from a stream of temporal edges. **STEP** combines *predictions* to the number of triangles a temporal edge is involved in, with a simple sampling strategy, leading to scalability, efficiency, and accurate approximation of all eight temporal triangle types simultaneously. We analytically prove that, by using a sublinear amount of memory, **STEP** obtains unbiased and very accurate estimates. In fact, even noisy predictions can significantly reduce the variance of **STEP**'s estimates. Our extensive experiments on massive temporal graphs with up to billions of edges demonstrate that **STEP** outputs high-quality estimates and is more efficient than state-of-the-art methods.

Keywords: Temporal networks · Temporal triangle counting · Streaming algorithm

1 Introduction

Temporal graphs model complex systems [13], including social networks [38] and databases [8], by associating each event in the system with its *timing* of occurrence. Temporal graph analysis provides a *deep understanding* of the underlying complex systems and their properties [14] through various problems such as

---

G. Venturin and I. Sarpe—contributed equally.

Supplementary Information The online version contains supplementary material available at https://doi.org/10.1007/978-3-032-06066-2_15.

temporal community detection [19], core decomposition [33], and pattern identification [10].

Temporal motifs and temporal triangles [21,29] are fundamental patterns defined by *i*) a subgraph representing a given *topological property*, *ii*) an ordering over the edges, capturing the timing of occurrence of the subgraph edges, and *iii*) a temporal proximity constraint assuring that all events occur close in time. The *counts* of temporal motifs and temporal triangles are crucial for a plethora of graph analyses such as graph classification [39], anomaly detection [2], dense subgraph identification [36], and more [10]. Counting *temporal* motifs can be much more challenging than counting static subgraphs. In fact, identifying a single star-shaped temporal motif is **NP**-hard, unlike static graphs where all star-shaped subgraphs can be counted in polynomial time [20,37].

Given the importance of *temporal triangle counting*, both exact [22,30] and approximate [34] algorithms have been developed. However, exact approaches do not scale to modern-sized temporal graphs [9,18,22,29,30]. In addition, approximate *sampling* methods, which often need *full-access* to the input data, require the processing of large sample sizes due to their pessimistic worst-case analysis, which is extremely *inefficient* and impractical [20,35,41]. Overall, both exact and approximate temporal triangle counting methods require substantial resources to handle large temporal graphs, and designing scalable and efficient algorithms is an extremely challenging open problem.

Main Contributions. We introduce STEP, a new algorithm for *approximate* temporal triangle counting in large temporal graphs. STEP processes temporal graph edges in a single pass *stream* [25], that is a challenging and practical setting. Streaming processing, in fact, enables analyzing massive temporal graphs, characterized by a high volume of interactions recorded over time [13,14], while limiting the memory available for storing the data. STEP uses a randomized sampling approach coupled with the information provided by a suitable *predictor* to identify and retain the most important edges over the stream. We prove that our design yields accurate estimates with sublinear memory and rigorous approximation guarantees, i.e., the output is a relative ε-approximation for small ε. Our extensive experimental evaluation shows that STEP saves up to 19× memory and 200× time compared to existing state-of-the-art methods while computing highly accurate estimates. Our key contributions are as follows:

1. We design STEP, a randomized, single-pass streaming algorithm to accurately estimate all temporal triangle counts simultaneously. STEP uses a sampling approach coupled with a predictor, resulting in low run time and memory usage.

2. We rigorously analyze STEP, proving that: *i*) it produces unbiased estimates independent of the prediction quality, *ii*) the predictor significantly decreases the variance of the estimates, and *iii*) estimates remain robust and of high quality even under reasonably noisy predictions.

3. We design a practical and efficient predictor that allows STEP to obtain high accuracy and small memory usage, despite being domain-agnostic.

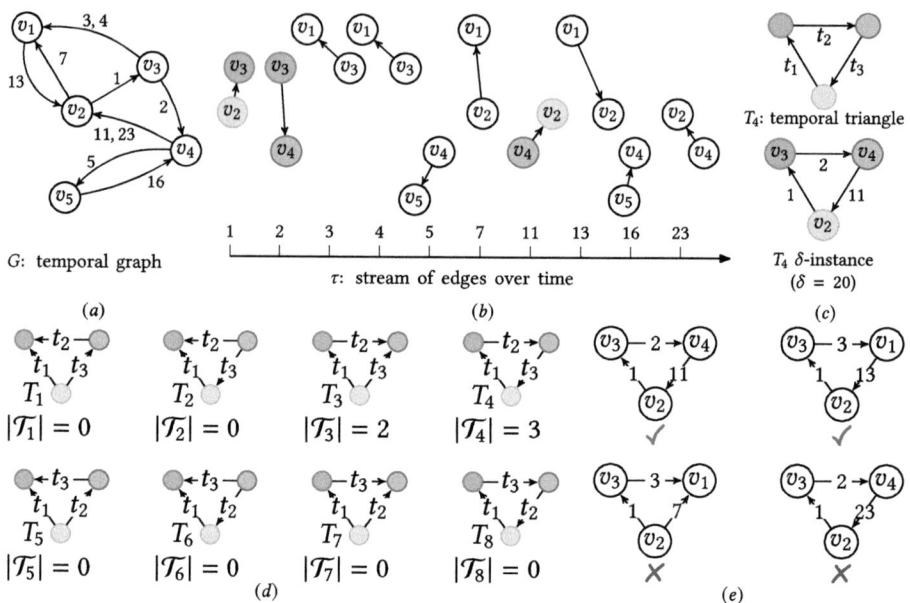

Fig. 1. (*a*): temporal graph $G = (V, E)$, with $V = \{v_1, \ldots, v_5\}$ and $E = \{(v_2, v_3, 1), \ldots\}$. (*b*): stream τ of the temporal edges of G. (*c*): the sequence $\langle (v_2, v_3), (v_3, v_4), (v_4, v_2) \rangle$ is a δ-instance of temporal triangle T_4 ($\delta = 20$). (*d*): all distinct temporal triangles and the number of their δ-instances in G ($\delta = 20$). Edge labels $t_i, i = 1, 2, 3$ (with $t_1 < t_2 < t_3$) denote the ordering of edges in the sequence σ (Def. 2). (*e*): some temporal triangles in G: δ-instances of T_4 for $\delta = 20$ are marked with ✓, while ✗ denotes edges that are not δ-instances.

4. We perform an extensive experimental evaluation on large temporal graphs to validate STEP and show that: *i*) it outperforms state-of-the-art (SotA) methods for temporal triangle counting, achieving highly accurate results while reducing resource usage by orders of magnitude; *ii*) STEP is the only method capable of obtaining accurate estimates on a three-billion-edge temporal graph; *iii*) STEP works in an online setting, using a predictor learned from historical data.

2 Preliminaries

We start by introducing the key definitions and concepts used in our work.

Definition 1. *A* temporal graph *is a pair* $G = (V, E)$ *where V is a set of n vertices and $E = \{(u_1, v_1, t_1), \ldots, (u_m, v_m, t_m) : u_i, v_i \in V, u_i \neq v_i \text{ and } t_i \in \mathbb{R}^+\}$ is a set of m directed* temporal edges. *Each temporal edge $e = (u, v, t) \in E$ has a* timestamp $t \in \mathbb{R}^+$ *denoting the time of the (static) interaction (u, v).*

Figure 1(a) shows an example of a temporal graph G with $n = 5$ and $m = 10$. We use the term *static edge* to denote an edge $(u, v) \in V^2$ with no timestamp.

Similarly, a graph formed by static edges is a *static* graph.[1] Our focus is to count *temporal triangles* [20,29], fundamental patterns for analyzing temporal graphs.

Definition 2 ([20,29]). *A temporal triangle is a pair $T = ((V_T, E_T), \sigma)$ where (V_T, E_T) is a static graph with $|V_T| = 3$ vertices and $|E_T| = 3$ edges, and σ is an ordering of the edges in E_T.*

A temporal triangle T captures *both* structural (i.e., a triadic interaction) and temporal properties (i.e., the temporal ordering of edges). We denote each distinct temporal triangle with $T_i, i \in [8]$[2] (see Fig. 1(d)), while T will denote an arbitrary temporal triangle.

Definition 3. *Let $T = ((V_T, E_T), \sigma)$ be a temporal triangle where $\langle(x_1, y_1), (x_2, y_2), (x_3, y_3)\rangle$ is the sequence of edges of E_T ordered according to σ. Given a temporal graph $G = (V, E)$ and a time duration $\delta \in \mathbb{R}^+$ we say that a sequence of temporally-ordered edges $S = \langle(u_1, v_1, t_1), (u_2, v_2, t_2), (u_3, v_3, t_3)\rangle$ from E is a δ-instance of the temporal triangle T if: 1) there exists a bijection f on the vertices such that $f(u_i) = x_i, f(v_i) = y_i$ for $i \in \{1, 2, 3\}$; 2) the time-duration of the sequence S is at most δ, that is $t_3 - t_1 \leq \delta$.*

Given a time-duration $\delta \in \mathbb{R}^+$, a δ-instance S represents an *occurrence* of the temporal triangle T within δ-time. See Fig. 1(c) and Fig. 1(e) for detailed examples. For $T_i, i \in [8]$, and a time-duration δ, we let $\mathcal{T}_i = \{\Delta \in E^3 : \Delta \text{ is a } \delta\text{-instance of } T_i \text{ in } G\}$ be the *set* of δ-instances of T_i in G, and $|\mathcal{T}_i|$ be the *count* of triangle T_i. Note that for a temporal graph with m temporal edges, the count $|\mathcal{T}_i|$ of a triangle T_i can be as large as $\Theta(m^3)$, and, in contrast to static graphs, m may not be polynomial in n (due to the edges timestamps).

Streaming Model. We consider the following restrictive *streaming* computational model: *1)* the temporal graph G is accessed as a stream τ of temporal edges; *2)* edges on the stream τ are *temporally ordered*, i.e., if $e_1 = (u_1, v_1, t_1)$ precedes $e_2 = (u_2, v_2, t_2)$ on τ, then $t_1 < t_2$; and *3)* each temporal edge can be processed only *once*, in a 1-pass over τ. See Fig. 1(b) for an example of a stream.

The streaming model we consider is a challenging and restrictive computational model for processing temporal graphs, of high practical utility. Our computational model is much more restrictive compared with existing works, that allow for *multiple passes* over τ [41], or *complete random access* to the graph [9,18,29,30]. In fact, modern temporal graphs have massive sizes, e.g., they are collected from high-throughput systems such as IP networks or social networks, requiring a streaming access model, as in our model [13].

Computational Problem. The *exact* computation of all temporal triangle counts is extremely challenging, inefficient, and resource demanding [9,22,29,30]. In contrast, we focus on computing *accurate estimates* of all counts $|\mathcal{T}_i|$ simultaneously, as formalized by the following problem.

---

[1] The static graph of $G = (V, E)$ is obtained by considering all edges in E as static.
[2] We use $i \in [a], a \in \mathbb{N}$ to denote $i \in \{1, \ldots, a\}$.

Problem 1 (Temporal triangle estimation problem). Given a 1-pass stream τ of a temporal graph G, a time-duration $\delta \in \mathbb{R}^+$, an approximation error $\varepsilon > 0$, and a small constant η, output estimates c_i such that $\mathbb{P}[||c_i - |\mathcal{T}_i|| \geq \varepsilon|\mathcal{T}_i|] \leq \eta, \forall i \in [8]$.

Prob. 1 requires the *simultaneous* computation of estimates c_i for triangle counts $|\mathcal{T}_i|, i \in [8]$, with guaranteed accuracy (i.e., relative ε-approximation) and bounded error probability η, over a challenging 1-pass stream τ. We also require that an algorithm for Prob. 1 must use *limited total memory* since temporal triangle counting is extremely memory-demanding [22,35,41]. Restricting the total memory to be sublinear is very common in streaming settings [27,42]. In our setting, we require a total memory *sublinear in* m_δ, i.e., the maximum number of temporal edges of the stream τ occurring in any time-window of length δ.

3 STEP Algorithm

3.1 Overview

We first introduce the techniques and design choices behind our algorithm STEP. We design STEP to achieve sublinear memory guarantees (see Sect. 3.3), by building on ideas from state-of-the-art streaming algorithms for sublinear counting of *static* triangles and subgraphs [37]. That is, *1)* STEP stores, probabilistically, a *small sample* of edges from the stream τ; *2)* STEP computes unbiased estimates c_i simultaneously for each count $|\mathcal{T}_i|, i \in [8]$ based on the retained *random* sample. The above approach allows STEP to use sublinear memory and to obtain *unbiased* estimates c_i, i.e., $\mathbb{E}[c_i] = |\mathcal{T}_i|$. However, the estimates c_i may be far from $|\mathcal{T}_i|$, especially when the random sample retained by STEP is not representative. To compute estimates c_i close to their expectations $|\mathcal{T}_i|$, we build on ideas from the Algorithms with Predictions literature for *static graphs* [4,7]: *i)* we empower STEP with a predictor $\mathcal{Q}(\cdot)$ that enables the identification of important edges on the stream τ—yielding representative samples retained by STEP and highly accurate estimates c_i; *ii)* we design a predictor for the *simultaneous estimation* of all temporal triangle counts, relating STEP's accuracy with the quality of predictions of $\mathcal{Q}(\cdot)$. We prove that perfect predictions as well as noisy predictions result in very accurate estimates c_i and sublinear space complexity (Thm. 1), improving over the state-of-the-art (that does not leverage predictions). In addition, we also design a *practical* and efficiently computable predictor $\mathcal{Q}(\cdot)$ for STEP.

All missing proofs and subroutines are in our extended version [40].

3.2 Algorithm Description

STEP leverages a randomized approach by sampling edges over the stream with a fixed probability $p \in (0, 1]$, similarly to state-of-the-art methods for estimating temporal subgraph counts [20,35,41]. In addition, STEP employs a *predictor* $\mathcal{Q}(\cdot)$, that classifies edges on the stream τ as either *heavy* or *light*. Heavy edges are those *predicted* to occur in many temporal triangles, and thus important to retain to collect a representative sample. The edge classification provided by $\mathcal{Q}(\cdot)$ is then

Algorithm 1: STEP

Input: Stream τ of temporal edges, time-duration δ, predictor $\mathcal{Q}(\cdot)$, sampling probability $p \in (0, 1]$.
Output: Estimates c_i of $|\mathcal{T}_i|$ for $i \in [8]$.

1   $H \leftarrow \emptyset; S_L \leftarrow \emptyset$;
2   $c_{i,0} \leftarrow 0; c_{i,1} \leftarrow 0; c_{i,2} \leftarrow 0$ for $i \in [8]$;
3   **foreach** $e = (u, v, t) \in \tau$ **do**
4      $H \leftarrow \texttt{CleanUp}(H, t - \delta); S_L \leftarrow \texttt{CleanUp}(S_L, t - \delta)$;
5      $\vee_{H,H}, \vee_{H,S_L}, \vee_{S_L,S_L} \leftarrow \texttt{CollectWedges}(H, S_L, e)$;
6      $c_{i,0} \leftarrow \texttt{UpdateCounts}(c_{i,0}, \vee_{S_L,S_L}, e)$ for $i \in [8]$;
7      $c_{i,1} \leftarrow \texttt{UpdateCounts}(c_{i,1}, \vee_{H,S_L}, e)$ for $i \in [8]$;
8      $c_{i,2} \leftarrow \texttt{UpdateCounts}(c_{i,2}, \vee_{H,H}, e)$ for $i \in [8]$;
9   **if** $\mathcal{Q}(e) = 1$ **then** $H \leftarrow H \cup \{e\}$;
10   **else if** $\mathit{BiasedCoin}(p) = true$ **then** $S_L \leftarrow S_L \cup \{e\}$;
11   **return** $c_i = \frac{c_{i,0}}{p^2} + \frac{c_{i,1}}{p} + c_{i,2}$ for $i \in [8]$;

used to obtain strong guarantees on small memory usage and high estimation accuracy. More in detail, STEP works as follows. First, it initializes two sets, H and S_L, for storing heavy and (sampled) light edges, respectively (line 1). It then initializes counters $c_{i,j}$ for each triangle type $T_i, i \in [8], j \in [0, 2]$ (line 2). All counters are used to output the unbiased estimates c_i for $|\mathcal{T}_i|$. STEP then processes the stream τ (line 3), and for each edge $e = (u, v, t)$: *1)* it removes edges from H and S_L with timestamps smaller than $t - \delta$ using the CleanUp procedure (line 4). The CleanUp procedure simply updates the sets H and S_L by retaining only edges $e' = (u', v', t')$ with t' within δ time from the timestamp of the current edge e, that is, $t - t' \leq \delta$. *2)* it collects all *wedges* in the sample $H \cup S_L$;[3] *3)* all collected wedges are partitioned into three subsets (line 5): $\vee_{H,H}$ (wedges with both edges in H), $\vee_{S_L,S_L}$ (both edges in S_L), and $\vee_{H,S_L}$ (one edge in H, the other in S_L); *3)* the counters $c_{i,j}$ are updated using the UpdateCounts procedure (lines 6-8), tracking occurrences of triangles T_i with 0, 1, or 2 heavy edges. STEP then calls the predictor $\mathcal{Q}(e)$ to determine whether e is heavy or light: if $\mathcal{Q}(e) = 1$, e is added to H (line 9); otherwise, e is added to S_L with probability p (line 10). Finally, STEP outputs estimates c_i for $i \in [8]$ by combining and weighting the counters $c_{i,j}, j = 0, 1, 2$ (line 11).

3.3 Analysis

Time Complexity. First, we briefly consider the *expected* time complexity of STEP. Given the input to Algorithm 1, the expected time complexity of STEP is $\mathcal{O}(m(pm_\delta + |H|)^2)$, where: m_δ is the maximum number of edges over τ that occur in any time-duration of length δ, and $|H|$ is the number of heavy edges in H during the execution of the algorithm (see our extended version [40]). When $|H| = o(m_\delta)$ and $p \ll 1$ (e.g., as in our experiments), STEP is much more efficient

---
[3] A wedge is a pair of distinct edges sharing a vertex.

than previous approaches (see Sect. 5). That is, STEP scales to large datasets, where previous approaches become impractical (see results in Sect. 4).

Unbiasedness. We prove that STEP computes *unbiased estimates* c_i of the counts $|\mathcal{T}_i|$, for $i \in [8]$, *independently* of the quality of the predictions of $\mathcal{Q}(\cdot)$.

Lemma 1. *Given a stream τ of a temporal graph $G = (V, E)$, a time-duration δ, and a predictor $\mathcal{Q}(\cdot)$, each estimate $c_i, i \in [8]$ reported by STEP is an unbiased estimate of the count $|\mathcal{T}_i|$, that is $\mathbb{E}[c_i] = |\mathcal{T}_i|$.*

Embedding Predictions. We now analyze the impact of the predictor $\mathcal{Q}(\cdot)$ for our algorithm STEP. We first propose a practical model for a predictor, formalizing a *ranking predictor*. Our model is motivated by the fact that most machine learning models are highly optimized for ranking metrics, e.g., Kendall's tau or Spearman's correlation [11,43]. More in detail, a ranking predictor ranks edges $e \in \tau$ according to their importance for counts $|\mathcal{T}_i|$. We show analytically that both a *perfect* ranking predictor and a *noisy* one yield *accurate* estimates and *sublinear space complexity* for STEP.

Perfect predictor. Let $\omega(e, \mathcal{T}_i) = |\{\Delta : e \in \Delta, \Delta \in \mathcal{T}_i\}|$ be the number of triangles in $\mathcal{T}_i, i \in [8]$ containing edge $e \in E$, and $W(e) = \sum_{i \in [8]} \omega(e, \mathcal{T}_i)$ be the total edge weight of e. Let $\mathbf{W} \doteq \langle e_1^W, \ldots, e_m^W \rangle$ be the edges in E ordered by *non-increasing* values of their weights $W(e)$, ties broken arbitrarily. Given two distinct edges $e, e' \in E$, we use $e \prec e'$ to denote that e comes before e' in the ordering $\mathbf{W}$. With a slight abuse of notation, we denote with $e_{\prec_j}$ the edge in the j-th position in $\mathbf{W}$, and with $\mathbf{W}(e, \prec)$ the position of edge $e \in E$ in $\mathbf{W}$.

(RANKING PREDICTOR) Given an integer value $K > 0$, a *ranking predictor* $\mathcal{Q}(\cdot)_K$ is such that $\mathcal{Q}(e)_K = 1$ iff $\mathbf{W}(e, \prec) \leq K$.

A ranking predictor requires as unique input a parameter K, i.e., the number of edges to classify as heavy. Clearly, K corresponds to the maximum number of edges to be retained deterministically by STEP.[4] A ranking predictor does not require the knowledge of a threshold over edge weights $W(e), e \in E$ to classify heavy edges, in contrast with previous literature [7]. That is our predictor model is required to output the ranking $\mathbf{W}$ without having explicit access to the weights $W(e), e \in E$, as this would not be practical.

We next introduce a more practical *noisy* ranking predictor.

Noisy predictor. Given two parameters α and K, we let $\Pi(\{1, \ldots, m\})_{(\alpha, K)}$ be the set of permutations of m elements where three blocks of elements are fixed, i.e., blocks $[1, \ldots, K - \alpha - 1]$, $[K - \alpha, \ldots, K + \alpha]$ and $[K + \alpha + 1, \ldots, m]$. That is, elements from one block can only be permuted inside the same block.

(NOISY RANKING PREDICTOR) Given a parameter $K > 0$ and $0 \leq \alpha \leq \min\{m - K + 1, K - 1\}$, an α-*noisy K-ranking predictor* outputs $\mathbf{W}_\pi = \langle e_{\pi_1}^W, \ldots, e_{\pi_{|E|}}^W \rangle$, that is the vector $\mathbf{W}$ permuted according to $\pi \sim \mathfrak{U}(\Pi(\{1, \ldots, m\})_{(\alpha, K)})$, where $\mathfrak{U}(\cdot)$ denotes the uniform distribution over the elements of a set.

---
[4] The set of heavy edges H used by STEP has size trivially bounded by K.

Therefore an α-noisy K-ranking predictor is such that it correctly classifies the top-$(K-\alpha-1)$ edges in $\mathbf{W}$, and the edges with small weight $W(e)$ (i.e., all edges in position $j \geq K+\alpha+1$). While, a noisy ranking predictor can be arbitrarily wrong in classifying edges in position $K-\alpha, \ldots, K+\alpha$ over $\mathbf{W}$. Where, α is a *noise parameter*: a larger value for α corresponds to a less accurate ranking predictor. Our noisy predictor definition closely reflects machine learning models or recommenders with high recall. Note that a 0-noisy predictor corresponds to a ranking predictor (without noise). Let $\nabla = \max_{i \in [1, m-1]}\{W(e_{\prec_i}) - W(e_{\prec_{i+1}})\}$ be the maximum difference of the weights for two adjacent edges in the vector $\mathbf{W}$. Finally let $\nabla_a = \nabla \cdot (a+1), a \geq 0$.

We now show that STEP computes a relative ε-approximation of all the temporal triangle counts $|\mathcal{T}_i|, i \in [8]$ with controlled error probability and sublinear memory usage in m_δ. We consider both perfect and noisy predictors.[5]

Theorem 1. *Consider an execution of STEP, with $\varepsilon > 0$ and $K = o(m_\delta)$. There exist constants $C > 1, \gamma \in (0, \frac{1}{2})$ such that:*

1. *when $\mathcal{Q}(\cdot)_K$ is a ranking predictor then if $p \geq \frac{C\sqrt{m_\delta}}{\varepsilon|\mathcal{T}_i|^{1/2-\gamma}}$, STEP uses $\mathcal{O}(\varepsilon^{-1} m_\delta^{3/2}/|\mathcal{T}_i|^{1/2-\gamma})$ memory in expectation;*
2. *when $\mathcal{Q}(\cdot)_K$ is an α-noisy K-ranking predictor for $\alpha \geq 1$ then if $p \geq \frac{C\sqrt{\nabla_\alpha m_\delta}}{\varepsilon|\mathcal{T}_i|^{1/2-\gamma}}$, STEP uses $\mathcal{O}\left(\varepsilon^{-1} m_\delta^{3/2} \sqrt{\nabla_\alpha}/|\mathcal{T}_i|^{1/2-\gamma}\right)$ memory in expectation.*

In both cases, STEP is a one-pass streaming algorithm with $\mathbb{P}[\exists i \in [8] : |c_i - |\mathcal{T}_i|| \geq \varepsilon|\mathcal{T}_i|] \leq 1/3$ using sublinear memory.

Consider case 1. and the following event E = "count $|\mathcal{T}_i|^{1/2-\gamma}$ is sufficiently large, for each $i \in [8]$". Then Thm. 1 indicates that the sampling probability p can be set to a sufficiently small value, as $\sqrt{m_\delta}/|\mathcal{T}_i|^{1/2-\gamma} \ll 1$ under E. Consequently, the expected memory usage of STEP becomes sublinear in m_δ, aligning with established results in concentration theory [5]. Clearly, if E does not hold, then counts $|\mathcal{T}_i|$ are small enough to be obtained with high accuracy using the set H identified through $\mathcal{Q}(\cdot)$. Now, consider case 2. from Thm. 1, under E, a noisy predictor increases STEP's expected memory usage by a factor $\sqrt{\nabla_\alpha}$ (compared to case 1.). That is STEP may miss some triangle counts due to noisy predictions, requiring a larger value for p to achieve the accuracy guarantees. Nonetheless, if the predictor effectively ranks important (heavy) edges (i.e., $\sqrt{\nabla_\alpha}$ is not too large), then STEP achieves accurate estimates with reduced variance compared to classical algorithms while maintaining an expected sublinear memory usage. In our extended version [40] we show, as a corollary of Thm. 1 case 1., that if the first K edges in $\mathbf{W}$ capture a sufficient number of triangles then $\mathrm{Var}[c_i]$ is a factor $\mathcal{O}(|\mathcal{T}_i|)$ smaller compared to when STEP does not use a predictor.

---

[5] We assume that there exists an arbitrarily large constant R for which $|\mathcal{T}_i| = R \cdot |\mathcal{T}_j|, i, j \in [8]$. Such assumption can be avoided replacing $|\mathcal{T}_i|$ with $\sum_i |\mathcal{T}_i|$.

3.4 A Simple and Practical Predictor

We now introduce a simple and practical noisy ranking predictor. That is, we describe a *temporal min-degree predictor* which can be built efficiently with a single pass on the input stream, and can be used within our algorithm STEP. We define the *temporal degree* of node $u \in V$ within a *time interval* $[t_a, t_b]$ as $d(u, t_a, t_b) = |\{(x, y, t') \in E : (x = u \text{ or } y = u) \text{ and } t' \in [t_a, t_b]\}|$. That is, the temporal degree is the number of edges incident to u within the given time interval. Next, given a temporal edge $e = (u, v, t) \in E$ and a time duration δ let $w_{\text{m-d}}(e) = \min\{d(u, t-\delta, t+\delta), d(v, t-\delta, t+\delta)\}$ be the *temporal min-degree weight*. That is, $w_{\text{m-d}}(e)$ is the minimum between the temporal degrees of the nodes of edge e. Intuitively, the temporal min-degree weight accounts for the temporal activity of nodes over the graph, which is crucial for our goal of designing a highly accurate predictor for STEP. Let $\mathbf{W}^{\text{m-d}}$ be the edges $e \in E$ ordered by non-increasing values of their weight $w_{\text{m-d}}(e)$, ties broken arbitrarily. Then, for any edge $e \in E$, the *temporal min-degree ranking predictor* classifies $\mathcal{Q}(e)_K = 1$ if e is within the first K edges of $\mathbf{W}^{\text{m-d}}$, and $\mathcal{Q}(e)_K = 0$ otherwise. Therefore, the temporal min-degree predictor uses the temporal min-degree weights $w_{\text{m-d}}(e)$ as a *proxy* for the unknown values $W(e)$ of a perfect predictor. Clearly, the temporal min-degree predictor may not be accurate when the rankings of $\mathbf{W}^{\text{m-d}}$ and $\mathbf{W}$ do not align. Note that the temporal min-degree predictor can be computed extremely efficiently, with a single pass over the stream, and avoiding exact temporal triangle counting. Finally, note that our temporal min-degree predictor leverages both *structural* and *temporal* properties in the data—in contrast with predictors for static triangle counting [4,7], that do not consider time. In our extended version [40], we provide an empirical comparison for STEP coupled with different predictors, showing the superior performance of our temporal min-degree predictor compared with state-of-the-art static predictors.

4 Experimental Evaluation

Our extensive experiments investigated the following questions:

Q1. How does STEP compare to SotA approaches in terms of accuracy of its estimates and computational resources (time and memory)?

Q2. What is the impact of the predictor $\mathcal{Q}(\cdot)$ on the estimates of STEP?

Q3. How does STEP perform in an *online setting*. Namely, when a predictor $\mathcal{Q}(\cdot)$ is learned on historical data, and then used on previously unseen data?

Datasets and Environment. We considered four massive publicly available temporal graphs (Table 1), which are extremely challenging for Problem 1 and used by previous works [9,28,30,36]. More details on the used datasets and the setting of our experiments can be found in our extended version [40]. Our code is publicly available online.[6]

---

[6] https://github.com/VandinLab/STEP.

Table 1. Datasets. We report: $n = |V|$ the number of nodes; $m = |E|$ the number of temporal edges; the *precision* of the timestamps; and the total *timespan*.

Dataset	n	m	precision	timespan
Stackoverflow (SO)	$2.6\,M$	$63.5\,M$	sec	7.60 years
Bitcoin (BI)	$48.1\,M$	$113.1\,M$	sec	7.08 years
Reddit (RE)	$8.4\,M$	$636.3\,M$	sec	10.06 years
EquinixChicago (EC)	$11.1\,M$	$3.3\,B$	μ-sec	62.00 mins

Baseline Methods. We compared STEP with the following SotA algorithms: Degeneracy [30], an *exact* algorithm for computing the counts of all temporal triangles; FAST-Tri [9], an *exact* algorithm specifically tailored to temporal triangles; MoTTo [18], a recent SotA *exact* algorithm for counting 3-nodes 3-edges motifs, including triangles; and EWS [41], the SotA *approximate* method for solving Prob. 1.[7] We also compared with the sampling approach of STEP *without* a predictor that we denote with NAIVE-S. Note that all exact approaches considered cannot process the input in streaming, requiring therefore large memory.

Memory and Runtime. We measured the peak RAM memory (in GB) of each algorithm over a representative run. The runtime is an average over ten runs, unless otherwise stated. Since EWS counts triangles independently, its runtime is an average of the aggregated time to process all triangles, across ten runs.

Parameters. We select a small, a medium, and a large value for the parameter δ according to the precision of each dataset. We set on SO, BI and RE $\delta \in \{3\,600, 86\,400, 259\,200\}$, while for EC we set $\delta \in \{1 \times 10^5, 2 \times 10^5, 3 \times 10^5\}$. We set the parameter K to $\frac{m}{100}$. The sampling probability p_{NS} of NAIVE-S is set to obtain, in *expectation*, the same number of edges retained by STEP (i.e., $|S_L| + |H|$). All the parameters used in our experiments are in the extended version [40].

Ranking Predictors. We considered two ranking predictors for STEP: *1)* a *perfect predictor* that exactly classifies the K edges with the highest weights $W(e), e \in E$ as defined in Sect. 3.3, and *2)* a *temporal min-degree* predictor, as described in Sect. 3.4. We denote the resulting methods with STEP$_P$ and STEP$_{TMD}$ respectively. The perfect predictor allows us to evaluate the performance of STEP when the edge weights correspond to the actual number of temporal triangles an edge is involved in—this is not of practical interest but provides a lower bound on the error of the estimates of STEP. The temporal min-degree predictor (TMD) is instead simple, general, domain-agnostic, and can be computed from simple

---

[7] EWS requires two parameters p_{EWS} and q_{EWS} that we set as suggested by the authors [41] (see [40] for further details).

structural properties in the data. The TMD uses the temporal min-degree as edge weight to classify the top-K most heavy edges to retain, as described in Sect. 3.4. The resulting method, STEP$_{\text{TMD}}$ is simple and of *practical* interest, given that the TMD can be computed efficiently.

Table 2. Peak RAM memory, in GB, of a representative run for the largest δ. *OOM* denotes out of memory.

Dataset	NAIVE-S	STEP$_P$	STEP$_{\text{TMD}}$	EWS	Degeneracy	FAST-Tri	MoTTo
SO	0.78	0.74	0.74	8.04	5.10	5.81	12.07
BI	1.70	1.81	1.74	27.05	15.40	17.43	34.08
RE	14.68	14.74	15.53	103.75	71.30	79.59	159.74
EC	63.46	62.70	63.47	*OOM*	*OOM*	*OOM*	*OOM*

4.1 Comparison with State-of-the-Art Methods

We first compared STEP with SotA baselines to answer question **Q1**. For such comparison, we fixed the parameters of all the approximation algorithms (STEP, NAIVE-S, and EWS) to ensure comparable runtime and MAE. Specifically, we ran STEP with the same sampling probability as EWS ($p = 0.01$) on all datasets except for SO, where $p = 0.1$ was used since STEP is much faster than EWS. When discussing results for STEP, we focus on STEP$_{\text{TMD}}$. Table 2 reports the peak memory usage for each algorithm, and Table 3 presents the runtime of all algorithms except STEP$_P$ and NAIVE-S (see [40] for additional results). Figure 2 shows the accuracy of each approximate method on SO, BI and RE datasets for the largest values of δ (exact methods always report 0 MAE). While Fig. 3 reports the accuracy of the STEP$_P$, STEP$_{\text{TMD}}$ and NAIVE-S approaches on the EC dataset (EWS is not reported since it violates the RAM budget, see Table 2). Results for other values of δ are available in the extended version [40]. On the SO dataset, STEP$_{\text{TMD}}$ requires substantially less memory than EWS, Degeneracy, FAST-Tri and MoTTo while achieving more accurate estimates than EWS for all values of δ and for most temporal triangle counts. On the RE dataset, STEP$_{\text{TMD}}$ similarly demonstrates a significant reduction in memory usage compared to EWS, Degeneracy, FAST-Tri and MoTTo, and often provides higher-quality estimates than EWS. On the BI dataset, STEP$_{\text{TMD}}$ is much more memory efficient compared to EWS, Degeneracy, FAST-Tri and MoTTo. For larger values of δ, when the estimation problem becomes more challenging, STEP$_{\text{TMD}}$ obtains more accurate estimates than EWS. For smaller values of δ, the estimates provided by STEP$_{\text{TMD}}$ are comparable but slightly less accurate than those of EWS. In terms of runtime, STEP$_{\text{TMD}}$ consistently outperforms Degeneracy, FAST-Tri and MoTTo, and, in most cases, also EWS, with the exception of $\delta = 259\,200$ on the BI dataset. The BI dataset contains almost 40 billion δ-instances, most of which are counted deterministically by STEP$_{TMD}$ (over H). Hence, STEP$_{TMD}$ outputs tight estimates but requires a high execution time (see our extended version [40] for further analyses on the time-accuracy trade-off). Finally, on the EC dataset, that has more than 3 billion temporal edges, all SotA baselines cannot terminate their execution within the maximum memory allowance (200GB). Instead, STEP$_{TMD}$ requires less than 65GB of memory, achieves an average MAE below 0.1, and runs in less than ten minutes, even for the largest δ. In summary, these results show that STEP$_{TMD}$ enables the *efficient* and *accurate* estimation of all temporal triangle counts with remarkably *small memory usage*, especially on massive datasets where existing SotA approaches cannot scale their computation due to high resource usage.

4.2 Impact of the Predictor

To answer **Q2**, we consider STEP$_P$, STEP$_{TMD}$, and NAIVE-S, and set their parameters so that they sample the same number of edges in expectation (see our extended version [40]). Figure 2 and Fig. 3 show that both STEP$_P$ and STEP$_{TMD}$ provide much more accurate estimates than NAIVE-S on all datasets, with the exception of $\delta = 3\,600$ for the BI dataset where STEP$_{TMD}$ and NAIVE-S are comparable (see our extended version [40]). Moreover, the variance of the estimates by both STEP$_P$ and STEP$_{TMD}$ is always smaller compared to NAIVE-S, especially for the larger datasets RE and EC. In terms of runtime, NAIVE-S is the fastest method (see [40]): in fact, NAIVE-S *counts fewer triangles* than STEP, yielding estimates with higher variance—highlighting a key trade-off, i.e., more accurate estimates require larger execution times for STEP. It is worth noting that on

Table 3. Average runtime (in sec). "✗" denotes out of RAM memory (200 GB). Exact algorithms are run once due to their high runtime, hence we do not show their variance. The best runtime is in bold. SU denotes the speed-up of STEP$_{TMD}$ compared to each baseline (N/A is used when the speed-up cannot be computed).

Dataset	δ	STEP$_{TMD}$	EWS		Degeneracy		FAST-Tri		MoTTo	
		Time	Time	SU	Time	SU	Time	SU	Time	SU
SO	3600	**4.9 ± 0.0**	30.4 ± 0.8	6.2×	348.4	71.1×	15.1	3.1×	174.5	35.6×
	86400	**6.3 ± 0.1**	32.0 ± 0.5	5.1×	355.2	56.4×	41.8	6.6×	254.5	40.4×
	259200	**7.5 ± 0.1**	35.6 ± 0.9	4.7×	356.3	47.5×	76.3	10.2×	378.9	50.5×
BI	3600	**6.1 ± 0.1**	67.7 ± 5.1	11.1×	422.1	69.2×	189.0	31.0×	1113.7	182.6×
	86400	**43.8 ± 0.4**	115.9 ± 1.7	2.6×	421.3	9.6×	4287.7	97.9×	18045.1	412.0×
	259200	278.2 ± 5.5	**198.5 ± 5.9**	0.7×	424.8	1.5×	13804.3	49.6×	55494.2	199.5×
RE	3600	**69.7 ± 2.0**	570.7 ± 50.3	8.2×	18656.8	267.7×	1708.7	24.5×	6406.0	92.0×
	86400	**103.5 ± 4.4**	943.1 ± 67.6	9.1×	18528.1	179.0×	7479.5	72.3×	23085.0	223.0×
	259200	**164.9 ± 2.1**	1121.8 ± 79.1	6.8×	18950.0	115.0×	11165.8	67.7×	29680.1	180.0×
EC	1×10^5	425.6 ± 16.8	✗	N/A	✗	N/A	✗	N/A	✗	N/A
	2×10^5	497.4 ± 8.6	✗	N/A	✗	N/A	✗	N/A	✗	N/A
	3×10^5	580.3 ± 0.9	✗	N/A	✗	N/A	✗	N/A	✗	N/A

the EC dataset, STEP$_{\text{TMD}}$ requires more time to execute than STEP$_\text{P}$, in contrast to all other datasets. This is due to the structure of the EC dataset, on which the temporal min-degree does not provide a good proxy for the weights $W(e)$ of temporal edges (see our extended version [40]). Nevertheless, STEP still computes more accurate estimates than NAIVE-S while being highly memory efficient. To summarize, by employing a predictor STEP$_\text{P}$ and STEP$_{\text{TMD}}$ significantly improve the accuracy and reduce the variance of NAIVE-S's estimates. However, such higher accuracy may lead to higher execution times compared to NAIVE-S, due to the processing of more occurrences.

4.3 Online Estimation

To address **Q3**, we developed a practical approach for learning a predictor from a *training stream* of temporal edges (τ^{tr}) and used it to estimate temporal triangle counts on a *test stream* (τ^{ts}). The training stream τ^{tr} consists of the first 75% of edges appearing on the stream τ. The predictor is based on a threshold value ϕ, obtained from the temporal min-degree weight (see Sect. 3.4) of the K-th edge in the non-decreasing ordering induced by $w_{\text{m-d}}(e), e \in \tau^{tr}$. When processing the test stream, edges in τ^{ts} with temporal degree $w_{\text{m-d}}(e) \geq \phi$ are classified as heavy and retained by the algorithm.[8] The underlying idea is that the threshold ϕ classifies important edges to retain over τ^{ts} whenever the training stream τ^{tr} is sufficiently representative (for τ^{ts}). The results for BI, RE and EC for the largest value of δ are shown in Fig. 4 (see the extended version [40]). We observe that STEP$_{\text{TMD}}$ provides more accurate estimates than NAIVE-S on the RE and BI datasets. On the EC dataset, STEP$_{\text{TMD}}$ and NAIVE-S achieve similar accuracy, as the learned predictor (i.e., ϕ) does not align well with a *perfect* classification over τ^{ts} (similarly to the results in Sect. 4.2). We study such aspects in the extended version [40]. Overall, our findings highlight that STEP effectively leverages simple predictors learned from historical data, often outperforming NAIVE-S in most configurations. Therefore, even under noisy and inaccurate predictions, STEP achieves good estimates, supporting its usage in practical applications.

5 Related Work

To the best of our knowledge, our work is the first to solve the *temporal* triangle counting problem *using predictions*. We now survey the works most relevant to this paper; for overviews on temporal motifs and algorithms with predictions see [10,21,26].

Temporal Motif and Triangle Counting. There exist several definitions of temporal motifs, including temporal triangles [21,23]. We adopt the definition introduced by Paranjape et al. [29], for which various counting algorithms exist.

---

[8] The predictor evaluates if $e = (u,v,t)$ should be retained or not at time $t + \delta$.

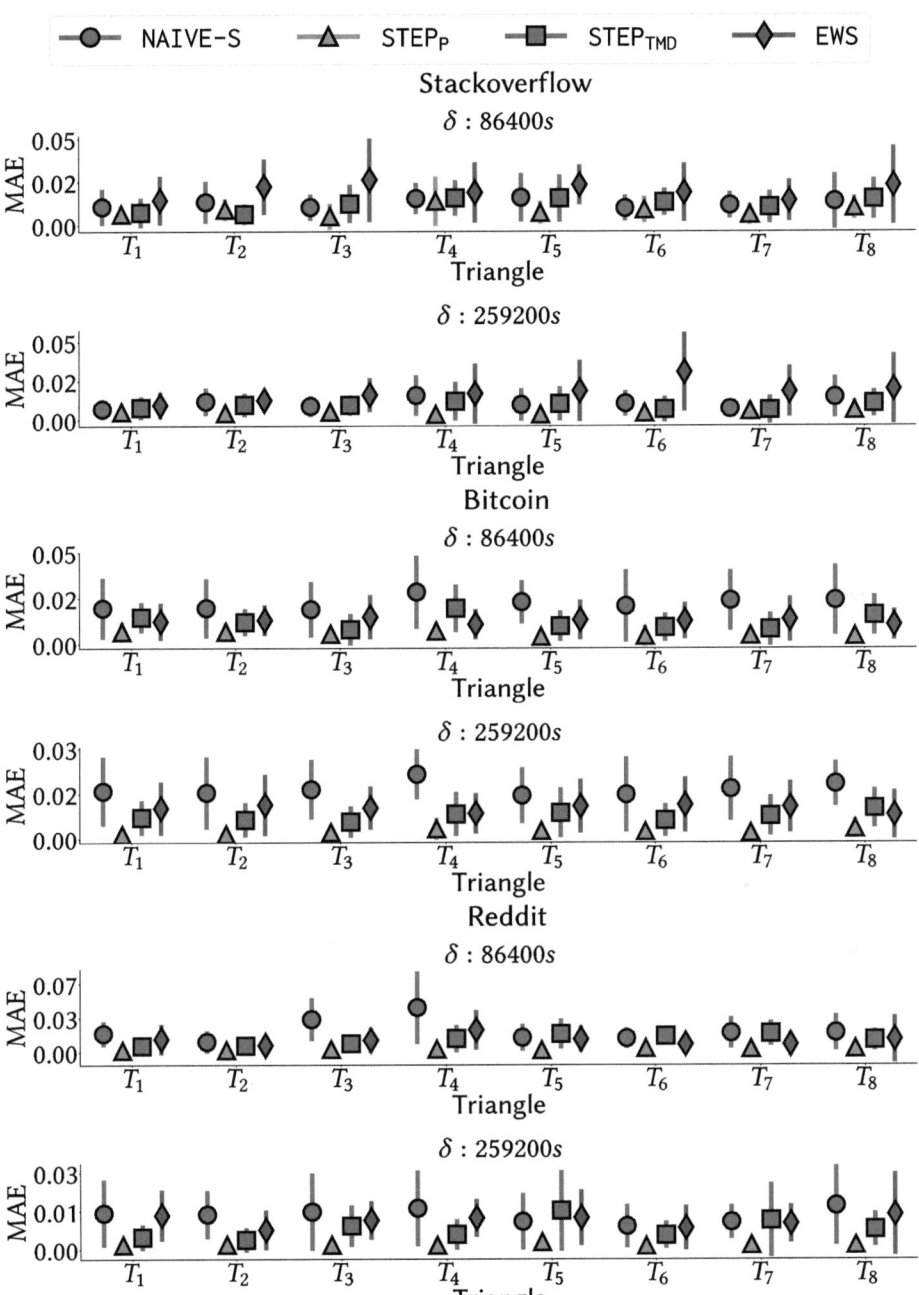

Fig. 2. MAE and standard deviation for STEP, NAIVE-S and EWS on SO, BI and RE datasets from Table 1, for the largest values of δ and for each temporal triangle (see Fig. 1(d)).

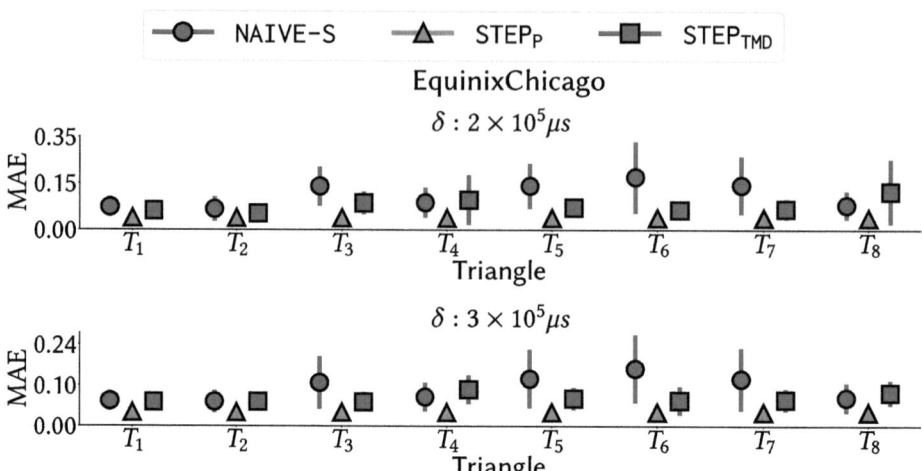

Fig. 3. MAE and standard deviation for STEP, NAIVE-S and EWS on EC dataset from Table 1, for the largest values of δ and for each temporal triangle (see Fig. 1(d)).

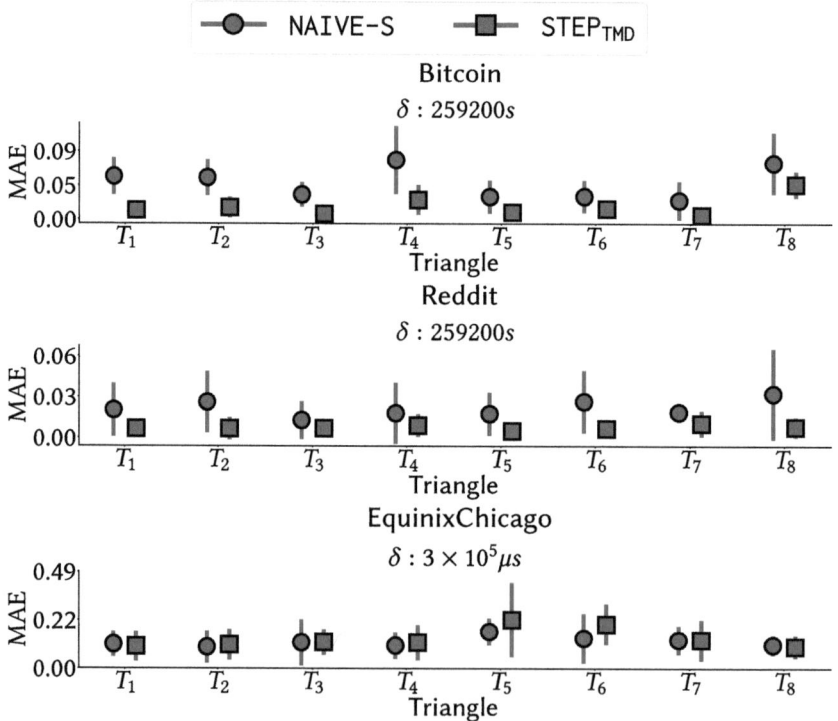

Fig. 4. Accuracy comparison (MAE and standard deviation) for online estimation over τ^{ts}, between NAIVE-S and STEP$_{\text{TMD}}$ (trained over the historical data τ^{tr}).

Exact Methods. Paranjape et al. [29] introduced a method with complexity $\mathcal{O}(|E'|^{3/2} + m|E'|^{3/4})$, where $|E'|$ is the number of edges in the static graph of a temporal graph, that is impractical on large temporal graphs. Gao et al. [9] and Li et al. [18] improved the work in [29] introducing various pruning techniques yielding a time-complexity of $\mathcal{O}(mm_\delta^2)$, matching the complexity of the exhaustive enumeration algorithm in [22]. In fact, most recent works do not scale to large temporal graphs [9,18], as shown by our experimental evaluation (Sect. 4). Pashanasangi and Seshadhri [30] developed an exact method with complexity $\mathcal{O}(m\kappa \log m)$, where κ is the degeneracy of the static graph [24]: such an approach can be impractical on large real-world graphs where κ is in the order of hundreds or thousands [30]. Moreover, all existing exact approaches remain computationally impractical and extremely memory-intensive, as they require access to the temporal graph, and cannot work in streaming [9,18,30].

Approximate Methods. Approximate approaches are based on randomized sampling. Most methods only approximate a *single* temporal motif count, either by collecting subgraphs within specific time windows [20,35] or by sampling temporal edges [41] or paths [28]. Some techniques can estimate *multiple* temporal motifs counts under specific constraints, such as shared static topology [34] or specific structure [32], but cannot process the graph as a stream. To our best knowledge, EWS by Wang et al. [41] is the only approximation algorithm designed for streaming processing. EWS uses edge sampling to obtain an estimate for an individual triangle count. However, EWS requires large computational resources, such as memory, not scaling on large temporal graphs (see Sect. 4).

Algorithms with Predictions (AwP) in Static Graphs. The AwP framework introduced in [26] enhances classical combinatorial algorithms with predictions obtained, for example, from machine learning models trained on historical data. Classical combinatorial algorithms benefit from predictions by improving their efficiency, e.g., runtime or memory usage, and retaining their worst-case complexity. Such new framework has been applied to clustering [15], graph problems [17], and more [1,3,6]. Related to our work, Chen et al. [7] developed a predictor-based sampling algorithm to estimate triangle and four-cycle counts in *static* graph streams. In addition to target *static* graphs, the work of Chen et al. [7] relies on the impractical assumption of a predictor knowing the number of triangles an edge participates in. Clearly, such an assumption is impractical: *i)* a perfect predictor can be obtained only by solving the triangle counting problem exactly; and *ii)* it cannot model the complex predictors used in practice. Recently, Boldrin and Vandin [4] improved the work in [7] and proposed a simple, domain-independent predictor that can be obtained with a single pass over the stream. Unfortunately, the idea in [4] is not suitable for solving the *temporal* triangle counting problem, as it makes STEP very inefficient, especially compared with our novel predictor (see our extended version [40]).

6 Conclusion

We studied the problem of counting temporal triangles in a stream of temporal edges. We introduced STEP, a sampling algorithm enhanced with a predictor, which provides highly accurate estimates while using minimal computational resources compared to SotA approaches. To the best of our knowledge, STEP is the *first algorithm* for temporal triangle counting using predictions. Experimental results show that STEP is much faster than SotA exact methods and requires significantly less resources than approximate SotA streaming algorithms, often obtaining more accurate estimates. Finally, we show how to efficiently compute a simple predictor, that can be also used for an online processing of the graph.

Future research includes the development of more advanced and domain-dependent predictors (e.g., learning specific edge-weights for the classification of important edges to retain over the stream), and extending STEP's approach to other temporal motifs [32,34].

Acknowledgments. This research is funded by the Ministry of University and Research within the Complementary National Plan PNC-I.1 "Research initiatives for innovative technologies and pathways in the health and welfare sector, D.D. 931 of 06/06/2022, PNC0000002 DARE - Digital Lifelong Prevention CUP: B53C22006440001" and PRIN Project n. 2022TS4Y3N "EXPAND: scalable algorithms for EXPloratory Analyses of heterogeneous and dynamic Networked Data". This research is also funded by the ERC Advanced Grant REBOUND (834862), and the Wallenberg AI, Autonomous Systems and Software Program (WASP) funded by the Knut and Alice Wallenberg Foundation.

Disclosure of Interests. The authors have no competing interests to declare that are relevant to the content of this article.

References

1. Azar, Y., Panigrahi, D., Touitou, N.: Online graph algorithms with predictions. SODA (2022)
2. Belth, C., Zheng, X., Koutra, D.: Mining persistent activity in continually evolving networks. KDD (2020)
3. Bernardini, G., Lindermayr, A., Marchetti-Spaccamela, A., Megow, N., Stougie, L., Sweering, M.: A universal error measure for input predictions applied to online graph problems. NeurIPS (2022)
4. Boldrin, C., Vandin, F.: Fast and accurate triangle counting in graph streams using predictions. ICDM (2024)
5. Boucheron, S., Lugosi, G., Bousquet, O.: Concentration Inequalities. Springer (2004)
6. Chen, J., Silwal, S., Vakilian, A., Zhang, F.: Faster fundamental graph algorithms via learned predictions. ICML (2022)
7. Chen, J.Y., et al.: Triangle and four cycle counting with predictions in graph streams. ICLR (2022)
8. Debrouvier, A., Parodi, E., Perazzo, M., Soliani, V., Vaisman, A.: A model and query language for temporal graph databases. VLDB Journal (2021)

9. Gao, Z., Cheng, C., Yu, Y., Cao, L., Huang, C., Dong, J.: Scalable motif counting for large-scale temporal graphs. ICDE (2022)
10. Gionis, A., Oettershagen, L., Sarpe, I.: Mining temporal networks. WWW (2024)
11. Heeg, F., Scholtes, I.: Using causality-aware graph neural networks to predict temporal centralities in dynamic graphs. NeurIPS (2024)
12. Hessel, J., Tan, C., Lee, L.: Science, AskScience, and BadScience: On the Coexistence of Highly Related Communities. ICWSM (2016)
13. Holme, P., Saramäki, J.: Temporal networks. Phys, Rep (2012)
14. Holme, P., Saramäki, J.: Temporal Network Theory. Publishing, Springer Int (2023)
15. Jiang, S.H.C., Liu, E., Lyu, Y., Tang, Z.G., Zhang, Y.: Online facility location with predictions. ICLR (2022)
16. Kondor, D., Csabai, I., Szüle, J., Pósfai, M., Vattay, G.: Inferring the interplay between network structure and market effects in bitcoin. New J. Phys. (2014)
17. Lattanzi, S., Ola, S., Sergei, V.: Speeding up Bellman-Ford via minimum violation permutations. ICML (2023)
18. Li, J., Qi, J., Huang, Y., Cao, L., Yu, Y., Dong, J.: MoTTo: Scalable motif counting with time-aware topology constraint for large-scale temporal graphs. CIKM (2024)
19. Lin, L., et al.: QTCS: Efficient query-centered temporal community search. PVLDB (2024)
20. Liu, P., Benson, A.R., Charikar, M.: Sampling methods for counting temporal motifs. WSDM (2019)
21. Liu, P., Guarrasi, V., Sariyuce, A.E.: Temporal network motifs: Models, limitations, evaluation. TKDE (2021)
22. Mackey, P., Porterfield, K., Fitzhenry, E., Choudhury, S., Chin, G.: A chronological edge-driven approach to temporal subgraph isomorphism. Big Data (2018)
23. Mang, Q., et al.: Efficient historical butterfly counting in large temporal bipartite networks via graph structure-aware index. arXiv (2024)
24. Matula, D.W., Beck, L.L.: Smallest-last ordering and clustering and graph coloring algorithms. JACM (1983)
25. McGregor, A.: Graph stream algorithms: a survey. SIGMOD (2014)
26. Mitzenmacher, M., Vassilvitskii, S.: Algorithms with predictions. CACM (2022)
27. Muthukrishnan, S., et al.: Data streams: algorithms and applications. In: Found. Trends®. Theor. Comput. Sci. (2005)
28. Pan, Y., Bhalerao, O., Seshadri, C., Talati, N.: Accurate and fast estimation of temporal motifs using path sampling. ICDM (2024)
29. Paranjape, A., Benson, A.R., Leskovec, J.: Motifs in temporal networks. WSDM (2017)
30. Pashanasangi, N., Seshadhri, C.: Faster and generalized temporal triangle counting, via degeneracy ordering. KDD (2021)
31. Porter, A., Mirzasoleiman, B., Leskovec, J.: Analytical models for motifs in temporal networks. WWW (2022)
32. Pu, J., Wang, Y., Li, Y., Zhou, X.: Sampling algorithms for butterfly counting on temporal bipartite graphs. arXiv (2023)
33. Qin, H., Li, R.H., Yuan, Y., Wang, G., Qin, L., Zhang, Z.: Mining bursting core in large temporal graphs. PVLDB (2022)
34. Sarpe, I., Vandin, F.: Oden: simultaneous approximation of multiple motif counts in large temporal networks. CIKM (2021)
35. Sarpe, I., Vandin, F.: PRESTO: Simple and scalable sampling techniques for the rigorous approximation of temporal motif counts. SDM (2021)
36. Sarpe, I., Vandin, F., Gionis, A.: Scalable temporal motif densest subnetwork discovery. KDD (2024)

37. Seshadhri, C., Tirthapura, S.: Scalable subgraph counting: The methods behind the madness. WWW (2019)
38. Tang, J., Musolesi, M., Mascolo, C., Latora, V.: Temporal distance metrics for social network analysis. SIGCOMM (2009)
39. Tu, K., Li, J., Towsley, D., Braines, D., Turner, L.D.: gl2vec: learning feature representation using graphlets for directed networks. ASONAM (2019)
40. Venturin, G., Sarpe, I., Vandin, F.: Efficient Approximate Temporal Triangle Counting in Streaming with Predictions (extended version). arXiv (2025)
41. Wang, J., Wang, Y., Jiang, W., Li, Y., Tan, K.L.: Efficient sampling algorithms for approximate motif counting in temporal graph streams. arXiv (2022)
42. Wang, P., Qi, Y., Sun, Y., Zhang, X., Tao, J., Guan, X.: Approximately counting triangles in large graph streams including edge duplicates with a fixed memory usage. PVLDB (2017)
43. Zhang, T., Fang, J., Yang, Z., Cao, B., Fan, J.: TATKC: A temporal graph neural network for fast approximate temporal Katz centrality ranking. WWW (2024)

Backdoor Attacks on Graph Classification via Data Augmentation and Dynamic Poisoning

Yadong Wang[1], Zhiwei Zhang[1(✉)], Pengpeng Qiao[2], Ye Yuan[1], and Guoren Wang[1]

[1] Beijing Institute of Technology, Beijing, China
bit.wangyd@gmail.com, {zwzhang, yuan-ye}@bit.edu.cn, wanggrbit@126.com
[2] Institute of Science Tokyo, Tokyo, Japan
peng2qiao@gmail.com

Abstract. Graph neural networks (GNNs) have gained widespread adoption in domains such as bioinformatics, social networks, and chemoinformatics, yet they remain susceptible to backdoor attacks. Existing backdoor attacks typically rely on subgraph triggers, which often introduce detectable anomalies and employ random poisoned sample selection, resulting in reduced stealthiness and efficiency. To address these limitations, we propose a novel backdoor attack framework that leverages data augmentation-based triggers and dynamic poisoned sample selection. Specifically, we design three alternative data augmentation strategies, edge modification guided by cosine similarity, edge removal based on degree centrality, and feature masking via gradient saliency, as backdoor triggers. Furthermore, we introduce a dynamic poisoned sample selection method informed by forgetting events. This method dynamically prioritizes high-impact poisoned samples to enhance attack efficiency while reducing the number of samples required to achieve the corresponding attack success rate (ASR). Experiments on four benchmark datasets, PROTEINS, NCI1, Mutagenicity, and ENZYMES, demonstrate the superiority of our method.

Keywords: GNNs · Graph Classification · Backdoor Attacks

1 Introduction

Graph classification has emerged as a fundamental research direction across multiple domains, particularly in bioinformatics and drug discovery [17], chemoinformatics [11], protein-protein interaction networks [10], and social network analysis [5]. With the rapid advancement of GNNs [1,2,9,14], the ability to model and process graph-structured data has significantly improved. By capturing high-order dependencies between nodes and edges, GNNs have demonstrated outstanding performance in graph classification tasks. However, the widespread adoption of GNNs in real-world applications has exposed critical security vulnerabilities, particularly in high-stakes domains where model reliability is crucial. In particular, backdoor attacks [7,8,20] on graph classification models pose a serious threat, enabling adversaries to manipulate model behavior while evading detection.

A backdoor attack occurs when an adversary secretly implants trigger patterns into training data. During inference, the model behaves normally on clean inputs but misclassifies inputs containing these triggers. This allows attackers to manipulate model predictions while evading detection. This attack is especially critical in graph classification due to the complex and high-dimensional nature of graph data. In such attacks, the adversary modifies the graph structure or perturbs node features in the training set, ensuring that the poisoned model behaves normally on clean inputs but misclassifies graphs that contain the embedded trigger. For example, in drug discovery, graph classification models are used to determine whether a molecular structure exhibits toxicity. An attacker could introduce a fixed molecular substructure as a trigger in the training data and alter the labels of these samples to "non-toxic". As a result, the backdoored model, when presented with a molecule containing the same trigger, incorrectly classifies it as non-toxic. Such manipulations could allow hazardous compounds to bypass safety checks or impair competitors by undermining model reliability. Given these high-stakes applications, studying backdoor attacks on graph classification models is essential.

Existing backdoor attack strategies in graph classification primarily rely on subgraph-based triggers. Zhang et al. [21] introduced a method where a fixed randomly generated subgraph is inserted into each poisoned sample. Xu et al. [18] further explored the impact of trigger placement by injecting subgraphs at both the most and least important positions in the graph. Xi et al. [15] proposed a more adaptive strategy that generates subgraph triggers via neural networks, varying their structural properties while keeping the number of injected nodes fixed. Despite their effectiveness, existing methods face two major limitations: (1) The injected subgraphs often introduce noticeable anomalies, making them susceptible to detection and mitigation [3]; (2) Existing methods randomly sample poisoned samples for trigger injection and label modification, resulting in a higher poisoning rate required to achieve the expected ASR.

To overcome these challenges, this paper introduces two backdoor attack designs: (1) *Data augmentation-based trigger*. Instead of injecting subgraph patterns, we leverage data augmentation [4,12,23] as backdoor triggers. Since data augmentation is commonly used to expand training datasets and enhance self-supervised learning (e.g., contrastive learning), it provides a natural way to conceal the trigger pattern. However, relying solely on random data augmentation is insufficient to enable the model to learn effective triggers. To address this limitation, we propose three data augmentation strategies, covering both topology- and feature-level transformations, to construct effective and stealthy backdoor triggers. (2) *Dynamic poisoned sample selection mechanism*. To further improve attack efficiency and reduce poisoning rate, we introduce a dynamic poisoned

Table 1. Methods for backdoor attacks on graph classification tasks.

Attack Name	Trigger Type	Injection Method	Sample Selection
Subgraph Backdoor[21]	fixed subgraph	subgraph injection	random
GNNExplainer[18]	fixed subgraph	subgraph injection	random
GTA[15]	adaptive subgraph	subgraph injection	random
TRAP[19]	perturbation-based	flip edges	random
Motif[22]	motif subgraph	subgraph injection	random
Ours	data augmentation	flip edges/mask features	dynamic selection

sample selection mechanism that prioritizes poisoned samples based on their contribution to the attack. This method identifies critical samples that have the highest impact on backdoor learning, ensuring that the model learns the trigger with minimal poisoned samples. The main contributions are as follows.

- We introduce a novel data augmentation-based trigger design that leverages topology-level or feature-level transformations to create stealthy and effective backdoor triggers for graph classification models.
- We introduce a dynamic poisoned sample selection strategy based on the occurrence of forgetting events, enabling the selection of poisoned samples that contribute more effectively to the backdoor attack.
- We conducted attack evaluations on GCN and GIN models across four benchmark datasets. The results demonstrate that our approach achieves better attack performance while maintaining a low clean accuracy drop (CAD).

2 Related Work

Backdoor attacks in graph classification remain an emerging area of research, with significant challenges yet to be addressed. Early research by [21] pioneered the idea of injecting predefined fixed subgraph patterns into training samples, prompting the GNN model to associate these subgraphs with attacker-designated target labels. Based on this, [18] further explored how the injection position of trigger subgraphs affects the attack performance, revealing that strategic placement at critical positions significantly influences attack success. [15] introduced an adaptive trigger generation approach using neural networks, producing triggers with fixed node counts but varied topologies, thereby enhancing the attack's flexibility and reducing detectability. [19] proposed perturbation-based triggers, leveraging meta-gradients computed on adjacency matrices to guide structural modifications. More recently, [22] investigated how different subgraph motifs influence the effectiveness of backdoor attacks from a motif-based perspective. Despite these advancements, existing methods have largely ignored the critical role of sample-level variations in backdoor attack effectiveness, leaving room for more efficient and stealthy approaches. We summarize and compare mainstream backdoor attack methods on graph classification tasks in Table 1.

3 Preliminaries and Problem Definition

3.1 Graph Classification and GNNs

A graph classification task operates on input graphs $G = (\mathcal{V}, \mathcal{E})$, where $\mathcal{V}$ denotes the node set with feature vectors $\{\mathbf{x}_i\}_{v_i \in \mathcal{V}}$ and $\mathcal{E}$ represents the set of edges capturing pairwise relationships between nodes. The goal is to learn a function $f : G \to y_G$ that maps structural and attribute information to a graph-level label y_G.

Modern approaches leverage GNNs, which iteratively refine node embeddings through neighborhood aggregation. At layer l, the embedding $\mathbf{h}_i^{(l)}$ of node v_i is updated via:

$$\mathbf{h}_i^{(l)} = \text{COMBINE}^{(l)} \left(\mathbf{h}_i^{(l-1)}, \text{AGGREGATE}^{(l)} \left(\{ \mathbf{h}_j^{(l-1)} \mid j \in \mathcal{N}(i) \} \right) \right),$$

where $\mathcal{N}(i)$ is the neighbor set of v_i, $\text{AGGREGATE}^{(l)}(\cdot)$ integrates neighboring embeddings, and $\text{COMBINE}^{(l)}(\cdot)$ fuses aggregated features with the node's current state.

To obtain graph-level predictions, a readout function aggregates the final-layer node embeddings $\{\mathbf{h}_i^{(L)}\}_{v_i \in \mathcal{V}}$ into a global graph representation:

$$\mathbf{z}_G = \text{READOUT} \left(\{\mathbf{h}_i^{(L)}\} \right),$$

where $\text{READOUT}(\cdot)$ is typically a pooling or summarization function that aggregates node-level embeddings from the final layer L into a single vector representation for the entire graph. The resulting graph embedding $\mathbf{z}_G$ is then fed into a classifier (e.g., multi-layer perceptron) to predict y_G.

This architecture enables GNNs to capture both *local structural patterns* (via neighborhood aggregation) and *global graph characteristics* (via readout operations), forming the foundation for modern graph classification systems.

3.2 Problem Formulation

Attacker's Knowledge and Capability. We analyze two attack scenarios, considering both white-box and black-box settings. In the white-box attack (as demonstrated in our experiments on the GCN model), the attacker employs a surrogate model with the same architecture as the victim model, enabling a more precise simulation of the target's behavior and thereby enhancing the attack's effectiveness. In contrast, the black-box attack (evaluated using our method on the GIN model) involves a surrogate model with a different architecture from the victim model, preventing the attacker from directly accessing the target's parameters or structural details. Instead, the attack relies on transferring adversarial patterns learned from the surrogate model. In both cases, the attacker manipulates a small portion of the training data by injecting structural or feature-based trigger patterns and modifying the corresponding labels, leading the victim model to misclassify inputs during inference.

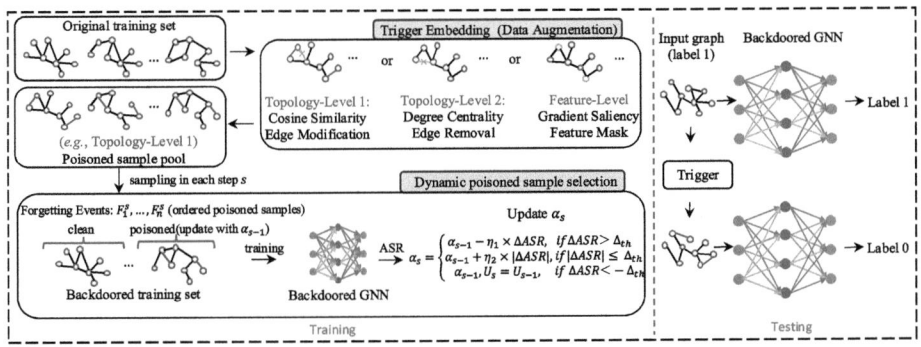

Fig. 1. The framework of our backdoor attack on graph classification task.

Adversary's Objective. Formally, given a GNN classifier F, a targeted attack class y_t, and a trigger graph denoted by G_{g_t}, the adversary aims to achieve two main objectives:

$$\begin{cases} F(G_{g_t}) = y_t, & \text{for trigger-embedded graphs } G_{g_t}, \\ F(G) = F_o(G), & \text{for clean graphs } G. \end{cases} \quad (1)$$

The first objective ensures the attack effectiveness: whenever the trigger g_t is embedded, the trojaned model F consistently classifies the input graph into the attacker-specified target class y_t. The second objective ensures attack evasiveness: the trojaned model F behaves identically to a clean model F_o on clean graphs, making the backdoor difficult to detect.

4 Method

We propose a novel backdoor attack framework for graph classification that comprises two designs: trigger construction via graph augmentation and dynamic poisoned sample selection based on forgetting events. As illustrated in Fig. 1, the attack process begins by applying a data augmentation-based strategy to generate poisoned samples, where each clean graph is perturbed using one of three predefined augmentation methods. Specifically, these methods include two topology-level strategies and one feature-level strategy. To preserve stealthiness, only one augmentation strategy is applied to each poisoned sample at a time.

Following augmentation, we adopt a dynamic poisoned sample selection strategy, which adaptively filters out low-impact poisoned samples and adjusts the selection process based on real-time ASR feedback. This enables the identification of high-value samples that maximize the effectiveness of the backdoor attack. During testing, we apply our designed trigger to clean samples, causing them to be classified as the target class by the backdoored GNN.

In the following sections, we first describe the three augmentation strategies used to construct backdoor triggers, and then detail our dynamic poisoned sample selection strategy.

4.1 Trigger Construction via Graph Augmentation

Topology-Level Augmentation. At the graph structure level, we employ two edge modification strategies.

Strategy 1: Edge Modification Based on Cosine Similarity. We utilize the cosine similarity between node feature vectors to guide edge addition and removal, ensuring that the modified edges blend naturally into the local structure. For any two unconnected nodes v_i and v_j, the cosine similarity between their feature vectors is computed as follows:

$$\text{Sim}(v_i, v_j) = \frac{\mathbf{x}_i \cdot \mathbf{x}_j}{\|\mathbf{x}_i\| \|\mathbf{x}_j\|}. \tag{2}$$

Based on these similarity values, we rank all possible node pairs. The top-k edges with the lowest similarity scores are removed if they exist, while the top-k edges with the highest similarity scores are added if they do not exist in the original graph.

Strategy 2: Edge Removal Based on Degree Centrality. To preserve the core structural and semantic information of the graph, we identify and remove edges with lower importance, as proposed in [23]. Specifically, we assign each existing edge an associated removal probability $p_{v_i v_j}$, reflecting its importance. We use the degree centrality of edges as the measure of their importance. According to the definition proposed in [23], the edge centrality based on node degree centrality is defined as the average of its two endpoints:

$$w_{v_i, v_j} = \frac{c(v_i) + c(v_j)}{2}, \tag{3}$$

where $c(v_i)$ and $c(v_j)$ denote the degree centrality values of the endpoints v_i and v_j, calculated as follows:

$$c(v_j) = \frac{\deg(v_j)}{|\mathcal{N}| - 1}, \tag{4}$$

with $\mathcal{N}$ representing the total number of nodes in the graph.

We apply a logarithmic transformation to the edge centrality to mitigate the dominant effect of high-degree nodes:

$$s_{v_i, v_j} = \log(w_{v_i, v_j}). \tag{5}$$

Finally, the edge removal probability is normalized to:

$$p_{v_i v_j} = \left(\frac{s_{\max} - s_{v_i, v_j}}{s_{\max} - s_{\min}} \right) \cdot p_e, \tag{6}$$

where p_e controls the overall probability of edge removal, $s_{\max}$ and $s_{\min}$ denote the maximum and minimum values of s_{v_i, v_j} respectively.

Feature-Level Augmentation. At the feature level, we employ the feature masking strategy.

Strategy 3: Feature Masking. For feature-level augmentation, we adopt a selective feature masking strategy based on degree centrality and gradient saliency masks, allowing us to protect critical features while perturbing less important ones.

First, we leverage degree centrality to distinguish between critical and non-critical nodes. High-centrality nodes retain all their features to preserve global information, whereas non-critical nodes undergo selective feature masking. We select the bottom $\rho\%$ of nodes with the lowest degree centrality for feature masking, ensuring that structurally less critical nodes undergo perturbation while preserving key graph information. The importance of each feature is determined using a gradient saliency mask, computed by backpropagating the gradients with respect to the node feature vector $\mathbf{x}_v$:

$$\mathbf{g}_v = \left|\frac{\partial \mathcal{L}}{\partial \mathbf{x}_v}\right|, \tag{7}$$

where $\mathcal{L}$ represents the model's loss function, and $\mathbf{g}_v$ measures the contribution of each feature dimension to the classification task. We then rank feature dimensions based on their importance scores and retain the top $(1 - q\%)$ of features while masking the remaining $q\%$ ones:

$$\tilde{\mathbf{x}}_v = \mathbf{x}_v \odot \mathbf{m}, \tag{8}$$

where $\mathbf{m} \in \{0, 1\}^F$ is the feature mask vector, defined as:

$$m_i = \begin{cases} 1, & i \in \text{Top-}(1 - q\%)(\mathbf{g}_v), \\ 0, & \text{otherwise.} \end{cases} \tag{9}$$

This method ensures that key discriminative features remain intact while introducing subtle noise by masking less significant features, making the attack more difficult to detect.

4.2 Dynamic Poisoned Sample Selection by Forgetting Events

The quality of poisoned samples directly influences the success rate and stealthiness of backdoor attacks. Traditional random sample selection methods often introduce redundant or low-impact samples, thereby reducing the ASR and increasing the risk of detection. Our objective is to identify a subset of samples that contribute significantly to the backdoor attack. Prior works [6,13] have indicated that forgetting samples reveal intrinsic data properties and play a crucial role in shaping the classifier's decision boundary, whereas samples that are rarely forgotten have a limited impact on the final model performance. [16] explored the influence of forgetting samples in image-based backdoor attacks and proposed the Filtering-and-Updating Strategy (FUS) to refine sample selection. Building upon this foundation, we investigate the effect of forgetting backdoor samples in graph-based data and enhance the FUS strategy by introducing a dynamic adjustment mechanism that adapts in real-time to sample performance, thereby efficiently selecting the most impactful poisoned samples for the attack.

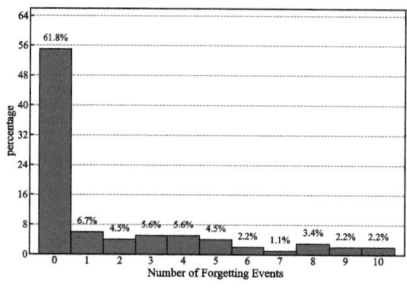
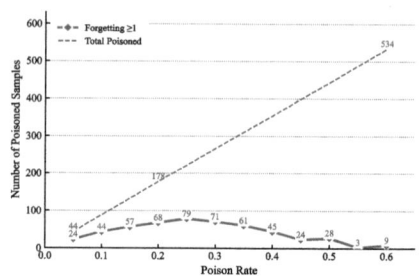

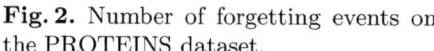

Fig. 2. Number of forgetting events on the PROTEINS dataset.

Fig. 3. Number of forgetting samples under different poisoning rates.

Definition of Forgetting Events. A forgetting event occurs when a model correctly classifies a sample at the time step r but subsequently misclassifies it in the time step $r+1$. Formally, the forgetting count F_n of poisoned sample n is defined as:

$$F_n = \sum_{r=1}^{R-1} \mathbb{I}(\hat{y}_n^r = y_t \text{ and } \hat{y}_n^{r+1} \neq y_t), \qquad (10)$$

where y_t represents the target label, $\hat{y}_n^r$ denotes the model's predicted label for sample n at the r-th training epoch, R denotes the total number of training epochs, and $\mathbb{I}(\cdot)$ is the indicator function.

Figure 2 illustrates an experiment conducted on the PROTEINS dataset. In this experiment, 61.8% of the data did not experience any forgetting events, while 38.2% of the data underwent at least one forgetting event. We refer to samples that have experienced at least one forgetting event as forgetting samples. [13] suggested that samples with frequent forgetting events contribute more significantly to the learning of backdoor patterns.

We further measure the number of forgetting samples under different poisoning rates, with the results shown in Fig. 3. It can be observed that as the poisoning rate increases, the number of forgetting samples initially increases and then decreases. Given a fixed poisoning rate, we aim to identify the most valuable forgetting samples for poisoning. We can achieve this goal by greedily retaining a large sample set of F_n, but it should be noted that only a small portion of the poisoned samples are recorded each time, and the forgetting events of the remaining clean training samples are not recorded. Therefore, this greedy retention method is local. According to the trend of change shown in Fig. 3, it is also infeasible to achieve this by expanding the poisoning set.

[13] employed the FUS strategy for image data sample selection. The FUS operates as follows: first, all training samples are poisoned to construct the poisoned sample pool $\mathcal{D}_{poisoned}$. The attacker randomly selects $U' \leftarrow p \cdot \mathcal{D}_{poisoned}$ samples from this poisoned sample pool based on a predefined poisoning rate p. The training process then iterates for S rounds, where in each round, a fixed proportion ($\alpha \cdot |U'|$) of the lowest-impact samples, ranked by F_n, are removed.

Subsequently, an equal number ($\alpha \cdot |U'|$) of new samples are randomly selected from the $\mathcal{D}_{poisoned} \setminus U'$. This iterative process continues until completion.

However, the FUS strategy has limitations: the filtering ratio α is fixed, and sample selection relies solely on direct removal without dynamic adjustment based on real-time sample performance. To address these issues, we propose a Dynamically Adjusted Filtering-and-Updating Strategy (DAFUS). We observe that the same poisoned sample may exhibit varying F_n when trained with different poisoned sample pools. Moreover, because we employ an early stopping mechanism during training, the number of training epochs can further influence the F_n value of a given poisoned sample. Therefore, instead of adjusting based on the average number of forgetting samples, we dynamically adapt the selection based on the attack success rate. We define the change in ASR as:

$$\Delta \text{ASR} = \text{ASR}_s - \text{ASR}_{s-1}. \tag{11}$$

The update ratio α for poisoned samples is dynamically adjusted as follows:

$$\alpha_s = \begin{cases} \alpha_{s-1} - \eta_1 \times (\Delta \text{ASR}), & \text{if } \Delta \text{ASR} > \Delta_{\text{th}}, \\ \alpha_{s-1} + \eta_2 \times (|\Delta \text{ASR}|), & \text{if } |\Delta \text{ASR}| \leq \Delta_{\text{th}}, \\ \alpha_{s-1}, \quad U_s = U_{s-1}, & \text{if } \Delta \text{ASR} < -\Delta_{\text{th}}. \end{cases} \tag{12}$$

where Δ_{th} represents a predefined threshold that distinguishes significant changes in ASR, η_1 and η_2 are adjustment rates that determine the magnitude of adjustments, and U_s denotes the backdoor training set at iteration s.

- When the ASR increases significantly ($\Delta \text{ASR} > \Delta_{\text{th}}$), the update ratio α is proportionally reduced based on the increase in ASR. This ensures that high-contribution samples are retained, preventing excessive replacement.
- When the change in ASR is insignificant ($|\Delta \text{ASR}| \leq \Delta_{\text{th}}$), the update ratio α increases proportionally according to the magnitude of the variation in ASR. This enhances exploration and mitigates the risk of being trapped in a local optimum.
- When the ASR decreases significantly ($\Delta \text{ASR} < -\Delta_{\text{th}}$), the poisoned sample set is immediately reverted to the previous iteration ($U_s = U_{s-1}$). This rollback mechanism helps restore attack effectiveness, which may have been compromised due to the removal of high-contribution samples.

We maintain an index of the poisoned samples for each iteration and ultimately select the sample set corresponding to the highest ASR as the final poisoning set. This strategy effectively balances exploration and exploitation by adaptively adjusting the update ratio of poisoned samples, leading to improved attack performance. We summarized the overall process of our attack framework in Algorithm 1.

Algorithm 1. Our backdoor attack framework

Input: Clean training set $\mathcal{D}_{\text{clean}}$, Poisoning rate p, Initial filter ratio α_0, Threshold Δ_{th}, Adjustment rates η_1, η_2, Max iterations S, Target class y_t
Output: Constructed poisoned training set $\mathcal{U}$

\# **Data Augmentation-based Triggers**
1: Generate poisoned sample pool $\mathcal{D}_{\text{poisoned}} \leftarrow \{(\text{augmentation}(G_i), y_t) \mid G_i \in \mathcal{D}_{\text{clean}}\}$ from topology-level or feature-level augmentation strategy
\# **Dynamic poisoned sample selection**
2: Initialize backdoor training set U from $\mathcal{D}_{\text{clean}}$ and $U' \leftarrow p \cdot \mathcal{D}_{\text{poisoned}}$
3: **for** $s = 1$ to S **do**
4:    Train model on U, record forgetting count $\{F_1, ..., F_n\}$ via Eq. 10
5:    Compute ASR_s and then calculate ΔASR via Eq. 11
6:    update filter ratio α_s via Eq. 12
7:    Sort U' by descending F_n
8:    Filter $\alpha_s \cdot |U'|$ samples with lowest F_n
9:    Randomly replenish same number from $\mathcal{D}_{\text{poisoned}} \setminus U'$
10:   update backdoor training set U
11: **end for**

5 Experiments

5.1 Experimental Setup

Datasets. We conduct experiments on four widely used graph classification datasets: PROTEINS, NCI1, Mutagenicity and ENZYMES. We split each dataset into 75% for training, 5% for validation, and 20% for testing. We summarize the key statistics of the datasets used in our experiments in Table 2.

Evaluation Metrics. We assess the effectiveness and evasiveness of our attack using the following two key metrics:

- **ASR**: The percentage of instances in the test set, originally belonging to non-target classes, that are successfully misclassified into the target class after embedding the backdoor trigger.
- **CAD**: The decrease in accuracy on clean test samples compared to a model trained without poisoning.

Hyperparameter Settings. We utilize two GNNs (GCN and GIN), each configured with a two-layers structure and ReLU activation function. The models are trained using the Adam optimizer with a learning rate of 0.01 and a weight decay of 5e-4. The maximum number of training epochs is set to 100, with an early stopping mechanism (patience=10) to prevent overfitting. During training, we use a batch size of 32 and apply a dropout rate of 0.1 for regularization. Table 3 shows the clean model accuracy of GCN and GIN on different datasets.

For the backdoor attack, we set the poisoning rate to 10%. In Data Augmentation Strategy 1, we set k = 2. In Strategy 2, the edge removal probability p_e is set to 0.8. In Strategy 3, we select the bottom 30% of nodes based on degree

Table 2. Summary of benchmark datasets.

Dataset	Graphs	Avg. Nodes	Avg. Edges	Classes
NCI1	4,110	29.8	32.3	2
PROTEINS	1,113	39.1	72.8	2
Mutagenicity	4,337	30.3	30.8	2
ENZYMES	600	32.6	62.1	6

Table 3. Clean model accuracy of GCN and GIN

Dataset	GCN	GIN
PROTEINS	0.7130	0.7264
NCI1	0.7251	0.7615
Mutagenicity	0.7707	0.8099
ENZYMES	0.3583	0.3833

centrality, and 15% of their features are masked. For the poisoned sample selection mechanism, we set the initial α to 0.5, the number of iterations S to 40, the ASR rollback threshold Δ_{th} to 0.05, and the adjustment rates η_1 and η_2 to 1.

For the baseline methods we compared, we adopt the parameter configuration specified in their original implementation.

Baseline Methods. Subgraph [21]: This method inserts a randomly generated fixed subgraph into a subset of training samples and assigns them to a target label. The trigger subgraph remains consistent across all poisoned samples. **Motif** [22]: This method utilizes frequent subgraph motifs as triggers, making them more naturally embedded in real-world datasets. **TRAP** [19]: TRAP flips edges in poisoned samples based on meta-gradients to create imperceptible perturbations that influence model predictions. **GTA** [15]: This method generates adversarial subgraphs using neural networks and injects them into poisoned samples, enhancing the attack's flexibility while maintaining stealthiness.

Our approach is named **Ours-Cos** when utilizing the first data augmentation strategy, **Ours-Deg** for the second, and **Ours-Mas** for the third.

5.2 Overall Performance of Backdoor Attacks

We use GCN as the backdoor model for trigger injection and sample selection. To evaluate our method, we measure the ASR and CAD on GCN models with the same architecture, representing a white-box attack scenario. Additionally, we assess the transferability of our attack by testing it on GIN models, which correspond to black-box attack settings.

Table 4 presents the experimental results. Among our three proposed strategies, Ours-Cos and Ours-Deg consistently achieve the highest ASR, while maintaining competitive or even lower CAD compared to baseline methods. This indicates that our method achieves better attack performance with comparable evasiveness to the baseline.

In comparison, Ours Cos has a slightly higher CAD, while Ours Deg achieves a better balance between ASR and CAD. Ours-Mas, which perturbs features rather than structure, shows the lowest ASR among our three strategies but still surpasses some baselines like Subgraph Backdoor and TRAP. This result suggests that structural perturbations are more effective than feature perturbations

Table 4. Comparison of Attack Performance on GCN and GIN.

Method	PROTEINS		NCI1		Mutagenicity		ENZYMES	
	ASR	CAD	ASR	CAD	ASR	CAD	ASR	CAD
Results on GCN								
Subgraph Backdoor	0.7263	0.0035	0.7288	0.0011	0.7698	0.0046	0.5254	**0.0083**
Motif	0.8842	0.0538	0.9733	0.0213	0.8544	0.0196	0.7288	0.0167
TRAP	0.8421	0.0179	0.8305	0.0284	0.8148	0.0276	0.6779	0.0250
GTA	0.8211	-0.0069	0.9612	0.0314	0.8968	0.0104	0.6949	0.0167
Ours-Cos	0.9474	0.0483	0.9758	0.0257	**0.9735**	0.0419	**0.8305**	0.0416
Ours-Deg	**0.9578**	0.0046	**0.9831**	0.0049	0.9656	−0.0081	0.7966	**0.0083**
Ours-Mas	0.9263	0.0404	0.9346	0.0173	0.9497	0.0150	0.7457	0.0167
Results on GIN								
Subgraph Backdoor	0.7215	−0.0011	0.7275	0.0018	0.7751	0.0042	0.5084	0.0083
Motif	0.8813	0.0571	0.9735	0.0199	0.8518	0.0191	0.7118	0.0167
TRAP	0.8401	0.0134	0.8306	0.0271	0.8201	0.0275	0.6613	0.0333
GTA	0.8184	0.0028	0.9686	0.0804	0.8941	0.0121	0.8779	0.0250
Ours-Cos	0.9443	0.0458	0.9782	0.0346	**0.9682**	0.0562	**0.8805**	0.0416
Ours-Deg	**0.9539**	0.0092	**0.9806**	0.0064	**0.9682**	0.0099	0.7796	**0.0083**
Ours-Mas	0.9225	0.0377	0.9370	0.0157	0.9523	0.0162	0.7288	0.0167

in attacking graph models, likely due to the greater impact of structural changes on model behavior.

Among the baseline methods, Motif and GTA perform well in ASR, while TRAP and Subgraph Backdoor exhibit moderate performance, indicating that the model does not effectively learn strong trigger patterns from these methods. However, due to its relatively moderate attack performance, its CAD is also correspondingly lower.

An interesting observation is that some methods, such as GTA, Subgraph Backdoor, and Ours-Deg, achieve negative CAD values on certain datasets. This indicates that, in some cases, the poisoned model slightly improves rather than degrades the clean accuracy. This phenomenon may be due to the way poisoned samples shift the decision boundary, inadvertently leading to a regularization effect that enhances model generalization.

5.3 Impact of Poisoning Rate

To analyze the impact of varying poisoning rates on the ASR, we evaluate three attack strategies of the GCN model on the NCI1 dataset under seven different poisoning rates: 0.02, 0.04, 0.06, 0.08, 0.10, 0.12, and 0.14. The experimental results are presented in Fig. 4.

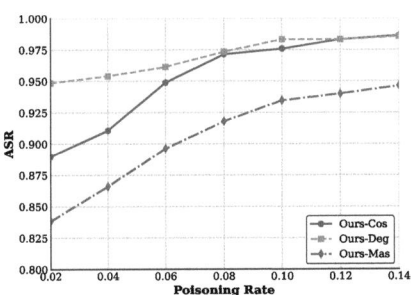 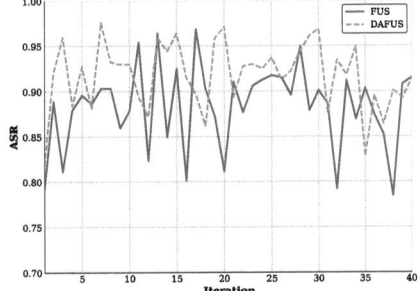

Fig. 4. Sensitivity of ASR to different poisoning rates.

Fig. 5. Sensitivity of ASR to different sample selection strategies.

As expected, increasing the poisoning rate consistently improves the ASR for all attack strategies. This is because a higher poisoning rate introduces more backdoored samples into the training process, allowing the model to learn the trigger pattern more effectively.

Among the three strategies, Ours-Deg demonstrates the best overall performance. Even at a low poisoning rate of 0.02, it maintains a high attack success rate, and as the poisoning rate increases, its ASR stabilizes, indicating its robustness in embedding backdoor triggers efficiently.

Ours-Cos performs slightly worse than Ours-Deg at lower poisoning rates but exhibits a rapid improvement as the poisoning rate increases. At 0.14, its ASR surpasses Ours-Deg, suggesting that cosine similarity-based modifications provide a more scalable and consistent impact across different contamination levels. Ours-Mas consistently shows the lowest ASR across all poisoning rates but follows an upward trend, indicating that feature-masking-based backdoors are effective, albeit requiring a higher poisoning rate to achieve performance comparable to structure-based triggers.

Notably, even at lower poisoning rates, our three attack strategies outperform some baseline methods at a 0.10 poisoning rate in Table 4, particularly TRAP and Subgraph Backdoor. This is attributed to our sample selection mechanism, which ensures that even with a low poisoning rate, only the most impactful samples are chosen for poisoning, thereby maintaining high ASR. This selective approach enables our method to achieve effective backdoor attacks with fewer poisoned samples, improving stealthiness while preserving attack performance.

5.4 Ablation Experiment

Impact of Poisoned Sample Selection Strategy. To evaluate the impact of different sample selection strategies on attack performance, we conducted experiments using three approaches: DAFUS, FUS, and Random Selection. Cosine similarity-based edge modifications from Strategy 1 were employed as the backdoor trigger. We measured their ASR performance on both GCN and GIN

Table 5. Comparison of ASR under different sample selection strategies

Sample Selection Strategy	PROTEINS		NCI1		Mutagenicity		ENZYMES	
	GCN	GIN	GCN	GIN	GCN	GIN	GCN	GIN
DAFUS	**0.9474**	**0.9443**	**0.9758**	**0.9782**	**0.9735**	**0.9682**	**0.8305**	**0.8805**
FUS	0.9023	0.8910	0.9104	0.9507	0.9456	0.9332	0.8105	0.8223
RANDOM	0.8761	0.8654	0.8886	0.9065	0.8924	0.8801	0.7967	0.7839

Table 6. Comparison of ASR under different Trigger

Augmentation Strategy	PROTEINS		NCI1		Mutagenicity		ENZYMES	
	GCN	GIN	GCN	GIN	GCN	GIN	GCN	GIN
Ours-Cos	0.9474	0.9443	0.9758	0.9782	**0.9735**	**0.9682**	**0.8305**	**0.8805**
Ours-Deg	**0.9578**	**0.9539**	**0.9831**	**0.9806**	0.9656	**0.9682**	0.7966	0.7796
Ours-Mas	0.9263	0.9225	0.9346	0.9370	0.9497	0.9523	0.7457	0.7288
Random-Edge	0.7676	0.7701	0.7789	0.7251	0.7265	0.6853	0.5103	0.5397
Random-Mask	0.6135	0.5846	0.5122	0.5346	0.6154	0.6452	0.4922	0.4135

models, with the results summarized in Table 5. DAFUS consistently outperforms both FUS and RANDOM. Compared to RANDOM, DAFUS improves ASR by 3.4%–9.7%, while FUS achieves an ASR improvement of 1.4%–5.3%. This demonstrates that forgetting-event-based poisoned sample selection effectively identifies more impactful poisoned samples for backdoor attacks. Furthermore, DAFUS outperforms FUS by an additional 2.0%–6.5%, highlighting that our dynamic adjustment mechanism enhances the efficiency and effectiveness of selecting critical samples.

Figure 5 illustrates the differences between FUS and DAFUS during iterations. As observed, FUS exhibits irregular fluctuations, with ASR varying unpredictably. In contrast, DAFUS employs a dynamic update rate and effectively rolls back samples when the attack success rate declines. This adaptive mechanism enables DAFUS to efficiently select the most relevant poisoned sample set based on real-time sample performance.

Impact of Data Augmentation Methods. To evaluate the effectiveness of our proposed data augmentation-based backdoor trigger, we compare it with two baseline augmentation strategies: Random-Edge (randomly modifying edges) and Random Feature Masking (randomly selecting nodes and applying random feature masks). The hyperparameter settings for these two baselines match those of Ours-Cos and Ours-Mas, respectively. All methods adopt the DAFUS strategy.

From the results in Table 6, we observe that our proposed backdoor attacks, based on three different data augmentation strategies, consistently outperform

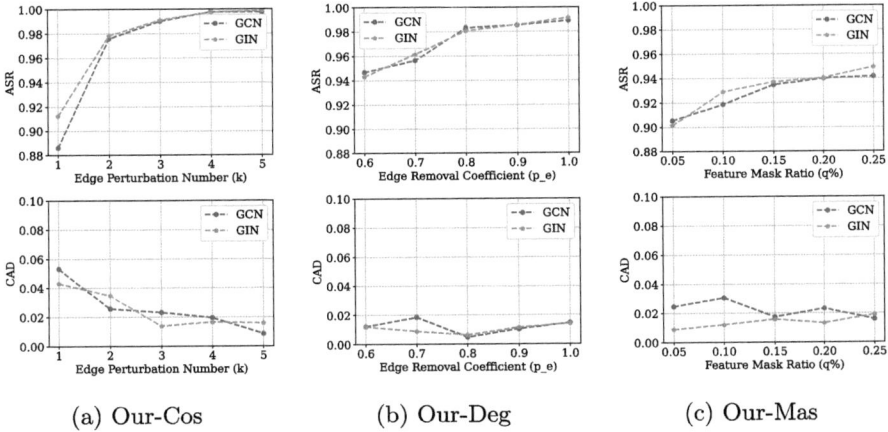

(a) Our-Cos (b) Our-Deg (c) Our-Mas

Fig. 6. Comparison of Different trigger parameters.

all baseline methods. This demonstrates that our data augmentation-based triggers effectively embed the trigger pattern into the model.

5.5 Impact of Trigger Parameters

In this section, we analyze the impact of trigger parameters (i.e., the amplitude of perturbation on a single sample) on experimental results. We conducted this experiment on the NCI1 dataset.

In Fig. 6, it can be observed that the ASR of the three methods exhibits a relatively consistent trend. Specifically, when the perturbation magnitude on the graph structure is small, the ASR remains relatively low. As the perturbation increases, the ASR rises rapidly in the initial stage and then gradually stabilizes. In contrast, the CAD does not follow a uniform pattern between the three methods. In most experimental settings, the CAD remains below 0.05, suggesting that these methods achieve high attack success rates while exerting minimal impact on the classification performance of clean samples.

6 Conclusion

This paper proposes a novel backdoor attack framework for graph classification. Our method introduces three alternative augmentation strategies and designs a sample selection mechanism to enhance attack efficiency and stealthiness.

Comprehensive experiments on four benchmark datasets demonstrate that our method outperforms existing backdoor attacks. Our approach achieves a higher ASR while maintaining a relatively low CAD. Among our three trigger strategies, Ours-Deg consistently balances ASR and CAD.

Overall, our study highlights the vulnerability of graph classification models to data augmentation-based backdoor attacks. Future work will focus on refining augmentation strategies and exploring more effective sample selection techniques to further improve attack efficiency and stealthiness.

Acknowledgment. This research was funded by the National Key R&D Program of China (Grant No.2024YFE0209000), the NSFC (Grant No.U23B2019).

Disclosure of Interests. The authors have no competing interests to declare that are relevant to the content of this article.

References

1. Bi, B., Zhang, Z., Qiao, P., Yuan, Y., Wang, G.: FedSig: a federated graph augmentation for class-imbalanced node classification. In: International Conference on Database Systems for Advanced Applications, pp. 474–490. Springer (2024)
2. Corso, G., Stark, H., Jegelka, S., Jaakkola, T., Barzilay, R.: Graph neural networks. Nature Rev. Meth. Prim. **4**(1), 17 (2024)
3. Dai, E., Lin, M., Zhang, X., Wang, S.: Unnoticeable backdoor attacks on graph neural networks. In: Proceedings of the ACM Web Conference 2023, pp. 2263–2273 (2023)
4. Ding, K., Xu, Z., Tong, H., Liu, H.: Data augmentation for deep graph learning: a survey. ACM SIGKDD Expl. Newsl **24**(2), 61–77 (2022)
5. Ianni, M., Masciari, E., Sperlí, G.: A survey of big data dimensions vs social networks analysis. J. Intell. Info. Syst. **57**, 73–100 (2021)
6. Katharopoulos, A., Fleuret, F.: Not all samples are created equal: deep learning with importance sampling. In: International Conference on Machine Learning, pp. 2525–2534. PMLR (2018)
7. Li, Y., Jiang, Y., Li, Z., Xia, S.T.: Backdoor learning: a survey. IEEE Trans. Neural Netw. Learn. Syst. **35**(1), 5–22 (2022)
8. Liu, Y., Ma, X., Bailey, J., Lu, F.: Reflection backdoor: a natural backdoor attack on deep neural networks. In: Vedaldi, A., Bischof, H., Brox, T., Frahm, J.-M. (eds.) ECCV 2020. LNCS, vol. 12355, pp. 182–199. Springer, Cham (2020). https://doi.org/10.1007/978-3-030-58607-2_11
9. Qiao, P., et al.: Tag: joint triple-hierarchical attention and GCN for review-based social recommender system. IEEE Trans. Knowl. Data Eng. **35**(10), 9904–9919 (2022)
10. Richards, A.L., Eckhardt, M., Krogan, N.J.: Mass spectrometry-based protein-protein interaction networks for the study of human diseases. Mol. Syst. Biol. **17**(1), e8792 (2021)
11. Rodríguez-Pérez, R., Bajorath, J.: Evolution of support vector machine and regression modeling in chemoinformatics and drug discovery. J. Comput. Aided Mol. Des. **36**(5), 355–362 (2022)
12. Sui, Y., et al.: A simple data augmentation for graph classification: a perspective of equivariance and invariance. ACM Trans. Knowl. Discov. Data **19**(2), 1–24 (2025)
13. Toneva, M., Sordoni, A., Combes, R.T.d., Trischler, A., Bengio, Y., Gordon, G.J.: An empirical study of example forgetting during deep neural network learning. arXiv preprint arXiv:1812.05159 (2018)
14. Wu, L., Cui, P., Pei, J., Zhao, L., Guo, X.: Graph neural networks: foundation, frontiers and applications. In: Proceedings of the 28th ACM SIGKDD Conference on Knowledge Discovery and Data Mining, pp. 4840–4841 (2022)

15. Xi, Z., Pang, R., Ji, S., Wang, T.: Graph backdoor. In: 30th USENIX Security Symposium (USENIX Security 21), pp. 1523–1540 (2021)
16. Xia, P., Li, Z., Zhang, W., Li, B.: Data-efficient backdoor attacks. arXiv preprint arXiv:2204.12281 (2022)
17. Xia, X.: Bioinformatics and drug discovery. Curr. Top. Med. Chem. **17**(15), 1709–1726 (2017)
18. Xu, J., Xue, M., Picek, S.: Explainability-based backdoor attacks against graph neural networks. In: Proceedings of the 3rd ACM Workshop on Wireless Security and Machine Learning, pp. 31–36 (2021)
19. Yang, S., et al.: Transferable graph backdoor attack. In: Proceedings of the 25th International Symposium on Research in Attacks, Intrusions and Defenses, pp. 321–332 (2022)
20. Zeng, Y., Park, W., Mao, Z.M., Jia, R.: Rethinking the backdoor attacks' triggers: a frequency perspective. In: Proceedings of the IEEE/CVF International Conference on Computer Vision, pp. 16473–16481 (2021)
21. Zhang, Z., Jia, J., Wang, B., Gong, N.Z.: Backdoor attacks to graph neural networks. In: Proceedings of the 26th ACM Symposium on Access Control Models and Technologies, pp. 15–26 (2021)
22. Zheng, H., Xiong, H., Chen, J., Ma, H., Huang, G.: Motif-backdoor: rethinking the backdoor attack on graph neural networks via motifs. IEEE Trans. Comput. Soc. Syst. **11**(2), 2479–2493 (2023)
23. Zhu, Y., Xu, Y., Yu, F., Liu, Q., Wu, S., Wang, L.: Graph contrastive learning with adaptive augmentation. In: Proceedings of the Web Conference 2021, pp. 2069–2080 (2021)

Healthcare and Bioinformatics

A CNN-Based Local-Global Self-attention via Averaged Window Embeddings for Hierarchical ECG Analysis

Arthur Buzelin[✉], Pedro Dutenhefner, Turi Rezende, Luisa G. Porfirio, Pedro Bento, Yan Aquino, Jose Fernandes, Caio Santana, Gabriela Miana, Gisele L. Pappa, Antonio Ribeiro, and Wagner Meira Jr.

Universidade Federal de Minas Gerais, Belo Horizonte, Brazil
{buzelin,turirezende,pedro.bento,yanaquino,caiosantana}@dcc.ufmg.br,
{pedroroblesduten,luisagont,josegeraldof}@ufmg.br, tom@hc.ufmg.br,
{glpappa,meira}@dcc.ufmg.br

Abstract. The high global mortality from cardiovascular diseases underscores the need for efficient diagnostic tools such as electrocardiograms (ECGs). Recent deep learning advances have greatly improved ECG analysis by capturing complex and informative patterns from the signals. CNNs remain the dominant architecture for this task, while transformers—despite their success in other domains—have yet to become the leading approach in ECG analysis. A key limitation is their difficulty in capturing local morphological features essential for accurate interpretation. In this regard, we propose a novel Local-Global Attention ECG model (LGA-ECG), which integrates convolutional inductive biases with global self-attention mechanisms. Our approach extracts queries by averaging embeddings obtained from overlapping convolutional windows, enabling fine-grained morphological analysis, while simultaneously modeling global context through attention to keys and values derived from the entire sequence. Experiments conducted on the CODE-15 dataset demonstrate that LGA-ECG outperforms state-of-the-art models and ablation studies validate the effectiveness of the local-global attention strategy. By capturing the hierarchical temporal dependencies and morphological patterns in ECG signals, this new design showcases its potential for clinical deployment with robust automated ECG classification PyTorch Implementation: https://github.com/pedroroblesduten/LGA-ECG.

Keywords: Electrocardiogram (ECG) · Transformer Model · Convolution · Classification · Local-global attention

1 Introduction

Cardiovascular diseases (CVDs) remain the leading cause of death globally, responsible for 17.9 million deaths in 2019, which corresponds to 32% of all

---
A. Buzelin, P. Dutenhefner, and T. Rezende—Equal contribution.

deaths worldwide, as reported by the World Health Organization (WHO) [19]. In light of this, electrocardiograms (ECGs), which are non-invasive and easy-to-perform examinations, are fundamental tools in the detection and monitoring of heart-related conditions. Their importance has only grown with the rise of digital health technologies [10]. In this context, artificial intelligence has become a valuable resource for automating ECG analysis, supporting clinical decision-making, reducing backlogs in telemedicine services, and enabling automated tasks such as disease classification [3], age estimation [9], and wave segmentation [5].

The rise of deep learning has transformed ECG signal analysis, with deep neural networks (DNNs) excelling in automatic feature extraction from raw ECG data, eliminating the need for manual engineering. Convolutional neural networks (CNNs) are particularly suited for this task, leveraging inductive biases such as spatial locality and translation equivariance [14, 15]. These properties enable CNNs to capture hierarchical temporal structures in ECG signals, from localized morphological features within heartbeats to global rhythm patterns. Moreover, translation equivariance ensures robust detection of clinically relevant features, regardless of their temporal positions.

Transformer architectures have shown significant success across various domains. However, the direct application of Vision Transformer (ViT)-based models to ECG data faces limitations due to their global attention mechanisms, which fail to adequately capture localized morphological features essential for accurate ECG interpretation. To address this limitation, hierarchical transformer models integrating local self-attention mechanisms have been proposed, demonstrating superior performance in ECG classification tasks [2, 8]. These models leverage the strengths of transformers in modeling temporal relationships while preserving locality bias, crucial for ECG signal interpretation. Building on these developments, this paper introduces a novel transformer architecture specifically tailored for ECG data.

Cardiology experts emphasize that effective ECG models must encompass multiple levels of temporal and contextual information, from individual waveform morphology to the overall rhythm structure [2]. Consequently, combining local feature extraction with global attention mechanisms emerges as a promising strategy for ECG analysis. Motivated by that, we propose a novel hierarchical transformer architecture that leverages overlapping convolutional projections to derive queries from local temporal segments. Specifically, each query vector is computed by averaging convolutional features within overlapping windows, inherently embedding convolutional inductive biases into the self-attention mechanism. These locally informed queries then attend to globally computed key and value vectors, allowing the model to simultaneously capture detailed morphological characteristics (such as waveform shapes and intervals) and broader contextual dependencies (such as inter-beat relationships) within ECG signals.

Our proposed Local-Global Attention ECG model (LGA-ECG) applies local convolutional inductive biases with global self-attention mechanisms, significantly improving ECG classification. Experimental results demonstrate that this hybrid approach outperforms state-of-the-art baseline methods, achieving superior performance in classification tasks.

2 Related Works

In this section, we review prior work on deep learning methods for ECG analysis, focusing on CNN-based approaches, hybrid CNN-transformer architectures, and local attention mechanisms; bridging the gap between local feature extraction and global sequence modeling.

2.1 Neural Networks for ECG

Automatic analysis of ECG signals has been extensively studied, with recent literature emphasizing deep learning methods, particularly Convolutional Neural Networks (CNNs), due to their inherent capacity for autonomously extracting morphological and temporal ECG features from raw data. Rajpurkar et al. [14] pioneered a deep CNN approach trained end-to-end on a large-scale dataset, achieving cardiologist-level accuracy in arrhythmia classification. Similarly, Ribeiro et al. [15] introduced deep neural networks with stacked convolutions, demonstrating strong generalization capabilities across multi-lead ECG data and surpassing cardiologist-level performance. Wang et al. [18] proposed a CNN-BiLSTM model for atrial fibrillation classification, using CNNs for morphology and BiLSTMs for temporal dependencies in ECG signals.

Recently, transformer-based architectures have increasingly been applied to ECG analysis, motivated by their success in sequence modeling tasks. Both Hu et al. [7] and El et al. [4] proposed hybrid CNN-Transformer approaches, where convolutional layers initially extract local morphological features, followed by transformer-based self-attention layers that model global temporal interactions. Building on [11], Liu et al.[8] proposed BaT, a beat-aligned framework leveraging local attention to process ECG signals progressively. BaT segments ECGs into beats, applying self-attention locally before merging representations to capture hierarchical features. However, it depends on complex preprocessing, where inaccuracies in beat segmentation may introduce biases or errors. Additionally, Dutenhefner et al. [2] proposed an approach that interleaves CNN and transformer blocks to create a hierarchical, multi-scale feature extraction pipeline.

2.2 Local Attention

Local attention mechanisms combine the modeling capabilities of self-attention with the structured inductive biases of convolution, benefiting tasks with spatial and sequential dependencies. Liu et al. [11] introduced the Swin Transformer, which improves efficiency through hierarchical local attention with shifting windows. However, its non-overlapping windows limit direct global context modeling, which is crucial for ECG analysis.

CoAtNet [1] addresses this problem by integrating convolutional inductive biases with global transformers via multi-scale relative attention. While effective, its predefined branches reduce flexibility and increase computational complexity. Similarly, Zhou et al. [20] introduced ELSA, enhancing local feature extraction with Hadamard attention and a ghost head module.

Building upon these strengths and addressing the limitations identified in previous works, the approach we propose introduces a novel local-global attention mechanism designed for ECG signals. Our method efficiently captures both local morphological variations and long-range dependencies while mitigating the computational burden. By leveraging adaptive attention windows and progressive feature aggregation, our approach also enhances ECG feature representation.

3 Methods

ECG analysis requires capturing information across multiple temporal scales: wave morphology (P, QRS, T), intra-heartbeat intervals (PR, QT), and inter-beat distances essential for rhythm analysis. We propose a novel self-attention mechanism tailored for ECG signals, which effectively balances fine-grained morphological details with global heartbeat patterns.

The proposed model first uses convolutional layers to project the ECG into an embedding space. Its core comprises layers of a novel windowed self-attention and feed-forward blocks with residual connections. Unlike traditional global self-attention, our method extracts queries (Q) from small overlapping windows to preserve local detail, while keys (K) and values (V) are computed globally, capturing long-range dependencies. Additionally, each self-attention block progressively reduces the sequence length, similar to convolutional pooling, allowing hierarchical abstraction from local waveform characteristics toward global rhythm and beat-to-beat features.

3.1 Local-Global Self-attention

The core innovation of our proposed transformer-based architecture lies in its novel local-global self-attention mechanism. Traditional self-attention mechanisms compute interactions uniformly across all tokens, which may overlook crucial local patterns in biomedical signals. In contrast, our method balances fine-grained local feature extraction and broader temporal context modeling.

Let us formally define the input tensor to this attention mechanism as $\mathbf{X}$, with dimensions:
$$\mathbf{X} \in \mathbb{R}^{B \times N \times D}, \tag{1}$$
where B is the batch size, N the sequence length, and D the embedding dimension.

Step 1: Normalization. First, we apply a standard layer normalization along the embedding dimension to stabilize and normalize the input:
$$\tilde{\mathbf{X}} = \text{LayerNorm}(\mathbf{X}), \quad \tilde{\mathbf{X}} \in \mathbb{R}^{B \times N \times D}. \tag{2}$$

Step 2: Local Windowed Query Generation. To effectively capture precise wave-level morphological details from ECG signals, we introduce a local window-based query generation strategy. Starting from the normalized input tensor $\tilde{\mathbf{X}} \in \mathbb{R}^{B \times N \times D}$, we extract a series of overlapping windows along the temporal dimension to form localized queries (**Q**).

Formally, given a window length l and stride s, we extract M overlapping windows from the sequence, where:

$$M = \left\lfloor \frac{N-l}{s} \right\rfloor + 1. \tag{3}$$

For each window indexed by $i \in \{0, 1, \ldots, M-1\}$, we select a contiguous subset of the input sequence:

$$\tilde{\mathbf{X}}^{(i)} = \tilde{\mathbf{X}}\left[:, (i \cdot s) : (i \cdot s + l), :\right], \quad \tilde{\mathbf{X}}^{(i)} \in \mathbb{R}^{B \times l \times D}. \tag{4}$$

Next, each extracted window $\tilde{\mathbf{X}}^{(i)}$ undergoes a convolutional projection along the temporal dimension. Specifically, we apply a 1D convolution with kernel size k_q, stride 1, padding p_q, and D output channels, obtaining:

$$\mathbf{Q}_{\text{conv}}^{(i)} = \text{Conv1D}_Q\left(\tilde{\mathbf{X}}^{(i)}\right), \quad \mathbf{Q}_{\text{conv}}^{(i)} \in \mathbb{R}^{B \times D \times l}. \tag{5}$$

The output $\mathbf{Q}_{\text{conv}}^{(i)}$ represents an enhanced embedding of the original local window, where each temporal position within the window has been projected into a new feature space through convolution.

To summarize this detailed local information into a single representative query vector per window, we then average these embeddings along the temporal dimension of length l. For each window i, the averaged query vector is calculated as:

$$\mathbf{Q}^{(i)} = \frac{1}{l}\sum_{t=1}^{l}\mathbf{Q}_{\text{conv}}^{(i)}[:,:,t], \quad \mathbf{Q}^{(i)} \in \mathbb{R}^{B \times D}. \tag{6}$$

Finally, stacking all the averaged queries across the M extracted windows results in the complete query tensor for attention:

$$\mathbf{Q} = \left[\mathbf{Q}^{(0)}, \mathbf{Q}^{(1)}, \ldots, \mathbf{Q}^{(M-1)}\right], \quad \mathbf{Q} \in \mathbb{R}^{B \times M \times D}. \tag{7}$$

To enhance stability and facilitate residual connections in deeper layers, we retain a copy of the query tensor as a residual term. This preserves local morphological details captured by convolution, ensuring stable gradients and improved convergence.

This process can be implemented in a simple and effective manner using a combination of a 1D convolutional layer that preserves the input shape, followed by an average pooling layer. The kernel size of the pooling operation determines the temporal compression factor. This approach is illustrated in Fig. 1.

Step 3: Global Key and Value Generation. In contrast to the localized queries, keys (**K**) and values (**V**) are computed from the entire normalized

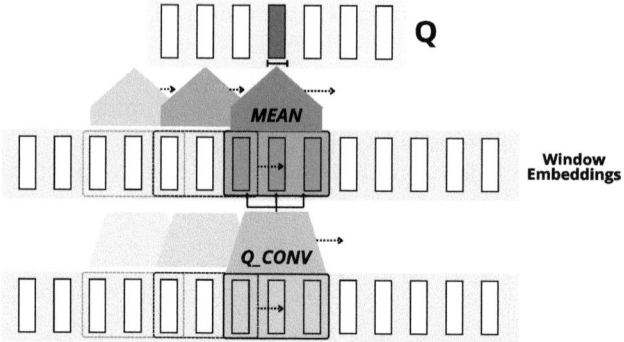

Fig. 1. Mean query extraction process for each ECG window.

sequence, enabling each local query to attend globally. We define these global projections using convolutional layers to retain a locality inductive bias while still allowing global context modeling:

$$\mathbf{K}_{\text{conv}} = \text{Conv1D}_K(\tilde{\mathbf{X}}), \quad \mathbf{V}_{\text{conv}} = \text{Conv1D}_V(\tilde{\mathbf{X}}), \tag{8}$$

both producing tensors of shape:

$$\mathbf{K}_{\text{conv}}, \mathbf{V}_{\text{conv}} \in \mathbb{R}^{B \times D \times N}. \tag{9}$$

We permute them back to match the original embedding format:

$$\mathbf{K} = \mathbf{K}_{\text{conv}}^\top \in \mathbb{R}^{B \times N \times D}, \quad \mathbf{V} = \mathbf{V}_{\text{conv}}^\top \in \mathbb{R}^{B \times N \times D}. \tag{10}$$

Step 4: Multi-Head Local-Global (LG) Attention Computation. We now apply a multi-head attention mechanism. For H attention heads, we split the embedding dimension D into H sub-dimensions of size $D_h = D/H$:

$$\mathbf{Q}_h \in \mathbb{R}^{B \times M \times D_h}, \quad \mathbf{K}_h, \mathbf{V}_h \in \mathbb{R}^{B \times N \times D_h}, \quad h = 1, \ldots, H. \tag{11}$$

For each head h, the scaled dot-product attention scores are computed as:

$$\mathbf{A}_h = \text{softmax}\left(\frac{\mathbf{Q}_h \mathbf{K}_h^\top}{\sqrt{D_h}}\right) \in \mathbb{R}^{B \times M \times N}. \tag{12}$$

Subsequently, we calculate the features as a weighted sum of values:

$$\mathbf{O}_h = \mathbf{A}_h \mathbf{V}_h \in \mathbb{R}^{B \times M \times D_h}. \tag{13}$$

Concatenating across all heads, we get the combined multi-head attention output:

$$\mathbf{O} = \text{concat}(\mathbf{O}_1, \ldots, \mathbf{O}_H) \in \mathbb{R}^{B \times M \times D}. \tag{14}$$

Step 5: Residual Connection and Sequence Reduction. Finally, we reintroduce the residual query information by adding back the previously stored queries $\mathbf{Q}_{\text{res}}$, maintaining strong local fidelity:

$$\mathbf{Y} = \mathbf{O} + \mathbf{Q}_{\text{res}}, \quad \mathbf{Y} \in \mathbb{R}^{B \times M \times D}. \tag{15}$$

The sequence length is effectively reduced from N to M by selecting a stride $s = 2$, ensuring $M = N/2$. This hierarchical summarization progressively condenses ECG features, capturing local and global information.

Our LG self-attention combines standard self-attention, convolution, and hierarchical transformers while overcoming their limitations. Unlike traditional self-attention, which lacks locality and scales quadratically, or convolutions, which struggle with long-range dependencies, our method extracts locally-informed queries via overlapping convolutional projections while maintaining global attention through sequence-wide keys and values. Additionally, convolutional projections inherently encode positional information, removing the need for explicit positional encodings. The local-global attentions is illustrated in Fig. 2.

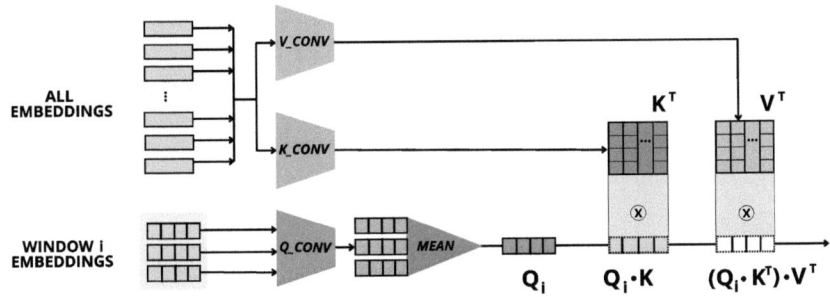

Fig. 2. Local-global self-attention operation for one ECG embedding window.

3.2 Transformer Block with Local-Global Self-attention

The Transformer Block integrates the local-global self-attention mechanism within a standard transformer architecture. It consists of two sub-layers: LGA and a feed-forward network, both with layer normalization and residual connections for stable training.

Given an input tensor $\mathbf{X} \in \mathbb{R}^{B \times N \times D}$, where B is the batch size, N is the sequence length, and D is the embedding dimension, the Transformer Block initially applies layer normalization along the embedding dimension:

$$\tilde{\mathbf{X}} = \text{LayerNorm}(\mathbf{X}), \quad \tilde{\mathbf{X}} \in \mathbb{R}^{B \times N \times D}. \tag{16}$$

Subsequently, the normalized sequence is processed by the local-global self-attention layer. Due to the windowed attention design, the spatial dimension N is effectively reduced approximately by half, from N to $M = N/2$, resulting in an output tensor $\mathbf{Y}_{\text{attn}}$:

$$\mathbf{Y}_{\text{attn}} = \text{LocalGlobalAttention}(\tilde{\mathbf{X}}), \quad \mathbf{Y}_{\text{attn}} \in \mathbb{R}^{B \times M \times D}. \tag{17}$$

To maintain a consistent residual connection despite the reduction in sequence length, we apply a pooling operation followed by a 1×1 convolution to the normalized input $\tilde{\mathbf{X}}$, ensuring dimensional compatibility:

$$\mathbf{X}_{\text{res}} = \text{Conv1D}\left(\text{MaxPool1D}\left(\tilde{\mathbf{X}}\right)\right), \quad \mathbf{X}_{\text{res}} \in \mathbb{R}^{B \times M \times D}. \tag{18}$$

Here, the max pooling operation reduces the temporal dimension by half, from N to M, while the 1×1 convolution adjusts embedding dimensions and reinforces the residual pathway. The resulting residual tensor $\mathbf{X}_{\text{res}}$ is added to the self-attention output, stabilizing training and enhancing gradient flow:

$$\mathbf{Z} = \mathbf{Y}_{\text{attn}} + \mathbf{X}_{\text{res}}, \quad \mathbf{Z} \in \mathbb{R}^{B \times M \times D}. \tag{19}$$

Next, we apply a second-layer normalization followed by a feed-forward neural network, often called the Multi-Layer Perceptron (MLP). This MLP consists of two linear layers with an intermediate non-linearity (ReLU). The dimensionality of the intermediate MLP layer, denoted as D_{MLP}, dynamically increases at each transformer block stage i, defined explicitly as $D_{\text{MLP}} = D_{\text{base}} \times 2 \times i$. Specifically, the MLP initially projects each embedding vector from the input dimension D to this expanded dimension D_{MLP}:

$$\mathbf{Z}_{\text{MLP}}^{(i)} = \text{ReLU}\left(\mathbf{Z}^{(i)} \mathbf{W}_1^{(i)} + \mathbf{b}_1^{(i)}\right), \quad \mathbf{Z}_{\text{MLP}}^{(i)} \in \mathbb{R}^{B \times M \times (D_{\text{base}} \times 2 \times i)}, \tag{20}$$

and subsequently project it back to the original embedding dimension D:

$$\mathbf{Z}_{\text{out}}^{(i)} = \mathbf{Z}_{\text{MLP}}^{(i)} \mathbf{W}_2^{(i)} + \mathbf{b}_2^{(i)}, \quad \mathbf{Z}_{\text{out}}^{(i)} \in \mathbb{R}^{B \times M \times D}. \tag{21}$$

This incremental expansion of the MLP dimensionality at successive transformer stages allows the model to progressively capture more complex and abstract features. A second residual connection then integrates the MLP output back into the main pathway, resulting in the final output tensor of each transformer block:

$$\mathbf{X}_{\text{final}}^{(i)} = \mathbf{Z}^{(i)} + \mathbf{Z}_{\text{out}}^{(i)}, \quad \mathbf{X}_{\text{final}}^{(i)} \in \mathbb{R}^{B \times M \times D}. \tag{22}$$

This staged expansion of the MLP dimension allows deeper layers to encode increasingly complex and abstract features, naturally aligning with the progressive shift from fine-grained morphological details to broader, long-range inter-beat relationships.

Each Transformer Block hierarchically condenses and enriches representations, aligning with clinical ECG analysis. Early layers capture fine-grained wave morphology, intermediate layers focus on intra-heartbeat intervals, and deeper layers model long-range dependencies across heartbeats, effectively identifying rhythm abnormalities. This structured progression inherently encodes clinically relevant inductive biases.

3.3 Overall Model Architecture

The overall architecture of the proposed model is illustrated in Fig. 3. It comprises two main components: a convolutional fron-tend and a sequence of transformer blocks equipped with the LGA mechanism. Initially, the multi-scale convolutional front-end transforms the raw ECG signals into a sequence of feature embeddings, capturing localized waveform details while reducing temporal dimensions. Subsequently, these embeddings are processed by a cascade of transformer blocks featuring the proposed local-global self-attention. These blocks hierarchically aggregate ECG features at progressively coarser temporal scales, effectively encoding wave-level morphologies, intra-beat intervals, and inter-beat rhythm relationships into comprehensive representations suitable for ECG analysis.

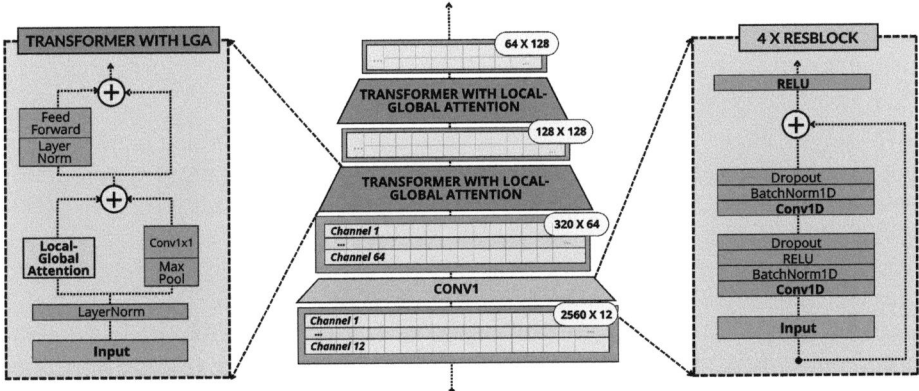

Fig. 3. Overall architecture of the proposed LGA network, integrating the convolutional front-end, composed of four repeated ResBlocks (right), with transformer blocks utilizing local-global self-attention (left).

4 Experiment Setup

4.1 Datasets

Our model was trained and evaluated using CODE-15, a publicly available 15% subset of the CODE (Clinical Outcomes in Digital Electrocardiography) dataset

[16]. CODE contains over 2 million ECGs from Minas Gerais, Brazil, annotated by cardiologists for six cardiac abnormalities: first-degree atrioventricular block (1st AVB), right bundle branch block (RBBB), left bundle branch block (LBBB), sinus bradycardia (SB), atrial fibrillation (AF), and sinus tachycardia (ST). These conditions indicate an increased risk for cardiovascular events, including stroke, heart failure, and sudden death, and require targeted clinical interventions. CODE-15 comprises 345,779 exams from 233,770 patients and has been widely adopted in ECG research, serving as a benchmark dataset for developing and evaluating deep learning models [15] [17].

We evaluated our model using the publicly available CODE-TEST dataset, also collected by the Telehealth Network of Minas Gerais (TNMG). CODE-TEST comprises 827 ECGs labeled by consensus among two or three cardiologists, covering the same six cardiac abnormalities. The high-quality, expert-consensus labels provide a robust benchmark for performance assessment.

For developing and validating the LGA-ECG model, the dataset is divided into four subsets by patient IDs: 90% of CODE-15 is used as the training set to train the model, while 5% of CODE-15 serves as the validation set for early stopping. An additional 5% of CODE-15 is designated as the development set, which is utilized for hyperparameter tuning and ablation studies. Finally, the entire CODE-TEST dataset is used as the test set to evaluate the final model performance against baseline methods.

4.2 Implementation Details and Benchmarks

For comparison, we assessed LGA-ECG against a suite of baseline models spanning diverse architectural families, including traditional CNN and transformer-based architectures. This selection ensured a rigorous and comprehensive evaluation across distinct modeling paradigms. The baselines were implemented using their original authors' codebases, with training settings configured according to their recommendations. All models were trained on the same Training Set and evaluated on the Test Set to ensure consistent comparisons. We employed standard classification metrics to evaluate the models: accuracy, F1-score, precision, and recall. These metrics were computed for each cardiac condition individually to provide a detailed understanding of model performance across different diseases, as well as averaged (macro).

The training process utilized the AdamW optimizer [12] and employed a cosine annealing learning rate schedule [13]. The initial learning rate was set to 0.0001 and was decreased cosine-wise to 0.00001 throughout the training. Additionally, early stopping was implemented, which terminates training if the validation error does not decrease for seven consecutive epochs. The training was conducted in parallel using 4 NVIDIA V100 GPUs.

5 Results

In this section, we analyze our model by comparing its performance to state-of-the-art models in ECG abnormality classification.

Table 1. Average performance of LGA-ECG when compared to other SOTA methods.

Metrics	ResNet-1	ResNet-2	ECG-Transform	BAT	ECG-DETR	HiT	LGA-ECG
Accuracy	0.991	0.989	0.981	0.991	0.9842	0.991	**0.994**
Precision	0.875	0.908	0.711	**0.918**	0.7768	0.909	0.907
Recall	0.778	0.743	0.687	0.799	0.6614	0.798	**0.872**
F1-Score	0.814	0.811	0.677	0.848	0.699	0.841	**0.885**

We first compare our model, LGA-ECG, with state-of-the-art methods for classifying six ECG abnormalities: AVB, RBBB, LBBB, SB, AF, and ST. The evaluated models include ResNet-1 [15], ResNet-2 [6], BAT [8], ECG-DETR [7], and HiT [2]. Due to class imbalance, accuracy may be inflated; thus, recall, precision, and particularly the F1-score will be our primary comparison metrics.

Analyzing recall first, LGA-ECG achieves 0.862, surpassing BAT (0.799) and becoming the first to exceed the 0.8 threshold. This marks a significant improvement in identifying positive cases, which is particularly critical in medical applications, where missing a diagnosis due to low recall (high false negatives) can lead to delayed treatments and severe consequences for patients. However, despite this substantial increase in recall, our model maintains a competitive precision of 0.907 – only slightly lower than BAT's 0.918. This demonstrates that the boost in recall did not come at the cost of a drastic drop in precision, ensuring a balanced performance that enhances overall reliability. This balance underscores its robustness for practical deployment in high-stakes scenarios.

Table 2. Per class F1-score of LGA-ECG and baseline methods in the test set.

Abnormality	ResNet-1	ResNet-2	ECG-Transform	BAT	ECG-DETR	HiT	LGA-ECG
1st AVB	0.661	0.719	0.489	0.689	0.631	0.682	**0.8**
RBBB	**0.924**	0.890	0.909	0.922	0.747	0.886	0.923
LBBB	0.927	0.843	0.886	0.945	0.826	0.909	**0.983**
SB	0.767	0.821	0.535	**0.836**	0.588	0.824	0.778
AF	0.703	0.758	0.478	0.818	0.563	0.833	**0.880**
ST	0.897	0.833	0.763	0.870	0.838	0.914	**0.946**
Avg. F1	0.814	0.811	0.677	0.848	0.699	0.841	**0.885**

Beyond recall and precision, F1-score provides a comprehensive measure of performance by balancing both metrics. LGA-ECG achieves a new record F1-score of 0.885, surpassing BAT, which reached 0.848, ensuring robust classification across all ECG abnormalities. Despite the class imbalance, our model also achieves a higher accuracy, scoring 0.994 compared to 0.991 from the closest competitor (BAT). By outperforming all baseline methods in all metrics, our approach demonstrates superior overall performance in distinguishing abnormal ECG patterns. All comparisons can be seen in Table 1.

Now, focusing solely on the F1-score, we can directly compare performance across different abnormalities. As shown in Table 2, LGA-ECG outperforms the baselines in four categories: ST, LBBB, AF, and 1st AVB. For RBBB, although the F1-score is slightly lower, it remains virtually equivalent to that of ResNet-1. The only class in which our model underperforms is SB. We hypothesize that this occurs due to the model's difficulty in accurately detecting longer intervals between consecutive R peaks (the prominent upward deflections in the ECG that indicate ventricular contractions). Further evaluation is necessary to confirm this limitation and guide appropriate improvements.

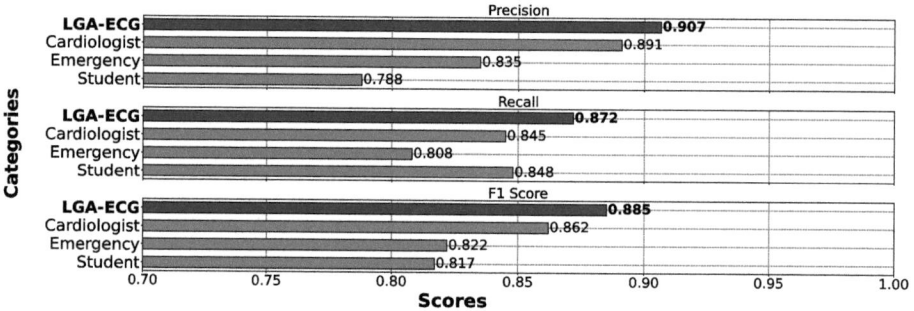

Fig. 4. Comparison of the average Precision, Recall, and F1 Score between the proposed LGA-ECG model and human performance.

The CODE-TEST dataset includes labels provided by cardiologists at different levels of training: (i) 4th-year cardiology residents (cardio.), (ii) 3rd-year emergency residents (emerg.), and (iii) 5th-year medical students (stud.). The reference labels used for calculating the evaluation metrics were determined by consensus among three experienced specialist cardiologists, who were excluded from the analysis. Using this expert consensus as the ground truth, we compared the labels assigned by professionals at different training levels with the predictions generated by the proposed LGA-ECG model. The results, presented in Fig. 4, show that the model outperformed all groups of cardiologists across all key metrics, demonstrating superior performance compared to individuals with varying levels of cardiology expertise.

6 Ablations

To assess the effectiveness of our proposed local-global attention mechanism, we perform a series of ablation studies to isolate its contributions and better understand its impact on ECG feature extraction.

6.1 Alternative Attention Mechanisms

First, we compare the proposed LGA against alternative attention strategies. Our goal is to evaluate how different query, key, and value configurations influence the model's ability to capture fine-grained ECG morphology and global contextual dependencies.

ViT-like: We begin by examining a standard ViT-like approach, which applies global self-attention across the entire sequence using linear projections for queries, keys, and values. While this method captures the global context effectively, it lacks local inductive biases.

Swin-like: Next, we compare our method with a local attention mechanism inspired by Swin Transformer [11], where self-attention is restricted to non-overlapping windows. This approach captures local features while progressively integrating global context through stacked local attention and inter-block pooling.

Global Q, K, V: We also analyze a global attention variant, which follows the standard attention mechanism but replaces linear projections with convolutional and average pooling layers. In this configuration, queries are computed in the same manner as keys and values, ensuring that all positions attend to each other globally. Although this setup preserves global context awareness, it may fail to efficiently encode localized waveform structures.

Local Q, K, V: Finally, we examine a fully localized variant, where the query Q is the mean of the embeddings within a window, while the keys K and values V correspond only to the embeddings of that window, without global context. We extract overlapping windows, ensuring that each window is condensed into a single embedding after the attention operation. This progressively reduces the data by half at each stage, establishing a hierarchical processing framework.

Table 3. Per class F1-score comparison between different attention mechanisms.

Abnormality	ViT-like	Swin-like	Global Q, K, V	Local Q, K, V	LGA-ECG
1st AVB	0.653	0.682	0.809	0.782	**0.800**
RBBB	0.862	0.886	0.925	**0.955**	0.923
LBBB	0.875	0.909	0.909	0.982	**0.983**
SB	0.768	**0.824**	0.733	0.750	0.778
AF	0.792	0.833	0.833	0.782	**0.880**
ST	0.887	0.914	0.870	0.885	**0.946**
Avg. F1	0.806	0.841	0.847	0.856	**0.885**

The results in Table 3 show that LGA-ECG achieves the highest F1-score (0.885), outperforming all alternative attention mechanisms. By integrating local convolutional inductive biases with global context, LGA-ECG surpasses both fully global (ViT-like, global QKV) and fully local (Swin-like, local QKV) approaches, demonstrating superior feature extraction for ECG classification.

6.2 Positional Encoding

We further evaluate whether convolutional biases introduced by the adapted projections sufficiently capture positional information, which is crucial in ECG analysis due to the diagnostic relevance of intervals between waves and heartbeats. Specifically, we investigate three positional encoding strategies:

Absolute Sinusoidal Positional Encoding: Predefined sinusoidal functions of varying frequencies are computed based on absolute positions and directly summed to the embeddings after the convolutional projection, explicitly embedding absolute positional information into each token.

Absolute Learnable Positional Encoding: A trainable embedding vector for each absolute position is learned during training and summed to the embeddings immediately after convolutional projection, enabling the model to adaptively capture position-specific patterns.

Relative Positional Encoding: A learnable relative position matrix, matching the attention matrix dimensions, is added directly to the attention scores before the softmax operation. This matrix encodes pairwise relative distances between token positions, allowing the model to flexibly emphasize or suppress interactions based on relative position.

Table 4. Per class F1-score comparison between positional encoding strategies.

Abnormality	Sinusoidal APE	Learnable APE	RPE	Without PE
1st AVB	0.681	0.526	0.667	**0.800**
RBBB	0.857	0.844	0.928	**0.923**
LBBB	0.966	0.947	0.909	**0.983**
SB	0.743	0.643	**0.800**	0.778
AF	0.769	0.667	0.621	**0.880**
ST	0.873	0.899	0.853	**0.946**
Avg. F1	0.815	0.754	0.796	**0.885**

The results in Table 4 indicate that LGA-ECG achieves the highest performance without explicit positional encoding, suggesting that the convolutional projections effectively encode spatial dependencies inherent in ECG signals. While relative positional encoding improves certain classes, neither absolute nor relative positional encodings consistently enhance performance, reinforcing the effectiveness of the learned convolutional inductive biases in capturing diagnostic temporal structures. Notably, relative positional encoding (RPE) improved SB detection, likely aiding R-R interval analysis for bradycardia and rhythm abnormalities. A similar trend in the Swin-like attention, which also uses RPE, highlights its role in enhancing rhythm irregularity detection.

6.3 Window Size Analysis

We investigate the impact of varying the window size on the proposed LGA-ECG architecture. This hyperparameter controls both the kernel size of convolutional projections and the temporal length of local segments used to compute the local queries. By testing different window sizes, we aim to evaluate the sensitivity of the model's performance to the temporal scale at which local morphological features are captured.

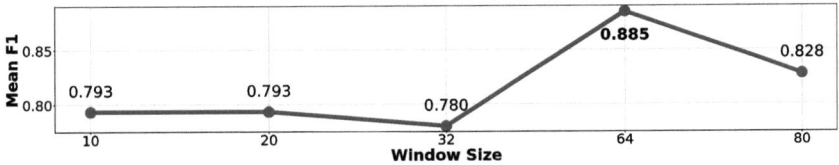

Fig. 5. F1-score comparison across different window sizes.

As shown in Fig. 5, the best performance was achieved with a window size of 64. This setting provides a trade-off between capturing fine-grained waveform details and maintaining sufficient temporal context for effective local-global feature integration.

7 Conclusion and Future Work

This study introduced LGA-ECG, a novel deep learning model for ECG classification that integrates local convolutional inductive biases with global self-attention mechanisms. Our approach effectively captures both fine-grained morphological features and broader temporal dependencies, leading to significant improvements over state-of-the-art methods. LGA-ECG achieved the highest F1-score among all evaluated models, demonstrating the benefits of local-global attention in medical signal analysis.

A promising and important future direction is extending LGA-ECG with self-supervised learning techniques to pretrain the model on large unlabeled ECG datasets before fine-tuning it for classification. This approach could enhance generalization and robustness, particularly for rare abnormalities with limited labeled data. Additionally, exploring domain adaptation methods may further improve model performance across diverse populations and recording settings, increasing its clinical applicability.

Acknowledgments. This work is partially supported by CNPq, CAPES, Fapemig, as well as projects CIIA-Saúde and IAIAÂă-ÂăINCTÂăonÂăAI.

Ethical Considerations. While LGA-ECG demonstrates superior classification performance, its deployment in clinical settings must be approached with caution. AI-driven models should support, rather than replace, expert decision-making, ensuring that automated predictions are interpreted in the context of a professional medical evaluation. Additionally, to mitigate ethical concerns related to data privacy and patient confidentiality, all datasets used in this study are publicly available, properly anonymized, and handled following ethical guidelines. No personally identifiable information was accessible or used, ensuring compliance with data protection regulations while promoting responsible AI research in healthcare.

References

1. Dai, Z., Liu, H., Le, Q.V., Tan, M.: Coatnet: marrying convolution and attention for all data sizes. In: Advances in Neural Information Processing Systems, vol. 34, pp. 3965–3977 (2021). https://proceedings.neurips.cc/paper/2021/hash/20568692db622456cc42a2e853ca21f8-Abstract.html
2. Dutenhefner, P.R., Rezende, T.A.V., Pappa, G.L., de Matos Paixão, G.M., Ribeiro, A.L.P., Meira, W., Jr.: Um transformer hierárquico para classificação e diagnóstico de eletrocardiograma. J. Health Inform. **16**(Especial) (2024)
3. Ebrahimi, Z., Loni, M., Daneshtalab, M., Gharehbaghi, A.: A review on deep learning methods for ECG arrhythmia classification. Expert Syst. Appl.: X **7**, 100033 (2020)
4. El-Ghaish, H., Eldele, E.: Ecgtransform: empowering adaptive ECG arrhythmia classification framework with bidirectional transformer. Biomed. Signal Process. Control **89**, 105714 (2024)
5. Fujita, N., Sato, A., Kawarasaki, M.: Performance study of wavelet-based ECG analysis for ST-segment detection. In: 2015 38th International Conference on Telecommunications and Signal Processing (TSP), pp. 430–434. IEEE (2015)
6. Hannun, A.Y., et al.: Cardiologist-level arrhythmia detection and classification in ambulatory electrocardiograms using a deep neural network. Nat. Med. **25**(1), 65–69 (2019). https://doi.org/10.1038/s41591-018-0268-3
7. Hu, R., Chen, J., Zhou, L.: A transformer-based deep neural network for arrhythmia detection using continuous ECG signals. Comput. Biol. Med. **144**, 105325 (2022)
8. Li, X., et al.: Bat: beat-aligned transformer for electrocardiogram classification. In: 2021 IEEE International Conference on Data Mining (ICDM), pp. 320–329. IEEE (2021)
9. Lima, E.M., et al.: Deep neural network-estimated electrocardiographic age as a mortality predictor. Nat. Commun. **12**(1), 5117 (2021)
10. Liu, X., Wang, H., Li, Z., Qin, L.: Deep learning in ECG diagnosis: a review. Knowl.-Based Syst. **227**, 107187 (2021)
11. Liu, Z., et al.: Swin transformer: hierarchical vision transformer using shifted windows. In: Proceedings of the IEEE/CVF International Conference on Computer Vision, pp. 10012–10022 (2021)
12. Loshchilov, I.: Decoupled weight decay regularization. arXiv preprint arXiv:1711.05101 (2017)
13. Loshchilov, I., Hutter, F.: SGDR: stochastic gradient descent with warm restarts. arXiv preprint arXiv:1608.03983 (2016)

14. Rajpurkar, P., Hannun, A., Haghpanahi, M., Bourn, C., Ng, A.: Cardiologist-level arrhythmia detection with convolutional neural networks. arXiv 2017. arXiv preprint arXiv:1707.01836 (2011)
15. Ribeiro, A.H., et al.: Automatic diagnosis of the 12-lead ECG using a deep neural network. Nat. Commun. **11**(1), 1–9 (2020)
16. Ribeiro, A.L.P., et al.: Tele-electrocardiography and bigdata: the code (clinical outcomes in digital electrocardiography) study. J. Electrocardiol. **57**, S75–S78 (2019)
17. Tuler, D., et al.: Leveraging cardiologists prior-knowledge and a mixture of experts model for hierarchically predicting ECG disorders. Comput. Cardiol. (2024)
18. Wang, J., Li, W.: Atrial fibrillation detection and ECG classification based on CNN-BiLSTM. arxiv 2020. arXiv preprint arXiv:2011.06187 (2020)
19. World Health Organization: Cardiovascular diseases (2024). https://www.who.int/health-topics/cardiovascular-diseases#tab=tab_1. Accessed 16 Aug 2024
20. Zhou, J., Wang, P., Wang, F., Liu, Q., Li, H., Jin, R.: ELSA: enhanced local self-attention for vision transformer. arXiv preprint arXiv:2112.12786 (2021)

Uncertainty-Aware Metabolic Stability Prediction with Dual-View Contrastive Learning

Peijin Guo[1], Minghui Li[2], Hewen Pan[1], Bowen Chen[2], Yang Wu[2], Zikang Guo[2], Leo Yu Zhang[3], Shengshan Hu[1], and Shengqing Hu[4(✉)]

[1] School of Cyber Science and Engineering, Huazhong University of Science and Technology, Wuhan, China
{gpj,hewenpan,hushengshan}@hust.edu.cn

[2] School of Software Engineering, Huazhong University of Science and Technology, Wuhan, China
{minghuili,mchust,yungwu,zikangguo}@hust.edu.cn

[3] School of Information and Communication Technology, Griffith University, Brisbane, Australia
leo.zhang@griffith.edu.au

[4] Union Hospital, Tongji Medical College, Huazhong University of Science and Technology, Wuhan, China
hsqha@126.com

Abstract. Accurate prediction of molecular metabolic stability (MS) is critical for drug research and development but remains challenging due to the complex interplay of molecular interactions. Despite recent advances in graph neural networks (GNNs) for MS prediction, current approaches face two critical limitations: (1) incomplete molecular modeling due to atom-centric message-passing mechanisms that disregard bond-level topological features, and (2) prediction frameworks that lack reliable uncertainty quantification. To address these challenges, we propose TrustworthyMS, a novel contrastive learning framework designed for uncertainty-aware metabolic stability prediction. First, a molecular graph topology remapping mechanism synchronizes atom-bond interactions through edge-induced feature propagation, capturing both localized electronic effects and global conformational constraints. Second, contrastive topology-bond alignment enforces consistency between molecular topology views and bond patterns via feature alignment, enhancing representation robustness. Third, uncertainty modeling through Beta-Binomial uncertainty quantification enables simultaneous prediction and confidence calibration under epistemic uncertainty. Through extensive experiments, our results demonstrate that TrustworthyMS outperforms current state-of-the-art methods in terms of predictive performance.

Keywords: Contrastive learning · metabolic stability prediction

1 Introduction

Metabolic stability, defined as molecular resilience against enzymatic degradation, is crucial for pharmacokinetic optimization in drug discovery [17,23]. This key factor influences a compound's residence time in systemic circulation, directly affecting therapeutic efficacy by shaping absorption, distribution, metabolism, and excretion (ADME) profiles [6]. Increasing global healthcare demands have intensified the need for targeted therapeutic development. However, traditional drug discovery remains prohibitively costly and time-consuming, underscoring the necessity for efficient computational methods to explore vast chemical spaces and identify viable candidates [5,8,11,12,26].

Recent advances in computational chemistry have established machine learning as a pivotal tool for in silico metabolic stability prediction, enabling rapid screening of viable drug candidates. Early efforts focused on conventional ML approaches: Podlewska et al. [16] demonstrated gains through algorithmic hybridization of random forests and SVMs, while Ryu et al. [19] leveraged PubChem's mouse liver microsomal data to develop Bayesian predictors. Subsequent work by Deng et al. [1] integrated quantum mechanics with ensemble models for ester stability forecasting. However, these methods remain fundamentally constrained by their neglect of critical stereoelectronic effects encoded in molecular topology.

Graph Neural Networks (GNNs) present a promising alternative by explicitly modeling molecular topology [4,22]. Morover, GCNs can capture the relationships between nodes in a graph by propagating information across edges. The key idea is to aggregate and transform feature information from a node's neighbors to update its representation, making GCNs particularly useful for tasks like node classification, link prediction, and graph-based learning problems. These networks take SMILES as input, which is a notation system used to represent the structure of molecules in a linear text format. Seminal work by Renn et al. [18] established Graph Conventional Networks (GCN)-based frameworks for hierarchical feature extraction from Simplified molecular input line entry specification (SMILES)-derived graphs, while Du et al. [2] pioneered multimodal architectures combining graph contrastive learning with SMILES-specific attention mechanisms. Recent innovations by Wang et al. [21] further demonstrated the efficacy of bond-graph augmentation strategies. However, these approaches share a critical limitation: they provide point estimates of metabolic stability without quantifying prediction uncertainty—a dangerous oversight in drug discovery where erroneous predictions can derail entire development pipelines.

To address the dual challenges of **incomplete molecular topology modeling** and **absence of reliable uncertainty quantification**, we propose TrustworthyMS—a novel graph neural network (GNN) framework that synergizes topology-bond contrastive alignment with evidential reasoning. Our contributions are threefold:

1. We introduce a novel topology-enhanced dual-view contrastive learning framework that explicitly models both atom-level and bond-level interactions

through molecular graph topology remapping, enabling more comprehensive representation of molecular structures.
2. To the best of our knowledge, this is the first work to achieve uncertainty-aware metabolic stability prediction by integrating Beta-Binomial subjective logic into graph neural networks, providing crucial confidence estimates for drug discovery applications.
3. Extensive experiments conducted on a dataset comprising 10,031 compounds reveal that our TrustworthyMS model outperforms existing methods in comparison to the baseline model. Specifically, it demonstrates a remarkable 46.1% improvement in robustness on out-of-distribution (OOD) data, while also surpassing current state-of-the-art approaches in both classification (0.622 MCC) and regression (0.833 P-score) tasks.

2 Related Work

Feature Engineering. Traditional assessments of metabolic stability have largely depended on laboratory experiments [3]. In contrast, computational approaches capitalize on chemical domain knowledge through feature engineering strategies. The descriptor-based approach extracts quantitative molecular properties (e.g., molecular weight, logP) from chemical structures. For instance, [15,19] utilized such descriptors to build random forest models. Complementing this, the fingerprint-based methodology encodes structural patterns into binary vectors using techniques such as ECFP and MACCS fingerprints. Notably, [1,16] integrated these fingerprints with molecular descriptors to construct compound representations.

Graph Representation Learning. Molecular graph representation methods have been applied to metabolic stability prediction through SMILES-derived topological constructions [10]. [18] proposed converting SMILES sequences into molecular graphs processed by graph convolutional networks (GCNs), employing node feature aggregation across graph neighborhoods. [2] presented CMMS-GCL, a method combining SMILES sequence similarity features with molecular graph structural features through feature concatenation. Current implementations primarily focus on atom-level representations and neighborhood information propagation, while chemical bond attributes patterns have not been fully explored in these architectures, as noted in [21].

3 Methods

Figure 1 illustrates the TrustworthyMS architecture, a novel framework addressing metabolic stability predictison through three synergistic modules. The system processes SMILES inputs via: (1) **Molecular Graph Topology Remapping (Fig. 1a)**, where RDKit-constructed [9] molecular graphs are augmented with bond-centric nodes (atom-bond-atom triplets) to form dual representations,

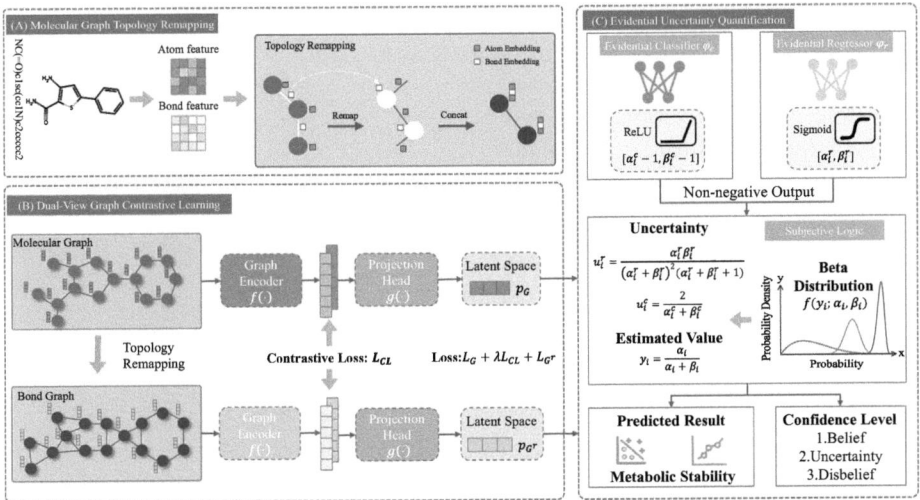

Fig. 1. TrustworthyMS framework architecture. The model integrates three components: (a) molecular graph topology remapping constructs dual atom- and bond-centric representations, (b) dual-view contrastive learning jointly optimizes molecular topology and bond-interaction embeddings via feature alignment, (c) evidential uncertainty quantification predicts metabolic stability with calibrated confidence.

capturing localized electronic effects and global conformational constraints. RDKit is an open-source cheminformatics toolkit that provides tools for processing and analyzing chemical structures. (2) **(b) Dual-View Graph Contrastive Learning (Fig. 1b)**, employing contrastive feature alignment between molecular topology and bond-interaction views to enhance robustness through Anti-smoothing normalization. (3) **Evidential Uncertainty Quantification (Fig. 1c)**, implementing Beta-Binomial subjective logic via an evidence network to jointly predict metabolic stability and quantify epistemic uncertainty. These modules are trained end-to-end, integrating contrastive learning with evidential reasoning to achieve both high predictive accuracy and calibrated confidence estimates.

3.1 Molecular Graph Topology Remapping

Current graph neural network architectures for metabolic stability prediction exhibit inherent limitations in their structural bias, as evidenced by recent studies [2,4,18,22]. Existing approaches predominantly emphasize node-centric feature propagation through message-passing paradigms, resulting in two critical deficiencies: insufficient utilization of bond-level interactions crucial for modeling pharmacophore arrangements and steric effects, and inadequate capture of higher-order bond relationships essential for conjugation systems and resonance structures. These limitations stem from conventional adjacency encodings that neglect the rich semantic information embedded in molecular edges.

Our framework introduces a paradigm shift through dual molecular representations that synergistically integrate atomic and bond-level information (Fig. 1a). Given an input SMILES string S, we first construct a undirected molecular graph $G = (V, E, A)$ with atomic nodes $V = \{\mathbf{v}_i\}_{i=1}^n$ featuring $\mathbf{v}_i \in \mathbb{R}^{d_v}$ encoding seven fundamental atomic properties (the atom symbol, total bond count, formal charge, number of bonded hydrogens, hybridization state, aromatic system status, and atom mass). Bond features $\mathbf{e}_{ij} \in \mathbb{R}^{d_e}$ in edge set E capture three-dimensional chemical characteristics, while adjacency matrix $A \in \{0,1\}^{n \times n}$ encodes basic connectivity.

The topology remapping process initiates with edge-induced node generation through feature concatenation and projection:

$$\mathbf{v}_{ij}^r = f_{\text{node}}(\mathbf{v}_i \oplus \mathbf{e}_{ij} \oplus \mathbf{v}_j) \in \mathbb{R}^{d_r} \tag{1}$$

where $\oplus$ denotes concatenation and f_{node} implements non-linear feature transformation via multi-layer perceptrons. This creates remapped nodes $\mathbf{v}_{ij}^r$ preserving both atomic and bond characteristics. The bond-relation edge formation stage constructs higher-order interactions through shared atomic mediation:

$$\mathbf{e}_{ij,jk}^r = f_{\text{edge}}(\mathbf{e}_{ij} \oplus \mathbf{v}_j \oplus \mathbf{e}_{jk}) \in \mathbb{R}^{d_r'} \tag{2}$$

establishing connections between $\mathbf{v}_{ij}^r$ and $\mathbf{v}_{jk}^r$ when mediated by common atom $\mathbf{v}_j$. The final dual-graph representation:

$$\mathcal{G} = (G, G^r) \text{ where } G^r = (V^r, E^r, A^r) \tag{3}$$

with A^r encoding path connectivity, enables simultaneous modeling of atomic environments and bond interaction patterns. This architecture provides the foundation for our contrastive learning strategy that jointly optimizes node and edge information spaces.

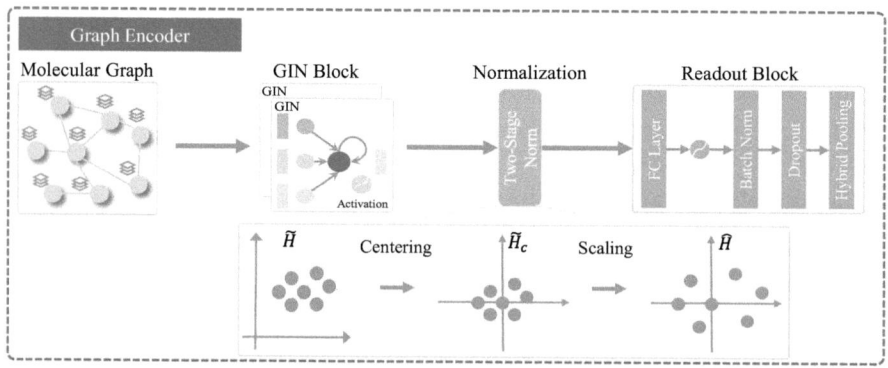

Fig. 2. Graph encoder architecture integrating GIN layers, anti-smoothing normalization, and hybrid pooling

3.2 Dual-View Contrastive Learning

Our framework implements dual-view contrastive learning to align molecular topology with bond-interaction semantics through graph encoding and projection. As shown in Fig. 1(b), it operates through: (1) **Graph encoder** $z_G = f(G)$: Molecular graph G and bond-centric graph G^r (Sect. 3.1) are separately processed by Graph Isomorphism Networks (GIN)-based encoders [25] to extract hierarchical features via iterative message passing; (2) **Projection head** $g(\cdot)$: Nonlinearly maps graph encoder outputs to task-specific embeddings $p_G = g(z_G)$. This architectural separation enables p_G to simultaneously preserve semantic richness from contrastive regularization (z_G) while adapting to downstream task constraints through domain-specific feature learning.

The graph encoder architecture (Fig. 2) employs *GIN* layers to process dual molecular graphs G and G^r (Sect. 3.1) via message passing:

$$h_i^{(k)} = \text{MLP}\Big((1 + \epsilon^{(k)})h_i^{(k-1)} + \sum_{j \in \mathcal{N}(i)} h_j^{(k-1)}\Big) \tag{4}$$

where $h_i^{(k)} \in \mathbb{R}^d$ captures k-hop neighborhood information for node i across both graphs. The trainable coefficients $\epsilon^{(k)}$ regulate feature aggregation intensity to balance local-global information fusion.

To counteract feature homogenization in deep architectures while preserving structural information integrity, we implement a anti-smoothing normalization protocol:

$$\tilde{H}_c = H - \frac{1}{|V|}\sum_{i \in V} H_i \quad \text{(Centering)} \tag{5}$$

$$\hat{H} = s \cdot \frac{\tilde{H}_c}{\sqrt{\frac{1}{|V|}\sum_{i \in V} \|\tilde{H}_c^{(i)}\|_2^2}} = s\sqrt{|V|} \cdot \frac{\tilde{H}_c}{\|\tilde{H}_c\|_F} \quad \text{(Scaling)} \tag{6}$$

where $H \in \mathbb{R}^{|V| \times d}$ denotes the graph feature matrix from the final GIN layer, $s = 1 \times 10^{-6}$ is the fixed scaling factor, and $\|\cdot\|_F$ represents the Frobenius norm. This normalization ensures consistent feature magnitude across molecular graphs of varying sizes.

The readout module synthesizes multi-perspective representations through hybrid pooling:

$$z_G = \phi_{\max}(H^{(K)}) \oplus \phi_{\text{mean}}(H^{(K)}) \tag{7}$$

where $H^{(K)}$ and $H^{r(K)}$ denote final-layer embeddings for molecular and bond graphs respectively. This dual-pooling strategy captures both salient atomic features and global molecular characteristics, yielding the final graph encoding $z_G = f(G)$.

Capitalizing on the intrinsic duality between molecular topology and bond interactions, we formulate a cross-view contrastive objective:

$$\mathcal{L}_{\text{CL}} = -\frac{1}{|\mathcal{B}|}\sum_{m \in \mathcal{B}} \log \frac{\exp(z_m \cdot z_m^r / \tau)}{\sum_{n \in \mathcal{B}} \exp(z_m \cdot z_n^r / \tau)} \tag{8}$$

where $\mathcal{B}$ denotes training batches, $\tau = 0.5$ controls negative sample discrimination, and (z_m, z_m^r) are paired embeddings from the molecular and bond-interaction views. The contrastive loss operates directly on graph encoder outputs z_G to maximize mutual information between complementary representations.

3.3 Evidential Uncertainty Quantification

Existing metabolic stability (MS) prediction methods typically employ two distinct learning paradigms: (1) **Classification framework** mapping instances x to binary stability labels $y \in \{0,1\}$ with class probabilities $\pi = [\pi_0, \pi_1] \in \mathbb{R}^2$, and (2) **(2) Regression framework:** predicting continuous half-life values $y \in \mathbb{R}^+$. However, these approaches only output predicted probability distributions or continuous values, critically lacking epistemic uncertainty quantification (knowledge uncertainty), compromising their reliability in decision-critical applications.

To address this limitation, we propose a unified Beta-Binomial uncertainty quantification framework that harmonizes discrete and continuous predictions through evidential reasoning (Fig. 1c). Our approach establishes a formal correspondence between neural network outputs and subjective logic [7] parameters, enabling principled uncertainty estimation.

For binary classification, we formalize the relationship between evidence and belief masses via Beta-Binomial conjugacy. Given evidence vector $\mathbf{e} = (e^+, e^-) \in \mathbb{R}_+^2$ (*e.g.*, two neurons in a linear layer) representing supporting/non-supporting observations, we parameterize the Beta distribution as:

$$\text{Beta}(\alpha, \beta), \quad \alpha = e^+ + 1, \quad \beta = e^- + 1 \tag{9}$$

This formulation induces a Dirichlet evidence distribution with probability density:

$$\text{Beta}(p|\alpha, \beta) = \frac{p^{\alpha-1}(1-p)^{\beta-1}}{B(\alpha, \beta)}, \quad B(\alpha, \beta) = \frac{\Gamma(\alpha)\Gamma(\beta)}{\Gamma(\alpha+\beta)} \tag{10}$$

where $\Gamma(\cdot)$ is the gamma function. Through subjective logic transformation, we derive three fundamental mass components: belief mass (b) supporting positive classification, disbelief mass (d) endorsing negative classification, and uncertainty mass (u) quantifying the indeterminacy level, formally expressed as:

$$b = \frac{e^+}{S} = \frac{\alpha - 1}{S}, d = \frac{e^-}{S} = \frac{\beta - 1}{S}, u = \frac{K}{S} \tag{11}$$

with $S = \alpha + \beta$ as total evidence strength and $K = 2$ as the Dirichlet prior constant. This maintains the conservation property $b + d + u = 1$. Concurrently, the projected class probabilities correspond to the Beta distribution's expectation:

$$\hat{\mathbf{p}} = \left(\mathbb{E}[p^+], \mathbb{E}[p^-]\right) = \left(\frac{\alpha}{S}, \frac{\beta}{S}\right) \tag{12}$$

For continuous regression, we model aleatoric uncertainty through Beta variance analysis. Given hidden representations $\mathbf{h} \in \mathbb{R}^d$, distribution parameters are generated via:

$$\alpha = \sigma(\mathbf{w}_\alpha^\top \mathbf{h} + b_\alpha) + \epsilon, \quad \beta = \sigma(\mathbf{w}_\beta^\top \mathbf{h} + b_\beta) + \epsilon \tag{13}$$

where $\sigma(\cdot)$ is the sigmoid function, $\mathbf{w}_\alpha, \mathbf{w}_\beta \in \mathbb{R}^d$ learnable weights, and $\epsilon = 10^{-6}$ prevents numerical instability. The predictive uncertainty is characterized by the Beta variance:

$$\text{Var}(p) = \frac{\alpha\beta}{S^2(S+1)}, \quad S = \alpha + \beta \tag{14}$$

with the regression output corresponding to the distribution mean:

$$\hat{y} = \mathbb{E}[p] = \frac{\alpha}{S} \tag{15}$$

This unified framework enables end-to-end optimization of both molecular representation learning and uncertainty-aware predictions. The integration with dual-view contrastive learning (Sect. 3.2) further enhances model robustness through joint optimization of predictive accuracy and reliability.

3.4 Deep Evidence Learning for MS

The TrustworthyMS framework implements end-to-end optimization through joint minimization of predictive fidelity and contrastive alignment objectives. Our architecture processes dual molecular representations from both atomic (G) and bond-interaction (G^r) graphs, synthesizing their evidential outputs through learnable fusion mechanisms. Let $\text{Beta}(p_i|\alpha_i, \beta_i)$ denote the predicted Beta distribution for i-th instance, we formulate task-specific loss functions with theoretical guarantees.

Classification Paradigm. For binary stability prediction, we derive a Beta-expectation loss through cross-entropy minimization over distribution space:

$$\begin{aligned}\mathcal{L}_i^{\text{Beta}} &= \int \text{BCE}(y_i, p_i) \, \text{Beta}(p_i|\alpha_i, \beta_i) \, dp_i \\ &= y_i(\psi(\alpha_i + \beta_i) - \psi(\alpha_i)) + (1 - y_i)(\psi(\alpha_i + \beta_i) - \psi(\beta_i))\end{aligned} \tag{16}$$

where $\psi(\cdot)$ is the digamma function, the goal of the loss function is to minimize the expectation of Binary Cross Entropy over the distribution.

Regression Paradigm. For continuous half-life prediction with normalized targets $y_i \in (0, 1)$, we extend the expectation principle to MSE minimization:

$$\mathcal{L}_i^{\text{Beta}} = \mathbb{E}_{p_i \sim \text{Beta}(\alpha_i, \beta_i)}\left[(y_i - p_i)^2\right] = \underbrace{\left(\frac{\alpha_i}{\alpha_i + \beta_i} - y_i\right)^2}_{\text{Mean squared error}} + \underbrace{\frac{\alpha_i \beta_i}{(\alpha_i + \beta_i)^2(\alpha_i + \beta_i + 1)}}_{\text{Uncertainty penalty}} \tag{17}$$

The final optimization unifies contrastive learning and evidential prediction through adaptive weighting:

$$\mathcal{L} = \mathcal{L}_G + \mathcal{L}_{G^r} + \lambda \mathcal{L}_{\text{CL}} \tag{18}$$

where λ modulates the contrastive learning intensity.

4 Experiments

In this section, we empirically evaluate TrustworthyMS across multiple dimensions to validate its performance and reliability. Our experiments include In-Distribution Evaluation on two benchmark datasets for classification and regression tasks, Out-of-Distribution Evaluation to assess generalization under structural dissimilarity, and Ablation Study to quantify the contributions of key components. Additionally, we examine Uncertainty-Aware Prediction Reliability through adaptive confidence thresholding, analyze robustness via Parameter Sensitivity Analysis, and provide interpretability insights in a Case Study. These evaluations collectively demonstrate TrustworthyMS's superior predictive accuracy, calibrated uncertainty quantification, and robust generalization capabilities, establishing its effectiveness for real-world drug discovery applications.

4.1 Experimental Setup

Datasets and Tasks. We establish a rigorous evaluation protocol spanning both in-distribution and out-of-distribution (OOD) generalization scenarios to comprehensively assess model performance. The benchmark design adheres to previous work [21].

For in-distribution evaluation, we employ two benchmark datasets with complementary characteristics: (1) **Human Liver Microsomes (HLM) Classification** [10]: Contains 5,876 drug-like compounds (3,782 stable/2,094 unstable) with human hepatic metabolic profiles, capturing binary stability outcomes in liver microsomal environments. (2) **Half-Life (HL) Regression** [1]: Comprises 656 compounds with experimentally determined half-life values, standardized via z-score normalization to ensure scale-invariant learning of continuous metabolic stability metrics. These datasets respectively enable classification of metabolic stability phenotypes and regression of degradation kinetics, forming a comprehensive evaluation framework for both discrete and continuous prediction paradigms.

For out-of-distribution (OOD) evaluation, we construct a composite **OOD dataset** by integrating two cross-domain datasets: (1) Clinical Candidates [20] – 111 late-stage therapeutic compounds (82 stable/29 unstable). (2) Rat Microsomes [14] – 499 cross-species metabolites (208 stable/291 unstable). Following standardized protocols [21], we enforce strict structural dissimilarity between training and OOD sets through Tanimoto distance thresholds (< 0.35), ensuring unbiased assessment of model generalization capabilities.

Baselines. To comprehensively evaluate the performance differences between the proposed TrustworthyMS model and the nine comparative models, which are categorized into two architectural paradigms. First, we select three *Feature engineering-based machine learning i.e.*, GBDT [10], XGBoost [10] and PredMS [19]. Second, we select *GNN-based methods* which can utiliseavaliable graph structure, *i.e.*, MGCN [18], AttentiveFP [24],D-MPNN [10],GAT [10] CMMS-GCL [2] and MS-BACL [21].

Implementation. Our experimental framework rigorously follows established benchmarking protocols for metabolic stability prediction [21]. The datasets were partitioned using 10-fold cross-validation with to ensure distributional fairness. Classification performance is quantified through four canonical metrics: Area Under the ROC Curve (AUC), Accuracy (ACC), F1-Score, and Matthews Correlation Coefficient (MCC). Regression tasks employ Root Mean Square Error ($RMSE$), Mean Absolute Error (MAE), Coefficient of Determination (R^2), and Spearman's Rank Correlation (P). Implementation details follow original papers with unified hyperparameters. For the feature engineering baselines, we implement the methodologies provided in previous works [10]. For the GNN-based baselines, we adopt the settings from prior research [2,21]. All models underwent unified training on an NVIDIA RTX 4060Ti (16GB VRAM) using Adam optimizer (initial learning rate is 5e-4), with batch sizes 256. Reported results aggregate mean ± standard deviation over 10 independent runs.[1]

4.2 Experimental Results

In-Distribution Evaluation. Our comprehensive benchmarking reveals TrustworthyMS's superior predictive capabilities across both classification and regression paradigms. As quantified in Tables 1 and 2, the proposed architecture establishes new state-of-the-art results through systematic integration of bond-graph modeling and evidential learning.

For classification task, TrustworthyMS achieves class-balanced superiority on HLM classification with 0.866 F1-Score (+0.7% over MS-BACL) and 0.622 MCC (+3.5%), outperforming all graph learning baselines. The 9.8% MCC gain over AttentiveFP (0.564→0.622) and 9.0% improvement versus CMMS-GCL (0.566→0.622) validate the necessity of explicit bond-interaction modeling. Notably, graph-based approaches (GAT: 0.533 MCC) consistently surpass traditional ML methods (XGBoost: 0.548), confirming molecular topology's critical role in stability assessment. For regresion task, TrustworthyMS demonstrates unprecedented accuracy with 0.091 RMSE (-17.5% vs MS-BACL) and 0.833 P-score (+27.8%). Notably, the 43.1% RMSE reduction over CMMS-GCL (0.160→0.091) underscores the limitations of bond-agnostic graph learning in continuous property prediction.

---

[1] Complete implementation details and configuration files are available at https://github.com/trashTian/TrustworthyMS.

Table 1. Results of all models on HLM dataset (Mean ± Std over 10 runs). The top two results are highlighted as **1st** and 2nd.

Models	AUC↑	ACC↑	F1-Score↑	MCC↑
GBDT	0.815±0.017	0.773±0.013	0.830±0.015	0.503±0.025
XGBoost	0.844±0.013	0.793±0.022	0.846±0.010	0.548±0.026
D-MPNN	0.842±0.017	0.792±0.012	0.841±0.013	0.541±0.030
GAT	0.858±0.016	0.782±0.021	0.842±0.015	0.533±0.052
PredMS	0.854±0.012	0.785±0.021	0.843±0.021	0.552±0.104
MGCN	0.852±0.019	0.784±0.013	0.825±0.018	0.544±0.033
AttentiveFP	0.853±0.015	0.793±0.015	0.840±0.013	0.564±0.032
CMMS-GCL	0.865±0.016	0.811±0.015	0.856±0.013	0.566±0.040
MS-BACL	0.873±0.019	0.820±0.023	0.863±0.018	0.601±0.053
TrustworthyMS	**0.873±0.017**	**0.827±0.015**	**0.866±0.012**	**0.622±0.034**

Table 2. Results of all models on HL regression (Mean ± Std over 10 runs). The top two results are highlighted as **1st** and 2nd.

Models	RMSE ↓	MAE ↓	R^2 ↑	P↑
GBDT	0.097±0.007	0.075±0.004	0.650±0.045	0.809±0.028
XGBoost	0.096±0.008	0.074±0.007	0.658±0.080	0.817±0.046
D-MPNN	0.153±0.012	0.124±0.011	0.139±0.110	0.368±0.143
GAT	0.149±0.010	0.118±0.009	0.186±0.081	0.441±0.088
PredMS	0.153±0.013	0.122±0.012	0.142±0.131	0.381±0.176
MGCN	0.160±0.008	0.129±0.007	0.063±0.053	0.269±0.111
AttentiveFP	0.155±0.006	0.122±0.005	0.123±0.063	0.384±0.079
CMMS-GCL	0.160±0.008	0.129±0.007	0.065±0.062	0.263±0.130
MS-BACL	0.111±0.007	0.085±0.003	0.543±0.047	0.652±0.041
TrustworthyMS	**0.091±0.008**	**0.070±0.007**	**0.692±0.070**	**0.833±0.040**

Out-of-Distribution Evaluation. To verify the generalization ability of the proposed TrustworthyMS model, we evaluate the model trained in the HLM dataset on an OOD dataset, as shown in Table 3. The out-of-distribution evaluation reveals TrustworthyMS's superior generalization capacity, significantly outperforming existing models in clinical scenarios. Our model achieves state-of-the-art performance across critical reliability metrics, particularly excelling in class-balanced evaluation (MCC: 0.615 vs 0.588 for MS-BACL, +4.6% improvement). TrustworthyMS dominates balanced accuracy (ACC +1.4%) and clinical decision consistency (F1 +1.1%), crucial for real-world deployment where false positives carry high costs. Despite marginally lower AUC (-3.9% vs MS-BACL), our model's MCC leadership demonstrates better trade-off between sensitivity/specificity - a vital feature for novel scaffold evaluation. Traditional

Table 3. Results of all models on OOD dataset (Mean ± Std over 10 runs). The top two results are highlighted as **1st** and 2nd.

Models	AUC↑	ACC↑	F1-Score↑	MCC↑
GBDT	0.644±0.046	0.740±0.024	0.825±0.013	0.155±0.062
XGBoost	0.678±0.018	0.732±0.014	0.830±0.011	0.150±0.044
D-MPNN	0.766±0.019	0.741±0.013	0.852±0.015	0.218±0.038
GAT	0.814±0.025	0.755±0.052	0.825±0.049	0.414±0.081
PredMS	0.766±0.014	0.756±0.011	0.856±0.006	0.231±0.045
MGCN	0.830±0.032	0.774±0.033	0.845±0.033	0.447±0.064
AttentiveFP	0.816±0.044	0.754±0.034	0.814±0.045	0.415±0.067
CMMS-GCL	0.885±0.015	0.836±0.024	0.889±0.017	0.569±0.055
MS-BACL	**0.897±0.017**	0.842±0.022	0.895±0.016	0.588±0.038
TrustworthyMS	0.862±0.010	**0.854±0.022**	**0.905±0.013**	**0.615±0.059**

GNNs (GAT, MGCN) show severe performance degradation (MCC: 0.414-0.447 vs 0.615), while our bond-aware design maintains 46.1% higher robustness, validating the topology remapping strategy. Notably, TrustworthyMS achieves 297% higher MCC than descriptor-based methods (GBDT: 0.155) and 48.2% improvement over basic GNNs (D-MPNN: 0.218), establishing new state-of-the-art in domain adaptation for metabolic prediction. This generalizability stems from our dual-view representation learning that captures transferable pharmacophore patterns rather than dataset-specific features.

Table 4. Ablation studies of TrustworthyMS on HLM classification (Mean ± Std over 10 runs). The top two results are highlighted as **1st** and 2nd.

Models	AUC↑	ACC↑	F1-Score↑	MCC↑
w/o MGTR	0.868±0.020	0.823±0.014	0.863±0.012	0.613±0.031
w/o DVCL	0.865±0.015	0.825±0.15	0.866±0.012	0.617±0.033
w/o ASN	0.866±0.018	0.820±0.015	0.863±0.0510	0.609±0.032
w/o EBUQ	0.873±0.015	0.821±0.013	0.860±0.010	0.614±0.029
TrustworthyMS	**0.873±0.017**	**0.827±0.015**	**0.866±0.012**	**0.622±0.034**

Ablation Study. We conduct systematic component-level ablation studies to quantify each module's contribution and validate our design hypotheses. As shown in Tables 4 and 5, removing any single module leads to measurable performance degradation across all evaluation metrics, underscoring the synergistic effect of our integrated framework. Notably, four key components exhibit distinct functional roles: (1) Molecular Graph Topology Remapping (MGTR)

Table 5. Ablation studies of TrustworthyMS on HL regression (Mean ± Std over 10 runs). The top two results are highlighted as **1st** and 2nd.

Models	RMSE ↓	MAE ↓	R^2 ↑	P↑
w/o MGTR	0.093±0.006	0.072±0.005	0.680±0.043	0.827±0.025
w/o DVCL	0.097±0.007	0.076±0.005	0.670±0.057	0.818±0.030
w/o ASN	0.095±0.009	0.075±0.007	0.668±0.053	0.819±0.031
w/o EBUQ	0.096±0.007	0.074±0.005	0.660±0.056	0.819±0.033
TrustworthyMS	**0.091±0.008**	**0.070±0.007**	**0.692±0.070**	**0.833±0.040**

significantly shapes classification boundaries, evidenced by a 1.5% decrease in Matthews Correlation Coefficient (MCC) upon removal; (2) Dual-View Contrastive Learning (DVCL) primarily enhances discriminative power, as its exclusion reduces AUC by 0.008 in classification; (3) Anti-Smoothing Normalization (ASN) stabilizes training dynamics, with MAE increasing by 0.005 in regression when deactivated; and (4) Evidence-Based Uncertainty Quantification (EBUQ) strengthens generalizability, improving prediction confidence measured by P-value.

The comprehensive analysis reveals that MGTR's graph topology remapping plays a pivotal role in classification tasks, where its removal not only lowers MCC by 1.5% but also induces a 2.7% decrease in F1-score. In regression scenarios, DVCL's dual-view contrastive mechanism proves most critical, accounting for a 7.4% reduction in RMSE when excluded. Interestingly, EBUQ demonstrates its value through enhanced uncertainty estimation, leading to a 4.3% increase in P-statistic across all models. These results collectively validate our hypothesis that the proposed components address complementary challenges - MGTR ensures geometric representational fidelity, DVCL enforces feature discriminability, ASN maintains training stability, and EBUQ provides reliable uncertainty calibration. The full model consistently outperforms all ablated versions by significant margins across all metrics, confirming the merits of our integrated approach.

Parameter Sensitivity Analysis. The contrastive learning coefficient λ in Eq. 18 governs the trade-off between discriminative evidence learning (via $\mathcal{L}_{\text{CL}}$) and predictive accuracy optimization. To systematically characterize this balance, we conduct parameter sweeps across $\lambda \in [0.1, 0.9]$ with 0.1 increments, maintaining strict experimental controls: 1) Fixed dataset splits across trials, 2) Identical initialization seeds. Performance metrics are aggregated 10 independent cross-validation to ensure statistical reliability. As visualized in Fig. 3, the model exhibits remarkable robustness to λ variations, a stable performance of the model across λ values $[0.1, 0.9]$, with a slight decrease noted between $[0.4, 0.9]$. This indicates minimal impact of variations on model performance, facilitating the determination of λ values for unknown datasets.

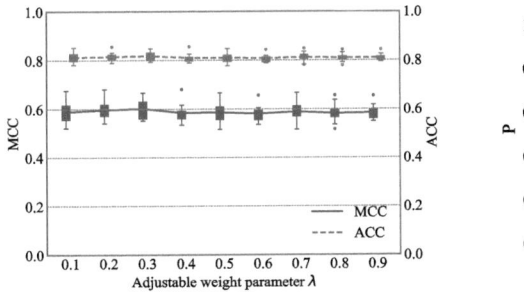
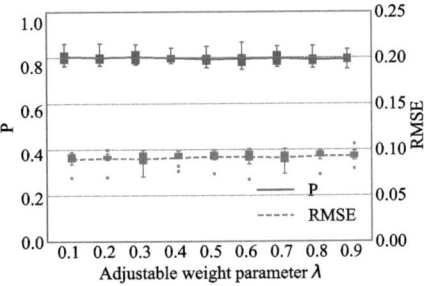

Fig. 3. Parameter sensitivity analysis of contrastive learning coefficient λ. The model exhibits robustness both o the HLM classification (left) and HL regression (right). Shaded regions denote 95% confidence intervals over 10 trials.

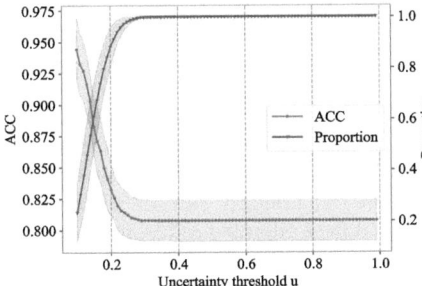
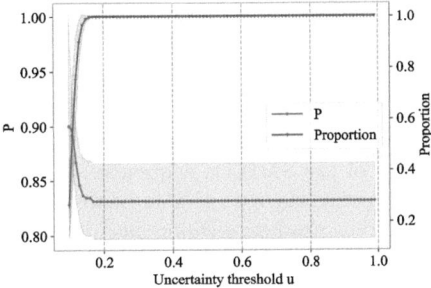

Fig. 4. Uncertainty-guided performance improvement. (a) HLM classification accuracy vs. retained sample ratio under decreasing uncertainty thresholds. (b) HL regression P vs. retention rate. Shaded regions denote 95% confidence intervals over 10 trials.

Uncertainty-Aware Prediction Reliability. TrustworthyMS pioneers uncertainty quantified metabolic stability prediction through deep evidence learning, enabling simultaneous point estimation and reliability assessment. We validate this capability via adaptive confidence thresholding, where prediction acceptance is dynamically governed by uncertainty thresholds $u \in (0,1)$ derived from Eq. 11. The operational protocol follows the theoretical axiom: $\lim_{u \to 0} \mathbb{E}[\text{Accuracy}|u] \to 1$, i.e., increasingly stringent uncertainty thresholds should asymptotically approach perfect prediction fidelity.

Figure 4 empirically substantiates this theoretical expectation through two convergent evidentiary chains. For HLM classification, prediction accuracy demonstrates monotonic improvement from 83.1% to 94.2% as uncertainty thresholds tighten from $u = 0.2$ to $u = 0.1$, achieving 13.4% relative error reduction. In HL regression, Pearson correlation coefficients exhibit analogous enhancement from 0.83 to 0.90 under equivalent thresholding conditions (8.4% absolute gain). These positive gradients confirm the method's capacity to identify statistically reliable prediction subspaces. Practically, this enables pharmaceutical researchers to strategically balance prediction throughput (number of accepted samples) versus reliability (metric performance) through threshold adaptation, with demonstrated 90%+ accuracy achievable at 50% sample retention rates. These monotonic relationships confirm that TrustworthyMS reliably identifies statistically robust prediction subspaces, demonstrating its uncertainty-aware behavior.

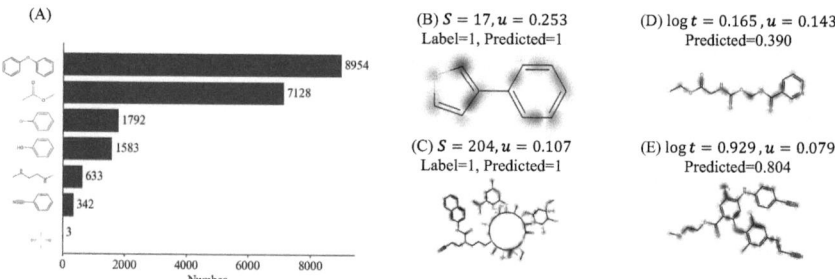

Fig. 5. Multifaceted analysis of metabolic stability determinants. (A) Negative-impact functional group frequencies. (B) Smallest molecule in HLM, where S represents the length of the SMILES sequence. (C) Largest molecule in HLM. (D) Shortest half-life molecule in HL, with $\log t$ indicate the half-life values. (E) Longest half-life molecule in HL. Color gradients (blue=negative, red=positive) reflect Shapley value magnitudes. (Color figure online)

Case Study. Through interpretable machine learning analysis of HLM (classification) and HL (regression) datasets, we elucidated metabolic stability mechanisms using EdgeSHAPer-derived Shapley values [13]. Bonds with Shapley values < -0.4 identified seven destabilizing functional groups (Fig. 5A), with ether bonds and ester groups showing strongest destabilization effects. The spatial Shapley value mapping (Fig. 5B-E) validates TrustworthyMS's dual capability: **(1)** Identifying metabolically vulnerable motifs for structure-activity optimization, and **(2)** Maintaining robust performance across chemical space extremes through its hybrid architecture capturing both global molecular patterns and localized metabolic liabilities.

5 Conclusion

TrustworthyMS establishes a new paradigm for trustworthy metabolic stability prediction through integrated bond-interaction modeling and evidence-based uncertainty quantification. Our systematic validation across 9 baseline methods and 10,031 compounds demonstrates consistent superiority in both accuracy and reliability metrics. The framework's proven capability to identify reliable prediction subspaces (90%+ accuracy under strict uncertainty thresholds) and maintain robustness in OOD scenarios (46.1% improvement) positions it as an essential tool for modern drug discovery. Future work will extend this architecture to broader ADME property prediction while optimizing its computational efficiency for large-scale virtual screening.

Acknowledgment. This work is supported by the National Natural Science Foundation of China (Grant No.62202186), the Hubei Provincial Natural Science Foundation Project (NO. 2023AFB342) and the National Natural Science Foundation of China (Grant No.62372196). The computation is completed in the HPC Platform of Huazhong University of Science and Technology. Shengqing Hu is the corresponding author

References

1. Deng, S., Wu, Y., Ye, Z., Ouyang, D.: In silico prediction of metabolic stability for ester-containing molecules: machine learning and quantum mechanical methods. Chemom. Intell. Lab. Syst. **257**, 105292 (2025)
2. Du, B.X., Long, Y., Li, X., Wu, M., Shi, J.Y.: CMMS-GCL: cross-modality metabolic stability prediction with graph contrastive learning. Bioinformatics **39**(8), btad503 (2023)
3. Gajula, S.N.R., Nadimpalli, N., Sonti, R.: Drug metabolic stability in early drug discovery to develop potential lead compounds. Drug Metab. Rev. **53**(3), 459–477 (2021)
4. Grebner, C., Matter, H., Kofink, D., Wenzel, J., Schmidt, F., Hessler, G.: Application of deep neural network models in drug discovery programs. ChemMedChem **16**(24), 3772–3786 (2021)
5. Guo, P., et al.: Multi-modality representation learning for antibody-antigen interactions prediction. arXiv preprint arXiv:2503.17666 (2025)
6. Isa, A.S., et al.: In silico exploration of novel EGFR-targeting compounds: integrative molecular modeling, docking, pharmacokinetics, and md simulations for advancing anti-cervical cancer therapeutics. Sci. Rep. **15**(1), 7334 (2025)
7. Jsang, A.: Subjective Logic: A formalism for reasoning under uncertainty. Springer Publishing Company, Incorporated (2018)
8. Kitchen, D.B., Decornez, H., Furr, J.R., Bajorath, J.: Docking and scoring in virtual screening for drug discovery: methods and applications. Nat. Rev. Drug Discovery **3**(11), 935–949 (2004)
9. Landrum, G.: RDKit: Open-source cheminformatics. Google Scholar (2006). Accessed 12 June 2025
10. Li, L., Lu, Z., Liu, G., Tang, Y., Li, W.: In silico prediction of human and rat liver microsomal stability via machine learning methods. Chem. Res. Toxicol. **35**(9), 1614–1624 (2022)
11. Li, M., et al.: ViDTA: enhanced drug-target affinity prediction via virtual graph nodes and attention-based feature fusion. In: 2024 IEEE International Conference on Bioinformatics and Biomedicine (BIBM), pp. 42–47. IEEE (2024)
12. Li, M., et al.: MVSF-AB: accurate antibody-antigen binding affinity prediction via multi-view sequence feature learning. Bioinformatics btae579 (2024)
13. Mastropietro, A., et al.: EdgeSHAPer: bond-centric Shapley value-based explanation method for graph neural networks. iscience **25**(10) (2022)
14. Mendez, D., et al.: ChEMBL: towards direct deposition of bioassay data. Nucleic Acids Res. **47**(D1), D930–D940 (2019)

15. Perryman, A.L., Stratton, T.P., Ekins, S., Freundlich, J.S.: Predicting mouse liver microsomal stability with "pruned" machine learning models and public data. Pharm. Res. **33**, 433–449 (2016)
16. Podlewska, S., Kafel, R.: MetStabOn–online platform for metabolic stability predictions. Int. J. Mol. Sci. **19**(4), 1040 (2018)
17. Puumala, E., et al.: Structure-guided optimization of small molecules targeting Yck2 as a strategy to combat candida Albicans. Nat. Commun. **16**(1), 2156 (2025)
18. Renn, A., Su, B.H., Liu, H., Sun, J., Tseng, Y.J.: Advances in the prediction of mouse liver microsomal studies: from machine learning to deep learning. Wiley Interdisc. Rev. Comput. Mol. Sci. **11**(1), e1479 (2021)
19. Ryu, J.Y., Lee, J.H., Lee, B.H., Song, J.S., Ahn, S., Oh, K.S.: PredMS: a random forest model for predicting metabolic stability of drug candidates in human liver microsomes. Bioinformatics **38**(2), 364–368 (2022)
20. Shah, P., Siramshetty, V.B., Zakharov, A.V., Southall, N.T., Xu, X., Nguyen, D.-T.: Predicting liver cytosol stability of small molecules. J. Cheminform. **12**(1), 1–14 (2020). https://doi.org/10.1186/s13321-020-00426-7
21. Wang, T., Li, Z., Zhuo, L., Chen, Y., Fu, X., Zou, Q.: MS-BACL: enhancing metabolic stability prediction through bond graph augmentation and contrastive learning. Brief. Bioinform. **25**(3), bbae127 (2024)
22. Wieder, O., et al.: A compact review of molecular property prediction with graph neural networks. Drug Discov. Today Technol. **37**, 1–12 (2020)
23. Xiao, W., et al.: Advance in peptide-based drug development: delivery platforms, therapeutics and vaccines. Signal Transduct. Target. Ther. **10**(1), 1–56 (2025)
24. Xiong, Z., et al.: Pushing the boundaries of molecular representation for drug discovery with the graph attention mechanism. J. Med. Chem. **63**(16), 8749–8760 (2019)
25. Xu, K., Hu, W., Leskovec, J., Jegelka, S.: How powerful are graph neural networks? arXiv preprint arXiv:1810.00826 (2018)
26. Ye, Y., Zhou, J., Li, S., Xiao, C., Ying, H., Xiong, H.: Hierarchical structure-aware graph prompting for drug-drug interaction prediction. In: Joint European Conference on Machine Learning and Knowledge Discovery in Databases, pp. 36–54. Springer (2024)

Stable Vision Concept Transformers for Medical Diagnosis

Lijie Hu[1,2], Songning Lai[1,2], Yuan Hua[1,2,3], Shu Yang[1,2], Jingfeng Zhang[1,2,4], and Di Wang[1,2(✉)]

[1] Provable Responsible AI and Data Analytics (PRADA) Lab, Thuwal, Saudi Arabia
lijie.hu@kaust.edu.sa
[2] King Abdullah University of Science and Technology, Thuwal, Saudi Arabia
[3] Tsinghua University, Beijing, China
[4] University of Auckland, Auckland, New Zealand

Abstract. Transparency is a paramount concern in the medical field, prompting researchers to delve into the realm of explainable AI (XAI). Among these XAI methods, Concept Bottleneck Models (CBMs) aim to restrict the model's latent space to human-understandable high-level concepts by generating a conceptual layer for extracting conceptual features, which has drawn much attention recently. However, existing methods rely solely on concept features to determine the model's predictions, which overlook the intrinsic feature embeddings within medical images. To address this utility gap between the original models and concept-based models, we propose **V**ision **C**oncept **T**ransformer (**VCT**). Furthermore, despite their benefits, CBMs have been found to negatively impact model performance and fail to provide stable explanations when faced with input perturbations, which limits their application in the medical field. To address this faithfulness issue, this paper further proposes the **S**table **V**ision **C**oncept **T**ransformer (**SVCT**) based on VCT, which leverages the vision transformer (ViT) as its backbone and incorporates a conceptual layer. SVCT employs conceptual features to enhance decision-making capabilities by fusing them with image features and ensures model faithfulness through the integration of Denoised Diffusion Smoothing. Comprehensive experiments on four medical datasets demonstrate that our VCT and SVCT maintain accuracy while remaining interpretability compared to baselines. Furthermore, even when subjected to perturbations, our SVCT model consistently provides faithful explanations, thus meeting the needs of the medical field.

Keywords: Explainable medical image classification · Explainability · Stability · Medical diagnosis

---

L. Hu, S. Lai, and Y. Hua—Equal contribution.

Supplementary Information The online version contains supplementary material available at https://doi.org/10.1007/978-3-032-06066-2_19.

1 Introduction

As the field of medical image analysis continues to evolve, deep learning models and methods have demonstrated excellent performance in tasks such as image recognition and disease diagnosis [9]. However, these advanced deep learning models are usually regarded as black boxes and lack credibility and transparency. Especially in the medical field, this opacity makes it difficult for physicians and clinical professionals to trust the predictions of the models. Thus, the requirement for interpretability of model decisions is more urgent in the medical field [17].

The healthcare field, characterized by stringent requirements for trustworthiness, necessitates models that not only exhibit high performance but are also comprehensible and can be trusted by practitioners. Therefore, Explainable Artificial Intelligence (XAI) has become one of the hotspots for research and development. By introducing interpretability, XAI tries to make the decision-making process of deep learning models more transparent and understandable. Some compelling interpretable methods, such as attention mechanisms [20], saliency maps [26], DeepLIFT and Shapley values [12], and influence functions [10], attempt to provide users with visual explanations about model decisions. However, while these post-hoc explanatory methods can provide useful information, there is still a certain disconnect between their explanations and model decisions, and these explanations are generated after model training and fail to participate in the model learning process. Some studies [17] have shown that post-hoc is sensitive to slight changes in the input, making the post-hoc methods misleading as they could provide explanations that do not accurately reflect the model's decision-making process.

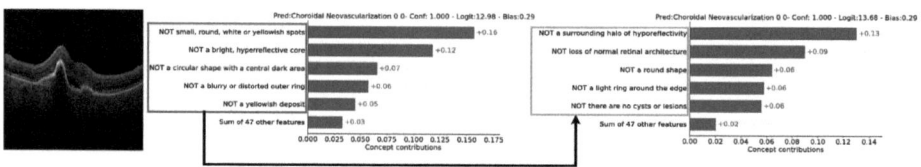

Fig. 1. An example of VCT framework on OCT2017 dataset [9]. The leftmost figure displays the input image, while the adjacent one on the left shows the concept output without perturbations. In contrast, the figure on the right presents the concept output after applying input perturbations, resulting in noticeable changes.

Therefore, researchers have shown interest in self-explained methods. Among them, concept-based methods have attracted a lot of attention. These approaches strive to incorporate interpretability into machine learning models by establishing connections between their predictions and concepts that are understandable to humans. As an illustration, the Concept Bottleneck Model (CBM) [11] initially forecasts an intermediate set of predefined concepts, subsequently utilizing these concepts to make predictions for the final output. [15] introduce Label-free CBM, a novel framework designed to convert any neural network into an interpretable CBM without the need for labeled concept data compared to the original CBM. These inherently interpretable methods provide concept-based explanations, which are generally more comprehensible than post-hoc approaches. However, many existing methods rely solely on concept features to determine the model's predictions. These approaches overlook the intrinsic feature embeddings within medical images. For instance, [18] solely utilizes concept labels to supervise the concept prediction results of the entire image. This oversight can lead to a decrease in classification accuracy, which is suggested to stem from the inefficient utilization of valuable medical information. Therefore, a significant challenge in the field of medical imaging is how to maintain a high level of accuracy while incorporating interpretability.

To address the aforementioned challenges, we propose Vision Concept Transformer (VCT), a novel medical image processing framework that is interpretable and maintains high performance. Vision Transformers (ViTs) [3] have achieved state-of-the-art performance for various vision tasks, showing good robustness in prediction. Thus, in the VCT framework, we utilize ViTs as the foundational network. To enhance interpretability, we employ a label-free methodology for generating the conceptual layer. Moreover, unlike previous CBMs, which only use conceptual features for prediction, in the VCT framework, we integrate conceptual features with image features, utilizing the conceptual layer as supplementary information to augment decision-making. This integration effectively addresses the issue of accuracy degradation associated with a singular label-free CBM, ensuring interpretability without compromising accuracy.

While VCT keeps the interpretability of CBMs, it also inherits their interpretability instability when facing perturbations or noise in the input. Specifically, adding slight noise to the input image can significantly change the top-k important concepts given by CBMs (see Fig. 1 for an example), i.e., the top k-indices of the concept vector. Instability is a common issue in deep learning interpretation methods, making it challenging to understand model reasoning [6], especially with unlabeled data and self-supervised training [4]. As in real medical scenarios, there is always natural and inherent noise or some adversarial examples manipulated by attackers [1]. Thus, VCT cannot be a faithful explainable tool for these applications.

To address the faithfulness issue, by using the Denoised Diffusion Smoothing method, we can smoothly and directly transform VCT into a Stable Vision Concept Transformer (SVCT) framework that is capable of providing stable interpretations despite perturbations to the inputs, the structure is shown in Fig. 2. Our contributions can be summarised as follows.

- We proposed the VCT framework, transforming ViTs into an interpretable CBM. VCT integrates conceptual features with image features, utilizing conceptual features as auxiliary decision-making components. This effectively addresses the performance degradation issue in existing CBMs due to inefficient utilization of medical information.
- To further enhance the interpretability stability of VCT, we propose a formal mathematical definition of an SVCT, which ensures that the top-k index of its conceptual vectors remains relatively stable under slight perturbations. We

utilize a Denoised Diffusion Smoothing (DDS) method to obtain an SVCT. Moreover, we theoretically proved that our method satisfies the properties of SVCT.
- We conducted extensive experiments on four medical datasets to validate the superiority of SVCT in the medical domain. First, we demonstrate that our SVCT is more accurate and interpretable than other CBM approaches. Secondly, we verified that the SVCT model still provides stable explanations under perturbations.

2 Related Work

Concept Bottleneck Models. Concept Bottleneck Model (CBM) [11] stands out as an innovative deep-learning approach applied to image classification and visual reasoning. It introduces a concept bottleneck layer into deep neural networks, enhancing model generalization and interpretability by learning specific concepts. However, CBM faces two primary challenges: its performance often lags behind that of original models lacking the concept bottleneck layer, attributed to incomplete information extraction from the original data to bottleneck features. Additionally, CBM relies on laborious dataset annotation [7]. Researchers have explored solutions to these challenges. [2] extend CBM into interactive prediction settings, introducing an interaction policy to determine which concepts to label, thereby improving final predictions. [14] address CBM limitations and propose a novel framework called Label-free CBM. This innovative approach enables the transformation of any neural network into an interpretable CBM without requiring labeled concept data, all while maintaining high accuracy [24]. However, most of the existing CBMs use only conceptual features for prediction, which can cause a degradation in prediction performance and make them unsuitable for medical scenarios.

Faithfulness in Explainable Methods. Faithfulness is an important property that should be satisfied by explanatory models, which ensures that the explanation accurately reflects the true reasoning process of the model [8]. Stability is crucial to the faithfulness of the interpretation. Some preliminary work has been proposed to obtain stable interpretations. For example, [23] theoretically analyzed the stability of post-hoc explanations and proposed the use of smoothing to improve the stability of explanations. They devised an iterative gradient descent algorithm for obtaining counterfactual explanations, which showed desirable stability. However, these techniques are designed for post-hoc explanations and cannot be directly applied to attention-based mechanisms like ViTs.

Interpretability in Medical Image Classification. In the research of interpretable artificial intelligence in medical image analysis, [21] proposes a new method to construct a robust and interpretable medical image classifier using natural language concepts, and it has been evaluated on multiple datasets. [18] focuses on self-explanatory deep models, introducing a model that implicitly learns conceptual explanations during training by adding an explanation generation module. These methods collectively enhance the interpretability of the model. However, the existing interpretability methods face two main issues. Firstly, they rely solely on concept features for decision-making, leading to insufficient utilization of valuable information in medical images and resulting in a performance decline in medical image processing. Secondly, existing methods exhibit instability when confronted with noise, failing to provide faithful explanations. Therefore, our work aims to ensure good performance while maintaining interpretability and providing faithful explanations to address these issues. See Appendix F for more details.

3 Stable Vision Concept Transformer

In this section, we propose the Stable Vision Concept Transformer (SVCT) framework. Specifically, we first leverage the Label-free Concept Bottleneck Model [15] to transform the ViT network into an interpretable CBM without concept labels, which is an automated, scalable, and efficient fashion to address the core limitations of existing CBMs. We then fuse the concept features with the ViTs features as decision-aiding features, which not only improves the interpretability of the model but also ensures a high degree of accuracy. To obtain an SVCT, we adopt Denoised Diffusion Smoothing (DDS) to turn it into an SVCT.

Our model consists of the following six steps, which are illustrated in Fig. 2 - **Step1:** The ViT model is trained on the target task, and VCT is transformed into SVCT by inserting the DDS method. **Step2:** We generate initial concept set based on the target task and filter out unwanted concepts using a series of filters. **Step3:** Compute embeddings by the backbone on the training dataset and obtain the concept matrix. **Step4:** Learn projection weights W_c to create a Concept Bottleneck Layer (CBL). **Step5:** Fuse the concept features with the ViTs features. **Step6:** Learn the weights W_F of the sparse final layer to make predictions. Detailed notations can be found in Table 6. We first introduce VCT for convenience.

3.1 Vision Concept Transformer

In this section, we introduce the vision concept transformer. Before that, it is necessary to pre-train the ViT model f on the target task dataset as a backbone for the VCT framework.

Label-Free CBMs. We use the label-free CBM [15] to get concept feature $f_c(X) \in \mathbb{R}^M$, where M is the number of concepts. Firstly, we obtain a concept set and use it as human-understandable concepts in the concept bottleneck layer (See Appendix D and E for details). Next, we need to learn how to project from the feature space $\mathbb{R}^{d_o}$ of the backbone network to an interpretable feature space $\in \mathbb{R}^M$ that corresponds to the set of interpretable concepts in the axial direction. We use a way of learning the projection weights $W_c \in \mathbb{R}^{M \times d_o}$ without any labeled

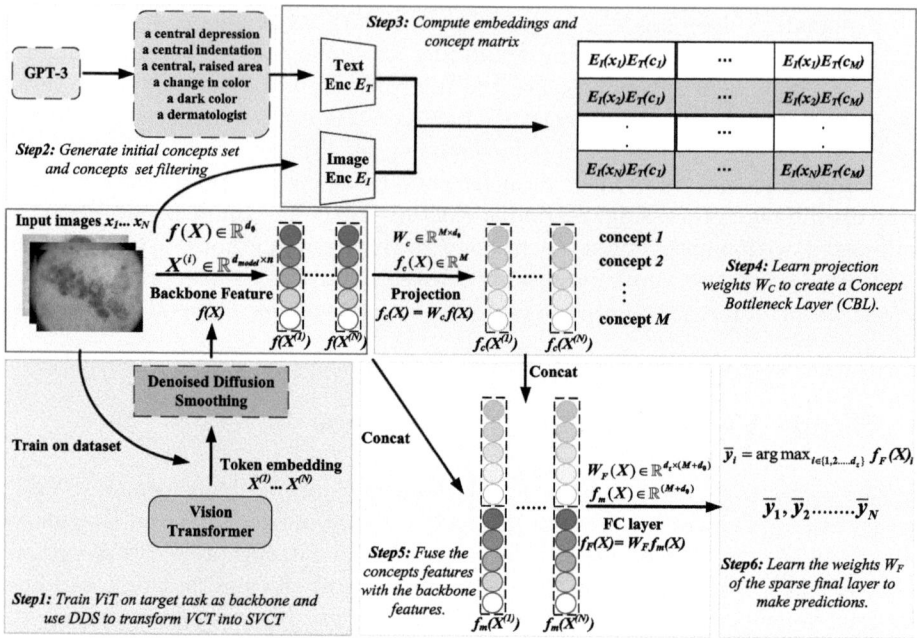

Fig. 2. Overview of our Stable Vision Concept Transformer (SVCT) model.

concept data by utilizing CLIP-Dissect [16]. We can learn about a bottleneck conceptual layer and get the concept feature

$$f_c(X) = W_c f(X) \in \mathbb{R}^M. \tag{1}$$

Concat ViT Feature and Concept Feature. Now that we have learned about the conceptual bottleneck layer and get $W_c \in \mathbb{R}^{M \times d_0}$. In VCT, the conceptual features are no longer used as the only features for classification. According to previous studies, based on the conceptual features alone will degrade the accuracy of the model. Therefore, here we use the conceptual features as the supplementary features, which are fused with the features extracted from the backbone network, and this feature fusion makes the VCT able to ensure accuracy improvement while having a better explanatory nature. Specifically, we define $f_m(X) = \text{concat}(f(X), f_c(X))$, where $f_m(X^{(i)}) \in \mathbb{R}^{M+d_0}$, and we define a feature of VCTs for prediction as follows:

$$F(X) = \text{concat}(f(X), W_c f(X)). \tag{2}$$

Final Classification Layer. The next goal is to learn the final predictor using the fully connected layer $W_F \in \mathbb{R}^{d_z \times (M+d_0)}$, where d_z represents the final number of predicted categories. For each input X, we have access to its predictive distribution through the final classification layer.

3.2 Stable VCT

As we mentioned in the introduction and Fig. 1, CBMs and VCT have an interpretation instability issue, i.e., a slight perturbation on the input could change the top-k concepts in the concept vector (concept feature in VCT). Here we aim to address the instability issue. We first give the definition of the top-k overlap ratio for two (concept) vectors,

Definition 1. *For vector $x \in \mathbb{R}^n$, we define the set of top-k component $T_k(\cdot)$ as*
$$T_k(x) = \{i : i \in [d] \text{ and } \{|\{x_j \geq x_i : j \in [n]\}| \leq k\}\}.$$
For two vectors x, x', their top-k overlap ratio $V_k(x, x')$ is defined as $V_k(x, x') = \frac{1}{k}|T_k(x) \cap T_k(x')|$.

Definition 2 (Stable VCTs). *Giving M number of concepts, a norm $\|\cdot\|$, and a divergence metric D, we call a function $g : \mathbb{R}^{d_{model} \times n} \to \mathbb{R}^M$ is an $(R, D, \gamma, \beta, k, \|\cdot\|)$-stable concept module for VCTs if for any given input data X and for all $X' \in \mathbb{R}^{d_{model} \times n}$ such that $\|X - X'\| \leq R$:*
(1) (Explanation Stability) $V_k(g(X'), g(X)) \geq \beta$.
(2) (Prediction Robustness) $D(\bar{y}(X), \bar{y}(X')) \leq \gamma$, where $\bar{y}(X), \bar{y}(X')$ are the prediction distribution of VCTs based on $g(X), g(X')$ respectively.

We call the models of VCTs based on g as SVCTs.

Intuitively, for input X, $g(X)$ is its concept vector. Thus, the first condition of SVCT ensures that the k-most important concepts will not change much, even if there are some perturbations on the input. The second one guarantees that the prediction of SVCT is also stable against perturbation, which inherits the good performance of VCT. For the parameters, R represents the stable radius. Within this radius, g is a stable concept module, D is the Rényi divergence between two distributions (we denote it as D_α). γ is a similarity coefficient, and as γ gets smaller, g is more robust. β is the stability coefficient, which measures the stability of the interpretation, and as β gets larger, g is more stable. In this paper, $\|\cdot\|$ is the ℓ_2-norm (if we consider X as a $d = d_{model} \times n$ dimensional vector). We can show if the prediction distribution is robust under Rényi divergence, then the prediction will be unchanged with perturbations on input (shown in Theorem 1).

Theorem 1. *If a function is a $(R, D_\alpha, \gamma, \beta, k, \|\cdot\|)$-stable concept module for VCTs, then if*
$$\gamma \leq -\log(1 - p_{(1)} - p_{(2)} + 2(\frac{1}{2}(p_{(1)}^{1-\alpha} + p_{(2)}^{1-\alpha}))^{\frac{1}{1-\alpha}}),$$
we have for all X' such that where $\|X - X'\| \leq R$,
$$\arg\max_{h \in \mathcal{H}} \mathbb{P}(\bar{y}(X) = h) = \arg\max_{h \in \mathcal{H}} \mathbb{P}(\bar{y}(X') = h),$$
where $\mathcal{H}$ is the set of classes, $p_{(1)}$ and $p_{(2)}$ refer to the largest and the second largest probabilities in $\{p_i\}$, where p_i is the probability that $\bar{y}(X)$ returns the i-th class.

Finding Stable Vision Concept Transformers. Motivated by [5], we propose a method called Denoised Diffusion Smoothing (DDS) to obtain SVCTs. The process is as follows: we use randomized smoothing to the VCT and then apply a denoised diffusion probabilistic model to the perturbed input. With this processing, we can transform a VCT into an SVCT, and its corresponding concept module becomes a stable concept module. Specifically, for a given input image x, its corresponding token embedding is X. We add some randomized Gaussian noise to X, i.e., $\tilde{X} = X + S$, where $S \sim \mathcal{N}\left(0, \sigma^2 I_{d_{model} \times n}\right)$. Then we will use some denoised diffusion models to denoise $\tilde{X}$ to get $\hat{X}$. We then take the obtained $\hat{X}$ as a new input to get concept feature $f_c(\hat{X})$ in (1) and go through the remaining structures of the VCT to get the final prediction.

Specifically, for a given input X, randomized smoothing is done by augmenting the data points of an image by adding additive Gaussian noise to the image, which we can denote as $X_{\text{rs}} \sim \mathcal{N}\left(X, \sigma^2 \mathbf{I}\right)$. Diffusion models rely on a particular form of noise modeling, denoted as $X_t \sim \mathcal{N}\left(\sqrt{\beta_t} X, (1-\beta_t) \mathbf{I}\right)$. Where β_t is a constant related to time step t. Thus, if we want to use a diffusion model for randomized smoothing, we need to establish a link between the parameters of the two noise models. The DDS model used in this paper multiplies X_{rs} by the factor $\sqrt{\beta_t}$, thus satisfying the requirement of the noise mean, and accordingly, in order to satisfy the requirement of the variance, we can obtain the equation $\sigma^2 = \frac{1-\beta_t}{\beta_t}$. As the time step changes, σ^2 changes as β_t changes because β_t is a constant with respect to the time step. But it can be computed at every time step, and by using this, we are able to obtain $X_{t^*} = \sqrt{\beta_{t^*}}(X + S)$, where $S \sim \mathcal{N}\left(0, \sigma^2 \mathbf{I}\right)$. Such a form of noise is consistent with the form on which the diffusion model depends, and we can use the diffusion model on X_{t^*} to obtain denoised sample $\hat{X} = \text{denoise}(X_{t^*}; t^*)$. In this paper, we repeat this process several times to improve robustness.

In the following, we show that $\tilde{w} = f_c(\hat{X})$ is a stable concept feature satisfying Definition 2 if σ^2 satisfies some condition. Before showing the results, we first provide some notations. For input image x, we denote $\tilde{w}_{i*}$ as the i-th largest component in $\tilde{w}(x)$. Let $k_0 = \lfloor (1-\beta)k \rfloor + 1$ as the minimum number of changes on $\tilde{w}(x)$ to make it violet the β-top-k overlapping ratio with $\tilde{w}(x)$. Let $\mathcal{S}$ denote the set of last k_0 components in top-k indices and the top k_0 components out of top-k indices. Then, we can prove the following upper bound. The details of the algorithm are in Algorithm 1.

Algorithm 1. SVCTs via Denoised Diffusion Smoothing

1: **Input:** X; A standard deviation $\sigma > 0$.
2: t^*, find t s.t. $\frac{1-\beta_t}{\beta_t} = \sigma^2$.
3: $X_{t^*} = \sqrt{\beta_{t^*}}(\tilde{X} + \mathcal{N}(0, \sigma^2 \mathbf{I}))$.
4: $\hat{X} = \text{denoise}(X_{t^*}; t^*)$.
5: $w = f_c(\hat{X})$, where f_c is in (1).
6: **Return:** Concept feature vector w.

Theorem 2. *Consider the function $\tilde{w}(X) = f_c(T(X + S))$, where f_c as the function in (1), T as the denoised diffusion model and $S \sim \mathcal{N}(0, \sigma^2 I_{d_{model} \times n})$. Then, it is an $(R, D_\alpha, \gamma, \beta, k, \|\cdot\|_2)$-stable concept module for VCTs for any $\alpha > 1$ if for any input image x we have*

$$\sigma^2 \geq \max\{\alpha R^2/2(\frac{\alpha}{\alpha-1}\ln(2k_0(\sum_{i \in \mathcal{S}} \tilde{w}_{i*}^\alpha)^{\frac{1}{\alpha}} +$$

$$(2k_0)^{\frac{1}{\alpha}} \sum_{i \notin \mathcal{S}} \tilde{w}_{i*}) - \frac{1}{\alpha-1}\ln(2k_0)), \alpha R^2/2\gamma\}.$$

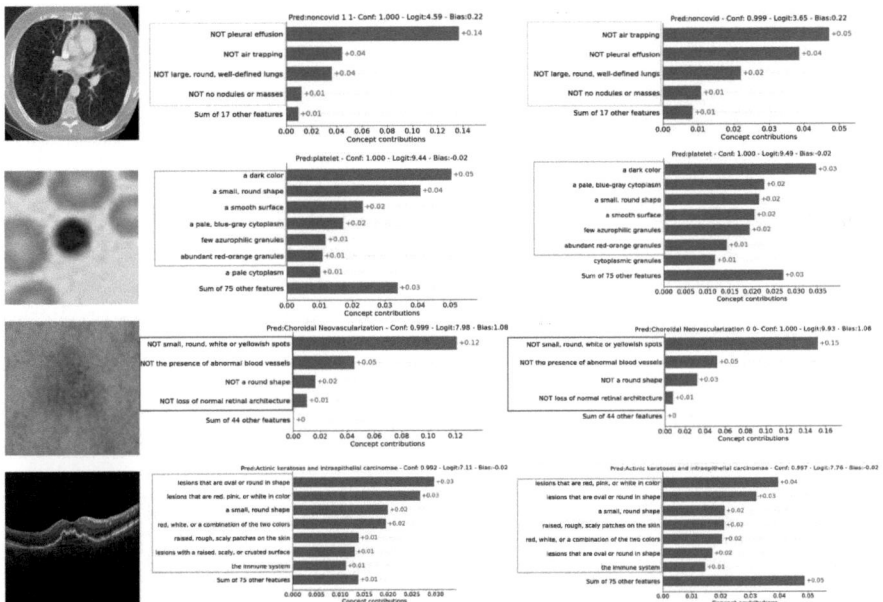

Fig. 3. Results of concept visualization. From left to right: one sample from each dataset, concept visualization results before perturbation, and concept visualization results after perturbation. Clear and enlarged pictures are shown in the Appendix L.

4 Experiments

4.1 Experimental Settings

Datasets. We conducted experiments on four medical datasets, including Human Against Machine with 10,015 training images (HAM10000) dataset [19], Covid19-CT dataset [25], BloodMNIST dataset [22], and Optical coherence tomography (OCT) 2,017 dataset [9]. Details are in Appendix G.

Table 1. Results of accuracy for the baselines and SVCT w/w.o perturbation.

Method	HAM10000	Covid19-CT	BloodMNIST	OCT2017
Standard (No interpretability)	99.13%	81.62%	97.05%	99.70%
Label-Free CBM (LF-CBM)	93.61%	79.75%	94.97%	97.50%
Post-hoc CBM (P-CBM)	97.60%	76.26%	94.83%	98.60%
Vision Concept Transformer (VCT)	99.00%	80.62%	96.21%	99.10%
Stable VCT(SVCT)	**99.05%**	**81.37%**	**96.96%**	**99.50%**
$\rho_u = 8/255$ - LF-CBM	90.08%	67.98%	80.53%	91.88%
$\rho_u = 8/255$ - P-CBM	90.96%	70.66%	77.55%	91.70%
$\rho_u = 8/255$ - VCT	95.80%	69.78%	89.45%	96.80%
$\rho_u = 8/255$ - **SVCT**	**97.97%**	**74.45%**	**94.07%**	**98.70%**
$\rho_u = 10/255$ - LF-CBM	88.70%	65.12%	75.63%	90.58%
$\rho_u = 10/255$ - P-CBM	90.21%	66.32%	74.27%	90.10%
$\rho_u = 10/255$ - VCT	95.28%	68.85%	87.71%	96.25%
$\rho_u = 10/255$ - **SVCT**	**97.24%**	**71.65%**	**92.65%**	**98.48%**

Baselines. In this paper, the standard model is ViT [3], which accomplishes the classification task by extracting image features, but the model itself is not interpretable. The baseline model is label-free CBM [15], which uses ViT as the backbone to generate a conceptual bottleneck layer and finally makes predictions through a linear layer.

Table 2. Results on CFS and CPCS for the baselines and SVCT under various perturbations.

Method	HAM10000		Covid19-CT		BloodMNIST		OCT2017	
	CFS	CPCS	CFS	CPCS	CFS	CPCS	CFS	CPCS
$\rho_u = 6/255$ - LF-CBM	0.3335	0.9405	0.6022	0.8117	0.5328	0.8511	0.3798	0.9254
$\rho_u = 6/255$ - VCT	0.3361	0.9394	0.6761	0.7650	0.5432	0.8436	0.3625	0.9314
$\rho_u = 6/255$ - **SVCT**	**0.1354**	**0.9900**	**0.5555**	**0.8359**	**0.3589**	**0.9320**	**0.3257**	**0.9468**
$\rho_u = 8/255$ - LF-CBM	0.3719	0.9256	0.6707	0.7710	0.6280	0.7947	0.3941	0.9196
$\rho_u = 8/255$ - VCT	0.4109	0.9098	0.8114	0.6743	0.7162	0.7328	0.3812	0.9240
$\rho_u = 8/255$ - **SVCT**	**0.1555**	**0.9867**	**0.6446**	**0.7818**	**0.4383**	**0.8977**	**0.3459**	**0.9387**
$\rho_u = 10/255$ - LF-CBM	0.4027	0.9123	0.7224	0.7336	0.6906	0.7545	0.4055	0.9145
$\rho_u = 10/255$ - VCT	0.4637	0.8844	0.8943	0.6155	0.8057	0.6670	0.3949	0.9179
$\rho_u = 10/255$ - **SVCT**	**0.1725**	**0.9836**	**0.7096**	**0.7389**	**0.5058**	**0.8625**	**0.3620**	**0.9321**

Perturbations. Perturbation refers to small changes or modifications made to input data. In this paper, we introduce perturbations to input images with different radius ρ_u to assess the stability and robustness of the SVCT model.

The range of perturbation radii ρ_u is [6/255, 10/255]. We employ the PGD [13] algorithm to craft adversarial examples with a step size of 2/255 and a total of 10 steps. As a default, we set the standard deviation $S = 8/255$ for the Gaussian noise in our method. All results are the average score running 10 times to reduce variance.

Evaluation Metrics. To demonstrate the utility of our approach, we report the classification accuracy on test data for classification tasks. We evaluate our model's stability using Concept Faithfulness Score (CFS) and Concept Perturbation Cosine Similarity (CPCS). CFS measures the stability of model interpretability between two concept weight vectors using Euclidean distance; we use c_1 to represent the concept weight vector without perturbation and c_2 to represent the concept weight after the perturbation. Then CFS is defined as CFS $= \|c_2 - c_1\|/\|c_1\|$. CPCS measures the cosine similarity between two concept weight vectors, which is defined as CPCS $= c_1 \cdot c_2 / \|c_1\|\|c_2\|$. The smaller the value of CFS, the less the conceptual weights change after being perturbed, and the more stable the model interpretability is. The closer the value of CPCS is to 1, the higher the similarity of conceptual weights before and after perturbation and the more stable interpretability of the model. More experimental details are in the Appendix G.

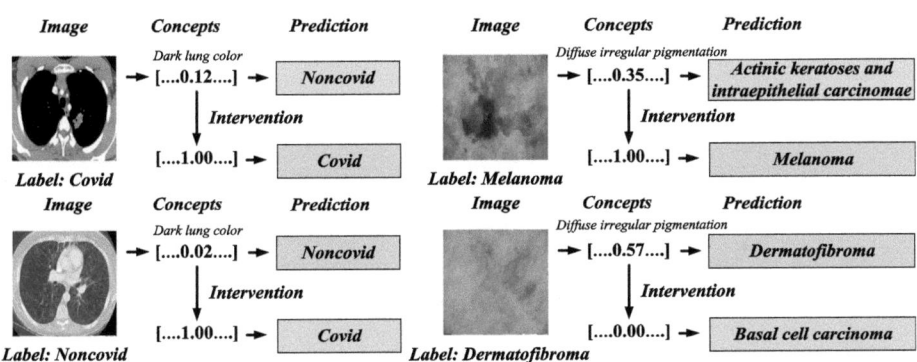

Fig. 4. Concept-intervention examples.

4.2 Utility Evaluation

Table 1 presents the accuracy results of our proposed SVCT method and the baseline approach on four datasets with different levels of perturbations. The table clearly shows that our method maintains a consistently high accuracy across all datasets without any noticeable variation or loss. This highlights the robustness of our approach in terms of accuracy preservation. Compared to Label-free CBM, our model can maintain higher accuracy while guaranteeing interpretability. Overall, the results in Table 1 show that our SVCT model successfully combines high accuracy and interpretability and maintains stability over multiple datasets.

Table 3. Results on sensitivity and specificity for the baselines and SVCT w/w.o perturbation.

Method	HAM10000		Covid19-CT		BloodMNIST		OCT2017	
	sensitivity	specificity	sensitivity	specificity	sensitivity	specificity	sensitivity	specificity
Label-free CBM	0.8878	0.9827	0.7984	**0.8608**	0.9407	0.9956	0.9750	0.9960
SVCT	**0.9899**	**0.9999**	**0.8191**	0.8037	**0.9667**	**0.9958**	**0.9950**	**0.9994**
$\rho_u = 10/255$ - LF CBM	0.6779	0.9615	0.5794	**0.9810**	0.5880	**0.9998**	0.8380	0.9880
$\rho_u = 10/255$ - **SVCT**	**0.9180**	**0.9932**	**0.7136**	0.9303	**0.8681**	0.9948	**0.9790**	**0.9923**

4.3 Stability Evaluation

Table 2 illustrates the experimental result for CFS and CPCS, assessing the stability of CBMs across various disturbance radii and comparing it with the baseline models. SVCT demonstrates superior stability concerning conceptual weights, showcasing minimal disparities pre and post-disturbance, signifying notable similarity. The prowess of SVCT in both CFS and CPCS exceeds that of the baseline model. These outcomes imply that SVCT maintains interpretability with robust resistance to perturbation, establishing it as a model with faithful explanations.

In order to represent the experimental results more intuitively, we first visualized the conceptual weight changes before and after the perturbation of each data. The results of these visualizations provide an intuitive explanation of the validity and stability of the SVCT's performance under the perturbation. The results in both Table 2 and Fig. 3 amply demonstrate that, compared with the baseline model, the SVCT is a model with superior stability while keeping interpretability to perturbation. These advantages make SVCT valuable in the medical field. Secondly, we also conducted repeated experiments in several conceptual spaces to verify the validity of SVCT. Details can be found in Appendix K.

4.4 Interpretability Evaluation

Faithfulness and Stability. SVCT introduces a DDS module while ensuring interpretability, which enables SVCT to provide faithful interpretations, and the results in Table 2 and Fig. 3 have shown that the stability performance of SVCT performs even better under input perturbations. Experimental results indicate that SVCT is a faithful model.

Test-Time Intervention. We envision that in practical applications, medical experts interacting with the model can intervene to "correct" concept values that

Table 4. Ablation study of SVCT on DDS module. We assess the efficacy of denoising and smoothing under input perturbations.

Method	Setting		HAM10000		Covid19-CT		BloodMNIST		OCT2017	
	Denosing	Smoothing	CFS	CPCS	CFS	CPCS	CFS	CPCS	CFS	CPCS
$\rho_u = 6/255$			0.3361	0.9394	0.6761	0.7650	0.5432	0.8436	0.3625	0.9314
		✓	0.3342	0.9405	0.6490	0.7789	0.5412	0.8462	0.3516	0.9362
	✓		0.2689	0.9607	0.5698	0.8221	0.3612	0.9288	0.3367	0.9425
	✓	✓	**0.1354**	**0.9900**	**0.5555**	**0.8359**	**0.3589**	**0.9320**	**0.3257**	**0.9468**
$\rho_u = 8/255$			0.4109	0.9098	0.8114	0.6743	0.7162	0.7328	0.3812	0.9240
		✓	0.3716	0.9255	0.7258	0.7288	0.6349	0.7862	0.3724	0.9279
	✓		0.3020	0.9503	0.6556	0.7710	0.4560	0.8724	0.3574	0.9343
	✓	✓	**0.1555**	**0.9867**	**0.6446**	**0.7818**	**0.4383**	**0.8977**	**0.3459**	**0.9387**
$\rho_u = 10/255$			0.4637	0.8844	0.8943	0.6155	0.8057	0.6670	0.3949	0.9179
		✓	0.4022	0.9119	0.7856	0.6884	0.6940	0.7453	0.3869	0.9217
	✓		0.3306	0.9402	0.7157	0.7320	**0.4988**	0.8421	0.3711	0.9283
	✓	✓	**0.1725**	**0.9836**	**0.7096**	**0.7389**	0.5058	**0.8625**	**0.3620**	**0.9321**

the model predicts incorrectly. During the inference process, we initially predict concepts and obtain corresponding concept scores. Subsequently, we intervene by altering concept values and generating output results based on the intervened concepts. In Fig. 4, we present several examples of interventions. In the example, we observed a significant darkening of the lung color, and the model gave an incorrect prediction, which, after our corrections, ended up being correct. When the model predicts correctly, we make the wrong corrections, which likewise causes the model to predict incorrectly. SVCT gives explanations that humans can understand and that humans can modify to achieve co-diagnosis. Besides, our SVCT can also improve its faithfulness in the test-time intervention under perturbations.

Sensitivity and Specificity. We also conducted sensitivity and specificity experiments on four datasets. Results are shown in Table 3. Sensitivity measures the proportion of actual positive cases that are correctly identified by the model and specificity measures the proportion of actual negative cases that are correctly identified by the model. Results show that SVCT consistently outperforms the LF CBM. For the Covid19-CT dataset, while LF CBM has the highest specificity (0.8608), SVCT demonstrates a higher sensitivity (0.8191), suggesting better detection of positive cases. When perturbation ($\rho_u = 10/255$), SVCT continues to show robust performance. For example, on the HAM10000 dataset, SVCT maintains high sensitivity (0.9180) and specificity (0.9932). These results demonstrate that SVCT not only performs well under standard conditions but also maintains high accuracy and robustness in the presence of data perturbations, making it a promising method for medical image analysis.

Table 5. Ablation study of SVCT on DDS module. We assess the efficacy of denoising and smoothing under input perturbations.

Method	Setting		HAM10000	Covid19-CT	BloodMNIST	OCT2017
	Denosing	Smoothing				
$\rho_u = 0$			99.00%	81.23%	96.81%	99.40%
		✓	98.33%	80.54%	95.88%	99.20%
	✓		98.88%	81.09%	96.33%	99.50%
	✓	✓	**99.05%**	**81.37%**	**96.96%**	**99.50%**
$\rho_u = 10/255$			92.56%	68.22%	80.59%	95.40%
		✓	92.66%	69.10%	81.14%	97.00%
	✓		96.11%	70.03%	90.21%	98.10%
	✓	✓	**97.24%**	**71.65%**	**92.65%**	**98.48%**

4.5 Ablation Study

Results are shown in Tables 4 and 5. The denoising diffusion model and randomized smoothing play an important role in SVCT. When we remove the denoising diffusion model, the performance of the model suffers significantly. While removing the randomized smoothing, the model performance degradation is small. When both modules are removed at the same time, the overall performance of the model decreases more significantly compared to removing a single module. This suggests that these two modules play a key role in maintaining conceptual stability while being able to provide faithful explanations. The ablation results show that without any one of the two modules, the performance of disease diagnosis may suffer. More ablation studies about the effect of feature fusion and DDS are shown in Appendix H, indicating that each module in our SVCT is necessary and efficient. The computational cost is shown in Appendix I, implying the efficiency of our SVCT.

5 Conclusion

In this paper, we propose the Vision Concept Transformer (VCT), and further propose the Stable Vision Concept Transformer (SVCT) framework. In SVCT, we utilize ViT as a backbone, generate the concept layer, and fuse the concept features and image features. SVCT mitigates the information leakage problem caused by CBM and maintains accuracy. Comprehensive experiments show that SVCT can provide stable interpretations despite perturbations to the inputs, with less performance degradation than CBMs and maintaining higher accuracy, indicating SVCT is a more faithful explanation tool.

Acknowledgements. This work is supported in part by the funding BAS/1/1689-01-01, URF/1/4663-01-01, REI/1/5232-01-01, REI/1/5332-01-01, and URF/1/5508-01-01 from KAUST, and funding from KAUST - Center of Excellence for Generative AI, under award number 5940.

References

1. Apostolidis, K.D., Papakostas, G.A.: A survey on adversarial deep learning robustness in medical image analysis. Electronics **10**(17), 2132 (2021)
2. Chauhan, K., Tiwari, R., Freyberg, J., Shenoy, P., Dvijotham, K.: Interactive concept bottleneck models. In: Proceedings of the AAAI Conference on Artificial Intelligence. vol. 37(5), pp. 5948–5955 (2023)
3. Dosovitskiy, A., et al.: An image is worth 16×16 words: transformers for image recognition at scale. In: International Conference on Learning Representations (2020)
4. Ghorbani, A., Abid, A., Zou, J.: Interpretation of neural networks is fragile (2018)
5. Ho, J., Jain, A., Abbeel, P.: Denoising diffusion probabilistic models (2020)
6. Hu, L., Liu, Y., Liu, N., Huai, M., Sun, L., Wang, D.: SEAT: Stable and explainable attention (2022)
7. Ismail, A.A., Adebayo, J., Bravo, H.C., Ra, S., Cho, K.: Concept bottleneck generative models. In: The Twelfth International Conference on Learning Representations (2023)
8. Jacovi, A., Goldberg, Y.: Towards faithfully interpretable NLP systems: How should we define and evaluate faithfulness? (2020)
9. Kermany, D.S., et al.: Identifying medical diagnoses and treatable diseases by image-based deep learning. Cell **172**, 1122–1131.e9 (2018). https://api.semanticscholar.org/CorpusID:3516426
10. Koh, P.W., Liang, P.: Understanding black-box predictions via influence functions (2020)
11. Koh, P.W., et al.: Concept bottleneck models. In: International Conference on Machine Learning, pp. 5338–5348. PMLR (2020)
12. Lundberg, S., Lee, S.I.: A unified approach to interpreting model predictions (2017)
13. Madry, A., Makelov, A., Schmidt, L., Tsipras, D., Vladu, A.: Towards deep learning models resistant to adversarial attacks. arXiv preprint arXiv:1706.06083 (2017)
14. Oikarinen, T., Das, S., Nguyen, L.M., Weng, T.W.: Label-free concept bottleneck models. In: The Eleventh International Conference on Learning Representations (2022)
15. Oikarinen, T., Das, S., Nguyen, L.M., Weng, T.W.: Label-free concept bottleneck models (2023)
16. Oikarinen, T., Weng, T.W.: CLIP-Dissect: Automatic description of neuron representations in deep vision networks (2023)
17. Rudin, C.: Stop explaining black box machine learning models for high stakes decisions and use interpretable models instead (2019)
18. Sarkar, A., Vijaykeerthy, D., Sarkar, A., Balasubramanian, V.N.: A framework for learning ante-hoc explainable models via concepts. In: Proceedings of the IEEE/CVF Conference on Computer Vision and Pattern Recognition, pp. 10286–10295 (2022)
19. Tschandl, P., Rosendahl, C., Kittler, H.: The HAM10000 dataset, a large collection of multi-source dermatoscopic images of common pigmented skin lesions. Sci. Data **5**(1) (2018). https://doi.org/10.1038/sdata.2018.161

20. Vaswani, A., et al.: Attention is all you need. Adv. Neural Inf. Process. Syst. **30** (2017)
21. Yan, A., et al.: Robust and interpretable medical image classifiers via concept bottleneck models. arXiv preprint arXiv:2310.03182 (2023)
22. Yang, J., et al.: MedMNIST v2 - a large-scale lightweight benchmark for 2D and 3D biomedical image classification. Sci. Data **10**(1) (2023).https://doi.org/10.1038/s41597-022-01721-8
23. Yeh, C.K., Hsieh, C.Y., Suggala, A.S., Inouye, D.I., Ravikumar, P.: On the (in)fidelity and sensitivity for explanations (2019)
24. Yuksekgonul, M., Wang, M., Zou, J.: Post-hoc concept bottleneck models (2023)
25. Zhao, J., Zhang, Y., He, X., Xie, P.: COVID-CT-dataset: a CT scan dataset about COVID-19. arXiv preprint arXiv:2003.13865 (2020)
26. Zhou, B., Khosla, A., Lapedriza, A., Oliva, A., Torralba, A.: Learning deep features for discriminative localization. In: 2016 IEEE Conference on Computer Vision and Pattern Recognition (CVPR), pp. 2921–2929 (2016). https://doi.org/10.1109/CVPR.2016.319

Gx2Mol: De Novo Generation of Hit-Like Molecules from Gene Expression Profiles

Chen Li[1(✉)] and Yoshihiro Yamanishi[2]

[1] D3 Center, Osaka University, Ibaraki, Osaka 567-0047, Japan
li.chen.d3c@osaka-u.ac.jp
[2] Graduate School of Informatics, Nagoya University, Nagoya 464-8601, Japan
yamanishi@i.nagoya-u.ac.jp

Abstract. *De novo* generation of hit-like molecules is a challenging task in the drug discovery process. Most methods in previous studies learn the semantics and syntax of molecular structures by analyzing molecular graphs or simplified molecular input line entry system (SMILES) strings; however, they do not take into account the drug responses of the biological systems consisting of genes and proteins. In this study we propose a deep generative model, Gx2Mol, which utilizes **g**ene e**x**pression profiles **to** generate **mol**ecular structures with desirable phenotypes for arbitrary target proteins. In the algorithm, a variational autoencoder is employed as a feature extractor to learn the latent feature distribution of the gene expression profiles. Then, a long short-term memory is leveraged as the chemical generator to produce syntactically valid SMILES strings that satisfy the feature conditions of the gene expression profile extracted by the feature extractor. Experimental results demonstrate that Gx2Mol produces new molecules with potential bioactivities and drug-like properties. The source code is available at: https://github.com/naruto7283/Gx2Mol.

Keywords: Gene expressions · Molecular generation · Deep learning

1 Introduction

Exploring the chemical space to discover molecules with therapeutic effects (e.g., anticancer drug production) is a time-consuming, costly, and high-risk task in the drug discovery field. Despite extensive premarket drug testing, the failure rate is still > 90% [13]. In general, drug development takes over 12 years and costs greater than $1.3 billion [3]. After identification of therapeutic target proteins for a disease of interest, researchers search for potential drug candidate molecules that can interact with the therapeutic target proteins. This process is referred to as hit identification [29]. The high-throughput screening of large-scale chemical

Supplementary Information The online version contains supplementary material available at https://doi.org/10.1007/978-3-032-06066-2_20.

compound libraries with various biological assays is often performed for the hit identification, but the experimental approach is expensive.

As an alternative to hit identification, computational methods such as virtual screening [9] and *de novo* molecular generation [20] can be used to accelerate the production of drug candidates. Virtual screening attempts to explore chemical databases containing massive volumes of molecules at minimal cost and obtain hit-like molecules through docking simulation [27]. *De novo* molecular generation attempts to generate new molecules with desired chemical properties or similar to known ligands [24]. Recently, artificial intelligence and deep learning-based generative models such as variational autoencoders (VAEs) [22] and generative adversarial networks (GANs) [18] have emerged for the *de novo* molecular generation. However, most methods in the previous studies focused on learning the syntax and semantics of molecular structures by analyzing molecular graphs or simplified molecular input line entry system (SMILES) strings.

The biological system is perturbed by drug treatment, thus, the use of biological data in addition to chemical data is desired for drug discovery. Omics data including transcriptome offer a comprehensive molecular landscape that can describe the cellular responses of human cells to drug treatment and the pathological histories of disease patients. Thus, omics data representing drug activities are important resources for current drug development. For example, the use of gene expression data in the preliminary stage of drug discovery is a promising approach [30], because it does not depend on prior knowledge of ligand structures or three-dimensional (3D) structural information of therapeutic target proteins [4]. However, omics-based drug discovery approach has severe limitations. The number of molecules with omics information is quite limited; thus, the method is applicable only to molecules for which omics data are measured. Deep learning methods using GANs [21] and VAEs [12] have been applied to generate molecules from gene expression data, but many generated compounds are chemically invalid or unrealistic, suggesting accuracy needs improvement.

In this study, we present a deep generative model, Gx2Mol, to analyze omics data and design new hit-like molecules. Specifically, a VAE is first used to extract low-dimensional features from gene expression profiles. These features then condition an LSTM-based generator [16] to produce valid SMILES strings aligned with the input profile. Gene expression features are used as conditions during LSTM training to guide the generation of molecules aligned with the target profile. The main contributions are as follows:

- **A novel idea**: unlike the previous methods on the generation of molecular chemical structures (e.g., SMILES strings and graphs), this study attempts to generate hit-like molecules from scratch using gene expression profiles.
- **A concise model**: combining simple generative models (i.e., VAE and LSTM) achieves the goal of molecular generation considering biological information.
- **Superior performance**: the experimental results demonstrate that the proposed method yields new molecules with potential bioactivities and drug-likeness properties, which can be utilized for further structure optimization.

2 Related Works

Traditional drug discovery relies on chemical intuition, medicinal chemistry, and structure-based design [1]. Chemists design molecules, build libraries, and use structural data for drug development. However, such methods are limited by high costs and time demands. Predicting bioactivity remains difficult, as conventional approaches struggle to capture complex structure-activity relationships [13].

2.1 Graph-Based Molecular Generation

Molecular graphs contain rich structural information and are often used for molecular generation [10]. Typically, a molecular graph is usually represented by an ensemble of atom vectors and bond matrices. VAEs attempt to approximate the distribution of molecular graphs to learn latent variables [6]. Generally, VAE-based models construct molecular graphs with a tree structure and employ an encoder to extract the molecular graph features and represent them as low-dimensional latent vectors. Then, the VAE decoder is employed as a molecular generator to reconstruct atoms in the tree into molecules via the latent vector representation. The design of graph-based generators is challenging; thus, GAN-based molecular generation models are rare. MolGAN [5] generates new graphs with the maximum likelihood of atoms and chemical bonds by sampling atomic features and chemical bond feature matrices. In addition, an actor-critic [19] reward network is used to calculate the property scores of the generated graphs. However, MolGAN suffers from a severe mode collapse, thereby causing its uniqueness to be less than 5%.

Flow-based molecular generative models, exemplified by MoFlow [34], initially produce bonds (edges) using a Glow-based model. Subsequently, atoms (nodes) are generated based on the established bonds through a novel graph conditional flow. Finally, these components are assembled into a chemically valid molecular graph, with posthoc validity correction. Diffusion models, such as DiGress [31], are based on a discrete diffusion process. Graphs are iteratively modified with noise through the addition or removal of edges and changes in categories.

2.2 SMILES-Based Molecular Generation

De novo drug design using SMILES strings attempts to generate new molecules with desired properties. For example, GrammarVAE [14] is a SMILES-based model that is used to generate molecular structures, where a VAE is used with a grammar-based decoder that generates syntactically valid SMILES strings. This model is trained on a dataset of existing molecules and generates new molecules with high structural diversity. In addition, TransORGAN [17] is a transformer-based GAN model designed to generate diverse molecules that are similar to the source molecules. The transformer and a one-dimensional convolutional neural network are employed as the generator and discriminator, respectively, and the Monte Carlo tree search-based policy gradient reinforcement learning algorithm [28] is used to explore new molecules with desired chemical properties.

2.3 Omics Data-Driven Molecular Generation

To date, most methods in previous studies generated hit-like molecules based on a learning set of ligand structures and bioactivities, where the structures are represented by graphs or SMILES strings. Diverging from conventional approaches, omics data-driven hit-like molecular generation endeavors to leverage omics data, specifically gene expression profiles. The overarching goal is to generate hit molecules that exhibit promising biological activities against specific targets, such as proteins associated with particular diseases. To our knowledge, there are limited studies that have explored drug design directly from omics data [12,21].

Generally, omics-based methods can generate hit-like molecules without prior knowledge of ligand structures and the 3D structure of the target proteins. A conditional Wasserstein GAN combined with a gradient penalty was proposed to generate hit-like molecules from noise using gene expression profile data [21], which is referred to as ConGAN in this study. However, the validity of the generated candidate molecules is not guaranteed, thereby limiting the hit identification ability. In addition, the prediction process of transcriptional correlation between ligands and targets is unclear. TRIOMPHE [12] is a VAE-based molecular generation model using transcriptional correlation between the gene expression profile with the perturbation of a therapeutic target protein and the gene expression profile with the treatment of small molecules. The most similar molecule is selected as the source molecule, the source molecule is projected to the latent space using a VAE encoder, and a decoder is used to sample and decode the latent vectors into new molecules. However, in their work, gene expression profiles were solely employed in correlation calculations for selecting SMILES strings before inputting them into the VAE model. During the molecular generation phase, gene expression profiles were not utilized to guide the generation of hit-like molecules. Consequently, the molecules generated using TRIOMPHE exhibited low Tanimoto coefficients compared to the corresponding known ligands. DRAGONET [33] generates drug candidates from patient gene expression profiles via a transformer-based VAE, integrating disease-related molecular substructures. It demonstrated effectiveness for diseases such as gastric cancer, atopic dermatitis, and Alzheimer's by producing molecules similar to approved drugs.

Unlike previous approaches, Gx2Mol generates hit-like compounds that exhibit potential biological activity against specific target proteins or therapeutic efficacy for particular diseases, leveraging gene expression profiles. Gx2Mol first extracts biological features from gene expression data using a VAE. Subsequently, these extracted features are utilized as conditional inputs to an LSTM, guiding the generation of hit-like molecules.

3 Gx2Mol

3.1 Extraction of Biological Features

The architecture of the Gx2Mol model is illustrated in Fig. 1. In phase (A), we initiate the process by training a VAE model, extracting essential biological features from gene expression profiles. The encoder network transforms the features

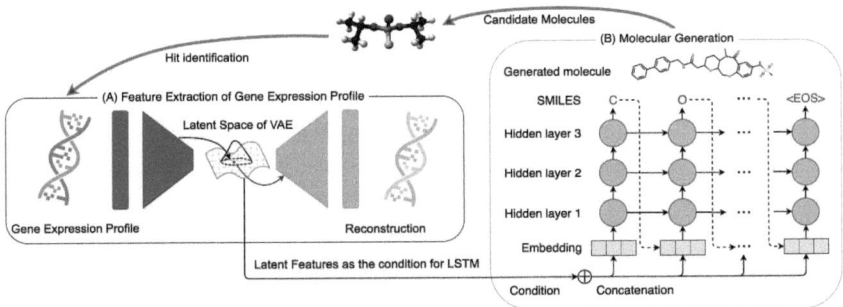

Fig. 1. Architecture of the Gx2Mol model. (A) A VAE is trained to extract the biological features of gene expression profiles. Here, a VAE encoder attempts to extract the latent feature vector of a gene expression profile, and a VAE decoder attempts to reconstruct the gene expression profile from the latent vector. (B) After the VAE training, the latent vector is utilized as a condition to an LSTM to generate SMILES strings. An extracted latent vector and a vector representation of a start token are concatenated to generate the first atom of a SMILES string. Then, the generated atom and the condition generate the next atom iteratively. This iterative process ends when the defined end token (i.e., <EOS>) is generated. Finally, all atoms are assembled into a SMILES string, which serves as a candidate molecule for hit identification in disease treatment.

of gene expression profiles into a low-dimensional latent space, which is subsequently reconstructed by the decoder. Post the training phase, only the encoder is utilized for subsequent downstream tasks.

Formally, let $\boldsymbol{G} = [g_1, g_2, \cdots, g_T]$ indicate the gene expression profile, where g_i represents the i-th gene with the maximum gene number of T. The VAE serves as a feature extractor in Gx2Mol, tasked with learning a latent feature distribution denoted as $p(z|\boldsymbol{G})$. The objective is to align this distribution as closely as possible to the reference distribution $p(z)$, characterized as an isotropic normal distribution. This alignment occurs through the approximation of observed gene expression profiles, while reinforcing the stochastic independence among latent variables. The utilization of the VAE in this manner facilitates the extraction of meaningful latent features from the input data, as demonstrated in Fig. 1 (A). This visualization offers a concrete representation of how the VAE captures key features within the gene expression profiles. High-dimensional gene expression profile reconstruction can be modeled by the integration of the low-dimensional feature space $p(z)$ and conditional distribution $p_{\boldsymbol{\theta}}(\boldsymbol{G}|z)$ parameterized by $\boldsymbol{\theta}$:

$$p_{\boldsymbol{\theta}}(\boldsymbol{G}) = \int p_{\boldsymbol{\theta}}(\boldsymbol{G}|z) p(z) dz. \tag{1}$$

To address the intractable issue of the posterior distribution $p_{\boldsymbol{\theta}}(z|\boldsymbol{G})$, the feature extractor replaces $p_{\boldsymbol{\theta}}(z|\boldsymbol{G})$ by an approximate variational distribution $q_{\boldsymbol{\theta}'}(z|\boldsymbol{G})$. Typically, $q_{\boldsymbol{\theta}'}(z|\boldsymbol{G})$ and $p_{\boldsymbol{\theta}}(\boldsymbol{G}|z)$ are used as the encoder and decoder of a VAE, respectively. According to the evidence lower bound [26], the loss function of the feature extractor can be formulated as

$$\mathcal{L}_F(\boldsymbol{\theta}, \boldsymbol{\theta}') = -\mathbb{E}_{z \sim q_{\theta'}(z|G)}[\log p_{\boldsymbol{\theta}}(\boldsymbol{G}|z)] + \beta \cdot D_{KL}(q_{\theta'}(z|\boldsymbol{G})||p(z)), \qquad (2)$$

where $\mathbb{E}[\cdot]$ and β indicate an expectation operation and the weight of the Kullback-Leibler divergence D_{KL} [11], respectively. The VAE encoder generates both a mean (μ) and a variance (σ^2) for each point in the latent space, typically following a Gaussian distribution. For a given gene expression profile $\boldsymbol{G}$, the approximate posterior distribution can be calculated as follows:

$$q_{\theta'}(z|\boldsymbol{G}) = \mathbf{N}\left(\mu(\boldsymbol{G}), \sigma^2(\boldsymbol{G})\right), \qquad (3)$$

where $\mu(\boldsymbol{G})$ and $\sigma^2(\boldsymbol{G})$ are the mean and variance functions parameterized by the encoder. The VAE then samples a point z from this distribution. Finally, the extracted latent vector of the gene expression profiles is as follows:

$$\boldsymbol{F}_{Gx} = \text{Encoder}(\boldsymbol{G}). \qquad (4)$$

3.2 Generation of Hit-Like Molecules

Here, an LSTM model is used as the chemical generator to produce syntactically valid SMILES strings that satisfy the feature conditions of the gene expression profiles extracted by the feature extractor. During phase (B), we incorporate the corresponding SMILES strings as inputs for LSTM training. The extracted features from gene expression profiles are fused with each SMILES token, serving as input for the model to iteratively generate the subsequent token.

Formally, let $\boldsymbol{X}_{1:n} = [\boldsymbol{x}_1, \boldsymbol{x}_2, \cdots, \boldsymbol{x}_n]$ denote a SMILES string of length n, where $\boldsymbol{x}_i$ is the i-th embedding vector of the SMILES string with the size of M. Then, $\boldsymbol{x}_i$ is concatenated with $\boldsymbol{F}_{Gx}$ as the input to the generator. The generator iteratively generates a character of the SMILES string at the current time step based on the previous time step. Let $\boldsymbol{Y}_{1:n} = [\boldsymbol{y}_1, \cdots, \boldsymbol{y}_n]$ indicate the predicted SMILES string for $\boldsymbol{X}_{1:n}$. According to the negative log likelihood, the loss function of the generator can be calculated as follows:

$$\mathcal{L}_G(\boldsymbol{X}_{1:n}, \boldsymbol{Y}_{1:n}) = -\sum_{i=1}^{n} \log p(\boldsymbol{y}_i|\boldsymbol{X}_{1:i-1}; \boldsymbol{\phi}), \qquad (5)$$

where $\boldsymbol{\phi}$ is the parameters of the chemical generator.

During the generation phase, the input to the VAE encoder exclusively comprises gene expression profiles for feature extraction. The resulting extracted features are subsequently employed to steer the process of generating hit-like molecules. Algorithm 1 summarizes the procedure of the Gx2Mol model. Here, sets of the gene expression profiles and SMILES strings are first used to train the feature extractor and chemical generator. In the training phase, the features of gene expression profiles are learned from a VAE-based feature extractor. The extracted features are used as conditions of the LSTM-based molecular generator. In the testing phase, the gene expression profile is employed to generate new hit-like molecules.

Algorithm 1. Procedure for the Gx2Mol model

1: **Data:** Gene expression profiles G and SMILES strings $X_{1:n}$
2: **Initialization:** the feature extractor F_θ, the molecule generator G_ϕ
3: // Train the feature extractor.
4: **for** $i = 1 \to f\_epochs$ **do**
5:     Update F_θ using G according to the loss function of Eq. (2).
6: **end for**
7: // Train the molecule generator.
8: **for** $i = 1 \to g\_epochs$ **do**
9:     Update G_ϕ using $X_{1:n}$ according to the loss function of Eq. (5).
10: **end for**
11: // Generate hit-like molecules from scratch.
12: Extract the features F_{Gx} using G according to Eq. (4).
13: Generate the corresponding SMILES representation from F_{Gx}.
14: // Test the generation task.
15: Calculate the Tanimoto coefficient using known ligands.
16: Select the molecule with the maximum Tanimoto coefficient score as the candidate molecule.

4 Experiments

Datasets. In this study, we used chemically induced gene expression profiles as training data to train the Gx2Mol model. In addition, we analyzed target protein-perturbed expression profiles with eight knockdown genes and two overexpressed genes to generate hit-like molecules, and disease reversal gene expression profiles as a case study to generate therapeutic molecules.

- **Chemically-induced gene expression profiles** were collected from the Library of Integrated Network-based Cellular Signatures (LINCS) database [7]. LINCS database stores the gene expression profiles with a dimension of 978 for 77 human cultured cell lines exposed to various molecules. We analyzed the gene expression profiles of the MCF7 cell line treated with 13,755 molecules whose SMILES string lengths were less than 80 at a concentration of 10 µM.
- **Target protein-perturbed gene expression profiles** were collected from the LINCS database. We analyzed the RAC-alpha serine / threonine-protein kinase (AKT1), RAC-beta serine / threonine-protein kinase (AKT2), Aurora B kinase (AURKB), cysteine synthase A (CTSK), epidermal growth factor receptor (EGFR), histone deacetylase 1 (HDAC1), mammalian target of rapamycin (MTOR), phosphatidylinositol 3-kinase catalytic subunit (PIK3CA), decapentaplegic homologue 3 (SMAD3), and tumor protein p53 (TP53), which have been verified to be useful therapeutic target proteins against cancers. The gene expression profiles for the first eight proteins were obtained from gene knockdown profiles of the MCF7 cell line, while those for the latter two proteins were obtained from gene overexpression profiles. When multiple profiles were measured under different experimental conditions for a

single protein, we averaged the multiple profiles of the same target protein to create target protein-specific profiles.
- **Disease-specific gene expression profiles** were obtained from the crowd extracted expression of differential signatures (CREEDS) database [32], which contains the expression profiles of 14,804 genes for 79 diseases. The disease-specific gene expression profiles were acquired by averaging the gene expression profiles from multiple patients with the same disease. Here, we extracted the most relevant 884 genes for gastric cancer, atopic dermatitis, and Alzheimer's disease from the disease-specific gene expression for model validation, and we created the disease reversal profiles by multiplying the disease-specific gene expression by -1. Note that the disease reversal profiles of a disease are considered to be associated with a therapeutic effect on that disease.

Hyperparameters. For the feature extractor, the encoder of the VAE included three feedforward layers with dimensions of 512, 256, and 128. The latent vector dimension was set to 64. Note that the dimensions of the decoder were the opposite dimensions of the encoder, i.e., 128, 256, and 512. The dropout probability and learning rate were set to 0.2 and 1e−4, respectively. The training of gene expression profiles was conducted with a batch size set at 64. For the generator, the embedding size was set to 128. The LSTM model contained three hidden layers with dimensions of 256. The dropout probability and learning rate were set to 0.1 and 5e−4, respectively. The maximum length of the generated SMILES strings was fixed to 100. The batch size for training LSTM was set to 64. In addition, the feature extractor and generator used the Adam optimizer, and the number of training epochs for the feature extractor and generator was set to 2000 and 300, respectively. All experiments were conducted on GPUs using CUDA.

Dataset Splitting and Model Selection. The dataset was partitioned into distinct sets for training (80%), validation (10%), and testing (10%) to ensure a robust evaluation of our Gx2Mol model. This division allows for effective model training on the training set, tuning of hyperparameters based on the validation set, and unbiased assessment of model performance on the test set. The selection of the optimal model was determined by monitoring the convergence of the total loss function of Gx2Mol during training. Convergence of the loss function indicates stability and optimal performance. This approach ensures the selection of a well-performing model based on its ability to minimize the defined loss and generalize effectively to unseen data.

4.1 Evaluation Measures

In this study, two essential chemical properties (quantitative estimate of drug-likeness (QED) [2] and synthesizability (SA) [8]) and the Tanimoto coefficient [25] were employed to assess hit-like molecules generated by the Gx2Mol.
- **QED** can be calculated by assigning different weights to eight molecular descriptors (i.e., molecular weight, octanol-water partition coefficient, number of hydrogen bond donors, number of hydrogen bond acceptors, molecular

polar surface area, number of rotatable bonds, number of aromatic rings, and number of structural alarms). where d_i and W_i represent the desirability function and weight of the i-th descriptor, respectively. Typically, the weights of the eight molecular descriptors were obtained through chemical experiments. In practice, the QED score was calculated by a function in the RDKit tool. The larger the QED score, the more drug-like the molecule.

- **Synthesizability (SA)** is assessed through the SA score, denoted as $SA = r_s - \sum_{i=1}^{5} p_i$. Here, r_s signifies the "synthetic knowledge," representing the ratio of contributions from all fragments to the total number of fragments in the molecule. In this study, r_s is computed from experimental results [8]. Each p_i ($i \in \{1, \cdots, 5\}$) corresponds to the ring complexity, stereo complexity, macrocycle penalty, size penalty, and bridge penalty, computed using the RDKit tool [15]. A higher SA score indicates greater ease of synthesizing the molecule.
- **Tanimoto coefficient**, which is calculated from the ECFP4 fingerprint [23] with a dimension of 2048. In practice, the ECFP4 and Tanimoto coefficients were calculated using the "GetMorganfingerprintAsBitVect" and "BulkTanimotoSimilarity" functions of the RDKit tool.

4.2 Gx2Mol Training

We evaluated the effectiveness of the VAE model in extracting the biological features from gene expression profiles and the capability of the LSTM model to generate new molecules experimentally.

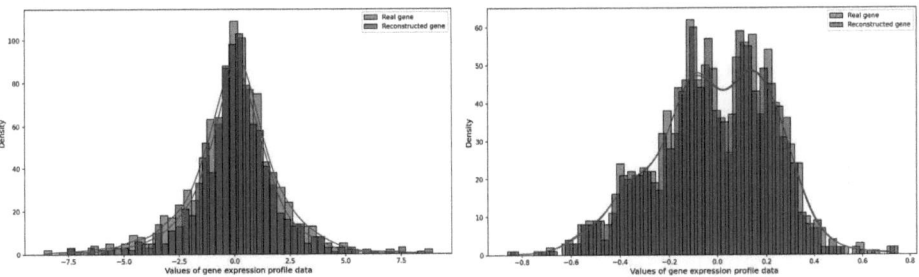

Fig. 2. Distribution of fold change values in the gene expression profile of the molecule "C17H25ClN2O3" exposed in the MCF7 cell. The original gene expression profile of "C17H25ClN2O3" (green) and the reconstructed gene expression profiles (red) have similar distributions. (Color figure online)

Fig. 3. Distribution of fold change values in the average gene expression profile of all molecules exposed in the MCF7 cell. The original gene expression profiles of the training set (green) and the reconstructed gene expression profiles (red) have similar distributions. (Color figure online)

Figure 2 shows a comparison of the distribution of fold change values in the gene expression profile of a molecule between the training set and the reconstructed set. Figure 3 shows a comparison of the distribution of fold change values in the average gene expression profile of all reconstructed molecules between the original set and the reconstructed set. Note that Fig. 2 shows the distribution of a gene expression profile of the molecule "C17H25ClN2O3" exposed in the MCF7 cell, whose SMILES representation is denoted as "CCC1=CC(=C(C(=C1 O)C(=O)NC[C@@ H]2CCCN2CC)OC)Cl." The distribution of the original gene expression profiles was similar to that of the reconstructed gene expression profiles acquired using the Gx2Mol. In other words, the VAE utilized in the Gx2Mol captures the biological features of the gene expression profiles and successfully reconstructs them into the original distribution.

Figure A.1 in the appendix[1] shows the training loss and the ratio of the generated valid molecules of the LSTM in the Gx2Mol. The loss decreased smoothly over the 300 training epochs and finally converges under 0.1. In contrast, the validity of the molecules generated by the conditional LSTM model gradually increased as training proceeds, with the final validity ratio converging at approximately 90%. Overall, the results indicate that the conditional LSTM utilized in the Gx2Mol can generate valid molecules effectively.

To further explore the ability of the Gx2Mol to generate molecules, we also compared the distribution of the QED scores of the molecules generated by Gx2Mol with molecules in the training data. Figure A.2 in the appendix shows that the generated molecules and the original molecules have similar QED distributions. The average QED scores of molecules in the training dataset and molecules generated by Gx2Mol were 0.60 and 0.61, respectively. The violin plots of the QED scores indicate that the Gx2Mol did not change the potential chemical property characteristics of the training data during the generation process, which demonstrates the LSTM's ability to generate molecules effectively.

Figures A.3 and A.4 in the appendix show the top-12 molecular structures with their QED scores for molecules in the training dataset and molecules generated by the Gx2Mol, respectively. It seems that all of the molecules are chemically valid and exhibit high QED scores.

Furthermore, we evaluated the QED scores for the top-k generated molecules using the Gx2Mol model. The results are presented in Table 1. The molecules generated by Gx2Mol exhibited QED scores that were higher yet comparable to those of the training data. These findings demonstrate that the Gx2Mol model generated molecules while preserving the QED properties.

Similarly, we present the top-12 molecular structures along with their synthesizability (SA) scores for molecules in the training dataset and those generated by Gx2Mol in Figures A.5 and A.6, respectively. The generated molecular structures indicate that our proposed Gx2Mol can produce valid molecules that are easy to synthesize. Moreover, the SA scores for the top-k generated molecules in Table 1 show that Gx2Mol effectively generated molecules with high SA scores.

---

[1] Additional appendices are available at: https://yamanishi.cs.i.nagoya-u.ac.jp/gx2mol/.

Table 1. Assessment of QED and SA scores for the top-k generated molecules.

Chemical Property	Data Source	Top-1	Top-10	Top-100	Top-1000
Drug-likeness (QED)	Compounds in training dataset	0.94	0.92	**0.85**	0.64
	Compounds generated by Gx2Mol	**0.95**	**0.93**	0.84	**0.65**
Synthesizability (SA)	Compounds in training dataset	1.00	0.94	0.85	0.47
	Compounds generated by Gx2Mol	**1.00**	**0.99**	**0.88**	**0.48**

4.3 Gx2Mol Generation

Generally, the gene expression profiles of knockdown and overexpression of target proteins correlate with the gene expression profiles of inhibitors and activators, respectively [12]. To generate molecules as candidates for inhibitory and activatory ligands of target proteins, the gene expression profiles of the eight knockdown and two overexpressed target proteins were considered in this study. The former includes AKT1, AKT2, AURKB, CTSK, EGFR, HDAC1, MTOR, and PIK3CA. The latter includes SMAD3 and TP53.

Table 2. Comparison of structural similarity scores of new molecules with known ligands for each target protein between baselines and Gx2Mol.

Therapeutic target protein	ConGAN	TRIOMPHE	Gx2Mol
AKT1	0.32	0.42	**0.53**
AKT2	0.29	0.35	**0.53**
AURKB	0.36	0.34	**0.67**
CTSK	0.31	0.29	**0.34**
EGFR	0.30	0.31	**0.72**
HDAC1	0.34	0.30	**0.42**
MTOR	0.39	**0.69**	0.46
PIK3CA	0.26	**0.32**	0.30
SMAD3	0.44	0.48	**0.85**
TP53	0.46	0.53	**0.55**

[⋆] The values in bold in gray cells are the maximum values.

We conducted experiments on the newly generated molecules by comparing their molecular structures with those of the known ligands (inhibitors and activators). If the newly generated molecules are meaningful, the newly generated

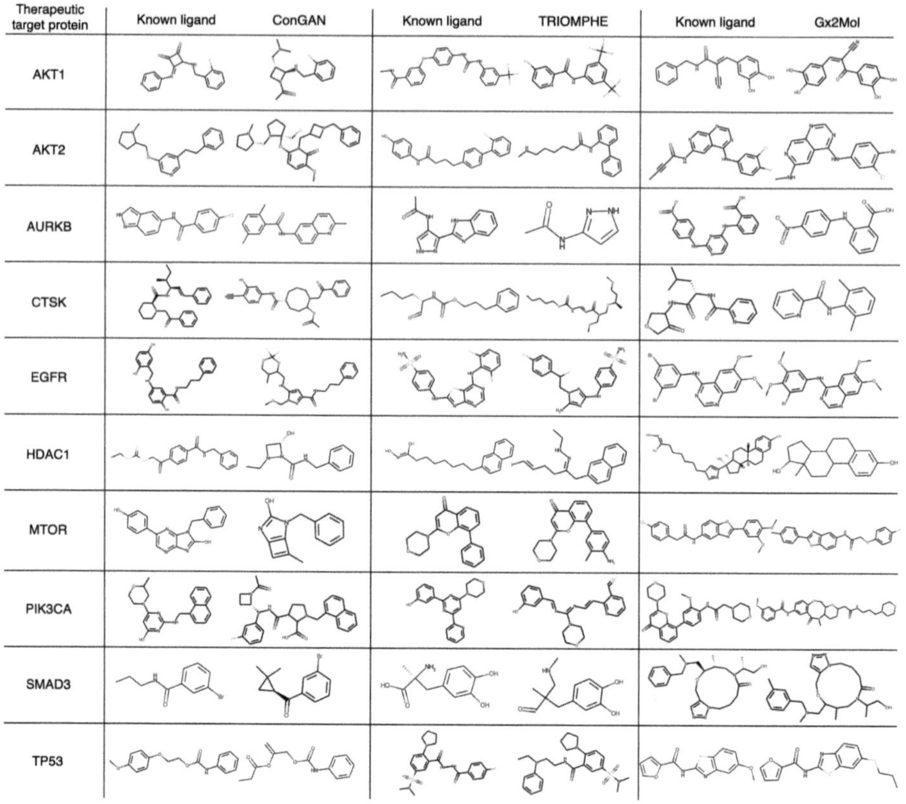

Fig. 4. Comparison of newly generated molecules from the baseline models and Gx2Mol with known ligands for each therapeutic target protein.

molecules should be structurally similar to known ligands of each target protein to some extent. To ensure a fair comparison with the TRIOMPHE baseline, the default sampling number for each gene expression profile of the target protein was set to 1000, consistent with the setting used in TRIOMPHE. Subsequently, we only retained the valid molecules from the 1000 generated samples to calculate structural similarity using Tanimoto coefficients. The results are presented in Table 2. ConGAN [21] and TRIOMPHE [12] are the two state-of-the-art (STOA) baselines that are related to the Gx2Mol. For the former eight knockdown target proteins, six of the calculated Tanimoto coefficients for the molecules generated by the Gx2Mol with inhibitory ligands (i.e., AKT1, AKT2, AURKB, CTSK, EGFR, and HDAC1) outperformed the baselines. For MTOR and PIK3CCA, the Tanimoto coefficients performed second only to TRIOMPHE. In addition, for both 2SMAD3 and TP53, i.e., the target proteins with gene overexpression perturbations, the Tanimoto coefficients of the generated molecules by the Gx2Mol were higher than those obtained by the baseline methods.

Furthermore, we analyzed the diversity metrics of the newly generated molecules. The diversity was computed based on molecular fingerprints generated using the Morgan algorithm (radius = 2, 2048 bits) as implemented in RDKit. The results are summarized in Table B.1. Notably, the maximum diversity values for all ten target proteins reach 1.0, while the average diversity values are consistently high (above 0.82) with low standard deviations, indicating a broad structural variety across the generated molecules.

Figure 4 shows the molecules generated by the baseline and Gx2Mol models and known ligands for each therapeutic target protein, where the newly generated molecular structures with the highest Tanimoto coefficients to the corresponding known ligands are shown. For the 10 target proteins, all generated molecules were structurally similar to the known ligands, compared with the baseline models. In summary, the Gx2Mol exhibited superior performance in terms of generating hit-like molecules from gene expression profiles via deep learning, and the proposed model outperformed the current SOTA baselines in most metrics.

4.4 Case Studies

Generally, gene expression profiles are altered in a patient with a disease state. A molecule that counteracts the disease state is considered to have therapeutic effects on the disease. As a case study, we generated molecules with therapeutic effects on a disease by considering disease-specific gene expression profiles.

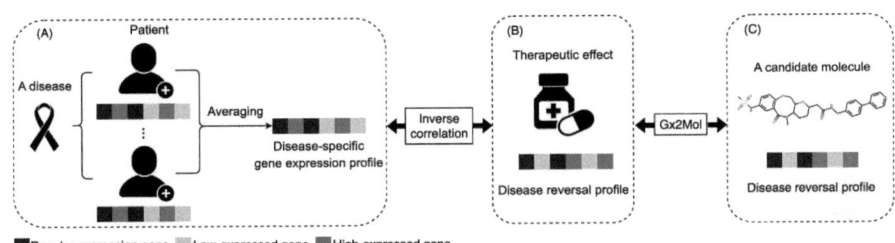

Fig. 5. Data processing of gene expression profiles for therapeutic molecular generation.

Figure 5 illustrates the data processing of a gene expression profile for the generation of molecules with therapeutic effects on a disease. First, as shown in Fig. 5 (A), a disease-specific gene expression profile is constructed by averaging the gene expression profiles of patients with a certain disease. Then, a gene expression profile that is inversely correlated with the disease-specific gene expression profile is constructed and defined as the disease reversal profile, as shown in Fig. 5 (B). Finally, the disease reversal profile is used as an input to the Gx2Mol to generate molecules with therapeutic effects (Fig. 5 (C)). The disease-specific gene expression profiles were obtained from the CREEDS database for patients with three diseases, i.e., gastric cancer, atopic dermatitis, and Alzheimer's disease.

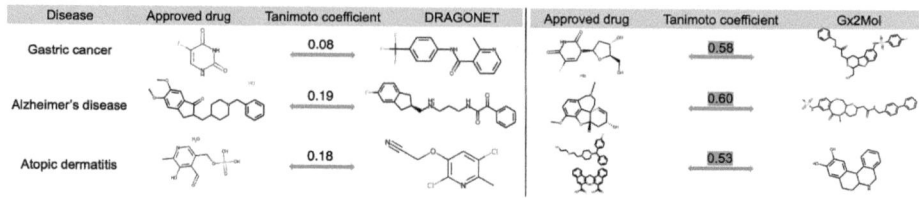

Fig. 6. Comparison of newly generated therapeutic molecules with approved drugs for each disease.

We examined the validity of the newly generated molecules by comparing the newly generated molecular structures with those of the approved drugs. If the newly generated molecules are meaningful, the newly generated molecules should be structurally similar to the approved drugs of each disease to some extent. We calculated the structural similarity using Tanimoto coefficients. Figure 6 illustrates the Tanimoto coefficients between approved drugs and newly generated molecules, comparing the results obtained from the SOTA DRAGONET [33] and our proposed Gx2Mol model, for each of the three diseases. Our proposed Gx2Mol model surpassed the SOTA DRAGONET in the therapeutic molecule generation for three diseases. Gx2Mol exhibited improved Tanimoto coefficients to approved drugs, reaching 0.58, 0.60, and 0.53 for gastric cancer, Alzheimer's disease, and atopic dermatitis. Additionally, fluorouracil (D04197) can be used in the treatment of liver metastases from gastrointestinal adenocarcinomas and also in the palliative treatment of liver and gastrointestinal cancers. When using the disease reversal profile of gastric cancer patients, the Tanimoto coefficient between the molecule generated by the Gx2Mol and fluorouracil was the largest. The Tanimoto coefficient of the Gx2Mol model-generated molecule with floxuridine was maximum using the disease reversal profile of gastric cancer patients. These results suggest that the generated molecules effectively capture the structural features of approved anti-gastric cancer drugs. In addition, the molecules generated for the other two diseases demonstrate structural features that are similar to those of the approved drugs. As a result, the molecules generated using the Gx2Mol have potential drug-like properties.

5 Conclusion

This study introduced the Gx2Mol model, designing to generate potential chemical structures of hit-like molecules from gene expression profiles using deep learning techniques. In the training phase, the Gx2Mol model first employed a VAE for feature extraction from high-dimensional gene expression profiles, and then the low-dimensional extracted features guided the generation of syntactically valid SMILES strings. In the generation phase, the VAE encoder served as the sole feature extractor, seamlessly combined with the generator to facilitate the generation of hit-like molecules. The results demonstrated the effectiveness of

Gx2Mol in generating hit-like molecules from gene expression profiles. Additionally, a case study illustrates the model's ability to generate potential chemical structures for therapeutic drugs related to gastric cancer, stress dermatitis, and Alzheimer's disease using patients' disease reversal profiles.

This study has a primary limitation. Since LSTMs are frequently employed in auto-regressive generation tasks, wherein the token at the next time step is generated based on the token at the current time step, there exists a potential constraint on the diversity of generated molecules when using LSTMs as generators. In future research, we aim to explore strategies to enhance the diversity of molecular generation within the Gx2Mol. Furthermore, the envisaged application of the Gx2Mol model involves integration into practical AI systems to assist chemists in generating diverse drug candidate hit-like molecules tailored for various diseases. This integration is anticipated to leverage the strengths of the Gx2Mol model and contribute to the advancement of drug discovery processes.

Acknowledgments. This research was supported by the International Research Fellow of the Japan Society for the Promotion of Science (Postdoctoral Fellowships for Research in Japan [Standard]), AMED under Grant Number JP23nk0101111 and JSPS KAKENHI [grant numbers 20H05797, 21H04915].

References

1. Akaji, K., Konno, H., Mitsui, H., Teruya, K., Shimamoto, Y., Hattori, Y., Ozaki, T., Kusunoki, M., Sanjoh, A.: Structure-based design, synthesis, and evaluation of peptide-mimetic sars 3cl protease inhibitors. J. Med. Chem. **54**(23), 7962–7973 (2011)
2. Bickerton, G.R., Paolini, G.V., Besnard, J., Muresan, S., Hopkins, A.L.: Quantifying the chemical beauty of drugs. Nat. Chem. **4**(2), 90–98 (2012)
3. Bongini, P., Bianchini, M., Scarselli, F.: Molecular generative graph neural networks for drug discovery. Neurocomputing **450**, 242–252 (2021)
4. Bung, N., Krishnan, S.R., Roy, A.: An in silico explainable multiparameter optimization approach for de novo drug design against proteins from the central nervous system. J. Chem. Inf. Model. **62**(11), 2685–2695 (2022)
5. De Cao, N., Kipf, T.: MolGAN: an implicit generative model for small molecular graphs. arxiv 2018. arXiv preprint arXiv:1805.11973 (2019)
6. Du, Y., Guo, X., Shehu, A., Zhao, L.: Interpretable molecular graph generation via monotonic constraints. In: Proceedings of the 2022 SIAM International Conference on Data Mining (SDM), pp. 73–81 (2022)
7. Duan, Q., et al.: Lincs canvas browser: interactive web app to query, browse and interrogate lincs 1000 gene expression signatures. Nucleic Acids Res. **42**(W1), W449–W460 (2014)
8. Ertl, P., Schuffenhauer, A.: Estimation of synthetic accessibility score of drug-like molecules based on molecular complexity and fragment contributions. Journal of cheminformatics **1**(1), 1–11 (2009)
9. Gimeno, A., et al.: The light and dark sides of virtual screening: what is there to know? Int. J. Mol. Sci. **20**(6), 1375 (2019)

10. Jin, W., Barzilay, R., Jaakkola, T.: Junction tree variational autoencoder for molecular graph generation. In: International Conference on Machine Learning, 2323–2332 (2018)
11. Joyce, J.M.: Kullback-leibler divergence. In: International Encyclopedia of Statistical Science, pp. 720–722 (2011)
12. Kaitoh, K., Yamanishi, Y.: Triomphe: transcriptome-based inference and generation of molecules with desired phenotypes by machine learning. J. Chem. Inf. Model. **61**(9), 4303–4320 (2021)
13. Kale, B., Clyde, A., Sun, M., Ramanathan, A., Stevens, R., Papka, M.E.: Chemograph: interactive visual exploration of the chemical space. Computer Graphics Forum **42**, 13–24 (2023)
14. Kusner, M.J., Paige, B., Hernández-Lobato, J.M.: Grammar variational autoencoder. In: International Conference on Machine Learning, pp. 1945–1954 (2017)
15. Landrum, G.: Rdkit documentation. Release **1**(1–79), 4 (2013)
16. Li, C., He, M., Qaosar, M., Ahmed, S., Morimoto, Y.: Capturing temporal dynamics of users' preferences from purchase history big data for recommendation system. In: 2018 IEEE International Conference on Big Data (Big Data), pp. 5372–5374 (2018)
17. Li, C., Yamanaka, C., Kaitoh, K., Yamanishi, Y.: Transformer-based objective-reinforced generative adversarial network to generate desired molecules. IJCAI, pp. 3884–3890 (2022)
18. Li, C., Yamanishi, Y.: SpotGAN: A reverse-transformer GAN generates scaffold-constrained molecules with property optimization. In: Joint European Conference on Machine Learning and Knowledge Discovery in Databases, pp. 323–338 (2023)
19. Lillicrap, T.P., et al.: Continuous control with deep reinforcement learning. arXiv preprint arXiv:1509.02971 (2015)
20. Lin, X., Li, X., Lin, X.: A review on applications of computational methods in drug screening and design. Molecules **25**(6), 1375 (2020)
21. Méndez-Lucio, O., Baillif, B., Clevert, D.A., Rouquié, D., Wichard, J.: De novo generation of hit-like molecules from gene expression signatures using artificial intelligence. Nat. Commun. **11**(1), 10 (2020)
22. Oliveira, A.F., Da Silva, J.L., Quiles, M.G.: Molecular property prediction and molecular design using a supervised grammar variational autoencoder. J. Chem. Inf. Model. **62**(4), 817–828 (2022)
23. Ortiz, A., Gorriz, J.M., Ramírez, J., Salas-Gonzalez, D., Initiative, A.D.N., et al.: Improving mri segmentation with probabilistic ghsom and multiobjective optimization. Neurocomputing **114**, 118–131 (2013)
24. Payne, C., Awalt, J.K., May, L.T., Tyndall, J.D., Jörg, M., Vernall, A.J.: Bifunctional tools to study adenosine receptors. Topics in Medicinal Chemistry, 1–43 (2022)
25. Rácz, A., Bajusz, D., Héberger, K.: Life beyond the tanimoto coefficient: similarity measures for interaction fingerprints. J. Cheminform. **10**(1), 1–12 (2018)
26. Ramapuram, J., Gregorova, M., Kalousis, A.: Lifelong generative modeling. Neurocomputing **404**, 381–400 (2020)
27. Shen, J., et al.: Discovery and structure-activity analysis of selective estrogen receptor modulators via similarity-based virtual screening. Eur. J. Med. Chem. **54**, 188–196 (2012)
28. Silver, D., Tesauro, G.: Monte-carlo simulation balancing. In: Proceedings of the 26th Annual International Conference on Machine Learning, pp. 945–952 (2009)

29. Stecula, A., Hussain, M.S., Viola, R.E.: Discovery of novel inhibitors of a critical brain enzyme using a homology model and a deep convolutional neural network. J. Med. Chem. **63**(16), 8867–8875 (2020)
30. Thomas, C.E., Will, Y.: The impact of assay technology as applied to safety assessment in reducing compound attrition in drug discovery. Expert Opin. Drug Discov. **7**(2), 109–122 (2012)
31. Vignac, C., Krawczuk, I., Siraudin, A., Wang, B., Cevher, V., Frossard, P.: DiGress: discrete denoising diffusion for graph generation. In: Proceedings of the 11th International Conference on Learning Representations (2023)
32. Wang, Z., et al.: Extraction and analysis of signatures from the gene expression omnibus by the crowd. Nat. Commun. **7**(1), 12846 (2016)
33. Yamanaka, C., Uki, S., Kaitoh, K., Iwata, M., Yamanishi, Y.: De novo drug design based on patient gene expression profiles via deep learning. Mol. Inf. **42**(8-9), 2300064 (2023)
34. Zang, C., Wang, F.: MoFlow: an invertible flow model for generating molecular graphs. In: Proceedings of the 26th ACM SIGKDD International Conference On Knowledge Discovery & Data Mining, pp. 617–626 (2020)

Alternate Geometric and Semantic Denoising Diffusion for Protein Inverse Folding

Chenglin Wang[1], Yucheng Zhou[2], Zhe Wang[1], Zijie Zhai[1], Jianbing Shen[2], and Kai Zhang[1](✉)

[1] East China Normal University, Shanghai, China
kzhang980@gmail.com
[2] SKL-IOTSC, CIS, University of Macau, Zhuhai, China
yucheng.zhou@connect.um.edu.mo, 52275901013@stu.ecnu.edu.cn

Abstract. Protein inverse folding is a fundamental problem in bioinformatics, aiming to recover the amino acid sequences from a given protein backbone structure. Despite the success of existing methods, they still have two limitations: (1) widely used topological modeling via GNNs may not effectively integrate geometric context of the entire protein 3D structure by focusing on only local residue message passing, and (2) current denoising processes primarily rely on geometric relations to update residue representations, while neglecting the semantic and functional correlations between different amino acid types. In this work, we propose an Alternate Geometric and Semantic Denoising Diffusion (**AGSDD**) that performs two types of denoising, i.e., geometric denoising and semantic denoising in turn, in the joint Geo-semantic residue representation space: (1) the geometric denoising module uses a geometric contextual aggregator to encode global contextual information from the entire protein structure and selectively distributes information to each residue; and (2) the semantic denoising module uses a learnable key-value dictionary of residue-types to facilitate communication between them so that learned residue features can be more accurately aligned to proper residue types. In experiments, we conduct extensive evaluations on the CATH4.2, TS50 and TS500 datasets, and observe that even without using any pre-trained protein language models, **AGSDD** still outperforms leading methods, achieving state-of-the-art performance and exhibiting strong generalization capabilities.

Keywords: Protein Inverse Folding · Diffusion Model · Alternate Denoising

1 Introduction

Protein inverse folding, a crucial task in bioinformatics and computational biology, aims to reversely explore possible amino acid (AA) sequences from a given protein 3D structure [15,24,43]. These predicted sequences can autonomously fold into functional proteins, enabling the design of novel proteins with desired structural and functional properties. Moreover, some of these designed proteins, which may not occur naturally, have significant applications in biological research, including drug design and antibody engineering [3,18,40].

Numerous studies have revealed the effective application of neural networks in analyzing protein [2,27,36,47]. Predicting AA sequences based on protein backbone structures is a 3D structure-to-sequence mapping problem. Numerous studies have utilized GNNs [30,33] to extract protein structural features (i.e., residue features and their connections) [3,15,16], followed by the Transformer to generate protein sequences in an autoregressive manner [4,38].

Recently, diffusion models have been extensively applied for generating meaningful contents in both vision and language [1,9,11,26,29,41,44], due to their ability to produce highly diverse yet faithful data from the desired distribution. Notably, diffusion models have shown promise in analyzing and interpreting protein structures. For instance, DPLM [39] adopted a discrete diffusion framework to train protein sequences, exhibiting the potential of the diffusion model for protein representation learning. Similarly, Grade-IF [42] proposed a graph diffusion model for protein inverse folding, effectively learning latent protein representations by capturing inter-residue interactions, which encapsulate various reasonable sequences for a given backbone structure.

Despite the wide application of diffusion models to proteins, current diffusion-based inverse folding has two challenges. First, existing methods typically employ GNNs to establish inter-residue interaction through geometry-driven denoising. However, the locality of GNN-based message passing fails to effectively integrate the contextual information across the entire protein chain, thereby limiting comprehensive residue representation learning. From a biological standpoint, the state of a protein chain is intrinsically linked to the collective contributions of its residues [28,31,32]. Viewing a protein chain as a steady-state system, each residue is vital for maintaining overall stability. Therefore, effective communication among residues is essential for protein representation learning. Furthermore, existing diffusion models predominantly rely on single-pattern geometry denoising that focuses on connection relationships between residues of the chain, while overlooking the impact of semantic correlations between different residue types on residue representation. In protein sequences, AA types are not merely discrete tokens but embody functional, biological, and evolutionary relationships between residues. Considering the semantic communication of the type of residue with all AA types can better update the residue representation and assign the residue to the most appropriate AA type.

To tackle these drawbacks, we propose an alternate geometric and semantic denoising process to perform more effective residue representation learning:

(1) **Geometric Denoising**: while preserving high-fidelity local structure modeling through GNNs, we introduce a Contextual Aggregator (CA) module. This module dynamically aggregates contextual information across the entire protein chain and distributes it selectively to each residue, enabling each residue to be aware of whole-chain geometric context and update. We

also call this protein-specific denoising because it depends on the chain-level structural specificity.
(2) **Semantic Denoising**: we construct a learnable residue key-value dictionary containing predefined semantic embeddings for all AA types and introduce a Semantic Alignment (SA) module. This module allows residue to dynamically aggregate type-specific semantic features through attention-based cross-type communication during denoising, facilitating flexible transformations between residue types and enhancing residue representation. We also call this protein-agnostic denoising because it operates on semantic features of AA and is independent of specific protein instances. Therefore, the alternate denoising process incorporates both a geometry-based learning channel that is protein-specific and a semantics-based learning channel that is protein-agnostic.

To evaluate the performance and generalization capacity of our method, we conduct experiments on the CATH4.2, TS50 and TS500 datasets [15,20]. Extensive experiments demonstrate that our method significantly outperforms baseline methods and achieves state-of-the-art performance. Finally, we provide detailed visualization and analysis to illustrate the effectiveness of our method.

The contributions of this work are summarized below:

- We introduce a diffusion model with an alternate geometric and semantic denoising strategy to achieve optimization based on both geometric context and semantic relationships for residue representation learning;
- We design a contextual aggregator module and a semantic alignment module, which enhance residue representations by using the context of the entire chain and facilitating communication between residue types;
- Our method demonstrates strong generalization and surpasses state-of-the-art approaches on the CATH4.2, TS50 and TS500 datasets.

2 Related Work

Protein inverse folding can be formulated as a structure-based conditional generation, where 3D structure can be encoded to a knn-graph. Node and edge features represent residues and their relationships. Previous work like Graph-Trans [15] extracted protein backbone features (e.g., angles and distances) for autoregressive sequence decoding. Recent works enhanced structural representation: GVP-GNN [16] introduced geometric vector perceptions to jointly model geometric and relational features, ProteinMPNN [3] incorporated virtual C_β atoms as additional input features for improved performance, PiFold [8] and VFN [22] leveraged virtual atoms to capture hidden structural patterns. Besides, to fully consider sequence information in the mapping process, ESM-IF [13] augmented training data and used this additional data to train, resulting in significant improvements. LM-Design [46] and KWDesign [6] employed pre-trained language models to refine amino acid sequences iteratively. These methods have achieved significant success in sequence recovery.

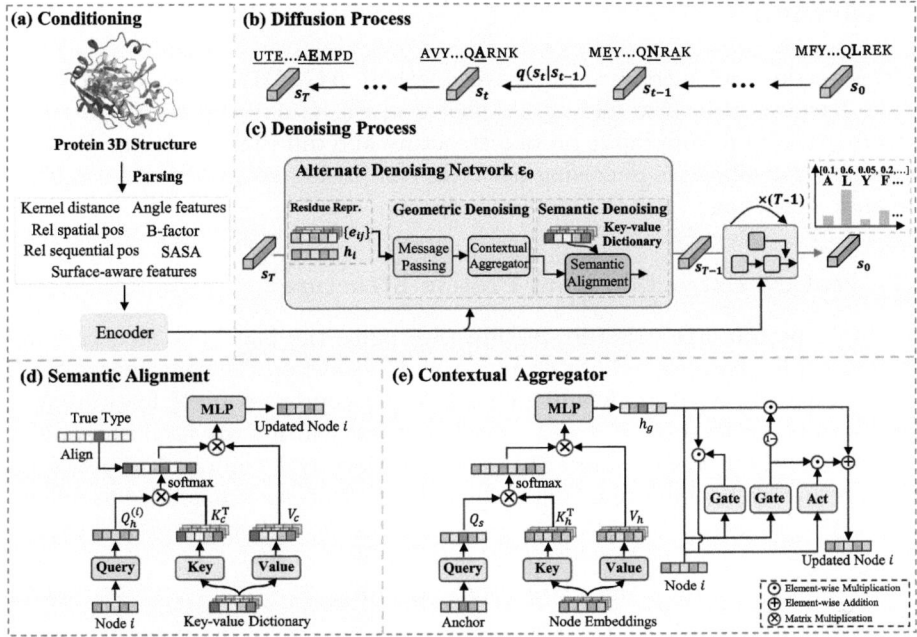

Fig. 1. Overview of **AGSDD** model, illustrated in (**a**), (**b**), (**c**). We take a certain residue type (highlighted in the figure) as an example. (**b**) The correct type (green) transforms to the incorrect noise type (underlined red). (**d**) We show the semantic alignment module in semantic denoising. The Key-value dictionary initializes the semantic features of all AA types. The true type is used to enforce the residue alignment to the proper type. (**e**) It is the contextual aggregator module in geometric denoising, where the anchor is initialized randomly to gather context of the protein-specific chain. (Color figure online)

In recent years, generative models have garnered significant attention [10, 19,35]. DDPM [11] utilized the Diffusion paradigm by progressively introducing Gaussian noise into images and learning its reverse process, which has achieved remarkable success in image generation. Furthermore, Latent Diffusion [29] and ControlNet [44] enhanced controllability by incorporating text as a condition for image generation. In Addition, D3PM [1] has extended the multinomial diffusion model by [12] to handle discrete data. DPLM [39] applied diffusion for unconditional protein sequence generation, leading to a better understanding of proteins. DiffPreT [45] pre-trained a protein encoder by sequence-structure joint diffusion modeling and enhanced by SiamDiff, a method to capture the correlation between different conformers of a protein. CPDiffusion-SS [14] is a latent graph diffusion model that generates protein sequences based on coarse-grained secondary structure, enhancing the reliability and diversity of the generated proteins. GRADE-IF [42] proposed an innovative graph denoising diffusion model for structure-based protein sequence design, demonstrating significant potential in generating diverse protein sequences.

3 Method

In this section, we introduce our novel method **AGSDD**, using the diffusion model for protein inverse folding. As shown in Fig. 1, our approach starts with feature extraction from input protein structure and diffusion modeling. We then delve into our alternate denoising network, comprising geometric denoising and semantic denoising.

3.1 Feature Extraction from Protein Structure

To obtain protein 3D structure features, we parse the backbone structure and construct a K-nearest neighbor graph $\mathcal{G}(\boldsymbol{X}, \boldsymbol{E})$ based on the coordinates of $\boldsymbol{C}_\alpha$ atoms, where K is 30 at default. The $\mathcal{G}(\boldsymbol{X}, \boldsymbol{E})$ comprises node features $\boldsymbol{X} \in \mathbb{R}^{N \times d_n}$ and edge features $\boldsymbol{E} \in \mathbb{R}^{M \times d_e}$, where these features are used to represent residues and their relationships, and N and M denote the numbers of nodes and edges, respectively. Following [42], node and edge features are defined as follows:

$$\boldsymbol{X} = \text{Encoder}_{\text{Node}}\left(\boldsymbol{X}_b; \boldsymbol{X}_{sasa}; \boldsymbol{X}_a; \boldsymbol{X}_s\right), \tag{1}$$

$$\boldsymbol{E} = \text{Encoder}_{\text{Edge}}\left(\boldsymbol{E}_k; \boldsymbol{E}_{sp}; \boldsymbol{E}_{se}\right), \tag{2}$$

where B-Factor $\boldsymbol{X}_b \in \mathbb{R}^{N \times 1}$ and solvent-accessible surface area (SASA) $\boldsymbol{X}_{sasa} \in \mathbb{R}^{N \times 1}$ are derived from the scalar values of $\boldsymbol{C}_\alpha$ atoms. B-Factor reflects the static stability of the protein, while SASA provides insights into protein folding and hydrophobicity. Angle features $\boldsymbol{X}_a \in \mathbb{R}^{N \times 4}$ contain the sine and cosine of backbone dihedral angles ψ and ϕ, i.e., local geometry of residues. Surface-aware features $\boldsymbol{X}_s \in \mathbb{R}^{N \times 5}$ are encoded as vectors according to a set of hyperparameters λ, representing the normalized distances between the central amino acid and its one-hop neighbors [5]. For edge features, kernel-based distances $\boldsymbol{E}_k \in \mathbb{R}^{M \times 15}$ are described using Gaussian radial basis functions (RBF) with varying bandwidths to capture distance information between connected residues at different scales, totaling 15 different distance features. $\boldsymbol{E}_{sp} \in \mathbb{R}^{M \times 12}$ are derived from the heavy atom positions of the corresponding residues, totaling 12 relative position features [42]. The relative sequence distances $\boldsymbol{E}_{se} \in \mathbb{R}^{M \times 66}$ use 65-dimensional one-hot vectors as bins to encode the relative sequence distance of two residues in the protein chain, along with a binary feature indicating whether the Euclidean distance between two connected residues is less than a specified threshold.

3.2 Diffusion Modeling

Our method is based on a diffusion modeling framework [1] for protein inverse folding, which includes both diffusion and denoising processes.

Diffusion Process. In the diffusion process, noise is introduced to the clean AA type $\boldsymbol{S}_0 \in \mathbb{R}^{N \times 20}$ of nodes. Specifically, at timestep t, each node's AA type $s_0 \in \mathbb{R}^{20}$ in the sequence transforms to other amino acid types using a probability transfer matrix $\boldsymbol{Q}_t = \alpha_t \boldsymbol{I} + (1 - \alpha_t)\mathbf{1}_k \mathbf{1}_k^\top / k, \boldsymbol{Q}_t \in \mathbb{R}^{20 \times 20}$ with $\boldsymbol{I}$ being the identity matrix and k being the number of AA types and $\mathbf{1}$ being the one vector of dimension k, i.e.,

$$p(\boldsymbol{s}_t|\boldsymbol{s}_{t-1}) = \boldsymbol{Q}_t \cdot \boldsymbol{s}_{t-1}, \tag{3}$$

where $\boldsymbol{s}_t$ and $\boldsymbol{s}_{t-1}$ represent node's noise AA type in step t and $t-1$, respectively. Similar to DDPM [11], we can compute node's noise AA type in step t from initial step, denoted as follows:

$$p(\boldsymbol{s}_t|\boldsymbol{s}_0) = \bar{\boldsymbol{Q}}_t \cdot \boldsymbol{s}_0. \tag{4}$$

$\bar{\boldsymbol{Q}}_t$ denotes transition probability from initial step to t directly, and $\boldsymbol{s}_0$ represents node's original AA type.

Denoising Process. In the denoising process, each node's noise AA type is sampled from the uniformly prior distribution and iterated back to the initial distribution. The transformation between distributions is sketched as follows:

$$p_\theta(\boldsymbol{s}_{t-1}|\boldsymbol{s}_t, \mathcal{G}) = \sum_{\hat{\boldsymbol{s}}_0} q(\boldsymbol{s}_{t-1}|\hat{\boldsymbol{s}}_0, \boldsymbol{s}_t, \mathcal{G}) p_\theta(\hat{\boldsymbol{s}}_0|\boldsymbol{s}_t, \mathcal{G}), \tag{5}$$

where $\hat{\boldsymbol{s}}_0$ is predicted AA type and $q(\boldsymbol{s}_{t-1}|\hat{\boldsymbol{s}}_0, \boldsymbol{s}_t, \mathcal{G})$ represent posterior that can be computed as follows:

$$q(\boldsymbol{s}_{t-1}|\hat{\boldsymbol{s}}_0, \boldsymbol{s}_t, \mathcal{G}) = \mathrm{DIST}\left(\boldsymbol{s}_{t-1}\Big|\frac{\boldsymbol{Q}_t^T \boldsymbol{s}_t \odot \bar{\boldsymbol{Q}}_{t-1}^T \hat{\boldsymbol{s}}_0}{\boldsymbol{s}_t^T \bar{\boldsymbol{Q}}_t \hat{\boldsymbol{s}}_0}\right), \tag{6}$$

where **DIST** is a categorical distribution over 20 AA types with probabilities computed by the posterior distribution [42].

3.3 AGSDD Denoising Network

As shown in Fig. 1, we propose **AGSDD**, including an alternate denoising network $\epsilon_\theta(\boldsymbol{S}_t, t, \mathcal{G})$ to predict the distribution $p_\theta(\hat{\boldsymbol{s}}_0|\boldsymbol{s}_t, \mathcal{G})$ of each node. The network includes two denoising phases: (1) geometric denoising consists of message passing and the contextual aggregator module, and (2) semantic denoising includes the semantic alignment module. We concatenate the corresponding $\boldsymbol{S}_t$ and $\boldsymbol{X}$ to form the initial node representation $\boldsymbol{H} = \{\boldsymbol{h}_1, ...\boldsymbol{h}_i, ...\boldsymbol{h}_N\}, \boldsymbol{H} \in \mathbb{R}^{N \times d}$.

Message Passing. The Message Passing module updates node representations using information from neighboring nodes and their relationships. Firstly, given a node $\boldsymbol{h}_i$ as an example, a gating mechanism within the **Cell** in Eq.(7-9), dynamically adjusts both node and edge features, producing the message $\boldsymbol{m}'_{ij}$. Specifically, the node $\boldsymbol{h}_i$ is concatenated with its neighboring node $\boldsymbol{h}_j$ as the message $\boldsymbol{m}_{ij}$, which is then merged with the edge features $\boldsymbol{e}_{ij}$ as gates, i.e.,

$$\boldsymbol{g}_{ij}^{(1)} = \sigma\left(\mathrm{Linear}\left([\boldsymbol{e}_{ij}; \boldsymbol{m}_{ij}]\right)\right), \; \boldsymbol{g}_{ij}^{(2)} = \sigma\left(\mathrm{Linear}\left([\boldsymbol{e}_{ij}; \boldsymbol{m}_{ij}]\right)\right), \tag{7}$$

where σ is the sigmoid function. $g_{ij}^{(1)}$ and $g_{ij}^{(2)}$ are two gates, which are used to update message m_{ij}, i.e.,

$$n_{ij} = \mathbf{Act}\left(\text{Linear}(e_{ij}) + g_{ij}^{(1)} \odot \text{Linear}(m_{ij})\right), \tag{8}$$

$$m'_{ij} = g_{ij}^{(2)} \odot m_{ij} + (1 - g_{ij}^{(2)}) \odot n_{ij}, \tag{9}$$

where $\mathbf{Act}(.)$ is the activation function. Subsequently, messages from all neighboring nodes are aggregated to update the central node's representation, i.e.,

$$h'_i = \mathbf{MLP}\left(h_i, \sum_{j \in \mathcal{N}_i} m'_{ij}\right), \tag{10}$$

where h'_i is the updated feature of node i, and $\mathcal{N}_i$ represents the set of neighbors of node i.

Contextual Aggregator. To effectively enhance representations for residues, we propose the contextual aggregator module, as shown in Fig. 1e, which integrates the contextual information of the entire protein chain and selectively distributes it to each residue for access. Specifically, a learnable virtual anchor $h_s \in \mathbb{R}^d$ is initialized at first. Subsequently, it is transformed to the query space, while the node representations updated from the Message Passing are transformed to the key and value spaces, i.e.,

$$Q_s = W_q^s \cdot h_s, \quad K_h = W_k^h \cdot H', \quad V_h = W_v^h \cdot H', \tag{11}$$

where $W_q^s \in \mathbb{R}^{d \times d}$, $W_k^h \in \mathbb{R}^{d \times d}$, $W_v^h \in \mathbb{R}^{d \times d}$ are the projection matrices. h_s is randomly initialized, and $H' = \{h'_1, ...h'_i, ...h'_n\}$ represents all nodes in the protein. We compute the attention score between them and use the score to adaptively aggregate information from the entire protein chain, i.e.,

$$h_g = \mathbf{Softmax}\left(\frac{Q_s \cdot K_h^T}{\sqrt{d}}\right) V_h, \tag{12}$$

where the output $h_g \in \mathbb{R}^d$, encapsulates the contextual information of the entire protein-specific structure, which is then provided to each residue for access. We employ the **Cell** module with a gating mechanism shown in Eqs. (13-15), which selectively receives the quantity of information based on the current node to enhance residue representation, i.e.,

$$g_i^{(1)} = \sigma(\text{Linear}([h'_i; h_g])), \quad g_i^{(2)} = \sigma(\text{Linear}([h'_i; h_g])), \tag{13}$$

where σ is the sigmoid function. $g_i^{(1)}$ and $g_i^{(2)}$ are two gates, which are used to receive information from the protein-specific contextual feature h_g according to node h'_i, i.e.,

$$c_i = \mathbf{Act}\left(\text{Linear}(h'_i) + g_i^{(1)} \odot \text{Linear}(h_g)\right), \tag{14}$$

$$\tilde{h}_i = g_i^{(2)} \odot h_g + (1 - g_i^{(2)}) \odot c_i, \tag{15}$$

where **Act**(.) is the activation function, $\widetilde{h}_i$ is the updated feature of node i.

Semantic Alignment. To make residue align to proper types more accurately during the denoising process, we introduce the semantic alignment module, in Fig. 1d. It adaptively integrates type-specific semantic features to enable cross-type communication. Firstly, all amino acid types are initialized as a learnable residue key-value dictionary $\boldsymbol{H}_c \in \mathbb{R}^{20 \times d}$. They are then mapped to the key and value spaces served as a reference, the node feature $\widetilde{h}_i$ is mapped to the query space served as a request, i.e.,

$$Q_h^{(i)} = \boldsymbol{W}_q \cdot \widetilde{h}_i, \quad \boldsymbol{K}_c = \boldsymbol{W}_k \cdot \boldsymbol{H}_c, \quad \boldsymbol{V}_c = \boldsymbol{W}_v \cdot \boldsymbol{H}_c, \tag{16}$$

where $\boldsymbol{W}_q \in \mathbb{R}^{d \times d}$, $\boldsymbol{W}_k \in \mathbb{R}^{d \times d}$, and $\boldsymbol{W}_v \in \mathbb{R}^{d \times d}$ are the projection matrices. We calculate the correlation between the node and the 20 AA types using scaled dot-product attention, i.e.,

$$\boldsymbol{p}(\boldsymbol{h}_i) = \textbf{Softmax}\left(\frac{Q_h^{(i)} \cdot \boldsymbol{K}_c^T}{\sqrt{d}}\right), \tag{17}$$

where $\boldsymbol{p}(\boldsymbol{h}_i) \in \mathbb{R}^{20}$ represents the correlation between the i-th node and the 20 AA types. The type semantic embeddings are then weighted to the node, i.e.,

$$\boldsymbol{h}_i^l = \boldsymbol{p}(\boldsymbol{h}_i) \cdot \boldsymbol{V}_c. \tag{18}$$

To ensure each node aligns with the corresponding AA type more accurately, we apply cross-entropy loss to constrain the correlation matrix, i.e.,

$$\mathcal{L}_{attn} = -\frac{1}{N}\sum_{i=1}^{N}\boldsymbol{p}(\boldsymbol{h}_{true}^{(i)})\log(\boldsymbol{p}(\boldsymbol{h}_i)), \tag{19}$$

where N is the number of nodes, and $\boldsymbol{p}(\boldsymbol{h}_{true}^{(i)}) \in \mathbb{R}^{20}$ is the ground truth AA types of node i. Finally, after two types of alternate denoising, the node representations are enhanced in each layer.

Following the diffusion framework [26], the time step t is mapped to γ and β to dynamically adjust the scale of features after computing the representation at each layer:

$$\boldsymbol{h}_i^l = \boldsymbol{h}_i^l * (\gamma + 1) + \beta, \tag{20}$$

γ and β denote scale and shift respectively. The dimensions of them are consistent with the node representation $\boldsymbol{h}_i^l$. The final node representation in layer m is mapped to the 20 AA types, which are associated with the secondary structure embedding ss [42]:

$$\boldsymbol{p}_i = \textbf{MLP}\left(\boldsymbol{h}_i^m + \textbf{Linear}(ss)\right), \tag{21}$$

where $\boldsymbol{p}_i \in \mathbb{R}^{20}$ represents the predicted amino acid type of the i-th node.

3.4 Training Objective

For the model training, we employed cross-entropy loss to optimize the model's final predictions for each node type, i.e.,

$$\mathcal{L}_{pred} = -\frac{1}{N}\sum_{i=1}^{N} p(h_{true}^{(i)}) \log(p_i), \tag{22}$$

$$\mathcal{L} = \alpha \cdot \mathcal{L}_{pred} + \lambda \cdot \mathcal{L}_{attn}, \tag{23}$$

where α and λ are weight coefficients, and $p(h_{true}^{(i)})$ represents the true type of the i-th residue, p_i represents the predicted type of the i-th residue and $\mathcal{L}$ represents the final loss, which includes the prediction cross-entropy loss $\mathcal{L}_{pred}$ and the constraint loss $\mathcal{L}_{attn}$ in semantic denoising.

4 Experiments

4.1 Dataset and Evaluation Metrics

In our experiments, we compare our method against other approaches on the CATH4.2 dataset, a widely-used benchmark categorized based on the CATH topology classification [25]. Following the data-splitting in previous works, e.g., GraphTrans [15], PiFold [8], and GRADE-IF [42], we divide the dataset into 18,024 proteins for training, 608 proteins for validation, and 1,120 proteins for testing. In addition, we extend our evaluation to the TS50 and TS500 datasets to validate the generalization capability of our model. We employ two evaluation metrics for assessing generated AA sequences, i.e., **Recovery** rate and **Perplexity**. The recovery rate quantifies the accuracy of the generated sequences compared to the ground truth, providing insight into the model's precision. Perplexity measures the uncertainty in the model's predictions, reflecting its confidence and ability to generalize to unseen data.

4.2 Experimental Setting

To comprehensively evaluate the model's performance to recover sequences, we divide the test data into three categories: "short", "single", and "all", as shown in Table 1. The "short" comprises proteins with AA sequence lengths fewer than 100, and "single" includes proteins composed of a single chain; "all" encompasses the entire test dataset. The denoising network consists of six stacked layers, and the timestep for the diffusion model is set to 500. The model is trained for a total of 70,000 steps with a batch size of 32 and gradient accumulation over two steps on an NVIDIA A6000 GPU. We employ the Adam optimizer with a learning rate of 0.0005 and a weight decay of 0.00001. The weight of α and λ are both 0.5. In the inference process, we utilize accelerated inference methods based on [34,42], with a skip interval of 500 and a single denoising step, striking a balance between recovery rate and perplexity.

Table 1. Experiment result on the CATH4.2 dataset.

Method	Perplexity↓			Recovery(%)↑		
	Short	Single	All	Short	Single	All
StructGNN [15]	8.29	8.74	6.40	29.44	28.26	35.91
GraphTrans [15]	8.39	8.83	6.63	28.14	28.46	35.82
GCA [37]	7.09	7.49	6.05	32.62	31.10	37.64
GVP [16]	7.23	7.84	5.36	30.60	28.95	39.47
AlphaDesign [7]	7.32	7.63	6.30	34.16	32.66	41.31
ProteinMPNN [3]	6.21	6.68	4.61	36.35	34.43	45.96
PiFold [8]	6.04	6.31	4.55	39.84	38.53	51.66
GRADE-IF [42]	5.49	6.21	4.35	45.27	42.77	52.21
VFN-IF [22]	5.70	5.86	4.17	41.34	40.98	54.74
AGSDD (ours)	**4.06**	**4.76**	**2.93**	**53.57**	**48.95**	**64.07**
w/ External Knowledge						
LM-Design [46]	6.77	6.46	4.52	37.88	42.47	55.65
KW-Design [6]	5.48	5.16	3.46	44.66	45.45	60.77

4.3 Main Results

To validate the effectiveness of our method, we compared it with other strong competitors using the CATH4.2 benchmark, and the results are shown in Table 1. Experimental results demonstrate that our model achieves state-of-the-art performance in AA sequence recovery and perplexity. To the best of our knowledge, our method is the first to achieve 60% recovery without external knowledge of pre-trained language models. In addition, compared to the VFN-IF model, our approach improves the recovery rate by 9.33%, confirming its superior performance. Compared with GRADE-IF, our method increases the recovery rate by 11.86%, indicating the effectiveness of semantic denoising in the denoising network for sequence recovery. Furthermore, while the LM-Design and KW-Design models utilize external knowledge from the pre-trained ESM [21], achieving recovery rates of 55.65% and 60.77%, respectively, our model improves the recovery rates by 8.42% and 3.30%. This demonstrates that our model delivers strong sequence recovery capabilities without external knowledge, thereby reducing computational complexity during the inference stage.

4.4 Generalization Capability Analysis

To verify the generalization capability of our model, we directly evaluated the trained model on the TS50 and TS500 datasets. The TS50 and TS500 datasets consist of 50 and 500 test proteins, respectively. As shown in Table 2, our model achieves state-of-the-art performance on both datasets, significantly outperforming existing methods. Specifically, our model achieves a perplexity (PPL) of 2.67

Table 2. Results of experiments on the TS50 and TS500 datasets. PPL refers to Perplexity, and Rec indicates Recovery (%).

Method	TS50 PPL	Rec	TS500 PPL	Rec
StructGNN [15]	5.40	43.89	4.98	45.69
GraphTrans [15]	5.60	42.20	5.16	44.66
GVP [16]	4.71	44.14	4.20	49.14
GCA [37]	5.09	47.02	4.72	47.74
AlphaDesign [7]	5.25	48.36	4.93	49.23
ProteinMPNN [3]	3.93	54.43	3.53	58.08
PiFold [8]	3.86	58.72	3.44	60.42
GRADE-IF [42]	3.71	56.32	3.23	61.22
VFN-IF [22]	3.58	59.54	3.19	63.65
AGSDD (ours)	**2.67**	**67.03**	**2.31**	**71.61**
w/ External Knowledge				
LM-Design [46]	3.50	57.89	3.19	67.78
KW-Design [6]	3.10	62.79	2.86	69.19

on TS50 and 2.31 on TS500, substantially outperforming existing approaches such as GRADE-IF and VFN-IF. For recovery rate (Rec), our model achieves 67.03% on TS50 and 71.61% on TS500. Notably, it is the first model, to our knowledge, that exceeds a recovery rate of 70% on the TS500 and over 65% on the TS50 without leveraging external knowledge in training. These results underscore the robustness and generalization capability of our approach. While models incorporating external knowledge in training, such as LM-Design [46] and KW-Design [6], also achieve competitive results, our model demonstrates that better performance can be reached purely through alternate denoising, thus reducing the reliance on external domain-specific information.

4.5 Ablation Study

To evaluate the impact of each module within the alternate denoising network, we conduct an ablation study, and the results are shown in Table 3. The performance metrics are evaluated across three datasets: CATH, TS50, and TS500. Firstly, removing the semantic alignment ("w/o SA") disrupts the model's understanding of various residue types, leading to a decline in performance across the CATH, TS50, and TS500 datasets. It demonstrates the necessity of the model's understanding of various residue types by aligning their representation during the denoising process. Similarly, excluding the contextual aggregator module ("w/o CA") also leads to a marked decline in performance. Without this module, the model is restricted to relying purely on graph neural network (GNN-based) neighbor inter-residue interactions, without leveraging holistic information from

Table 3. Ablation study. "w/o SA" indicates the model without semantic alignment, "w/o CA" refers to the model without contextual aggregator in the geometric denoising, "w/o ALL" denotes the model without SA, CA and the cell module in message passing.

Model	CATH		TS50		TS500	
	Rec	PPL	Rec	PPL	Rec	PPL
AGSDD	64.07	2.93	67.03	2.67	71.61	2.31
w/o SA	63.13	3.00	64.46	2.80	70.32	2.39
w/o CA	61.60	3.16	64.24	2.89	68.74	2.52
w/o SA & CA	61.48	3.17	63.68	2.92	68.73	2.51
w/o ALL	60.96	3.21	63.61	2.95	68.36	2.54

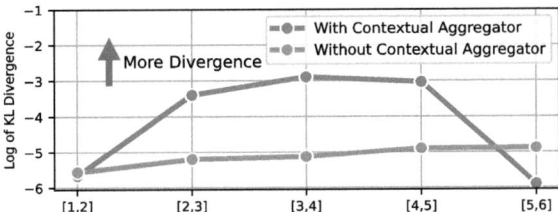

Fig. 2. Nonlinear features analysis of contextual aggregator module on layer output. The x-axis shows two adjacent layers, and the y-axis represents the logarithm of KL divergence, which measures changes in node feature distributions. The polyline depicts nonlinear divergences in node representations for 50 randomly selected protein cases from CATH4.2 test set with or without the CA module. Arrows indicate the direction towards nodes with stronger nonlinear features.

the entire protein chain. This limitation hinders the model's ability to contextualize residue interactions, as evidenced by decreased recall and increased perplexity across all datasets. These results confirm the effectiveness of integrating global chain-level information to enrich residue representations and improve predictive accuracy. When both the semantic alignment and contextual aggregator module are simultaneously removed ("w/o SA & CA"), the model suffers further performance degradation. This reinforces the complementary contributions of these two components, highlighting that both are indispensable for capturing complex residue dependencies within the denoising network. Lastly, we explore the role of the Cell module within the Message Passing part, which integrates node and edge representations from neighboring nodes. When the Cell module is replaced with a MLP, model performance declines, indicating the crucial role of the Cell module in effectively integrating neighboring node and edge representations.

4.6 Nonlinear Analysis in Contextual Aggregator

To better understand the effectiveness of the CA module, we examine its influence on the nonlinear characteristics of layer outputs. In Fig. 2, we compare two scenarios: one where the CA module is used and another where it is not. The y-axis represents the logarithm of the KL divergence, which quantifies the changes in feature distributions between adjacent layers. A higher value indicates a greater divergence, suggesting more pronounced nonlinear transformations. The results reveal that incorporating the CA module significantly increases the KL divergence across layers, especially in the earlier stages. This indicates that CA enhances the model's ability to capture and propagate complex nonlinear patterns, thereby improving its representation of inter-residue relationships. In contrast, without the CA module, the divergence remains consistently lower, suggesting limited capacity for nonlinear feature extraction. Thus, the CA module's impact is particularly beneficial for tasks that require nuanced representation of protein structures.

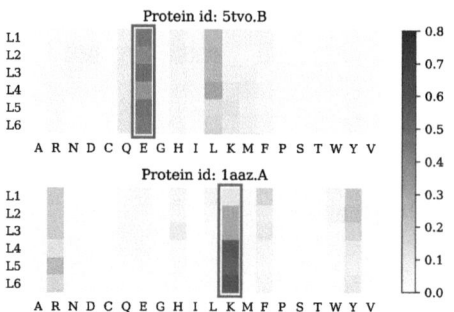

Fig. 3. How a specific position in the sequence attends to all AA types across layers in semantic alignment module. (**vertical**: different layers, **horizontal**: 20 AA types). The specific residue can incorporate the semantic information of the correct type as the layer goes deeper.

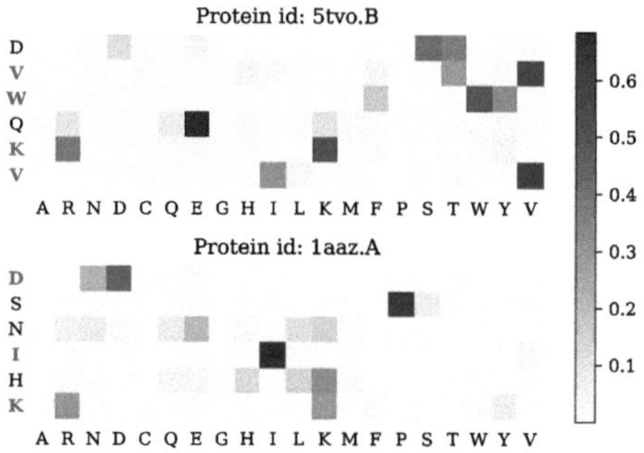

Fig. 4. How each position in the sequence attends to the correct type at the final layer in the semantic alignment module. (**Vertical**: prediction types of a segment, **horizontal**: 20 AA types). Residues with accurately predicted types (red) align to corresponding type semantic features.

4.7 Visualization of Semantic Alignment

To investigate the impact of the semantic alignment module, we present visualization results of attention between residues and semantic features of all type. Specifically, we analyze the AA types to which individual residues attend across different layers of the denoising network, as shown in Fig. 3. We also show the AA types attended to by multiple residues in a continuous segment at the final layer, in Fig. 4. In Fig. 3, the vertical axis (L1 to L6) represents the network layers, while the horizontal axis represents the 20 AA types. The values indicate the attention weights computed in the semantic denoising phase for the specific residue and each of the 20 AA types. For the 5tvo.B protein, the true type of

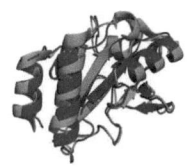  

Recovery: 0.679 (PDB ID: 3fkf) Recovery: 0.663 (PDB ID: 4u13) Recovery: 0.654 (PDB ID: 2bng)
RMSD: 0.917; avg.pLDDT: 90.39 RMSD: 0.565; avg.pLDDT: 95.39 RMSD: 0.923; avg.pLDDT: 89.63

Fig. 5. Comparison of the folding between predicted (Blue) and native (Green) structures, where the predicted structures are generated using AlphaFold2 based on **AGSDD**-designed AA sequences. (Color figure online)

the randomly chosen residue is glutamic acid (E), and for the 1aaz. A protein, it is lysine (K). The results demonstrate that as the number of layers increases, the attention weight for the node corresponding to the true AA type features of each residue gradually rises. By the final layer, the residue aligns with its true AA type, suggesting that the model effectively aligns residues with the semantic information of their true AA types and incorporates this information into the residue to facilitate flexible transition of types to enhance representation. In addition, Fig. 4 visualizes the attention of multiple residues in the model's final layer. These residues are from a randomly selected continuous segment. The horizontal axis represents the 20 AA types, while the vertical axis represents the predicted amino acid types of these residues, where the red represents accurate prediction. The visualization shows that the correctly predicted residues have the highest attention weights for their true types in the semantic alignment module, which indicates that injecting type semantic information into the residue representations is beneficial for prediction.

4.8 Folding Ability

We further explore the folding ability of the generated amino acid sequences to verify its rationality. Specifically, we randomly select test proteins 3fkf, 4u13 and 2bng from the CATH4.2 test set and utilize the protein structure prediction method ColabFold [23], which offers user-friendly access to AlphaFold2 [17] for predicting the 3D structures of the generated amino acid sequences. These predicted structures are then aligned with the corresponding PDB structures. As shown in Fig. 5, the recovery rate of the generated sequences 3fkf is 0.679, and secondary structure elements such as α-helices and β-sheets are effectively formed. The average pLDDT score is 90.39, and the RMSD is 0.917, where the average pLDDT score assesses confidence in the predicted structure, and the RMSD measures the deviation between the predicted and fixed structures. These results demonstrate the validity and rationality of our model in generating new sequences based on fixed backbone structures.

5 Conclusion

In this paper, we propose an alternate geometric and semantic denoising diffusion **AGSDD** that performs protein-specific geometric denoising and protein-agnostic semantic denoising for protein inverse folding. Firstly, after local structure modeling through GNNs, our method integrates contextual information from the entire 3D structure and assigns it selectively to each residue to maintain inter-residue communication, enhancing the residue representation. Moreover, we introduce a semantic denoising that use a learnable key-value dictionary of residue-types to facilitate communication between them in the denoising process. In addition, our cell module effectively decouples and computes the relevance of adjacent node and edge information. In experiments, our method surpasses existing leading approaches on the CATH4.2, TS50 and TS500 datasets.

Acknowledgements. This work is supported by the national key research and development program 2022YFC3400501, and national natural science foundation of China 62276099.

References

1. Austin, J., Johnson, D.D., Ho, J., Tarlow, D., Van Den Berg, R.: Structured denoising diffusion models in discrete state-spaces. In: NeurIPS (2021)
2. Chen, W., Wang, X., Wang, Y.: FFF: Fragment-guided flexible fitting for building complete protein structures. In: CVPR (2023)
3. Dauparas, J., et al.: Robust deep learning–based protein sequence design using proteinmpnn. Science (2022)
4. Devlin, J., Chang, M.W., Lee, K., Toutanova, K.: Bert: Pre-training of deep bidirectional transformers for language understanding. In: NAACL (2019)
5. Ganea, O., et al.: Independent se(3)-equivariant models for end-to-end rigid protein docking. In: ICLR (2022)
6. Gao, Z., et al.: KW-design: Pushing the limit of protein design via knowledge refinement. In: ICLR (2024)
7. Gao, Z., Tan, C., Li, S.Z.: Alphadesign: a graph protein design method and benchmark on alphafold DB (2023)
8. Gao, Z., Tan, C., Li, S.Z.: Pifold: toward effective and efficient protein inverse folding. In: ICLR. OpenReview.net (2023)
9. Gong, S., Li, M., Feng, J., Wu, Z., Kong, L.: Diffuseq: Sequence to sequence text generation with diffusion models. In: ICLR (2023)
10. Goodfellow, I., Pouget-Abadie, J., Mirza, M., Xu, B., Warde-Farley, D., Ozair, S., Courville, A., Bengio, Y.: Generative adversarial nets. In: NeurIPS, vol. 27 (2014)
11. Ho, J., Jain, A., Abbeel, P.: Denoising diffusion probabilistic models. In :NeurIPS (2020)
12. Hoogeboom, E., Nielsen, D., Jaini, P., Forré, P., Welling, M.: Argmax flows and multinomial diffusion: learning categorical distributions. In: NeurIPS (2021)
13. Hsu, C., et al.: Learning inverse folding from millions of predicted structures. In: ICML (2022)

14. Hu, Y., Tan, Y., Han, A., Zheng, L., Hong, L., Zhou, B.: Secondary structure-guided novel protein sequence generation with latent graph diffusion. CoRR (2024)
15. Ingraham, J., Garg, V., Barzilay, R., Jaakkola, T.: Generative models for graph-based protein design. In: NeurIPS (2019)
16. Jing, B., Eismann, S., Suriana, P., Townshend, R.J.L., Dror, R.O.: Learning from protein structure with geometric vector perceptrons. In: ICLR (2021)
17. Jumper, J., et al.: Highly accurate protein structure prediction with alphafold. Nature (2021)
18. Khoury, G.A., Smadbeck, J., Kieslich, C.A., Floudas, C.A.: Protein folding and de novo protein design for biotechnological applications. Trends in biotechnology (2014)
19. Kingma, D.P., Welling, M.: Auto-encoding variational bayes. In: ICLR (2014)
20. Li, Z., Yang, Y., Faraggi, E., Zhan, J., Zhou, Y.: Direct Prediction of Profiles of Sequences Compatible with a Protein Structure By Neural Networks With Fragment-based Local And Energy-based Nonlocal Profiles. Structure, Function, and Bioinformatics, Proteins (2014)
21. Lin, Z., et al.: Evolutionary-scale prediction of atomic-level protein structure with a language model. Science (2023)
22. Mao, W., et al.: De novo protein design using geometric vector field networks. In: ICLR. OpenReview.net (2024)
23. Mirdita, M., Schütze, K., Moriwaki, Y., Heo, L., Ovchinnikov, S., Steinegger, M.: Colabfold: making protein folding accessible to all. Nature methods (2022)
24. O'Connell, J., et al.: Spin2: Predicting Sequence Profiles from Protein Structures Using Deep Neural Networks. Structure, Function, and Bioinformatics, Proteins (2018)
25. Orengo, C.A., Michie, A.D., Jones, S., Jones, D.T., Swindells, M.B., Thornton, J.M.: Cath–a hierarchic classification of protein domain structures. Structure (1997)
26. Peebles, W., Xie, S.: Scalable diffusion models with transformers. In: ICCV (2023)
27. Quan, R., Wang, W., Ma, F., Fan, H., Yang, Y.: Clustering for protein representation learning. In: CVPR (2024)
28. Rackovsky, S.: Global characteristics of protein sequences and their implications. In: Proceedings of the National Academy of Sciences (2010)
29. Rombach, R., Blattmann, A., Lorenz, D., Esser, P., Ommer, B.: High-resolution image synthesis with latent diffusion models. In: CVPR (2022)
30. Satorras, V.G., Hoogeboom, E., Welling, M.: E (n) equivariant graph neural networks. In: ICML. PMLR (2021)
31. Scheraga, H.A., Rackovsky, S.: Homolog detection using global sequence properties suggests an alternate view of structural encoding in protein sequences. In: Proceedings of the National Academy of Sciences (2014)
32. Scheraga, H.A., Rackovsky, S.: Global informatics and physical property selection in protein sequences. In: Proceedings of the National Academy of Sciences (2016)
33. Schütt, K., Unke, O., Gastegger, M.: Equivariant message passing for the prediction of tensorial properties and molecular spectra. In: ICML. PMLR (2021)
34. Song, J., Meng, C., Ermon, S.: Denoising diffusion implicit models. arXiv preprint arXiv:2010.02502 (2020)
35. Song, Y., Sohl-Dickstein, J., Kingma, D.P., Kumar, A., Ermon, S., Poole, B.: Score-based generative modeling through stochastic differential equations. In: ICLR. OpenReview.net (2021)
36. Sverrisson, F., Feydy, J., Correia, B.E., Bronstein, M.M.: Fast end-to-end learning on protein surfaces. In: CVPR (2021)

37. Tan, C., Gao, Z., Xia, J., Hu, B., Li, S.Z.: Global-context aware generative protein design. In: ICASSP (2023)
38. Vaswani, A., et al.: Attention is all you need. In: NeurIPS (2017)
39. Wang, X., Zheng, Z., Ye, F., Xue, D., Huang, S., Gu, Q.: Diffusion language models are versatile protein learners. arXiv preprint arXiv:2402.18567 (2024)
40. Watson, J.L., et al.: De novo design of protein structure and function with rfdiffusion. Nature **620** (2023)
41. Wu, T., et al.: Ar-diffusion: Auto-regressive diffusion model for text generation. NeurIPS **36** (2023)
42. Yi, K., Zhou, B., Shen, Y., Lió, P., Wang, Y.: Graph denoising diffusion for inverse protein folding. In: NeurIPS (2023)
43. Yue, K., Dill, K.A.: Inverse protein folding problem: designing polymer sequences. In: Proceedings of the National Academy of Sciences (1992)
44. Zhang, L., Rao, A., Agrawala, M.: Adding conditional control to text-to-image diffusion models. In: ICCV (2023)
45. Zhang, Z., Xu, M., Lozano, A.C., Chenthamarakshan, V., Das, P., Tang, J.: Pre-training protein encoder via Siamese sequence-structure diffusion trajectory prediction. In: NeurIPS 2023 (2023)
46. Zheng, Z., Deng, Y., Xue, D., Zhou, Y., Ye, F., Gu, Q.: Structure-informed language models are protein designers. In: ICML (2023)
47. Zhong, Z., Mottin, D.: Efficiently predicting mutational effect on homologous proteins by evolution encoding. In: ECML PKDD (2024)

Images and Computer Vision

Self-generated Cross-Modal Prompt Tuning

Guiming Cao[1], Zonghan Wu[2], Huan Huo[1], Yuming Ou[1], and Guandong Xu[1,3](✉)

[1] University of Technology Sydney, Sydney, Australia
Guiming.Cao@student.uts.edu.au, Guandong.Xu@uts.edu.au
[2] East China Normal University, Shanghai, China
[3] The Education University of Hong Kong, Hong Kong, China

Abstract. Training prompt tuning models on task-specific data is a common method for adapting vision-language model knowledge to image recognition downstream tasks. Despite recent advancements in prompt tuning, achieving superior generalization to heterogeneous images, across a wide range of visual characteristics in style, format, and source, remains a significant challenge. To this end, we propose a novel method, namely Self-generated Cross-modal Prompt tuning (SCP), which generates pseudo prompts by applying the frozen knowledge in both the initialization and optimization stages to guide training. Consequently, the model can be trained on available datasets while effectively generalizing to heterogeneous image data in a wide spectrum of textual classes and visual characteristics. Extensive experiments on four benchmarks indicate that our proposed SCP significantly outperforms well-known baselines in generalization performance across a broad spectrum of downstream tasks. Notably, our proposed SCP exhibits significant improvements in both Cross-Dataset and Domain-Shift Generalization, with performance gains of at least 3.63% and 11.71%, respectively. Our code is available at https://github.com/Ghosttimber/Academic.

Keywords: Computer Vision · Multi-Modal · Prompt Tuning

1 Introduction

Recently developed vision-language models (VLMs) interpret and connect data across a variety of modalities, representing a significant leap forward from the traditional paradigm in multi-modal downstream tasks. Such a model, exemplified by CLIP [28], aligns image and text in a shared space, achieving superior generalization performance without task-specific training. Building upon CLIP, Context Optimization (CoOp) [43] prepends learnable tokens into the prompt of

Supplementary Information The online version contains supplementary material available at https://doi.org/10.1007/978-3-032-06066-2_22.

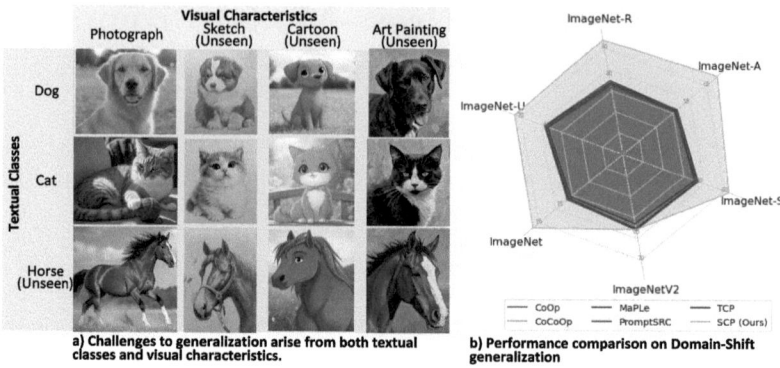

Fig. 1. Challenges addressed by our proposed SCP and its performance compared to the well-known baselines.

VLMs (learnable prompt), demonstrating improved generalization performance. This paradigm, termed prompt tuning, tailors VLMs to task-specific datasets, broadening the applicability of VLMs to a wide range of downstream tasks.

Expanding upon the foundation laid by CoOp, several subsequent approaches (KgCoOp [36], PromptSRC [16] and TCP [37]) have focused on unlocking the potential of prompt tuning in downstream tasks, retrieving the frozen knowledge lost in training by establishing alignment between the prompted embedding (i.e. the embedding carrying the learnable token) and the frozen CLIP embedding. This mechanism facilitates the knowledge transfer from the training distribution to out-of-distribution, thereby mitigating overfitting to the unseen textual classes from the training data. As a result, further improved generalizability is attainable. Despite the advancement in prompt tuning, a remaining critical challenge stems from achieving superior generalization to heterogeneous images, which encompasses diverse visual characteristics such as style, format, and source, reflecting real-world scenarios as illustrated in Fig. 1(a). In other words, the challenge lies in finding a learnable prompt against heterogeneous images.

Motivated by the challenges, we have found that transforming a textual prompt into its counterpart in the image space results in pseudo prompts independent of visual characteristics. Consequently, incorporating such pseudo prompts as guidance in training enhances the ability to achieve superior generalization across a broader range of downstream tasks as illustrated in Fig. 1(b). Accordingly, based on the aforementioned observation, we propose a novel prompt tuning model agnostic to both textual classes and visual characteristics, and it is referred to as Self-generated Cross-modal Prompt Tuning (SCP).

In essence, SCP systematically leverages frozen CLIP knowledge in both the initialization and optimization phases. In the initialization, the optimal matching embeddings between the textual and visual prompt are selected by the frozen CLIP model and incorporated into learnable prompts representation. The main purpose is to mitigate the negative effects of biases arising from the specificity of textual class and visual characteristics. Consequently, robust learnable prompts can be attained to enhance generalization capability. We refer to this initialization strategy as Cascade Propagation Prompt Initialization (CPPI). As for the optimization, the learnable prompt is aligned with the pseudo prompt embedding (i.e. proxy representation) derived from frozen CLIP knowledge in a cross-modal manner. Note that the proxy representation holds a different role regarding the modality of the learnable prompt in the alignment. The proxy representation aligned with the visual learnable prompt is generated from the textual prompt of frozen CLIP, serving as pseudo prompts in the image space. We found that it remains independent of visual characteristics. Clearly this enables visual learnable prompts to acquire a robust representation. Similarly, the proxy representation aligned with the textual learnable prompt comes from the visual prompt of frozen CLIP. It offers sufficient samples for the training in alignment while existing baselines rely on limited samples or hand-crafted samples. This optimization strategy is referred to as Self-generated Proxy Alignment (SPA).

In addition, building upon the cross-modal nature of SPA and following [27], we adopt the Euclidean loss in the alignment to reduce the modality gap between textual and visual representations to a desirable level. To mitigate the information loss [15] in the modality conversion of learnable prompts, we propose an Entropy-Regulation (ER) module, which, combined with the adoption of Euclidean loss, further improves the generalization performance.

In summary, this paper makes four major contributions:

- We propose a novel prompt tuning method (Self-generated Cross-modal Prompt tuning), that trains on limited readily available images, adapting prompt tuning to a much broader array of downstream applications.
- In our method, we take advantage of textual and visual knowledge from frozen CLIP into both the initialization and optimization process in a cross-modal manner, conducive to superior generalization capability.
- We introduce the Euclidean loss and the ER to improve the generalization capability, mitigating the challenge discussed by the existing research.
- Extensive experiments on four benchmarks clearly demonstrate that our proposed SCP significantly outperforms the well-known baselines in generalization capability across a wide range of downstream tasks.

2 Related Work

Vision Language Models. Recently, several methods, including BAN [17], Intra-Inter [10], and MCAN [38], adopt the VLMs with the attention-based framework, showing that the utilization of VLMs significantly improves the performance across a wide spectrum of downstream tasks. Subsequently, the methods (ViLBERT [22], LXMERT [32] and UNITER [2]) explore the potential of VLMs models based on BERT-like architectures, attaining further improvement. Methods proposed thereafter, namely CLIP [28] and ALIGN [14], are trained to align a considerable amount of web-scale image-text pair data in a multi-modal

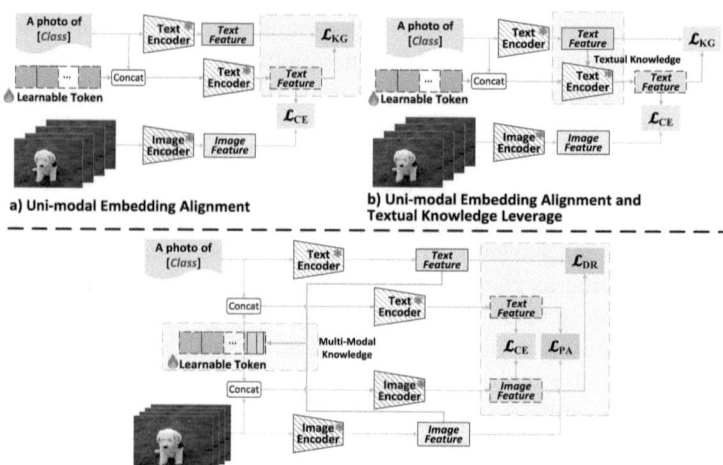

Fig. 2. Schematic architecture of two typical baselines and our proposed method. Compared to (a) and (b), (c) utilizes multi-modal knowledge of frozen CLIP and aligned prompted embedding with frozen CLIP embedding in a cross-modal manner to direct the learnable prompt to obtain a robust representation.

architecture, leaping forward the generalization capability to a new level. Meanwhile, this training mechanism has been widely adopted in image recognition [9,41], object detection [8,23,33,39], and segmentation [6,20,29].

Prompt Learning. As a new paradigm to leverage VLMs, prompt tuning manages to significantly address the challenges of CLIP arising from the fact that the hand-crafted text is insufficient for specialized tasks regarding training time and the sensitivity of prompt design. On the other hand, a recent prompt tuning method, Distribution-Aware Prompts tuning (DAPT) [3], optimize the learnable prompt by minimising the intra-dispersion and maximizing the inter-dispersion to obtain better generalization performance. Alternatively, Read-only Prompt Optimization (RPO) [19] proposes a set of read-only prompts aiming to avoid the impact on the internal representation of CLIP by using masked attention. Another approach, Decoupled Prompt Tuning (DePT) [40], enhances generalization performance by isolating task-specific knowledge from the channels of feature representation and preserving the shared knowledge.

More recently, two mechanisms, i.e. the multi-modal architecture and the retrieval of frozen CLIP knowledge, are introduced to prompt tuning. Among MaPLe, RPO, DAPT and PromptSRC [16], MaPLe [15] is the early method to apply multi-modal architecture to utilise the knowledge in both text and image encoders. PromptSRC applies the architecture, and concurrently aligns its learnable prompt embedding with frozen CLIP knowledge, which is another pathway to improve the generalization. Alternatively, several methods improve generalization by only retrieving frozen CLIP knowledge, including ProGrad, KgCoOp and TCP. While ProGrad [44] only optimizes the prompt whose gradient is aligned (or non-conflicting) to the frozen CLIP knowledge. KgCoOp [36] explicitly addresses the gap between the embedding of learnable prompts and that of frozen CLIP as shown in Fig. 2(a). As an alternative, TCP further leverages the frozen CLIP knowledge by injecting its text embeddings into the encoder illustrated as Fig. 2(b), enhancing the generalization performance. Note that, these three methods only retrieve the textual knowledge from frozen CLIP. Besides, methods like PromptKD [21] and HPT [34] apply extra knowledge from fine-tuned models and large language models are not covered in this study.

3 Methodology

In this paper, we propose a novel method, referred to as SCP, to achieve superior generalization by leveraging the frozen CLIP knowledge in both the initialization and optimization stage of the learnable prompt as its schematic architecture shown in Fig. 2(c). Before delineating on SCP, to facilitate understanding, we first review the fundamental knowledge from the existing baseline framework.

3.1 Existing Baseline Framework

The existing baseline, such as CoOp, adopts CLIP for image recognition downstream tasks by prepending learnable tokens to the prompt context. Note that, the pre-trained encoders in CLIP, both image and text, convert the prompt context and the image sample into corresponding embeddings, which are then paired based on the contrastive loss to ensure optimal matching. In specific, the hand-crafted template with c class labels, e.g. "a photo of a $\{Class\}$", $Class : C \in \{1, 2, ...c\}$, is embedded into vectorized textual tokens $T = \{t_i\}_{i=1}^{c}$, and the b learnable tokens $P = \{p_i\}_{i=1}^{b}$ are initialized in text modality space. Then, the text encoder $\mathcal{B}(\cdot)$ interprets the combination of learnable tokens and vectorized textual tokens into the text embedding $W^p = \mathcal{B}([P, T]) = \{w_i^p\}_{i=1}^{c}$. To infer P, the cosine similarity score $sim(\cdot)$ needs to be maximized. Equivalently, the contrastive loss, between the image embedding x and the prompted text embedding w_y^p, is calculated as

$$\mathcal{L}_{ce} = \frac{\exp(sim(\mathrm{x}, \mathrm{w}_y^p/\tau))}{\sum_{i=1}^{c} \exp(sim(\mathrm{x}, \mathrm{w}_i^p/\tau))}. \tag{1}$$

Here, τ refers to the temperature parameter.

To further unlock the potential of CLIP, MaPLe extends learnable prompts to the image side and takes advantage of multiple transformer blocks in the learning process. Specifically, the prompted image embedding is generated as $X^p = \mathcal{V}([\widetilde{P}, Z])$. Here, $\widetilde{P} = \mathcal{F}(P)$ is the operation that converts learnable token to image modality space by a projection function $\mathcal{F}(\cdot)$, Z refers to the vectorized visual tokens. Following Maple [15], the operation for processing prompted text and image embeddings through J transformer layers is

$$W_{j+1}^p = \mathcal{B}_{j+1}([P_j, T_j]) \tag{2}$$

and

$$X^p_{j+1} = \mathcal{V}_{j+1}([\widetilde{P_j}, Z_j]) = \mathcal{V}_{j+1}([\mathcal{F}(P_j), Z_j]), \tag{3}$$

respectively, where $j \in (0, 1, \cdots, J-1)$. Accordingly, the contrastive loss in MaPLe is calculated as

$$\mathcal{L}_{ce} = \frac{\exp(sim(\mathrm{x}^p, \mathrm{w}^p_y/\tau))}{\sum_{i=1}^{c} \exp(sim(\mathrm{x}^p, \mathrm{w}^p_i/\tau))}. \tag{4}$$

Alternatively, KgCoOp [36] proposed new loss function, i.e.

$$\mathcal{L}_{kg} = \left\| W^{frozen} - W^p \right\|_2^2, \tag{5}$$

to account for the distribution gap between the text embedding of frozen CLIP and that of prompted model. Therefore, KgCoOp has the final loss function as

$$\mathcal{L}_{Total} = \mathcal{L}_{ce} + \omega \mathcal{L}_{kg}, \tag{6}$$

where ω serves as a crucial weighting hyper-parameter.

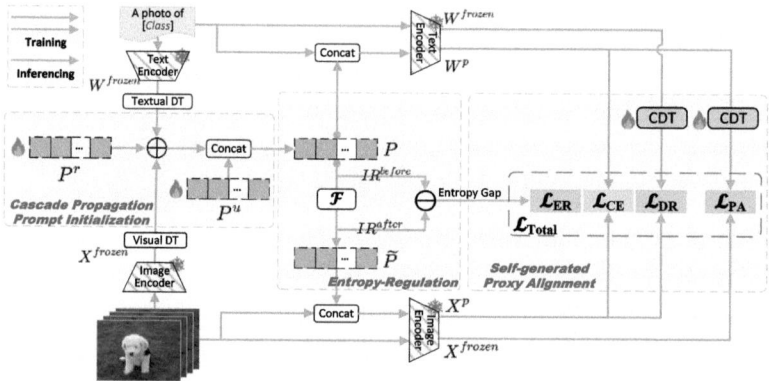

Fig. 3. The framework of Self-generated Cross-model Prompt tuning. Here, Textual DT and Visual DT perform intra-modal dimension transformation, while P^r and P^u refer to restricted tokens and unrestricted tokens, respectively. $\mathcal{F}$ refers to the projection function, and CDT refers to the cross-modal dimension transformation module. In addition, $\mathcal{L}_{CE}$ is the standard cross-entropy loss, $\mathcal{L}_{ER}$ is the proposed Entropy-Regulation constraint to minimize information during the projection function. $\mathcal{L}_{DR}$ and $\mathcal{L}_{PA}$ are the constraints for the proposed Self-generate Proxy Alignment to minimize the discrepancy between the corresponding prompted embedding and frozen CLIP embedding.

3.2 Self-generated Cross-Modal Prompt Tuning

In the existing framework, the learnable prompts obtain task-specific knowledge to learn a representation space that potentially overfits the training data.

Clearly, it degrades the generalization capability when the data is not present in training. Recent baselines, such as KgCoOp, PromptSRC, and TCP, draw upon the frozen CLIP knowledge in intra-modal to retrieve the generalization capability of CLIP lost in such training. However, such a mechanism is insufficient to direct the learnable prompt to learn a representation that manages to generalize the heterogeneous images, resulting in a minor improvement in the related evaluation, i.e. Cross-Dataset generalization and Domain-Shift generalization. Accordingly, our proposed method, Self-generated Cross-modal Prompt tuning (SCP), taps the frozen CLIP knowledge in a cross-modal manner to generate the pseudo prompts. Consequently, robust learnable prompts are achieved by aligning pseudo prompts in training, leading to the superior generalization capability on the image recognition downstream task. It mainly consists of three major modules, as shown in Fig. 3, each of which is introduced in the sequel.

Cascade Propagation Prompt Initialization (CPPI). In initialization, CPPI introduces two learnable tokens (restricted tokens P^r and unrestricted tokens P^u) to dynamically leverage the frozen CLIP knowledge, allowing the learnable prompt to learn a robust representation for a wide range of scenarios. Specifically, the text and image are first encoded by the frozen CLIP encoder. Then, the optimal matching embeddings between the textual and visual prompts are selected by the frozen CLIP model, referred to as W^{frozen} and X^{frozen}. The resulting embeddings are projected by Dimension Transformation (DT) and further reshaped into the size of the restricted tokens $P^r \in \mathbb{R}^{C \times b \times 512}$. Note that, there are visual DT and textual DT for corresponding modality, and both of them are built with a two-layer bottleneck structure (Linear-ReLU-Linear), with the hidden layer reducing the input layer to 64 and 128 as middle dimensions for visual DT and textual DT, respectively. The output size of both DTs is raised to $b \times 512$, depending on learnable token length b.

After that, the first element-wise addition is conducted between the text embedding with a specific class, which has the highest similarity identified by the frozen CLIP, and the image embedding. Next, a second element-wise addition is performed between the modified embedding and P^r to generate the knowledge-based learnable tokens P^{kr}. Subsequently, P^{kr} and P^u are combined as $P = [P^{kr}, P^u]$. Finally, P undergoes the process outlined in Eqs. 2 and 3.

Entropy-Regulation. As discussed in [15], the direction of modality conversion in learnable tokens affects generalization performance, likely due to information loss. Therefore, we propose a module, namely Entropy-Regulation (ER), to mitigate the information loss and balance the generalization performance between the directions. In specific, both before and after the projection function, we employ the Fast Fourier Transform (FFT) on learnable tokens, Then the entropy of the learnable token is calculated as

$$\textbf{Entropy}(q_i) = -\sum_{i=1}^{512} q_i \log_2(q_i + \epsilon), \qquad (7)$$

serving as the information recorder IR. Here, the input q_i represents the probability of occurrence of the i-th elements of each learnable token after the operation of FFT. ϵ is a small positive number. To account for the entropy gap between before and after the conversion for every learnable token involved, including the unrestricted and restricted learnable tokens in each transformer layer, we have

$$\mathcal{L}_{ER} = IR^{before} - IR^{after}. \tag{8}$$

Self-generated Proxy Alignment. Self-generated Proxy Alignment (SPA) mechanism is introduced to generate a proxy representation by transforming the frozen CLIP knowledge into cross-modal space for the training. Specifically, the text embedding W^{frozen} from frozen CLIP is mapped into the image modality space by the Cross-modal Dimension Transformation (CDT), which has the same structure as DT with different settings in terms of the dimensions. Note that, the mapped embedding from text modality space potentially remains independent of image modality-specific information. The alignment between the mapped embedding and the prompted image embedding X^p manages to develop a robust representation for X^p, facilitating the improvement of generalization capability. This operation is referred to as Domain Resistance (DR).

In addition, SPA generates sufficient embedding samples from the frozen CLIP knowledge in image modality space to address the insufficient training process on text learnable prompts that occurred in existing methods. Such an operation is referred to as Prompt Argumentation (PA). The prompted text embedding W^p is mapped into the image modality space by the CDT. Then the alignment between the resulting embedding and image embeddings X^{frozen} from frozen CLIP provides sufficient training for W^p.

Moreover, SPA employs the Euclidean distance (i.e. non-contrastive loss) on training to reduce the intra-modal gap and consequently enhance the generalization performance further. Thus, to account for the distribution gap in the alignment of both DR and PA can be calculated as

$$\mathcal{L}_{DR} = \left\| CDT(W^{frozen}) - X^p \right\|_2^2, \tag{9}$$

$$\mathcal{L}_{PA} = \left\| CDT(W^p) - X^{frozen} \right\|_2^2, \tag{10}$$

to prompt the synergy from the marriage of transforming frozen knowledge in a cross-modal manner and non-contrastive loss. Here, $CDT(\cdot)$ performs cross-modal dimension transformation. Finally, we have the total loss as

$$\mathcal{L}_{Total} = \mathcal{L}_{CE} + \mathcal{L}_{ER} + \lambda_1 \mathcal{L}_{DR} + \lambda_2 \mathcal{L}_{PA}, \tag{11}$$

where λ_1 and λ_2 refer to the weighting factors associated with corresponding loss and are set to 5 and 7, respectively. Consequently, SPA empowers SCP to tap the potential of CLIP, conducive to superior generalization capability.

4 Experiments

In this section, we first assess our SCP effectiveness in generalization capability. In specific, we compare our proposed SCP with thirteen well-known prompt tuning methods on four benchmarks widely used in previous studies, including Base-to-New class generalization, Cross-Dataset generalization, Domain-Shift generalization and Few-Shot classification. Then, the extended experiments are conducted to analyse the effectiveness of modules used in our SCP.

Table 1. Comparison of the Base-to-New generalization with 13 existing approaches. 'Uni', 'Multi', 'FC' denotes the 'uni-modal prompt tuning', 'multi-modal prompt tuning' and 'frozen CLIP knowledge', respectively. Δ refers to the gap between our proposed SCP and TCP.

Datasets	Sets	CLIP (IJCV22)	CoOp (CVPR22)	CoCoOp (ICCV23)	DAPT (ICCV23)	ProGrad (CVPR22)	ProDA (CVPR23)	KgCoOp (ICCV23)	RPO (ICLR23)	PLOT (ICCV23)	MaPLe (CVPR23)	DePT (CVPR24)	PromptSRC (ICCV23)	TCP (CVPR24)	SCP	Δ
		-	Uni	Uni+FC	Multi	Uni+FC	Uni	Uni+FC	Multi	Uni	Multi	Uni	Multi+FC	Uni+FC	Multi+FC	
Average	Base	69.34	82.38	80.47	83.18	82.48	81.56	80.73	81.13	83.98	82.28	83.62	84.12	84.13	86.48	+2.35
	New	74.22	67.96	71.69	69.27	70.75	72.30	73.60	75.00	71.72	75.14	75.04	75.02	75.36	76.11	+0.75
	HM	71.70	74.48	75.83	75.59	76.16	76.65	77.00	77.78	77.37	78.55	79.10	79.31	79.51	80.97	+1.46
ImageNet	Base	72.43	76.46	75.98	76.83	77.02	75.40	75.83	76.60	77.30	76.66	77.03	77.75	77.27	82.34	+5.07
	New	68.14	66.31	70.43	69.27	66.66	70.23	69.96	71.57	69.87	70.54	70.13	70.70	69.87	76.91	+7.04
	HM	70.22	71.02	73.10	72.85	71.46	72.72	72.78	74.00	73.42	73.47	73.42	74.06	73.38	79.53	+6.15
Caltech101	Base	96.84	97.80	97.96	97.83	98.02	98.27	97.72	97.97	98.53	97.74	98.30	98.13	98.23	97.42	-0.81
	New	94.00	93.27	93.81	93.07	93.89	93.23	94.39	94.37	92.80	94.36	94.60	93.90	94.67	89.85	-4.82
	HM	95.40	95.48	95.84	95.39	95.91	95.68	96.03	96.03	95.58	96.02	96.41	95.97	96.42	93.48	-2.94
Oxford Pets	Base	91.17	94.47	95.20	95.00	95.07	95.43	94.65	94.63	94.50	95.43	94.33	95.50	94.67	98.11	+3.44
	New	97.26	96.00	97.69	95.83	97.63	97.83	97.76	97.50	96.83	97.76	97.23	97.40	97.20	99.40	+2.20
	HM	94.12	95.23	96.43	95.41	96.33	96.62	96.18	96.05	95.65	96.58	95.76	96.44	95.92	98.75	+2.83
Standford Cars	Base	63.37	75.67	70.49	75.80	77.68	74.70	71.76	73.87	79.07	72.94	79.13	78.40	80.80	78.72	-2.08
	New	74.89	67.53	73.59	64.93	68.63	71.20	75.04	75.53	74.80	74.00	75.47	74.73	74.13	68.83	-5.30
	HM	68.65	71.37	72.01	69.36	72.88	72.91	73.36	74.69	76.88	73.47	77.26	75.52	77.32	73.44	-3.88
Flowers	Base	72.08	97.27	94.87	96.97	95.54	97.70	95.00	94.13	97.93	95.92	98.00	97.90	97.73	95.35	-2.38
	New	77.80	67.13	71.75	60.90	71.87	68.68	74.73	76.67	73.53	72.46	76.37	76.77	75.57	77.49	+1.92
	HM	74.83	79.44	81.71	74.81	82.03	80.66	83.65	84.50	83.99	82.56	85.84	86.06	85.23	85.50	+0.27
Food101	Base	90.10	89.37	90.70	90.37	90.37	90.30	90.50	90.33	89.80	90.71	90.50	90.63	90.57	98.93	+8.36
	New	91.22	88.77	91.29	91.30	88.59	88.57	91.70	90.83	91.37	92.05	91.60	91.50	91.37	98.43	+7.06
	HM	90.66	89.07	90.99	90.83	89.98	89.43	91.09	90.58	90.58	91.38	91.05	91.06	90.97	98.68	+7.71
FGVC Aircraft	Base	27.19	39.67	33.41	39.77	40.54	36.90	36.21	37.33	42.13	37.44	43.20	41.97	41.40	40.83	-0.57
	New	36.29	31.23	23.71	29.80	27.57	34.13	33.55	34.20	33.73	35.61	34.83	36.97	34.43	34.87	+0.44
	HM	31.09	34.50	27.74	34.14	32.82	35.46	34.83	35.70	37.46	36.50	38.57	39.46	37.83	37.86	+0.03
SUN397	Base	69.36	80.85	79.74	80.97	81.26	78.67	80.29	80.60	82.20	80.82	82.33	82.83	82.63	90.73	+8.10
	New	75.35	68.34	76.86	76.97	74.17	76.93	76.53	77.80	73.63	78.70	77.80	79.00	78.20	85.43	+7.23
	HM	72.23	74.07	78.27	77.55	77.79	77.36	79.18	77.68	79.75	80.00	80.87	80.35	88.00	+7.65
DTD	Base	53.24	79.97	77.01	82.23	77.35	80.67	77.55	76.70	81.97	80.36	82.20	82.60	82.77	84.76	+1.99
	New	59.90	48.60	56.00	54.23	52.35	56.48	54.99	62.13	43.80	59.18	59.13	57.50	58.07	64.41	+6.34
	HM	56.37	60.46	64.85	65.36	62.45	66.44	64.35	68.61	57.09	68.16	68.78	67.80	68.25	73.20	+4.95
EuroSAT	Base	56.48	90.10	87.49	94.73	90.11	83.90	85.64	86.63	93.70	94.07	89.03	92.40	91.63	95.35	+3.72
	New	64.05	53.00	60.04	50.33	60.89	66.00	64.34	68.97	62.67	73.23	71.07	68.43	74.73	62.20	-12.53
	HM	60.03	66.74	71.21	65.74	72.67	73.88	73.48	76.79	75.11	82.30	79.04	78.63	82.32	75.29	-7.03
UCF101	Base	70.53	84.33	82.33	84.3	84.33	85.23	82.89	83.67	86.60	83.00	85.80	86.93	87.13	88.20	+1.07
	New	77.50	67.37	73.45	76.33	74.94	71.97	76.67	75.43	75.90	78.66	77.23	78.33	80.77	79.39	-1.38
	HM	73.85	74.98	77.67	80.12	79.35	78.04	79.65	79.34	80.90	80.77	81.29	82.41	83.83	83.56	-0.27

4.1 Experiment Setup

Datasets. To implement the comparisons, as same as the well-known methods [9,15,41–43], eleven image datasets are used in Base-to-New class generalization, Cross-Dataset generalization and Few-Shot classification. Specifically, FGVCAircraft [24], Flowers102 [25], Food101 [1], OxfordPets [26] and Stanford-Cars [18] refer to fine-grained image datasets; Caltech101 [7] and ImageNet [5] refer to generic-object; DTD [4] refers to texture and EuroSAT [11] refers to satellite. While SUN397 [35] refers to the scene recognition task and UCF101 [31] refers to the action recognition task. As for Domain-Shift generalization, another four datasets from the ImageNet family with the shifted domain are included, i.e. ImageNet-Sketch [33], ImageNet-V2 [30], ImageNet-A [13] and ImageNet-R [12].
Baseline. In this paper, thirteen well-known prompt tuning methods are

involved as the baseline, all of which do not leverage the external model but the original CLIP as frozen knowledge. The thirteen well-known baselines with validated results are CLIP, CoOp, CoCoOp, DAPT, ProGrad, ProDA, KgCoOp, RPO, PLOT, MaPLe, DePT, PromptSRC, and TCP.

Training and Evaluation. In the comparisons, we use the CLIP with the backbone of ViT-B/16 in a 16-shot learning manner. The length b of both P^r and P^u learnable tokens is set to 2. Both P^r and P^u are first initialized with "a photo of Class" in the text modality space. The deep transformer layer depth J is set to 8. Besides, the SGD optimizer is used for training with a batch size of 4, a learning rate of 3.5e-3, and 30 training epochs. The evaluation metric is the average accuracy over 3 runs (random seeds 1, 2, and 3). Note that, in Cross-Dataset and Domain-Shift generalization, we train SCP with J modified to 3, training epoch set to 2, and a learning rate of 2.6e-3 to reduce computational cost. Similarly, in ablation experiments, we optimize the training epoch to 5.

4.2 Base-To-New Class Generalization

In the Base-to-New class generalization, every single dataset is divided into two groups (base and new). Each group contains mutually exclusive classes for training and evaluation, respectively. Then, this evaluation could assess if, after learning from the base group, the model could transfer the knowledge to the new group within one dataset. Thus, the evaluation metrics for generalization performance include the accuracies of both groups and their Harmonic Mean (HM). Note that, it can be seen from Table 1 that the recent significant progress in generalization performance occurred in methods that apply multi-modal prompt tuning and frozen CLIP knowledge in the training stage (i.e. PromptSRC and TCP). Thus, we compare our proposed SCP with the well-known baselines from the perspectives regarding these two prompt tuning mechanisms in the sequel.

Multi-modal Prompt Tuning. It can be observed in Table 1 that the best average performances among the 4 multi-modal prompt tuning baselines are 84.12% (PromptSRC), 75.12% (MaPLe), and 79.31% (PromptSRC) for Base, New, and HM, respectively. In comparison, our proposed SCP achieves 86.48%, 76.11%, and 80.97%, respectively. The result represents a significant improvement of 2.36%, 0.99%, and 1.66%, respectively, surpassing the best generalization performance provided by the multi-modal prompt tuning baselines.

Prompt Tuning with Fozen CLIP Knowledge. For prompt tuning that leverages frozen CLIP knowledge, Table 1 clearly demonstrates that the TCP performs the best among the 5 baselines (CoCoOp, ProGrad, KgCoOp, PromptSRC, and TCP), achieving 84.13%, 75.36% and 79.51% for Base, New and HM metrics, respectively. In fact, it can be clearly seen that TCP outperforms all the other 12 listed baselines. In contrast, our proposed SCP achieves 86.48%,

76.11%, and 80.97%, respectively, representing an improvement of 2.35%, 0.75% and 1.46%, respectively. Note that, for all three metrics, our proposed SCP obtains the best generalization performance in 5/11 datasets (ImageNet, DTD, Food101, OxfordPets and SUN397). Furthermore, in Food101 and OxfordPets datasets, SCP achieves outstanding generalization performance. For example, in terms of *HM*, Food101 and OxfordPets achieve 98.68% and 98.75%, respectively, indicating a significant improvement of 7.30% and 2.13% over the best baseline performance of 91.38% (MaPLe) and 96.62% (ProDA) for these specific datasets.

Overall, through the extensive comparison of the Base-to-New class generalization in Table 1, it is clearly illustrated our SCP consistently outperforms the thirteen baselines regarding the generalization performance. It shows that, with the aid of frozen CLIP knowledge in a cross-modal manner, SCP shows superior generalization capability in a wide range of image recognition downstream tasks.

4.3 Cross-Dataset Generalization

Table 2. Comparison of Cross-Dataset generalization. Δ refers to the gap between our proposed SCP and TCP.

	Source	Target									
	ImageNet	Caltech	Pets	Cars	Flowers	Food	Aircraft	SUN	DTD	EuroSAT	UCF	Avg.
CoOp	71.51	93.70	89.14	64.51	68.71	85.30	18.47	64.15	41.92	46.39	66.55	63.88
CoCoOp	71.02	94.43	90.14	65.32	71.88	86.06	22.94	67.36	45.73	45.37	68.21	65.74
MaPLe	70.72	93.53	90.49	65.57	72.23	86.20	24.74	67.01	46.49	48.06	68.69	66.30
PromptSRC	71.27	93.60	90.25	65.70	70.25	86.15	23.90	67.10	46.87	45.50	68.75	65.81
TCP	69.88	94.25	90.46	65.24	71.88	86.78	24.99	67.12	45.00	44.67	68.10	65.85
SCP	87.97	93.67	93.21	60.74	70.51	96.93	27.75	82.98	52.88	50.05	70.52	69.93
Δ	+18.09	-0.58	+2.75	-4.50	-1.37	+10.15	+2.76	+15.86	+7.88	+5.38	+2.42	+4.08

For Cross-Dataset generalization, the model is trained on ImageNet as the source dataset and evaluated on 10 target datasets that potentially contain heterogeneous images not presented in ImageNet. Compared to the Base-to-New class generalization, this evaluation imposes stricter standards for the generalization capability regarding domain generalization. However, it can be seen from Table 2 that SCP consistently outperforms the baselines regarding the generalization performance. Note that these baselines excel in the Base-to-New class generalization. Specifically, significant performance advantages are achieved on the source dataset (ImageNet) and 7 out of 10 target datasets. Notably, it can be calculated that SCP obtains significant improvements of 16.46%, 10.15%, 15.62%, and 6.01% over existing best results on the source dataset and target datasets (Food, SUN and DTD), respectively. Clearly, this analysis indicates that SCP achieves a significant generalization performance improvement for the scenario containing heterogeneous images that are not present in the training.

4.4 Domain-Shift Generalization

In the Domain-Shift generalization, in contrast to Cross-Dataset generalization, the model is still trained on ImageNet but evaluated on the dataset with the shifted domain from ImageNet. Note that, this evaluation focuses on assessing the domain generalization capability of the model while all classes have been included in the training. As shown in Table 3, SCP significantly outperforms the existing best baseline in 3 out of 4 target datasets and is only marginally inferior to the best result in the remaining one (ImageNet-V2). Table3 clearly shows the superiority of the SCP on Domain-Shift generalization. Significantly, the striking improvement suggests that SCP offer a novel pathway to advance prompt tuning for recognizing heterogeneous images in the downstream application.

Table 3. Comparison of Domain-Shift generalization. Δ refers to the performance gap between our proposed SCP and TCP.

	Source	Target				
	ImageNet	-V2	-Sketch	-A	-R	Average
CoOp	71.51	64.20	47.99	49.71	75.21	59.28
CoCoOp	71.02	64.07	48.75	50.63	76.18	59.91
MaPLe	70.72	64.07	49.15	50.90	76.98	60.28
PromptSRC	71.27	**64.35**	49.55	50.90	77.80	60.65
TCP	69.88	63.14	48.39	50.22	76.22	59.49
SCP	**87.97**	64.25	**61.73**	**70.28**	**93.18**	**72.36**
Δ	+18.10	+1.12	+13.34	+20.07	+16.95	+12.87

Table 4. Comparison of Few-Shot classification with 4-shot samples. Δ refers to the gap between our proposed SCP and TCP.

Datasets	CoOp	CoCoOp	ProGrad	KgCoOp	MaPLe	DAPT	PLOT	PromptSRC	TCP	SCP	Δ
ImageNet	69.37	70.55	70.21	70.19	70.67	70.80	70.40	70.80	70.48	**84.32**	+13.84
Caltech101	94.44	94.98	94.93	94.65	94.30	94.23	**95.13**	94.77	95.00	94.62	-0.38
OxfordPets	91.30	93.01	93.21	93.20	92.05	92.17	92.55	93.23	91.90	**96.38**	+4.48
StandfordCars	72.73	69.10	71.75	71.98	68.70	74.40	74.93	71.83	**76.30**	74.58	-1.72
Flowers	91.14	82.56	89.98	90.69	80.80	92.37	92.93	91.31	**94.40**	84.46	-9.94
Food101	82.58	86.64	85.77	86.59	86.90	83.60	86.46	86.06	85.30	**98.49**	+13.19
FGVCAircraft	33.18	30.87	32.93	32.47	29.03	32.47	35.29	32.80	36.20	**38.64**	+2.44
SUN397	70.13	70.50	71.17	71.79	71.47	72.20	70.42	72.80	72.11	**85.84**	+13.73
DTD	58.57	54.79	57.72	58.31	54.73	61.37	62.43	60.64	63.97	**66.19**	+2.22
EuroSAT	68.62	63.83	70.84	71.06	54.87	72.73	**80.70**	75.02	77.43	80.40	+2.97
UCF101	77.41	74.99	77.82	78.40	73.70	79.40	79.76	79.35	80.83	**83.12**	+2.29
Avg.	73.59	71.98	74.21	74.48	70.66	75.07	76.45	75.33	76.72	**80.64**	+3.92

4.5 Few-Shot Classification

Having evaluated the generalization capability of our proposed SCP with 16-shot training, Table 4 presents a similar evaluation for a more challenging scenario where fewer samples are available. In specific, the models are trained on 11 datasets with a 4-shot labelled source image and evaluation is conducted within the same class space. It can be observed that the proposed SCP outperforms all the baselines in average performance, and significantly so in 7 out of 11 datasets. This clearly indicates that SCP also enjoys superb generalization capability for image recognition downstream tasks with few-shot learning conditions.

4.6 Ablation Analysis

In ablation analysis, we evaluate the effectiveness of various modules introduced by the proposed SCP regarding the performance in Base-to-New class generalization.

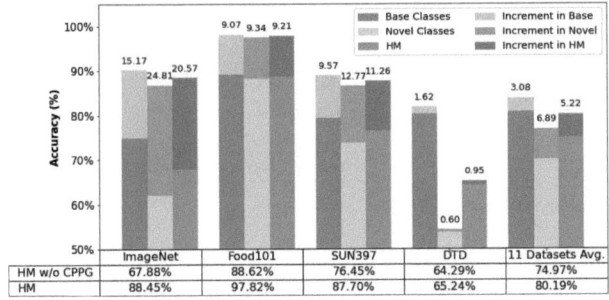

Fig. 4. Analysis of Cascade Propagation Prompt Initialization.

Effect of Cascade Propagation Prompt Initialization (CPPI). Figure 4 examines the impact of CPPI on 4 datasets (ImageNet, Food101, SUN397 and DTD) and average performance across 11 datasets. For instance, the average Base, New and HM results with CPPI module improve the performance from 80.73%, 69.98% and 74.97% to 83.81%, 76.87% and 80.19%, respectively. This result clearly suggests that CPPI effectively embeds the frozen CLIP knowledge into the learnable prompts, addressing overfitting to the training data.

Effect of Entropy-Regulation Module. To verify the effectiveness of the Entropy-Regulation (ER) for modality conversion, we disentangle the ER in our SCP and leverage it on an existing multi-modal method, MaPLe. A modified SCP and MaPLe are employed in this study to minimize the effect of the script. In Table 5, The absolute value, $|\Delta|$, demonstrates the performance gap between converting text to image and the reverse process. The average value across 11

Table 5. Analysis on Entropy-Regulation. Δ refers to the gap between different directions of modality conversion within the same model.

Model	Prompt Proj.	ImageNet	Caltech101	OxfordPets	StandfordCars	Flowers	Food101	FGVCAircraft	SUN397	DTD	EuroSAT	UCF101	Average
1. MaPLe	$P \to \tilde{P}$	72.63	96.12	96.67	72.82	81.55	90.83	29.79	79.03	61.90	80.93	80.40	
	$\tilde{P} \to P$	73.23	96.01	96.68	72.87	82.45	91.08	35.96	79.21	65.74	63.30	81.16	
	$|\Delta|$	0.60	0.11	0.01	0.05	0.90	0.25	6.17	0.18	3.84	17.63	0.76	2.77
2. MaPLe w/ ER	$P \to \tilde{P}$	72.58	96.58	96.67	72.31	81.98	91.13	29.16	78.90	61.42	80.60	80.59	
	$\tilde{P} \to P$	73.30	95.95	96.57	72.59	82.00	91.25	29.46	79.46	66.87	61.07	80.18	
	$|\Delta|$	0.72	0.63	0.10	0.28	0.02	0.12	0.30	0.56	5.45	19.53	0.41	2.56
3. SCP w/o ER	$P \to \tilde{P}$	90.53	90.12	97.82	70.23	80.57	98.80	37.81	89.66	67.86	72.70	82.96	
	$\tilde{P} \to P$	89.26	92.35	97.03	70.61	84.32	96.13	37.28	90.87	70.30	75.32	81.62	
	$|\Delta|$	1.27	2.23	0.79	0.38	3.75	2.67	0.53	1.21	2.44	2.62	1.34	1.75
4. SCP	$P \to \tilde{P}$	90.02	91.49	97.53	70.70	82.05	99.21	37.81	89.82	68.41	74.46	82.74	
	$\tilde{P} \to P$	90.13	91.70	97.70	70.99	81.63	98.51	34.92	90.92	71.50	72.16	80.93	
	$|\Delta|$	0.11	0.21	0.17	0.29	0.42	0.70	2.89	1.10	3.09	2.30	1.81	1.19

datasets indicates that the groups employing the ER exhibit a reduced disparity across different directions of modality conversion for both the SCP and MaPLe. Besides, we compare ER with a non-ER group and a modified energy-based regulation version instead of entropy-based as illustrated in Table 6. The results shows that entropy-based ER effectively enhances generalization performance.

Table 6. Analysis on ER for various mechanisms.

Regulation	Base	New	HM
w/o ER	83.91	76.95	80.28
Energy-based	54.13	52.73	53.42
Entropy-based	84.41	77.45	80.78

Table 7. Analysis on Self-generated Proxy Alignment.

Domain Resist.	Prompt Augment.	Base	New	HM
-	-	81.91	73.04	77.22
✓	-	83.46	77.11	80.16
-	✓	81.19	72.08	76.37
✓	✓	83.81	76.87	80.19

Effect of Self-generated Proxy Alignment. Table 7 explore all four combinations in terms of the adoption of two modules (Domain Resistance and Prompt Augmentation). It can be clearly seen that solely employing the DR appears to enhance generalization capability, in contrast to the less favourable performance of only using PA. However, the combination of both DR and PA achieves higher generalization performance in the Base and HM than others.

Table 8. Analysis on the initialization templates.

Templates	Base	New	HM
"a photo of a"	83.81	76.87	80.19
"this is a picture of"	83.89	76.94	80.26
"X X X X"	84.79	78.67	81.62

Effect of different initialization templates. We analyze the effect of the initialization template for learnable tokens by comparing three different templates, "a photo of a {}", "this is a picture of {}" and random initialization template "X X X X {}". Table 8 shows a marginal difference between the two handcrafted templates. More importantly, the random initialization template further empowers SCP to achieve superior generalizability, although it necessitates much stricter standards for the training of learnable prompts. This analysis indicates that SCP is robust against the effect associated with the initialization template.

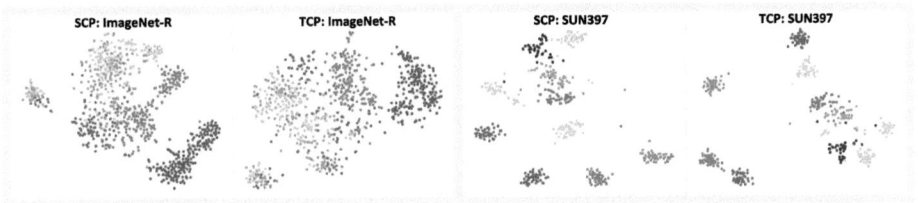

Fig. 5. t-SNE plots of image embeddings in SCP and TCP.

5 Visualization

To facilitate understanding of the superior generalization performance achieved by SCP, in Fig. 5, the image embeddings prepended with the learnable token from our proposed SCP and TCP are visualized in t-SNE, while colours differentiate classes in the dataset. SCP display more distinct discriminative clustering than those from TCP in both Cross-Dataset and Domain-Shift Generalization.

6 Conclusion

Prompt tuning effectively adapts fundamental vision-language models to the image recognition downstream tasks. However, prompt tuning methods suffer from overfitting to training data, limiting the potential improvement of generalization capability, significantly so for heterogeneous images that differ from the training data. In this study, we address this challenge from the perspective of finding a robust representation of learnable prompts. To obtain such a representation, we propose to train the learnable prompt by aligning pseudo prompts generated from self-knowledge in a cross-modal manner. The resulting representation is able to adapt to various textual classes and visual characteristics, consequently enhancing the generalization capability. Extensive experiments on four benchmarks clearly show that SCP outperforms well-known baselines in generalization performance. In particular, our proposed SCP achieves a striking improvement of generalization performance on Cross-Dataset and Domain-Shift generalization, revealing its superiority of generalization capability across a wide range of scenarios where the heterogeneous images are not present in the training data. Crucially, this paper provides a new avenue for expanding the applicability of prompt tuning to a broader spectrum of downstream applications.

References

1. Bossard, L., Guillaumin, M., Van Gool, L.: Food-101 - mining discriminative components with random forests. In: Fleet, D., Pajdla, T., Schiele, B., Tuytelaars, T. (eds.) Computer Vision - ECCV 2014, pp. 446–461. Springer International Publishing, Cham (2014)
2. Chen, Y.C., Li, L., Yu, L., Kholy, A.E., Ahmed, F., Gan, Z., Cheng, Y., Liu, J.: Uniter: Universal image-text representation learning (2020)
3. Cho, E., Kim, J., Kim, H.J.: Distribution-aware prompt tuning for vision-language models. In: Proceedings of the IEEE/CVF International Conference on Computer Vision (ICCV), pp. 22004–22013 (October 2023)
4. Cimpoi, M., Maji, S., Kokkinos, I., Mohamed, S., Vedaldi, A.: Describing textures in the wild (2013)
5. Deng, J., Dong, W., Socher, R., Li, L.J., Li, K., Fei-Fei, L.: Imagenet: A large-scale hierarchical image database. In: 2009 IEEE Conference on Computer Vision and Pattern Recognition, pp. 248–255 (2009)
6. Ding, J., Xue, N., Xia, G.S., Dai, D.: Decoupling zero-shot semantic segmentation (2022)
7. Fei-Fei, L., Fergus, R., Perona, P.: Learning generative visual models from few training examples: An incremental bayesian approach tested on 101 object categories. In: 2004 Conference on Computer Vision and Pattern Recognition Workshop, pp. 178–178 (2004). https://doi.org/10.1109/CVPR.2004.383
8. Feng, C., et al.: Promptdet: Towards open-vocabulary detection using uncurated images (2022)
9. Gao, P., et al.: Clip-adapter: Better vision-language models with feature adapters (2021)
10. Gao, P., Lu, J., Li, H., Mottaghi, R., Kembhavi, A.: Container: Context aggregation network (2021)
11. Helber, P., Bischke, B., Dengel, A., Borth, D.: Eurosat: A novel dataset and deep learning benchmark for land use and land cover classification (2019)
12. Hendrycks, D., et al.: The many faces of robustness: a critical analysis of out-of-distribution generalization (2021)
13. Hendrycks, D., Zhao, K., Basart, S., Steinhardt, J., Song, D.: Natural adversarial examples (2021)
14. Jia, C., et al.: Scaling up visual and vision-language representation learning with noisy text supervision (2021)
15. Khattak, M.U., Rasheed, H., Maaz, M., Khan, S., Khan, F.S.: Maple: multi-modal prompt learning. In: Proceedings of the IEEE/CVF Conference on Computer Vision and Pattern Recognition, pp. 19113–19122 (2023)
16. Khattak, M.U., Wasim, S.T., Naseer, M., Khan, S., Yang, M.H., Khan, F.S.: Self-regulating prompts: Foundational model adaptation without forgetting. In: Proceedings of the IEEE/CVF International Conference on Computer Vision (ICCV), pp. 15190–15200 (October 2023)
17. Kim, J.H., Jun, J., Zhang, B.T.: Bilinear attention networks (2018)

18. Krause, J., Stark, M., Deng, J., Fei-Fei, L.: 3D object representations for fine-grained categorization. In: 2013 IEEE International Conference on Computer Vision Workshops, pp. 554–561 (2013). https://doi.org/10.1109/ICCVW.2013.77
19. Lee, D., Song, S., Suh, J., Choi, J., Lee, S., Kim, H.J.: Read-only prompt optimization for vision-language few-shot learning. In: Proceedings of the IEEE/CVF International Conference on Computer Vision (ICCV), pp. 1401–1411 (2023)
20. Li, B., Weinberger, K.Q., Belongie, S., Koltun, V., Ranftl, R.: Language-driven semantic segmentation (2022)
21. Li, Z., Li, X., Fu, X., Zhang, X., Wang, W., Chen, S., Yang, J.: Promptkd: unsupervised prompt distillation for vision-language models. In: Proceedings of the IEEE/CVF Conference on Computer Vision and Pattern Recognition, pp. 26617–26626 (2024)
22. Lu, J., Batra, D., Parikh, D., Lee, S.: Vilbert: Pretraining task-agnostic visiolinguistic representations for vision-and-language tasks (2019)
23. Maaz, M., Rasheed, H., Khan, S., Khan, F.S., Anwer, R.M., Yang, M.H.: Class-agnostic object detection with multi-modal transformer (2022)
24. Maji, S., Rahtu, E., Kannala, J., Blaschko, M., Vedaldi, A.: Fine-grained visual classification of aircraft (2013)
25. Nilsback, M.E., Zisserman, A.: Automated flower classification over a large number of classes. In: 2008 Sixth Indian Conference on Computer Vision, Graphics and Image Processing, pp. 722–729 (2008).https://doi.org/10.1109/ICVGIP.2008.47
26. Parkhi, O.M., Vedaldi, A., Zisserman, A., Jawahar, C.V.: Cats and dogs. 2012 IEEE Conference on Computer Vision and Pattern Recognition pp. 3498–3505 (2012). https://api.semanticscholar.org/CorpusID:383200
27. Qian, Q., Xu, Y., Hu, J.: Intra-modal proxy learning for zero-shot visual categorization with clip. In: Oh, A., Naumann, T., Globerson, A., Saenko, K., Hardt, M., Levine, S. (eds.) Advances in Neural Information Processing Systems, vol. 36, pp. 25461–25474. Curran Associates, Inc. (2023)
28. Radford, A., et al.: Learning transferable visual models from natural language supervision (2021)
29. Rao, Y., et al.: Denseclip: Language-guided dense prediction with context-aware prompting (2022)
30. Recht, B., Roelofs, R., Schmidt, L., Shankar, V.: Do imagenet classifiers generalize to imagenet? (2019)
31. Soomro, K., Zamir, A.R., Shah, M.: Ucf101: A dataset of 101 human actions classes from videos in the wild (2012)
32. Tan, H., Bansal, M.: Lxmert: Learning cross-modality encoder representations from transformers (2019)
33. Wang, H., Ge, S., Xing, E.P., Lipton, Z.C.: Learning robust global representations by penalizing local predictive power (2019)
34. Wang, Y., Jiang, X., Cheng, D., Li, D., Zhao, C.: Learning hierarchical prompt with structured linguistic knowledge for vision-language models. In: Proceedings of the AAAI Conference on Artificial Intelligence, vol. 38, pp. 5749–5757 (2024)
35. Xiao, J., Hays, J., Ehinger, K.A., Oliva, A., Torralba, A.: Sun database: Large-scale scene recognition from abbey to zoo. In: 2010 IEEE Computer Society Conference on Computer Vision and Pattern Recognition, pp. 3485–3492 (2010)
36. Yao, H., Zhang, R., Xu, C.: Visual-language prompt tuning with knowledge-guided context optimization. In: Proceedings of the IEEE/CVF Conference on Computer Vision and Pattern Recognition (CVPR), pp. 6757–6767 (June 2023)

37. Yao, H., Zhang, R., Xu, C.: Tcp:textual-based class-aware prompt tuning for visual-language model. In: Proceedings of the IEEE/CVF Conference on Computer Vision and Pattern Recognition (CVPR), pp. 23438–23448 (June 2024)
38. Yu, Z., Yu, J., Cui, Y., Tao, D., Tian, Q.: Deep modular co-attention networks for visual question answering (2019)
39. Zang, Y., Li, W., Zhou, K., Huang, C., Loy, C.C.: Open-Vocabulary DETR with Conditional Matching, pp. 106–122. Springer Nature Switzerland (2022)
40. Zhang, J., Wu, S., Gao, L., Shen, H.T., Song, J.: Dept: decoupled prompt tuning. In: Proceedings of the IEEE/CVF Conference on Computer Vision and Pattern Recognition (CVPR), pp. 12924–12933 (June 2024)
41. Zhang, R., et al.: Tip-adapter: Training-free clip-adapter for better vision-language modeling (2021)
42. Zhou, K., Yang, J., Loy, C.C., Liu, Z.: Conditional prompt learning for vision-language models (2022)
43. Zhou, K., Yang, J., Loy, C.C., Liu, Z.: Learning to prompt for vision-language models. Int. J. Comput. Vision **130**(9), 2337–2348 (2022)
44. Zhu, B., Niu, Y., Han, Y., Wu, Y., Zhang, H.: Prompt-aligned gradient for prompt tuning (2024)

Quality-Preserving Extreme Image Compression: Using Interpretable Conditioning Inputs with Diffusion Models

Shayan Ali Hassan[✉], Danish Humair, Ihsan Ayyub Qazi, and Zafar Ayyub Qazi

Department of Computer Science, Lahore University of Management Sciences, Lahore, Pakistan
{25100165,25100183,ihsan.qazi,zafar.qazi}@lums.edu.pk

Abstract. Diffusion models have revolutionized image synthesis, but their potential for image compression remains underexplored. We introduce PLIC (Pseudo-Lossy Image Compression), a compression framework leveraging diffusion models and conditioning inputs to achieve high compression ratios while maintaining strong perceptual similarity and superior image quality. Unlike traditional neural compressors using abstract latent representations, our approach uses interpretable conditioning inputs (text prompts, canny edges, color palettes) to guide diffusion-based image reconstruction. Grounded in rate-distortion-perception theory, PLIC prioritizes minimizing bitrate and distortions over pixel-perfect reconstruction, allowing diffusion models to fill in plausible details during decompression which still results in high perceptual similarity. Evaluating on 490 real-world images, we demonstrate superior compression ratios (0.004 bits per pixel and 0.197 bits per pixel on average) while maintaining excellent image quality (mean BRISQUE=23.36, mean CPBD=0.60) and high perceptual similarity. Our approach scales effectively with increasing image resolution, with compression advantages growing at the most common image resolutions. We analyze practical implications including benefits for internet affordability, archival storage, and deployment considerations. Our project code can be found at: https://github.com/PseudoLossy/PLIC.

Keywords: Image Compression · Diffusion Models · Conditioning Inputs

1 Introduction

Image compression is widely used for reducing the data footprint of images while maintaining acceptable visual quality. Without image compression, many

---

S. A. Hassan and D. Humair—Contributed equally to this work.

digital applications such as web browsing, video streaming, and cloud storage would not be possible at scale. Traditional lossless image compression algorithms, such as those used by PNG, can achieve compression ratios of up to 3:1 (66% compression), while lossy formats like JPEG and WebP can reach up to 20:1 (95% compression) [11]. However, at such high compression levels, image quality often degrades significantly due to severe compression artifacts and distortions.

With the rise in popularity of deep learning models during the last decade, neural network architectures have been extensively applied to image compression tasks, achieving state-of-the-art performance. Generally, neural image compressors involve extracting high-level features from an image using a network and transforming them into a latent space representation. This representation achieves compression by exploiting spatial and semantic redundancies to distill only the most important information. The latent space representation is then provided as input to another network in order to obtain a reconstruction of the original image. Leveraging image features in this manner to reconstruct images has been shown to produce images with fewer visual distortions and greater perceptual fidelity compared to algorithmic codecs [26].

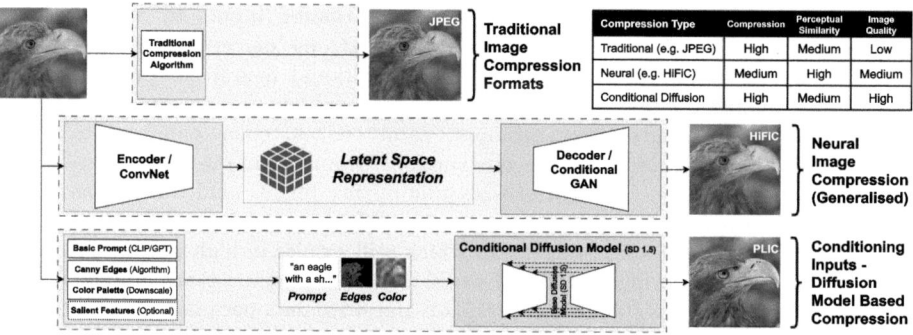

Fig. 1. Overview of how using conditioning inputs in tandem with diffusion models to compress images (our methodology) differs from traditional codecs and neural image compressors. Blue regions indicate compression steps, while red regions indicate decompression steps, while the width of each region provides an estimate of the computational demands. Notice the symmetrical and asymmetrical computational demand of neural compressors and our method respectively. (Color figure online)

More recently, denoising probabilistic diffusion models such as Stable Diffusion have shown remarkable performance in generating high-quality, realistic images [9,15]. Architectures such as ControlNet [43] use "conditioning inputs" to control diffusion model outputs by conditioning them to adhere to structural guides. These inputs inherently encode perceptually important information about an image, and unlike abstract latent space representations, conditioning inputs explicitly extract interpretable spatial information such as color, structure, and depth, suggesting their potential utility beyond mere generation control.

We propose to re-imagine these conditioning inputs as components of a novel compression paradigm. We term our framework as PLIC (Pseudo-Lossy Image Compression). PLIC is grounded in rate-distortion-perception theory, strategically selecting ControlNet conditioning inputs that minimize bitrate and minimize distortions (maximizing quality), deliberately deprioritizing pixel-perfect reconstruction. This allows diffusion models to leverage their learned priors to "fill in" perceptually plausible details during reconstruction, effectively outsourcing part of the reconstruction process to the model's understanding of visual reality. This can result in exceptional compression ratios and higher image quality while still maintaining high perceptual similarity, a significant departure from the predominant focus on latent space representations in current compression literature. The differences between PLIC and traditional image compression formats and neural image compressors are illustrated in Fig. 1.

Through extensive experimentation on a carefully curated dataset of 490 real-world images from the top 1,000 globally visited domains, we demonstrate that using just three interpretable conditioning inputs (text prompts, canny edges, and color palettes) is sufficient to outperform neural compression baselines. Our evaluation includes three key experiments: (1) assessing the perceptual benefits of increasing the number of conditioning inputs, (2) analyzing image quality, perceptual similarity, and compression ratios against existing approaches, and (3) evaluating the feasibility of our framework with current technology. We evaluate our method across diverse image types and various resolutions (333×687 to 4032×2030), revealing that compression advantages scale better at common image sizes, despite computational overhead during decoding.

Taken together, we make three key contributions in this work:

- We introduce a novel compression framework grounded in rate-distortion-perception theory, which uses conditioning inputs to deliberately prioritize image quality and compression efficiency over pixel-perfect reconstruction.
- We demonstrate that our conditioning-inputs-based compression method, using three conditioning inputs (text prompts, canny edges, and color palettes) achieves exceptional *compression ratios* of 0.004 bits per pixel at minimum and 0.197 bits per pixel on average while having the best average *image quality* (mean BRISQUE=23.36, mean CPBD=0.60). While PLIC currently incurs higher *computation times*, it produces reconstructions with high *perceptual similarity*. Through extensive experiments against a neural framework that maximizes perceptual similarity and a neural framework that maximizes compression, we show our approach outperforms most previous baselines despite its significantly smaller data footprint.
- We provide a detailed analysis of the method's practical implications, including its scalability benefits across common image resolutions, its potential to increase internet affordability without degrading user experience, advantages for long-term archival storage, and considerations regarding computational requirements and ease of deployment.

2 Related Work

2.1 Neural Image Compression

Most traditional image compression techniques based on neural networks employ some form of either a variational autoencoder (VAE) [19] or generative adversarial network (GAN) [12]. VAEs use a predefined network known as an encoder to transform the input, in this case an image, into a probabilistic latent space. This distribution of the image within the latent space is the compressed form, and a predefined decoder is used to transform the latent space distribution back into the input space. GANs utilize a generator and discriminator network to generate new data indistinguishable from the original input data's distribution. Since both architectures try to reconstruct an image from a smaller latent representation, there is some loss in information during the encoding and decoding steps, thus both suffer from the rate-distortion-perception tradeoff [5,8]. The rate-distortion-perception tradeoff states that in low bitrate contexts, such as compression, minimizing the distortions in images will lead to less perceptually pleasing images due to noise and other factors, and vice-versa. VAEs are known to induce blurriness in images for this reason [45].

There have been many proposed improvements and modifications to such neural networks in order to tailor them for image compression with higher realism, such as using less computationally expensive decoding activations in VAEs [37,40], semantically decoupling an image into multiple independent regions before encoding them [10], using Conditional-GANs trained on labelled data instead [25], and using a text encoder to inform the image encoder which details are perceptually the most important [21].

2.2 Diffusion Models for Image Compression

Diffusion models, also referred to as diffusion denoising probabilistic models (DDPMs) [15], have gained prominence as a powerful class of generative models, known for their high-quality image synthesis. Such models rely on the denoising autoencoder, which is repeatedly sampled while supervised by input features (such as text features in the case of text-to-image diffusion models) in order to incorporate random noise into an image, allowing for iterative generation of a high quality image. Latent diffusion models which shift the diffusion process to a lower-dimensional latent space have helped to substantially reduce computational demands [34]. Furthermore, ControlNet [43]; a neural network architecture designed to add spatial conditioning controls to large, pre-trained text-to-image diffusion models allows for even greater fidelity and controllability in generations. Using image conditioning inputs that are easily understood by humans such as edge maps, depth maps, segmentation masks, among others, users are able to modify the image structure and style as needed.

Unsurprisingly, using diffusion models to compress images is emerging as an area of research interest due to their learned knowledge about both high-level and low-level visual concepts, allowing them to reconstruct image details at higher fidelity and perceptual quality for a given bitrate [46]. However, these models are known for their generative diversity [1,16] therefore in the context of image compression where the generated image must obey a ground truth, recent work has focused on controlling the output of these models while optimizing them for compression. This includes introducing additional latent variables to guide the denoising process [39], removing redundant processes in the denoising steps to increase performance [33] and using short text embedding generated from the original image itself instead of a prompt to generate the image [30]. While all of these methods score well on perceptual metrics, their use of latent vectors as the condition for the diffusion model prevents them from outperforming existing methods in terms of compression. Furthermore, the easily interpretable conditioning inputs typically employed in ControlNet are not explored as a means of compression. While [22] investigates the use of sketches as a conditioning input to preserve structural information for compression, and [7] uses simple image descriptions in conjunction with latent image representations, the similarity of the reconstructed images is lacking with respect to the originals, especially for perceptually important details.

To the best of our knowledge, this is the first work that thoroughly investigates the potential of using simple, non-vector conditioning inputs as a means of compressing images.

3 Methodology

Supported by the rate-distortion-perception theory, we propose to choose conditioning inputs that aim to minimize bitrate and maximize perceptual similarity with the original image, thus forgoing minimization of pixel-level differences and spatial distortions [4]. While this would render reference-based pixel-wise metrics unsuitable for evaluation, this is preferable as most conditioning inputs supported by ControlNet versions of diffusion models capture a facet of the most perceptually meaningful information only, tending to ignore finer details at the pixel-level. Furthermore, diffusion models will be able to judiciously "fill in" the gaps at the pixel-level, such as texture, due to their learned knowledge about the world, allowing for the reconstructed images to still be of higher quality even if there are pixel-level differences. With the prioritized optimizations in mind, we extract the semantic, structural and color information from the original image via the following conditioning inputs:

1. Text prompt: The prompt serves as a description of the image and is sufficient to provide semantic information. We opt to use the GPT-4-vision API to generate the prompt from the original images, as this allows us to tweak human-friendly zero-shot instructions which can help prevent misuse as well as leverage a Large Language Model (LLM) to only describe perceptually and contextually important information.

2. Canny Edges: Canny edges can provide the structural information [6], ensuring that reconstructions have the same composition as the original image. This approach strikes a balance between minimal bitrate and improved accuracy, as the canny edgemaps are compact due to being monochrome.

3. Color Palettes: A color palette further contextualizes the information provided to the diffusion model by providing general information of how the colors were distributed in the image, ensuring accurate color replications. It can be obtained by downsizing an image to a small resolution such as 32 × 32.

3.1 Additional Optimizations

In order to increase perceptual similarity in a compression maximizing manner, we propose three further optimizations to the aforementioned conditioning inputs:

Due to edge detection, most pixels in a Canny edge bitmap have the same value, representing negative space between thin, edge outlines, allowing further optimization. We exploit this by using lossless JBIG2, the industry standard compression algorithm for bi-level images, typically used in fax machines and black-and-white PDFs. JBIG2 outperforms other algorithms by reducing bi-level images by a factor of 2-5 [17]. Testing on 490 images scraped from the Web (Sect. 4), we see that JBIG2 provides significant lossless compression, allowing the canny edges to be up to 99.95% and on average 90% smaller than the original image. The results are presented in Fig. 2.

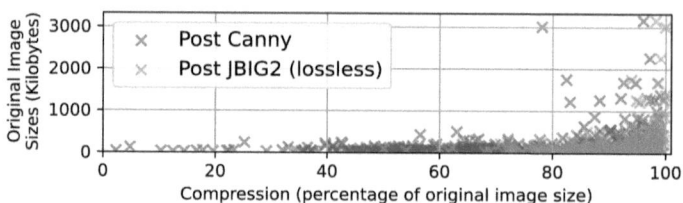

Fig. 2. Using JBIG2 on canny edges provides significant lossless compression.

The color map is encoded via WebP, which provides significantly reduced compression artifacting compared to JPEG [11], ensuring that the colors extracted from the original image are provided to the diffusion model accurately.

Lastly, we propose using segmentation masks to preserve finer perceptual details across compression and reconstruction. Stable Diffusion Inpainting allows using a black and white mask to indicate which sections of an image should be recreated, and which sections should be left untouched, thus allowing for the preservation of critical, *salient features*, such as faces, small text and small logos [42]. The cropped salient features are stored unmodified as part of the compressed form, hence the total compression becomes indirectly proportional to the area of salient features in the original image. However, since only small, important details are at risk of being distorted and thus marked as salient [22,33], compression is expected to still be significant. Salient features can be masked very quickly and automatically by leveraging Meta's Segment Anything Model

[20] to identify various segments in an image and using Grounding DINO [23] to identify segments with small, salient features.

Our approach extracts only the most high-level and perceptually important features as conditioning inputs to serve as the compressed state of an image. This method guarantees the preservation of information in these conditioning inputs during reconstruction while allowing a diffusion model to 'fill in' missing details autonomously–a technique we term as *'Pseudo-Lossy' Image Compression*. Therefore, for the sake of brevity we shall refer to our proposed methodology of compressing images via conditioned diffusion models as **PLIC**. Figure 1 provides an overview of the conditioning inputs in PLIC and how it differs from traditional methods.

4 Experiments and Results

To evaluate the efficacy of PLIC in real-world scenarios, we scraped images from the top 1000 globally visited domains using the Google Chrome UX Report (CRUX) lists [36] and manually removed pages with inappropriate content, resulting in a final set of 600 pages. Given the imbalance in image quantity across websites, each website was categorized into one of seven main categories derived from Cloudflare's domain categorizations [35]: E-Commerce, Informational, Business/Company, News, Social Media, Video Streaming, and other.

From each category, we randomly sampled 70 images, resulting in a dataset of 490 images.[1] A minimum resolution of 512 × 256 in either orientation was set because (i) lower-resolution images lack the necessary detail and structure needed by current text-to-image models to generate high-quality, coherent outputs [32] and (ii) such images do not provide much compression due to their already small size. Thus, in our dataset, the resolution of collected images ranged from 333 × 687 to 4032 × 2030.

We conduct 3 different types of experiments:

- Evaluating the perceptual benefits of increasing conditioning inputs.
- Detailed analysis of image quality, perceptual similarity and compression ratios against existing approaches.
- Exploring how the generation costs scale up in two different use cases.

4.1 Ablation Study of Conditioning Inputs

We validate the choice of conditioning inputs by compressing all images in the dataset to their conditioning inputs, reconstructing them and evaluating the perceptual similarity of the reconstructions with respect to the original images.

---

[1] Images with transparent pixels were excluded to prevent processing inconsistencies. Many image models are optimized for RGB channels and may mishandle the alpha channel for transparency. This ensures consistent data processing and avoids potential artifacts during model training and inference.

We repeat this experiment 4 times, each time adding another conditioning input to evaluate the contribution of each to the perceptual similarity, (prompts only, prompts + canny edges, prompts + canny edges + color maps, prompts + canny edges + color maps + salient feature preservation enabled). We used Stable Diffusion 1.5 (SD1.5) as the diffusion model in conjunction with two ControlNet pipelines to condition the input, where one conditioned the image generation based on structure and color and the other used inpainting to generate all parts of the image other than the selected region.

The extent of compression is measured in two ways; (i) via comparing the size of the original image against the compressed state (i.e. the sum of prompt size, canny edges size after JBIG2 compression, color palette size, segmentation mask size and salient features size) and (ii) bits per pixel (bpp). For the perceptual similarity evaluation metric, we use DINOv2, a self-supervised Vision Transformer that achieves state-of-the-art performance on many computer vision tasks [29]. DINOv2 creates visual feature embeddings which are well-suited to capture important semantic information about images. Furthermore, since DINOv2 is self-supervised, it has learned visual features that can generalize across various image distributions, even outside of its training set. The cosine similarity between the embeddings of the original and the reconstructed image can be used as an accurate measure of perceptual similarity [44]. The results are presented in Fig. 3 and the summary statistics are provided in Table 1.

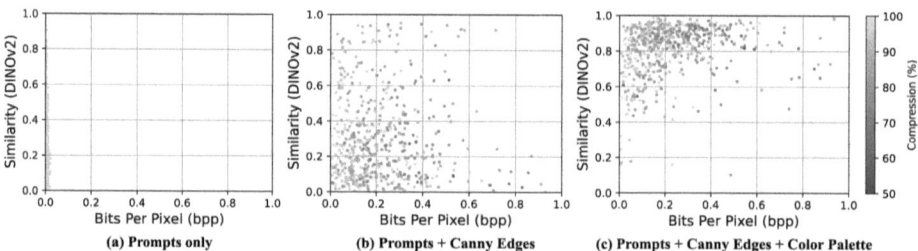

Fig. 3. Tradeoff between bpp and perceptual similarity as conditioning inputs increase.

Table 1. Summary statistics of the ablation study.

EXP	DINOv2			Compression (%)			Compression (bpp)		
	Median	Min	Max	Median	Min	Max	Median	Min	Max
Prompt	**0.16**	0.00	0.90	**99.78**	84.00	99.998	**0.0004**	0.0001	0.02
+ Canny	**0.24**	0.00	0.95	**91.14**	54.00	99.95	**0.17**	0.0001	0.93
+ Color	**0.85**	0.10	0.99	**90.47**	52.91	99.94	**0.18**	0.01	0.94
+ Salient	**0.89**	0.58	0.98	**77.85**	0.00	96.82	**0.33**	0.05	1.45

Fig. 4. Perceptual gains of increasing the number of conditioning inputs.

As we add more conditioning inputs, we see weaker compression ratios as the median bpp increases from 0.0004 to 0.33. However, looking at compression as the percentage reduction in size instead we see that the images are still being heavily compressed in all cases. Furthermore, adding more conditioning inputs results in a consistent increase in perceptual similarity score, increasing from 0.16 as a baseline to 0.89, referencing the rate-perception tradeoff. Due to salient preservation targeting small regions from an image, the perceptual similarity score does not improve much between the salient feature preservation test and the previous test. Figure 4 visually shows the effects of our salient feature step on critical details, as well as the effects of increasing conditioning inputs generally.

4.2 Detailed Image Analysis

Next, we evaluate PLIC against two neural image compression frameworks:

- **HiFiC** [25]: HiFiC is a popular conditional-GAN-based image compressor that achieves state-of-the-art results in many image compression on various metrics such as PSNR (Peak signal-to-noise ratio), MS-SSIM (Multiscale - structural similarity index measure) and FID (Fréchet inception distance) [14] at very low bitrates. In order to ensure a fair comparison, we aim to keep the compression ratios between PLIC and HiFiC as close as possible hence we specifically use HiFiC-Low as it achieves the highest compression ratios as compared to HiFiC-Medium or HiFiC-High, at the cost of some loss in similarity.
- **TACO** [21]: TACO is an image compression framework which utilizes a text encoding to guide a diffusion encoder for creating a latent representation of an image, instead of directly using a text prompt to guide the encoder instead. It also achieves state-of-the-art results in LPIPS (Learned Perceptual Image Patch Similarity) [44], a widely used perceptual similarity metric. Similarly

to HiFiC, we use TACO with the hyper-parameter $\lambda = 0.015$ which results in the most aggressive compression.

To ensure a more robust evaluation, we use PLIC with not just SD1.5 but also Flux.1, a recent transformer based text-to-image diffusion model that has gained considerable popularity, in order to draw any insights between consistent behavior in diffusion models (we did not provide color palettes as a conditioning input to Flux as it was recently released at the time of experimentation and a well-trained canny + color conditioned version of the model did not exist yet). Furthermore, instead of just using DINOv2 as the perceptual similarity metric, we also evaluate all images using the LPIPS metric, due to its high alignment with human ratings [44].

As mentioned previously in Sect. 3, while our methodology produces largely perceptually similar reconstructions, they are different at the pixel-level since fine, noisy details are not captured at any point. Since PLIC is not constraint to exactly reconstruct pixel-level textures, the reconstructed images do not suffer from compression artifacts/blockiness/blurriness as the diffusion model makes no attempt to reconstruct exact details from compressed data and is free to generate the output from it's own learned distributions. To measure this increase in *image quality*, a no-reference (NR) image quality assessment (IQA) model is required since providing the original image as a reference would lead to poor scores due to the pixel-wise differences being interpreted as reconstruction loss. To measure reconstruction quality, we use BRISQUE (blind/referenceless image spatial quality evaluator) [27], which uses luminance coefficients to quantify possible losses of 'naturalness' in the image due to the presence of compression distortions, and CPBD (cumulative probability of blur detection) [28], which uses a probabilistic model to measure levels of blur at each edge in an image.

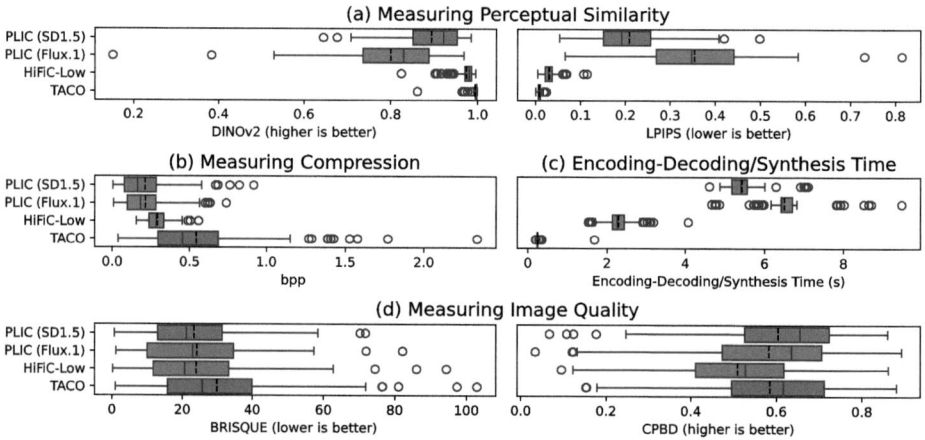

Fig. 5. Comparison of perceptual similarity, compression strength, computational time and image quality between PLIC (SD1.5, Flux.1), HiFiC-Low and TACO.

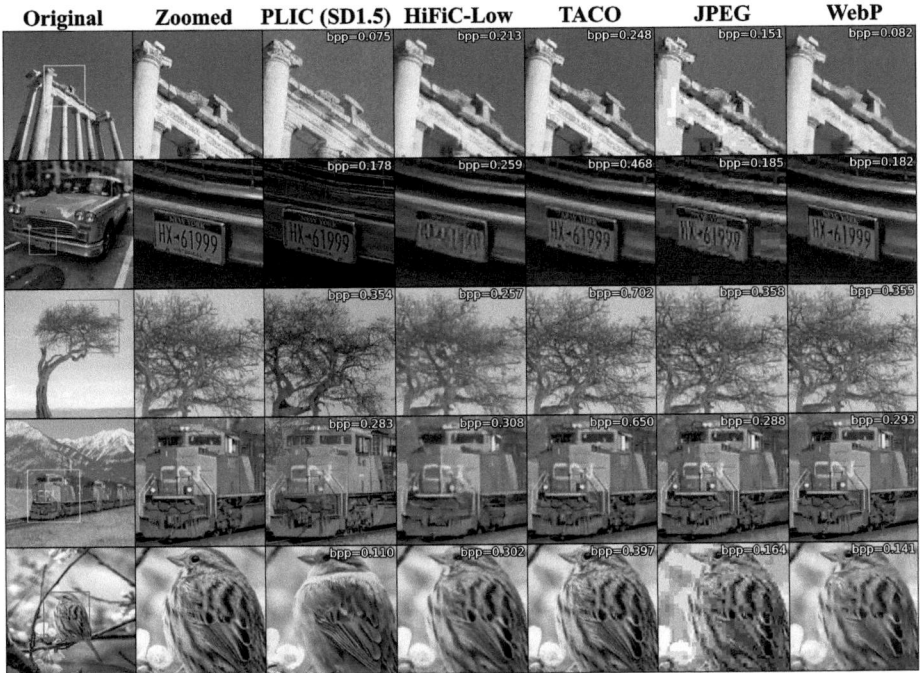

Fig. 6. Visual comparison showing the superiority of PLIC and conditioning inputs + diffusion model compression in general to reconstruct higher quality and fidelity of images that are still perceptually similar in the extremely low bitrate regime. JPEG & WebP images were compressed with maximum strength in order to bring the compression extents as close as possible to PLIC. HiFiC and TACO were also used at maximum compression strength as previously mentioned.

We evaluate all methodologies against each other across 6 dimensions: perceptual similarity with DINOv2 and LPIPS, compression, encoding–decoding/synthesis times, and image quality with BRISQUE and CPBD, on a 150 image subset of our dataset for each sub-experiment. The results are provided in Fig. 5. While HiFiC-Low and TACO achieve better perceptual similarity scores, the scores for PLIC with SD1.5 are still reasonably good, with an average of 0.90 DINOv2 score and 0.21 LPIPS score (perceptual similarity for PLIC with Flux is slightly lower as expected due to the lack of color palettes). However, the compression ratios achieved by PLIC are noticeably better, with an average bpp of 0.20 for SD1.5, which is lower than the 25th percentile bpp for both HiFiC and TACO. As for image quality, the BRISQUE score distributions show average scores of 23.36, 23.91 and 29.90 for SD1.5, HiFiC and TACO respectively, indicating TACO has more spatial distortions than the other two. Meanwhile, the CPBD score distributions show average scores of 0.60, 0.51 and 0.58 for SD1.5, HiFiC and TACO respectively, indicating HiFiC images to be more blurry compared to the other two. While HiFiC images suffer from blurriness and TACO

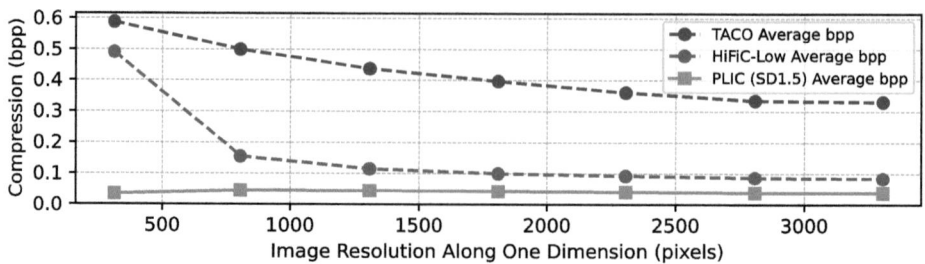

Fig. 7. Comparison of average bpp after compression across image resolutions.

images suffer from distortions and noise, PLIC with SD1.5 minimizes both distortions and bluriness, performing the best when evaluated by the BRISQUE and CPBD metrics. Hence, PLIC demonstrates the best image quality and visually pleasing reconstructions (given that the viewer is fine with a non-exact pixel-level yet still perceptually similar overall reconstruction). This becomes evident in Fig. 6 too, as the PLIC reconstructions look much sharper and defined, free of compression artifacts. In the computational time analysis, a clear weakness of PLIC is shown as HiFiC and TACO are much faster at encoding and decoding images, while the diffusion models are slower due to their highly iterative nature.

Lastly for the detailed image analysis, we investigate how the average bpp changes as image dimensions/resolution changes. High-resolution images (at least 3000 pixels along any dimension) were sampled from our dataset, downsized versions of various resolutions were created for each and each version was compressed and decompressed using PLIC with SD1.5, HiFiC and TACO. The results are shown in Fig. 7. We find that the PLIC average bpp is not dependent upon the original/reconstructed image size. This makes sense as prompts are negligible in size and generated according to what the image is depicting thus they are similar irrespective of resolution. Color palettes are always obtained by reducing the image to a constant 32×32 resolution, thus they have negligent impact on the bpp. Canny edges meanwhile are the same size as the original dimensions and are thus the amount of bits needed to encode the information for one pixel remains proportionately the same, especially after JBIG2 compression. Only varying level of salient features cause small deviations for PLIC. Overall, for image dimensions of about 500 to 1500 pixels especially, PLIC scales better at compressing images when compared to a GAN or diffusion-encoder based compressors such as HiFiC or TACO, which proportionately require a larger latent vectors to represent an image at lower resolutions.

4.3 Cost Analysis Across File Sizes and Storage Duration

In this section, we evaluate the overall cost implications of our framework by examining two distinct scenarios: (i) on-demand image delivery, where both network egress and GPU decoding costs matter, and (ii) long-term archival storage, where storage fees and time before access dominate.

On-Demand Transfer and Decoding: Figure 8a shows the ratio of original transfer cost to our method's total cost (i.e., PLIC transfer *plus* decoding). A ratio above 1 indicates that using PLIC is cheaper. We bin images by their original file size, and apply a common egress fee ($0.09/GB on AWS [2]), as well as a GPU rental rate ($1/hour for an A100 on Vast.ai [38]). Notably, our GPU VRAM was heavily underutilized and rental prices include a significant premium, so the per-image decoding cost could be even lower when amortized over larger batches or shared GPU usage. Across bins, we observe higher cost savings (ratio up to ×45) as image size increases. This stems from the fact that our compressed conditioning data does not grow significantly with resolution, as seen in Fig. 7. Furthermore, larger image files in our dataset were likely to be less optimized beforehand, granting our framework more competitive savings, whereas smaller image files were already heavily compressed and showed a ratio lower than 1, but at the cost of much lower fidelity.

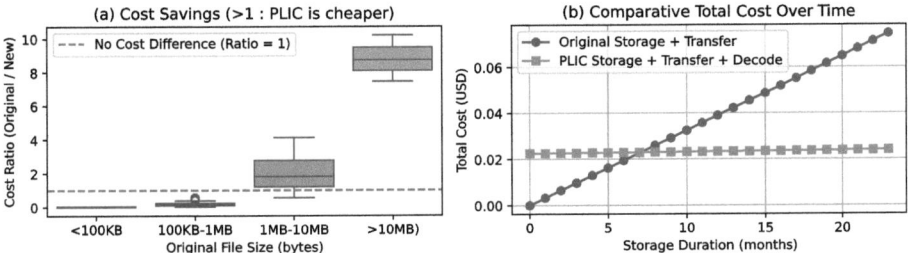

Fig. 8. (a) *Immediate cost ratio* of storing/transferring original images vs. using PLIC, binned by file size. Ratios above 1.0 indicate that PLIC is cheaper. (b) *Cumulative cost over time* for long-term storage, comparing original images to PLIC's reduced representations.

Long-Term Storage and Decoding: In many real-world scenarios, images remain stored for extended periods, making the *storage footprint* at least as important as immediate transfer and decoding cost. Figure 8b compares the cumulative cost of retaining and eventually transferring the original images versus storing PLIC's smaller conditioning inputs and decoding them on-demand. We apply a common storage rental rate ($0.023/GB/month for Amazon S3 [3]), and assume the same egress fees and GPU rental as before. Over time, the modest decode overhead is overshadowed by significant storage savings, especially as the image set grows or is retained for periods longer than 6 to 12 months. Therefore, PLIC provides substantial operational benefits for archival or on-demand use cases (high-write, low-read scenarios), even under conservative GPU cost assumptions, due to it's asymmetrical computational demands and the compression step being quite inexpensive as the diffusion model remains un-involved.

5 Discussion

In this section, we would like to discuss other aspects, contributions and limitations of our method that were not explored in the previous sections:

Bandwidth Savings and Internet Affordability: Webpage sizes have increased by roughly 13 times over the last decade, in large part due to the use of more and higher quality images [13]. Simultaneously, 94 developing countries fail to meet the target for affordable broadband services due to Internet plan costs exceeding 2% of the monthly Gross National Income (GNI) per capita [18]. Given the extreme levels of compression, PLIC-based image compression can be a viable pathway towards increasing bandwidth savings for end users, thus making the internet much more affordable. PLIC can also enhance the user experience during web browsing given that in most cases, image quality is enhanced compared to traditional image codecs and neural compression frameworks, while still preserving high perceptual similarity with respect to the original images. Due to the combination of high image quality and perceptual similarity, but lower pixel-level similarity, we expect such compression to excel in 'semantic imagery contexts', where images serve primarily to evoke or illustrate broad concepts, rather than to provide detailed visual information. Examples of such contexts include news articles, educational materials, and stock photos.

High-Write, Low-Read Scenarios: PLIC is attractive for workloads where images are written or uploaded frequently but accessed only sporadically. Backups, archives, long-tail media libraries, and even "cold" portions of personal photo galleries fall into this category. In such settings, traditional storage tiers often force a painful trade-off: either keep full-fidelity images and incur recurring capacity fees, or delete them outright to reclaim space. PLIC offers a third option. Because encoding is lightweight while decoding is heavyweight, write time remains minimal yet stored footprint is reduced significantly compared to other compression methods. Reads remain possible albeit with a compute penalty. This "compress instead of delete" path allows users to retain access to rarely viewed or lower-value images that would otherwise be purged, deferring costly storage upgrades for cloud providers and individual users alike.

Client-Side Reconstruction: Currently, due to the computational demands of diffusion models, we assume the image to be transmitted over a network in it's compressed state and being reconstructed at the edge, such as through a content delivery network (CDN) server, where adequate compute is available. While this can help to reduce costs for CDN providers and generally decrease ingress bandwidth over the internet, end-users can not currently receive the affordability benefits. However, recent trends indicate running deep neural networks on client devices such as smartphones and laptops may soon become feasible. Apple has recently made improvements to iPhone hardware allowing them to run language models such as OpenELM [24]. Additionally, one-step image generators such as DMD2 [41], based on knowledge distillation, allow high-quality images to be synthesized at extremely low inference times.

Ease of Deployment: As long as the image model supports text, canny, color inputs and inpainting, similar extents of compression and image quality can be achieved regardless of the image model at the core. Thus PLIC offers flexibility for a wide range of tasks where one model may be better than another. Furthermore, unlike existing neural compression frameworks, PLIC requires no additional model training to use whatsoever. We were able to experiment with the proposed methodology immediately because versions of popular image models that accept conditioning inputs will already be trained by community contributors for artistic purposes and use in a variety of image generation tasks. This 'out-of-the-box' approach can allow developers to immediately deploy PLIC, unlike GAN and encoder-based methodologies such as HiFiC and TACO which must be extensively trained first, are only limited to the specific task of image compression, and must be re-trained again to incorporate improvements in neural network understanding.

Ethical Considerations: PLIC based compression, if used properly, is also able to account for any societal biases in diffusion models, as evident by the example in Fig. 4. As more conditioning inputs are provided, the model gains context and a better understanding of the features such as in this case, the person's skin tone, refining the output to match the original. Conversely, this also means a malicious actor could falsify canny edges / color palettes or add misleading words to prompts to intentionally produce inaccurate or negatively biased reconstructions. Past instances show that people are understandably sensitive to offensive content generated by image models, such as when Google's Gemini model in an attempt to curb societal biases ended up generating images with obvious historical inaccuracies, causing controversy [31].

6 Conclusion

In this paper, we investigated a novel image compression approach using conditioning inputs for diffusion models, providing a compelling alternative to traditional neural compression methods. By leveraging text prompts, canny edges, color palettes, and salient feature preservation, our method achieves extreme compression while maintaining high perceptual similarity, effectively navigating the rate-distortion-perception tradeoff. Experiments on real-world images demonstrate superior compression ratios and image quality, with scalability benefits at common resolutions. While decoding remains computationally intensive, the flexibility and ease of deployment make this approach promising for future compression solutions, with potential applications in bandwidth optimization, energy/storage efficiency, and real-time image reconstruction.

Acknowledgments. We thank Rania Yakub Khan, Zaeem Khan and Ayesha Mirza for assisting with the experiments, verifying our results and for providing invaluable feedback.

Disclosure of Interests. The authors have no competing interests to declare that are relevant to the content of this article.

References

1. Aithal, S.K., Maini, P., Lipton, Z., Kolter, J.Z.: Understanding hallucinations in diffusion models through mode interpolation. Adv. Neural. Inf. Process. Syst. **37**, 134614–134644 (2025)
2. Amazon Web Services: Amazon EC2 On-Demand Pricing. https://aws.amazon.com/ec2/pricing/on-demand/. Accessed 17 Mar 2025
3. Amazon Web Services: Amazon S3 Pricing. https://aws.amazon.com/s3/pricing/. Accessed 17 Mar 2025
4. Bachard, T., Bordin, T., Maugey, T.: Coclico: extremely low bitrate image compression based on clip semantic and tiny color map. In: 2024 Picture Coding Symposium (PCS), pp. 1–5. IEEE (2024)
5. Blau, Y., Michaeli, T.: Rethinking lossy compression: the rate-distortion-perception tradeoff. In: International Conference on Machine Learning, pp. 675–685. PMLR (2019)
6. Canny, J.: A computational approach to edge detection. IEEE Trans. Pattern Anal. Mach. Intell. **PAMI-8**(6), 679–698 (1986)
7. Careil, M., Muckley, M.J., Verbeek, J., Lathuilière, S.: Towards image compression with perfect realism at ultra-low bitrates. In: The Twelfth International Conference on Learning Representations (2023)
8. Cover, T.M.: Elements of information theory. John Wiley & Sons (1999)
9. Croitoru, F.A., Hondru, V., Ionescu, R.T., Shah, M.: Diffusion models in vision: a survey. IEEE Trans. Pattern Anal. Mach. Intell. **45**(9), 10850–10869 (2023)
10. Feng, R., Gao, Y., Jin, X., Feng, R., Chen, Z.: Semantically structured image compression via irregular group-based decoupling. In: Proceedings of the IEEE/CVF International Conference on Computer Vision, pp. 17237–17247 (2023)
11. Ginesu, G., Pintus, M., Giusto, D.D.: Objective assessment of the webp image coding algorithm. Signal Process.: Image Commun. **27**(8), 867–874 (2012)
12. Goodfellow, I., et al.: Generative adversarial nets. In: Advances in Neural Information Processing Systems, vol. 27 (2014)
13. Habib, R., et al.: A framework for improving web affordability and inclusiveness. In: Proceedings of the ACM SIGCOMM 2023 Conference, pp. 592–607 (2023)
14. Heusel, M., Ramsauer, H., Unterthiner, T., Nessler, B., Hochreiter, S.: Gans trained by a two time-scale update rule converge to a local nash equilibrium. In: Advances in Neural Information Processing Systems, vol. 30 (2017)
15. Ho, J., Jain, A., Abbeel, P.: Denoising diffusion probabilistic models. Adv. Neural. Inf. Process. Syst. **33**, 6840–6851 (2020)
16. Hoogeboom, E., Agustsson, E., Mentzer, F., Versari, L., Toderici, G., Theis, L.: High-fidelity image compression with score-based generative models. arXiv preprint arXiv:2305.18231 (2023)
17. Howard, P.G., Kossentini, F., Martins, B., Forchhammer, S., Rucklidge, W.J.: The emerging jbig2 standard. IEEE Trans. Circuits Syst. Video Technol. **8**(7), 838–848 (1998)

18. ITU: Measuring digital development: Ict price trends 2019 (2020)
19. Kingma, D.P., Welling, M., et al.: Auto-encoding variational bayes (2013)
20. Kirillov, A., et al.: Segment anything. In: Proceedings of the IEEE/CVF International Conference on Computer Vision, pp. 4015–4026 (2023)
21. Lee, H., Kim, M., Kim, J.H., Kim, S., Oh, D., Lee, J.: Neural image compression with text-guided encoding for both pixel-level and perceptual fidelity. arXiv preprint arXiv:2403.02944 (2024)
22. Lei, E., Uslu, Y.B., Hassani, H., Bidokhti, S.S.: Text+ sketch: image compression at ultra low rates. arXiv preprint arXiv:2307.01944 (2023)
23. Liu, S., et al.: Grounding dino: marrying dino with grounded pre-training for open-set object detection. In: European Conference on Computer Vision, pp. 38–55. Springer (2024)
24. Mehta, S., et al.: Openelm: An efficient language model family with open training and inference framework. In: Workshop on Efficient Systems for Foundation Models II@ ICML2024 (2024)
25. Mentzer, F., Toderici, G.D., Tschannen, M., Agustsson, E.: High-fidelity generative image compression. In: Advances in Neural Information Processing Systems, vol. 33 (2020)
26. Mishra, D., Singh, S.K., Singh, R.K.: Deep architectures for image compression: a critical review. Signal Process. **191**, 108346 (2022)
27. Mittal, A., Moorthy, A.K., Bovik, A.C.: No-reference image quality assessment in the spatial domain. IEEE Trans. Image Process. **21**(12), 4695–4708 (2012)
28. Narvekar, N.D., Karam, L.J.: A no-reference image blur metric based on the cumulative probability of blur detection (cpbd). IEEE Trans. Image Process. **20**(9), 2678–2683 (2011)
29. Oquab, M., et al.: Dinov2: Learning robust visual features without supervision. arXiv preprint arXiv:2304.07193 (2023)
30. Pan, Z., Zhou, X., Tian, H.: Extreme generative image compression by learning text embedding from diffusion models. arXiv preprint arXiv:2211.07793 (2022)
31. Raghavan, P.: Gemini image generation got it wrong. we'll do better (2024). https://blog.google/products/gemini/gemini-image-generation-issue (2024)
32. Ramesh, A., Dhariwal, P., Nichol, A., Chu, C., Chen, M.: Hierarchical text-conditional image generation with clip latents. arXiv preprint arXiv:2204.06125 **1**(2), 3 (2022)
33. Relic, L., Azevedo, R., Gross, M., Schroers, C.: Lossy image compression with foundation diffusion models. In: European Conference on Computer Vision, pp. 303–319. Springer (2024)
34. Rombach, R., Blattmann, A., Lorenz, D., Esser, P., Ommer, B.: High-resolution image synthesis with latent diffusion models. In: Proceedings of the IEEE/CVF Conference on Computer Vision and Pattern Recognition, pp. 10684–10695 (2022)
35. Ruth, K., et al.: A world wide view of browsing the world wide web. In: Proceedings of the 22nd ACM Internet Measurement Conference, pp. 317–336 (2022)
36. Ruth, K., Kumar, D., Wang, B., Valenta, L., Durumeric, Z.: Toppling top lists: Evaluating the accuracy of popular website lists. In: Proceedings of the 22nd ACM Internet Measurement Conference, pp. 374–387 (2022)
37. Tao, L., Gao, W., Li, G., Zhang, C.: Adanic: towards practical neural image compression via dynamic transform routing. In: Proceedings of the IEEE/CVF International Conference on Computer Vision, pp. 16879–16888 (2023)
38. Vast.ai: GPU Pricing for A100 SXM4. https://cloud.vast.ai/?gpu_option=A100%20SXM4 Accessed 17 Mar 2025

39. Yang, R., Mandt, S.: Lossy image compression with conditional diffusion models. Adv. Neural. Inf. Process. Syst. **36**, 64971–64995 (2023)
40. Yang, Y., Mandt, S.: Computationally-efficient neural image compression with shallow decoders. In: Proceedings of the IEEE/CVF International Conference on Computer Vision, pp. 530–540 (2023)
41. Yin, T., Gharbi, M., Park, T., Zhang, R., Shechtman, E., Durand, F., Freeman, W.T.: Improved distribution matching distillation for fast image synthesis. In: NeurIPS (2024)
42. Yu, T., et al.: Inpaint anything: segment anything meets image inpainting. arXiv preprint arXiv:2304.06790 (2023)
43. Zhang, L., Rao, A., Agrawala, M.: Adding conditional control to text-to-image diffusion models. In: Proceedings of the IEEE/CVF international conference on computer vision, pp. 3836–3847 (2023)
44. Zhang, R., Isola, P., Efros, A.A., Shechtman, E., Wang, O.: The unreasonable effectiveness of deep features as a perceptual metric. In: Proceedings of the IEEE Conference on Computer Vision and Pattern Recognition, pp. 586–595 (2018)
45. Zhao, S., Song, J., Ermon, S.: Towards deeper understanding of variational autoencoding models. arXiv preprint arXiv:1702.08658 (2017)
46. Zhao, W., Rao, Y., Liu, Z., Liu, B., Zhou, J., Lu, J.: Unleashing text-to-image diffusion models for visual perception. In: Proceedings of the IEEE/CVF International Conference on Computer Vision, pp. 5729–5739 (2023)

Beyond General Edge Utilization: Edge Attention Mean Teacher for Semi-Supervised Medical Image Segmentation

Kaiwei Sun, Luhan Wang(✉), and Jin Wang

Key Laboratory of Data Engineering and Visual Computing, Chongqing University of Posts and Telecommunications, Chongqing, China
{sunkw,wangjin}@cqupt.edu.cn, s230201109@stu.cqupt.edu.cn

Abstract. Deep learning has achieved substantial success in the field of semi-supervised medical image segmentation. Current researches mainly concentrate on enhancing pseudo-label generation process and refining consistency regularization architectures. However, the edge information, which is essential for medical image segmentation but scarce in semi-supervised scenario, is often overlooked. To address this problem, we present an edge attention mean teacher (EAMT) method that goes beyond general edge extraction to better leverage the edge information for improved segmentation performance. Particularly, based on a novel definition of edge, we propose a new edge extraction method to boost the edge extraction capability of model. Furthermore, we elaborately design an edge-aware loss function that uses the extracted edges as additional supervision for labeled data and as masks for unlabeled data. The EAMT method is characterized by its capability to extract and leverage robust edge information to promote the learning process for both labeled and unlabeled data. We evaluate the segmentation performance of the proposed EAMT method on two public 3D datasets (LA and Pancreas-CT). Experimental results demonstrate that EAMT achieves superior segmentation performance compared to several state-of-the-art methods in semi-supervised medical image segmentation.

Keywords: Semi-supervised learning · Medical image segmentation · Edge attention · Mean teacher

1 Introduction

Medical image segmentation, such as computed tomography (CT) and magnetic resonance imaging (MRI), is essential for many clinical applications [8,23,36]. Recent years have witnessed the remarkable success of deep learning in fully supervised scenario. These supervised methods heavily rely on a large number of annotated medical images to guarantee their segmentation performance.

However, well annotation of medical images is time-consuming. Semi-supervised learning aims at learning robust models with only a little labeled data along with a large amount of unlabeled data, making it more data-efficient.

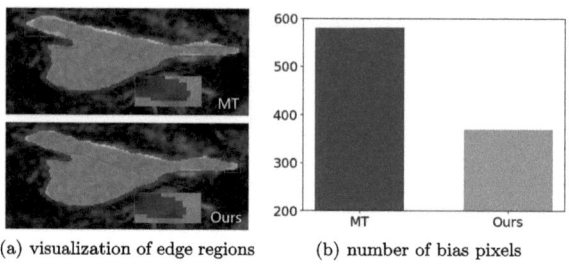

(a) visualization of edge regions   (b) number of bias pixels

Fig. 1. Edge information is crucial to medical image segmentation. In figure(a), red pixels mean the predictions while white pixels are the ground-truth. The predictions on bias areas marked with red rectangles are key to differentiate the segmentation performance. Figure(b) shows the number of the bias pixels predicted by MT method and our proposed EAMT method. (Color figure online)

The core issue in semi-supervised learning is how to effectively utilize unlabeled data. Currently, two mainstream techniques, consistency regularization and pseudo-labeling, are widely recognized for their excellent performance. Most semi-supervised methods incorporate dual networks to get additional features from unlabeled data [8]. Mean Teacher (MT) [18] serves as a foundational benchmark for consistency regularization, and its variants [19,25,33] have a significant impact on medical image segmentation. Another approach is pseudo-labeling, which focuses on enhancing the quality of pseudo-labels [24]. Despite the promising outcomes of these methods, they usually overlook the edge information, which is crucial for accurate segmentation of medical images, as depicted in Fig. 1(a). However, the edge regions, which usually encompass the ground-truth and the background, pose a significant challenge for model to accurately segment. In computer vision, conventional wisdom has it that the shallow layers of deep convolutional neural network (CNN) architectures are rich in edge information. Moreover, due to the robust feature extraction abilities of attention modules, numerous studies have integrated attention blocks into their works to bolster the extraction of edge information [20,35]. Owing to the accessibility of a large number of labeled medical images, these supervised methods have successfully harnessed edge information. However, edge information has not yet been effectively adapted to the semi-supervised learning domain.

In the context of semi-supervised medical image segmentation, maximizing the use of edge information can be achieved by prompting the model to capture extensive edge cues from labeled data, which can then be utilized to inform the segmentation of unlabeled data. We accomplish this by introducing a novel definition of edge and proposing the EAMT method. Specifically, the EAMT method is built on a typical MT architecture and employs the V-Net [14] as backbone. We incorporate an edge attention module within the top two layers of the encoder. Furthermore, we introduce an edge extraction method to get edge from labeled data, which is further utilized as additional supervision for labeled data and as masks for unlabeled data. We also develop a novel edge-aware loss function that leverages edge information to enhance learning from labeled data and imposes edge consistency to promote learning from unlabeled data. As shown in Fig. 1(b), our proposed EAMT method obtains much less predicted bias pixels than MT. We further evaluate the performance of the proposed EAMT method on two benchmark 3D datasets in semi-supervised medical image segmentation: LA dataset and Pancreas-CT dataset.

In summary, our work makes the following contributions:

- Based on the MT architecture, we propose the EAMT method that aims at leveraging edge information to enhance segmentation performance.
- We present a novel definition of edge, which goes beyond the general edge extraction to gain more robust edge information.
- Based on the new definition of edge, we develop an edge extraction module that leverages attention mechanism to extract rich edge information.
- We design an edge-aware loss function that utilizes edge information to promote learning from unlabeled data, and uses the edge information as additional supervision to strengthen learning from labeled data.
- We validate our proposed EAMT method on two public benchmark datasets, and the experimental results show that EAMT outperforms several state-of-the-art methods, demonstrating the effectiveness of our method.

2 Related Work

2.1 Semi-supervised Medical Image Segmentation

Consistency regularization based methods are prevalent in semi-supervised medical image segmentation. These methods build upon the smoothness assumption that minor perturbations should not significantly alter the outputs of model. The pioneering work MT [18] adds noise to teacher network and utilizes an exponential moving average (EMA) to update the parameters of teacher network, which is formulated as:

$$\theta'_t = \lambda \theta'_{t-1} + (1-\lambda)\theta_t, \qquad (1)$$

where θ'_t denotes the parameters of the teacher network at time step t, θ_t denotes the parameters of the student network, and λ is the smoothing hyperparameter that regulates the degree of smoothing between the new and old parameters. Another common approach is pseudo-labeling, where a segmentation network first generates predictions for the unlabeled data, and these predictions are subsequently used as pseudo-labels to guide the supervised learning process [31].

Whether employing consistency regularization or adopting pseudo-labeling, mainstream methods in semi-supervised medical image segmentation adopt a structure with dual networks to better leverage unlabeled data. For instance, in the work of ABD [5], an adaptive bidirectional displacement mechanism is utilized to mitigate the limitations that mixed perturbations impose on two subnets. The MCF framework [24] allows two networks to learn from each other by a mutual correction mechanism. The BCP [1] uses two networks and a bidirectional copy-paste technique to learn common features from unlabeled data. The UAMT [33] explores uncertainty information, which improves the performance of general MT. Luo et al. [13] use two different types of subnets to obtain more robust information. The SAMT-PCL [3] constructs one encoder with dual decoders to obtain predictions and uncertainty maps from different perspectives. Despite their success, those methods usually overlook the valuable edge information. Our proposed EAMT places greater emphasis on edge information and employs a robust attention module to enhance the model's capability of edge feature extraction.

2.2 Edge-Related Works

Edge information, which is widely recognized as a critical feature in computer vision, is extensively utilized in supervised medical image segmentation. In the ET-Net [35], an edge guidance module is incorporated to extract edge details from the encoder, and this extracted edge information is subsequently utilized in a weight aggregation module. In the DCAN [2], a CNN is employed to handle substantial changes in appearance and produce detailed probabilistic maps with high accuracy. The EANet [20] designs an edge attention module to enhance the edge information extraction ability of model. Cheng et al. [4] utilized directional feature maps to tackle the blurred margins problem. In their work, Yang et al. [32] developed an improved active contour model, which is capable of extracting robust edge information from images. Despite the advancements, edge extraction strategies prevalent in supervised scenario have not been extended to the semi-supervised medical image segmentation domain.

2.3 Attentions in Computer Vision

Attention mechanisms have demonstrated remarkable efficacy in Natural Language Processing (NLP) tasks and have been increasingly integrated into Computer Vision (CV) tasks. The applications of attention in CV can be categorized into three primary categories: spatial attention, channel attention, and hybrid attention. In CNNs, each layer generates a feature map. Spatial attention focuses on learning a weight for each pixel across all channels within the feature map. The non-local neural networks [22] calculate the response at a specific location by taking a weighted sum of the features. The SMSA module [17] captures spatial information from each feature channel, thereby improving the network's capacity to discern fine details. The channel attention approach involves learning distinct weights for each channel. In the milestone work SENet [9], inter-channel relationships are modeled to adjust the feature responses on a per-channel basis. The ECA-Net [21] improves the structure of SENet and gets lower model complexity. In BA-Net [34], a bridge attention module is proposed, which amplifies channel attention through the integration of feature information from various convolutional layers. The hybrid attention, which represents a synergistic application of different attentions, has been explored in numerous studies [6,17,26]. Attention mechanisms have exhibited extraordinary feature extraction capabilities; however, simply stacking these attentions is far from being effective. Our proposed edge attention module strategically employs channel attention solely in the shallow layers of the encoder.

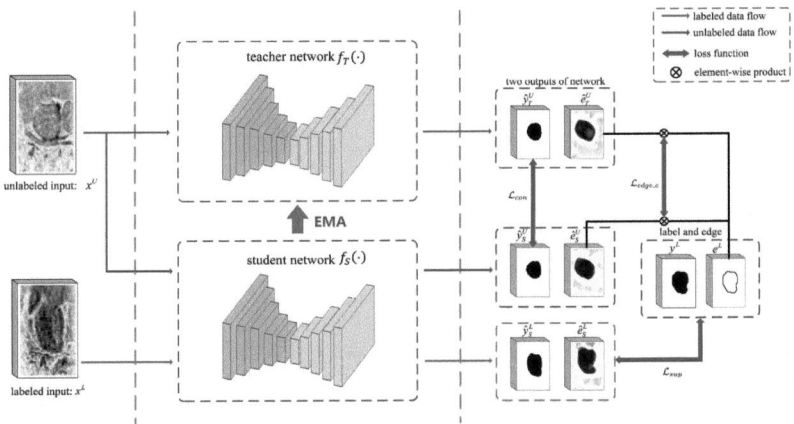

Fig. 2. Architecture of the proposed EAMT method.

3 Methodology

3.1 Overview of EAMT Method

In the semi-supervised medical image segmentation scenario, we assume that the training data consists of a labeled dataset $\mathcal{D}_L = (x_i^L, y_i^L)_{i=1}^{N}$, and an unlabeled dataset $\mathcal{D}_U = (x_i^U)_{i=N+1}^{N+M}$. The number of labeled images is much less than that of unlabeled images, i.e. $N \ll M$. Here, $x_i \in \mathbb{R}^{H \times W \times D}$ represents the medical image, $y_i \in \{0,1\}^{H \times W \times D}$ is the corresponding ground-truth. In our proposed EAMT method, we integrate the extracted edge $e_i \in \{0,1\}^{H \times W \times D}$ into labeled dataset, and reformulate the labeled dataset as $\mathcal{D}_L = (x_i^L, y_i^L, e_i^L)_{i=1}^{N}$. The proposed EAMT method is built upon the MT architecture, with a well designed edge attention module equipped within both teacher network $f_T(\cdot)$ and student network $f_S(\cdot)$. Moreover, a novel edge-aware loss function is also integrated into the EAMT. The architecture of EAMT is shown in Fig. 2.

During the training phase, both labeled and unlabeled data are fed into the student network. While only the unlabeled data is fed into the teacher network.

The outputs of two networks include segmentation prediction $\hat{y}$ and edge prediction $\hat{e}$:

$$\hat{y}_S^L, \hat{e}_S^L, \hat{y}_S^U, \hat{e}_S^U = f_S((x^L, x^U)), \quad (2)$$

$$\hat{y}_T^U, \hat{e}_T^U = f_T(x^U + \epsilon), \quad (3)$$

where the subscripts S and T denote the student network and teacher network, respectively, ϵ represents the random noise (perturbations).

The loss function of EAMT comprises both supervised loss and unsupervised loss. And the loss function is utilized to update the parameters of student network while parameters of teacher network are updated by EMA (see Eq. 1).

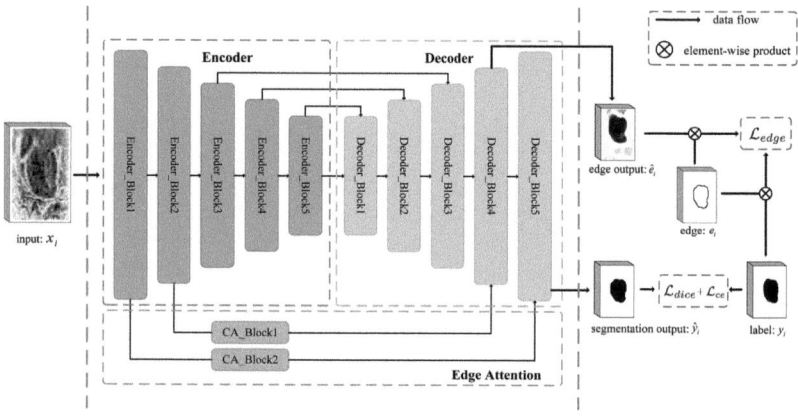

Fig. 3. Improved network structure.

3.2 Edge Extraction Module

Robust edge information extraction holds a core position in our proposed EAMT. The design of edge extraction module comprises two parts: a novel definition of edge and an edge attention block.

Definition of Edge. The general edge is defined as the outermost one pixel along the boundary, containing only a few pixels. Consequently, the edge extracted by conventional methods tends to be sparse and is very sensitive to noise. To achieve more robust edge extraction, we present a novel edge definition. Specifically, instead of viewing the outermost one pixel as edge, we define the outermost boundary as b_i and consider its surrounding 26 pixels as edge. The new definition of edge is explained in Fig. 4(a) and formulated as follows:

$$b_i(p) = (1 \in \mathcal{N}(p)) \land (0 \in \mathcal{N}(p)) \land (x_i^L(p) == 1), \quad (4)$$

$$e_i^L(p) = b_i(p) \lor (\exists_{p' \in \mathcal{N}(p)} b_i(p')), \quad (5)$$

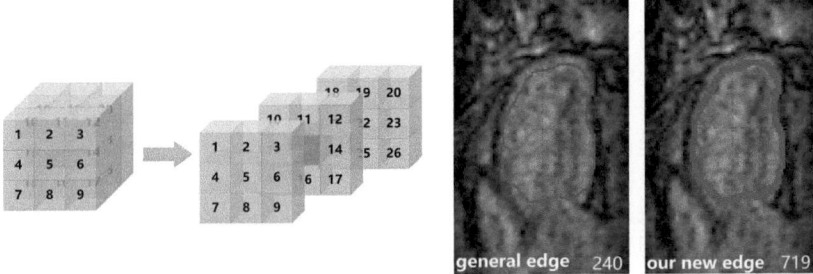

(a) explanation of new edge definition (b) visualization of extracted edge

Fig. 4. A novel definition of edge. In figure (a), each element in the cube represents a pixel. The value of this central orange pixel in the edge map is determined by all 27 pixels within a larger cube. The left side of figure (b) shows the general edge extracted by conventional method, the outermost edge contains only 240 pixels over 10000 pixels, while the right side of figure (b) depicts the edge extracted by our method, which contains 719 pixels (more than 5%). (Color figure online)

where p and p' represent a pixel, $x_i^L(\cdot)$ denotes the value of the pixel in the image, $e_i^L(\cdot)$ denotes the value of the pixel in the edge, b_i signifies the general edge, and $b_i(\cdot)$ indicates the value of the pixel, $\mathcal{N}(\cdot)$ refers to the 26 neighbouring pixels of a given pixel. By considering more neighbouring pixels along the boundary, the newly defined edge can encompass more pixels along the boundary, improving the robustness of edge. The difference between general edge and edge extracted by our method is shown in Fig. 4(b).

Edge Attention. Inspired by the success of attention mechanism, we propose to displace the standard residual connections between the first two layers of encoder and last two layers of decoder with an edge attention module that comprises two channel attention (CA) blocks, which consists of three layers: an average pooling layer, a linear layer with ReLU, and a linear layer with Sigmoid. The average pooling layer ensures that every pixel of a channel contributes to the weight of this channel, and then two linear layers are used to calculate the weights of channels, which are also viewed as attention scores. The calculation of channel attention block is formulated as:

$$\mathbf{Y} = \mathbf{X} \times \sigma\left(\text{Linear}_2(\text{ReLU}(\text{Linear}_1(\text{AvgPool}(\mathbf{X}))))\right), \tag{6}$$

where $\mathbf{X}$ is the input of channel attention block, $\mathbf{Y}$ is the output of channel attention block, $\sigma(\cdot)$ represents the sigmoid function, Linear$(\cdot)$ denotes a linear transformation, and AvgPool$(\cdot)$ means average pooling.

3.3 Edge-Aware Loss Function

The edge extraction module can extract robust edge information. Subsequently, another core issue is how to leverage the edge information to promote the learning. To this end, we elaborately design an edge-aware loss function, which is a combination of supervised loss $\mathcal{L}_{sup}$ and unsupervised loss $\mathcal{L}_{unsup}$:

$$\mathcal{L}_{overall} = \mathcal{L}_{sup} + \alpha \mathcal{L}_{unsup}, \tag{7}$$

where α is a balancing factor that controls the weight of inherent consistency.

For labeled data, we use the combination of Dice loss [14] and cross entropy loss to supervise the model training, as done in many medical image segmentation researches [1,24,33]. Beyond that, we utilize edge information extracted from the labeled data as additional supervision. Thus, the loss function on labeled data is formulated as follows:

$$\mathcal{L}_{sup}(\hat{y}_S^L, y^L, \hat{e}_S^L, e^L) = 0.5 \left(\mathcal{L}_{dice}(\hat{y}_S^L, y^L) + \mathcal{L}_{ce}(\hat{y}_S^L, y^L) \right) + \beta \mathcal{L}_{edge}, \tag{8}$$

$$\mathcal{L}_{edge} = \frac{\text{SUM}\left(\left((\hat{e}_S^L - y^L) \cdot e^L\right)^2\right)}{\sum_{p=1}^{P} e^L(p)}, \tag{9}$$

where $\hat{y}_S^L$ is the predicted segmentation, y^L is the ground-truth, $\hat{e}_S^L$ is the edge prediction, e^L is the edge, $\mathcal{L}_{dice}(\hat{y}_S^L, y^L)$ denotes the Dice loss, $\mathcal{L}_{ce}(\hat{y}_S^L, y^L)$ represents the cross entropy loss, β is a balancing factor, $\mathcal{L}_{edge}$ is edge loss, function SUM($\cdot$) is the sum of the pixel-level values in a feature map, P represents the total number of pixels in the image, and p signifies an individual pixel within that image, the calculation of $e^L(p)$ is shown in Eq. 5. From Fig. 3, we can see that the edge output is extracted from the penultimate decoder, which obtains edge information from the edge attention module. Therefore, the loss $\mathcal{L}_{edge}$ helps to update the parameters of edge attention module. Additionally, to avoid redundant computations, the loss $\mathcal{L}_{edge}$ only takes into account the edge regions that are crucial for medical image segmentation.

For unlabeled data, we calculate the consistency loss between student network and teacher network. Specifically, the consistency loss consists of segmentation consistency loss $\mathcal{L}_{con}$ and edge consistency loss $\mathcal{L}_{edge\_c}$. The loss function $\mathcal{L}_{unsup}$ on unlabeled data is formulated as:

$$\mathcal{L}_{unsup}(\hat{y}_S^U, \hat{y}_T^U, \hat{e}_S^U, \hat{e}_T^U, e^L) = \mathcal{L}_{con}(\hat{y}_S^U, \hat{y}_T^U)$$
$$+ \gamma \mathcal{L}_{edge\_c}(\hat{e}_S^U, \hat{e}_T^U, e^L), \tag{10}$$

$$\mathcal{L}_{con}(\hat{y}_S^U, \hat{y}_T^U) = \left(\hat{y}_S^U - \hat{y}_T^U\right)^2, \tag{11}$$

$$\mathcal{L}_{edge\_c}(\hat{e}_S^U, \hat{e}_T^U, e^L) = \frac{\text{SUM}\left(\left((\hat{e}_S^U - \hat{e}_T^U) \cdot e^L\right)^2\right)}{\sum_{p=1}^{P} e^L(p)}, \tag{12}$$

where γ is also a balancing factor, $\hat{y}$ represents the segmentation prediction, the subscripts S and T denote student network and teacher network, respectively, and the superscript U means unlabeled data. From Eq. 12, we can see that the edge e^L extracted from the labeled data are utilized as masks for unlabeled data. By imposing edge consistency between student and teacher networks, the learning from unlabeled data can leverage the edge information from labeled data to achieve better segmentation. By utilizing the edge extracted from labeled data as masks, a synergistic learning framework between labeled and unlabeled data is created, where edge information from labeled data can promote learning from unlabeled data and unlabeled data can provide more details about edge regions to help robust edge extraction on labeled data.

4 Experiments

4.1 Datasets

Two public datasets are used in our experiments, including the LA dataset [30], which contains 100 3D MRI images, and the Pancreas-CT dataset [15], which comprises 82 CT scans. For fair comparison, we preprocess the two datasets following the previous works [1,16]. We also compare the segmentation performance of our proposed EAMT method with that of several state-of-the-art methods for semi-supervised medical image segmentation.

4.2 Implementation and Experimental Setting

Implementation Configurations. Our proposed EAMT is implemented using PyTorch and trained on an NVIDIA 4070 GPU. We employ the 3D V-Net architecture as the backbone, which is a de facto choice for many medical image segmentation tasks. We utilize the SGD optimizer with a weight decay of 0.0001 and a momentum factor of 0.9. The initial learning rate is set to 0.01, and we adopt a polynomial decay strategy to adjust the learning rate at each iteration.

For the LA dataset, we set the maximum number of iterations to 15k. We set the batch size to 8, comprising 4 labeled and 4 unlabeled samples. For the Pancreas-CT dataset, we set the maximum iteration to 10k, and a batch size of 4, with 2 labeled and 2 unlabeled samples. The parameter α in Eq. 7 is set following the work in [18]. The parameter β in Eq. 8 is setting to 0.1 for Pancreas-CT and 0.5 for LA dataset, besides, every 1.5k iterations, we will multiply this parameter for the LA dataset by 0.5. And γ in Eq. 10 is set to 1.0 for both two datasets.

Following previous works in semi-supervised medical image segmentation [1,5,10,33], our experiments were conducted with two typical semi-supervised settings, i.e. training with 10% labeled data and training with 20% labeled data. Four metrics were adopted to evaluate the segmentation performance: Dice similarity coefficient (Dice), Jaccard similarity coefficient (Jaccard), 95% Hausdorff Distance (95HD), and Average Surface Distance (ASD).

Table 1. Segmentation Results on LA dataset

Method	Volumes Used		Dice(%)↑	Jaccard(%)↑	95HD(voxel)↓	ASD(voxel)↓
	Labeled	Unlabeled				
V-Net	8(10%)	0	82.74	71.72	3.26	13.35
V-Net	16(20%)	0	86.03	76.06	3.51	14.26
V-Net	80(100%)	0	91.65	83.82	1.60	5.28
MT	8(10%)	72	83.50	72.72	2.67	12.74
UAMT	8(10%)	72	84.25	73.48	3.36	13.84
DTC	8(10%)	72	87.42	**78.06**	**2.40**	**8.37**
CAML	8(10%)	72	**87.54**	77.95	2.57	10.76
SASSNet	8(10%)	72	86.79	76.90	4.10	14.56
EAMT(ours)	8(10%)	72	**89.93**	**81.86**	**1.74**	**7.02**
UMCT	16(20%)	64	89.36	81.01	2.60	7.25
MT	16(20%)	64	88.22	79.20	2.73	10.75
UAMT	16(20%)	64	88.59	79.67	2.14	8.51
DTC	16(20%)	64	89.42	80.98	2.10	7.32
UPC	16(20%)	64	89.65	81.36	2.15	6.71
MC-Net	16(20%)	64	90.34	82.48	1.77	**6.00**
CAML	16(20%)	64	**90.71**	83.07	**1.59**	6.08
SASSNet	16(20%)	64	89.17	80.69	2.86	8.57
EAMT(ours)	16(20%)	64	**90.95**	**83.51**	**1.71**	6.61

↑: the higher the better; ↓: the lower the better; best two results are marked in bold.

4.3 Experimental Results

Segmentation Results on LA Dataset. We compared the segmentation performance of our proposed EAMT method with that of the benchmark semi-supervised learning method MT [18] and several state-of-the-art methods, including UMCT [28], UAMT [33], DTC [12], UPC [11], MC-Net [27], CAML [7] and SASSNet [10]. The segmentation results of our proposed EAMT and the comparing methods are presented in Table 1, where the best two results in terms of four evaluation metrics are marked in bold. Overall, in 10% labeled data setting, EAMT achieves the best segmentation performance in terms of four evaluation metrics. The proposed EAMT improves the Dice from 82% to almost 90% with only 10% labeled data, and yields nearly identical Jaccard scores compared with fully supervised learning methods when using 20% labeled data. In both 10% and 20% settings EAMT outperforms several state-of-the-art semi-supervised methods, which demonstrates the superiority of our method. Moreover, EAMT significantly outperforms MT which is the base architecture of EAMT, indicating its effectiveness in leveraging edge information. In Fig. 5, we have visualized the segmentation results on LA dataset. Compared with other edge-cutting methods, the proposed EAMT method can yield more accurate segmentation, especially for complex region areas.

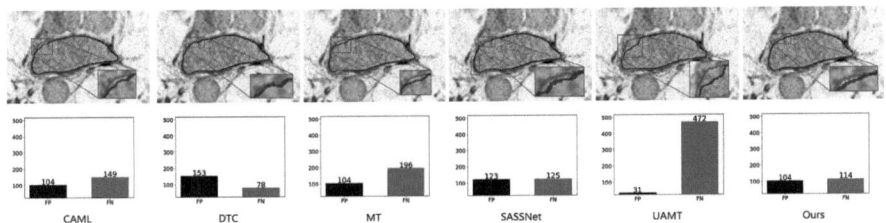

Fig. 5. Visualization of segmentations on LA dataset. The blue line represents predicted segmentation and the red line means the ground-truth. The bias areas are highlighted by red rectangles. We also count the FP and FN pixels in each slice. (Color figure online)

Table 2. Segmentation results on Pancreas-CT dataset

Method	Volumes Used		Dice(%)↑	Jaccard(%)↑	95HD(voxel)↓	ASD(voxel)↓
	Labeled	Unlabeled				
V-Net	6	0	58.41	46.81	18.43	50.03
V-Net	12	0	71.63	56.81	8.67	19.54
V-Net	62	0	82.46	69.65	1.42	6.76
UMCT	6	56	67.74	53.59	7.41	16.34
MT	6	56	65.13	51.98	7.03	23.06
UAMT	6	56	66.44	51.02	**5.19**	20.42
DTC	6	56	67.58	52.79	6.16	**15.57**
FUSSNet	6	56	**68.32**	**54.01**	5.85	17.46
EAMT(ours)	6	56	**70.20**	**55.51**	**2.57**	**14.17**
UMCT	12	50	76.42	62.98	5.40	14.34
MT	12	50	75.82	62.03	3.37	13.09
UAMT	12	50	78.26	62.72	**3.09**	10.43
DTC	12	50	77.19	63.75	4.25	**9.36**
FUSSNet	12	50	**79.25**	**63.71**	3.47	9.52
EAMT(ours)	12	50	**79.60**	**66.57**	**2.18**	**8.22**

Segmentation Results on Pancreas-CT Dataset. We compare the proposed EAMT method with several state-of-the-art and milestone works, including UMCT [28], MT, UAMT [33], DTC [12], and FUSSNet [29]. The segmentation results in terms of four evaluation metrics are reported in Table 2. Overall, the proposed EAMT method yields the best segmentation results over four evaluation metrics in both semi-supervised settings, which indicates the effectiveness of our proposed EAMT method in semi-supervised medical image segmentation. The visualization of segmentation results is shown in Fig. 6. It can be observed that as the number of training iterations increases, the model's segmentation performance on edges improves progressively.

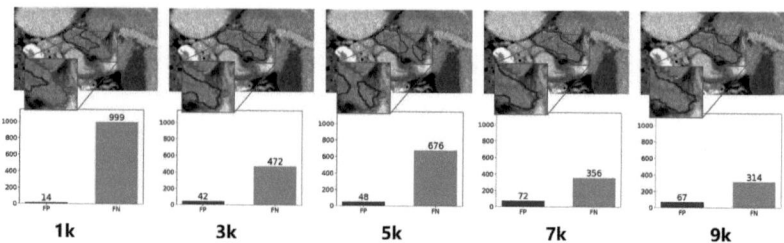

Fig. 6. Visualization of segmentations on Pancreas-CT dataset with different iterations. The blue line represents predicted segmentation and the red line means the ground-truth. The bias areas are highlighted by red rectangles. We also count the FP and FN pixels in each slice. (Color figure online)

4.4 Ablation Study

To verify the effectiveness of our EAMT, we conducted several ablation experiments. The experimental settings were kept consistent: two datasets (20% labeled and 80% unlabeled).

Table 3. Segmentation results with different attention block numbers

Block Numbers	dataset	Dice(%)↑	Jaccard(%)↑
0	LA dataset	89.63	81.37
1	LA dataset	90.16	82.28
2	LA dataset	**90.95**	**83.51**
3	LA dataset	90.47	82.74
4	LA dataset	90.71	83.12
0	Pancreas-CT	77.41	64.13
1	Pancreas-CT	78.32	65.10
2	Pancreas-CT	**79.60**	**66.57**
3	Pancreas-CT	77.63	64.60
4	Pancreas-CT	78.30	64.95

The Effect of Edge Attention. We conducted experiments on the edge attention module in two dimensions: the number of attention blocks and the types of attention modules. Firstly, we have conducted with different numbers, the results are presented in Table 3. We can see that setting the number to 2 yields the best performance, and an increased number of attention blocks does not directly lead to better performance. This can be attributed to the fact that a single layer attention block is insufficient for capturing robust edge information, while 3 and 4 layers tend to capture more abstract features rather than concrete edge details.

Table 4. Segmentation results with different types of attention block

attention types	dataset	parameters↓	dice(%)↑
Spatial Attention	LA dataset	1372	89.05
Channel Attention	LA dataset	**374**	**90.95**
Spatial Attention	Pancreas-CT	1372	77.51
Channel Attention	Pancreas-CT	**374**	**79.60**

Furthermore, we have investigated the impact of different types. The segmentation results are reported in Table 4. We can observe that the channel attention block not only has fewer parameters but also outperforms the spatial attention block, making it a more suitable choice for our application.

Edge Extraction. In order to verify the robustness of our edge extraction method, we conducted experiments on two datasets. From Table 5, we can observe that our designed edge extraction method obtains superior segmentation performance than the general edge extraction method. Furthermore, from Fig. 7, we can see that our proposed EAMT method produces more accurate segmentation over the complex edge regions, which also demonstrates the robustness of our edge extraction method.

Table 5. Segmentation results with different edge extraction methods

method	dataset	Dice(%)↑	Jaccard(%)↑
general edge	LA dataset	89.32	80.93
our edge	LA dataset	**90.95**	**83.51**
general edge	Pancreas-CT	70.67	56.85
our edge	Pancreas-CT	**79.60**	**66.57**

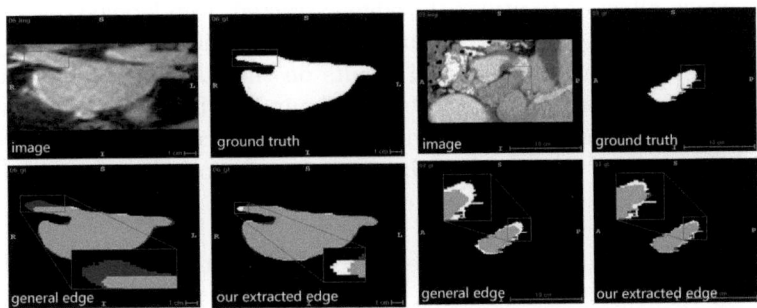

(a) segmentation on LA dataset (b) segmentation on Pa dataset

Fig. 7. Visualization of segmentations using general edge and our proposed new edge.

Edge-Aware Loss Function. In order to verify the importance of edge-aware loss functions, we conducted four ablation experiments. The results are presented in Table 6. We can observe that both types of edge-aware loss functions perform effectively, yielding improved segmentation performance compared to the baseline model, which does not utilize edge-aware loss functions. Moreover, the combination of the two edge-aware functions results in an augmented effect.

Table 6. Segmentation results with different loss functions

$\mathcal{L}_{edge}$	$\mathcal{L}_{edge\_c}$	dataset	Dice(%)↑	Jaccard(%)↑
✗	✗	LA dataset	88.84	80.47
✓	✗	LA dataset	89.87	81.80
✗	✓	LA dataset	89.70	81.67
✓	✓	LA dataset	**90.95**	**83.51**
✗	✗	Pancreas-CT	77.63	64.42
✓	✗	Pancreas-CT	78.68	65.64
✗	✓	Pancreas-CT	78.28	64.92
✓	✓	Pancreas-CT	**79.60**	**66.57**

5 Conclusion

The edge attention mean teacher (EAMT) method presented in this study aims to enhance the performance of semi-supervised medical image segmentation by effectively harnessing edge information. Our approach introduces several innovative methods and modules to achieve this goal. We define a novel edge segmentation task that can be addressed by a plug-and-play edge attention module. Notably, we introduce a new edge extraction method and an edge-aware loss function, which allow us to utilize the edge extracted from labeled data for both supervising the learning process on labeled data and guiding the learning process on unlabeled data. The experimental results on the LA dataset and Pancreas-CT dataset substantiate the effectiveness of our EAMT method in leveraging edge information. This work underlines the significance of edge information in the field of semi-supervised medical image segmentation. And future work will focus on optimizing these methods.

Acknowledgments. The authors have no competing interests to declare that are relevant to the content of this article.

References

1. Bai, Y., Chen, D., Li, Q., Shen, W., Wang, Y.: Bidirectional copy-paste for semi-supervised medical image segmentation. In: 2023 IEEE/CVF Conference on Computer Vision and Pattern Recognition (CVPR), pp. 11514–11524 (2023)
2. Chen, H., Qi, X., Yu, L., Dou, Q., Qin, J., Heng, P.A.: Dcan: deep contour-aware networks for object instance segmentation from histology images. Med. Image Anal. **36**, 135–146 (2017)
3. Chen, Y., Chen, F., Huang, C.: Combining contrastive learning and shape awareness for semi-supervised medical image segmentation. Expert Syst. Appl. **242**, 122567 (2024)
4. Cheng, F., et al.: Learning directional feature maps for cardiac MRI segmentation. In: Martel, A.L., et al. (eds.) MICCAI 2020. LNCS, vol. 12264, pp. 108–117. Springer, Cham (2020). https://doi.org/10.1007/978-3-030-59719-1_11
5. Chi, H., Pang, J., Zhang, B., Liu, W.: Adaptive bidirectional displacement for semi-supervised medical image segmentation. In: 2024 IEEE/CVF Conference on Computer Vision and Pattern Recognition (CVPR), pp. 4070–4080 (2024)
6. Fu, J., et al.: Dual attention network for scene segmentation. In: 2019 IEEE/CVF Conference on Computer Vision and Pattern Recognition (CVPR), pp. 3141–3149 (2019)
7. Gao, S., Zhang, Z., Ma, J., Li, Z., Zhang, S.: Correlation-aware mutual learning for semi-supervised medical image segmentation. In: Medical Image Computing and Computer Assisted Intervention - MICCAI, vol. 14220, pp. 98–108 (2023)
8. Han, K., Sheng, V.S., Song, Y., Liu, Y., Qiu, C., Ma, S., Liu, Z.: Deep semi-supervised learning for medical image segmentation: a review. Expert Syst. Appl. **245**, 123052 (2024)
9. Hu, J., Shen, L., Albanie, S., Sun, G., Wu, E.: Squeeze-and-excitation networks. IEEE Trans. Pattern Anal. Mach. Intell. **42**, 2011–2023 (2020)
10. Li, S., Zhang, C., He, X.: Shape-aware semi-supervised 3d semantic segmentation for medical images. In: Martel, A.L., et al. (eds.) MICCAI 2020. LNCS, vol. 12261, pp. 552–561. Springer, Cham (2020). https://doi.org/10.1007/978-3-030-59710-8_54
11. Lu, L., Yin, M., Fu, L., Yang, F.: Uncertainty-aware pseudo-label and consistency for semi-supervised medical image segmentation. Biomed. Signal Process. Control **79**, 104203 (2023)
12. Luo, X., Chen, J., Song, T., Wang, G.: Semi-supervised medical image segmentation through dual-task consistency. In: Proceedings of the AAAI Conference on Artificial Intelligence, vol. 35, pp. 8801–8809 (2021)
13. Luo, X., Hu, M., Song, T., Wang, G., Zhang, S.: Semi-supervised medical image segmentation via cross teaching between cnn and transformer. In: International Conference on Medical Imaging with Deep Learning, vol. 172, pp. 820–833 (2022)
14. Milletarì, F., Navab, N., Ahmadi, S.A.: V-net: fully convolutional neural networks for volumetric medical image segmentation. In: 2016 Fourth International Conference on 3D Vision (3DV), pp. 565–571 (2016)
15. Roth, H.R., et al.: DeepOrgan: multi-level deep convolutional networks for automated pancreas segmentation. In: Navab, N., Hornegger, J., Wells, W.M., Frangi, A.F. (eds.) MICCAI 2015. LNCS, vol. 9349, pp. 556–564. Springer, Cham (2015). https://doi.org/10.1007/978-3-319-24553-9_68
16. Shi, Y., et al.: Inconsistency-aware uncertainty estimation for semi-supervised medical image segmentation. IEEE Trans. Med. Imaging **41**, 608–620 (2022)

17. Si, Y., et al.: Scsa: exploring the synergistic effects between spatial and channel attention. arXiv preprint arXiv:2407.05128 (2024)
18. Tarvainen, A., Valpola, H.: Mean teachers are better role models: weight-averaged consistency targets improve semi-supervised deep learning results. In: Proceedings of the 31st International Conference on Neural Information Processing Systems, pp. 1195–1204 (2017)
19. Wang, K., et al.: Semi-supervised medical image segmentation via a tripled-uncertainty guided mean teacher model with contrastive learning. Med. Image Anal. **79**, 102447 (2022)
20. Wang, K., Zhang, X., Zhang, X., Lu, Y., Huang, S., Yang, D.: Eanet: iterative edge attention network for medical image segmentation. Pattern Recogn. **127**, 108636 (2022)
21. Wang, Q., Wu, B., Zhu, P., Li, P., Zuo, W., Hu, Q.: Eca-net: efficient channel attention for deep convolutional neural networks. In: 2020 IEEE/CVF Conference on Computer Vision and Pattern Recognition (CVPR), pp. 11531–11539 (2020)
22. Wang, X., Girshick, R., Gupta, A., He, K.: Non-local neural networks. In: 2018 IEEE Conference on Computer Vision and Pattern Recognition (CVPR), pp. 7794–7803 (2018)
23. Wang, Y., Zhou, Y., Shen, W., Park, S., Fishman, E.K., Yuille, A.L.: Abdominal multi-organ segmentation with organ-attention networks and statistical fusion. Med. Image Anal. **55**, 88–102 (2019)
24. Wang, Y., Xiao, B., Bi, X., Li, W., Gao, X.: Mcf: mutual correction framework for semi-supervised medical image segmentation. In: 2023 IEEE/CVF Conference on Computer Vision and Pattern Recognition (CVPR), pp. 15651–15660 (2023)
25. Wang, Z., Zheng, J.Q., Voiculescu, I.: An uncertainty-aware transformer for mri cardiac semantic segmentation via mean teachers. In: Medical Image Understanding and Analysis, vol. 13413, pp. 494–507 (2022)
26. Woo, S., Park, J., Lee, J.-Y., Kweon, I.S.: CBAM: convolutional block attention module. In: Ferrari, V., Hebert, M., Sminchisescu, C., Weiss, Y. (eds.) ECCV 2018. LNCS, vol. 11211, pp. 3–19. Springer, Cham (2018). https://doi.org/10.1007/978-3-030-01234-2_1
27. Wu, S., Li, J., Liu, C., Yu, Z., Wong, H.S.: Mutual learning of complementary networks via residual correction for improving semi-supervised classification. In: 2019 IEEE/CVF Conference on Computer Vision and Pattern Recognition (CVPR), pp. 6493–6502 (2019)
28. Xia, Y., et al.: 3d semi-supervised learning with uncertainty-aware multi-view co-training. In: 2020 IEEE Winter Conference on Applications of Computer Vision (WACV), pp. 3635–3644 (2020)
29. Xiang, J., Qiu, P., Yang, Y.: Fussnet: fusing two sources of uncertainty for semi-supervised medical image segmentation. In: Medical Image Computing and Computer Assisted Intervention – MICCAI 2022, vol. 13438, pp. 481–491 (2022)
30. Xiong, Z., Xia, Q., Hu, Z., Huang, N., Zhao, J.: A global benchmark of algorithms for segmenting the left atrium from late gadolinium-enhanced cardiac magnetic resonance imaging. Med. Image Anal. **67**, 101832 (2021)
31. Yang, X., Song, Z., King, I., Xu, Z.: A survey on deep semi-supervised learning. IEEE Trans. Knowl. Data Eng. **35**, 8934–8954 (2023)
32. Yang, Y., Hou, X., Ren, H.: Efficient active contour model for medical image segmentation and correction based on edge and region information. Expert Syst. Appl. **194**, 116436 (2022)

33. Yu, L., Wang, S., Li, X., Fu, C.-W., Heng, P.-A.: Uncertainty-aware self-ensembling model for semi-supervised 3d left atrium segmentation. In: Shen, D., et al. (eds.) MICCAI 2019. LNCS, vol. 11765, pp. 605–613. Springer, Cham (2019). https://doi.org/10.1007/978-3-030-32245-8_67
34. Zhang, R., et al.: Ba-net: bridge attention in deep neural networks. arXiv preprint arXiv:2410.07860 (2024)
35. Zhang, Z., Fu, H., Dai, H., Shen, J., Pang, Y., Shao, L.: ET-Net: a generic edge-aTtention guidance network for medical image segmentation. In: Shen, D., et al. (eds.) MICCAI 2019. LNCS, vol. 11764, pp. 442–450. Springer, Cham (2019). https://doi.org/10.1007/978-3-030-32239-7_49
36. Zhao, X., et al.: Rcps: rectified contrastive pseudo supervision for semi-supervised medical image segmentation. IEEE J. Biomed. Health Inform. **28**, 251–261 (2024)

Interpretability and Explainability

Queryable and Interpretable PU Learning Through Probabilistic Circuits

Sieben Bocklandt[1,2(✉)], Vincent Derkinderen[1,2], Koen Vanderstraeten[3], Wouter Pijpops[3], Kurt Jaspers[3], Luc De Raedt[1,2,4], and Wannes Meert[1,2]

[1] Department of Computer Science, KU Leuven, Leuven, Belgium
sieben.bocklandt@kuleuven.be
[2] Leuven.AI - KU Leuven Institute for AI, Leuven, Belgium
[3] Tunify, Beringen, Belgium
[4] Center for Applied Autonomous Systems, Örebro University, Örebro, Sweden

Abstract. We introduce a novel concept learning scenario that involves only positive and unlabeled (PU) data and focuses on interpretable models. Our scenario is motivated by a real-world application learning concepts for music playlists (e.g., 'relaxing music'). These concepts must be understood by humans and used as database queries. We demonstrate that probabilistic circuits offer a compelling solution for PU learning as they can effectively learn to represent joint probability distributions without the need for negative examples. However, achieving interpretability and seamless conversion into database queries presents additional challenges. To address these, we propose a novel approach that transforms a learned probabilistic circuit into a logic-based discriminative model. Notably, this is the first study to investigate probabilistic circuits in a PU learning framework, contributing two key innovations: (1) a new description length metric called aggregated entropy as a measure for interpretability; and (2) PUTPUT, an algorithm designed to prune low-probability regions from the circuit before converting it into a logic-based model, optimizing for both F_1-score and aggregated entropy.

1 Introduction

Our work is motivated by an application in the music streaming industry, in which music playlists play a crucial role. The automated curation of playlists is an active area of research [1,4,5,24,28]. A particularly effective approach is to represent a playlist as a concept (e.g., 'relaxing music') rather than as a fixed collection of songs. When a playlist is represented as a discriminative model, it can be automatically populated, allowing for the inclusion of newly released songs that fit the concept.

Learning a concept in this context involves meeting the following criteria: (i) it is a PU learning task, i.e., the data is exclusively positive and unlabeled [3]; (ii)

Supplementary Information The online version contains supplementary material available at https://doi.org/10.1007/978-3-032-06066-2_25.

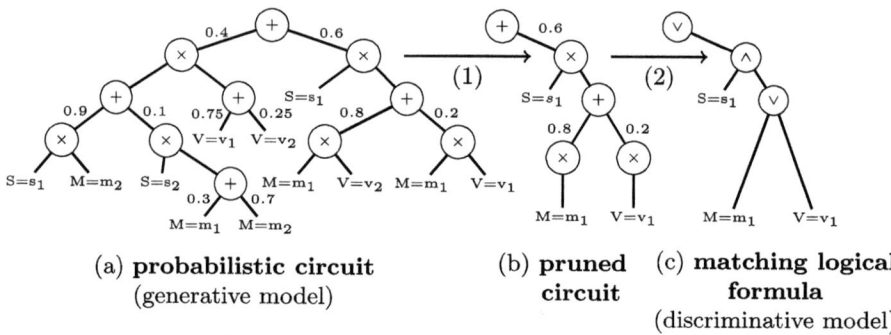

Fig. 1. Overview of our approach (in the context of a music playlist). (1) A probabilistic circuit over variables $Style(S)$, $Mood(M)$ and $Version(V)$ is pruned to only contain the high probability regions. (2) This smaller circuit is transformed into a logic formula, acting as a discriminative model that is easier to inspect and verify by a domain expert, and can be turned into a database query.

the learned model must be convertible into a database query; and (iii) the model must be interpretable, allowing a music expert to inspect and validate it. The importance of interpretability is particularly crucial in a business setting. For instance, Tunify[1] provides a music streaming service specifically designed for businesses, in which they must ensure the quality of each playlist. In this context, even a single inappropriate song can disrupt the atmosphere in environments like wellness centres or funeral homes.

To meet all these criteria, we focus on models that are well-suited to a PU setting and can be converted into a logic formula. Decision trees and rule learning algorithms fulfil these requirements, but require that we first augment the dataset with negative examples while taking into account the PU-learning setting. For instance, the Rocchio classification approach identifies reliable negatives by selecting examples close to a prototype learned from the unlabeled data [3].

We focus on probabilistic circuits (see Fig. 1a) as a competitive alternative, as they do not require negative examples and are therefore more directly applicable to and appropriate for the PU learning. These circuits [6] form a unified framework for tractable probabilistic models, representing a joint probability distribution while being capable of tractably handling various tasks. However, these circuits are more challenging to inspect and convert into a database query. To address this, we propose a new approach that extracts a logical formula (the discriminative model) from a learned probabilistic circuit, **leading to the following contributions.**

1. To the best of our knowledge, we are the first to study probabilistic circuits in an interpretable PU setting.
2. We propose the aggregated entropy as a new description length that measures the ease with which a domain expert can inspect the extracted formula.

---

[1] www.tunify.com.

3. More importantly, we introduce PUTPUT (Probabilistic circuit Understanding Through Pruning Underlying logical Theories). This is a new method that prunes the low probability regions from the circuit (see Fig. 1b), as these are less likely to be part of the intended concept, whilst also considering the impact on interpretability (the aggregated entropy). After pruning these regions, we can easily extract a matching logical formula from the circuit (see Fig. 1c) that can be inspected and can function as a database query.

Our evaluation demonstrates the effectiveness of our approach on a real-world use case of music playlist generation. Furthermore, a user study shows that aggregated entropy is better fit to measure human interpretability than the standard description length and evaluation on open-source datasets confirms that the method is more generally applicable beyond this use case.

The remainder of the paper is structured as follows. First, we provide the necessary background information and the problem statement in respectively Sects. 2 and 3. Then, in Sects. 4 and 5, we introduce our new description length called aggregated entropy, and our method, called PUTPUT. The empirical evaluation of these is presented afterwards, in Sect. 6. Finally, we discuss related work in Sect. 7 and conclude in Sect. 8.

2 Background

We first provide a brief primer on logic formulas, probabilistic circuits and PU learning.

2.1 Logic Formulas

A *literal* is a Boolean variable v or its negation $\neg v$. A *propositional logic formula* ψ is inductively defined as a literal, the negation of logic formula $\neg \psi_1$, the conjunction (read 'and') of two logic formulas $\psi_1 \wedge \psi_2$, or a disjunction (read 'or') $\psi_1 \vee \psi_2$, with the expected semantics. A *clause* $\mathcal{C}$ is a literal or disjunction of literals, such as $v_1 \vee \neg v_2$. A formula ψ is said to be in *conjunctive normal form* (CNF) iff it is a conjunction of clauses, such as $(v_1 \vee \neg v_2) \wedge (\neg v_1)$. A formula ψ is said to be in *disjunctive normal form* (DNF) iff it is a disjunction of conjunctions of literals, such as $(v_1 \wedge \neg v_2) \vee (\neg v_1)$.

We support categorical variables by admitting Boolean variables that represent equalities. That is, a Boolean variable could represent *style=jazz*, while another variable represents *style=rock*. We assume an implicit theory that forbids both variables to be true at the same time. For convenience, we may write *style=jazz* rather than $v_{style=jazz}$. An *example* in our context is a value assignment to each categorical variable.

The *dual graph* $G_d(\psi)$ of a CNF formula ψ is a graph that connects clauses iff they share the same variable [29]. In our context we slightly change this definition to reason over categorical and binary variables. More formally, two clauses $\mathcal{C}$ and $\mathcal{C}'$ are joined by an edge iff there is a categorical or binary variable that is present in both clauses.

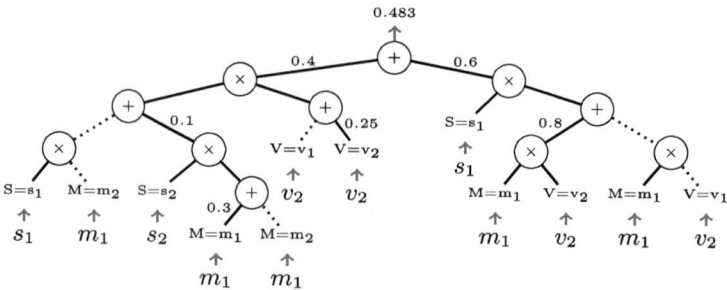

Fig. 2. Generation of a probability with given input $\{m_1, v_2\}$. We marginalise over S, as no value is assigned to S. Dashed lines indicate edges whose weight is irrelevant for the given input. After performing addition and multiplying with the relevant weights, the final result, $P(Mood = m_1, Version = v_2)$, is given at the root node.

2.2 Probabilistic Circuits

A probabilistic circuit (PC) $\mathcal{M} := (\mathcal{G}, \theta)$ is a probabilistic model, representing a joint probability distribution $P(\mathbf{X})$ over random variables $\mathbf{X}$ through a directed acyclic graph (DAG) $\mathcal{G}$ parameterised by θ [6]. Each node in the DAG defines a computational unit, which is one of three types – an input, sum, or product node. Every leaf in $\mathcal{G}$ constitutes an input node, while every inner node is either a sum or a product node. An example of a probabilistic circuit is given in Fig. 1a.

In our setting, each input node of a PC represents a distribution over a categorical random variable X. Furthermore, we assume without loss of expressivity that the distribution has all probability mass over a single value $x \in X$. In other words, an input node labeled $X = x$ in Fig. 1a outputs the probability (0 or 1) that the input is equal to x. Each product node represents a factorisation of incoming distributions over different random variables, and each sum node represents a mixture, i.e., a weighted sum over the distributions leading into it. The weights of the mixture are indicated on the edges in Fig. 1a.

Figure 2 shows an evaluation of the PC to compute $P(Mood = m_1, Version = v_2)$, marginalising over $Style$. First, we set the input of the PC. For example, each input node associated to M has input m_1, leading them to output 1 for $M=m_1$ and 0 for $M=m_2$. We marginalise over $Style$, denoted as S, thus each input node $S=s$ receives input s and outputs 1. These outputs propagate through the PC, performing the sum- and product operations, resulting in the output probability at the root node.

A probabilistic circuit $\mathcal{M}$ can easily be converted into a logic formula ψ that captures the nonzero probability input instances of the circuit. Assuming only nonzero weights on the edges, ψ can be extracted from $\mathcal{M}$ by replacing every product node with $\wedge$, every sum node with $\vee$, and removing the weights of every edge. Additionally, the input nodes are converted into literals such as $S=s_1$. Figure 3 shows the logic formula ψ extracted from Fig. 1a.

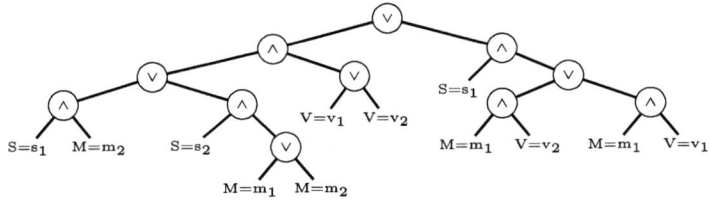

Fig. 3. Formula derived from the circuit in Fig. 1a.

2.3 Learning from Positive and Unlabeled Data

PU learning methods address the task of learning from positive and unlabeled data [3]. Neural networks, support vector machines, bagging approaches and density estimators can all be used in this setting [17,21,37,38]. These approaches however do not result in a classifier that is easily convertable into a database query and inspectable by a domain expert. As an alternative approach, one can first enhance the dataset with reliable negative examples before learning a decision tree or a ruleset – both of which are easier to convert into a query and inspect. For instance, Rocchio classification identifies reliable negative examples as examples that are close to a prototype learned on the unlabeled data [3]. A similar approach, that was also used in the context of music playlist generation, considers the likelihood to identify reliable negative examples [15].

3 Problem Statement

The motivating use case of our work is a problem occurring in the workflow of music streaming provider *Tunify*. They have a database of annotated music where each song is represented by a fixed set of categorical features. These can be objective (*BPM, Year, Lyricist, ...*) or subjective (*Mood, Feel, ...*). As one of their services, they provide a predefined selection of playlists. These playlists are represented as logical formulas ψ that can be used as queries on a database to obtain the songs currently matching ψ.

However, *Tunify* must also be able to assure customers that all playlists are safe, e.g., to avoid a black metal song appearing in a playlist intended as happy songs for children, or for a funeral home. Therefore, to enable easier inspection by a music expert, we wish to extract an interpretable formula ψ that acts as a discriminative classifier covering the high probability regions of the learned probabilistic circuit. The focus on high probability regions allows ψ to cover only the most relevant examples.

Given: a probabilistic circuit $\mathcal{M}$ as described in Sect. 2, a set of examples $\mathcal{E}$, a description length DL and a nonzero probability threshold t.

Objective: $\mathcal{E}_{HPR} \subseteq \mathcal{E}$ are examples in the high probability regions of $\mathcal{M}$, i.e., the examples $e \in \mathcal{E}$ for which $P_{\mathcal{M}}(e) \geq t$. Using $\mathcal{E}_\psi$ to indicate all examples in $\mathcal{E}$ that are covered by ψ, the goal is to find formula ψ such that:

1. $\mathcal{E}_\psi$ is as close to $\mathcal{E}_{HPR}$ as possible[2]:

$$\arg\max_{\psi} F_1(\mathcal{E}_\psi, \mathcal{E}_{HPR}) \tag{1}$$

2. whilst minimising the description length of ψ:

$$\arg\min_{\psi} DL(\psi) \tag{2}$$

4 A New Description Length

The approach that we will propose captures the high probability regions of a probabilistic circuit as a logical formula that is easier to inspect and understand by a domain expert. The standard description length, i.e., the number of literals in the formula, is not fine-grained enough to fully capture interpretability. This description length fails to account for subtle variations in how users perceive complexity, leading to weaker alignment with interpretability trends. To address this limitation, we introduce a new description length measure called *aggregated entropy*. Before describing it in detail, we first provide the motivation for its introduction.

4.1 Motivation of Aggregated Entropy

First, consider that nested logic formulas consisting of multiple levels of $\wedge$ and $\vee$ are more complex than flat forms such as CNF and DNF. Second, consider that DNFs are more complex to inspect once categorical variables are involved. This is due to what Ryszard Michalski, one of the founders of the field of machine learning, called an internal disjunction: a disjunction over a categorical variable to indicate its possible values, for example '*style=jazz* $\vee$ *style=rock*'. He argued for their interpretability from a cognitive perspective in a concept learning setting [20]. We illustrate this using the following example from our application.

$$\begin{aligned}&(style = jazz \wedge feel = happy) \vee (style = jazz \wedge feel = exciting) \vee \\ &(style = rock \wedge feel = happy) \vee (style = rock \wedge feel = exciting)\end{aligned} \tag{3}$$

In this case, a CNF representation is preferred.

$$(style = jazz \vee style = rock) \wedge (feel = happy \vee feel = exciting) \tag{4}$$

An additional advantage of CNF formulas is that they can easily be extended to remove undesired examples e (e.g., songs) as examples are conjunctions of attributes: $\psi \wedge \neg e$ which is equal to $\psi \wedge (\neg v_1 \vee \cdots \vee \neg v_n)$.

---

[2] Note that F_1-score is preferred over accuracy here, as there can be significantly more true negatives than true positives.

Description lengths provide a quantitative measure of complexity for the information content within data or models. DUCE [22] and BoolXAI [27], for instance, use the literal count as a description length for formulas in DNF and CNF respectively. Similarly, description length finds an application in information theory, as illustrated by the Huffman encoding which minimises the number of bits required to describe a sentence [16]. These description lengths capture the length of a logical formula.

Naturally, a longer formula is less desirable from an interpretability standpoint. Still, we argue these description lengths are insufficient in the context of this work because they neither consider the complexity that arises when variables are present in multiple clauses, nor do they consider the categorical variables. We therefore propose a new description length that we call the aggregated entropy of a CNF formula.

4.2 Aggregated Entropy

This new description length is based on information theory and keeps two principles in mind:

- A CNF formula is easier to understand when a variable is present in only a few clauses.
- A CNF formula is easier to understand when a categorical variable allows either very few or many values. As an example, consider a formula that expresses that a music style is only allowed to be metal, or one that expresses everything except metal.

Aggregated entropy approximates this by quantifying the number of bits needed to represent a clause and its directly linked clauses, as a proxy for how much a user needs to memorise when reading the model.

Definition 1 (Entropy of a variable within a clause). *The entropy of a categorical variable X within a clause $\mathcal{C}$ and with $\phi(\alpha) = -\alpha \, log_2(\alpha)$ is defined as*

$$E_{var}(\mathcal{C}, X) = \phi(\frac{|\mathcal{C}(X)|}{|X|}) + \phi(\frac{|X| - |\mathcal{C}(X)|}{|X|}), \tag{5}$$

with $\mathcal{C}(X)$ the set of Boolean variables in $\mathcal{C}$ that are associated with X, and $|X|$ the total number of possible values for X. In other words, $|\mathcal{C}(X)|/|X|$ is the fraction of possible values for X that are mentioned within clause $\mathcal{C}$.

Definition 2 (Aggregated entropy of a clause). *The aggregated entropy $DL_{cl}(\mathcal{C})$ of a clause $\mathcal{C}$ is a description length that aggregates the entropy of its variables,*

$$DL_{cl}(\mathcal{C}) = \sum_{X \in \mathcal{C}} E_{var}(\mathcal{C}, X), \tag{6}$$

where we use $X \in \mathcal{C}$ to consider the categorical variables that are present in clause $\mathcal{C}$.

The ease with which a CNF formula ψ is understood decreases when variables are present in multiple clauses. Therefore, while considering the aggregated entropy for each clause $\mathcal{C}$ within ψ, we also consider the aggregate of its neighbouring clauses, i.e., the clauses $\mathcal{C}'$ with whom $\mathcal{C}$ shares variables.

Definition 3 (Aggregated entropy of a CNF). *The aggregated entropy $DL(\psi)$ of a CNF formula ψ is*

$$DL(\psi) = \sum_{\mathcal{C} \in \psi} \left[DL_{cl}(\mathcal{C}) + \sum_{\mathcal{C}' \in \psi | e(\mathcal{C},\mathcal{C}') \in G_d(\psi)} DL_{cl}(\mathcal{C}') \right], \quad (7)$$

with $e(\mathcal{C}, \mathcal{C}') \in G_d(\psi)$ denoting the clause neighbour relationships through the dual graph defined in Sect. 2.

Example of Aggregated Entropy. Given formula ψ over categorical variables $\{A, B, X\}$ with $|A| = 5$, $|B| = 6$, and $|X| = 7$.

$$\psi = \underbrace{(a_1 \vee a_2 \vee a_3)}_{\mathcal{C}_1} \wedge \underbrace{(a_1 \vee b_1 \vee b_2)}_{\mathcal{C}_2} \wedge \underbrace{(x_1 \vee x_2 \vee x_3)}_{\mathcal{C}_3}$$

We compute $DL(\psi)$ using the following clause entropies:

$$DL_{cl}(\mathcal{C}_1) = \phi(\tfrac{3}{5}) + \phi(\tfrac{2}{5}), \; DL_{cl}(\mathcal{C}_2) = \phi(\tfrac{1}{5}) + \phi(\tfrac{4}{5}) + \phi(\tfrac{2}{6}) + \phi(\tfrac{4}{6})$$
$$DL_{cl}(\mathcal{C}_3) = \phi(\tfrac{3}{7}) + \phi(\tfrac{4}{7})$$

with $\phi(\alpha) = -\alpha log_2(\alpha)$. Clauses $\mathcal{C}_1$ and $\mathcal{C}_2$ both mention categorical variable A, resulting in an edge $e(\mathcal{C}_1, \mathcal{C}_2)$ in the dual graph of ψ. This results in
$DL(\psi) = \underbrace{DL_{cl}(\mathcal{C}_1) + DL_{cl}(\mathcal{C}_2) + DL_{cl}(\mathcal{C}_3)}_{\text{clause entropies}} + \underbrace{DL_{cl}(\mathcal{C}_2)}_{e(\mathcal{C}_1,\mathcal{C}_2)} + \underbrace{DL_{cl}(\mathcal{C}_1)}_{e(\mathcal{C}_2,\mathcal{C}_1)} \approx 6.21$

In the rest of this paper we minimise $DL(\psi)$ to obtain more preferred CNF formulas ψ.

4.3 User Study

To evaluate whether our newly proposed description length better captures human interpretability compared to using the number of literals, we conducted a user study. Participants (N = 46) were asked to answer 12 questions. In each question, they were given i) a playlist description in the form of a CNF formula, and ii) a set of songs, each represented as a list of categorical attributes, after which they were asked to select all songs that were covered by the playlist.

We posit that descriptions that are less interpretable, lead to a longer response time.

Furthermore, a description length should align with this, similarly assigning a higher length. Therefore, we compare the aggregated entropy and the classic description length that is based on the number of literals, by their ability to align with the trend in response time.

The Spearman correlation between the response time is 0.63 for the aggregated entropy, and 0.55 for the number of literals, indicating the presence of correlation for both. To determine whether the difference in strengths is statistically significant, we apply Steiger's Z-test for dependent correlations, obtaining a p-value of 0.03. Since $p < 0.05$, we conclude that the correlation with aggregated entropy is significantly stronger, and thus, that it is a more appropriate measure for human interpretability.

Our results further show in a pairwise comparison that the aggregated entropy aligned with user response trends in 77% of cases, compared to 61% for the number of literals metric. The full questionnaire and additional details about the user study can be found in Appendix D.

5 Method

The input probabilistic circuit $\mathcal{M}$ is a generative model that can be transformed into a discriminative one: given an example e, we can compute $P_{\mathcal{M}}(e) \geq t$ (with t the given threshold). However, because the discriminative model must function as a database query and be inspectable by a domain expert, we instead consider extracting a logical formula ψ from the circuit using the approach described in Sect. 2.2.

Importantly, the resulting formula would be too general as it covers any nonzero probability instance of the circuit. To solve this problem, we propose to first prune the probabilistic circuit $\mathcal{M}$ in a way that only the high probability regions remain. Afterwards, we can extract a logical formula ψ from the pruned circuit and convert it to a CNF. This formula then acts as a discriminative classifier that indicates whether a given example belongs to the high probability region of the input probabilistic circuit $\mathcal{M}$.

We propose PUTPUT, a new two-step approach that prunes a probabilistic circuit while considering the F_1-score and aggregated entropy. The first step eliminates circuit edges that originate from sum nodes, using existing pruning functions. This results in a circuit only covering the high probability regions. A second step eliminates input nodes to further decrease the aggregated entropy, while maintaining the F_1-score of the first step as a lower bound.

5.1 Step 1: Pruning Sum Nodes

Pruning Functions. Dang, Liu, and Van den Broeck (2022) proposes four pruning functions for a probabilistic circuit. The first function randomly eliminates sum node inputs, while the second approach eliminates them based on their corresponding mixture weight. Both of these functions were identified as less performant so we do not consider them. The third function is based on generative significance, pruning those sum node inputs that contribute the least to

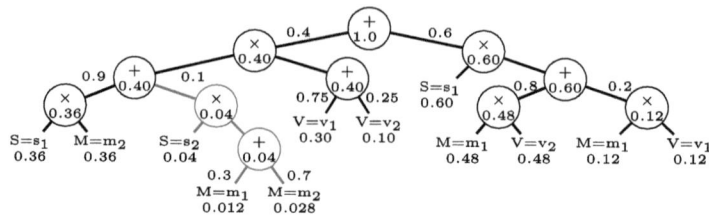

Fig. 4. The result after pruning the probabilistic circuit from Fig. 1a, with the generative significance method set to eliminate the five nodes with the lowest top down probabilities (shown in blue). (Color figure online)

Algorithm 1. Step 2: Pruning input nodes in PC

Require: Pruned PC $\mathcal{M}'$, high-probability examples $\mathcal{E}_{HPR}$, examples $\mathcal{E}$
Ensure: $\mathcal{M}'$ with pruned input nodes
1: $lower\_bound = F_1(\mathcal{E}_{\mathcal{M}'}, \mathcal{E}_{HPR})$
2: **repeat**
3:   **for** each input node n in $\mathcal{M}'$ **do**
4:     $\mathcal{M}'' \leftarrow \mathcal{M}'/n$ ◁ Prunes node n
5:     **if** $F_1(\mathcal{E}_{\mathcal{M}''}, \mathcal{E}_{HPR}) \geq lower\_bound$ **then**
6:       $\mathcal{M}' \leftarrow \mathcal{M}''$
7: **until** $\mathcal{M}'$ has not changed
8: **return** $\mathcal{M}'$
---

the circuit output. In Fig. 4 we show its application on the circuit of Fig. 1a, annotating each node by its top down probability, i.e., the probability that the node will be visited when unconditionally drawing samples from the circuit. This function is parameterised by the number of edges it must eliminate. The fourth approach is based on circuit flows, which works similar to the third approach but it first adjusts the sum node mixture weights by conditioning on a given dataset. In this way, it considers how many samples from the dataset flow through each node. This pruning function is parameterised by the number of edges it must eliminate and the dataset on which to condition.

Applying Pruning Functions. PUTPUT first identifies the preferred values of the parameters (i.e., the number of edges to eliminate) of the pruning function that lead to the highest F_1-score (Eq. 1). This can be achieved exhaustively or by using a search function such as golden section search [25]. We used the latter in our evaluation to conclude that pruning based on circuit flows is the preferred pruning function. The result of step 1 is a pruned probabilistic circuit such that the F_1-score is maximised (see Fig. 4).

5.2 Step 2: Pruning Input Nodes

The first step already decreases the aggregated entropy due to its correlation with circuit size. The second step decreases this even further by considering for each input node whether it is beneficial to prune them. While the first step prunes some sum node inputs, the second step prunes them further and in addition also prunes input nodes that lead into product nodes.

The F_1-score resulting from the first step is used as a lower bound in this second step. Pruning children of a product node may influence whether it is beneficial to prune a node that was previously considered. PUTPUT therefore employs an iterative procedure that reconsiders all input nodes until no more changes are made. The pseudocode for this step is shown in Algorithm 1. The circuit resulting from step 1 is denoted as $\mathcal{M}'$, while $\mathcal{E}_{\mathcal{M}'}$ are the examples $e \in \mathcal{E}$ for which $P'_{\mathcal{M}}(e) > 0$, as these are the examples covered by the logical formula derived from $\mathcal{M}'$ (see Section 2.2). Note that probability threshold t is implicitly present in $\mathcal{E}_{HPR}$. If we apply this second step on Fig. 4, we obtain Fig. 5.

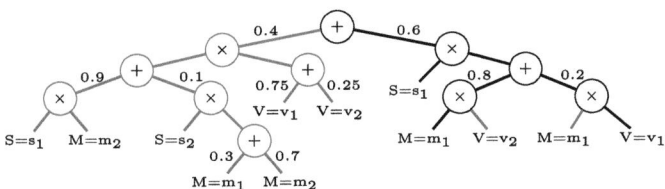

Fig. 5. The circuit after applying step 2 of PUTPUT, with $\mathcal{E}_{HPR} = \{(s_1, m_1, v_1), (s_1, m_1, v_2), (s_1, m_2, v_1)\}$.

6 Evaluation

The proposed PUTPUT method is empirically evaluated to answer the following research questions:

1. Which pruning function results in the highest F_1-score (step 1)?
2. Does pruning of the input nodes improve the aggregated entropy (step 2)?
3. How does PUTPUT perform more generally, including on the music playlist generation task?

6.1 Setup

Given a dataset of positive and unlabeled examples $\mathcal{E}$, we first learn a probabilistic circuit $\mathcal{M}$ using the Hidden Chow Liu Tree method [18] available in the JUICE package [10]. Next, we find the probability threshold t that identifies the high probability regions. A higher threshold t leads to a smaller, more precise region. However, if the threshold t is too high, the resulting formula will overfit, leading to lower recall and thus reduced F_1-score. The user's choice of t, which dictates the trade-off, is therefore important. As this depends on a specific use case, we instead determine an appropriate value for t through a more generalized approach, using the elbow method on the generated posterior probabilities, which is inspired by work on finding the reject threshold in pattern recognition [7].

The elbow method selects a probability threshold t by first ordering all examples based on their probability, in descending order. More formally, we use $\mathcal{E}$ to denote a set of examples, $\mathcal{M}$ to denote a probabilistic circuit, and $p(e)$ to denote the probability of $e \in \mathcal{E}$ according to $\mathcal{M}$. Let $\mathcal{L} = [e_1, ..., e_n]$ be the examples in $\mathcal{E}$, ordered according to probability $p(e)$, such that e_1 has the highest probability and e_n the lowest. The elbow method then finds threshold t by searching for a sudden sharper decrease in probability. I.e., find example e_i such that

$$i = \arg\min_{x=1..|\mathcal{E}|}(x \mid \frac{p(e_{x+1}) - p(e_x)}{p(e_x) - p(e_{x-1})} \geq 0.3), \tag{8}$$

after which the threshold is defined as $t = p(e_i)$. The value of 0.3 in the elbow method is a user-specified parameter. We decided this value by analysing the results of the music use case in collaboration with a music expert of *Tunify*. Since there is no expert for the open-source datasets, we reuse the same threshold t throughout the experiments (Fig. 6).

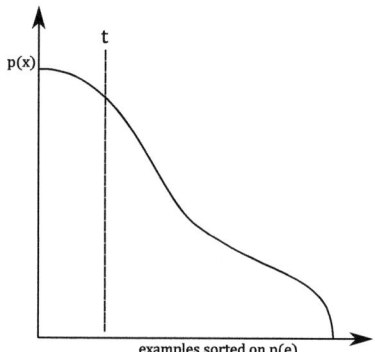

Fig. 6. The elbow method selects threshold t, identifying high probability regions.

Using this threshold t, we determine the high probability region examples $\mathcal{E}_{HPR} \subseteq \mathcal{E}$. Afterwards, we apply PUTPUT to prune $\mathcal{M}$, leading to the discriminative formula ψ.

6.2 Datasets

- *Tunify* provided real-world data, 360 000 songs, annotated with 14 categorical features having 7 to 120 possible values, and a set of intended playlist concepts. From this private data 15 classes where constructed, each representing a different playlist concept that has to be learned. We consider two types of concepts, based on the playlists used by customers from *Tunify*.

- *Single playlist concept*: 5 known product playlist concepts with their respective songs, e.g., Rock.
- *Disjunctive playlist concepts*: 10 combinations of two known concepts that have a disjunctive form, e.g., Rock or Easy Lounge.
– the *FMA* music dataset [12] used for genre classification (8 classes, 9217 examples), which is the open source dataset that is most similar to the *Tunify* dataset.
– black and white images of
  - MNIST (10 classes, 2500 examples) [13],
  - fashionMNIST (10 classes, 2500 examples) [36],
  - EMNIST letters (26 classes, 2600 examples) [8].
– the *mushrooms* (2 classes, 8124 examples) [31] and *splice* (3 classes, 3190 examples) [32] datasets of the UCI machine learning repository.

Setup. A class in a dataset determines the positive labels. We consider a PU learning setting wherein most of the examples are unlabeled. More specifically, for each class in each dataset, we create 10 subsets of the data and randomly label only 5% of the positively labeled examples, resulting in 740 PUTPUT datasets. We evaluate on the full dataset.

Example. We provide a small example to motivate our goal of extracting a discriminative classifier, and to illustrate the general applicability beyond music playlist generation. We learned a probabilistic circuit on black and white images of MNIST data containing 13 positively labeled examples representing the digit 0. We then applied PUTPUT to obtain the following logical formula ψ with (W=White, B=Black).

$$p_{12,22}=W \wedge p_{14,15}=B \wedge p_{14,16}=B \wedge (p_{8,15}=W \vee p_{8,17}=W) \wedge (p_{15,9}=W \vee p_{13,12}=B)$$

Apparently, the high probability region of the learned probabilistic circuit only considers seven of the 784 pixels to predict whether an MNIST digit depicts a 0. Figure 7 shows two MNIST digits that match ψ and are part of the high probability regions of the probabilistic circuit. The latter can be verified by evaluating the probabilistic circuit for the given image. In addition to being more interpretable, the domain expert can also use description ψ as a starting point to further refine their intended concept.

6.3 Experiments

Experiment 1: Comparing Pruning Methods. To address research question 1, we evaluate the first step of PUTPUT with the two previously described pruning functions on the open-source benchmarks. Table 1 indicates that pruning by circuit flows results in the best average F_1-score and circuit size, the latter of which likely leads to a decreased aggregated entropy. In the following experiments, we therefore use pruning by circuit flows.

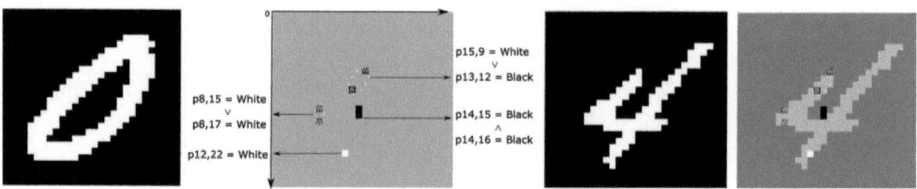

Fig. 7. Two MNIST images matching the logical formula ψ extracted by PUTPUT from a learned probabilistic circuit.

Table 1. Results of experiment 1 after the first step of PUTPUT, showing the average F_1-score and circuit size (and standard deviations) in relation to $\mathcal{E}_{HPR}$. The abbreviation gen. sign. refers to the generative significance method.

Function	F_1-score	Circuit size (# nodes)
no pruning		3086 ± 1163
circuit flows	0.313 ± 0.23	1812 ± 812
gen. sign.	0.285 ± 0.24	2281 ± 904

Experiment 2: Effect of PUTPUT's Step 2. The second step of PUTPUT prunes the input nodes to further lower the aggregated entropy. Table 2 shows the results of PUTPUT applied on the open-source benchmarks. We conclude for the second research question, that the second step significantly decreased the aggregated entropy. Furthermore, it also increased the F_1-score and recall.

Experiment 3: evaluation of PUTPUT. For all datasets, we evaluate using the ground truth labels rather than $\mathcal{E}_{HPR}$. To the best of our knowledge, the only other work that operates in a PU learning scenario and produces an interpretable model that is convertible into a database query, is the work by Goyal et al. [15]. They learn a decision tree (DT) by first enhancing the dataset with negative examples, via either the Rocchio (r) or Likelihood (l) method [3]. In addition to replicating their work, we also extend their idea by considering inductive logic programming (ILP): instead of learning a decision tree, we learn logical rules using RIPPER [9]. Because those methods are not easily convertable into CNF, but are easily convertable into DNF, we apply them on the reliable negatives as the positive class, converting the resulting DNF into CNF by negation. Afterwards, we compare the CNF to the one produced by our method, PUT-

Table 2. Results of experiment 2, showing average and standard deviation for various metrics, in relation to examples $\mathcal{E}_{HPR}$, after PUTPUT step 1 and 2.

Step	F_1-score	Aggregated entropy	Precision	Recall	PC size (# nodes)	LC size (# nodes)
1	0.313 ± 0.23	10168 ± 45798	0.341 ± 0.25	0.363 ± 0.27	1812 ± 812	1168 ± 1242
2	0.362 ± 0.23	287 ± 454	0.341 ± 0.26	0.381 ± 0.26	523 ± 294	92 ± 73

PUT. To summarize, we evaluate PUTPUT by comparing to both DT and ILP approaches, using either the Rocchio (r) or Likelihood (l) method.

Figure 8 shows the critical difference diagrams of the experiment. A more detailed visualization of the results is presented in Appendix B and C. The most important metric is the F_1-score, as the best aggregated entropy can be trivially achieved with a formula ψ that is always true. This highlights that PUTPUT outperforms other approaches on the *Tunify* data. They failed to learn a meaningful theory, as shown by the mean F_1-score: 0.73 for PUTPUT versus a max mean of 0.125 for l+ilp. On open-source benchmarks, PUTPUT matches r+DT in F_1-score while outperforming in aggregated entropy. These results show that PUTPUT is broadly applicable beyond the *Tunify* use case.

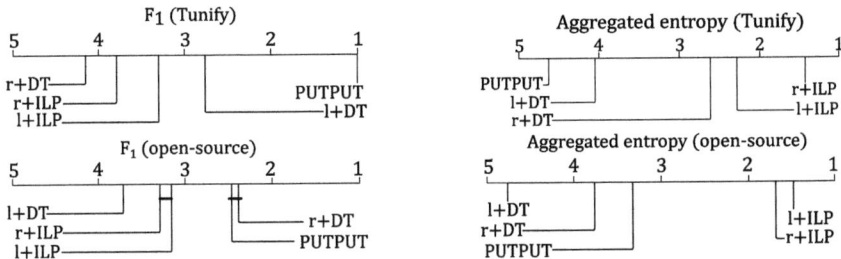

Fig. 8. The critical decision diagrams of experiment 3. Results closer to 1 are better.

7 Related Work

Probabilistic Circuits. Dang et al. proposed several pruning functions for a probabilistic circuit, functions that we utilise within PUTPUT [11]. They used these functions while devising a prune+grow approach to learn more meaningful probabilistic circuits: insignificant parts are pruned before again growing the remaining part. An earlier application of probabilistic circuits in the field of explainable AI is by Wang et al., who used them to find explanations that have a high probability of being correct [35]. Verreet et al. have used probabilistic circuits to explicitly model PU assumptions, improving the identification of reliable negatives [33]. In contrast to our work, the PC structure was not learned on data, nor was it used to learn the final model.

Explainability in AI can be tackled in different ways. (1) By limiting to interpretable models, possibly sacrificing accuracy [23]; (2) By transforming a learned model into a more interpretable one. For example by compiling a Bayesian network classifier into a logical classifier [30]; (3) By transforming part of a model into an interpretable version. This is the approach followed by LIME [26] and SHAP [19] where linear models are generated around a point of interest; (4) By querying the model to identify edge cases or adversarial examples [14]. In this work we focused on the second strategy, such that the resulting model can easily be transformed into a database query, and inspected by a domain expert.

Pattern Mining. Finding a description of a given set of examples is a problem setting that occurs in the field of data mining. KRIMP [34] is a pattern mining algorithm that uses the minimum description length principle to find a code table that compresses the data. Unfortunately, converting this code table into a comprehensive logical formula is not trivial. Another example of the use of pattern mining to find descriptions, is constraint-based querying to explore Bayesian networks [2]. The patterns mined in this work are used to answer explorative queries explaining the Bayesian network representation.

8 Conclusions

Motivated by a real-world music playlist generation task, we made three key contributions to queryable, interpretable PU learning. First, we are the first to apply probabilistic circuits for learning interpretable models from positive and unlabeled data. Second, we introduced aggregated entropy, a novel description length that measures the ease with which domain experts can inspect and understand the extracted logical formulas. Our primary contribution, however, is PUTPUT, a method that prunes low-probability regions of a probabilistic circuit to facilitate the extraction of interpretable logic formulas. Evaluation shows that PUTPUT outperforms competing methods on the playlist generation use case and that it is broader applicable through experiments on open-source datasets.

Acknowledgments. This research received funding from the Flemish Government under the "Onderzoeksprogramma Artificiële Intelligentie (AI) Vlaanderen" programme and from the KU Leuven Research Funds (STG/20/052, iBOF/21/075). LDR is also supported by the Wallenberg AI, Autonomous Systems and Software Program (WASP) funded by the Knut and Alice Wallenberg Foundation.

Code and Appendix. The source code and appendices are found on https://github.com/ML-KULeuven/PUTPUT.

Disclosure of Interests. Authors KV, WP and KJ are employed by Tunify, who have provided the music playlist dataset.

References

1. Aucouturier, J., Pachet, F.: Scaling up music playlist generation. In: Proceedings of the 2002 IEEE International Conference on Multimedia and Expo, ICME. vol. 1, pp. 105–108. IEEE Computer Society (2002). https://doi.org/10.1109/ICME.2002.1035729
2. Babaki, B., Guns, T., Nijssen, S., De Raedt, L.: Constraint-based querying for bayesian network exploration. In: Fromont, E., De Bie, T., van Leeuwen, M. (eds.) IDA 2015. LNCS, vol. 9385, pp. 13–24. Springer, Cham (2015). https://doi.org/10.1007/978-3-319-24465-5_2

3. Bekker, J., Davis, J.: Learning from positive and unlabeled data: a survey. Mach. Learn. **109**(4), 719–760 (2020). https://doi.org/10.1007/s10994-020-05877-5
4. Bonini, T., Gandini, A.: "first week is editorial, second week is algorithmic": platform gatekeepers and the platformization of music curation. Soc. Media + Society **5**(4) (2019). https://doi.org/10.1177/2056305119880006
5. Bonnin, G., Jannach, D.: Automated generation of music playlists: survey and experiments. ACM Comput. Surv. **47**(2), 26:1–26:35 (2014)
6. Choi, Y., Vergari, A., Van den Broeck, G.: Probabilistic circuits: a unifying framework for tractable probabilistic models. UCLA. http://starai.cs.ucla.edu/papers/ProbCirc20.pdf (2020)
7. Chow, C.K.: On optimum recognition error and reject tradeoff. IEEE Trans. Inf. Theory **16**(1), 41–46 (1970)
8. Cohen, G., Afshar, S., Tapson, J., van Schaik, A.: EMNIST: extending MNIST to handwritten letters. In: IJCNN, pp. 2921–2926. IEEE (2017)
9. Cohen, W.W.: Fast effective rule induction. In: Twelfth International Conference on Machine Learning, pp. 115–123. Morgan Kaufmann (1995)
10. Dang, M., Khosravi, P., Liang, Y., Vergari, A., Van den Broeck, G.: Juice: a julia package for logic and probabilistic circuits. In: AAAI, pp. 16020–16023. AAAI Press (2021)
11. Dang, M., Liu, A., Van den Broeck, G.: Sparse probabilistic circuits via pruning and growing. In: NeurIPS (2022)
12. Defferrard, M., Benzi, K., Vandergheynst, P., Bresson, X.: FMA: a dataset for music analysis. In: 18th International Society for Music Information Retrieval Conference (ISMIR) (2017), https://arxiv.org/abs/1612.01840
13. Deng, L.: The MNIST database of handwritten digit images for machine learning research [best of the web]. IEEE Signal Process. Mag. **29**(6), 141–142 (2012)
14. Devos, L., Meert, W., Davis, J.: Versatile verification of tree ensembles. In: ICML. Proceedings of Machine Learning Research, vol. 139, pp. 2654–2664. PMLR (2021)
15. Goyal, K., et al.: Automatic generation of product concepts from positive examples, with an application to music streaming. In: BNAIC/BENELEARN. Communications in Computer and Information Science, vol. 1805, pp. 47–64. Springer (2022)
16. Huffman, D.A.: A method for the construction of minimum-redundancy codes. Proc. IRE **40**(9), 1098–1101 (1952). https://doi.org/10.1109/JRPROC.1952.273898
17. Li, T., Wang, C., Ma, Y., Ortal, P., Zhao, Q., Stenger, B., Hirate, Y.: Learning classifiers on positive and unlabeled data with policy gradient. In: ICDM, pp. 399–408. IEEE (2019)
18. Liu, A., Van den Broeck, G.: Tractable regularization of probabilistic circuits. In: NeurIPS, pp. 3558–3570 (2021)
19. Lundberg, S.M., Lee, S.: A unified approach to interpreting model predictions. In: NIPS, pp. 4765–4774 (2017)
20. Michalski, R.S.: A theory and methodology of inductive learning. Artif. Intell. **20**(2), 111–161 (1983)
21. Mordelet, F., Vert, J.: A bagging SVM to learn from positive and unlabeled examples. Pattern Recognit. Lett. **37**, 201–209 (2014)
22. Muggleton, S.H.: Duce, an oracle-based approach to constructive induction. In: IJCAI, pp. 287–292. Morgan Kaufmann (1987)
23. Murdoch, W., Singh, C., Kumbier, K., Abbasi Asl, R., Yu, B.: Definitions, methods, and applications in interpretable machine learning. Proceedings of the National Academy of Sciences **116**, 201900654 (2019). https://doi.org/10.1073/pnas.1900654116

24. Pichl, M., Zangerle, E., Specht, G.: Understanding playlist creation on music streaming platforms. In: IEEE International Symposium on Multimedia, ISM, pp. 475–480. IEEE Computer Society (2016). https://doi.org/10.1109/ISM.2016.0107
25. Pronzato, L., Wynn, H., Zhigljavsky, A.: A generalized golden-section algorithm for line search. IMA J. Math. Control Inf. **15** (1998). https://doi.org/10.1093/imamci/15.2.185
26. Ribeiro, M.T., Singh, S., Guestrin, C.: Why should I trust you?: Explaining the predictions of any classifier. In: KDD, pp. 1135–1144. ACM (2016)
27. Rosenberg, G., et al.: Explainable artificial intelligence using expressive boolean formulas. Mach. Learn. Knowl. Extract. **5**(4), 1760–1795 (2023). https://doi.org/10.3390/make5040086, https://www.mdpi.com/2504-4990/5/4/86
28. Sakurai, K., Togo, R., Ogawa, T., Haseyama, M.: Controllable music playlist generation based on knowledge graph and reinforcement learning. Sensors **22**(10), 3722 (2022)
29. Samer, M., Szeider, S.: Algorithms for propositional model counting. J. Discrete Algorithms **8**(1), 50–64 (2010)
30. Shih, A., Choi, A., Darwiche, A.: A symbolic approach to explaining bayesian network classifiers. In: IJCAI, pp. 5103–5111. ijcai.org (2018)
31. Mlr, U.C.I.: Mushroom. UCI Machine Learning Repository (1987). https://doi.org/10.24432/C5959T
32. Mlr, U.C.I.: Molecular biology (Splice-junction Gene Sequences). UCI Mach. Learn. Repository (1992). https://doi.org/10.24432/C5M888
33. Verreet, V., De Raedt, L., Bekker, J.: Modeling PU learning using probabilistic logic programming. Mach. Learn. **113**(3), 1351–1372 (2024)
34. Vreeken, J., van Leeuwen, M., Siebes, A.: Krimp: mining itemsets that compress. Data Min. Knowl. Discov. **23**(1), 169–214 (2011)
35. Wang, E., Khosravi, P., Van den Broeck, G.: Probabilistic sufficient explanations. In: IJCAI, pp. 3082–3088. ijcai.org (2021)
36. Xiao, H., Rasul, K., Vollgraf, R.: Fashion-MNIST: a novel image dataset for benchmarking machine learning algorithms. CoRR **abs/1708.07747** (2017)
37. Yuan, Y., Bai, F.: Absolute value inequality svm for the pu learning problem. Mathematics **12**, 1454 (2024). https://doi.org/10.3390/math12101454
38. Zhang, H., Chen, Q., Zou, Y., Pan, Y., Wang, J., Stevenson, M.: Document set expansion with positive-unlabeled learning: a density estimation-based approach. CoRR arXiv:2401.11145 (2024)

Interpretable Hybrid-Rule Temporal Point Processes

Yunyang Cao, Juekai Lin, Hongye Wang, Wenhao Li[✉], and Bo Jin[✉]

Tongji University, 200092 Shanghai, China
{whli,bjin}@tongji.edu.cn

Abstract. Temporal Point Processes (TPPs) are widely used for modeling event sequences in various medical domains, such as disease onset prediction, progression analysis, and clinical decision support. Although TPPs effectively capture temporal dynamics, their lack of interpretability remains a critical challenge. Recent advancements have introduced interpretable TPPs. However, these methods fail to incorporate numerical features, thereby limiting their ability to generate precise predictions. To address this issue, we propose Hybrid-Rule Temporal Point Processes (HRTPP), a novel framework that integrates temporal logic rules with numerical features, improving both interpretability and predictive accuracy in event modeling. HRTPP comprises three key components: basic intensity for intrinsic event likelihood, rule-based intensity for structured temporal dependencies, and numerical feature intensity for dynamic probability modulation. To effectively discover valid rules, we introduce a two-phase rule mining strategy with Bayesian optimization. To evaluate our method, we establish a multi-criteria assessment framework, incorporating rule validity, model fitting, and temporal predictive accuracy. Experimental results on real-world medical datasets demonstrate that HRTPP outperforms state-of-the-art interpretable TPPs in terms of predictive performance and clinical interpretability. In case studies, the rules extracted by HRTPP explain the disease progression, offering valuable contributions to medical diagnosis. The supplementary material is available at https://github.com/yy-c/HRTPP0.

Keywords: Temporal point processes · Interpretability · Event sequence modeling · Logic rules

1 Introduction

Event sequence data is prevalent in various domains, especially healthcare, including disease onset prediction [3,21], progression analysis [6,14], and clinical decision support [10,20], where events occur asynchronously over time. Unlike traditional continuous-time series, which record values at regular intervals, event

---

J. Lin and H. Wang— Contributed equally to this work.

sequence data consists of discrete events with irregular time stamps, highlighting the necessity of specialized methods for discrete temporal data processing. Numerical features often accompany event sequences, providing crucial contextual information such as intensity, magnitude, or categorical attributes, which are essential for capturing complex temporal dependencies and enhancing predictive performance [18].

Temporal Point Processes (TPPs) are widely used for modeling event sequence data due to their ability to capture the stochastic nature of event occurrences over time. Traditional point process models, such as the Poisson process [13], Hawkes process [9], and self-correcting process [11], rely on predefined parametric intensity functions, which often struggle to capture complex temporal dependencies and require strong assumptions about the underlying data distribution. To address these limitations, neural point processes, including models based on recurrent neural networks (RNNs) [5], transformer architectures [29], and continuous normalizing flows [25], have been proposed to learn flexible, data-driven representations of event dynamics. However, these learning-based approaches often lack interpretability and require large amounts of training data to generalize effectively.

The interpretability of temporal point processes is crucial for many real-world applications, especially in healthcare, where understanding the underlying event dynamics is as important as making accurate predictions. For example, in medical diagnostics, an interpretable TPP model can assist doctors in analyzing disease progression by identifying key rules influencing the timing of medical events. Recent advancements have introduced interpretable TPPs, incorporating rule-based mechanisms [14,15,23] or sparse attention structures [17]. However, these methods typically sacrifice key advantages of numerical features, thereby limiting their ability to generate precise predictions. Thus, existing approaches face several limitations: traditional TPP models [4,9], though capable of utilizing numerical features, often lack the flexibility to capture complex temporal dependencies; neural TPP models [5], though powerful, are typically considered black boxes with limited transparency; and interpretable models [14,17], while offering some level of interpretability, often fail to incorporate rich numerical features effectively, reducing their predictive accuracy and rule reliability.

An urgent issue is ensuring both interpretability and accuracy. To address these issues, we propose Hybrid-Rule Temporal Point Processes (HRTPP), a novel framework that integrates rule-based mechanisms with numerical feature enhancement. HRTPP integrates three key intensity components: basic intensity, rule-based intensity, and numerical feature intensity, which together determine the overall intensity. The numerical feature intensity captures the influence of continuous-valued attributes. The rule-based intensity encodes temporal dependencies through predefined logic rules, which are optimized via a structured rule mining process involving Bayesian optimization. The best rule set is finally selected by a two-stage mining strategy.

The **contributions** of this paper are as follows:

- A rule-guided numerical augmentation framework is proposed, integrating rule-based mechanisms with numerical features to enhance TPP modeling.

- A two-phase rule mining strategy is introduced to balance search space complexity and predictive performance.
- A comprehensive evaluation paradigm for interpretable temporal point process models is established, incorporating multiple criteria to assess both predictive performance and rule reliability.

2 Related Work

Temporal Point Processes. Temporal Point Process (TPP) models provide a probabilistic framework for capturing event sequences in continuous time. A key challenge in TPP research lies in designing intensity functions that are both expressive and interpretable. Efforts to improve interpretability in TPPs have led to the development of attention-based and rule-based approaches. Attention-based approaches such as SA-HP [28] and THP [29] incorporate self-attention mechanisms to capture long-range dependencies in event sequences. ITHP [19] further explains THP by algebraic operations. Although these methods improve flexibility, the trade-off between accuracy and interpretability remains an open problem. Rule-based TPP models focus on enhancing interpretability through structured rule sets. TLPP [16] first introduces logic rules to model event intensities and defines temporal rules as a combination of temporal predicates and relations. TELLER [15] introduces a principled approach to mine rules that explain temporal dependencies. Based on this, CLUSTER [14] and NS-TPP [27] design different deep neural network structures to accelerate rule mining. Clock Logic Neural Network (CLNN) [24] incorporates weighted clock logic formulas as rules to model event interactions. The recent trend in TPP research highlights the need to balance both explainable and effective aspects, integrating structured rule-based approaches with deep learning models for more explainable and effective event modeling.

Rule Mining. Rule mining focuses on automatically discovering logical rules from event sequence data to explain event occurrence patterns. Traditional methods for rule discovery primarily identify frequent patterns, but struggle with capturing temporal dependencies. Apriori [1] efficiently extracts frequent event sets but fails to model event order. Sequential pattern mining techniques, such as CM-SPADE [7] and VGEN [8], attempt to incorporate temporal orders but face difficulties in handling fine-grained timestamps. To overcome these limitations, TELLER [15] formulates rule discovery as a maximum likelihood problem to generate high quality rules, but requires a lot of computation. CLUSTER [14] introduces an iterative framework based on the Expectation-Maximization algorithm to improve rule mining efficiency. NS-TPP [27] represents predicates and logic rules as vector embeddings and introduces a neural-symbolic framework for rule mining. Clock Logic Neural Network (CLNN) [24] utilizes weighted clock logic formulas to introduce three novel rule forms and incorporate numerical values into the rules. HyperLogic [26] proposes the integration of if-then logic rules within neural network architectures.

3 Background

TPPs are widely used to interpret complex event sequences over time. For example, in intensive care unit (ICU) monitoring, physicians analyze the progression of symptoms and lab results to make decisions. Understanding the logic rules among medical events is crucial for accurate diagnosis and treatment. This section briefly reviews temporal point processes and temporal logic rules.

3.1 Temporal Point Processes

Temporal Point Process (TPP) is mathematically defined as a stochastic process $\{t_i\}_{i=1}^{N}$ where each t_i denotes the timestamp of an event, and N is the number of observed events. The core component of TPPs is the conditional intensity function $\lambda(t)$, which defines the instantaneous rate of event occurrence at time t, conditioned on the history $\mathcal{H}_t = \{t_1, t_2, \ldots, t_i\}$ up to but not including t:

$$\lambda(t|\mathcal{H}_t) = \lim_{\Delta t \to 0} \frac{\mathbb{P}\left(N(t+\Delta t) - N(t) = 1 \mid \mathcal{H}_t\right)}{\Delta t}. \tag{1}$$

Here, Δt is a small time interval, and $N(t)$ denotes the counting process up to t. This intensity function governs the likelihood of an event happening at a particular time. The overall dynamics are characterized by the joint distribution. By modeling $\lambda(t|\mathcal{H}_t)$, TPPs can describe a wide range of event patterns, including those influenced by past occurrences, external features, or domain-specific rules.

3.2 Temporal Logic Rules

Temporal logic rules consist of two parts: temporal predicates and relations. Define a set of predicates as $\mathcal{X} = \{X_1, X_2, \ldots, X_n, Y\}$, where each predicates X_u is an independent variable, Y is a target variable. Define a set of temporal relations as $\mathcal{C}$, which define how the variables are related over time. Rules are in the form of "if-then". A generalized temporal logic rule R can be expressed as:

$$R : C_i(\psi_1, \psi_2) \to Y, \tag{2}$$

where $C_i \in \mathcal{C}$ represents a temporal relation, and ψ_1, ψ_2 are expressions that can either be variables from $\mathcal{X}$ or recursively defined temporal rules. For example, ψ can represent the variable "high heart rate" or the rule "high heart rate before hypertension". The temporal relations between two temporal points can be divided into four types: *and, before, equal, after* [2]. Actually, "X_1 before X_2" and "X_2 after X_1" are equivalent, so the final set of temporal relations is $\mathcal{C} = \{and, before, equal\}$.

4 Methodology

This section introduces the framework of Hybrid-Rule Temporal Point Processes (HRTPP), shown in Fig. 1. Given an event sequence $\mathcal{S} = \{(t_i, k_i, v_i)\}_{i=1}^{N}$ consisting of N events, each event type $k_i \in \{1, 2, \ldots, K\}$ is associated with an

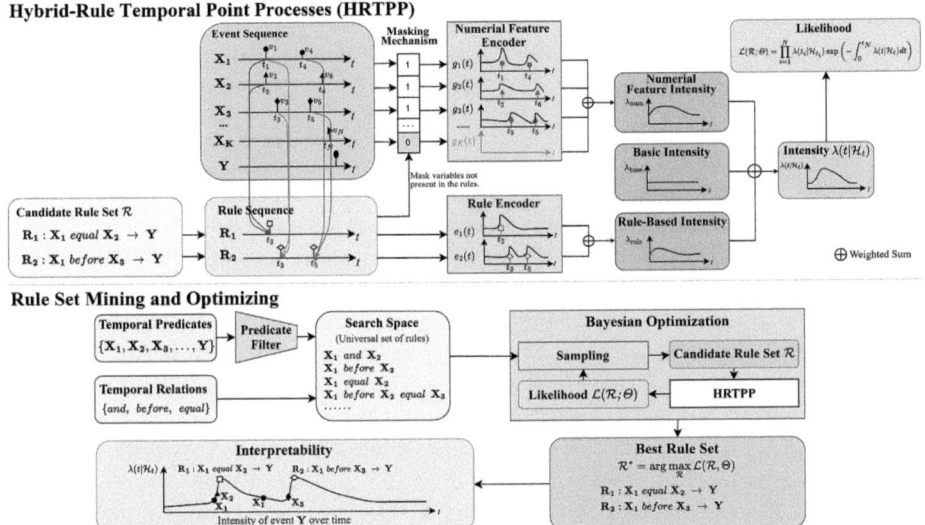

Fig. 1. The framework of model. In the HRTPP component, given a candidate rule set and event sequences, the model can compute the likelihood of the intensity function. The model integrates three key intensity components: basic intensity, rule-based intensity, and numerical feature intensity, which together determine the overall event intensity function $\lambda(t|\mathcal{H}_t)$. The numerical feature intensity captures the influence of continuous-valued attributes using a numerical feature encoder and a masking mechanism. The rule-based intensity encodes temporal dependencies through predefined rule set. In the rule set mining and optimizing component, Bayesian optimization iteratively refines the rule set by utilizing HRTPP computed likelihoods to guide the sampling distribution over the search space. The selected rules provide interpretable explanations of critical events via their impact on the intensity function dynamics.

independent variable X_k and a numerical feature v_i, providing contextual information. For instance, in ICU monitoring, an event k_i "elevated heart rate" at $t_i = 2$ hours may have $v_i = 120$ bpm. The conditional intensity function $\lambda(t|\mathcal{H}_t)$ is extended to incorporate temporal logic rules alongside numerical attributes, formulated as follows:

$$\lambda(t|\mathcal{H}_t) = f(\mathcal{S}_t; \Theta, \mathcal{R}), \tag{3}$$

where $\mathcal{H}_t$ represents the historical event information, $\mathcal{S}_t = \{(t_i, k_i, v_i)\}_{t_i < t}$ denotes the observed event sequence, Θ is the set of model parameters, and $\mathcal{R}$ comprises the extracted temporal logic rules that govern event dependencies.

4.1 Rule-Based Feature Construction

Temporal logic rules are essential in medical diagnosis, particularly in ICU monitoring, where capturing symptom progression is crucial for informed clinical decision-making. We propose a rule-based feature construction framework that integrates structured temporal rules with numerical features. This approach encodes event dependencies into numerical representations, ensuring a balance between explainability and data-driven modeling.

Definitions of Temporal Rules. Temporal rules formally define the logical relationships between different events over time, which consists of temporal predicates and temporal relations. In this study, we categorize the temporal relations between two time points into three types: *before, equal, and*.

Given two predicates X_u and X_v with timestamps t_u and t_v, along with a target event Y occurring at $t_y > \max(t_u, t_v)$ and the indicator function $\mathbb{I}(\cdot)$, the three types of temporal rules are mathematically defined as follows. *Before*, where X_u occurs before X_v within a small time tolerance δ, formulated as $\mathcal{C}_{before}(X_u, X_v) = \mathbb{I}(t_u - t_v < -\delta)$. *Equal*, where X_u and X_v occur approximately at the same time, formulated as $\mathcal{C}_{equal}(X_u, X_v) = \mathbb{I}(|t_u - t_v| \leq \delta)$. *And*, which simply states that both events occur without temporal constraints, formulated as $\mathcal{C}_{and}(X_u, X_v) = 1$. These temporal rules provide a structured mechanism for capturing event dependencies.

Rule Encoder. To effectively incorporate temporal rules into the TPP framework, we encode hybrid-rule information into a continuous vector space. Based on the definitions of temporal rules, we construct hybrid-rule event sequences. For instance, consider the temporal rule "X_u before $X_v \rightarrow Y$". The corresponding hybrid-rule event sequence records the timestamps when the condition X_u before X_v is satisfied. Specifically, this sequence tracks each moment where the constraint $\mathcal{C}_{before}(X_u, X_v)$ transitions from 0 to 1. The encoding function for a rule R_j is defined as:

$$e_j(t) = \sum_{t_j \in \mathcal{T}_j} d_{\text{rule}}(t - t_j), \qquad (4)$$

where d_{rule} is the decay function, and $\mathcal{T}_j$ denotes the set of timestamps when rule R_j is triggered. The choice of the decay function depends on real-world dynamics. For example, an exponential decay function, defined as $d_{rule}(t) = e^{-t}$ for $t \geq 0$, can model the diminishing influence of past rule activations over time.

Numerical Feature Encoder. Numerical features provide quantitative insight into the condition of a patient. The numerical feature encoder captures the dynamic influence of numerical attributes over time. Given an event sequence $\mathcal{S} = \{(t_i, k_i, v_i)\}_{i=1}^N$, the sequence corresponding to the predicate X_k is expressed as $\{(t_i, k_i, v_i)\}_{k_i=k}$. Generally, not all predicates directly influence the target event. Therefore, we introduce a masking mechanism to filter out irrelevant predicates. The mask is defined according to the given rule set, where only the predicates appearing in rules associated with the target event remain active, ensuring that the retained variables are indeed the relevant ones. Formally, the mask set is denoted as $\mathcal{M} = \{m_k\}_{k=1}^K$, and the valid predicate set $\mathcal{X}_V \subset \mathcal{X}$

denotes the collection of all variables appearing in the rules. The mask function is defined as $m_k = 1$ if $X_k \in \mathcal{X}_V$, and $m_k = 0$ otherwise. Using this masking mechanism and the sequence $\{(t_i, k_i, v_i)\}_{k_i=k}$, we define the numerical feature encoding function for predicate X_k as:

$$g_k(t) = m_k \sum_{i:k_i=k} v_i d_{\text{num}}(t - t_i), \tag{5}$$

where d_{num} is a time decay function, that models the influence of past numerical observations. The mask m_k ensures consistency within the HRTPP framework.

4.2 Hybrid-Rule Temporal Point Processes

HRTPP extends classical TPP by integrating rule-based dependencies and numerical features. The overall intensity function is composed of three key components. First, basic intensity models fundamental event patterns. Second, rule-based intensity encodes temporal logic rules. Third, numerical feature intensity incorporates clinical measurements to refine event prediction.

Basic Intensity. The basic intensity component λ_{base} captures the time independent information. This component reflects the inherent likelihood of events occurring. Mathematically, the basic intensity is expressed as: $\lambda_{\text{base}} = \lambda_0$, where λ_0 is a learnable parameter.

Rule-Based Intensity. The rule-based intensity component integrates domain expertise and temporal dependencies into the event modeling process. Given a predefined set of temporal rules $\mathcal{R}$, the rule-based intensity function is defined as:

$$\lambda_{\text{rule}}(t) = \sum_{R_j \in \mathcal{R}} \alpha_j e_j(t), \tag{6}$$

where α_j is a learnable parameter representing the weight associated with rule R_j. $e_j(t)$ denotes the encoding function, shown in Eq. (4). By incorporating rule-based intensity, HRTPP ensures that predictions align with medically interpretable dependencies rather than relying solely on data-driven patterns.

Numerical Feature Intensity. Numerical features such as heart rate and blood pressure provide an essential context for event predictions. The numerical feature intensity component modulates event occurrence probabilities based on these continuously valued attributes. The intensity function is defined as:

$$\lambda_{\text{num}}(t) = \sum_{k=1}^{K} \beta_k g_k(t), \tag{7}$$

where β_k is a learnable parameter representing the weight associated with predicate X_k. $g_k(t)$ is the numerical feature encoder, which is shown in Eq. (5). For example, if a patient's blood pressure remains high, it may increase the likelihood of a hypertension-related event. The numerical feature dynamically modulates event probabilities, providing a richer representation of patient status.

The overall intensity function integrates all three intensity components. In order to ensure that the overall intensity function remains positive, we apply the softplus transformation. The softplus function is defined as: Softplus$(x) = \gamma \log(1 + \exp(x/\gamma))$, where $\gamma > 0$ is a learnable parameter. By incorporating Eqs.(4)-(7), the final expression for the overall intensity function is as follows:

$$\lambda(t|\mathcal{H}_t) = \text{Softplus}\left(\lambda_{\text{base}}(t) + \lambda_{\text{rule}}(t) + \lambda_{\text{num}}(t)\right)$$

$$= \text{Softplus}\left(\lambda_0 + \sum_{R_j \in \mathcal{R}} \alpha_j \sum_{t_j \in \mathcal{T}_j} d_{\text{rule}}(t - t_j) + \sum_{k=1}^{K} \beta_k m_k \sum_{i:k_i = k} v_i d_{\text{num}}(t - t_i)\right). \tag{8}$$

where $\boldsymbol{\alpha} = \{\alpha_j\}_{j=1}^{|\mathcal{R}|}$ is the set of weights associated with temporal rules, $\boldsymbol{\beta} = \{\beta_i\}_{i=1}^{K}$ is the set of weights associated with numerical features. The learnable parameters set is denoted as $\Theta = \{\boldsymbol{\alpha}, \boldsymbol{\beta}, \gamma, \lambda_0\}$. This overall intensity function serves as the foundation for modeling event occurrences in HRTPP framework, enabling robust modeling in event prediction and rule mining.

4.3 Training and Prediction

To effectively learn the parameters of the HRTPP model and enable accurate event prediction, we design a training framework based on likelihood maximization and employ our learned intensity function for future event forecasting.

Loss Function. The HRTPP model is trained by maximizing the likelihood of observed event sequences within the temporal point process framework. Given an event sequence $\mathcal{S} = (t_i, k_i, v_i)_{i=1}^{N}$ and a rule set $\mathcal{R}$, the likelihood function is formulated as $\mathcal{L}(\Theta) = \prod_{i=1}^{N} \lambda(t_i|\mathcal{H}_{t_i}) \exp\left(-\int_0^{t_N} \lambda(t|\mathcal{H}_t)dt\right)$, where Θ is the set of learnable model parameters. To facilitate optimization, we minimize the negative log-likelihood (NLL) as the loss function:

$$\mathcal{L}_{\text{NLL}}(\Theta) = -\sum_{i=1}^{N} \log \lambda(t_i|\mathcal{H}_{t_i}) + \int_0^{t_N} \lambda(t|\mathcal{H}_t)dt. \tag{9}$$

This loss function ensures that the model learns to assign higher intensities to observed events while also maintaining proper event distributions over time.

Event Prediction. HRTPP model can be used to predict the timing of future events based on the learned intensity function. Given a history $\mathcal{H}_t$ up to time t, the next event time $\hat{t}$ is sampled from the conditional density function:

$$p(\hat{t}|\mathcal{H}_t) = \lambda(\hat{t}|\mathcal{H}_t) \exp\left(-\int_t^{\hat{t}} \lambda(s|\mathcal{H}_s)ds\right). \tag{10}$$

By minimizing the loss function, HRTPP effectively learns the underlying intensity function of event occurrences. By predicting the timing of the next event, HRTPP can capture the evolving dynamics of the sequence, offering valuable insights and data-driven support for medical diagnosis.

4.4 Rule Mining and Optimization

To efficiently extract temporal logic rules, a two-phase rule mining strategy is employed, incorporating rule candidate generation and Bayesian optimization.

Rule Candidate Generation. Temporal rules are derived from historical event sequences to construct a structured search space. Without constraints, the combination of predicates and relations can be excessively large. For instance, any rule containing m predicates interconnected by $(m-1)$ relations yields a combinatorial space of $K^m C^{m-1}$ possible configurations, with K and C being the total number of the predicates and relations respectively. To address this, rule length is restricted, and predicate filtering is applied. Firstly, rule length significantly impacts interpretability. Overly complex rules hinder comprehension, whereas single-predicate rules lack temporal expressiveness. Based on medical guidelines, a maximum of two or three predicates is imposed. Secondly, predicate filtering is conducted via pre-training using a rule-free TPP model as a baseline. Each predicate is evaluated individually, and those reducing model loss are retained. The resulting filtered predicates are used to generate candidate rules, ensuring that each rule contains at least one valid predicate. This process refines the search space, facilitating efficient rule selection.

Rule Optimization via Bayesian Optimization. Following candidate generation, Bayesian optimization is utilized to refine the rule set and maximize predictive performance, avoiding the infeasibility of exhaustive searches. The objective is to identify the optimal rule subset $\mathcal{R}^*$ that maximizes the model log-likelihood:

$$\mathcal{R}^* = \arg\max_{\mathcal{R}} \log \mathcal{L}(\mathcal{R}; \Theta), \tag{11}$$

where $\log \mathcal{L}(\mathcal{R}; \Theta)$ denotes the model likelihood given the rule set $\mathcal{R}$. To maintain efficiency and interpretability, the rule set size $|\mathcal{R}|$ is constrained to a fixed constant.

Bayesian optimization iteratively updates the rule set in three steps: (1) sampling candidate subsets using a probabilistic acquisition function, (2) evaluating model performance, and (3) refining the posterior distribution to guide further searches. This approach efficiently identifies high-quality rules while mitigating overfitting and redundancy, ensuring an optimal balance between model accuracy and interpretability. Unlike brute-force search methods, Bayesian optimization efficiently explores the parameter space.

5 Experiments

5.1 Experimental Setup

Datasets. We use four real-world disease-specific datasets: AKI (Acute Kidney Injury), Stroke, Sepsis, and CAD (Coronary Artery Disease). These medical datasets are extracted from MIMIC-IV [12], a large-scale medical database that contains electronic health records. Table 1 presents the statistical information of these datasets. The number sign # denotes a summation operation. As shown in the table, these four datasets increase in size from top to bottom. In the AKI dataset, disease progression to Phase III serves as the target event. The Stroke dataset focuses on patients transitioning from moderate to severe conditions. In the Sepsis dataset, the occurrence of low urine output is tracked as a target of organ failure. In the CAD dataset, patient mortality is defined as the target event.

Baselines. We adopted three state-of-the-art models with explicit rule-mining capabilities: TEmporal Logic rule LearnER (TELLER) [15], Clock Logic Neural Network (CLNN) [24], and CLUSTER [14].

Evaluation Metrics. To assess the performance of the models, we conducted comprehensive experiments. Each dataset is randomly split into an 80% training set and a 20% test set. The evaluation metrics used to measure predictive performance include *Negative Log-Likelihood (NLL)*, *Root Mean Squared Error (RMSE)* and *Rule Accuracy (Acc)*. Rule accuracy means the proportion of correct rules.

Table 1. Datasets statistics.

Dataset	# Sequences	# Types	# Events	Seq. Length	Avg. Length
AKI	2327	38	58k	[3, 123]	24.93
Stroke	4951	48	447k	[2, 2207]	97.47
Sepsis	20081	66	1375k	[2, 1406]	68.46
CAD	12459	56	3519k	[6, 7955]	282.45

5.2 Performance Analysis

In this section, we compare the performance of model fitting, event occurrence time prediction, and rule accuracy using three evaluation metrics. The results shown in Table 2 demonstrate that HRTPP outperforms baseline models. The lowest NLL indicates that HRTPP effectively captures and models uncertainty. HRTPP also achieves the lowest RMSE, suggesting precise event time predictions and enhancing reliability in medical applications. High rule accuracy of HRTPP demonstrates the extraction of medically relevant rules, improving interpretability and supporting transparent decision-making. Among the two most accurate models, HRTPP is computationally more efficient, consistently completing training in under 16 h on all datasets, whereas TELLER requires over 48 h.

Table 2. Comparisons of main results.

	AKI			Stroke			Sepsis			CAD		
	NLL↓	RMSE↓	Acc↑	NLL↓	RMSE↓	Acc↑	NLL↓	RMSE↓	Acc↑	NLL↓	RMSE↓	Acc↑
TELLER	12.9	8.1	80%	21.8	8.4	100%	23.4	4.4	75%	203.8	5.3	80%
CLNN	277.5	10.4	83%	178.9	13.2	70%	207.2	5.9	67%	177.1	4.2	71%
CLUSTER	79.0	10.4	60%	36.3	13.2	65%	37.5	8.8	65%	98.9	10.4	55%
HRTPP	7.4	5.4	100%	15.1	4.3	100%	12.7	2.7	80%	5.8	3.7	100%

5.3 Rule Analysis

In this section, we analyze the quality of the rules from the perspectives of rule expression, correctness, reliability, and distribution, thereby verifying the interpretability of the model. We take the CAD dataset as an example. Table 3 shows top 10 rules of four models. The full results are shown in the supplementary material.

Rule Expression Analysis. In the CAD dataset, we set mortality as the target variable and compare HRTPP with baseline models. The correctness of the rules was determined by referencing medical guidelines jointly issued by authoritative medical bodies [22]. Table 3 shows the rules, weights, and correctness. The weights of HRTPP are α_j in Eq. (8), demonstrating the importance of rules. Different rules are connected by logical disjunction relationships. From the experimental results, TELLER and CLNN rely on simple variables and discover few rules, missing complex physiological interactions. CLUSTER offers more flexible rules but is highly sensitive to noise, making it difficult to extract correct medical indicators. In contrast, HRTPP uncovers clinically meaningful rules, such as "if a high anion gap occurs before low heart rate, then death occurs", highlighting the link between metabolic disorders and circulatory failure. These rules enhance accuracy and align with medical logic, aiding clinical decision-making.

Rule Distribution Analysis. Understanding mortality risk indicators in CAD patients is crucial for better management and prediction. To analyze these factors, we created a graph network based on medical guidelines [22], visually mapping their hierarchical relationships in Fig. 2. As shown in the Fig. 2, arterial blood pressure, heart rate, C-reactive protein and cholesterol directly effect

Table 3. Rules on the CAD dataset. The predicates in green boxes are direct indicators, and those in blue boxes are indirect indicators.

Model	Rule	Weight	Correctness
TELLER	Respiratory Rate High → Dead	0.2859	Correct
	Arterial Blood Pressure diastolic Low → Dead	0.2202	Correct
	Heart Rate High → Dead	0.1614	Correct
	Arterial Blood Pressure mean Low → Dead	0.1400	Correct
	O2 saturation pulseoxymetry Low → Dead	0.1283	Incorrect
CLNN	c_Glucose High - c_Dead > -0.25	1.03	Correct
	c_BUN High - c_Dead > -0.63	1.01	Correct
	c_INR Low - c_BUN High > 0.01	0.99	Incorrect
	c_Glucose High - c_AST Low > -0.08	0.99	Incorrect
	c_Albumin High - c_Glucose High > 0.02	0.97	Correct
	c_BUN High - c_C-Reactive-Protein High > -0.14	0.96	Correct
	c_Brain Natiuretic Peptide High - c_BUN High > 0.41	0.94	Correct
CLUSTER	BUN Low equal Lactic Acid Low	-	Incorrect
	Hemoglobin High equal Hematocrit High	-	Incorrect
	Brain Natiuretic Peptide High after ALT Low	-	Correct
	Heart Rate High before AST Low	-	Correct
	Calcium ionized High equal Total Bilirubin High	-	Incorrect
	CK-MB fraction High equal Calcium ionized Low	-	Correct
	Calcium ionized Low equal Cholesterol High	-	Correct
	Temperature Low equal Hemoglobin High	-	Correct
	Hematocrit Low equal Total Bilirubin Low	-	Incorrect
	Glucose Low before Anion gap Low	-	Incorrect
HRTPP	Heart Rate Low equal Arterial Blood Pressure diastolic High → Dead	2.4073	Correct
	Anion gap High before Heart Rate Low → Dead	1.7742	Correct
	Heart Rate Low equal Potassium High → Dead	1.6257	Correct
	Potassium Low before O2 saturation pulseoxymetry Low → Dead	1.3959	Correct
	Respiratory Rate Low before Potassium High → Dead	1.1533	Correct
	Arterial Blood Pressure mean Low before Arterial Blood Pressure diastolic Low → Dead	1.1312	Correct
	Anion gap Low equal O2 saturation pulseoxymetry Low → Dead	1.1303	Correct
	Glucose Low equal Arterial Blood Pressure systolic Low → Dead	0.5603	Correct
	Heart Rate Low equal INR High → Dead	0.4213	Correct
	Temperature High and Respiratory Rate High → Dead	0.3194	Correct

mortality, while other indicators influence mortality through them. Hence, we classify the rules into direct or indirect rules according to their relationships. Table 3 shows direct indicators in green and indirect indicators in blue. HRTPP identifies the most direct rules, showing strong ability in capturing key CAD mortality factors. HRTPP also balances direct and indirect rules well, focusing on major factors without omitting minor details, thus enhancing its applicability in medical decision-making.

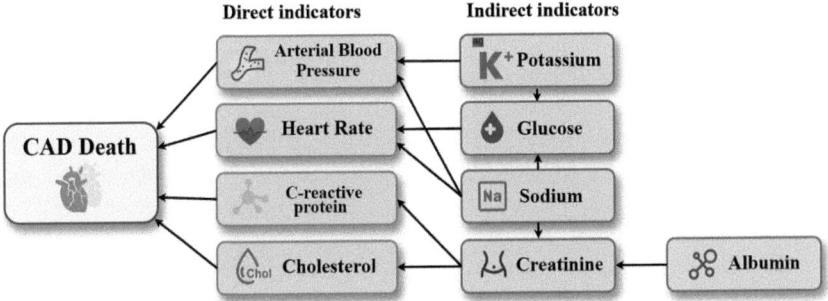

Fig. 2. Hierarchical relationships of CAD indicators. The indicators in green boxes are direct indicators, and those in blue boxes are indirect indicators. Arrows denote dependencies between indicators in a cause-effect manner. (Color figure online)

5.4 Stability Analysis

Model stability is crucial in medical decision support, ensuring consistency across conditions. To evaluate model stability, we recorded the frequency of four direct CAD indicators in five runs, using a five-fold cross-validation. Figure 3 presents the results, where HR, ABP, Cho, and CRP denote Heart Rate, Arterial Blood Pressure, Cholesterol, and C-reactive Protein, respectively. As shown in the figure, HRTPP has the highest frequency of direct rules, which shows the best stability and consistency. Clinically, its stability ensures interpretable results by minimizing fluctuations caused by minor data changes, thereby enhancing decision-making accuracy and supporting personalized treatment.

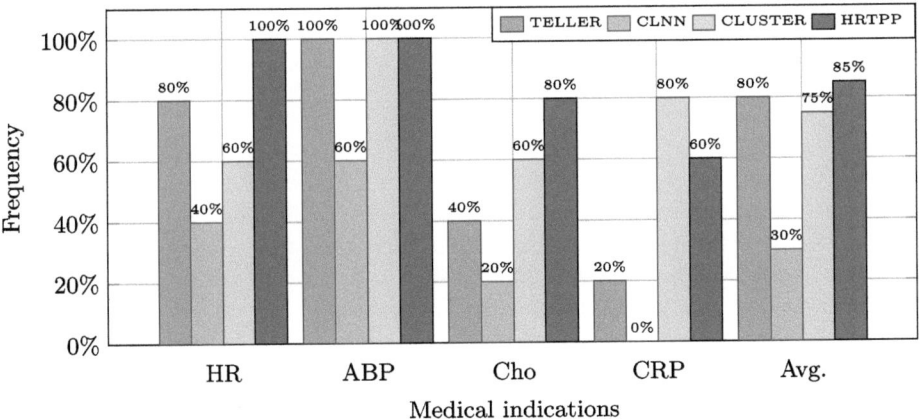

Fig. 3. Frequency of direct rules in five runs.

5.5 Case Study

In this section, we show the mechanism by which rules and events affect the target. When a rule is triggered, its strength increases instantaneously, reflecting the potential risk associated with the condition. Figure 4 shows the intensity curve of a CAD patient. In this figure, abnormalities in physiological indicators triggered key rules over time. At 17.19h, high blood glucose and creatinine appeared, followed by infection-related signs, increasing rule strength. At 60.26h, metabolic imbalance was triggered by an elevated anion gap and low heart rate. At 92.43h, high INR (International Normalized Ratio) and low heart rate indicated coagulation abnormalities. Finally, at 123.58h, decreased oxygen saturation and increased blood pressure triggered the end-event rule, leading to a sharp rise in intensity and death.

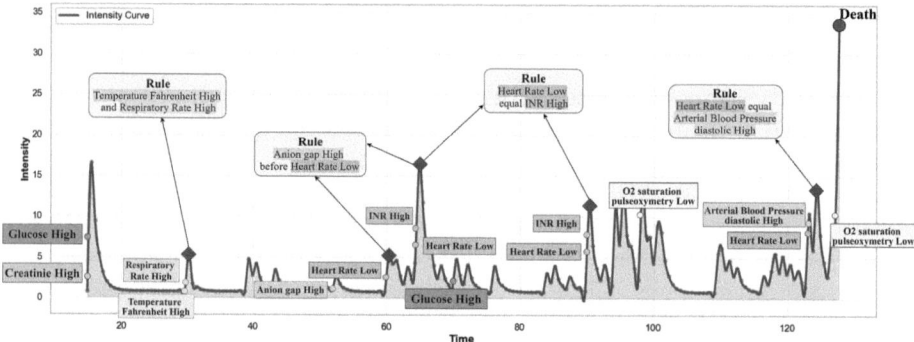

Fig. 4. Overall intensity over time for a CAD patient. The red curve represents the intensity of the target variable, reflecting the probability of death. Key events affecting the mortality are annotated below the curve, while the timing of logic rules is marked above. The entire figure illustrates the patient's full clinical progression in the ICU. (Color figure online)

This mechanism enables real-time monitoring and early warning of high-risk conditions while providing interpretable analysis of disease progression to support clinical decisions. By applying rule-guided dynamic analysis, we identify key causal relationships in CAD progression and detect turning points in disease deterioration, allowing clinicians to intervene precisely at critical moments. These rules are not just data-driven predictions but verifiable medical reasoning, ensuring transparency and reliability in CAD treatment.

5.6 Ablation Study

We conducted an ablation study to assess the impact of Numerical Feature Augmentation (NFA) on model performance. We classify models into two categories. Category I uses only basic intensity, like probabilistic TPP models. Category II uses basic and rule-based intensity. Table 4 shows the NLL of two categories. The introduction of NFA universally improve model performance across datasets, with the sole exception of AKI. The standard metrics employed in AKI evaluation underrepresent clinically significant intermediate events. This limitation is compounded by NFA focus on global rule coverage rather than domain-specific critical pattern recognition. These findings validate the effectiveness of numerical intensity in medical event modeling.

Table 4. Ablation study of NFA for NLL performance.

Category	State	AKI	Stroke	Sepsis	CAD
Category I	w/o NFA	**7.41**	15.26	12.83	6.30
	with NFA	**7.41**	**15.24**	**12.73**	**5.96**
Category II	w/o NFA	**7.43**	15.26	12.77	6.12
	with NFA	**7.43**	**15.14**	**12.72**	**5.84**

6 Conclusion

This paper proposes Hybrid-Rule Temporal Point Processes (HRTPP), a novel framework that integrates rule-based reasoning with numerical feature modeling. The proposed approach effectively incorporates domain expertise through temporal logic rules, while leveraging numerical feature encoder to capture complex event dependencies. By integrating a structured rule mining and optimization strategy, HRTPP refines the rule search process, ensuring both efficiency and robustness in modeling event sequences. Experimental results demonstrate that HRTPP achieves superior predictive accuracy and interpretability compared to baseline methods, making it a valuable tool for medical diagnosis. Future work will focus on adaptive rule learning mechanisms to improve flexibility and generalization.

Acknowledgements. This work is supported by National Natural Science Foundation of China (62406270), Shanghai Rising-Star Program (24YF2748800).

References

1. Agrawal, R., Srikant, R.: Fast algorithms for mining association rules. In: Proceedings of the 20th International Conference on Very Large Data Bases, vol. 1215, pp. 487–499 (1994)
2. Bruce, B.C.: A model for temporal references and its application in a question answering program. Artif. Intell. **3**, 1–25 (1972)
3. Che, Z., Purushotham, S., Cho, K., Sontag, D., Liu, Y.: Recurrent neural networks for multivariate time series with missing values. Sci. Rep. **8**(1), 6085 (2018)

4. Di Crescenzo, A., Martinucci, B., Zacks, S.: Compound poisson process with a poisson subordinator. J. Appl. Probab. **52**(2), 360–374 (2015)
5. Du, N., Dai, H., Trivedi, R., Upadhyay, U., Gomez-Rodriguez, M., Song, L.: Recurrent marked temporal point processes: Embedding event history to vector. In: Proceedings of the 22nd ACM SIGKDD Conference on Knowledge Discovery and Data Mining, pp. 1555–1564 (2016)
6. Fan, Z., et al.: Construction and validation of prognostic models in critically ill patients with sepsis-associated acute kidney injury: interpretable machine learning approach. J. Transl. Med. **21**(1), 406 (2023)
7. Fournier-Viger, P., Gomariz, A., Campos, M., Thomas, R.: Fast vertical mining of sequential patterns using co-occurrence information. In: Advances in Knowledge Discovery and Data Mining: 18th Pacific-Asia Conference, pp. 40–52. Springer (2014)
8. Fournier-Viger, P., Gomariz, A., Šebek, M., Hlosta, M.: Vgen: fast vertical mining of sequential generator patterns. In: Data Warehousing and Knowledge Discovery: 16th International Conference, pp. 476–488. Springer (2014)
9. Hawkes, A.G.: Spectra of some self-exciting and mutually exciting point processes. Biometrika **58**(1), 83–90 (1971)
10. Hayat, N., Geras, K.J., Shamout, F.E.: Medfuse: multi-modal fusion with clinical time-series data and chest x-ray images. In: Machine Learning for Healthcare Conference, pp. 479–503. PMLR (2022)
11. Isham, V., Westcott, M.: A self-correcting point process. Stochastic Process. Appl. **8**(3), 335–347 (1979)
12. Johnson, A.E.W., Stone, D.J., Celi, L.A., Pollard, T.J.: The mimic code repository: enabling reproducibility in critical care research. J. Am. Med. Inform. Assoc. **25**(1), 32–39 (2018)
13. Jorgenson, D.W.: Multiple regression analysis of a poisson process. J. Am. Stat. Assoc. **56**(294), 235–245 (1961)
14. Kuang, Y., Yang, C., Yang, Y., Li, S.: Unveiling latent causal rules: a temporal point process approach for abnormal event explanation. In: International Conference on Artificial Intelligence and Statistics, pp. 2935–2943. PMLR (2024)
15. Li, S., et al.: Explaining point processes by learning interpretable temporal logic rules. In: International Conference on Learning Representations (2021)
16. Li, S., et al.: Temporal logic point processes. In: International Conference on Machine Learning, pp. 5990–6000. PMLR (2020)
17. Li, Z., Sun, M.: Sparse transformer Hawkes process for long event sequences. In: Joint European Conference on Machine Learning and Knowledge Discovery in Databases, pp. 172–188. Springer (2023)
18. Meng, Z., et al.: Transfeat-tpp: An interpretable deep covariate temporal point processes. arXiv preprint arXiv:2407.16161 (2024)
19. Meng, Z., Wan, K., Huang, Y., Li, Z., Wang, Y., Zhou, F.: Interpretable transformer Hawkes processes: Unveiling complex interactions in social networks. In: Proceedings of the 30th ACM SIGKDD Conference on Knowledge Discovery and Data Mining, pp. 2200–2211 (2024)
20. Palma, J., Juarez, J.M., Campos, M., Marin, R.: Fuzzy theory approach for temporal model-based diagnosis: an application to medical domains. Artif. Intell. Med. **38**(2), 197–218 (2006)
21. Renc, P., et al.: Zero shot health trajectory prediction using transformer. NPJ Digital Med. **7**(1), 256 (2024)

22. Virani, S.S., et al.: 2023 aha/acc/accp/aspc/nla/pcna guideline for the management of patients with chronic coronary disease: a report of the american heart association/american college of cardiology joint committee on clinical practice guidelines. J. Am. Coll. Cardiol. **82**(9), 833–955 (2023)
23. Walzer, K., Schill, A., Löser, A.: Temporal constraints for rule-based event processing. In: Proceedings of the ACM first Ph. D. Workshop in CIKM, pp. 93–100 (2007)
24. Yan, R., et al.: Weighted clock logic point process. In: International Conference on Learning Research (2023)
25. Yang, G., Huang, X., Hao, Z., Liu, M.Y., Belongie, S., Hariharan, B.: Pointflow: 3D point cloud generation with continuous normalizing flows. In: Proceedings of the IEEE/CVF International Conference on Computer Vision, pp. 4541–4550 (2019)
26. Yang, Y., Ren, W., Li, S.: Hyperlogic: enhancing diversity and accuracy in rule learning with hypernets. Adv. Neural. Inf. Process. Syst. **37**, 3564–3587 (2024)
27. Yang, Y., Yang, C., Li, B., Fu, Y., Li, S.: Neuro-symbolic temporal point processes. In: International Conference on Machine Learning (2024)
28. Zhang, Q., Lipani, A., Kirnap, O., Yilmaz, E.: Self-attentive Hawkes process. In: International Conference on Machine Learning, pp. 11183–11193. PMLR (2020)
29. Zuo, S., Jiang, H., Li, Z., Zhao, T., Zha, H.: Transformer Hawkes process. In: International Conference on Machine Learning, pp. 11692–11702. PMLR (2020)

SVEBI: Towards the Interpretation and Explanation of Spiking Neural Networks

Jasper De Laet, Hamed Behzadi-Khormouji, Lucas Deckers, and Jose Oramas[✉]

University of Antwerp, SqIRL/IDLab, Imec, Antwerp, Belgium
jose.oramas@uantwerpen.be

Abstract. Artificial Neural Networks have demonstrated the versatility to adapt to different problems while at the same time achieving high predictive performance. A characteristic of these models is their high-computation demands, which translates into high energy consumption. Spiking Neural Networks (SNN) have been proposed as an energy-efficient alternative with promising results in several tasks. Despite being a promising alternative that could motivate massive deployment, research on the interpretation of these models is almost non-existent. To address this problem, we propose SVEBI, a method that extracts insights on the representation encoded by SNNs, via the analysis of sparse relevant internal units that drive the decision-making process. In addition, we show the use of the relevant units as a means to justify, i.e. explain, the predictions made by an SNN for a given input. In this explanation/justification task, our experiments show SVEBI is comparable, if not superior, to existing methods.

Keywords: Spiking Neural Networks · Interpretability · Explainability

1 Introduction

Artificial Neural Networks (ANNs) have demonstrated broad applicability, frequently matching or even surpassing human performance. ANNs show their strength in several topics including, but not limited to, speech recognition [3,46], image/video recognition [5,17,31], natural language processing [21,40] or in domains like finance [13] or healthcare [33]. However, the computational cost associated with ANNs is undeniably substantial, not only during training but also during inference and deployment. As task complexity increases, so does the complexity of the models, leading to higher computational demands in both training and real-world usage [38]. A high computational cost implies a high energy consumption which leads to limitations regarding the applicability of ANNs. This indicates that utilizing a more energy-efficient neural network design could become necessary for continuous improvement in the field of AI.

In the biological neural networks found inside the brain, information is propagated between neurons through spikes (i.e., discrete binary events). It is known

---

J. De Laet and H. Behzadi-Khormouji—Equal Contribution.

© The Author(s), under exclusive license to Springer Nature Switzerland AG 2026
R. P. Ribeiro et al. (Eds.): ECML PKDD 2025, LNAI 16015, pp. 460–477, 2026.
https://doi.org/10.1007/978-3-032-06066-2_27

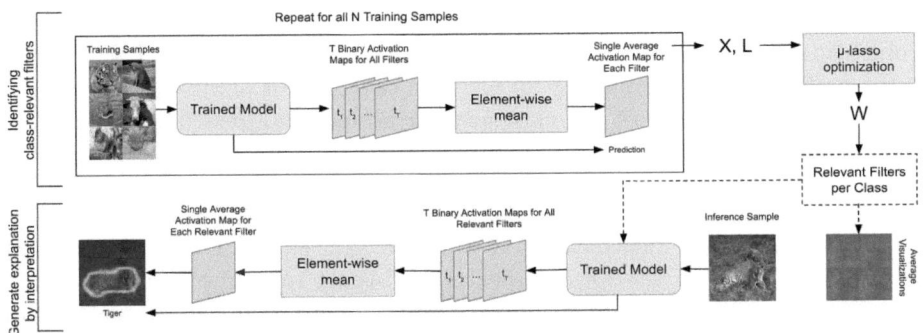

Fig. 1. Overview of the proposed methodology for the interpretation and explanation of SNNs. This includes identifying class-relevant filters, followed by the generation of average visualizations for interpretability and explanatory heatmaps.

that these spikes are sparse in time, which means that individual spikes encode a high amount of information [2,37]. The fact that just a few spikes are necessary to convey information throughout the brain contributes to the observation that the brain uses a low amount of energy in proportion to the tasks it can perform when compared to ANNs [2,39,45]. Spiking Neural Networks (SNNs) are neural networks whose design is inspired from the spiking nature of biological neural networks. SNNs use spikes to propagate information through the network over time. It has been demonstrated that SNNs, when implemented through neuromorphic hardware, can achieve significantly higher energy efficiency compared to traditional ANNs. Intel's Loihi neuromorphic chip has demonstrated energy consumption up to 16 times lower than AI models running on conventional hardware [9,28]. Likewise, IBM's TrueNorth processor achieves a remarkable efficiency gain, using up to 100,000 times less energy per synaptic operation compared to traditional CPU/GPU-based neural networks [1,6]. Moreover, SNNs have proven capable of achieving competitive results in various tasks, such as image classification [15,41,48].

As SNNs are proposed as a possible replacement for traditional ANNs, there is demand for the interpretability of SNNs, i.e. understanding its inner-workings. Understanding what an SNN learns comes down to discovering what is exactly encoded in the SNN after training. Due to the opaque characteristics of neural networks this is not an obvious task. Despite the fact that there exist numerous works dedicated to investigating the encoded features in non-spiking ANNs, a similar analysis in the context of SNNs remains limited. In this study, we endeavor to find a means for determining what a trained SNN has actually learned, i.e., the interpretation of SNNs. Towards this goal, we leverage existing well-studied interpretation methods (namely [25]) for non-spiking ANNs, while taking into account the fundamental differences between SNNs and traditional ANNs. Furthermore, comparable to the traditional ANNs, the need for justifications (explanations) towards the decisions made by a model also applies for SNNs. This introduces our secondary goal where we also aim for the explanation of SNNs. Targeting these goals, this work proposes a new approach, SVEBI, for the interpretation as well as explanation of SNNs trained on image classification problems (see Fig. 1). In summary, we develop a method that provides insights on the representation encoded by an SNN via the analysis of filters that are critical for the performance of the classification problem addressed by the model. This method results in our two main contributions, which can be outlined as follows: (i) Considering the identified filters, we achieve interpretation of SNNs through visualizations that reveal the features that were learned by the model (ii) In addition, these identified filters are used as a basis for the generation of visual explanations in the form of heatmaps. Apart from three notable works [4,16,24], there has been limited direct research focused on the interpretability and explainability of SNNs.

This paper is organized as follows: Sect. 2 summarizes existing literature related to our work. Section 3 explains some fundamental concepts related to the contributions of this work. Then in Sect. 4, we present the proposed method and describe its operation. In Sect. 5 we validate the proposed method and discuss the corresponding results. Section 6 outlines its limitations. We provide closing remarks in Sect. 7.

2 Related Work

Interpretation of Neural Networks. In the field of computer vision, there exist multiple interpretation methods that concern themselves with the extraction of features and concepts learned by a traditional ANN. These methods can be split up into two categories, interpretable-by-design methods and post-hoc methods. The interpretable-by-design methods (e.g., [8,22]) are ANN models that are designed and structured in such a way that after training it is automatically possible to analyze and understand, to a certain degree, what they have actually learned. The post-hoc methods (e.g., [25,42]) are generally methods that are applied on already trained "non-interpretable" ANN models, such that this will yield some insights regarding internal encodings of these models.

Since SNNs use spikes to propagate information through the network over time, instead of instantaneous continuous values as in traditional ANN designs, these existing interpretation methods are not directly applicable to SNNs. This motivates our objective, wherein we focus on developing an interpretation method that considers both the spiking nature and temporal dimension of SNNs. On this context, to the best of our knowledge, there is no method that provides this capability for SNNs.

Explanation Techniques for Neural Networks. In general, explanation of neural networks refers to justifying the outputs produced by the model. For image classification tasks, this often comes down to finding and investigating what information in the input was of greater importance for the model to generate a prediction for a specific input sample [27,29,32,47]. Regarding this task, we focus on explanation through visualizations in the format of heatmaps. There exist model-agnostic methods like LIME [29] and RISE [27] that can be directly applied to SNNs as they do not depend on the internal workings or structure of the model. However, methods like this require perturbing the input data where each perturbation needs to be evaluated by the model. This approach can be quite computationally expensive, which is not scalable. Moreover, their application would come at the cost of the low-energy consumption benefits of SNNs. While there are several heatmap methods available for the explanation of ANNs that are more computationally efficient, such as CAM [47] or Grad-CAM [32], directly applying these to SNNs is not a straightforward task due to the difference between the internal workings of traditional ANNs and SNNs. These methods do not take the temporal dynamics of SNNs into account. On top of this, methods like Grad-CAM require computing the gradient, which is not obvious for SNNs considering their non-differentiable nature and the use of surrogate gradients.

However, there exists a work that adapts gradient-based methods using a surrogate gradient [4]. These methods are presented in two distinct forms: one tailored for event-driven data (SNN-Grad3D and SNN-IG3D) and the other designed for 2D image classification data (SNN-Grad2D and SNN-IG2D). Following our focus on 2D image classification problems, we only consider the 2D methods in this work. SNN-Grad2D is inspired by the original saliency map from [34]. In SNN-Grad, the output attribution map represents the output class scores with respect to the input. This results in an attribution map for each timestep of the SNN. To convert this to the 2D matrix, the maps are summed over the time dimension. SNN-IG2D is based on the integrated gradients approach from [36]. This involves generating a monotonous path that gradually transforms a baseline image into the original input image in a specific number of steps. They start with a fully black image as baseline. Following this, they compute the SNN gradients with respect to the input (using surrogate gradient) for each individual step in the path, which are then integrated along the path. Here, to produce a single attribution map, the maps computed at different time-stamps are added.

Different from the above, Spike Activation Map (SAM) [16] produces heatmap visualizations per layer for each timestep. In contrast to SNN-Grad and SNN-IG, it does not need any gradients to produce its visualizations, which is advantageous because of the non-differentiable characteristics of the LIF neurons that compose SNNs. SAM is based on the temporal dynamics of SNNs to assign neuronal contribution scores in forward propagation using the history of previous spikes. It does not use any class labels, which means that the generated explanation visualization does not necessarily highlight regions of the image specific to a predicted class. Instead, the generated heatmap highlights the regions that the network focused on to generate a prediction given any image. This means that the heatmaps do not necessarily guarantee that a region of interest relevant to the predicted class is highlighted. Temporal Spike Attribution (TSA) [24] extends SAM by combining neuron spike timings, model weights, and output layer information during a forward pass to compute a final score. In contrast to SAM, TSA indirectly uses the prediction by including the membrane potentials of the output layer which define the final prediction of an SNN. However, TSA was not directly developed to be applied on convolutional neural networks, as where we specifically focus on 2D image classification tasks. Like SAM, but in contrast to SNN-Grad2D and SNN-IG2D, we present a method that is capable of producing explanation heatmaps without the need for computing gradients. However, our method uses the predictions of the model to steer the generation of the explanations. In contrast to SAM but similar to SNN-Grad2D and SNN-IG2D, our method produces a single heatmap for all timesteps together based on the class predicted by the model, which ensures that the highlighted region is relevant to the predicted class.

3 Background

In this section, we first introduce key concepts essential for understanding the contributions made by this work (Sect. 3.1). This is followed by background information on the post-hoc interpretation method proposed in [25] since our work can be seen as an extension to the SNN domain of that method (Sect. 3.2).

3.1 Spiking Neural Networks

Artificial Neural Networks (ANNs) were originally inspired by the biological neural networks present in the brain [20,30]. However, significant differences exist between traditional ANNs and biological neural networks in terms of structure, neural computations, learning rules, and the way information propagates between neurons [37]. These differences result in traditional ANNs consuming significantly more energy, which motivates the development of designs that align more closely with the biological counterpart. One of the most prominent examples of this are Spiking Neural Networks (SNNs), which use spikes (discrete events) to propagate information over time, emulating the spiking nature of biological neurons. A spike can be represented as a 1, and the absence of a spike as a 0. In SNNs, time is defined by timesteps T over which a single input is fed to the network. In this work, feeding a single input to an SNN means recurrently presenting the input to the network at each timestep. In our case, the input can be regarded as an image as we focus on image classification. These concepts are implemented through a spiking neuron model. Various spiking neuron models exist, but in this work the Leaky Integrate-and-Fire (LIF) model is used [18].

Leaky Integrate-and-Fire Neuron: Similar to neurons in non-spiking ANNs, LIF neurons operate by summing weighted inputs. However, instead of pushing it through an activation function, the weighted sum is added to an internal state called the membrane potential $U[t]$. When this potential reaches a threshold θ, an output spike is generated. This behaviour can be described by the Heaviside step function, where the input is the membrane potential minus the threshold value ($U[t] - \theta$). Considering that $S_{out}[t]$ denotes the output spike value at timestep t, this function can be reformulated regarding the spiking neuron as:

$$S_{out}[t] = \begin{cases} 1, & \text{if } U[t] > \theta \\ 0, & \text{otherwise} \end{cases} \quad (1)$$

After spiking, the membrane potential experiences a reset which can be a soft reset (subtraction by some defined value) or a hard reset (set to zero). In our case, we use a soft reset. Inherent to the LIF neuron model, the membrane potential leaks over time as well. The behaviour of the membrane potential with regard to the previous timestep can be characterized by the following discrete formula:

$$U[t] = \beta U[t-1] + WX[t] - S_{out}[t-1]\theta \tag{2}$$

where β determines the leakage and $WX[t]$ denotes the weighted input. See Fig. 2 for a schematic representation of the LIF neuron.

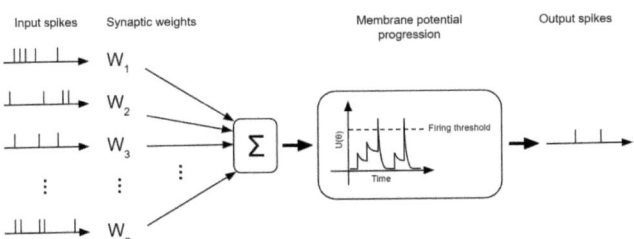

Fig. 2. Illustration of a LIF neuron. Input spikes are multiplied by their respective synaptic weights before being added to the membrane potential. The membrane potential progresses over time, where it produces a single output spike when reaching a certain threshold value. After spiking, the membrane potential experiences a reset [18]

Network Structure: To form a network, multiple spiking neurons are grouped together in a similar way as with traditional ANNs. The spiking neurons are grouped together to form layers. Then, multiple layers can be stacked to produce a deep SNN.

Spike Encoding: When data is fed to an SNN, it needs to be converted into a spike representation such that the information can propagate through the network. There are several ways to do this [11], here we choose to not use an explicit input encoding technique. On the contrary, we feed our input data (continuous values) directly to the network and in this way let the network come up with its own encoding strategy in the input layer. Regarding the output of an SNN, it is necessary to convert the output of the last layer such that it represents the format of the expected output. We follow the common approach of having the number of output neurons to be equal to the number of output classes and then the neuron with the highest membrane potential after the last timestep represents the final output of the SNN [15,19,41]. Here, the membrane potentials of the last layer do not experience a reset after exceeding θ such that they do not emit any spikes. The loss of a prediction with regard to a target can be computed through the same loss functions used for training non-spiking ANNs. In our case, we used the cross-entropy loss.

Surrogate Gradient: At last, training SNNs can be challenging due to the non-differentiable nature of the Heaviside step function. In this work, we use the surrogate gradient method [23] to handle this. This means using the Heaviside step function in the forward pass, but replacing it by a differentiable function for computing the gradient in the backward pass. Similarly to [15], we use a sigmoidal approximation of the derivative of the step function.

3.2 ANN Interpretation and Explanation Method

When designing an interpretation method or an explanation method, it is important to base the method on attributes derived directly from the model. As explained in Sect. 3.1, the non-differentiable nature of the LIF-neuron prevents us from computing the gradients of the model. While computing gradients using a surrogate gradient function during training has shown to be effective, these are not the actual gradients of the model. This motivates our decision to adopt an activation-based approach, as the activations can be easily obtained from an SNN. In addition to this, it has been shown that SNNs following architectures and topologies inspired from non-spiking ANNs can achieve reasonable results [15,37,41,44,48]. Consequently, we opt to develop a post-hoc interpretation method, as it eliminates the need to design a new SNN architecture.

The Visual Explanation By Interpretation (VEBI) method, proposed in [25], is capable of both achieving a level of interpretation as well as explanation of ANNs. Both the interpretation and explanation are based on a post-hoc approach to identify a set of internal relevant filters per class for a given pretrained model. This method consists out of two main steps. First, the extraction of the input-wise internal responses from the network F for all N images, where N denotes the number of images used to train the model F. The second step includes using these image-wise responses to obtain a matrix $W \in \mathbb{R}^{m \times C}$ that indicates what layer-filter pairs are relevant to what class by solving a μ-lasso problem (Eq. 3). Here, m denotes the total number of considered filters (or features in general) and C the total number of classes.

$$W^* = argmin_W \|X^T W - L^T\|_F^2 \qquad (3)$$

Here, X is a matrix containing the input-wise responses for all N images where $X \in \mathbb{R}^{m \times N}$. L is a matrix containing the predicted labels (in one-hot encoding format) for all N inputs where $L \in \{0,1\}^{C \times N}$. In order to enforce that only a subset of the most relevant features are selected by W, a sparsity constraint μ is added in the following manner $\|w_j\|_1 \leq \mu, \forall j \in \{1, 2, ..., C\}$. This makes it a μ-lasso problem.

Model Interpretation: This is achieved by producing via visualizations that aim to depict the visual patterns encoded by the extracted relevant features. In [25], these visualizations are produced via average images computed from the top-k 100 images for which the identified relevant filters have the highest responses. Prior to the average operation, these images are cropped to the size of the receptive field of the relevant filter centered at the location that has the maximum activation in the filter response.

Model Explanation: This is achieved by accompanying the class label predicted by the model with heatmap visualizations derived from the set of relevant filters supporting the prediction. Since in [25] the generation of these explanations involves computing the gradient through backpropagation — a process not directly feasible for SNNs, as outlined in Sect. 3.1—we have not further extended the explanation method presented in [25]. Instead, we have come up with our own method for generating visual explanations (Sect. 4.2).

4 Proposed Method

We propose SVEBI, a pipeline capable of both achieving interpretability and explainability of SNNs. It is composed out of two core elements. First, a method for the identification and inspection of features that are of importance to the classes of interest. This is achieved by finding the relationship between internal activations and predicted class labels (Sect. 4.1). Second, an approach for estimating layer-level responses which can serve as means for explanation by aggregating the average activation maps of filters relevant to the predicted class (Sect. 4.2). SVEBI can be considered an SNN counterpart of VEBI.

4.1 Identifying Class-Relevant Filters

We devise a method for identifying class-relevant filters by extending the method from VEBI [25] (see Sect. 3.2). Our method is an adaptation that allows for producing the W matrix that indicates the relevant layer-filter pairs per class by taking into account the disparities between non-spiking ANNs and SNNs.

The main difference lies in the first step, the extraction of input-wise responses x_i for every i^{th} training image which involves the collection of the internal responses of each filter in the architecture. For non-spiking ANNs, this means collecting a single activation map containing continuous values for each filter. However, an SNN uses spikes over time to propagate information through the network. This means that the filter responses of a single filter are activation maps consisting of binary events. Furthermore, passing a single image through the network is done over a number of timesteps T. Thus, when passing a single image through an SNN G, each filter in G produces an activation map for each timestep. We approach this difference in the following manner: When passing the ith image through G, we collect T activation maps for each filter. We denote an activation map as S_{it}^f per filter f, where $t \in \{1, 2, 3, ..., T\}$. We squeeze the resulting T activation maps by defining a single average activation map $\bar{S}_i^f$ for filter f. As the activation maps can be seen as matrices, we obtain this by computing the element-wise mean as follows:

$$\bar{S}_i^f = \frac{1}{T} \sum_{t=1}^{T} S_{it}^f \qquad (4)$$

This is done for each filter, followed by the subsequent steps described in VEBI [25]. Consequently, this average activation map forms the SNN equivalent for the single activation map that is collected per filter for non-spiking ANNs. As before, the above is repeated for all N training images which is followed by using the N input-wise responses to define the matrix $X \in \mathbb{R}^{m \times N}$ and then estimate $W \in \mathbb{R}^{m \times C}$ by solving the μ-lasso problem (see Eq. 3). As described in Sect. 3.2, sparsity is enforced via the constraint μ.

4.2 Generating Explanatory Heatmaps

We generate visual explanations for SNNs in the form of heatmap visualizations using the relevant filters identified by our method (Sect. 4.1) as a basis. The heatmap visualization is based on the spiking behaviour within the identified relevant filters of a layer with respect to a single input image belonging to a specific class.

This begins by passing an image i through the SNN G and collecting the output activation map S_{it}^f of the specific relevant filter f for all $t \in \{1, 2, 3, ..., T\}$. Analogous to the previous sections, this is followed by producing a single average activation map $\bar{S}_i^f$ (via Eq. 4). This is then repeated for all class-relevant filters of a single layer for the predicted class, after which we add all resulting average activation maps together. We can produce the heatmap explanation by upscaling the summed activation map to the size of the input image i, applying normalization, and then superimposing on the input image i.

4.3 Computational Considerations

The most significant computational cost introduced by our method arises during the identification of relevant filters, as this step requires processing the entire training set with the model. The generation of explanation heatmaps at inference time results in only minimal overhead, comparable to a standard forward pass through the model, as it involves collecting activation maps and executing a set of lightweight computations.

5 Evaluation

We evaluate our methods by conducting several experiments. First, we investigate the impact of the identified relevant filters on the performance of the model. This experiment serves as a fundamental sanity check that determines whether the identified filters are indeed critical for the decision-making process (Sect. 5.2). Secondly, we assess the layer-wise distribution of the identified relevant filters of the model (Sect. 5.3). This is followed by a qualitative analysis of the identified relevant filters by generating visual feedback. The objective of this experiment is to understand what the model has learned, thereby achieving model interpretation (Sect. 5.4). Then, we present our explanatory heatmaps, which we qualitatively evaluate by comparing to the maps produced by SNN-Grad2D and SNN-IG2D (Sect. 5.5) [4]. At last, we perform a quantitative evaluation of our explanation method by using the insertion/deletion evaluation protocol [27] where we again compare to SNN-Grad2D and SNN-IG2D (Sect. 5.6).

5.1 Experimental Setup

We evaluate our methods using a shallow SNN consisting of 2 convolutional layers and 2 fully connected layers trained on MNIST [10]. From here on, we refer to this as the *shallow SNN*. In addition, we also consider a spiking equivalent of the popular CNN architecture VGG19 [35], which we refer to as *SVGG19*. For this, we consider the classification task on the AwA2 dataset [43], where the goal is to predict which animal is present in each image. AwA2 consists of 50 animal classes which comes down to 37.322 images (resized to 224x224). We used an 80/20 split for training and testing. For the shallow SNN, we trained for 5 epochs using 10 timesteps, a batch size of 100 and a learning rate of 0.3, resulting in a training accuracy of 98.96% and a best test accuracy of 98.79%. As an initial step for the SVGG19, we used the pre-trained weights provided by PyTorch [26], derived from training a non-spiking VGG19 on the ImageNet dataset [17]. Since SVGG19 shares an identical topology (in terms of layer and neuron structure) with the non-spiking VGG19, these pre-trained weights can be seamlessly transferred to SVGG19. This was followed by a training phase consisting of 50 epochs without freezing any layers, using 25 timesteps, a batch size of 8 and a learning rate of 0.003, achieving a training accuracy of 99.89% and a test accuracy of 89.83%. For both models, a spiking threshold ($\theta = 1$) is used, and the input is fed directly into the network, allowing it to autonomously develop an encoding strategy within the input layer (see Sect. 3.1). Our implementation is publicly available in our Github repository[1].

5.2 Impact of Identified Relevant Filters

To measure the impact of the identified filters on the model performance, we analyze the magnitude of the contributions of the identified filters to the model's classification accuracy. We do this by inspecting the classification results of the models when ablating the filters and comparing this to the full model performance per class. We ablate filters from a specific class and compute performance for that class, then average the results over all classes. Ablating filters is done by setting their output to zero. To verify whether the impact of a relevant filter is greater than just any filter, we compare to the classification results of the model when ablating randomly selected filters per class. The number of randomly selected filters is equal to the number of identified relevant filters. For this experiment, we do not narrow down to a specific sparsity constraint (μ), but instead identify the relevant filters for all $\mu \in \{1, 2, ..., 50\}$ and use these results for our analysis. We then repeat the above for all the values considered for the μ sparsity parameter. The average classification results over all classes of

---
[1] https://github.com/JasperDeLaet/SVEBI.

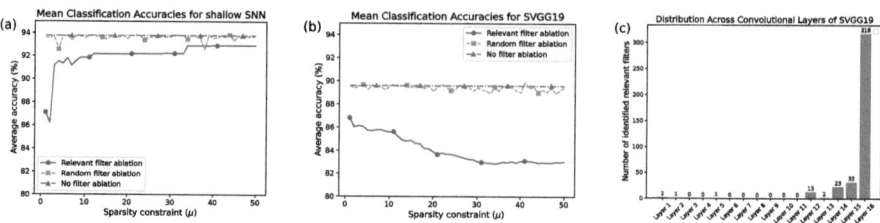

Fig. 3. (a,b) Classification results for shallow SNN and SVGG19 over different μ values, respectively. This includes the accuracy when all filters in the model are considered (green), when the output of relevant filters is ablated (blue) and when the output of random filters is ablated (orange). (c) Layer-wise distribution of the identified relevant filters over the 16 convolutional layers of the SVGG19. (Color figure online)

this experiment can be found in Figs. 3 (a,b). We observe for both models that for all μ, the accuracy when ablating relevant filters is always substantially lower than when ablating randomly selected filters. This suggests that our method is capable of identifying filters that have a greater impact on the decision-making process of the model than just any filter. The sparsity constraint μ can be considered a tunable hyperparameter, for which we use $\mu = 2$ for the shallow SNN and $\mu = 20$ for the SVGG19 in all subsequent experiments.

5.3 Layer-Wise Distribution of Identified Relevant Filters

We assess the distribution of the identified relevant filters over the layers of the model. For the shallow SNN, relevant filters are found in the first convolutional layer for classes 0, 1, 4 and 6 and are present in the second convolutional layer for all classes. Figure 3 (c) shows that the identified relevant filters for the SVGG19 exhibit a skewed distribution, with a high concentration in the later layers of the model, while there are fewer relevant filters in the earlier and middle layers. This is in line with observations in the literature that state that earlier layers learn more generic features (edges, textures, and basic shapes), and that later layers focus on more complex class-specific features.

5.4 Qualitative Interpretation Feedback

Following the previous experiment, we perform a qualitative analysis in which we aim to determine what features the identified relevant filters have learned. In this way, we develop an understanding of what the model has actually learned, i.e. interpretation of the model. This qualitative analysis is performed by generating interpretation feedback in the form of average visualizations for multiple relevant filters which are resized to the input image size (Sect. 3.2). This experiment is conducted only for the SVGG19 model on the AwA2 dataset, as the low resolution of MNIST results in overly coarse visualizations that do not yield

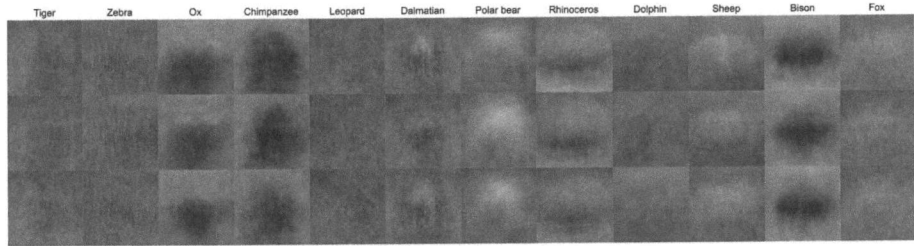

Fig. 4. Average visualizations (resized to input image size) for multiple identified relevant filters of the SVGG19 over the AwA2 dataset.

meaningful insights into the learned filter representations. Representative examples of the resulting visualizations for the identified relevant filters are shown in Fig. 4. We observe that the average visualizations generally depict features that are specific to the classes for which the identified filters are relevant. For example, the average visualizations for animals with distinctive fur patterns clearly show some representation of these patterns (tiger, zebra, leopard, and dalmatian). For the ox, a head with horns can be discerned, while for the chimpanzee, a silhouette emerges. In addition to the animal-specific features, we notice that some average visualizations show characteristics of the environment in which the corresponding animal is often encountered (e.g., the polar bear or dolphin). These results generally confirm the suggestion made in Sect. 5.3, as the average visualizations show quite complex features.

5.5 Qualitative Assessment of Explanation Feedback

We examine the visual quality of our explanation heatmaps and compare them to the output of SNN-Grad2D and SNN-IG2D. Since SVEBI is capable of producing explanations for any identified relevant filter regardless of which layer the filter belongs to, we can explain the internal activations of the model for multiple layers. This provides deeper insights into how the model arrives at a specific prediction, leading to enhanced explainability. However, since not all layers contain relevant filters, we present SVEBI explanations for only a subset of the layers in Fig. 5. The explanations generated for the MNIST samples by SVEBI tend to highlight regions corresponding to parts of the digits. For example, the results for class 6 clearly show higher focus towards the top curve of the number 6. For the SVGG19, the explanations produced by SVEBI coming from later layers clearly show a region of interest highlighted in a manner that effectively differentiates it from the surrounding regions. Evidently, the explanations from the earlier layers show a focus on larger and less specific regions. For example, the explanations for the dolphin class sample indicate a high importance attributed to the water in the background in the first and second layers of the model. However, when considering the explanations from the final layer, it becomes evident that the model focuses on parts of the dolphin itself. Similarly for the leopard, we observe that in layer 12 the model has an interest for patches of the fur pattern of the leopard, where in layer 16 the focus lies on the full head of the leopard.

Compared to the gradient-based explanations produced by SNN-Grad2D and SNN-IG2D, the SVEBI output is more widespread and smooth, while the gradient-based explanations are notably sparse. This trend is most clearly observed in the explanations generated for SVGG19. This aligns with existing literature, where it is commonly found that gradient-based heatmaps tend to be sparse [34,36].

5.6 Quantitative Evaluation of Explanation Techniques

There are different approaches for quantitatively evaluating heatmap explanations, [7,12,14,27]. However, we use the two automatic evaluation metrics (insertion/deletion) proposed by [27]. These evaluation metrics can be applied to a single heatmap, producing quantitative values that reflect the quality of the heatmap–specifically, whether it effectively highlights regions with high contribution to the model's prediction. In short, insertion operates by starting from a baseline image and gradually inserting pixels from the input sample based on decreasing importance determined by the heatmap. For every insertion, the performance of the model is measured. Essentially, after this procedure, the AUC of the obtained model predictions scores forms the quality score. Deletion works in a similar fashion but starts from the full input image and gradually deletes pixels from this image based on pixel importance determined by the heatmap. Again, the AUC of the model prediction scores forms the quality score. For insertion, a higher AUC score indicates better performance, as it means that the most important pixels are inserted first. Conversely, for deletion, a lower AUC score is preferred, as it suggests that the most important pixels are deleted first. In our case, the insertion baseline for AwA2 was a blurred version of the original input sample, whereas for MNIST, we used a black image (all-zero pixels). For the deletion protocol in both datasets, pixels were 'deleted' by replacing them with black pixels (i.e., setting the pixel values to zero).

To quantitatively evaluate our method and compare it to the existing SNN-Grad2D and SNN-IG2D approaches, we compute the average insertion and deletion scores over 9,920 test samples from the MNIST dataset and 7,056 test samples from the AwA2 dataset. Figure 6 shows the performances of the models over the complete insertion and deletion procedures. Table 1 presents the corresponding AUC scores. Regarding the shallow SNN on MNIST, we observe that SVEBI outperforms the gradient-based methods in the insertion metric. For deletion, SVEBI performs comparably to SNN-Grad2D but is outperformed by SNN-IG2D. In the case of SVGG19 on AwA2, SVEBI significantly surpasses the gradient-based methods in terms of insertion scores. For deletion, SVEBI shows comparable performance, with SNN-IG2D yielding the best result. For the SVGG19-AwA2 explanations, the poor insertion results, but rather good deletion results for SNN-Grad2D and SNN-IG2D compared to SVEBI could be attributed to the sparsity of the gradient-based explanations. During the insertion procedure, this sparsity causes the model to be first presented with

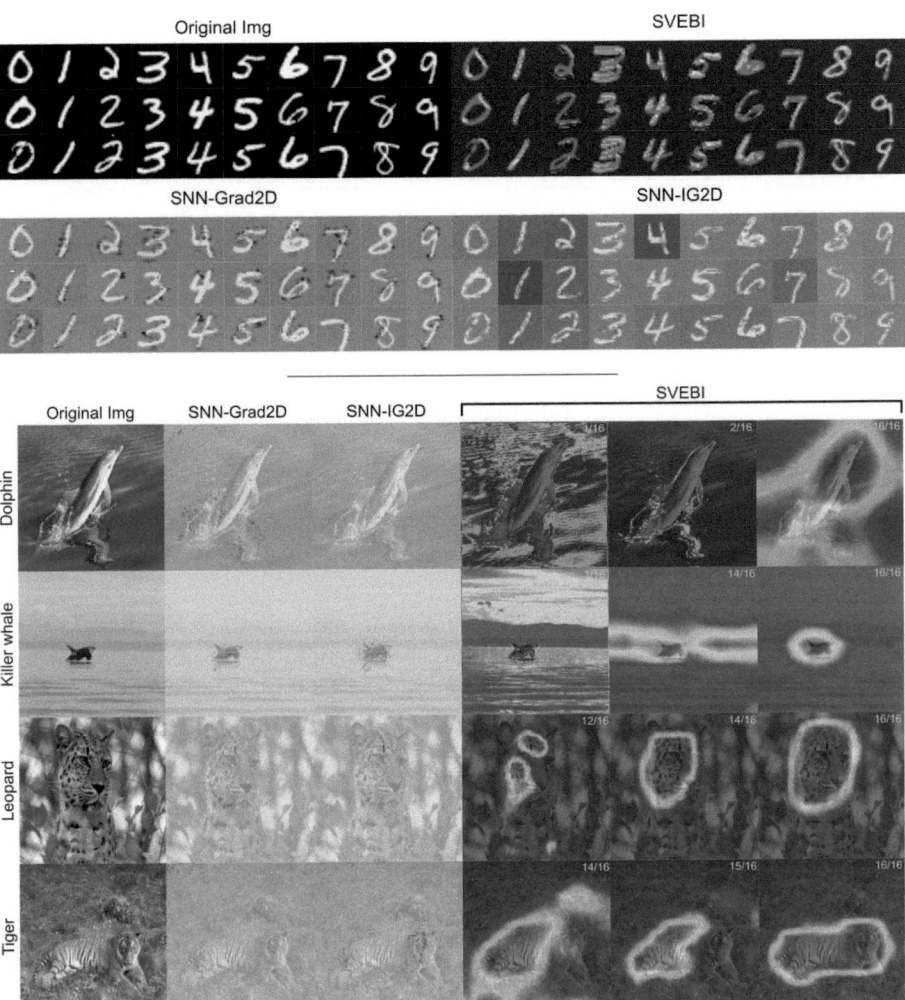

Fig. 5. Explanation heatmaps examples for a shallow SNN trained on MNIST (top) and SVGG19 trained on AwA2 (bottom). SVEBI Explanations for MNIST focus on layer 2 while those for AwA2 come from those where the relevant features/filters with highest activation are located.

important pixels that are more spread out, which lowers the model's ability to capture spatial information. This results in the model not being able to perform as well as opposed to when it is introduced with more smooth and continuous patches of pixels, which is the case for the SVEBI explanations. However, during the deletion procedure, the smoother nature of our explanation heatmaps cause the deletion of pixels to more likely focus on one region before moving to another location within the input image. Here, the sparsity of the explanations of the gradient-based methods enables a better exploration of the spatial

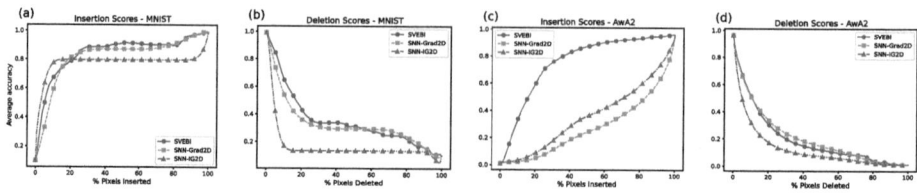

Fig. 6. Insertion/deletion scores for models trained on the MNIST (a,b) and AwA2 (c,d) datasets.

Table 1. Insertion and Deletion AUC scores over MNIST and AwA2 datasets.

Method	MNIST		AwA2	
	Insertion	Deletion	Insertion	Deletion
SNN-Grad2D	0.8199	0.3285	0.2752	0.2088
SNN-IG2D	0.7814	**0.1678**	0.3590	**0.1281**
SVEBI (ours)	**0.8459**	0.3516	**0.7582**	0.1969

extent of the image which results in attenuating more distinct regions. The difference between the results of MNIST and AwA2 could be attributed to the fact that for AwA2 we use a much deeper model (SVGG19) compared the shallow SNN used for MNIST. As the gradient-based methods use a surrogate gradient, the increased model depth could negatively affect the output explanations, as a deeper model requires additional operations when computing the surrogate gradients. This may increase the cumulative error arising from the use of surrogate gradients, which approximate the model's actual gradients. A more rigorous analysis is needed to validate this hypothesis, suggesting possible future research on the comparison of gradient-based and activation-based explanation methods in SNNs.

6 Limitations

For both the identification of relevant filters and the generation of explanatory heatmaps we obtain a single activation map per filter for each sample pushed through the network by performing an averaging operation over the time dimension. Here, we assume equal importance for each timestep which could cause loss of temporal information. Possible future work could include combining this averaging operation with some temporal weighting approach. In addition, we focus solely on 2D image classification, which suggests possible future directions for adapting SVEBI to classification/regression of neuromorphic datasets.

7 Conclusion

We proposed SVEBI, a method for the analysis of the representations learned by SNNs (model interpretability) and the explainability of the outputs they produce. Our results suggest that on the interpretation side, the proposed method is capable of accurately identifying the features learned by the SNN which are important for its decision-making process. On the explainability side, quantitatively-speaking, the explanations produced by SVEBI seem to be superior to those of existing methods. On the qualitative side, the visualizations produced by our method are denser and smooth compared to the sparse heatmaps produced by previous efforts. These results show the potential of SVEBI towards assisting the study of the internal workings of existing and future SNN models. This opens the door for deeper SNN studies regarding Bias Analysis, Fairness, and other aspects that are critical for the deployment of AI technology.

Acknowledgments. This work is supported by the UAntwerp BOF DOCPRO4-NZ Project (id 41612) "Multimodal Relational Interpretation for Deep Models".

Disclosure of Interests. The authors have no competing interests to declare that are relevant to the content of this article.

References

1. Akopyan, F., et al.: Truenorth: design and tool flow of a 65 mw 1 million neuron programmable neurosynaptic chip. IEEE Trans. Comput. Aided Des. Integr. Circuits Syst. **34**(10), 1537–1557 (2015)
2. Attwell, D., Laughlin, S.B.: An energy budget for signaling in the grey matter of the brain. J. Cerebral Blood Flow Metabolism **21**(10), 1133–1145 (2001)
3. Bhushan, C., Kamble: Speech recognition using artificial neural network – a review. Int. J. Comput., Commun. Instrument. Eng. **3** (2016)
4. Bitar, A., Rosales, R., Paulitsch, M.: Gradient-based feature-attribution explainability methods for spiking neural networks. Front. Neurosci. **17** (2023)
5. Carreira, J., Zisserman, A.: Quo vadis, action recognition? a new model and the kinetics dataset. In: CVPR (2017)
6. Cassidy, A.S., et al..: Real-time scalable cortical computing at 46 giga-synaptic ops/watt with 100× speedup in time-to-solution and 100,000× reduction in energy-to-solution. In: SC (2014)
7. Chattopadhay, A., Sarkar, A., Howlader, P., Balasubramanian, V.N.: Gradcam++: Generalized gradient-based visual explanations for deep convolutional networks. In: WACV (2018)
8. Chen, C., Li, O., Tao, C., Barnett, A.J., Su, J., Rudin, C.: This looks like that: deep learning for interpretable image recognition. In: CVPR (2019)
9. Davies, M., et al.: Loihi: a neuromorphic manycore processor with on-chip learning. IEEE Micro **38**(1), 82–99 (2018)
10. Deng, L.: The mnist database of handwritten digit images for machine learning research. IEEE Signal Process. Mag. **29**(6), 141–142 (2012)
11. Eshraghian, J.K., et al.: Training spiking neural networks using lessons from deep learning. In: Proceedings of the IEEE (2023)
12. Gomez, T., Fréour, T., Mouchère, H.: Metrics for saliency map evaluation of deep learning explanation methods. In: ICPRAI (2022)
13. Huang, J., Chai, J., Cho, S.: Deep learning in finance and banking: a literature review and classification. Front. Business Res. China **14** (12 2020)

14. Jung, H., Oh, Y.: Towards better explanations of class activation mapping. In: ICONIP (2023)
15. Kim, Y., Panda, P.: Revisiting batch normalization for training low-latency deep spiking neural networks from scratch. Front. Neurosci. **15** (2021)
16. Kim, Y., Panda, P.: Visual explanations from spiking neural networks using inter-spike intervals. Nature Scientific Reports (2021)
17. Krizhevsky, A., Sutskever, I., Hinton, G.E.: Imagenet classification with deep convolutional neural networks. In: NeurIPS (2012)
18. Lapicque, L.: Recherches quantitatives sur l'excitation électrique des nerfs traitée comme une polarisation. J. Physiol. Pathol. Gen. **9**, 620–635 (1907)
19. Malcolm, K., Casco-Rodriguez, J.: A comprehensive review of spiking neural networks: Interpretation, optimization, efficiency, and best practices. In: arXiv:2303.10780 (2023)
20. McCulloch, W.S., Pitts, W.: A logical calculus of the ideas immanent in nervous activity. Bull. Math. Biophys. **5**(4), 115–133 (1943)
21. Min, B., et al.: Recent advances in natural language processing via large pre-trained language models: a survey. ACM Comput. Surv. **56**(2) (2023)
22. Nauta, M., van Bree, R., Seifert, C.: Neural prototype trees for interpretable fine-grained image recognition. In: CVPR (2021)
23. Neftci, E.O., Mostafa, H., Zenke, F.: Surrogate gradient learning in spiking neural networks. IEEE Signal Process. Mag. **36** (2019)
24. Nguyen, E., Nauta, M., Englebienne, G., Seifert, C.: Feature attribution explanations for spiking neural networks. In: 2023 IEEE 5th International Conference on Cognitive Machine Intelligence, pp. 59–68 (2023)
25. Oramas, J., Wang, K., Tuytelaars, T.: Visual explanation by interpretation: Improving visual feedback capabilities of deep neural networks. In: ICLR (2019)
26. Paszke, A., Gross, S., Massa, F., Lerer, A., Bradbury, J., et al.: Pytorch: an imperative style, high-performance deep learning library. In: NeurIPS (2019)
27. Petsiuk, V., Das, A., Saenko, K.: Rise: Randomized input sampling for explanation of black-box models. In: BMVC (2018)
28. Plank, P., Rao, A., Wild, A., Maass, W.: A long short-term memory for ai applications in spike-based neuromorphic hardware. Nature Intelligence (2022)
29. Ribeiro, M.T., Singh, S., Guestrin, C.: "why should i trust you?": Explaining the predictions of any classifier. In: KDD (2016)
30. Rosenblatt, F.: The perceptron: a probabilistic model for information storage and organization in the brain. Psychol. Rev. **65**(6), 386–408 (1958)
31. Sanghvi, K., Aralkar, A., Sanghvi, S., Saha, I.: A survey on image classification techniques. SSRN Electron. J. (01 2021)
32. Selvaraju, R.R., Cogswell, M., Das, A., Vedantam, R., Parikh, D., Batra, D.: Gradcam: visual explanations from deep networks via gradient-based localization. Int. J. Comput. Vision **128**(2), 336–359 (2019)
33. Shahid, N., Rappon, T., Berta, W.B.: Applications of artificial neural networks in health care organizational decision-making: a scoping review. PLoS ONE **14** (2019)
34. Simonyan, K., Vedaldi, A., Zisserman, A.: Deep inside convolutional networks: Visualising image classification models and saliency maps. In: ICLR (2014)
35. Simonyan, K., Zisserman, A.: Very deep convolutional networks for large-scale image recognition. In: arXiv:1409.1556 (2014)
36. Sundararajan, M., Taly, A., Yan, Q.: Axiomatic attribution for deep networks. In: ICML (2017)

37. Tavanaei, A., Ghodrati, M., Kheradpisheh, S.R., Masquelier, T., Maida, A.S.: Deep learning in spiking neural networks. Neural Netw. **111** (2019)
38. Thompson, N.C., Greenewald, K., Lee, K., Manso, G.F.: The computational limits of deep learning. In: arXiv:2007.05558 (2022)
39. Tripp, C.E., Perr-Sauer, J., Gafur, J., Nag, A., Purkayastha, A., et al.: Measuring the energy consumption and efficiency of deep neural networks: an empirical analysis and design recommendations. In: arXiv:2403.08151 (2024)
40. Vaswani, A., et al.: Attention is all you need. In: NeurIPS (2017)
41. Vicente-Sola, A., Manna, D.L., Kirkland, P., Caterina, G., Bihl, T.: Keys to accurate feature extraction using residual spiking neural networks. Neuromorphic Comput. Eng. **2**(4), 044001 (2022)
42. Wang, Y., Su, H., Zhang, B., Hu, X.: Interpret neural networks by extracting critical subnetworks. IEEE Trans. Image Process. **29**, 6707–6720 (2020)
43. Xian, Y., Lampert, C.H., Schiele, B., Akata, Z.: Zero-shot learning-a comprehensive evaluation of the good, the bad and the ugly. IEEE Trans. Pattern Anal. Mach. Intell. **41**(9), 2251–2265 (2019)
44. Yamazaki, K., Vo-Ho, V.K., Bulsara, D., Le, N.T.H.: Spiking neural networks and their applications: a review. Brain Sci. **12** (2022)
45. Zambrano, D., Nusselder, R., Scholte, H.S., Bohté, S.M.: Sparse computation in adaptive spiking neural networks. Front. Neurosci. **12** (2019)
46. Zhang, Y., Chan, W., Jaitly, N.: Very deep convolutional networks for end-to-end speech recognition. In: ICASSP (2016)
47. Zhou, B., Khosla, A., Lapedriza, A., Oliva, A., Torralba, A.: Learning deep features for discriminative localization (2015)
48. Zhou, C., et al.: Spikingformer: Spike-driven residual learning for transformer-based spiking neural network. In: arXiv:2304.11954 (2023)

Towards Better Generalization and Interpretability in Unsupervised Concept-Based Models

Francesco De Santis[1](✉), Philippe Bich[1], Gabriele Ciravegna[1,2], Pietro Barbiero[3], Tania Cerquitelli[1], and Danilo Giordano[1]

[1] Politecnico di Torino, Torino 10129, Italy
{francesco.de.santis,philippe.bich,gabriele.ciravegna,tania.cerquitelli,
danilo.giordano}@polito.it
[2] CENTAI Institute, Torino 10138, Italy
gabriele.ciravegna@centai.eu
[3] Universita' della Svizzera Italiana, Lugano 6900, Switzerland
pietro.barbiero@usi.ch

Abstract. To increase the trustworthiness of deep neural networks, it is critical to improve the understanding of how they make decisions. This paper introduces a novel unsupervised concept-based model for image classification, named Learnable Concept-Based Model (LCBM) which models concepts as random variables within a Bernoulli latent space. Unlike traditional methods that either require extensive human supervision or suffer from limited scalability, our approach employs a reduced number of concepts without sacrificing performance. We demonstrate that LCBM surpasses existing unsupervised concept-based models in generalization capability and nearly matches the performance of black-box models. The proposed concept representation enhances information retention and aligns more closely with human understanding. A user study demonstrates the discovered concepts are also more intuitive for humans to interpret. Finally, despite the use of concept embeddings, we maintain model interpretability by means of a local linear combination of concepts.

Keywords: CBM · XAI · Interpretable AI

1 Introduction

Understanding the *reason* why Deep Neural Networks (DNNs) make decisions is critical in today's society, as these models are increasingly deployed and affect people's lives. This concern has also led regulatory institutions to mandate interpretability and the possibility of challenging the decisions of deep neural networks as prerequisites for Artificial Intelligence (AI)

Supplementary Information The online version contains supplementary material available at https://doi.org/10.1007/978-3-032-06066-2_28.

Systems [27,38]. EXplainable AI (XAI) methods have emerged to address this challenge [2,12,30]. However, several papers argue that feature importance explanations (such as saliency maps [33,45]) have failed to achieve this goal, since showing where a network is looking is insufficient to explain the reasons behind its decisions [1,31]. To truly explain what the network has seen, many XAI methods are shifting toward explanations in terms of human-understandable attributes, or *concepts* [1,10,14,28]. Concepts can be either extracted post-hoc [11] or directly inserted within the network representation to create a so-called concept-based model (CBMs, [16]).

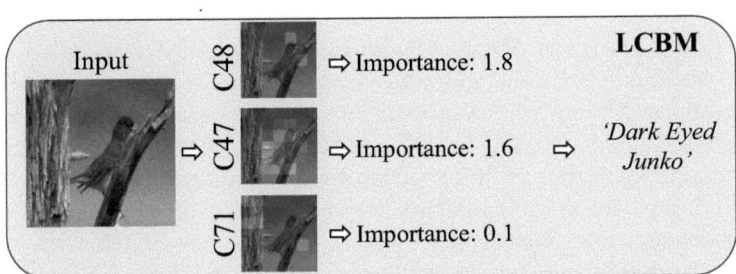

Fig. 1. Learnable Concept-Based Model (LCBM) learns a dictionary of unsupervised concepts. Unlike black-box models, LCBM classifies images interpretably using these concepts. Here, the image is correctly classified as *Dark-eyed junco* by leveraging concepts C48 (eyes/beak), C47 (wings), and C71 (trunk/tree). Notably, C71, while present, is less relevant to bird species classification.

CBMs can be created in a supervised way [4,8,16] or through a dedicated unsupervised learning process [3,6,40]. The latter approach enables the use of CBMs in contexts where concept annotations are unavailable and large language models (LLMs) [26,41] lack sufficient knowledge. Yet, a fundamental challenge persists: standard unsupervised approaches rely on single-neuron activations to represent each concept, thereby limiting the amount of information that can be captured. This limitation creates a trade-off between interpretability and accuracy. The issue becomes even more pronounced when concise explanations are needed to avoid cognitive overload for users [7,19,24]. As demonstrated in our experiments, standard unsupervised approaches exhibit a significant performance gap compared to end-to-end methods in such scenarios, making unsuitable their effective deployment. In this paper, we demonstrate that by using unsupervised concept embeddings, we can create a highly effective Learnable Concept-Based Model (LCBM) employing a limited number of concepts. Our experiments show that this approach: i) overcomes the limited generalization of compared models, almost matching the performance of black-box models; ii) increases the representation capability of standard unsupervised concept layers in terms of information retention and alignment with human representation; iii) ensures that the extracted concepts are more interpretable, as highlighted by a user study; and iv) by providing the task prediction through a local linear combination of concepts, it retains task interpretability[1].

2 Related Work

Concept-based XAI (C-XAI) aims to provide human-understandable explanations by using concepts as intermediate representations [14,28,31]. While supervised approaches [8,16] rely on predefined symbols, unsupervised models autonomously extract concepts by modifying a network's internal representation through unsupervised learning, prototypical representations, or hybrid techniques [3,16].

Unsupervised Concept Basis. These methods learn disentangled representations in the model's latent space by grouping samples based on fundamental characteristics. They typically achieve this via input reconstruction [3,40] or unsupervised losses [40,46]. In [46], convolutional filters act as unsupervised concepts, maximizing mutual information between images and filter activations. SENN [3] employs an autoencoder to derive clustered representations and generate class-concept relevance scores. BotCL [40] enhances SENN with attention-based concept scoring and contrastive loss. Compared to these, LCBM introduces concept embeddings for richer representations, improving the generalization-interpretability trade-off.

Prototype Concepts. This approach encodes training example traits as prototypes within the network, comparing them to input samples for prediction. [21] explains predictions via prototype similarity, using an autoencoder for dimensionality reduction. ProtoPNet [6] extracts prototypes representing image subparts, while HPNet [13] organizes prototypes hierarchically for classification across taxonomy levels. Despite providing useful example-based explanations, these models constrain representation capacity. Our approach enhances performance by leveraging richer representations while retaining prototype-based interpretability, as shown in concept dictionaries.

Hybrid Approaches. Recent research explores hybrid models that integrate supervised and unsupervised concepts [23,32] or leverage pre-trained LLMs [26,41,44]. The variational approach in [23] shares similarities with ours but relies on single neurons and partial supervision, limiting scalability. Methods leveraging LLMs assume sufficient knowledge for zero-shot concept annotations, yet this depends on the underlying model [35]. For instance, CLIP [29], despite its popularity, exhibits low concept accuracy even in contexts similar to its pre-training, as confirmed by our experiments.

3 Methodology

In an unsupervised concept-based setting, the objective is to make predictions using a set of abstract, human-interpretable concepts that are not predefined but

---
[1] Code to reproduce the proposed model is available at https://github.com/LCBM.

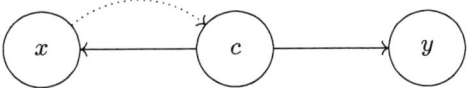

Fig. 2. Probabilistic Graphical Model. Solid arrows represent the data generating process. Dotted arrows represent inference.

must be directly inferred from the data. To address this challenge, we propose a set of desiderata that define the required properties of the learned concepts:

- *Representativity* [5]: Concepts should capture key features of the input data.
- *Completeness* [43]: Concepts should support strong task generalization.
- *Alignment* [28]: Concepts should correspond to human-understandable constructs.

If concepts do not accurately represent the input data, they cannot be trusted for either inference or explainability. As a result, *Representativity*, a common requirement in representation learning [5], is a necessary but not sufficient condition for an interpretable unsupervised concept-based model: *Completeness* is also essential to ensure the concepts are useful for making task-specific predictions. Ultimately, interpretability is achieved only with an *Alignment* with a human-defined representation. While this property is always met in supervised CBMs, in unsupervised contexts it is a major challenge.

3.1 Learnable Concept-Based Model

In a supervised learning context, a CBM is trained to approximate the joint distribution $p(x, c, y)$, where x, c, and y correspond to realizations of the random variables X (images), C (concepts), and Y (class labels), respectively. In contrast to the supervised setting, where these variables are fully observable during training, the unsupervised scenario lacks knowledge about C. Therefore, it is only through marginalizing over C that we can account for the combined effect of all possible values of C on the relationship between X and Y:

$$p(x,y) = \int_c p(x,c,y)\,dc \qquad (1)$$

In order to address this problem, we introduce the Learnable Concept-Based Model (LCBM), a latent variable model enabling explanations and interventions in terms of a set of unsupervised concepts. Following [25], LCBM considers a data generating process in which concepts C represent latent factors of variation for both X and Y, as shown in the probabilistic graphical model in Fig. 2. Thus, the joint distribution factorizes as:

$$p(x,y) = \int_c p(x,c,y)dc = \int_c p(x\mid c)p(y\mid c)p(c)dc \qquad (2)$$

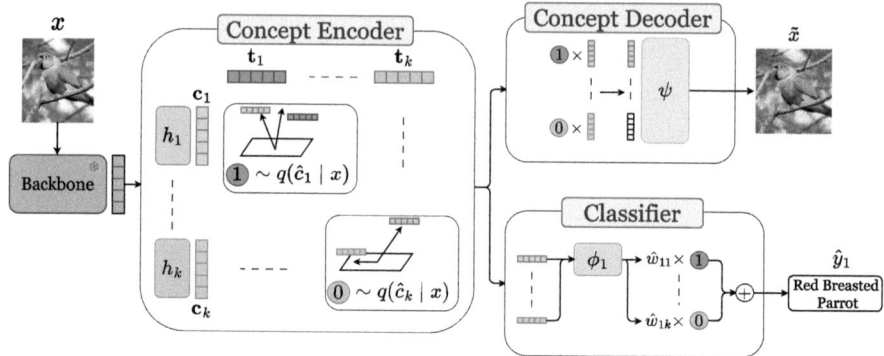

Fig. 3. LCBM schema. The concept encoder $q(c \mid x)$ provides the probability for each learnt concept $\hat{c}_j$ and the associated embeddings $\mathbf{c}_j$. Both concept scores and embeddings are used to predict the output class $p(y \mid c)$ and to reconstruct the input $p(x \mid c)$.

where $p(y \mid c)$ is modelled as a categorical distribution parametrized by the task predictor f; $p(x \mid c)$ as a Gaussian distribution parametrized by the concept decoder ψ. Finally, $p(c)$ is a prior distribution over a set of unsupervised concepts.

During training, LCBM assumes to observe realizations of the random variables X and Y which hold new evidence we can use to update the prior $p(c)$. Since the computation of the true posterior $p(c \mid x, y)$ is intractable, LCBM amortizes inference needed for training by introducing an approximate posterior $q(c \mid x)$ parametrized by a neural network. Since at test time we can only observe X, we condition the approximate only on this variable.

Optimization Problem. LCBMs are trained to optimize the log-likelihood of tuples (x, y). Following a variational inference approach, we optimize the evidence lower bound (ELBO) of the log-likelihood, which results as follows:

$$\text{ELBO} = \overbrace{E_q[\log p(x|c)]}^{\text{Representativity}} + \overbrace{E_q[\log p(y|c)]}^{\text{Completeness}} - \overbrace{KL(q(c|x) \parallel p(c))}^{\text{Alignment}} \quad (3)$$

This likelihood has three components: a reconstruction term $p(x|c)$, whose maximization ensures concepts' *Representativity*; a classifier $p(y \mid c)$, which quantifies concepts' *Completeness*; and a KullbackLeibler divergence term that encourages the approximate posterior $q(c \mid x)$ to remain close to a defined prior $p(c)$, promoting an *Alignment* to human representations. To achieve all the desired properties, we must define a sufficiently rich concept representation. We describe the latter together with its prior in Sect. 3.2, the classifier in Sect. 3.3 and the decoder in Sect. 3.4. For an overall visualization of LCBM, see Fig. 3.

3.2 Unsupervised Concept Representation

To model each concept in the concept representation c in an unsupervised way, we define it as following a Bernoulli distribution. This choice reflects a discrete, binary nature of a 'concept' as an atomic unit of knowledge, inducing *Alignment* and facilitating its comprehension and modification through human interventions. However, Bernoulli distributions may not be able to represent both the input and output distributions, ultimately creating a bottleneck in the representation of the model.

To solve this issue, we associate each concept with a corresponding unsupervised concept embedding $\mathbf{c}_j \in \mathbf{C} \subseteq \mathbb{R}^d$. This embedding provides a richer representation of the concept, capturing further nuances (e.g., 'color' and 'size' if the concept represents a 'vehicle'). The concept embedding $\mathbf{c}_j$ is derived as a composition of two neural modules $h \circ g$. The latter is a frozen pre-trained backbone $g : X \to E$ mapping input X into an intermediate embedding space $E \subseteq \mathbb{R}^s$, while the first module, $h_j : E \to \mathbf{C}$, is a per-concept MLP producing the concept embedding $\mathbf{c}_j = h_j(g(x))$. To ensure that this embedding is representative of the intended concept and allows interventions, we assign each concept a prototype $\mathbf{t}_j \in \mathbb{R}^d$, which serves as a learned reference within the embedding space of $\mathbf{c}_j$. To compute the concept score $\hat{c}_j$, we first calculate the alignment between the concept embedding $\mathbf{c}_j$ and its prototype $\mathbf{t}_j$ through their dot product $\mathbf{c}_j \cdot \mathbf{t}_j$, and transform it into a probability $\pi_j = \sigma(\mathbf{c}_j \cdot \mathbf{t}_j) \in [0, 1]$ via a sigmoid function σ. Using π_j as the probability parameter, we sample from a Bernoulli distribution applying the reparametrization trick [22] to obtain the concept score $\hat{c}_j$. Thus, the final concept score is sampled from the following distribution:

$$\hat{c}_j \sim q(\hat{c}_j \mid x) = \text{Bern}(\hat{c}_j; \pi_j) \cdot p(\mathbf{c}_j \mid x), \qquad (4)$$

where $p(\mathbf{c}_j \mid x)$ is the probability distribution parametrized by $h(g(x))$ and can be modelled either via Gaussian distributions [15], or through a degenerate Dirac delta distribution, without assuming any uncertainty. For the sake of simplicity, we choose the second approach.

Batch Prior Regularization. The parameter α parameterizes the Bernoulli prior in the KL term of Eq. 3, and determines the activation probability of each concept for every sample. It is fundamental to optimize KL divergence over a batch of sample rather than for each sample. Indeed, by setting $\alpha = 0.2$, and performing the optimization for each sample, we force each concept to activate for each sample with 20% confidence. This behaviour is far from optimal as we want LCBM to be sure about the presence or absence of a certain concept in a specific sample, i.e., producing $\pi_j \approx 1$ for a sample which contains a specific concept and $\pi_j \approx 0$ otherwise. To address this, we shift the KL divergence optimization at the batch level by averaging the activation probabilities for a concept j across the batch: $\bar{\pi}_j = \frac{1}{B}\sum_{z=1}^{B}\pi_{jz}$, where B is the batch size.

3.3 Interpretable Classifier

The classifier $f(\mathbf{c}, \hat{c})$ leverages both concept embeddings and concept scores to boost prediction accuracy without sacrificing interpretability. Specifically, each class prediction $\hat{y}_i$ is represented as a linear combination of concept scores $\hat{c}_j$

and associated weights $\hat{w}_{ij} \in \mathbb{R}$, where the weights are predicted over the concept embedding, i.e., $\hat{w}_{ij} = \phi_i(\mathbf{c}_j)$, and ϕ_i is a class-specific function parameterized by a neural network. The output prediction $\hat{y}$ is then computed as $\hat{y} = \underset{i}{\mathrm{argmax}}\, p(y_i|c) = \underset{i}{\mathrm{argmax}} \sum_j \hat{w}_{ij} \cdot \hat{c}_{ij}$. Note that $\hat{w}_{ij}$ depends on the concept embedding $\mathbf{c}_j = g(x)$ predicted for a specific sample. This means that while the final prediction is provided by means of a linear classification over the concept scores, thus preserving locally the interpretability of standard CBMs, the network ϕ can predict different weights $\hat{w}_{mj}$ for different samples, thus overcoming the representation bottleneck of standard CBMs.

3.4 Concept Decoder

As previously introduced, we parametrize the decoding function with a neural network ψ. To improve the image reconstruction capabilities, also in this case we rely on the concept embeddings $\mathbf{c}$. However, to still take into account the associated concept predictions $\hat{c}$, we multiply the embeddings $\mathbf{c_j}$ by the corresponding concept prediction $\hat{c}_j$ before feeding them to the concept decoder. As a result, the input is reconstructed as $\hat{x} = \psi(\hat{c} \cdot \mathbf{c})$.

4 Experiments

In this section, we present the experiments conducted to evaluate our proposed methodology. The experiments are designed to address the following key research questions:

1. **Generalization:** How effectively does the model generalize for classification tasks? Is the concept representation *complete*?
2. **Concept Representation Evaluation:** How much information is captured from c with respect to both the input image x and the label y? Are the learnt concepts *representative* of the data?
3. **Concept Interpretability:** How interpretable are the learnt concepts produced? Are they *aligned* with human representations?
4. **Model Interpretability:** Are the final predictions interpretable in terms of the discovered concepts? Can a user modify the concept prediction to extract counterfactual predictions?

4.1 Experimental Setting

In the following we report the dataset, metrics and baselines that we consider for evaluating and comparing our model. We conducted experiments using two backbones g: ResNet-18 and ViT-base-patch32. Instead, we always use a decoder ψ composed by five transposed convolutional layers.

Dataset. This study uses seven image classification datasets of varying complexity. We employ two MNIST [20] variants, *Even/Odd* (digit parity) and *Addition*

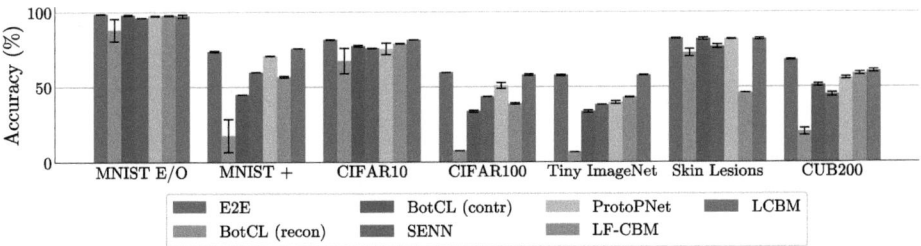

Fig. 4. Comparison of the generalization performance across the evaluated datasets. LCBM consistently provides the highest generalization accuracy across concept-based models, closing the gap with end-to-end black box ones.

(paired digits summed as labels). *CIFAR-10* and *CIFAR-100* contain 10 and 100 natural image classes, with models extracting 15 and 20 macro-class concepts, respectively [17]. *Tiny ImageNet* includes 200 classes but is tested on 30 concepts for added challenge [42]. *Skin Lesions* classifies dermatoscopic images into 4 macro categories [37]. Finally, *CUB-200* [39] covers 200 bird species with species and attribute annotations.

Metrics. We use specific metrics to address each research question. All results are reported with the mean and standard deviation, computed over the test sets by repeating the experiments with three different initialization seeds.

1. **Generalization:** To assess the classification generalization performance, we compute the *Task Accuracy*.
2. **Concept Representation Evaluation:** We employ the *Information Plane* approach [36] to analyze the information retained in the different concept representations. The information plane reports the evolution of the mutual information between the concept representation and both the input x ($I(C, X)$) and the label y ($I(C, Y)$) as the training epoch increases. For models reconstructing the input from the concepts, we assess the *Input Reconstruction Error* by computing the Mean Squared Error (MSE) between the inputs x and their reconstructions $\hat{x}$.
3. **Concept Interpretability:** For datasets with annotated concepts, we assess their alignment with the learnt concepts using the macro *Concept F1 Score* (best-match approach) and the *Concept Alignment Score (CAS)* [8] for concept representation alignment. Additionally, we conducted a user study with 72 participants, each answering 18 questions. The study evaluated *Plausibility* by asking users to (i) select an image that best represents a given concept and (ii) identify an intruder image among those representing a single concept. It also assessed *Human Understanding* by having participants assign a name to a set of images illustrating a concept. Finally, we provide qualitative insights through *Concept Dictionaries*, showcasing images with the strongest activations for each concept.
4. **Model Interpretability:** We perform *Concept Interventions* [16] to observe how model predictions change when concept predictions are modified. As posi-

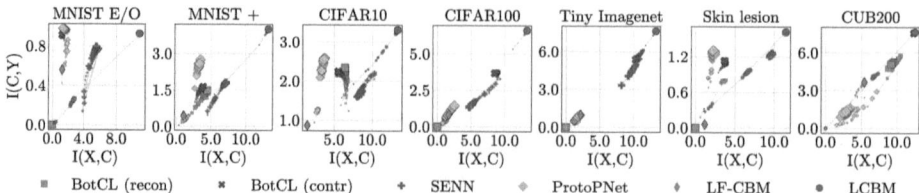

Fig. 5. Information Plane for the different models in terms of Mutual information between concept and input variables $I(X, C)$, and between the concept and output variables $I(C, Y)$. The size of the markers is proportional to the training epoch.

Table 1. We report the Input Reconstruction Error in terms of MSE for those methods that explicitly reconstruct the input.

	MNIST E/O	MNIST Add.	CIFAR10	CIFAR100	Tiny ImageNet	Skin Lesion	CUB200
BotCL	1.40 ± 0.09	1.57 ± 0.03	0.87 ± 0.02	0.82 ± 0.01	1.35 ± 0.06	0.72 ± 0.02	0.07 ± 0.01
SENN	0.62 ± 0.02	0.93 ± 0.03	0.81 ± 0.04	0.74 ± 0.01	1.10 ± 0.02	0.61 ± 0.04	0.05 ±≤0.01
LCBM	**0.32±≤0.01**	**0.71±0.11**	**0.51±≤0.01**	**0.55±≤0.01**	**0.72±≤0.01**	**0.32±≤0.01**	**0.05±≤0.01**

tive concept interventions are non-trivial in unsupervised concept settings, we perform negative interventions [8]. Negative interventions involve randomly swapping the values of the concept scores with a given probability, expecting model accuracy to decrease as intervention probability increases. For LCBM, to switch a concept to inactive, we set $\hat{c}_j = 0$, while to activate it, we set $\hat{c}_j = 1$ and replace the concept embedding with the concept prototype $\bar{c}_j = \mathbf{t_j}$. Additionally, we provide *Qualitative Explanations* generated by LCBM using as concept importances the predicted weights multiplied by the concept predictions $w_{ij} \cdot \hat{c}_j$.

Baselines. To compare the performance of the proposed approach, we test it against unsupervised approaches like *SENN* [3] and two variants of a SOTA model BotCL [40]: *BotCL (Recon)*, which employs an autoencoder-based approach to reconstruct the input image from the concept bottleneck, and *BotCL (Contr)*, which applies a contrastive term to the loss to encourage distinct concept activations for different classes. Also, we consider a prototype based approach *ProtoPNet* [6] and Label-Free CBM (LF-CBM) [26] a recent hybrid approach. If the concepts were known (e.g., MNIST Addition), we used CLIP to align the model with concept captions (e.g., this image contains the digit 4). If the concepts were unknown, we used the LLM to generate a list of possible concepts. Finally, we compare with a standard black-box model trained end-to-end (E2E).

4.2 Generalization

LCBM is the most accurate interpretable model (Fig. 4). The proposed methodology significantly outperforms the baselines. In the most challenging scenario (Tiny ImageNet with only 30 concepts), it achieves up to a 50% increase in task accuracy compared to the worst baseline (BotCL (recon)) and up to a 17% improvement over the runner-up model, ProtoPNet. Our model consistently delivers the best generalization accuracy across all datasets, with higher gaps in challenging gaps with lower concept-class ratios. This result is valid even when we compare LCBM with LF-CBM which exploit the pre-existing knowledge within a VLM to extract concept annotations. Only in the very simple MNIST Even/Odd dataset a few methods perform better, by a few decimals. We attribute this improvement to the unsupervised concept embeddings, which allows learning more *complete* representations for task prediction.

LCBM closes the gap with black-box models (Fig. 4). Figure 4 also shows that LCBM achieves results comparable to the E2E black-box model. The generalization loss is always less than 1–2%. Notably, on the MNIST addition dataset, a setting where reasoning capabilities over concepts are required, our approach outperforms the black-box model with a task accuracy improvement of 2%. Overall, LCBM demonstrates its capability to achieve high interpretability without sacrificing accuracy in unsupervised concept learning settings.

4.3 Concept Representation Evaluation

LCBM concept representation retains more information regarding both the input and the output (Fig. 5). The concept representation obtained through unsupervised concept embedding is significantly richer than that derived from simple concept scores. As training progresses, most baselines experience a reduction in mutual information with the input $I(X, C)$ while increasing the mutual information with the output $I(Y, C)$. This observation supports the conclusion that unsupervised CBM models tend to lose input-related information while attempting to optimize task performance [34], even for those models that explicitly require concepts to be representative of the input, such as SENN and BotCL (Recon). On the contrary, LCBM overcome this limitation by means of concept embeddings, which facilitate a better balance between competing objectives, as evidenced by the monotonic increase in mutual information with both the input and output during training.

LCBM allows better input reconstruction (Table 1). To understand why the mutual information $I(X, C)$ of LCBM is consistently higher compared to other reconstruction-based unsupervised CBMs, we assess the Input Reconstruction Error in terms of MSE. As shown in Table 1, LCBM achieves lower MSE in image reconstruction compared to the runner-up model (usually SENN), with values ranging from 0.18 to 0.38. We believe that concept embeddings facilitate more accurate and efficient reconstruction by allowing more information to flow to the decoder network when a concept is active ($\hat{c}_j = 1$). Unlike other unsupervised models that can only pass a single value ($\hat{c}_j$), LCBM passes the entire associated concept embedding ($\bar{c}_j$) to the decoder.

Table 2. Macro F1-score for candidate concepts with respect to existing human-representations for datasets on which the latter are available.

	MNIST E/O	MNIST Add.	CIFAR100	Skin	CUB200
BotCL (recon)	0.47 ± 0.01	0.41 ± 0.01	0.38 ± 0.03	0.47 ± 0.02	0.34± 0.01
BotCL (contr)	0.47 ± 0.02	0.45 ± 0.02	0.40 ± 0.04	0.44 ± 0.03	0.37± 0.02
SENN	0.61 ± 0.02	0.58 ± 0.01	0.44 ± 0.02	0.52 ± 0.02	0.41± 0.02
ProtoPNet	0.26 ± 0.01	0.24 ± 0.01	0.31 ± 0.01	0.16 ± 0.02	0.28± 0.03
LF-CBM	0.52± 0.01	0.50 ± 0.03	0.45 ± 0.01	0.58 ± 0.01	0.45 ± 0.01
LCBM (ours)	**0.88±0.08**	**0.81±0.04**	**0.60±≤0.01**	**0.58±≤0.01**	**0.55±≤0.01**

Fig. 6. Tiny-Imagenet dictionary produced by LCBM. Each column of images represents the set of 7 images that mostly activate each concept. Concept numbers are reported on top of each column.

4.4 Concept Interpretability

LCBM concepts are more aligned to human-defined representations (Table 2). For datasets with human-defined concept representations, we evaluate the alignment between these representations and those extracted by the compared concept learning methods. In Table 2, we observe that LCBM learns concepts that are significantly more aligned with human-defined representations than existing methods. After matching the concept predictions with the concept annotations using the Hungarian algorithm [18], LCBM achieves an F1 score that is up to +0.36 higher than the runner-up, which is always LF-CBM. We remind, however, that this model has a huge intrinsic advantage, as the employed VLM is prompted to predict the concepts of each datasets. The fact that LCBM without any concept supervision achieves higher concept F1 scores than LF-CBM is impressive, but consistent with recent literature reporting poor LF-CBM concept accuracy [35].

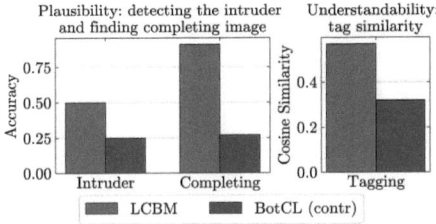 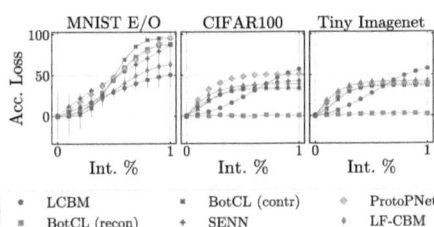

Fig. 7. User study results. Left, user accuracy in detecting the intruder image and the image completing a set of images representing a concept. Right, the similarity of the tags employed by users to describe an extracted concept.

Fig. 8. Negative interventions: percentage accuracy loss when increasing the intervention probability. The higher the accuracy loss, the higher the sensitivity of the model to human interventions.

LCBM concepts are qualitatively distinguishable (Fig. 6). While we quantitatively demonstrated that the LCBM concepts align with those of datasets equipped with annotations, for datasets lacking annotations, we examine the dictionaries representing the images that most strongly activate each concept, as proposed in [3]. Figure 6 presents the dictionary generated by the model for the Tiny ImageNet dataset. Each column (concept) exhibits a recurring and distinguishable pattern. For example, concept $C0$ encompasses images of flowers and plants, whereas $C2$ appears to correspond to long, slender objects. Concept $C4$ includes large mammals such as bison and bears, while $C7$ represents close-up images of small animals.

LCBM concepts are more plausible and understandable to humans (Fig. 7). To quantitatively assess the quality of the representations, we conducted a user study comparing the plausibility and human-understandability of the concept extracted by our method and BotCL the SOTA baseline for unsupervised concept learning. Figure 7 shows that LCBM concepts enable users to find the intruder image and to complete the set of images much better than BotCL concepts, with an accuracy up to +25% in terms of finding the right intruder image and up to +64% in terms of selecting the completing image. Also, when assessing the understandability of the concepts we see a higher similarity up to +.35 of the embeddings of the terms employed to tag the concepts provided by LCBM than those of BotCL. The embeddings are generated using the multilingual sentence encoder "all-MiniLM-L6-v2".

4.5 Model Interpretability

LCBM is sensitive to concept interventions (Fig. 8). Figure 8 shows that our methodology responds to interventions similarly to other baselines, except MNIST Even-Odd, where the precision drops only to 50%. In all other datasets,

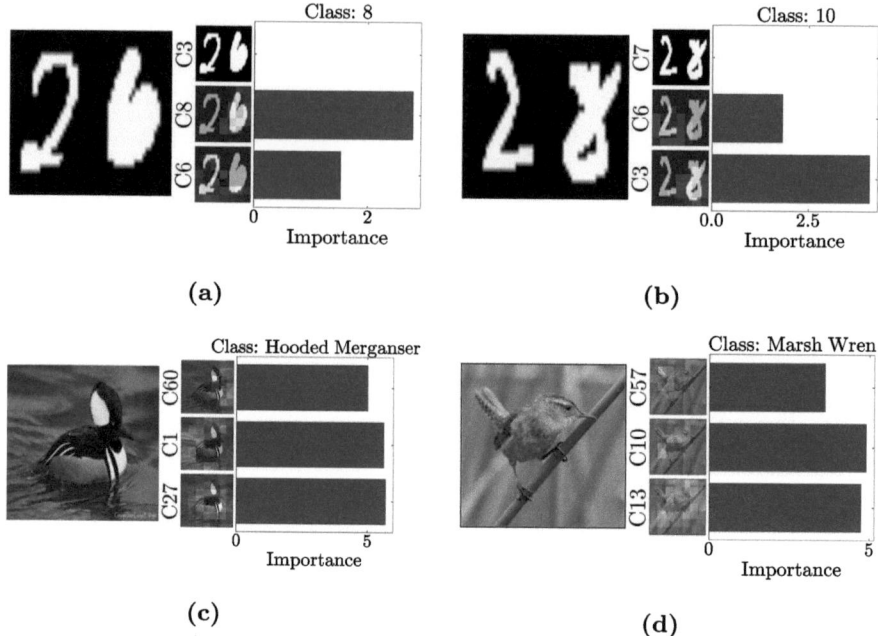

Fig. 9. Example of interpretable prediction on different datasets. We provide the concept importance together with the Grad-CAM for the most important concepts.

concept interventions are effective, with LCBM generally experiencing one of the highest accuracy losses when fully intervened, particularly on CIFAR100 and Tiny ImageNet. This is notable since embedding-based supervised CBMs typically resist interventions and require specialized training [9], whereas LCBM does not, suggesting its potential for more effective interventions in supervised settings.

LCBM provides interpretable predictions (Fig. 9). Finally, we present sample explanations generated by LCBM. As illustrated in Fig. 9.a, the image contains a "two" and a "six," with the model correctly predicting the sum as eight. The model identifies concepts $C6$ and $C8$ as important, which correspond to the learned concepts "two" and "six", and further validated by the Grad-CAM results (shown on the y-axis), highlighting the respective digits in the image. Concept $C3$, which does not appear in the image, has an importance value of 0. Figure 9.c illustrates how an image of a bird is classified as a Hooded Merganser based on a triplet of concepts: $C27$ focuses on the orange wing, $C1$ on the crest extending from the back of the head, and $C60$ on the black beak.

5 Conclusion

This paper introduced a novel unsupervised concept learning model that leverages unsupervised concept embeddings. This approach enables improved generalization accuracy compared to traditional unsupervised Concept-Based Models (CBMs), while also enhancing the representation of concepts. Our experiments demonstrate that the extracted concepts better represent the input data and align more closely with human representations, as evidenced by the F1-score metric, CAS, and the findings from the user study.

Limitations and Future work. The first limitation of this work lies in the employed CNN decoder. While it helps extract meaningful unsupervised concept representations, it struggles to effectively decode the learned concepts. While our model reduces the human effort in understanding learned concepts, some manual inspection is still required. Vision Language Models (VLMs) could help fully automate concept labeling by using representative images, but this approach may be less effective in contexts where VLMs lack knowledge, which is the primary area of application for unsupervised CBMs. Finally, our experiments have been limited to image classification tasks. Extending the model to generative tasks presents a challenge and could be explored in future work.

References

1. Achtibat, R., et al.: From attribution maps to human-understandable explanations through concept relevance propagation. Nature Mach. Intell. **5**(9), 1006–1019 (2023)
2. Adadi, A., Berrada, M.: Peeking inside the black-box: a survey on explainable artificial intelligence (xai). IEEE access **6**, 52138–52160 (2018)
3. Alvarez Melis, D., Jaakkola, T.: Towards robust interpretability with self-explaining neural networks. In: Advances in Neural Information Processing Systems, vol. 31 (2018)
4. Barbiero, P., Ciravegna, G., Giannini, F., Lió, P., Gori, M., Melacci, S.: Entropy-based logic explanations of neural networks. In: Proceedings of the AAAI Conference on Artificial Intelligence. vol. 36, pp. 6046–6054 (2022)
5. Bengio, Y., Courville, A., Vincent, P.: Representation learning: a review and new perspectives. IEEE Trans. Pattern Anal. Mach. Intell. **35**(8), 1798–1828 (2013)
6. Chen, C., Li, O., Tao, D., Barnett, A., Rudin, C., Su, J.K.: This looks like that: deep learning for interpretable image recognition. Adv. Neural Inform. Process. Syst. **32** (2019)
7. Ciravegna, G., et al.: Logic explained networks. Artif. Intell. **314**, 103822 (2023)
8. Espinosa Zarlenga, M., et al.: Concept embedding models: Beyond the accuracy-explainability trade-off. In: Koyejo, S., Mohamed, S., Agarwal, A., Belgrave, D., Cho, K., Oh, A. (eds.) Advances in Neural Information Processing Systems. vol. 35, pp. 21400–21413. Curran Associates, Inc. (2022)
9. Espinosa Zarlenga, M., Collins, K., Dvijotham, K., Weller, A., Shams, Z., Jamnik, M.: Learning to receive help: Intervention-aware concept embedding models. In: Advances in Neural Information Processing Systems, vol. 36 (2024)

10. Fel, T., et al.: Craft: Concept recursive activation factorization for explainability. In: Proceedings of the IEEE/CVF Conference on Computer Vision and Pattern Recognition, pp. 2711–2721 (2023)
11. Ghorbani, A., Wexler, J., Zou, J.Y., Kim, B.: Towards automatic concept-based explanations. In: Advances in Neural Information Processing Systems, vol. 32 (2019)
12. Guidotti, R., Monreale, A., Ruggieri, S., Turini, F., Giannotti, F., Pedreschi, D.: A survey of methods for explaining black box models. ACM Comput. Surv. (CSUR) **51**(5), 1–42 (2018)
13. Hase, P., Chen, C., Li, O., Rudin, C.: Interpretable image recognition with hierarchical prototypes. In: Proceedings of the AAAI Conference on Human Computation and Crowdsourcing, vol. 7, pp. 32–40 (2019)
14. Kim, B., Wattenberg, M., Gilmer, J., Cai, C., Wexler, J., Viegas, F., et al.: Interpretability beyond feature attribution: Quantitative testing with concept activation vectors (tcav). In: International Conference on Machine Learning, pp. 2668–2677. PMLR (2018)
15. Kim, E., Jung, D., Park, S., Kim, S., Yoon, S.: Probabilistic concept bottleneck models. In: Proceedings of the 40th International Conference on Machine Learning. ICML'23, JMLR.org (2023)
16. Koh, P.W., Nguyen, T., Tang, Y.S., Mussmann, S., Pierson, E., Kim, B., Liang, P.: Concept bottleneck models. In: International Conference on Machine Learning, pp. 5338–5348. PMLR (2020)
17. Krizhevsky, A., et al.: Learning multiple layers of features from tiny images (2009)
18. Kuhn, H.W.: The hungarian method for the assignment problem. Naval Res. Logist. Quart. **2**(1–2), 83–97 (1955)
19. Lakkaraju, H., Kamar, E., Caruana, R., Leskovec, J.: Faithful and customizable explanations of black box models. In: Proceedings of the 2019 AAAI/ACM Conference on AI, Ethics, and Society, pp. 131–138 (2019)
20. Lecun, Y., Bottou, L., Bengio, Y., Haffner, P.: Gradient-based learning applied to document recognition. Proc. IEEE **86**(11), 2278–2324 (1998). https://doi.org/10.1109/5.726791
21. Li, O., Liu, H., Chen, C., Rudin, C.: Deep learning for case-based reasoning through prototypes: A neural network that explains its predictions. In: Proceedings of the AAAI Conference on Artificial Intelligence, vol. 32 (2018)
22. Maddison, C.J., Mnih, A., Teh, Y.W.: The concrete distribution: a continuous relaxation of discrete random variables. In: International Conference on Learning Representations (2022)
23. Marconato, E., Passerini, A., Teso, S.: Glancenets: interpretable, leak-proof concept-based models. Adv. Neural. Inf. Process. Syst. **35**, 21212–21227 (2022)
24. Miller, G.A.: The magical number seven, plus or minus two: some limits on our capacity for processing information. Psychol. Rev. **63**(2), 81 (1956)
25. Misino, E., Marra, G., Sansone, E.: Vael: bridging variational autoencoders and probabilistic logic programming. Adv. Neural. Inf. Process. Syst. **35**, 4667–4679 (2022)
26. Oikarinen, T., Das, S., Nguyen, L.M., Weng, T.W.: Label-free concept bottleneck models. In: The Eleventh International Conference on Learning Representations (2023). https://openreview.net/forum?id=FlCg47MNvBA
27. Panigutti, C., et al.: The role of explainable AI in the context of the AI act. In: Proceedings of the 2023 ACM Conference on Fairness, Accountability, and Transparency, pp. 1139–1150 (2023)

28. Poeta, E., Ciravegna, G., Pastor, E., Cerquitelli, T., Baralis, E.: Concept-based explainable artificial intelligence: a survey. arXiv preprint arXiv:2312.12936 (2023)
29. Radford, A., et al.: Learning transferable visual models from natural language supervision. In: International Conference on Machine Learning, pp. 8748–8763. PMLR (2021)
30. Ribeiro, M.T., Singh, S., Guestrin, C.: " why should i trust you?" explaining the predictions of any classifier. In: Proceedings of the 22nd ACM SIGKDD International Conference On Knowledge Discovery and Data Mining, pp. 1135–1144 (2016)
31. Rudin, C.: Stop explaining black box machine learning models for high stakes decisions and use interpretable models instead. Nature Mach. Intell. **1**(5), 206–215 (2019)
32. Sawada, Y., Nakamura, K.: Concept bottleneck model with additional unsupervised concepts. IEEE Access **10**, 41758–41765 (2022)
33. Selvaraju, R.R., Cogswell, M., Das, A., Vedantam, R., Parikh, D., Batra, D.: Gradcam: visual explanations from deep networks via gradient-based localization. In: Proceedings of the IEEE International Conference on Computer Vision, pp. 618–626 (2017)
34. Shwartz-Ziv, R., Tishby, N.: Opening the black box of deep neural networks via information. arXiv preprint arXiv:1703.00810 (2017)
35. Srivastava, D., Yan, G., Weng, L.: Vlg-cbm: training concept bottleneck models with vision-language guidance. Adv. Neural. Inf. Process. Syst. **37**, 79057–79094 (2024)
36. Tishby, N., Pereira, F.C., Bialek, W.: The information bottleneck method. arXiv preprint physics/0004057 (2000)
37. Tschandl, P., Rosendahl, C., Kittler, H.: The ham10000 dataset, a large collection of multi-source dermatoscopic images of common pigmented skin lesions. Sc. Data **5**(1), 1–9 (2018)
38. Veale, M., Zuiderveen Borgesius, F.: Demystifying the draft eu artificial intelligence act–analysing the good, the bad, and the unclear elements of the proposed approach. Comput. Law Rev. Int. **22**(4), 97–112 (2021)
39. Wah, C., Branson, S., Welinder, P., Perona, P., Belongie, S.: The caltech-ucsd birds-200-2011 dataset. Tech. Rep. CNS-TR-2011-001, California Institute of Technology (2011)
40. Wang, B., Li, L., Nakashima, Y., Nagahara, H.: Learning bottleneck concepts in image classification. In: Proceedings of the IEEE/CVF Conference on Computer Vision and Pattern Recognition, pp. 10962–10971 (2023)
41. Yang, Y., Panagopoulou, A., Zhou, S., Jin, D., Callison-Burch, C., Yatskar, M.: Language in a bottle: Language model guided concept bottlenecks for interpretable image classification. In: Proceedings of the IEEE/CVF Conference on Computer Vision and Pattern Recognition, pp. 19187–19197 (2023)
42. Yao, L., Miller, J.: Tiny imagenet classification with convolutional neural networks. CS 231N **2**(5), 8 (2015)
43. Yeh, C.K., Kim, B., Arik, S., Li, C.L., Pfister, T., Ravikumar, P.: On completeness-aware concept-based explanations in deep neural networks. Adv. Neural. Inf. Process. Syst. **33**, 20554–20565 (2020)
44. Yuksekgonul, M., Wang, M., Zou, J.: Post-hoc concept bottleneck models. In: ICLR 2022 Workshop on PAIR2Struct: Privacy, Accountability, Interpretability, Robustness, Reasoning on Structured Data (2022). https://openreview.net/forum?id=HAMeOIRD_g9

45. Zeiler, M.D., Fergus, R.: Visualizing and understanding convolutional networks. In: Fleet, D., Pajdla, T., Schiele, B., Tuytelaars, T. (eds.) ECCV 2014. LNCS, vol. 8689, pp. 818–833. Springer, Cham (2014). https://doi.org/10.1007/978-3-319-10590-1_53
46. Zhang, Q., Wu, Y.N., Zhu, S.C.: Interpretable convolutional neural networks. In: Proceedings of the IEEE Conference on Computer Vision and Pattern Recognition, pp. 8827–8836 (2018)

Tree-Based OWL Class Expression Learner over Large Graphs

Caglar Demir[✉][iD], Moshood Yekini[iD], Michael Röder[iD], Yasir Mahmood[iD], and Axel-Cyrille Ngonga Ngomo[iD]

Data Science Research Group, Department of Computer Science, Paderborn University, Paderborn, Germany
{caglar.demir,moshood.olawale.yekini,michael.roeder,
yasir.mahmood,axel.ngonga}@upb.de

Abstract. Learning continuous vector representations for knowledge graphs has significantly improved state-of-the-art performances in many challenging tasks. Yet, deep-learning-based models are only post-hoc and locally explainable. In contrast, learning Web Ontology Language (OWL) class expressions in Description Logics (DLs) is ante-hoc and globally explainable. However, state-of-the-art learners have two well-known limitations: scaling to large knowledge graphs and handling missing information. Here, we present a decision-tree-based learner (TDL) to learn Web Ontology Languages (OWLs) class expressions over large knowledge graphs, while imputing missing triples. Given positive and negative example individuals, TDL firstly constructs unique OWL expressions in $\mathcal{SHOIN}$ from concise bounded descriptions of individuals. Each OWL class expression is used as a feature in a binary classification problem to represent input individuals. Thereafter, TDL fits a CART decision tree to learn Boolean decision rules distinguishing positive examples from negative examples. A final OWL expression in $\mathcal{SHOIN}$ is built by traversing the built CART decision tree from the root node to leaf nodes for each positive example. By this, TDL can learn OWL class expressions without exploration, i.e., the number of queries to a knowledge graph is bounded by the number of input individuals. Our empirical results show that TDL outperforms the current state-of-the-art models across datasets. Importantly, our experiments over a large knowledge graph (DBpedia with 1.1 billion triples) show that TDL can effectively learn accurate OWL class expressions, while the state-of-the-art models fail to return any results. Finally, expressions learned by TDL can be seamlessly translated into natural language explanations using a pre-trained large language model and a DL verbalizer.

Keywords: Decision Tree · OWL Class Expression Learning · Description Logic · Knowledge Graph · Large Language Model · Verbalizer

1 Introduction

Explainability is quintessential to establish trust in Artificial Intelligence (AI) decisions [32]. Its significance becomes particularly pronounced when AI algorithms rely on large amounts of data, e.g., the Web – an extensive and widely utilized information infrastructure that serves over 5 billion users worldwide. For instance, the recent success of large language models is built upon a crawled Web corpus comprising raw web page data, metadata extracts, and text extracts [5,17,30,34]. A key development over the last decade has been the increasing availability of Web data in the form of large-scale Resource Description Framework (RDF) Knowledge Graphs (KGs) [16]. According to the 2022 crawl of WebDataCommons, roughly 50% of the Web sites now contain (fragments of) RDF KGs.[1] The giant joint Knowledge Graph (KG) that can be extracted from the Web is known to contain at least 82 billion triples [4]. However, when analyzing or processing such a large graph, explainability and scalability remain challenging. For example, while learning continuous vector representations for knowledge graphs has significantly improved state-of-the-art performances in many challenging tasks [10,29], many deep-learning-based models that such solutions rely on, are only post-hoc and locally explainable [25]. In contrast, OWL class expression learning is ante-hoc explainable and showed good performance in areas like ontology engineering [21], bio-medicine [24], and Industry 4.0 [8]. However, most symbolic class expression learners cannot operate well on large KGs having millions of triples.

Our work contributes to a wider domain of designing scalable and explainable Machine Learning (ML) approaches for learning OWL class expressions over large RDF knowledge graphs. An OWL class expression represents a set of individuals by formally specifying conditions on the properties of individuals [26]. Such class expressions[2] in description logic syntax are ante-hoc explainable and intrinsically human-readable, e.g.,$\exists$award.{NobelPrizeInPhysics} represents a set of individuals being awarded a Nobel prize in physics. At the same time, they can be used by machines, e.g., the set of individuals satisfying this expression in the DBpedia KG can be retrieved via the following SPARQL query [12]:

```
SELECT DISTINCT ?x WHERE
{
    ?x dbo:award ?s_1 .
    FILTER (?s_1 IN
        (dbr:Nobel_Prize_in_Physics))
}
```

---

[1] 1.51 billion of the 3.20 billion URLs crawled by the Web Data Commons contained RDF, see http://webdatacommons.org/structureddata, accessed on April 25th, 2024.
[2] An OWL class expression can also be called a Description Logic (DL) concept. We will stick to the first term throughout this paper.

Thus the given class expression can be seen as a human-readable, interpretable, and binary descriptor, identifying a set of 163 individuals as positive within the DBpedia KG.[3]

Learning class expressions relies on two sets of given examples: a set of positive examples (E^+) that the target class expression should describe while differentiating them from a set of negative examples (E^-).[4] For example, given the positive examples $E^+ = \{$Roger Penrose, Paul Dirac$\}$ and the negative examples $E^- = \{$Barack Obama, George R. R. Martin$\}$, a class expression learning algorithm using the DBpedia KG may return the class expression provided above, since the expression's entailment holds for Penrose and Dirac but not for Obama and Martin. However, although state-of-the-art approaches effectively tackle the class expression learning problem on benchmark datasets, their deployment in large-scale applications remains unrealized. Early approaches reformulate the learning problem as a search problem in an infinite, quasi-ordered search space [21,23]. Therein, the search begins by applying a downward refinement operator to the root state (i.e., the most general class expression $\top$). Thereafter, the search is guided by a heuristic function. However, recent results suggest that search-based symbolic learners do not scale well on large KGs [9]. This limitation arises from the fact that search-based symbolic learners must explore the space of OWL class expressions to identify an accurate one. The potentially vast search space introduces significant challenges, serving as the principal barrier to learning class expressions over large KGs [3,9].

In this work, we present a solution to the search space exploration problem in state-of-the-art models. Our proposal is a decision tree-based learner (TDL) that can tackle the class expression learning problem over large KGs by performing retrieval operations (i.e., retrieving qualifying individuals of a class expression) only at most $|E^+ \cup E^-|$ times. More specifically, $\forall e \in E^+ \cup E^-$, TDL first retrieves the first hop information about examples (elucidated in 4). From these $|E^+ \cup E^-|$ sets of triples, TDL constructs unique class expressions using $\mathcal{SHOIN}$ Description Logic (DL). These expressions are then treated as features in a binary classification problem to describe examples numerically (as detailed in 4). Subsequently, TDL fits a CART decision tree to distinguish E^+ from E^- within the created feature space. The final class expression is built by traversing the built CART decision tree from the root node to leaf nodes for each positive example. Overall, our experimental results over three benchmark datasets with four state-of-the-art models indicate that TDL learns more accurate class expressions under a time constraint and generalizes better than state-of-the-art models including Drill [9] and EvoLearner [13]. Importantly, we show that TDL can learn OWL class expressions over knowledge graphs involving more than 1.1 billion triples in less than 2 min, while all other baselines lead to out-of-memory errors. Finally, we further improve the explainability by integrating a large language model and a verbalizer to translate potentially complex domain-specific class expressions into natural language sentences.

---

[3] https://dbpedia.org/sparql.
[4] We give a formal definition for class expression learning in Sect. 2.3.

The main contributions of this paper are as follows:

1. We propose an explainable and scalable ML approach (TDL) to learn OWL class expressions over large RDF KGs.
2. We conducted extensive experiments to benchmark the learning and generalization performance of our proposal against state-of-the-art models.
3. To the best of our knowledge, TDL is the first OWL class expression learner integrating a pre-trained language model and a verbalizer to translate domain-specific expressions into plain natural language sentences.

In the following Section, we introduce background knowledge about RDF, DLs, and class expression learning. After that, we present related work in Sect. 3 before explaining our approach in detail in Sect. 4. The evaluation and its results are described in Sect. 5 and discussed in Sect. 6. We conclude the paper in Sect. 7.

2 Background

2.1 RDF Knowledge Graphs and OWL

RDF is a formal language for describing structured information [15]. The goal of RDF is to enable applications to exchange data on the Web while still preserving their original meaning. OWL is designed to model the semantics of RDF KGs that facilitates machine interpretability of Web content by providing additional expressive power along with formal semantics [15]. OWL has three sublanguages: OWL Full (the most expressive but undecidable), OWL DL (expressive and decidable), and OWL Lite (decidable, less expressive). OWL Full contains OWL DL and OWL Lite, while OWL DL contains OWL Lite. OWL DL coincides with $\mathcal{SHOIN}(D)$ DL [15]. Note that any RDF KG forms an OWL Full ontology [2].

2.2 Description Logics

Description Logics (DLs) are fragments of first-order predicate logic using only unary and binary predicates [1,15,27]. A DL knowledge base corresponding to an OWL ontology is often defined as a pair $\mathcal{K} = (\mathcal{T}, \mathcal{A})$, where $\mathcal{T}$ denotes the set of terminological axioms describing the relationships between defined DL concepts. Every terminological axiom is of the form of $A \sqsubseteq B$ or $A \equiv B$ where A and B are DL concepts and $A, B \in N_C$. N_C denotes a set of atomic concepts corresponding to OWL named classes. $\mathcal{A}$ denotes the set of assertions describing relationships among DL individuals $a, b \in N_I$ via roles $r \in N_R$ as well as instantiation relationships. N_I and N_R denote the set of individuals and the set of DL roles corresponding to OWL properties, respectively. Thus $\mathcal{A}$ contains an assertion of the form $A(a)$ or $r(a,b)$, where $A \in N_C, r \in N_R$, and $a, b \in N_I$. Within this work, we focus on $\mathcal{SHOIN}$ DL. Table 1 depicts the syntax and semantics for $\mathcal{SHOIN}$ concepts.

Table 1. Syntax and semantics for concepts in $\mathcal{SHOIN}$ following Lehmann et al. [21]. $\mathcal{I} = (\Delta^{\mathcal{I}}, \cdot^{\mathcal{I}})$ is an interpretation where $\Delta^{\mathcal{I}}$ is its domain and $\cdot^{\mathcal{I}}$ is the interpretation function.

Construct	Syntax	Semantics
Atomic concept	A	$A^{\mathcal{I}} \subseteq \Delta^{\mathcal{I}}$
Role	r	$r^{\mathcal{I}} \subseteq \Delta^{\mathcal{I}} \times \Delta^{\mathcal{I}}$
Nominals	$\{o\}$	$o^{\mathcal{I}} \subseteq \Delta^{\mathcal{I}}, |o^{\mathcal{I}}| = 1$
Inverse Role	r^-	$\{(b^{\mathcal{I}}, a^{\mathcal{I}}) \in \Delta^{\mathcal{I}} \times \Delta^{\mathcal{I}} \mid (a^{\mathcal{I}}, b^{\mathcal{I}}) \in r^{\mathcal{I}}\}$
Top concept	$\top$	$\Delta^{\mathcal{I}}$
Bottom Concept	$\bot$	$\emptyset$
Negation	$\neg C$	$\Delta^{\mathcal{I}} \setminus C^{\mathcal{I}}$
Disjunction	$C \sqcup D$	$C^{\mathcal{I}} \cup D^{\mathcal{I}}$
Conjunction	$C \sqcap D$	$C^{\mathcal{I}} \cap D^{\mathcal{I}}$
Exists Restriction	$\exists r.C$	$\{a^{\mathcal{I}} \in \Delta^{\mathcal{I}} \mid \exists b^{\mathcal{I}} \in C^{\mathcal{I}}, (a^{\mathcal{I}}, b^{\mathcal{I}}) \in r^{\mathcal{I}}\}$
Universal Restriction	$\forall r.C$	$\{a^{\mathcal{I}} \in \Delta^{\mathcal{I}} \mid \forall b^{\mathcal{I}}, (a^{\mathcal{I}}, b^{\mathcal{I}}) \in r^{\mathcal{I}} \Rightarrow b^{\mathcal{I}} \in C^{\mathcal{I}}\}$
Atmost Restriction	$\geq n\, r.C$	$\{a^{\mathcal{I}} \in \Delta^{\mathcal{I}} \mid |\{b^{\mathcal{I}} \in C^{\mathcal{I}} : (a^{\mathcal{I}}, b^{\mathcal{I}}) \in r^{\mathcal{I}}\}| \geq n\}$
Atleast Restriction	$\leq n\, r.C$	$\{a^{\mathcal{I}} \in \Delta^{\mathcal{I}} \mid |\{b^{\mathcal{I}} \in C^{\mathcal{I}} : (a^{\mathcal{I}}, b^{\mathcal{I}}) \in r^{\mathcal{I}}\}| \leq n\}$

2.3 OWL Class Expression Learning

Definition 1 (OWL Classical Learning Problem). *Given a DL knowledge base $\mathcal{K}$, a set of positive individuals $E^+ \subset N_I$, and a set of negative OWL individuals $E^- \subset N_I$ s.t. $E^+ \cap E^- = \emptyset$, the learning problem is to find an OWL class expression H s.t.*

$$\forall p \in E^+ : \mathcal{K} \models H(p) \text{ and } \forall n \in E^- : \mathcal{K} \not\models H(n). \tag{1}$$

Traditionally, this learning problem is transformed into a search problem within a quasi-ordered concept space $(\mathcal{C}, \preceq)$ [21], where $\mathcal{C}$ denotes all valid OWL class expressions in a DL. An OWL class expression learner (e.g. OCEL, CELOE [22]) applies a downward refinement operator $\rho : \mathcal{C} \rightarrow 2^{\mathcal{C}}$ to traverse in $\mathcal{C}$, e.g., Mother $\preceq \rho$(Female). To steer the search starting from $\top$ to H satisfying 1, a fixed heuristic function is often applied. Most heuristic functions are based on the quality of the traversed OWL class expressions. One of these metrics is the F1 score, which is defined as

$$F_1(H) = \frac{|E^+ \cap \mathcal{R}(H)|}{|E^+ \cap \mathcal{R}(H)| + \frac{1}{2}(|E^- \cap \mathcal{R}(H)| + |E^+ \setminus \mathcal{R}(H)|)}, \tag{2}$$

where $\mathcal{R}$ denotes a concept retrieval operation that maps a class expression to a subset of N_I. As the size of $\mathcal{K}$ grows, computing the quality of a class expression becomes a bottleneck due to this mapping process [3,9,20]. Recent state-of-the-art models (e.g. Drill [9], EvoLearner [13]) apply reinforcement learning or evolutionary algorithms to find H as elucidated in Sect. 3. In contrast, our proposed approach only needs a refinement operator to generate its training data and does not make use of the mapping process.

3 Related Work

DL-Learner [21] is regarded as the most mature and recent system for class expression learning [6,9]. DL-Learner comprises several state-of-the-art approaches, including OCEL and CELOE [22]. Both consider the OWL class expression learning problem as a search problem in a quasi-ordered space of OWL class expressions in DLs. To traverse the search space, OCEL and CELOE apply a downward refinement operator while relying on different statistical heuristic functions. During the search, CELOE prioritizes syntactically shorter expressions. CELOE and OCEL apply the redundancy elimination and the expression simplification rules to decrease their runtimes. Although applying such fixed rules may reduce the number of explored expressions, long runtimes and extensive memory requirements still prohibit large-scale applications of such refinement-operators-based approaches [9,11,14]. Rizzo et al. [31] follow the general idea of a refinement-operator-based approach but focus on a small number of class expressions, which are used to create several decision trees that are combined similar to a random forest. Recent works often focus on accelerating the learning process. DRILL [9] uses a deep Q-network instead of a fixed heuristic function to steer the search more efficiently towards accurate OWL class expressions. CLIP [18] prunes the search space by introducing an upper bound on the length of the OWL class expressions. NCES [19,20] uses deep neural networks to learn mappings between sets of examples and class expressions without a search process. EvoLearner [13] is based on evolutionary algorithms and initializes its population (i.e., class expressions) by random walks on the input RDF KG.

Compared to the state-of-the-art models, TDL uses multi-hop information about E^+ and E^- to detect relevant OWL class expressions. Such expressions are then used as binary features for a supervised binary classification problem. TDL builds a decision tree algorithm (e.g. CART) to tackle this supervised binary classification problem, where a node corresponds to OWL class expression. Therefore, TDL learns Boolean rules to distinguish positive and negative examples. Instead of using a fixed handcrafted heuristic, TDL can use the Shannon information gain to recursively partition the feature space (i.e., the extracted class expression space) such that the positive examples are grouped together.

4 Methodology

Supervised Binary Classification. Given two ordered sets $E^+, E^- \subset N_I$ with $E^+ \cap E^- = \emptyset$ and a knowledge base $\mathcal{K}$, we firstly extract the first hop information as

$$\mathcal{F} = \bigcup_{x \in E} \{(x, p, o) \mid (x, p, o) \in \mathcal{K}\}, \tag{3}$$

where $E = E^+ \cup E^-$. Given $\mathcal{F}$, a set of relevant atomic concepts can be defined as

$$\mathcal{FC} = \bigcup_{(s,p,o)\in\mathcal{F}} \{o \mid o \in N_C\}. \tag{4}$$

Similarly, relevant restrictions over N_I and N_C can be defined as

$$\mathcal{FRO} = \bigcup_{(s,p,o)\in\mathcal{F} \,\wedge\, o\in N_I} \{\exists p.\{o\}\} \cup \{\forall p.\{o\}\} \tag{5}$$

and

$$\mathcal{FRC} = \bigcup_{(s,p,o)\in\mathcal{F} \,\wedge\, o\in N_I} \{\exists p.\text{type}(o)\} \cup \{\forall p.\text{type}(o)\}, \tag{6}$$

where type : $N_I \to N_C$ returns a subset of N_C that a given OWL individual belongs to. Since an individual can belong to multiple atomic concepts, a complex conjunctive concept can be constructed and included in $\mathcal{FRC}$. Similarly, since an individual can appear with other nominals with same property, a complex restriction involving multiple nominals can also be included in $\mathcal{FRO}$. Multi-hop expression can be extracted by extending the fillers in $\mathcal{FRO}$ and $\mathcal{FRC}$. By introducing counting over $\mathcal{FRO}$ and $\mathcal{FRC}$, Atmost and Atleast restrictions can be obtained.

Through these extractions over first-hop information about E, we enable a decision tree to leverage multi-hop information for the learning problem. Through $\mathcal{FC}$, $\mathcal{FRO}$ and $\mathcal{FRC}$, we firstly build the training data $\mathbf{X} \in \mathbb{R}^{|E|\times(|\mathcal{FC}|+|\mathcal{FRO}|+|\mathcal{FRC}|)}$ and $\mathbf{y} \in \{0,1\}^{|E|}$ where the j-th feature corresponds to a Boolean feature (e.g. $\exists$hasChild.{Julia}) of $\mathbf{X}_{i,j} \in \{1.0, 0.0\}$ for the i-th individual in E. After $\mathbf{X}, \mathbf{y}$ are constructed, we fit a decision tree to learn binary decision rules to distinguish the positive individuals E^+ from the negative individuals E^-.

Running Example. Fig. 1 visualizes an example tree built on $\mathbf{X}$ and $\mathbf{y}$ for the Aunt benchmark learning problem. The rationale of using a decision tree is that it can be seen as a piece-wise constant approximation, where each decision is ante-hoc explainable [32]. For instance, being a Female and having a sibling being Mother can be important to distinguish E^+ from E^-. The entropy decreases from 1.0 to 0.0 when classifying 25 positive individuals $\mathbf{x} \in E^+$ as positive class, each of them fulfilling the following: (i) (x, type, Female) $\wedge$ (x, hasSibling, y) $\wedge$ and (ii) (y, hasChild, z) $\wedge$ (z, type, Person), where $y, z \in N_I$ and hasSibling, hasChild, type $\in N_R$. Importantly, with a decision tree, we can rank class expressions in descending order w.r.t. their normalized total reduction of entropy.

From a Decision Tree to a DL Concept. After creating a decision tree $T(\cdot)$ using $\mathbf{X}$ and $\mathbf{y}$, we construct a class expression. Let N be the set of decision nodes of $T(\cdot)$ and let the elements of N have two types: leaf nodes L and decision nodes D with $L \cup D = N$. A leaf node $l \in L$ contains a class label $c \in \{-1, +1\}$. We describe a decision node $d_i \in D$ as triple $d_i = (\sigma_i, n_i^+, n_i^-)$, where σ_i is a condition based on a feature in $\mathcal{F}$, while n_i^+ and n_i^- are child nodes of d_i in the tree.

Building Conjunctive DL Concepts. When classifying a given individual, the decision tree algorithm starts at the root node and traverses the tree. The traversal depends on whether the current node is a leaf node or a decision node. If it is a leaf node, the node's class is assigned to the example. If it is a decision node, the example is tested against the node's condition. If the example fulfills the condition, the algorithm traverses to the n_i^+ child node. Otherwise, the traversal continues with the n_i^- child node. We consider each node as a class expression; hence, for a given positive individual, we construct a conjunctive class expression from all nodes seen along the respective traversal. For a given $e \in E^+$, let $\pi = \{n_1, ..., n_{|\pi|} | n_{|\pi|} \in L, \forall i < |\pi| : n_i \in D\}$ denote a sequence of qualifying nodes starting from the root node and ending with a leaf node. From π, a conjunctive class expression can be obtained as

$$C_\pi = \prod_{i=1} \sigma_i, \qquad (7)$$

where $C_\pi(e)$ is the observed explainable features of e at inference by the decision tree classifier. Let Π denote a set of conjunctive class expressions constructed for E^+. For the running example shown in Fig. 2, Π contains the following three class expressions:

$$\text{Female} \sqcap (\exists \text{ hasSibling.Father}) \qquad (8)$$
$$\text{Female} \sqcap (\neg(\exists \text{ hasSibling.Father}) \sqcap (\exists \text{ married.Brother}) \qquad (9)$$
$$\text{Female} \sqcap (\neg(\exists \text{ hasSibling.Father})) \sqcap (\neg(\exists \text{ married.Brother})) \sqcap$$
$$(\exists \text{ hasSibling.Mother}) \qquad (10)$$

Note that since Π is a set, only distinct sequences of decision tree nodes are transformed into class expressions. By this, we aim to reduce redundancy, i.e., the length of generated concepts.

Disjunction of Conjunctive DL Concepts. A final prediction for a given class expression learning problem is then computed as

$$H = \bigsqcup_{C_\pi \in \Pi} C_\pi. \qquad (11)$$

For the running example, H corresponds to the disjunction of Equations (8) to (10). Hence, TDL can tackle a class expression learning problem **without a single retrieval operation**. Recall that as the size of the input knowledge base grows, performing retrieval operations to compute the quality of a class expression becomes a computational bottleneck.

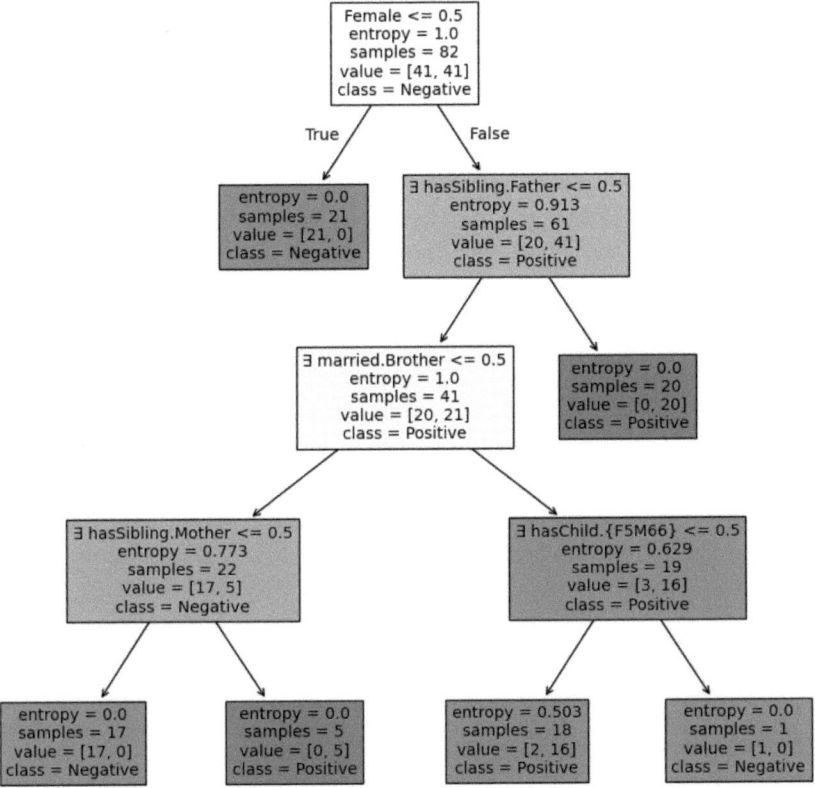

Fig. 1. The built decision tree for the Aunt benchmark learning problem. Outgoing arrows mark the path of examples that either fulfill or neglect the originating node's condition, and `value` array shows counts of observed negative and positive examples

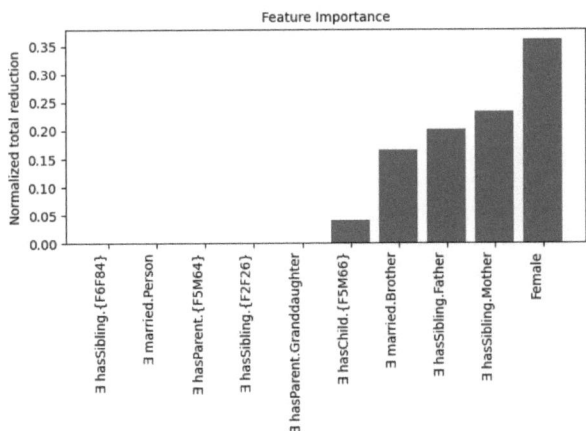

Fig. 2. Normalized total entropy reduction of important features for the Aunt benchmark learning problem with generated goal concept as: `Aunt` ≡ `Female` ⊓ (∃ `hasSibling.Mother` ⊔ ∃`hasSibling.Father` ⊔ (∃textttmarried.Brother(∃`hasChild`.⊤))).

From DL Concepts to Natural Language Sentences. We investigate techniques to translate a predicted class expression into natural language sentences. Therewith, we aim to enable non-domain experts to interpret predictions. To this end, we applied a large language model with or without an OWL verbalizer. We explored several system prompts and used the following one:

You are an expert. Be concise in your answers and translate this description logic concept into English sentences.
Provide no explanations: $

where $ is replaced with a class expression.

5 Experiments

5.1 Datasets

We use three benchmark datasets—Family, Carcinogenesis, and Mutagenesis— obtained from [9]. In addition, we use the English DBpedia as example of a large KG together with three example learning problems created manually using prominent politicians.[5] Table 2 gives an overview of datasets.

Table 2. Overview of benchmark datasets and total learning problems. $|\mathcal{K}|$, $|N_I|$, $|N_C|$, $|N_R|$ and LP denote the number of triples, individuals, concepts, roles, and learning problems, respectively.

Dataset	$|\mathcal{K}|$	$|N_I|$	$|N_C|$	$|N_R|$	LP
Family	2,032	202	18	4	18
Mutagenesis	62,067	14,145	86	11	1
Carcinogenesis	96,939	22,372	142	21	1
DBpedia	1,151,575,981	42,042,875	1,568	1,194	3

5.2 Experimental Setup

We base our experimental setup on [9] and use all learning problems provided by the datasets. We compare approaches based on their F1-scores for predicted class expression and their runtimes. On each dataset, each model is initialized once. For each learning problem, the time needed for the inference of the class expression is measured as runtime. We use two standard stopping criteria for all approaches. (i) We set the maximum runtime to 30 s (60 min for the DBpedia). (ii) Approaches were configured to terminate as soon as they find a goal state (i.e., a state with F1-score = 1.0). Note that (i) is a soft constraint as the runtime

---
[5] We use the English DBpedia version 2022-12.

criterion is not checked during all the steps of some of the evaluated approaches. If models do not find a goal state, the most accurate state is retrieved.

In a second experiment, we quantify the generalization performance of all approaches using a 10-fold cross-validation on the provided learning problems of the first three datasets. All experiments have been executed on a DELL Precision 3591 with an Intel Core Ultra 7 165H CPU, 64GB RAM, and Ubuntu 22.05. We provide an open-source implementation of TDL, including scripts for training and evaluation to ensure the reproducibility of our results using the ONTOLEARN framework [7].[6]

5.3 Experimental Results

Learning Class Expressions Under Time Restriction. Table 3 reports the concept learning results on the three benchmark datasets with benchmark learning problems as previously done in [9]. Overall, TDL outperforms OCEL, CELOE, Evolearner, and Drill w.r.t. F1-score and runtimes. On all 18 learning problems of the Family dataset, TDL reaches the goal state while requiring less runtime. Compared to OCEL, CELOE, and Drill, EvoLearner underperforms considerably. After these results, we delved into the implementation of EvoLearner and analyzed the learning problems on each datasets. We made the following two observations: (i) If the input knowledge base is not reloaded from the disk into memory for each learning problem, the performance of EvoLearner degenerates. (ii) Goal concepts for some of the benchmark learning problems (e.g. Brother, Daughter, Father, Sister) on the Family benchmark dataset can be found via a linear search over the set of defined class expressions, i.e., a class expression satisfying 1 is already defined in $\mathcal{K}$. In some of these cases, EvoLearner fails in identifying these existing concepts as solutions. To address (1), we reran our experiments on the Family dataset for EvoLearner and we reload the knowledge base for each learning problem. Although this setting increases the runtimes by 1.3 s on average, EvoLearner finds a goal concept having F1-score of 1.0 for all 18 learning problems on the Family benchmark dataset.

The learning problems created for the DBpedia KG and the evaluation results are listed in Table 4. TDL is the only algorithm that is able to solve the learning problems. All other approaches terminate with an out-of-memory error due to the size of the graph and the intermediate results they retrieve from it.

K-Fold Cross Validation. Tables 5 and 6 report the 10-fold cross-validation results on the benchmark datasets. Overall, results indicate that TDL outperforms OCEL, CELOE, Drill, and Evolearner in nearly all metrics. Only for the Mutagenesis dataset, TDL achieves a slightly lower F1-score than OCEL and CELOE. The results also show that the generalization performance of OCEL, CELOE, Drill and TDL do not fluctuate, whereas the generalization performance of Evolearner differs extremely (up to 50% F1-score differences between learning problems).

---
[6] https://github.com/dice-group/Ontolearn/tree/tdl

Table 3. Class expression learning results on the benchmark datasets with benchmark learning problems. F1 and RT denote the F1-score of learned concept w.r.t. E^+ and E^- and runtime in seconds, respectively. Maximum runtime is set to 30 s. Goal concepts with † denote that the respective concept is defined in $\mathcal{K}$, i.e., a goal concept can be found via a linear search over $\mathcal{K}$. Bold and underlined results indicate the best results and second best results.

Dataset	Goal Concept	OCEL		CELOE		EvoLearner		Drill		NCES		TDL	
		F1	RT	F1	RT	F1	RT	F1	RT	F1	RT	F1	RT
Family	Aunt	0.837	15.008	0.911	8.101	1.000	1.523	0.863	30.036	0.804	1.622	1.000	0.061
	Uncle	0.905	19.639	0.905	7.339	0.483	0.254	0.927	30.038	0.884	1.853	1.000	0.043
	Cousin	0.721	12.067	0.793	8.972	0.348	0.335	0.826	30.047	0.686	1.870	1.000	0.060
	Grandgranddaughter	1.000	0.003	1.000	0.001	1.000	0.299	1.000	0.003	1.000	1.902	1.000	0.024
	Grandgrandfather	1.000	0.846	1.000	0.182	0.829	0.295	1.000	0.408	0.944	1.726	1.000	0.032
	Grandgrandmother	1.000	2.506	1.000	0.259	1.000	0.272	1.000	0.400	0.944	1.790	1.000	0.037
	Grandgrandson	1.000	2.082	1.000	0.198	0.486	0.365	1.000	0.224	0.923	1.707	1.000	0.030
	Brother†	1.000	0.033	1.000	0.007	1.000	0.394	1.000	0.051	1.000	1.699	1.000	0.036
	Daughter†	1.000	0.026	1.000	0.009	1.000	0.366	1.000	0.048	1.000	1.752	1.000	0.052
	Father†	1.000	0.004	1.000	0.002	1.000	0.340	1.000	0.008	1.000	1.946	1.000	0.178
	Granddaughter†	1.000	0.003	1.000	0.001	1.000	0.301	1.000	0.005	1.000	1.879	1.000	0.043
	Grandfather†	1.000	0.003	1.000	0.001	1.000	0.277	1.000	0.005	1.000	1.915	1.000	0.037
	Grandmother†	1.000	0.008	1.000	0.002	1.000	0.290	1.000	0.008	0.921	1.648	1.000	0.041
	Grandson†	1.000	0.004	1.000	0.002	1.000	0.336	1.000	0.007	1.000	1.783	1.000	0.043
	Mother†	1.000	0.004	1.000	0.002	0.000	0.277	1.000	0.007	1.000	1.843	1.000	0.055
	PersonWithASibling†	1.000	0.003	1.000	0.001	0.700	0.331	0.737	30.031	1.000	1.985	1.000	0.073
	Sister†	1.000	0.003	1.000	0.001	0.955	0.291	1.000	0.033	1.000	1.939	1.000	0.046
	Son†	1.000	0.005	1.000	0.002	0.905	0.293	1.000	0.008	0.905	1.843	1.000	0.052
	Avg. Results	0.970	2.903	<u>0.978</u>	1.393	0.817	<u>0.380</u>	0.964	6.743	0.945	1.817	**1.000**	**0.052**
Mutagenesis	Unknown	0.916	32.30	0.916	30.04	**0.980**	31.31	0.704	30.17	0.704	<u>8.324</u>	<u>0.919</u>	**4.050**
Carcinogenesis	Unknown	0.734	30.42	0.734	30.13	<u>0.807</u>	30.98	0.705	30.19	0.705	<u>8.528</u>	**0.973**	3.370

Translation Into Natural Language. We used Qwen2.5 32B Instruct-AWQ [33,35] and a verbalizer LD2NL [28] to translate the complex, learned class expressions into plain text. The LLM only gets the class expression while LD2NL needs $\mathcal{K}$ as additional input. The outputs of the verbalization given by Qwen2.5 32B Instruct-AWQ and LD2NL for the class expression prediction from TDL for the Aunt learning problem as an example.

Qwen2.5 32B Instruct-AWQ.

- Female who either has a sibling who is a Father and is married to a Brother or has a sibling who is a Mother and is not married to a Brother.'
- Female who has a sibling who is a Father, is married to a Brother or has a child who is F5M66, and Female who does not have a Father sibling, does not marry a Brother, and has a Mother sibling.

Table 4. Learning OWL class expression over 1.1 billion triples. F1 and RT denote the F1-score of learned concept w.r.t. E^+ and E^- and runtime in seconds, respectively. – denotes no results provided due to the out-of-memory error.

Learning Problem	OCEL		CELOE		Evo		Drill		TDL	
	F1	RT	F1	RT	F1	RT	F1	RT	F1	RT
$E^+ = \{$B. Obama$\}$, $E^- = \{$A. Merkel$\}$	–	–	–	–	–	–	–	–	1.000	62.18
$E^+ = \{$B. Obama,A. Merkel$\}$, $E^- = \{$E. Macron$\}$	–	–	–	–	–	–	–	–	1.000	67.33
$E^+ = \{$B. Obama,A. Merkel,E. Macron$\}$, $E^- = \{$P. Sánchez$\}$	–	–	–	–	–	–	–	–	1.000	71.41

Table 5. 10-fold cross-validated class expression learning results for the learning problems of the Family dataset. F1 and RT denote the average F1-scores of learned concepts on the 10-test folds and runtime in seconds, respectively. Maximum runtime is set to 30 s. Goal concepts with † denote that the respective concept is defined in $\mathcal{K}$, i.e., a goal concept can be found via a linear search over $\mathcal{K}$. Bold and underlined results indicate the best results and second best results.

Dataset	Goal Concept	OCEL		CELOE		EvoLearner		Drill		NCES		TDL	
		F1	RT	F1	RT	F1	RT	F1	RT	F1	RT	F1	RT
Family	Aunt	0.631	16.190	0.855	16.190	1.000	2.723	0.791	30.106	0.812	3.696	1.000	0.107
	Cousin	0.708	12.520	0.789	12.520	0.344	0.279	0.784	30.105	0.557	4.090	0.956	0.153
	Uncle	0.891	20.731	0.891	20.731	0.642	0.276	0.899	30.161	0.877	4.551	0.986	0.103
	Grandgranddaughter	1.000	0.010	1.000	0.010	0.800	0.236	1.000	0.003	1.000	4.202	1.000	0.077
	Grandgrandfather	1.000	0.657	1.000	0.657	0.860	0.195	1.000	0.795	0.947	4.118	0.913	0.079
	Grandgrandmother	1.000	5.060	1.000	5.060	1.000	0.233	1.000	0.816	0.947	4.314	0.880	0.076
	Grandgrandson	1.000	1.826	1.000	1.826	0.463	0.199	1.000	0.722	0.931	4.108	0.862	0.083
	Brother†	1.000	0.006	1.000	0.006	1.000	0.314	1.000	0.008	1.000	4.022	1.000	0.091
	Daughter†	1.000	0.006	1.000	0.006	0.900	0.323	1.000	0.015	0.967	3.966	1.000	0.113
	Father	1.000	0.004	1.000	0.004	1.000	0.280	1.000	0.007	1.000	4.225	1.000	0.109
	Granddaughter†	1.000	0.003	1.000	0.003	0.700	0.244	1.000	0.005	1.000	4.140	1.000	0.103
	Grandfather†	1.000	0.003	1.000	0.003	0.780	0.256	1.000	0.005	0.980	4.088	1.000	0.088
	Grandmother†	1.000	0.003	1.000	0.003	0.556	0.240	1.000	0.005	0.964	4.563	1.000	0.088
	Grandson†	1.000	0.004	1.000	0.004	0.666	0.240	1.000	0.007	1.000	4.377	1.000	0.107
	Mother†	1.000	0.004	1.000	0.004	0.625	0.219	1.000	0.007	0.929	4.441	1.000	0.113
	PersonWithASibling†	1.000	0.004	1.000	0.004	0.564	0.244	0.725	30.072	0.976	4.680	1.000	0.145
	Sister†	1.000	0.003	1.000	0.003	0.731	0.247	1.000	0.008	1.000	4.361	1.000	0.103
	Son†	1.000	0.004	1.000	0.004	0.710	0.212	1.000	0.007	0.943	4.363	1.000	0.106
Avg. Results		0.957	3.170	<u>0.974</u>	3.170	0.741	<u>0.387</u>	0.955	6.820	0.935	4.239	**0.978**	**0.102**

Table 6. 10-fold cross-validated class expression learning results on the Mutagenesis and Carcinogenesis datasets. F1 and RT denote the average F1-scores of learned concepts on the 10-test folds and runtime in seconds, respectively. Maximum runtime is set to 30 s.

Dataset	Goal Concept	OCEL		CELOE		Evo		Drill		NCES		TDL	
		F1	RT	F1	RT	F1	RT	F1	RT	F1	RT	F1	RT
Mutagenesis	Unknown	**0.918**	31.551	**0.918**	31.551	0.742	32.317	0.704	30.046	0.704	**10.062**	0.855	<u>11.467</u>
Carcinogenesis	Unknown	0.706	30.899	0.701	30.899	0.707	33.059	0.704	30.280	<u>0.714</u>	**9.844**	**0.747**	<u>10.670</u>

– A female who either has a sibling who is a father, is married to a brother but has no children, or has a sibling who is a mother but is not married to a brother and has no children.

LD2NL. Every predicted individual is that something that a female that has not as sibling has as child a person and that marries something that has as sibling a mother or that a female that has as sibling something that has as child a person or that something that a female that has not as sibling has as child a person and that does not marry has as sibling a mother and that marries something that has as sibling a son. Although the translation via Qwen2.5 32B Instruct-AWQ arguably is more fluent than the translation of LD2NL, LD2NL verbalizes the input at least 10 times faster and requires less memory.

6 Discussion

Although TDL finds more accurate concepts in less time in most of cases, the length of the extracted class expressions created from the decision tree can grow quite large in comparison to the results of the other approaches. A large, complex class expression may require more domain expert knowledge for the interpretation. Moreover, TDL currently does not support datatype properties, data values, or data types. Consequently, we expect that TDL may perform poorly if a goal concept is based on the usage of one of these features, e.g., the class of persons that are taller than 1.80 m.

We conjecture that the performance of TDL can be further improved in an iterative fashion. More specifically, after $\mathcal{F}$ is constructed and a decision tree is built, the most important features can be refined through a refinement operator and the refinements can be added into $\mathcal{F}$. Consider married.Brother.hasChild as shown in Fig. 2, many possible feature candidates can be inferred depending on schema design of $\mathcal{K}$, e.g. ($\exists$married.Brother($\exists$hasChild.Male))) or ($\exists$married.Brother($\exists$hasChild.Person))) provided Male $\sqsubseteq$ Person. Although this iterative process may allow the creation of a decision tree to find more compact rules to distinguish E^+ from E^-, it may require more careful hyperparameter optimization to alleviate possible overfitting.

7 Conclusion

In this work, we proposed TDL—a decision-tree-based learner for OWL class expressions. We explained how we use the decision tree to learn Boolean rules from a feature space comprising class expressions. Furthermore, we illustrated that the Boolean rules learned by said tree can be adeptly converted into class expressions. Additionally, we showed that domain-specific class expressions can be seamlessly translated into natural language sentences by employing a sophisticated language model enhanced with a verbalizer. Our evaluation showed that our approach TDL outperforms previous state-of-the-art approaches on all benchmarking datasets except one case. We also were able to show that TDL is the only approach that is able to provide results for learning problems on a large KG comprising 1.1 billion triples. In future work, we want to improve TDL further to cover its shortcomings discussed in Sect. 6. For example, we plan to extend the feature generation to be able to learn class expression in the $\mathcal{SHOIN}(D)$ DL.

Acknowledgements. This work has been supported by the European Union's Horizon Europe research and innovation programme within the project ENEXA under the grant No. 101070305, the Deutsche Forschungsgemeinschaft (DFG, German Research Foundation): TRR 318/1 2021 - 438445824, the Ministry of Culture and Science of North Rhine-Westphalia (MKW NRW) within projects SAIL under the grant No. NW21-059D and WHALE (LFN 1-04) funded under the Lamarr Fellow Network programme.

References

1. Baader, F.: The description logic handbook: Theory, implementation and applications. Cambridge university press (2003)
2. Bechhofer, S., et al.: OWL Web Ontology Language. W3c recommendation, W3C (February 2004). https://www.w3.org/TR/2004/REC-owl-ref-20040210/
3. Bin, S., Bühmann, L., Lehmann, J., Ngonga Ngomo, A.C.: Towards sparql-based induction for large-scale rdf data sets. In: ECAI 2016, pp. 1551–1552. IOS Press (2016)
4. Bizer, C., Meusel, R., Primpeli, A., Brinkmann, A.: Web data commons – rdfa, microdata, embedded json-ld, and microformats data sets – october 2022. https://webdatacommons.org/structureddata/2022-12/stats/stats.html (2022). Accessed 15 May 2023
5. Brown, T., et al.: Language models are few-shot learners. Adv. Neural. Inf. Process. Syst. **33**, 1877–1901 (2020)
6. Bühmann, L., Lehmann, J., Westphal, P., Bin, S.: Dl-learner structured machine learning on semantic web data. In: Companion Proceedings of the The Web Conference 2018. pp. 467–471. WWW '18, International World Wide Web Conferences Steering Committee, Republic and Canton of Geneva, Switzerland (2018)
7. Demir, C., et al.: Ontolearn–a framework for large-scale owl class expression learning in python. J. Mach. Learn. Res. **26**(63), 1–6 (2025)
8. Demir, C., Himmelhuber, A., Liu, Y., Bigerl, A., Moussallem, D., Ngomo, A.C.N.: Rapid explainability for skill description learning. In: ISWC (Posters/Demos/Industry) (2022)
9. Demir, C., Ngomo, A.C.N.: Neuro-symbolic class expression learning. In: Proceedings of the Thirty-Second International Joint Conference on Artificial Intelligence, pp. 3624–3632 (2023)
10. Dettmers, T., Minervini, P., Stenetorp, P., Riedel, S.: Convolutional 2d knowledge graph embeddings. In: Proceedings of the AAAI Conference on Artificial Intelligence, vol. 32 (2018)
11. d'Amato, C.: Machine learning for the semantic web: lessons learnt and next research directions. Semantic Web **11**(1), 195–203 (2020)

12. Harris, S., Seaborne, A., Prud'hommeaux, E.: SPARQL 1.1 Query Language. Recommendation, W3C (March 2013). http://www.w3.org/TR/2013/REC-sparql11-query-20130321/
13. Heindorf, S., et al.: Evolearner: Learning description logics with evolutionary algorithms. In: Proceedings of the ACM Web Conference 2022, pp. 818–828 (2022)
14. Hitzler, P., Bianchi, F., Ebrahimi, M., Sarker, M.K.: Neural-symbolic integration and the semantic web. Semantic Web **11**(1), 3–11 (2020)
15. Hitzler, P., Krotzsch, M., Rudolph, S.: Foundations of semantic web technologies (2009)
16. Hogan, A., et al.: Knowledge graphs. ACM Comput. Surv. (Csur) **54**(4), 1–37 (2021)
17. Jiang, A.Q., et al.: Mistral 7b. arXiv preprint arXiv:2310.06825 (2023)
18. Kouagou, N.J., Heindorf, S., Demir, C., Ngonga Ngomo, A.: Learning concept lengths accelerates concept learning in ALC. In: ESWC. Lecture Notes in Computer Science, vol. 13261, pp. 236–252. Springer (2022)
19. Kouagou, N.J., Heindorf, S., Demir, C., Ngonga Ngomo, A.: Neural class expression synthesis in *ALCHIQ(D)*. In: ECML/PKDD (4). Lecture Notes in Computer Science, vol. 14172, pp. 196–212. Springer (2023)
20. Kouagou, N.J., Heindorf, S., Demir, C., Ngonga Ngomo, A.C.: Neural class expression synthesis. In: European Semantic Web Conference, pp. 209–226. Springer (2023)
21. Lehmann, J.: Learning OWL class expressions, vol. 22. IOS Press (2010)
22. Lehmann, J., Auer, S., Bühmann, L., Tramp, S.: Class expression learning for ontology engineering. J. Web Seman. **9**(1), 71–81 (2011). https://doi.org/10.1016/j.websem.2011.01.001,https://www.sciencedirect.com/science/article/pii/S1570826811000023
23. Lehmann, J., Hitzler, P.: Concept learning in description logics using refinement operators. Mach. Learn. **78**(1–2), 203 (2010)
24. Lehmann, J., Völker, J.: Perspectives on ontology learning, vol. 18. IOS Press (2014)
25. Marques-Silva, J., Ignatiev, A.: Delivering trustworthy AI through formal XAI. In: Thirty-Sixth AAAI Conference on Artificial Intelligenc, pp. 12342–12350. AAAI Press (2022)
26. Motik, B., Patel-Schneider, P.F., Parsia, B.: OWL 2 Web Ontology Language Structural Specification and Functional-Style Syntax (Second Edition). Recommendation, W3C (December 2012). http://www.w3.org/TR/2012/REC-owl2-syntax-20121211/
27. Nardi, D., Brachman, R.J., et al.: An introduction to description logics. Descrip. Logic Handbook **1**, 40 (2003)
28. Ngomo, A.C.N., Moussallem, D., Bühmann, L.: A Holistic Natural Language Generation Framework for the Semantic Web. In: Proceedings of the International Conference Recent Advances in Natural Language Processing, pp. 8. ACL (Association for Computational Linguistics) (2019)
29. Nickel, M., Murphy, K., Tresp, V., Gabrilovich, E.: A review of relational machine learning for knowledge graphs. Proc. IEEE **104**(1), 11–33 (2015)
30. Radford, A., Wu, J., Child, R., Luan, D., Amodei, D., Sutskever, I., et al.: Language models are unsupervised multitask learners. OpenAI blog **1**(8), 9 (2019)
31. Rizzo, G., d'Amato, C., Fanizzi, N., Esposito, F.: Tree-based models for inductive classification on the web of data. J. Web Semantics **45**, 1–22 (2017). https://doi.org/10.1016/j.websem.2017.05.001, https://www.sciencedirect.com/science/article/pii/S1570826817300173

32. Rudin, C.: Stop explaining black box machine learning models for high stakes decisions and use interpretable models instead. Nature Mach. Intell. **1**(5), 206–215 (2019)
33. Team, Q.: Qwen2.5: A party of foundation models (September 2024). https://qwenlm.github.io/blog/qwen2.5/
34. Touvron, H., et al.: Llama 2: Open foundation and fine-tuned chat models. arXiv preprint arXiv:2307.09288 (2023)
35. Yang, A., et al.: Qwen2 technical report. arXiv preprint arXiv:2407.10671 (2024)

Smooth InfoMax - Towards Easier Post-Hoc Interpretability

Fabian Denoodt[1](✉), Bart de Boer[2], and José Oramas[1]

[1] University of Antwerp, IDLab-imec, sqIRL Prinsstraat 13, 2000 Antwerp, Belgium
fabian.denoodt@uantwerpen.be
[2] Vrije Universiteit Brussel, Pleinlaan 2, 1050 Brussels, Belgium

Abstract. We introduce Smooth InfoMax (SIM), a self-supervised representation learning method that incorporates interpretability constraints into the latent representations at different depths of the network. Based on β-VAEs, SIM's architecture consists of probabilistic modules optimized locally with the InfoNCE loss to produce Gaussian-distributed representations regularized toward the standard normal distribution. This creates smooth, well-defined, and better-disentangled latent spaces, enabling easier post-hoc analysis. Evaluated on speech data, SIM preserves the large-scale training benefits of Greedy InfoMax while improving the effectiveness of post-hoc interpretability methods across layers. Our code is available via <u>GitHub</u>.

Keywords: Self-Supervised Representation Learning · Contrastive Learning · Post-Hoc Interpretability

1 Introduction

Black-box models, particularly deep neural networks (NNs), have shown remarkable performance in recent years. However, despite their impressive success, their lack of interpretability poses a significant challenge, limiting their use in high-stakes decision environments. Consequently, various post-hoc interpretability techniques have been explored. Notable contributions include the work of [28], which aims to find the input image that maximally activates a specific neuron in the network, and the research by [33], which focuses on highlighting the regions in the input that a particular neuron is sensitive to.

However, the effectiveness of these post-hoc methods decreases in complex models due to the large number of neurons that must be analyzed. Additionally, as argued by [1], the internal semantic concepts learned by these neurons are typically highly entangled throughout the network. This makes the interpretation of a neuron particularly difficult, as multiple neurons may work as a whole and together be sensitive to a given semantic concept while other neurons may not be contributing anything at all. For these reasons, it is likely impossible to fully understand these NNs with just the existing post-hoc interpretability techniques. In contrast, inherently interpretable models (e.g., logistic regression and decision trees) offer more transparency but may struggle with complex problems.

Another challenge with NNs is that they are typically trained end-to-end, which requires significant memory, especially as models grow larger. This can pose hardware constraints, as training must fit within the available memory of the device. Additionally, deeper networks can be more susceptible to the vanishing gradient problem [13].

To address these issues, we propose Smooth-InfoMax, a self-supervised representation learning method that integrates two existing paradigms: Greedy InfoMax (GIM) [18] and β-Variational Autoencoders (β-VAEs) [5]. This integration improves the post-hoc interpretability of the NN while enabling large-scale distributed training, combining benefits not achievable by either paradigm alone.

SIM's learning objective is based on contrastive learning and does not require labels or a decoder for training. Building upon GIM, SIM splits the architecture into modules, each trained greedily with a novel loss based on the InfoNCE bound [25]. As such, we preserve benefits such as large-scale distributed training of architectures that would otherwise not fit in memory and reduced vanishing gradients issues [18].

Furthermore, SIM incorporates the latent-space regularization properties of β-VAEs across various depths in the network. This helps create smooth and well-structured latent spaces that encourage disentanglement [5,12,27]. As a result, small changes in the latent space correspond to small changes in the input space, making post-hoc interpretability easier. However, unlike β-VAEs, SIM does not require a decoder during training, reducing memory usage. Another key difference is that SIM applies this regularization across different layers, making it easier to analyze representations throughout the network, rather than β-VAEs where the regularization typically is only applied at a single layer. A decoder can then be used as a post-hoc interpretability tool by traversing a latent space in the network, revealing the information that a particular neuron is sensitive to. Obtaining meaningful insights with such a procedure would be a lot harder if the spaces were not as well structured, as is typically the case in conventional NNs [3,7].

Our contributions are the following:

1. Introducing SIM, a framework with a novel loss function and probabilistic architecture for easier interpretable latent spaces, evaluated on sequential speech data. Although a relatively straightforward integration of existing methods, this proposed combination provides specific benefits not achievable by either approach alone.
2. We show, via a decoder, that SIM produces latent spaces that are easier to analyze. This also leads to a new metric for quantifying the number of dimensions required for successful reconstructions.
3. Empirically showing that ideas from β-VAE extend to other frameworks and can be repeated at different depths without significant performance loss.

Reproducibility: Our code and commands to replicate the experiments are all available via GitHub.

2 The Starting Point Greedy InfoMax

Greedy InfoMax (GIM) learns representations from sequential data without the need for labels by exploiting the assumption of slowly varying data [31]. This assumption is for instance applicable to speech signals where the conveyed information at time step t and $t+k$ contains redundancy, such as the speaker's identity, the conveyed emotion and the pronounced phonemes [18]. Meanwhile, this information may not necessarily be shared with random other patches of speech. An encoder can then be optimized to create representations that maximally preserve the shared information between the representations of temporally nearby patches [18], while at the same time discarding low-level information and noise that is more local [25]. It has been shown that such a strategy creates highly competitive representations for downstream tasks in various domains [4,11,18,19,24,25,29].

The Network Architecture. An audio sequence is split up into patches $\mathbf{x}_1 \ldots \mathbf{x}_T$ where each $\mathbf{x}_t$ is a vector of fixed length, containing for instance 10ms of speech. Each patch $\mathbf{x}_t$ is encoded by passing it through a series of M encoder modules: $g_{enc}^1(\cdot), g_{enc}^2(\cdot), \ldots, g_{enc}^M(\cdot)$. An encoder module consists of one or more convolution layers. The final representation $\mathbf{z}_t^M$ is then obtained by propagating $\mathbf{x}_t$ through each module as follows:

$$g_{enc}^M(\ldots g_{enc}^2(g_{enc}^1(\mathbf{x}_t))) = \mathbf{z}_t^M. \tag{1}$$

As such, each module's output is the input of the successive module: $g_{enc}^m(\mathbf{z}_t^{m-1}) = \mathbf{z}_t^m$. For tasks where context-related information is required, the final module g_{enc}^M can be replaced by an autoregressive module $g_{ar}(\mathbf{z}_1^{M-1} \ldots \mathbf{z}_t^{M-1}) = \mathbf{c}_t$. The autoregressive module can for instance be represented as a Gated Recurrent Unit (GRU). Both $\mathbf{z}_t^M$ or $\mathbf{c}_t$ may serve as the representation for downstream tasks and can be pooled into a single vector if needed.

The Loss Function. Given a representation $\mathbf{z}_t^m$ and a set $X = \{\mathbf{z}_1^m, \mathbf{z}_2^m, \ldots\} \cup \{\mathbf{z}_{t+1}^m, \ldots, \mathbf{z}_{t+K}^m\}$ consisting of random encoded audio patches and K subsequent samples of $\mathbf{z}_t^m$, respectively, GIM learns to preserve the information between temporally nearby representations by learning to discriminate the subsequent *positive* samples $\mathbf{z}_{t+k}^m$ from the *negative* random samples $\mathbf{z}_j^m$ using a function $f_k^m(\cdot)$ which scores the similarity between two latent representations [18]. This function is defined as follows:

$$f_k^m(\mathbf{z}_{t+k}^m, \mathbf{z}_t^m) = \exp(\mathbf{z}_{t+k}^m{}^T W_k^m \mathbf{z}_t^m), \tag{2}$$

where W_k is a weight matrix which is learned. Intuitively, due to the slowly varying data assumption, the similarity score for positive patches should be high and small for negative patches. The InfoNCE loss, used to optimize an *individual* module $g_{enc}^m(\cdot)$ and its respective W_k^m is shown below:

$$\mathcal{L}_{\text{NCE}}^m = -\sum_k \mathbb{E}_X \left[\log \frac{f_k^m(\mathbf{z}_{t+k}^m, \mathbf{z}_t^m)}{\sum_{\mathbf{z}_j^m \in X} f_k^m(\mathbf{z}_j^m, \mathbf{z}_t^m)} \right]. \tag{3}$$

One can prove that minimizing the InfoNCE loss is equivalent to maximizing a lower bound on the mutual information between $\mathbf{z}_t^m$ and $\mathbf{z}_{t+k}^m$ [25]:

$$I(\mathbf{z}_{t+k}^m; \mathbf{z}_t^m) \geq \log(N) - \mathcal{L}_{\text{NCE}}^m. \tag{4}$$

As a result of GIM's greedy approach, a conventional neural network architecture can be divided into modules. These modules can be trained either in parallel on distributed devices or sequentially, enabling the training of models larger than device memory and reducing the vanishing gradient problem. In the following section, we discuss how we can preserve these benefits in SIM, while also allowing for better interpretability.

3 Smooth InfoMax

While optimizing for the InfoNCE bound, as done in GIM, is remarkably successful for downstream classification, analyzing the learned representations remains difficult. In what follows we introduce Smooth InfoMax (SIM), maintaining the computational benefits obtained from optimizing the InfoNCE objective, while introducing easily traversable latent spaces and better disentangled representations at different depths in the network due to techniques borrowed from β-VAEs.

3.1 Towards Decoupled Training for Probabilistic Representations

The architecture is again based on modules, where the modules $g_{enc}^1(\cdot)$, $g_{enc}^2(\cdot)$, ..., $g_{enc}^M(\cdot)$ are each greedily optimized without gradients flowing between them. However, rather than producing a single deterministic point $\mathbf{z}_t^m$, the output from $g_{enc}^m(\cdot)$ is now a multivariate Gaussian distribution $q(\mathbf{z}_t^m \mid \mathbf{z}_t^{m-1})$, parameterized by the mean vector $\boldsymbol{\mu}$ and covariance matrix $\text{diag}(\boldsymbol{\sigma})$. More precisely, we have:

$$g_{enc}^m(\mathbf{z}_t^{m-1}) = q(\mathbf{z}_t^m \mid \mathbf{z}_t^{m-1}) = \mathcal{N}(\boldsymbol{\mu}, \text{diag}(\boldsymbol{\sigma})), \tag{5}$$

with $\boldsymbol{\mu}$ and $\boldsymbol{\sigma}$ dependent on $\mathbf{z}_t^{m-1}$. A point $\mathbf{z}_t^m$ is then obtained by sampling from this distribution, denoted respectively, as follows:

$$\mathbf{z}_t^m \sim q^m(\cdot \mid \mathbf{z}_t^{m-1}). \tag{6}$$

The encoding modules are thus stochastic and obtaining two representations from the same input will not necessarily produce the same result. This is in contrast to GIM's latent representations which remain fixed with respect to the input.

We obtain these stochastic modules by defining each module $g_{enc}^m(\cdot)$ consisting of two blocks. The first block receives as input $\mathbf{z}_t^{m-1}$ and predicts the parameters $\boldsymbol{\mu}$ and $\boldsymbol{\sigma}$. The second block samples $\mathbf{z}_t^m \sim q^m(\cdot \mid \mathbf{z}_t^{m-1})$ from this distribution and produces an output representation. In practice, sampling from q^m is achieved through a reparameterization trick, as introduced in [16]. The equation to compute $\mathbf{z}_t^m$ then becomes:

$$\mathbf{z}_t^m = \boldsymbol{\mu} + \boldsymbol{\sigma} \odot \boldsymbol{\epsilon},$$

where ϵ corresponds to a sampled value $\epsilon \sim \mathcal{N}(\mathbf{0}, \mathbf{I})$ and $\odot$ is element-wise multiplication. The two blocks are depicted in Fig. 1. The optional autoregressive module $g_{ar}(\cdot)$ has been untouched, and remains identical as in GIM, resulting in deterministic representations.

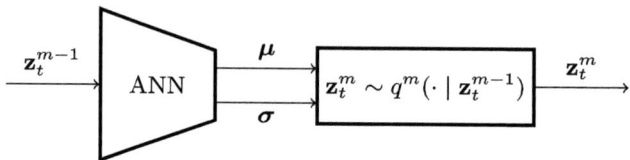

Fig. 1. A single module.

3.2 The Loss Function

Instead of training the NN's modules end-to-end with a global loss function, each module is optimized greedily with its own loss. Through the introduction of the *Smooth-InfoNCE* loss, mutual information between temporally nearby representations is maximized, while regularizing the latent space to be approximate to the standard Gaussian $\mathcal{N}(\mathbf{0}, \mathbf{I})$. This loss is defined as follows:

$$\mathcal{L}_{\text{S-NCE}}^m = -\sum_k \underbrace{\mathbb{E}_{\substack{\mathbf{z}_{t+k}^m \sim q^m(\cdot|\mathbf{z}_{t+k}^{m-1}) \\ \mathbf{z}_t^m \sim q^m(\cdot|\mathbf{z}_t^{m-1})}} \left[\log \frac{f_k^m(\mathbf{z}_{t+k}^m, \mathbf{z}_t^m)}{\sum_{\mathbf{z}_j^m \in X} f_k^m(\mathbf{z}_j^m, \mathbf{z}_t^m)} \right]}_{\text{Maximize } I(\mathbf{z}_{t+k}^m, \mathbf{z}_t^m)} + \beta \underbrace{D_{KL}\left(q^m(\cdot|\mathbf{z}_t^{m-1}) \parallel \mathcal{N}(\mathbf{0},\mathbf{I})\right)}_{\text{Regularisation}}. \quad (7)$$

Here, $m \in \mathbb{N}$ refers to the m'th module and $k \in \mathbb{N}$ the number of follow-up patches the similarity score $f_k^m(\mathbf{z}_{t+k}^m, \mathbf{z}_t^m)$ must rate. The latent representations $\mathbf{z}_{t+k}^m$ and $\mathbf{z}_t^m$ are encoded samples produced by $g_{enc}^m(\mathbf{z}_{t+k}^{m-1})$ and $g_{enc}^m(\mathbf{z}_t^{m-1})$, respectively and X is a set of samples $\{\mathbf{z}_{t+k}^m, \mathbf{z}_1^m, \mathbf{z}_2^m, \dots\}$ where $\mathbf{z}_j^m$ with $j \neq t+k$ are random samples. In practice, the set can be based on the training batch. The parameter $\beta \geq 0$ is a hyper-parameter indicating the relative importance between the two terms. When $\beta = 0$, SIM is identical to GIM but with an altered architecture supporting probabilistic representations. The similarity score $f_k^m(\cdot)$ remains identical as in GIM:

$$f_k^m(\mathbf{z}_{t+k}^m, \mathbf{z}_t^m) = \exp(\mathbf{z}_{t+k}^{m}{}^T W_k^m \mathbf{z}_t^m). \quad (8)$$

$\mathcal{L}_{\text{S-NCE}}^m$ consists of two terms. The first term ensures that latent representations of temporally nearby patches maximally preserve their shared information. The second pushes the latent representations close to the origin.

The Gradient. To estimate the expectation term in $\mathcal{L}_{\text{S-NCE}}$, we apply the same approximation method as in VAEs, achieved through Monte Carlo estimates [16]. The first term in $\mathcal{L}_{\text{S-NCE}}$ then becomes:

$$-\sum_k \frac{1}{L} \left[\sum_{l=1}^{L} \log \frac{f_k^m(\mathbf{z}_{t+k}^{m\,(l)}, \mathbf{z}_t^{m\,(l)})}{\sum_{\mathbf{z}_j^m \in X} f_k^m(\mathbf{z}_j^m, \mathbf{z}_t^{m\,(l)})} \right].$$

Here, L refers to the number of samples drawn. Each $\mathbf{z}_{t+k}^{m\,(l)}$ and $\mathbf{z}_t^{m\,(l)}$ are different samples produced by their respective distributions. However, similar to [16], we can set $L = 1$ without significantly hurting performance.

With regards to the second term in $\mathcal{L}_{\text{S-NCE}}$, since $q^m(\cdot \mid \mathbf{z}_t^{m-1})$ is a Gaussian defined by parameters $\boldsymbol{\mu}$ and $\boldsymbol{\sigma}$, a closed-form solution exists [16]. The closed-form equation is the following:

$$D_{KL}\left(q^m(\cdot \mid \mathbf{z}_t^{m-1}) \parallel \mathcal{N}(\mathbf{0}, \mathbf{I})\right) = \frac{1}{2} \sum_{i=1}^{D} \left(-\log \sigma_i^2 - 1 + \sigma_i^2 + \mu_i^2\right).$$

The variable D refers to the number of dimensions of $\boldsymbol{\mu}$ and $\boldsymbol{\sigma}$. This term can thus, be directly computed and does not need to be approximated through Monte Carlo estimates. The gradient for the two terms can then be computed using automatic differentiation tools such as PyTorch.

3.3 Properties of the Latent Space

Here, we present two conjectures regarding the structure of the latent space defined by each of SIM's modules. They will serve as the main argument for why SIM's representations are more easily analyzable. Meanwhile, alternative contrastive approaches such as GIM lack these benefits.

Conjecture 1. $\mathcal{L}_{\text{S-NCE}}$ *enforces an uninterrupted and well-covered space around the origin.*

In SIM, a latent representation $\mathbf{z}_t^m \in \mathcal{Z}^m$ of a data point $\mathbf{z}_t^{m-1} \in \mathcal{Z}^{m-1}$ is a sample from a Gaussian distribution. Thus, encoding the same $\mathbf{z}_t^{m-1}$ an infinite number of times results in a spherical region (around a particular mean $\boldsymbol{\mu}$) in $\mathcal{Z}^m$ that is covered by the latent representations corresponding to $\mathbf{z}_t^{m-1}$, without any interruptions in this region. This is different from GIM where a data point merely covers a single point of the latent space (and not an entire region). Furthermore, because the KL divergence requires each region to be close to the origin, the regions are more likely to utilize the limited space efficiently around the origin, resulting in a lower chance of obtaining gaps between two regions from different data points.

Conjecture 2. $\mathcal{L}_{\text{S-NCE}}$ *enforces smooth and consistent transitions in the latent space with respect to the shared information between temporarily nearby patches.*

The argument on why this holds true is similar to the argument made for VAEs [16]. In the case of a VAE, a smooth space implies that a small change to z should result in a small change to its corresponding reconstruction, such that:

$$\mathbf{z} \approx \mathbf{z}' \implies p(\mathbf{x} \mid \mathbf{z}) \approx p(\mathbf{x} \mid \mathbf{z}'). \tag{9}$$

Indeed, one can observe that the KL-divergence will encourage the region of latent points that a data point $\mathbf{x}$ can map to be large. Meanwhile, the reconstruction error in a VAE encourages all the latent points falling in this region to be as close as possible to the initial data point $\mathbf{x}$. In SIM, the same argument can be used to obtain:

$$\mathbf{z}_t^m \approx \mathbf{z}_t^{m'} \implies f(\mathbf{z}_{t+k}^m, \mathbf{z}_t^m) \approx f(\mathbf{z}_{t+k}^m, \mathbf{z}_t^{m'}), \tag{10}$$

resulting in a smooth space with respect to the shared information between temporally nearby patches. Additionally, if a decoder is trained on SIM's representations, for the same reason, we obtain:

$$p(\mathbf{x}_t \mid \mathbf{z}_t^m) \approx p(\mathbf{x}_t \mid \mathbf{z}_t^{m'}). \tag{11}$$

Traversability of the Space. As a result of the smooth and well-defined shape, one can make small changes to $\mathbf{z}_t^m$ and observe what happens through a decoder with a much smaller risk of having abrupt changes to the corresponding $\mathbf{x}$, or obtaining out-of-distribution latent points that correspond to non-meaningful reconstructions due to gaps in the latent space. This results in an easily traversable latent space with a predictable structure, which is not guaranteed in conventional NNs, as they typically do not enforce these additional constraints.

Disentanglement. GIM poses no direct constraints on disentanglement risking having many dimensions of the representation together contribute a small amount to the contained information of an individual concept. However, as argued by [12], setting the prior $p(\mathbf{z})$ of the β-VAE's loss to an isotropic Gaussian encourages disentanglement in the representations. This results in each dimension from the encoding to capture a different property of the original data. In the case of $\mathcal{L}_{\text{S-NCE}}$, the prior corresponds to the standard normal $\mathcal{N}(\mathbf{0}, \mathbf{I})$, and thus, this theorem is also applicable to SIM, and choosing a large value for β in $\mathcal{L}_{\text{S-NCE}}$ applies more pressure for the representations to be better disentangled.

4 Experiments and Evaluation

We evaluate SIM's latent representations on raw speech data and compare them against GIM as a baseline. The goal is to measure the impact of β-VAE regularization in terms of raw performance and to analyze how effectively post-hoc interpretability techniques would perform. Since this work uses the well-established properties of β-VAEs, we do not aim to independently revalidate them. β-VAE's disentanglement, in particular, has been extensively confirmed [6,12,15] and benchmarked against other methods in prior work [17].

4.1 Setup

Dataset. We use two publicly available speech datasets. The first is an artificial dataset[1] with a known and predictable structure, chosen because it provides a clear expectation of what a learning system should capture. The second, following GIM, is the 100-hour subset of the large-scale LibriSpeech dataset [18,26]. The artificial dataset contains 851 fixed-length (640 ms) audio files, sampled at 16 kHz and split into 80% training and 20% test sets. Each file consists of a single spoken sound composed of alternating consonants and vowels (e.g., "gi-ga-bu").

Architecture. SIM's architecture consists of three probabilistic CNN-based encoder modules and one autoregressive GRU module. Each CNN layer in these modules has 512 hidden dimensions. In g_{enc}^1, two convolutions (kernel: 10, 8; stride: 5, 4; padding: 2) are followed by parallel μ and σ convolution layers (kernel: 1, stride: 1, no padding). g_{enc}^2 contains two convolutions (kernel: 4; stride: 2; padding: 2), followed by μ and σ convolutions (kernel: 1, no padding). g_{enc}^3 has one convolution (kernel: 4, stride: 2, padding: 1) followed by μ and σ convolutions (kernel: 1, no padding). The final module, g_{ar}, is a GRU with an output of size 64 × 256. ReLU is applied after each convolution except in the μ and σ layers. The total downsampling factor is 160, producing a feature vector for every 10 ms of speech. Batch norm is applied to LibriSpeech but not to the artificial dataset. While it wasn't strictly necessary for LibriSpeech, it significantly increased training speed, which is beneficial given the dataset's large size. All modules are trained in parallel without gradients flowing between modules.

Training Procedure. SIM is trained with the Adam optimizer (learning rate: 2×10^{-4}, batch size: 8). The maximum number of patches to predict in the future K is set to 10, with 1000 epochs on the artificial dataset and 100 on LibriSpeech. The regularization weight β is set to 0.01 on the artificial dataset to encourage interpretability and 0.001 on LibriSpeech to balance interpretability and performance. Implementation details regarding drawing negative samples for $f_k^m(\cdot)$ remain identical to the audio experiment from ([18]).

4.2 Classification Performance

We evaluate SIM's representations by training a fully connected linear layer on top of SIM's frozen pretrained backbone for classification tasks. Classifiers are trained on temporally-average-pooled representations for 10 epochs using Cross-Entropy and the Adam optimizer ($lr = 0.001$). Tasks include vowel (3 labels) and syllable (9 labels) classification on the artificial dataset, and phoneme (41 labels) and speaker (251 labels) classification on LibriSpeech.

Results. A known drawback of β-VAE regularization is increased performance degradation, as greater emphasis is placed on disentanglement through the

---

[1] Available at https://github.com/fdenoodt/Artificial-Speech-Dataset.

Table 1. Accuracy for classification tasks on the artificial speech and LibriSpeech datasets. [a]Baseline results from [18].

Artificial Speech Dataset		
Method	Vowel Classification (%)	Syllable Classification (%)
Supervised	91.19 ± 1.56	83.32 ± 2.06
Random Backbone	32.44 ± 4.44	9.88 ± 2.12
GIM	95.24 ± 0.60	50.0 ± 1.55
SIM	92.58 ± 2.06	44.53 ± 1.77
LibriSpeech Dataset		
Method	Speaker Classification (%)	Phone Classification (%)
Supervised[a]	98.90	77.70
Random Backbone[a]	1.90	27.60
GIM	98.60	61.80
SIM	96.02	60.22

hyperparameter β [15]. Interestingly, Table 1 shows that this trade-off is quite manageable, especially considering that SIM applies this regularizer across different layers. Both SIM and CPC achieve high accuracy on speaker (96.02%, 98.60%) and vowel (92.58%, 95.24%) classification but perform worse on syllable (44.53%, 50.00%) and phoneme (60.22%, 61.80%) classification. This suggests that the InfoNCE objective favors global sequence features while preserving less local information. Adding a hidden layer improved training accuracy for the syllable task but did not improve test performance, indicating that consonant information may no longer be fully retained in the representations. Meanwhile, the randomly initialized backbone performs poorly across all tasks, confirming that SIM learns meaningful representations.

4.3 Representation Analysis

Qualitative Assessment of Latent Space Smoothness. To gain a notion of the smoothness of SIM's latent space, we train a decoder $D(\mathbf{z}_t^3) = \tilde{\mathbf{x}}_t$ on the artificial dataset, using representations from $g_{enc}^3(\cdot)$ to decode interpolations between two latent representations. Two audio signals, "bidi" and "baga" are encoded into their respective latent representations, $\mathbf{z}_{bidi}^3$ and $\mathbf{z}_{baga}^3$ (64 × 512). Interpolated representations $\mathbf{z}_\alpha^3 = (1-\alpha)\mathbf{z}_{bidi}^3 + \alpha \mathbf{z}_{baga}^3$ are decoded for values of α between 0 and 1.

Results. Fig. 2 shows the decoded signals smoothly transitioning as α varies, with no abrupt changes or nonsensical outputs. Exploring other interpolated audio signals than the one presented here, is possible via our demo. When decoding real samples (non-interpolated), we noted that vowel sounds were consistently correct, but consonants were often unclear or incorrect, which aligns with our discussion in 4.2 that consonant information may be less represented.

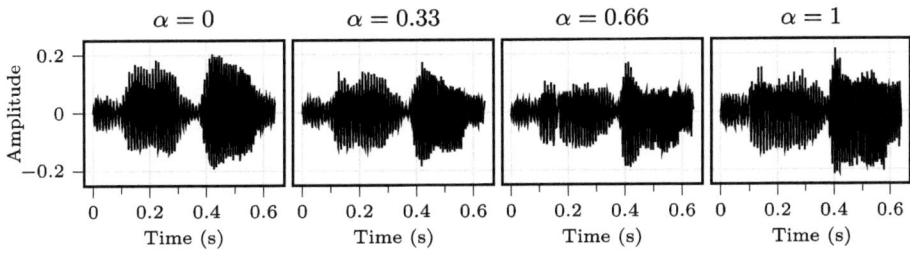

Fig. 2. Interpolated latent representations between two audio signals ("bidi" and "baga") using SIM. Each plot shows the decoded signal for different interpolation factors α. Listen to the decoded audio, among others, on Google Colab.

Quantitative Evaluation of Specific Information Spread. To assess how vowel and speaker information is distributed across latent dimensions, we train linear classifiers (without bias) on average-pooled representations from $g^1_{enc}(\cdot)$, $g^2_{enc}(\cdot)$, and $g^3_{enc}(\cdot)$. Classifier weights indicate the relevance of each dimension, with large magnitudes signifying high importance.

Results. As shown in Fig. 3, SIM concentrates vowel/speaker information in fewer dimensions, which is beneficial for interpretability. GIM, on the other hand, spreads this information more broadly thereby requiring a larger number of neurons to be studied. Accuracy for vowel identification in GIM: 95.94%, 92.81%, 94.06%, and in SIM: 87.5%, 93.44%, 91.87%. For speaker identification, GIM: 88.29%, 97.83%, 98.56%, and SIM: 68.36%, 91.76%, 94.32%.

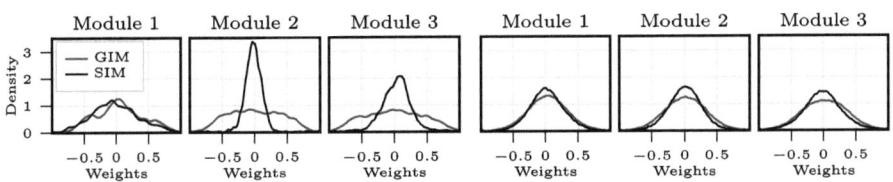

Fig. 3. Distribution of linear classifier weights for vowel prediction (artificial dataset, left) and speaker identification (LibriSpeech, right), trained on representations from $g^1_{enc}(\cdot), g^2_{enc}(\cdot), g^3_{enc}(\cdot)$. SIM's classifiers show more weights near zero, indicating that vowel and speaker information is concentrated in fewer dimensions.

Quantitative Evaluation of General Information Spread. To further observe the impact on interpretability through unit analysis and to analyze whether our representations align with the known disentanglement properties from β-VAE's regularizer [6,12,15], we introduce a metric to measure how effectively a decoder $D : \mathcal{Z}^m \to \mathcal{X}$ can reconstruct a target signal when only the most relevant latent dimensions are modified. This serves as a proxy for entanglement, especially given that the artificial dataset has only a few ground truth factors, requiring far fewer dimensions than the available 512.

For each pair of starting and target representations $\left(\mathbf{z}_{\text{start}}^m, \mathbf{z}_{\text{target}}^m\right)$, we define an interpolated representation, $\mathbf{z}_{\alpha=1}^m$, where only the N most important dimensions (those with the greatest average difference over 64 time frames) are altered to match $\mathbf{z}_{\text{target}}^m$. The similarity between the decoded $\mathbf{z}_{\alpha=1}^m$ and $\mathbf{z}_{\text{target}}^m$ measures how many dimensions are needed to transform the signal. The relative error is computed as:

$$\delta = \frac{\text{MAE}\left(D(\mathbf{z}_{\text{target}}^m), D(\mathbf{z}_{\alpha=1}^m)\right)}{\text{MAE}\left(D(\mathbf{z}_{\text{start}}^m), D(\mathbf{z}_{\alpha=1}^m)\right)} \tag{12}$$

Here, δ ranges from 0 (exact match to target) to 1 (no effect from altering dimensions).

Decoder Details. Each decoder $D(\mathbf{z}_t^m)$ is trained for 50 epochs on representations from a specific module $g_{enc}^m(\cdot)$, using the MSE loss, a learning rate of 2×10^{-4}, and batch size 8. The decoder mirrors the encoder architecture, but for the first module, two additional layers (kernel size 3, padding 1, stride 1) were added to improve reconstruction.

Results. Table 2 shows the relative errors. Across all depths, SIM reconstructs the target signal using fewer dimensions than GIM. For the artificial dataset, GIM needs at least half of the dimensions for successful reconstruction, whereas SIM achieves similar results with just 1/8th. Given the limited information in this dataset, which theoretically requires far fewer than 512 dimensions, multiple of GIM's dimensions seem sensitive to similar attributes. This implies a more entangled representation, which aligns with earlier findings in Fig. 3. For LibriSpeech, SIM consistently requires fewer dimensions, averaging around half the number used by GIM, showing potential to scale well to more complex datasets.

Table 2. Relative reconstruction error δ (%) when only the N most important dimensions out of 512 are active. Lower values are preferred. GIM distributes relevant information across more dimensions than SIM.

Module	Method	\multicolumn{8}{c	}{Artificial Speech Dataset}	\multicolumn{8}{c}{LibriSpeech Dataset}
		2	4	8	16	32	64	128	256	512	2	4	8	16	32	64	128	256	512
g_{enc}^1	GIM	99.32	98.71	97.6	95.46	91.2	82.35	62.96	24.33	0	95.55	91.77	87.47	81.12	71.65	58.02	39.52	16.8	0
	SIM	84.01	62.5	37.42	29.45	23.64	17.96	11.97	5.66	0	88.02	79.83	64.92	36.93	15.55	10.62	6.96	3.53	0
g_{enc}^2	GIM	98.86	97.91	96.17	93.07	87.58	77.8	59.81	27.46	0	97.35	94.88	90.82	84.7	76.6	67.02	54.25	31.32	0
	SIM	89.89	81.78	65.96	39.26	28.04	20.98	14.0	6.97	0	88.75	82.32	74.74	65.83	49.4	32.47	22.44	12.39	0
g_{enc}^3	GIM	99.01	98.16	96.59	93.9	89.29	81.09	65.23	31.76	0	94.37	90.65	85.08	78.1	71.47	65.68	57.0	35.95	0
	SIM	92.74	87.44	77.56	59.27	39.89	27.96	17.55	7.73	0	86.76	81.14	75.54	70.96	64.75	52.02	39.23	23.38	0

Qualitative Analysis of Latent Shape. To evaluate the structure of SIM's latent space, we first compute the representations $\mathbf{z}_t^3 = g_{enc}^3(\mathbf{x}_t)$ for each sample from the test set. For each of their 512 dimensions, we construct a histogram with 100 bins, showing how all activations of the dataset for an individual dimension are spread. Figure 4 displays the histograms for a selected set of dimensions. SIM's activations consistently follow a Gaussian distribution, aligning with our design goal of regularizing the latent space toward a standard normal distribution. This predictable structure helps post-hoc interpretability tools by clearly describing the regions of interest. In contrast, the latent representations produced by GIM show greater variation. In particular, dimension 9 for the artificial dataset, and dimensions 13 and 14 for LibriSpeech are shifted away from the origin or differ from the other dimensions. Note that in GIM's current implementation, the latent spaces are implicitly constrained to center around the origin due to the use of a bias-free discriminator in Eq. 2. If the discriminator were non-linear or had a bias term, the shape of the latent space could potentially be even less predictable.

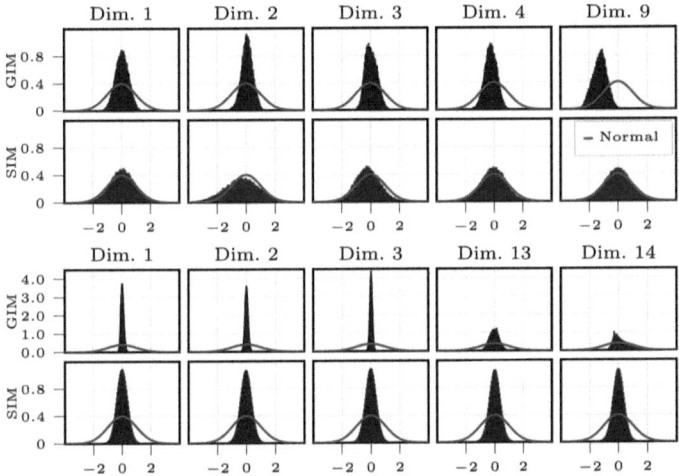

Fig. 4. Top rows: Artificial Dataset, bottom: LibriSpeech. Distribution of activations per dimension. SIM's activations have a consistent shape across dimensions, whereas GIM enforces no latent space constraints, resulting in greater variation in certain dimensions. Other dimensions are available here.

5 Related Work

This work uses the benefits of β-VAE's regularization, applying them across multiple layers to improve post-hoc analysis of the network.

In terms of *interpretability through regularization*, various approaches have been explored. For instance, sparsity regularization in the activations of hidden representations [2,10,30] has been shown to improve the compression of information into fewer dimensions, reducing the number of neurons to analyze, yet this does not encourage disentanglement or smoothness. Similarly, [22] improves model interpretability through regularization of activations, modifying the model's behavior such that existing explainability methods produce explanations that better align with human perception. Another notable method involves tree regularization [32], which constrains neural networks to be well-approximated by decision trees, thereby improving interpretability. While effective, its applications are typically limited to simpler tasks where decision trees can easily be formed. In contrast, SIM relies on post-hoc tools for its analysis but is able to model complex audio or vision tasks. Regarding disentanglement, traditional methods have typically focused on regularizing a single layer in the architecture [6,9,12,14,15], whereas SIM applies one of these approaches in a new context and across multiple layers.

For *post-hoc interpretability*, SIM's decoder is similar to approaches like [8, 28], which reconstruct inputs from latent representations but rely on gradient ascent rather than a learned decoder. However, since NNs are not typically bijective, the reconstructions found do not necessarily map to a similar point from the dataset, resulting in often noisy and unclear reconstructions [8,28]. To improve intelligibility, recent feature-activation-based methods incorporate human priors [20,21,23], guiding reconstructions toward more interpretable outputs. Decoders offer an alternative by directly learning to reconstruct inputs, implicitly encoding priors from the training data. However, they may introduce hallucinations that do not fully reflect the original model. Nonetheless, both gradient-based and decoder-based approaches could benefit from SIM's structured latent spaces due to their encouraged smoothness, better disentanglement, and well-defined shapes.

6 Discussion

We presented Smooth InfoMax, a self-supervised representation learning approach that incorporates interpretability requirements into the design of the model. Our proposal demonstrates how β-VAE regularization can be integrated into GIM's contrastive learning framework at various depths in the network. As such, SIM enjoys GIM's computational advantages—such as decoder-less training, large-scale distributed training for architectures that would otherwise not fit in memory, and reduced vanishing gradients—while also preserving the well-structured latent space properties of β-VAEs across layers. Remarkably, this is achieved without significantly compromising performance. SIM enables more effective post-hoc interpretability, bringing us closer to understanding the internal workings of these neural networks.

Limitations and Future Work. Although the latent space properties of β-VAEs improve post-hoc interpretability, the overall success still depends on the faithfulness of the generated explanations and the clarity of the information encoded in the representations. Additionally, SIM shows a small performance gap relative to its baseline, suggesting that integrating recent advances in disentanglement could be beneficial. While our evaluation focuses on sequential speech data (an XAI domain less exhaustively explored than vision), SIM's InfoNCE-based architecture is easily adaptable to other modalities, such as vision and natural language. Finally, SIM could be valuable beyond GIM as its probabilistic architecture and regularization can be integrated into other frameworks too, including end-to-end NNs as shown in this toy example.

Acknowledgments. This research was funded by the Department of Computer Science at the University of Antwerp and by the Vrije Universiteit Brussel.

Disclosure of Interests. The authors have no competing interests to declare that are relevant to the content of this article.

References

1. Bau, D., Zhou, B., Khosla, A., Oliva, A., Torralba, A.: Network Dissection: Quantifying Interpretability of Deep Visual Representations. In: Proceedings of the IEEE Conference on Computer Vision and Pattern Recognition, pp. 6541–6549 (2017)
2. Bengio, Y.: Learning deep architectures for ai. Found. Trends Mach. Learn. **2**(1), 1–127 (2009)
3. Bengio, Y., Courville, A., Vincent, P.: Representation learning: a review and new perspectives. IEEE Trans. Pattern Anal. Mach. Intell. **35**(8), 1798–1828 (2013)
4. Bhati, S., Villalba, J., Zelasko, P., Moro-Velázquez, L., Dehak, N.: Segmental contrastive predictive coding for unsupervised word segmentation. In: Hermansky, H., Cernocký, H., Burget, L., Lamel, L., Scharenborg, O., Motlícek, P. (eds.) 22nd Annual Conference of the International Speech Communication Association, Interspeech 2021, Brno, Czechia, August 30 - September 3, 2021, pp. 366–370. ISCA (2021)
5. Burgess, C.P., et al.: Understanding disentangling in β-vae. arXiv preprint arXiv:1804.03599 (2018)
6. Chen, R.T., Li, X., Grosse, R.B., Duvenaud, D.K.: Isolating sources of disentanglement in variational autoencoders. In: Advances in Neural Information Processing Systems, vol. 31 (2018)
7. Doersch, C.: Tutorial on variational autoencoders. arXiv preprint arXiv:1606.05908 (2016)
8. Erhan, D., Bengio, Y., Courville, A., Vincent, P.: Visualizing higher-layer features of a deep network. Univ. Montreal **1341**(3), 1 (2009)
9. Ge, Y., Xu, Z., Xiao, Y., Xin, G., Pang, Y., Itti, L.: Encouraging disentangled and convex representation with controllable interpolation regularization. In: IEEE/CVF Winter Conference on Applications of Computer Vision, WACV 2023, Waikoloa, HI, USA, January 2-7, 2023, pp. 4750–4758. IEEE (2023)
10. Glorot, X., Bordes, A., Bengio, Y.: Deep sparse rectifier neural networks. In: Gordon, G.J., Dunson, D.B., Dudík, M. (eds.) Proceedings of the Fourteenth International Conference on Artificial Intelligence and Statistics, AISTATS 2011, Fort Lauderdale, USA, April 11-13, 2011. JMLR Proceedings, vol. 15, pp. 315–323. JMLR.org (2011)

11. Hénaff, O.J.: Data-efficient image recognition with contrastive predictive coding. In: Proceedings of the 37th International Conference on Machine Learning, ICML 2020, 13-18 July 2020, Virtual Event. Proceedings of Machine Learning Research, vol. 119, pp. 4182–4192. PMLR (2020)
12. Higgins, I., et al.: Beta-VAE: learning basic visual concepts with a constrained variational framework. In: International Conference on Learning Representations (Jul 2022)
13. Hochreiter, S.: The vanishing gradient problem during learning recurrent neural nets and problem solutions. Int. J. Uncertain. Fuzziness Knowl. Based Syst. **6**(2), 107–116 (1998)
14. Hsu, W., Zhang, Y., Glass, J.R.: Unsupervised learning of disentangled and interpretable representations from sequential data. In: Advances in Neural Information Processing Systems 30: Annual Conference on Neural Information Processing Systems 2017, December 4-9, 2017, Long Beach, CA, USA. pp. 1878–1889 (2017)
15. Kim, H., Mnih, A.: Disentangling by factorising. In: International conference on machine learning, pp. 2649–2658. PMLR (2018)
16. Kingma, D.P., Welling, M.: Auto-encoding variational bayes. In: Bengio, Y., LeCun, Y. (eds.) 2nd International Conference on Learning Representations, ICLR 2014, Banff, AB, Canada, April 14-16, 2014, Conference Track Proceedings (2014)
17. Locatello, F., et al.: Challenging common assumptions in the unsupervised learning of disentangled representations. In: international Conference on Machine Learning, pp. 4114–4124. PMLR (2019)
18. Löwe, S., O'Connor, P., Veeling, B.S.: Putting an end to end-to-end: Gradient-isolated learning of representations. In: Advances in Neural Information Processing Systems 32: Annual Conference on Neural Information Processing Systems 2019, NeurIPS 2019, December 8-14, 2019, Vancouver, BC, Canada, pp. 3033–3045 (2019)
19. Lu, M.Y., Chen, R.J., Wang, J., Dillon, D., Mahmood, F.: Semi-supervised histology classification using deep multiple instance learning and contrastive predictive coding. arXiv preprint arXiv:1910.10825 (2019)
20. Mahendran, A., Vedaldi, A.: Visualizing deep convolutional neural networks using natural pre-images. Int. J. Comput. Vis. **120**(3), 233–255 (2016)
21. Mordvintsev, A., Olah, C., Tyka, M.: Inceptionism: Going deeper into neural networks (2015). https://research.googleblog.com/2015/06/inceptionism-going-deeper-into-neural.html
22. Moshe, O., Fidel, G., Bitton, R., Shabtai, A.: Improving interpretability via regularization of neural activation sensitivity. Mach. Learn. **113**(9), 6165–6196 (2024)
23. Nguyen, A.M., Dosovitskiy, A., Yosinski, J., Brox, T., Clune, J.: Synthesizing the preferred inputs for neurons in neural networks via deep generator networks. In: Lee, D.D., Sugiyama, M., von Luxburg, U., Guyon, I., Garnett, R. (eds.) Advances in Neural Information Processing Systems 29: Annual Conference on Neural Information Processing Systems 2016, December 5-10, 2016, Barcelona, Spain, pp. 3387–3395 (2016)
24. Nhem, T., Denoodt, F., Weyn, M., Peeters, M., Oramas, J., Berkvens, R.: Label-efficient learning for radio frequency fingerprint identification. In: IEEE Wireless Communications and Networking Conference, WCNC 2025 (2025), to appear
25. Oord, A.v.d., Li, Y., Vinyals, O.: Representation learning with contrastive predictive coding. arXiv preprint arXiv:1807.03748 (2018)
26. Panayotov, V., Chen, G., Povey, D., Khudanpur, S.: Librispeech: an asr corpus based on public domain audio books. In: 2015 IEEE International Conference on Acoustics, Speech and Signal Processing (ICASSP), pp. 5206–5210. IEEE (2015)

27. Sikka, H., Zhong, W., Yin, J., Pehlevant, C.: A Closer Look at Disentangling in β-VAE. In: 2019 53rd Asilomar Conference on Signals, Systems, and Computers, pp. 888–895 (Nov 2019)
28. Simonyan, K., Vedaldi, A., Zisserman, A.: Deep inside convolutional networks: Visualising image classification models and saliency maps. In: Bengio, Y., LeCun, Y. (eds.) 2nd International Conference on Learning Representations, ICLR 2014, Banff, AB, Canada, April 14-16, 2014, Workshop Track Proceedings (2014)
29. Stacke, K., Lundström, C., Unger, J., Eilertsen, G.: Evaluation of contrastive predictive coding for histopathology applications. In: Alsentzer, E., McDermott, M.B.A., Falck, F., Sarkar, S.K., Roy, S., Hyland, S.L. (eds.) Proceedings of the Machine Learning for Health NeurIPS Workshop. Proceedings of Machine Learning Research, vol. 136, pp. 328–340. PMLR (11 Dec 2020)
30. Vincent, P., Larochelle, H., Bengio, Y., Manzagol, P.A.: Extracting and composing robust features with denoising autoencoders. In: Proceedings of the 25th International Conference On Machine Learning, pp. 1096–1103 (2008)
31. Wiskott, L., Sejnowski, T.J.: Slow feature analysis: unsupervised learning of invariances. Neural Comput. **14**(4), 715–770 (2002)
32. Wu, M., Parbhoo, S., Hughes, M.C., Roth, V., Doshi-Velez, F.: Optimizing for interpretability in deep neural networks with tree regularization. J. Artif. Intell. Res. **72**, 1–37 (2021)
33. Zeiler, M.D., Fergus, R.: Visualizing and understanding convolutional networks. In: Fleet, D., Pajdla, T., Schiele, B., Tuytelaars, T. (eds.) ECCV 2014. LNCS, vol. 8689, pp. 818–833. Springer, Cham (2014). https://doi.org/10.1007/978-3-319-10590-1_53

Conformalized Exceptional Model Mining: Telling Where Your Model Performs (Not) Well

Xin Du[1,2,3,4], Sikun Yang[1,2,3,4(✉)], Wouter Duivesteijn[5], and Mykola Pechenizkiy[5]

[1] School of Computing and Information Technology, Great Bay University, 523000 Dongguan, China
{duxin,sikunyang}@gbu.edu.cn
[2] Great Bay Institute for Advanced Study, Great Bay University, Dongguan, China
[3] Guangdong Provincial Key Laboratory of Mathematical and Neural Dynamical Systems, Great Bay University, Dongguan, China
[4] Dongguan Key Laboratory for Intelligence and Information Technology, Great Bay University, Dongguan, China
[5] Data and Artificial Intelligence Cluster, Department of Mathematics and Computer Science, Eindhoven University of Technology, 5600MB Eindhoven, the Netherlands
{w.duivesteijn,m.pechenizkiy}@tue.nl

Abstract. Understanding the nuanced performance of machine learning models is essential for responsible deployment, especially in high-stakes domains like healthcare and finance. This paper introduces a novel framework, Conformalized Exceptional Model Mining, which combines the rigor of Conformal Prediction with the explanatory power of Exceptional Model Mining (EMM). The proposed framework identifies cohesive subgroups within data where model performance deviates exceptionally, highlighting regions of both high confidence and high uncertainty. We develop a new model class, mSMoPE (multiplex Soft Model Performance Evaluation), which quantifies uncertainty through conformal prediction's rigorous coverage guarantees. By defining a new quality measure, Relative Average Uncertainty Loss (RAUL), our framework isolates subgroups with exceptional performance patterns in multi-class classification and regression tasks. Experimental results across diverse datasets demonstrate the framework's effectiveness in uncovering interpretable subgroups that provide critical insights into model behavior. This work lays the groundwork for enhancing model interpretability and reliability, advancing the state-of-the-art in explainable AI and uncertainty quantification.

Keywords: Exceptional Model Mining · Conformal Prediction · Uncertainty Quantification · Explainability

Supplementary Information The online version contains supplementary material available at https://doi.org/10.1007/978-3-032-06066-2_31.

1 Introduction

As deep learning techniques continue to advance across various fields such as healthcare [2] and financial data science [39], it becomes increasingly important to ensure that these models are both responsible and explainable when deployed [6]. For example, in the case of a deep learning model used for disease diagnosis, medical professionals may need to understand the conditions under which the model provides highly confident predictions, as well as situations where it exhibits significant uncertainty. To meet these demands, uncertainty quantification methods are essential [43], while techniques such as Exceptional Model Mining (EMM) can offer interpretable insights [12,17,34]. Therefore, developing a conformalized exceptional model mining approach is crucial for helping users gain a deeper understanding of their model's performance [44].

EMM focuses on modeling multivariate interactions (captured in a *model class*), and discovering cohesive subgroups where these interactions are exceptional compared with these interactions across the whole dataset [17]. EMM has been widely applied to the analysis of classification, regression tasks for tabular datasets [16], structural interaction for the network datasets [28], and transition behavior for sequential datasets [35]. EMM practitioners have applied this framework on more complex datasets and diverse scenarios, including explainable machine learning research where EMM is employed to analyze the behavior of classifiers to provide responsible and explainable results [38]. However, existing classification model classes in EMM only focus on the binary classification problem: application for regression and multi-class classification (especially for the softmax based classifiers) is still underexplored. We develop a new model class for EMM to understand the behavior of regressors and multi-class classifiers.

Conformal prediction is a versatile framework designed to provide rigorous guarantees for uncertainty quantification [4]. Given a heuristic probability estimate from any pre-trained model —whether for classification, regression, or other tasks—- conformal prediction leverages a small hold-out dataset to transform this heuristic estimate into a statistically valid probability measure with guaranteed coverage. Specifically, in a classification scenario, conformal prediction generates a prediction set that contains the true label with a certain confidence level. This prediction set serves as a measure of uncertainty, offering insights into the classifier's reliability. A smaller prediction set indicates higher confidence in the model's predictions, while a larger set reflects greater uncertainty.

We strive to generate explainable results that identify cohesive subgroups and provide insights into the model's performance, through a method that can be applied to any classifier or regressor. To do so, we must address two major difficulties. On the one hand, due to the multi-output nature of multi-class classifiers using the softmax function, it is crucial to design a model class capable of handling complex interactions between multiple variables. On the other hand, integrating the validity in conformal prediction within concepts of interestingness within EMM presents another significant challenge. To address these issues, we propose a novel model class called mSMoPE (multiplex Soft Model Performance Evaluation), which introduces the average size of uncertainty sets as a new target variable for the EMM framework. This allows input attributes to be leveraged in forming cohesive subgroups that capture the relationship between the attributes and the target variable.

In this work, we utilize conformal prediction across various tasks, including classification and regression on tabular data [3]. Based on these applications, we introduce a general framework that demonstrates how conformalized exceptional models can be applied to diverse data mining scenarios to uncover meaningful cohesive patterns. These patterns, represented as conjunctions of attribute-value conditions, offer valuable insights into the behavior of machine learning models. Furthermore, by incorporating deep learning models such as multilayer perceptrons (MLPs), our framework enables a deeper understanding of deep learning models for tabular datasets, facilitating comprehensive performance analysis in tabular tasks.

1.1 Main Contributions

We propose a general framework for exceptional model mining with conformal prediction named conformalized exceptional model mining. This framework allows the user to generate a rigorous output about the model's performance with uncertainty measurement. Our main contributions are:

- we present mSMoPE: multiplex Soft Model Performance Evaluation, a new model class for EMM. This model class processes the input attributes, distilling a rigorous uncertainty set that captures the uncertainty of the model's output;
- based on the proposed new model class, we define a new quality measure that measures the average uncertainty loss between subgroups and the entire dataset. The proposed quality measure allows us to represent the discrepancy quantitatively so that the exceptional interplay between the input attributes and the uncertainty set can be revealed;
- we conduct experiments qualitatively and quantitatively on several public datasets. The results effectively demonstrate the interpretable subgroups that are exceptional in terms of predictive uncertainty.

2 Related Work

Exceptional Model Mining (EMM) [12,17,34] is a subfield of pattern mining, itself a branch of data mining, that focuses on identifying patterns in subsets of data rather than the dataset as a whole. Pattern mining is distinct in that it seeks to describe only specific portions of the data, often with a predefined description language, while ignoring the coherence of the remaining data. A subset of the data is considered "interesting" based on some criteria of interest, and EMM builds on this principle. In pattern mining, such subsets are often described using a conjunction of conditions on dataset attributes. For instance, in a dataset where records describe people, a pattern might look like "Age $\geq$ 30 AND Smoker = yes $\rightarrow$ interesting". By restricting patterns to conditions that relate to attributes of the data, the results become more interpretable to domain experts, as they align with familiar quantities. Such subsets, expressed in terms of these conditions, are called *subgroups*.

One of the best-known forms of pattern mining is Frequent Itemset Mining [1], which identifies subgroups that co-occur unusually often in an unsupervised manner: "Age $\geq$ 30 AND Smoker = yes $\rightarrow$ high frequency". In supervised settings, the focus shifts to identifying subgroups based on their relationship to a specified target attribute. This is the foundation of Subgroup Discovery (SD) [7,24,30,49], which aims to find subgroups where the distribution of a binary target attribute is unusual: "Smoker = yes $\rightarrow$ Lung cancer = yes". EMM extends Subgroup Discovery by considering multiple target attributes simultaneously. Rather than focusing on unusual distributions of a single target attribute, EMM investigates unusual interactions between several target attributes. EMM achieves this by defining a *model class* to represent the type of unusual interaction between targets, and a quality measure to quantify the interestingness of subgroups. The aim is to find subgroups where this quality measure is maximized, thereby uncovering patterns that exhibit exceptional relationships within the data.

Existing work has explored the identification of subgroups exhibiting unusual interactions among multiple targets, through established EMM model classes such as correlation, regression, Bayesian networks, and classification [17,18,34]. Among these, the classification model class [Subsect.3.3]ch31leman2008exceptional bears particular relevance to the mSMoPE model class, though they differ in two key aspects. First, their definitions establish distinct relationships between subgroup descriptions and the classifier's search space. In the classification model class, both the input and output attributes of the classifier are treated as targets, preventing these attributes from appearing in subgroup descriptions; exceptional subgroups are thus described using attributes excluded from the classifier. In contrast, the mSMoPE model class permits all input attributes (excluding outputs) to define subgroups, directly linking discovered subgroups to subspaces within the classifier's search space. Second, the model classes pursue different goals: the classification model class analyzes classifier behavior without a ground truth, whereas the mSMoPE model class evaluates performance in the presence of a ground truth during the calibration stage. The closest work to this paper is SCaPE [19]. This model class studies soft classifiers for a binary target, seeking subgroups of the classifier input space where the soft classifier outputs are exceptionally well or badly aligned with the binary ground truth. Conversely, in this paper, we focus on the performance of a multi-class classifier or a regressor. We construct the target variable based on the concept of conformal prediction, for which the terms of uncertainty have been included in the target.

Several Local Pattern Mining tasks share similarities with SD, including Contrast Set Mining [8] and Emerging Pattern Mining [11]. These tasks do not address multiple target attributes simultaneously, and do not explicitly model unusual interactions. Distribution Rules [27] represent an approach where a deviating model over a single numeric target is sought, identifying subgroups where the target's distribution deviates most from the overall dataset distribution. While this can be viewed as an early form of EMM with a single target, it does not account for multi-target interactions. In contrast, Umek et al. [47] consider SD with multiple targets, but their method reverses the attribute partitioning approach used in EMM. They generate candidate subgroups through agglomerative clustering of the targets and use predictive modeling on the descriptors to find matching subgroup descriptions. However, this approach does not allow for flexible expressions of unusual target interactions. Redescription Mining [21] identifies multiple descriptions that induce the same subgroup, modeling unusual interactions within the descriptor space rather than the target space. None of these methods explicitly evaluate the performance of a classifier or a regressor.

Many studies focus on accurately estimating predictive uncertainty in neural networks. Initially, the standard approach involved training Bayesian neural networks to learn a distribution over network weights, which required both computational and algorithmic modifications [20,31]. Alternative methods circumvent these challenges through ensembles [32] or approximate Bayesian inference [42]. However, these approaches have limitations, such as the need to train multiple neural network copies adversarially. Consequently, the most commonly used technique remains the ad-hoc calibration of softmax scores using Platt scaling [22]. Conformal prediction offers a different perspective by generating predictive sets that satisfy the coverage property [48]. We employ a practical data-splitting variant known as split conformal prediction, which enables the application of conformal prediction techniques to virtually any predictor [33]. Unlike traditional calibration methods, conformal prediction operates within a general framework rather than a specific algorithm. Therefore, key design choices must be made to optimize performance for different contexts. In this paper, our primary contribution is the integration of the conformal prediction framework into EMM, equipping the latter with the ability to quantify prediction confidence.

3 Conformalized Exceptional Model Mining

We assume a dataset $\Omega = (X, Y)$, where X stems from a k-dimensional *input space* $\mathcal{X} = \times_{i=1}^{k} \mathcal{X}^i$, and Y stems from an *output space* $\mathcal{Y}$, to be instantiated later. We also assume a *predictor* $\mu : \mathcal{X} \to \mathcal{Y}$. We denote the number of records in Ω by N, and we allow each $\mathcal{X}^i$ to have any reasonable domain: binary, categorical, ordinal, numeric. We partition the N records of Ω into two parts: the *calibration set* $\Omega_{\text{calib}} = (X_{\text{calib}}, Y_{\text{calib}})$ and the *test set* $\Omega_{\text{test}} = (X_{\text{test}}, Y_{\text{test}})$. We denote the number of records in Ω_{calib} by n, leaving $N - n$ records for Ω_{test}.

3.1 Conformal Prediction

Conformal Prediction (CP) is a distribution-free framework in machine learning and statistical modeling that provides valid confidence estimates, prediction sets, or prediction intervals for predictive models. In this work, we focus on the computationally efficient split CP method [48]. It performs as a wrapper around a trained base model and uses a set of exchangeable hold-out / calibration data to construct prediction sets or intervals. Given a predefined miscoverage rate $\alpha \in [0,1]$, the method follows three main steps. Firstly, it computes non-conformality scores, which quantify the degree to which a given output deviates from expected predictions. CP defines a non-conformality score function $S : \mathcal{X} \times \mathcal{Y} \to \mathbb{R}$, which captures uncertainty in the model's predictions. Intuitively, $S(x,y)$ measures how y "conforms" to the prediction at x; in classification, this could be the predicted probability of class y, while in regression, it may be the residual value $S(x,y) = |y - \hat{\mu}(x)|$ for a predictor $\hat{\mu} : \mathcal{X} \to \mathcal{Y}$. Secondly, it computes the $(1 - \alpha)$ quantile of the non-conformality scores on the calibration set. For $\Omega_{\text{calib}} = \{(X_i, Y_i)\}_{i=1}^n$, $\hat{q}$ can be computed as Quantile($\{S(X_1, Y_1), \ldots, S(X_n, Y_n)\}, [(1 - \alpha)(n + 1)]/n)$. Thirdly, for any $(X_{n+1}, Y_{n+1}) \in \Omega_{\text{test}}$, Conformal Prediction constructs a prediction set or interval $\hat{T}(X_{n+1}) = \{y \in \mathcal{Y} : S(X_{n+1}, y) \leq \hat{q}\}$. Additionally, if $\{X_i, Y_i\}_{i=1}^{n+1}$ are exchangeable, then $S_{n+1} := S(X_{n+1}, Y_{n+1})$ is exchangeable with $\{S_i\}_{i=1}^n$ since $\hat{\mu}$ is given. Hence, $\hat{T}(X_{n+1})$ contains the true label with predefined coverage rate [48]: $P\{Y_{n+1} \in \hat{T}(X_{n+1})\} = \mathbb{P}\{S_{n+1} \geq \text{Quantile}(\{S_1, \ldots, S_{n+1}\}, 1 - \alpha)\} \geq 1 - \alpha$ due to exchangeability of $\{S_i^{n+1}\}$. This framework works with any non-conformality score; we discuss one for multi-class classification, and one for regression.

Adaptive Prediction Set (APS). In classification tasks, general methods generating prediction sets usually create smallest average sizes, but tend to undercover hard subgroups and overcover easy ones. Adaptive Prediction Set (APS) is proposed to avoid this problem; we use the non-conformality score in APS proposed by [41]. The cumulative sum of ordered class probabilities was taken till the true class. As motivation for this procedure, note that if the softmax outputs $\hat{\mu}(X_{\text{test}})$ were a perfect model of $Y_{\text{test}}|X_{\text{test}}$, we would greedily include the top-scoring classes until their total mass exceeds $1 - \alpha$. Formally, we can describe this oracle algorithm as $\{\pi_1, \ldots, \pi_k\}$, where $k = \inf\{k' : \sum_{j=1}^{k'} \hat{\mu}(X_{\text{test}})_{\pi_j} \geq 1 - \alpha\}$, and π is the permutation of $\{1, \ldots, K\}$ that sorts $\hat{\mu}(X_{\text{test}})$ from most likely to least likely. Because we never know whether $\hat{\mu}(X_{\text{test}})$ is any good, this procedure fails to provide coverage. Hence, we need to use CP to transform the heuristic notion of uncertainty into a rigorous notion. We define a score function as $s(x,y) = \sum_{j=1}^{k} \hat{\mu}(x)_{\pi_j}$, where $y = \pi_k$. That is to say, we greedily include classes in our set until we reach the true label, then we stop. This procedure considers the softmax outputs of all classes rather than just the true class. Then we conduct the conformal procedure to set

$\hat{q} = \text{Quantile}(\{S_1, \ldots, S_n\}, [(1-\alpha)(n+1)]/n)$, and formulate the prediction set as $\mathcal{T}(x) = \{\pi_1, \ldots, \pi_k\}$, where $k = \inf\{k' : \sum_{j=1}^{k'} \hat{\mu}(x)_{\pi_j} \geq \hat{q}\}$.

Conformalized Quantile Regression (CQR). Conformalized Quantile Regression (CQR) [40] is a widely recognized CP method for constructing prediction intervals, known for its simplicity and effectiveness. CQR is based on quantile regression that acquires heuristic estimates $\hat{\mu}_{\alpha/2}(x)$ and $\hat{\mu}_{1-\alpha/2}(x)$ for the $(\alpha/2)$ and $(1-\alpha/2)$ conditional quantile functions of Y given $X = x$. The non-conformality score is computed using the calibration set as: $S_i = \max\{\hat{\mu}_{\alpha/2}(X_i) - Y_i, Y_i - \hat{\mu}_{1-\alpha/2}(X_i)\}$, for each $(X_i, Y_i) \in \Omega_{\text{calib}}$. Then the scores are employed to calibrate the plug-in prediction interval $\hat{\mathcal{T}}(x) = [\hat{\mu}_{\alpha/2}(x), \hat{\mu}_{1-\alpha/2}(x)]$. To be specific, we let $\hat{q}$ be the $([(|\Omega_{\text{calib}}| + 1)(1-\alpha)]/|\Omega_{\text{calib}}|)$ empirical quantile of $\{S(X_1, Y_1), \ldots, S(X_{|\Omega_{\text{calib}}|}, Y_{|\Omega_{\text{calib}}|})\}$; the prediction interval for new input data X_{test} is then constructed as $\mathcal{T}(X_{\text{test}}) = [\hat{\mu}_{\alpha/2}(X_{\text{test}}) - \hat{q}, \hat{\mu}_{1-\alpha/2}(X_{\text{test}}) + \hat{q}]$.

3.2 Soft and Hard Model Outputs

Suppose that we have a multi-class classification problem: any record of the dataset belongs to exactly one of the K available classes. Let us denote those classes by $\{1, \ldots, K\}$. For such a problem, two particular types of classification algorithms can be distinguished. On the one hand, a hard classifier outputs for each record in the test set a decision to which class it thinks the record belongs: the output is one of the K values. On the other hand, a soft classifier outputs for each record in the test set a real-valued K−plex vector (typically but not necessarily a probability): the output can be any value in $\mathbb{R}$, and higher values for the output correspond to a higher confidence that the records should be assigned class corresponding to the indicator.

Next, suppose that we have a real-valued regression problem: any record of the dataset could be mapped to exactly real-valued numbers. Let us denote those numbers by Y. For such a problem, two particular types of regression algorithms can be distinguished. On the one hand, a hard regressor outputs for each record in the test set a decision to which number it thinks the record can be mapped to: the output is a real-valued number. On the other hand, a soft regressor outputs for each record in the test set an interval with which one represents the lower quantile in the conditional distribution function of Y, and the other represents the upper quantile. Fix the lower and upper quantiles to be equal to $\alpha_{\text{lo}} = \alpha/2$ and $\alpha_{\text{hi}} = 1 - \alpha/2$. We will have an interval that covers the true value Y with miscoverage rate α, with the lower and upper pair of conditional quantile functions as $q_{\alpha_{\text{lo}}}(x)$ and $q_{\alpha_{\text{hi}}}(x)$, as $\mathcal{T}(x) = [q_{\alpha_{\text{lo}}}(x), q_{\alpha_{\text{hi}}}(x)]$. By construction, this interval satisfies $\mathbb{P}\{Y \in \mathcal{T}(X)|X = x\} \geq 1 - \alpha$. The length of the prediction interval $\mathcal{T}(x)$ can vary substantially depending on the value of X. This variation naturally captures the uncertainty in predicting Y, with wider intervals indicating greater uncertainty [36, 46].

Hard regressors estimate the test response Y_{n+1} given the record $r^{n+1} = x$ by minimizing the sum of squared residuals on the n training points: $\hat{\mu}(x) = \mu(x, \hat{\theta})$,

$\hat{\theta} = \arg\min_\theta \frac{1}{n} \sum_{i=1}^n (Y_i - \mu(X_i; \theta))^2 + \mathcal{R}(\theta)$. Here θ are the parameters of the regression model and $\mu(x;\theta)$ is the regression function, and $\mathcal{R}$ is a potential regularizer. Conversely, soft regressors like quantile regression estimate a conditional quantile function q_α of Y_{n+1} given $X_{n+1} = x$. This can be cast as the optimization problem $\hat{q}_\alpha(x) = f(x; \hat{\theta})$, $\hat{\theta} = \arg\min_\theta \frac{1}{n} \sum_{i=1}^n \rho_\alpha(Y_i, f(X;\theta)) + \mathcal{R}(\theta)$, where $f(x;\theta)$ is the quantile regression function and the loss function ρ_α is the "pinball loss" defined by

$$\rho_\alpha(y, \hat{y}) := \begin{cases} \alpha(y - \hat{y}) & \text{if } y - \hat{y} > 0, \\ (1 - \alpha)(\hat{y} - y) & \text{otherwise.} \end{cases}$$

This makes quantile regression widely applicable. In a concrete setting with a dataset at hand, we have information about each record r^i, whose true label or true response can be used as the perfect output of the hard model output. At the same time, we can also extract input attribute information to compute the soft model output. We investigate unusual interplay between these classifiers and regressors in an Exceptional Model Mining setting.

3.3 The mSMoPE Model Class for EMM

Traditional EMM assumes a dataset Ω, which is a bag of N records of the form $(a_1, \ldots, a_k, r)$. Candidate subgroups are generated by a guided search through the space spanned by the *descriptors* $a_1, \ldots, a_k$, and generated candidates are evaluated by a quality measure φ that assesses the candidate for exceptional behavior on the target space r; see [17, Algorithm 1] for an algorithm performing this task. As k EMM descriptors, we can simply employ the k-dimensional input space as introduced near the start of Sect. 3. The remaining challenge is to extract a useful target space r out of the conformal predictions in the preceding sections, and define a quality measure φ that sensibly determines whether generated candidate subgroups display exceptional conformal predictive behavior.

The goal of the mSMoPE model class for EMM is to let r capture the size of prediction set or the interval of regressing prediction, which represent the uncertainty level of how the model performs, and seek subgroups where this uncertainty is extreme: one can parameterize the model class to seek highly certain subgroups or highly uncertain subgroups. We are interested in such summarization on the entire dataset to see the whole uncertainty level, and on the subgroups to see how the descriptive information interplays with the uncertainty information. We use these measures to define a quality measure for the mSMoPE model class, that gauges how exceptional the uncertainty set is on a subgroup compared to the uncertainty set on the entire dataset.

Generating r for Classification Models. Suppose that the model that we are analyzing is a classification model and the dataset is a classification dataset. Firstly, we take the softmax output of the model as the soft outputs. Then we can set the conformal score $s_i = 1 - \hat{\mu}(X_i)_{Y_i}$ to be one minus the softmax output of the true class. Because we do not know whether the probability of softmax output is any good, we can only treat it as the heuristic notion of the uncertainty. Secondly, we define $\hat{q}$ to be the $[(n+1)(1-\alpha)]/n$ empirical quantiles of $\{s_1, \ldots, s_n\}$ on Ω_{calib}. Thirdly, for Ω_{test}, we can create a prediction set $\mathcal{T}(X_{\text{test}}) = \{y : \hat{\mu}(X_{\text{test}}) \geq 1 - \hat{q}\}$ that includes all classes with a high enough softmax output. Finally, for each record $(X_i, Y_i) \in \Omega_{\text{test}}$, we set $r = |\mathcal{T}(X_i)|$: the size of its prediction set. The larger r is, the less certain the model is of its prediction.

Generating r for Regression Models. Suppose that the model we are analyzing is a regression model and the dataset is a regression dataset. Firstly, we use the quantile regression model to get an initialized interval as $[\hat{t}_{\alpha/2}(x), \hat{t}_{1-\alpha/2}(x)]$. With the quantile output, we can define the score function to be the projective distance from y onto the interval as: $s(x, y) = \max\{\hat{t}_{\alpha/2}(x) - y, y - \hat{t}_{1-\alpha/2}(x)\}$. Here the scores are computed using Ω_{calib}. Secondly, we compute $\hat{q} = \text{Quantile}(s_1, \ldots, s_n; [(n+1)(1-\alpha)]/n)$ and formulate the valid prediction set by taking $\mathcal{T}(x) = [\hat{t}_{\alpha/2}(x) - \hat{q}, \hat{t}_{1-\alpha/2}(x) + \hat{q}]$. Intuitively, the set $\mathcal{T}$ just grows or shrinks the distance between the quantiles by $\hat{q}$ to achieve coverage. Finally, for each record $(X_i, Y_i) \in \Omega_{\text{test}}$, we set r equal to the length of the interval for $\mathcal{T}(X_i)$. The larger r is, the more difficult the model finds the input data.

Quality Measures Over r. For the entire dataset or a given subgroup, we have a distribution of target variable r, which represents the distribution of uncertainty on the population level. In practice, we extract the average value of the distribution as the representation of the target variable, denoted as Average Uncertainty Loss.

Definition 1 (Average Uncertainty Loss). *Given a (sub-)population S of records in a dataset, the average uncertainty loss (AUL) is given by:*

$$AUL(S) = \frac{1}{|S|} \sum_{(X_i, Y_i) \in S} r^i$$

Here, r^i represents the computed size of prediction set or the length of interval for record i.

In Exceptional Model Mining, we strive to find subgroups for which the target interaction captured by the model class is exceptional. Exceptionality does not occur in a vacuum: the behavior on a subgroup can only be exceptional when contrasted with a reference behavior that represents normality. Often, target behavior across the full dataset is used for this reference behavior, and so we define the following quality measure for the mSMoPE model class.

Definition 2 (Relative Average Uncertainty Loss). *Given a subgroup S of Ω, its Relative Average Uncertainty Loss, φ_{raul}, is given by:*

$$\varphi_{raul}(S) = AUL(\Omega) - AUL(S)$$

To find subgroups for which the model is highly certain about its prediction, i.e., subgroups for which the soft model works very well, one should maximize φ_{raul}; positive values for φ_{raul} indicate that the soft model performs better than usual on this subgroup. It is because the efficiency of conformal prediction is higher than usual. To find subgroups for which the soft model does not work, one should minimize φ_{raul}; negative values for φ_{raul} indicate that the soft model performs worse than usual on this subgroup. It is because the efficiency of the conformal prediction is lower than usual. Alternatively, one could find a list of subgroups for which the soft model performs exceptionally in general, by maximizing $|\varphi_{\text{raul}}|$. The resulting list of subgroups could be partitioned into poorly- and well-classified subgroups in a post-processing step. In this paper, however, we maintain the strict separation of bad and good subgroups by presenting results of φ_{raul}-maximizing and -minimizing runs separately.

The definitions of these quality measures themselves are trivial. The main contributions of Conformalized EMM and the mSMoPE model class for EMM lie not so much in convoluted quality measure formulas, but instead in the path taken through Conformal Prediction methodologies in order to arrive at meaningful definitions of r (to subsequently be incorporated in quality measures for EMM).

4 Experimental Setup

We evaluate the performance of Conformalized EMM in several experiments, performed on several real-world datasets, and demonstrating the exceptional subgroups Conformalized EMM can discover. By doing this, we aim to show the effective performance through the newly defined model class mSMoPE and the associated quality measure φ_{raul}. The contents are organized as follows. Firstly, we introduce the datasets used in this paper. We introduce the source of the data, the detailed composition of the data and the tasks in the data. Secondly, we introduce the base model μ that is required to conduct Conformalized EMM. Thirdly, we introduce the results, by listing the subgroups discovered in the datasets. Source code for reproducing the experiments are released https://github.com/octeufer/ConformEMM. Through the experiments, we aim to answer the following questions:

1. Is Conformalized Exceptional Model Mining sufficient to tell where your model performs (not) well?
2. Can Conformalized Exceptional Model Mining efficiently discover meaningful subgroups from multiple datasets?
3. How does the performance of Conformalized Exceptional Model Mining vary across models and datasets?

4.1 Datasets

We use a diverse set of public datasets. These datasets are: **Wine quality**, for which the goal is to model wine quality based on physicochemical tests [29].

Online News Popularity, which summarizes a heterogeneous set of features about the articles published by Mashable in a period of two years. The goal is to predict the level of shares in social networks [29]. **Helena**, an anonymized dataset for the classification task, including 100 classes [23]. **Covertype**, classification into forest cover types based on characteristics such as elevation, aspect, slope, hillshade, and soil type [10]. **MimicIII**, a large database comprising deidentified health-related data associated with over forty thousand patients who stayed in critical care units of the Beth Israel Deaconess Medical Center [26]. **California Housing**, real estate data [37]. **Year, the Million Song Dataset**, a collection of audio features and metadata for a million contemporary popular music tracks [9]. Table 1 lists metadata of all these datasets.

Table 1. Dataset metadata, with the average uncertainty loss for the MLP model.

i	Ω_i	N	k	Task	AUL(Ω_i)
1	Wine Quality	4 898	11	classification	2.471
2	News Popularity	39 644	59	classification	8.377
3	Helena	65 196	27	classification	33.277
4	Cover Type	581 012	54	classification	1.085
5	MimicIII	7 414	19	regression	319.305
6	CA Housing	20 640	8	regression	279 400.923
7	Year	515 345	90	regression	25.161

4.2 Setting Up the Predictor

Conformalized EMM requires a predictor function μ, whose conformal predictions lead to the generation of the EMM target space r, which ought to represent the uncertainty regarding the performance of the model (for classification or regression tasks). We employ a Multi-Layer Perceptron (MLP) as this base model. The MLP that we implement follows common design principles. We compose the model from multiple MLP blocks, each constructed by a linear fully-connected layer with batch normalization [25], ReLU [5], and dropout [45]. We select this NN architecture because it can handle all types of available attributes (binary, nominal, numeric). Moreover, the architecture is flexible in the design so that it can handle softmax outputs and quantile regression outputs.

4.3 Parameterization

As outlined in Sect. 3.3, we implement the CP algorithms so that the size of the prediction set and the length of the prediction interval can be computed based on the MLP model. The mSMoPE model class and the φ_{raul} quality measure are implemented following [13,14], where we restrict the search to a refinement depth of 2, i.e., we allow the resulting subgroups to be defined on two condition of the descriptors. This setting explores the expressive power of the resulting subgroups and enhances their potential for the interpretation by domain experts. Nothing restricts the use of the mSMoPE model class to subgroups defined by only two attributes. We opt for this limitation to maintain a balance between expressiveness and interpretability: exploring subgroups with more attributes would be computationally feasible at the cost of less-interpretable results. The search space is defined based on the types of attributes. For a binary attribute a_i, we consider the subgroups $a_i = 0$ and $a_i = 1$. If a_i is a nominal attribute with m distinct values $v_1, \ldots, v_m$, we examine m subgroups of the form $a_i = v_j$. For a real-valued attribute, we explore multiple intervals using the dataset's observed values as interval endpoints. Among these, only two subgroups are reported: the highest-scoring subgroup of the form $a_j \leq v_j$ and the highest-scoring subgroup of the form $a_i > v_j$. Finally, we use a parameter λ to bound the minimum subgroup size, to combat overfitting: we only report subgroups that contain at least $\lambda\%$ of the records in the dataset.

We run our algorithms twice for each dataset: once maximizing φ_{raul} in order to find subgroups on which the model performs well, with high certainty about its outputs, and once minimizing φ_{raul} in order to find subgroups on which the model performs poorly, with high uncertainty. In each run, we only report subgroups whose AUL outperforms the baseline set by the AUL of the entire dataset: the maximizing run reports only subgroups with $\varphi_{\text{raul}} \geq 0$, and the minimizing run reports only subgroups with $\varphi_{\text{raul}} \leq 0$.

5 Experimental Results

For each dataset, the top-3 most certain subgroups found while maximizing φ_{raul} are reported in Table 2, along with their qualities. When comparing the final columns of Tables 1 and 2, the values for the datasets Wine Quality (Ω_1) and Cover Type (Ω_4) stand out. For the subgroups found on these datasets, we see that φ_{raul} is smaller than $\text{AUL}(\Omega_i)$ by precisely 1, which implies that the average uncertainty loss of the top-ranked subgroups is just less than the average uncertainty loss on the whole dataset. I.e.: Conformalized EMM discovered subgroups for which the classifiers are highly confident about their prediction set so that the label is just the only one in the set. Even for datasets News Popularity and Helena, the size of prediction set in the subgroups that we found is limited to 2 and 3 in average uncertainty loss. We can see that the average uncertainty loss on the whole datasets for these datasets are 8.377 and 33.277. It shows that Conformalized EMM discovers subgroups that are extremely certain about their predictions comparing with the average uncertainty loss on the entire datasets. For the regression tasks, we see that our algorithms found subgroups that decrease the uncertainty prediction interval from 319.305 by 136.275, from 279 400.923 by 51 232.926, and from 25.161 by 10.106. This is a substantial drop. More results and visualizations of our findings can be found in the supplementary material [15].

Table 2. Top-3 subgroups per dataset maximizing φ_{raul}.

Ω_i	Most certain subgroups $\mathbf{S}$	$\varphi_{\text{raul}}(\mathbf{S})$
Ω_1	free sulfur dioxide > 130.444 and alcohol > 10.756	1.471
	free sulfur dioxide > 130.444 and sulphates ≤ 0.507	1.471
	free sulfur dioxide > 130.444 and sulphates ≤ 0.411	1.471
Ω_2	self reference max shares > 562 200.000 and self reference avg shares ≤ 76 711.111	7.082
	self reference max shares > 749 600.000 and min negative polarity ≤ −0.667	6.532
	self reference max shares > 562 200.000 and num self hrefs > 25.778	6.282
Ω_3	V12 > 226.693 and V10 ≤ 170.078	30.025
	V21 ≤ −14.767 and V12 > 198.388	29.809
	V21 ≤ −14.767 and V19 > 77.927	29.612
Ω_4	Hillshade Noon ≤ 56.444 and Horizontal Distance To Fire Points ≤ 7 173.000	0.085
	Hillshade Noon ≤ 56.444 and Horizontal Distance To Fire Points ≤ 6 376.000	0.085
	Hillshade Noon ≤ 56.444 and Horizontal Distance To Fire Points ≤ 5 579.000	0.085
Ω_5	GLUCOSE > 538.333 and SODIUM ≤ 135.667	136.275
	GLUCOSE > 538.333 and ALBUMIN > 3.133	133.106
	GLUCOSE > 538.333 and CHLORIDE ≤ 106.000	132.774
Ω_6	population > 3 967.333 and households ≤ 1 352.333	51 232.926
	population > 3 967.333 and total rooms ≤ 8 432.000	51 137.378
	longitude > −115.426 and median income ≤ 2.111	49 965.760
Ω_7	V35 ≤ −342.419 and V6 ≤ −1.723	10.106
	V35 ≤ −342.419 and V1 > 41.529	9.671
	V3 ≤ −94.950 and V35 ≤ −201.227	9.655

On the other hand, when comparing the final columns of Tables 1 and 3, the values for the datasets Wine Quality (Ω_1) and News Popularity (Ω_2) stand out. For the subgroups found on these datasets, we see that φ_{raul} is smaller than AUL(Ω_i), which implies that the average uncertainty loss of the top-ranked subgroups is just larger than average uncertainty loss on the entire dataset. I.e.: Conformalized EMM discovered subgroups for which the classifiers are highly unconfident about their prediction set. We notice that for News Popularity dataset, the discovered subgroups demonstrate an uncertainty set of size 10, which is the largest set we encountered within our experiments: Conformalized EMM identified the prediction that contains all the possible labels in the prediction set, which shows the most uncertain performance.

Table 3. Top-3 subgroups per dataset minimizing φ_{raul}.

Ω_i	Most uncertain subgroups S	$\varphi_{\text{raul}}(\mathbf{S})$
Ω_1	sulphates > 0.984 and total sulfur dioxide > 152.667	−2.529
	sulphates > 0.984 and free sulfur dioxide ≤ 33.889	−1.529
	chlorides > 0.271 and sulphates ≤ 0.507	−1.529
Ω_2	LDA 04 > 0.927 and abs title sentiment polarity ≤ 1.000	−1.622
	LDA 04 > 0.927 and abs title sentiment polarity > 0.333	−1.622
	LDA 04 > 0.927 and abs title sentiment polarity > 0.222	−1.622
Ω_3	V11 ≤ 28.576 and V2 ≤ 0.342	−17.820
	V11 ≤ 28.576 and V6 ≤ 0.371	−17.276
	V2 ≤ 0.122 and V10 ≤ 56.849	−17.271
Ω_4	Horizontal Distance To Fire Points > 6 376.000 and Hillshade 3pm > 225.778	−0.790
	Horizontal Distance To Fire Points > 6 376.000 and Hillshade 9am ≤ 112.889	−0.790
	Elevation ≤ 2 525.333 and Horizontal Distance To Fire Points > 5 579.000	−0.665
Ω_5	BUN > 87.667 and ALBUMIN ≤ 2.600	−114.185
	ALBUMIN ≤ 2.067 and HEMOGLOBIN > 10.867	−108.213
	ALBUMIN ≤ 2.067 and HEMATOCRIT > 32.100	−98.418
Ω_6	median income > 6.944 and housing median age > 46.333	−117 202.286
	median income > 6.944 and housing median age > 40.667	−115 196.680
	median income > 8.556 and housing median age > 46.333	−114 451.983
Ω_7	V6 > 8.905 and V2 ≤ −164.854	−18.338
	V3 > 214.741 and V35 ≤ 118.308	−17.146
	V3 > 214.741 and V24 ≤ 1054.198	−17.146

6 Conclusion

We introduce Conformalized Exceptional Model Mining (Conformalized EMM): a method to discover subgroups in a dataset where a multi-class classifier or regressor is exceptionally certain or uncertain about its own prediction. We express this (un)certainty in terms of the size of the Adaptive Prediction Set for multi-class classification problems, and the interval length in Conformalized Quantile Regression for regression problems. The (un)certainty expression is subsequently fed to the mSMoPE (multiplex Soft Model Performance Evaluation) model class for EMM, discovering exceptional subgroups evaluated by the Average Uncertainty Loss, a quantity expressing how well the soft model outputs can represent the confidence of the model predictions. The quality measure φ_{raul} is designed to find coherent subspaces of the dataset where the soft model performs highly certain (when maximizing φ_{raul}), highly uncertain (when minimizing φ_{raul}) or exceptional (when maximizing $|\varphi_{\text{raul}}|$). Since EMM results in easily interpretable subgroups, our focus is not on letting the machine improve the machine: the primary goal in the mSMoPE model class for EMM is to provide a better understanding to the domain expert.

We illustrate the findings one could expect from the mSMoPE model class by experiments on seven datasets. Some discovered subgroups are troublesome for our model, and some subgroups are found where our model has barely any problems. The mSMoPE model class highlights as a particularly troublesome area a subgroup in News Popularity dataset whose characterizing feature is associated with all the classes in the dataset, and as a particularly benign area a subgroup that is associated with one particular class. Overall, when maximizing φ_{raul}, one easily finds small subgroups on which the soft model performs highly certain; the subgroups on which the soft model performs highly uncertain are typically less trivial, hence they demand further attention. The mSMoPE model class for EMM helps to understand multi-class classification and regression, which leads to ideas on how to improve the overall classifier or regressor performance.

Acknowledgments. This work was supported by National Natural Science Foundation of China (NSFC) under Grant No.62476047. This work was partly supported by H2020 SmartChange project, funded within EU's Horizon Europe research program (GA No. 101080965) and NWO EDIC project.

Disclosure of Interests. The authors have no competing interests to declare that are relevant to the content of this article.

References

1. Agrawal, R., Srikant, R.: Fast algorithms for mining association rules in large databases. In: Proceedings of the VLDB, pp. 487–499 (1994)
2. Ahmad, M.A., Eckert, C., Teredesai, A.: Interpretable machine learning in healthcare. In: ICBCHI, pp. 559–560 (2018)
3. Angelopoulos, A.N., Bates, S., Fannjiang, C., Jordan, M.I., Zrnic, T.: Prediction-powered inference. Science **382**(6671), 669–674 (2023)
4. Angelopoulos, A.N., Bates, S., Jordan, M., Malik, J.: Uncertainty sets for image classifiers using conformal prediction. In: ICLR (2020)
5. Arora, R., Basu, A., Mianjy, P., Mukherjee, A.: Understanding deep neural networks with rectified linear units. In: ICLR (2018)
6. Arrieta, A.B., et al.: Explainable artificial intelligence (xai): concepts, taxonomies, opportunities and challenges toward responsible ai. Inform. Fusion **58**, 82–115 (2020)
7. Atzmueller, M.: Subgroup discovery. WIREs Data Mining Knowl. Discov. **5**(1), 35–49 (2015)
8. Bay, S.D., Pazzani, M.J.: Detecting group differences: mining contrast sets. DMKD **5**, 213–246 (2001)
9. Bertin-Mahieux, T., Ellis, D.P., Whitman, B., Lamere, P.: The million song dataset. In: ICMIR (2011)

10. Blackard, J.A., Dean, D.J.: Comparative accuracies of artificial neural networks and discriminant analysis in predicting forest cover types from cartographic variables. Comput. Electron. Agric. **24**(3), 131–151 (1999)
11. Dong, G., Li, J.: Efficient mining of emerging patterns: Discovering trends and differences. In: KDD, pp. 43–52 (1999)
12. Du, X.: The Uncertainty in Exceptional Model Mining. Ph.D. thesis, Technische Universiteit Eindhoven (2020)
13. Du, X., Pei, Y., Duivesteijn, W., Pechenizkiy, M.: Fairness in network representation by latent structural heterogeneity in observational data. AAAI **34**(04), 3809–3816 (2020)
14. Du, X., Ramamoorthy, S., Duivesteijn, W., Tian, J., Pechenizkiy, M.: Beyond discriminant patterns: on the robustness of decision rule ensembles. arXiv (2021)
15. Du, X., Yang, S., Duivesteijn, W., Pechenizkiy, M.: Supplementary Material to "Conformalized Exceptional Model Mining: Telling Where Your Model Performs (Not) Well" (6 2025). https://doi.org/10.6084/m9.figshare.29306939.v1
16. Duivesteijn, W., Feelders, A., Knobbe, A.: Different slopes for different folks: mining for exceptional regression models with Cook's distance. In: KDD, pp. 868–876 (2012)
17. Duivesteijn, W., Feelders, A.J., Knobbe, A.: Exceptional model mining: supervised descriptive local pattern mining with complex target concepts. DMKD **30**, 47–98 (2016)
18. Duivesteijn, W., Knobbe, A., Feelders, A., van Leeuwen, M.: Subgroup discovery meets Bayesian networks — an exceptional model mining approach. In: ICDM, pp. 158–167. IEEE (2010)
19. Duivesteijn, W., Thaele, J.: Understanding where your classifier does (not) work- the SCaPE model class for EMM. In: ICDM, pp. 809–814. IEEE (2014)
20. Gal, Y.: Uncertainty in deep learning. Ph.D. thesis, University of Cambridge (2016)
21. Galbrun, E., Miettinen, P.: From black and white to full color: extending redescription mining outside the boolean world. Stat. Anal. Data Mining: ASA Data Sci. J. **5**(4), 284–303 (2012)
22. Guo, C., Pleiss, G., Sun, Y., Weinberger, K.Q.: On calibration of modern neural networks. In: ICML, pp. 1321–1330. PMLR (2017)
23. Guyon, I., et al.: Analysis of the automl challenge series. Autom. Mach. Learn. **177**, 177–219 (2019)
24. Herrera, F., Carmona, C.J., González, P., del Jesus, M.J.: An overview on subgroup discovery: foundations and applications. Knowl. Inf. Syst. **29**(3), 495–525 (2011)
25. Ioffe, S.: Batch normalization: Accelerating deep network training by reducing internal covariate shift. arXiv preprint arXiv:1502.03167 (2015)
26. Johnson, A.E., et al.: MIMIC-III, a freely accessible critical care database. Sci. Data **3**(1), 1–9 (2016)
27. Jorge, A.M., Azevedo, P.J., Pereira, F.: Distribution rules with numeric attributes of interest. In: PKDD, pp. 247–258. Springer (2006)
28. Kaytoue, M., Plantevit, M., Zimmermann, A., Bendimerad, A., Robardet, C.: Exceptional contextual subgraph mining. Mach. Learn. **106**(8), 1171–1211 (2017). https://doi.org/10.1007/s10994-016-5598-0
29. Kelly, M., Longjohn, R., Nottingham, K.: The UCI machine learning repository. https://archive.ics.uci.edu
30. Klösgen, W.: Explora: A multipattern and multistrategy discovery assistant. In: Fayyad, U.M., Piatetsky-Shapiro, G., Smyth, P., Uthurusamy, R. (eds.) Advances in Knowledge Discovery and Data Mining, pp. 249–271. AAAI/MIT Press (1996)

31. Kuleshov, V., Fenner, N., Ermon, S.: Accurate uncertainties for deep learning using calibrated regression. In: ICML, pp. 2796–2804. PMLR (2018)
32. Lakshminarayanan, B., Pritzel, A., Blundell, C.: Simple and scalable predictive uncertainty estimation using deep ensembles. In: NeurIPS, 30 (2017)
33. Lei, J., G'Sell, M., Rinaldo, A., Tibshirani, R.J., Wasserman, L.: Distribution-free predictive inference for regression. JASS **113**(523), 1094–1111 (2018)
34. Leman, D., Feelders, A., Knobbe, A.: Exceptional model mining. In: ECMLPKDD, pp. 1–16. Springer (2008)
35. Lemmerich, F., Becker, M., Singer, P., Helic, D., Hotho, A., Strohmaier, M.: Mining subgroups with exceptional transition behavior. In: KDD, pp. 965–974 (2016)
36. Meinshausen, N., Ridgeway, G.: Quantile regression forests. JMLR **7**(35), 983–999 (2006)
37. Pace, R.K., Barry, R.: Sparse spatial autoregressions. Stat. Probab. Lett. **33**(3), 291–297 (1997)
38. Proença, H.M., Grünwald, P., Bäck, T., van Leeuwen, M.: Robust subgroup discovery: discovering subgroup lists using mdl. DMKD **36**(5), 1885–1970 (2022)
39. Provost, F., Fawcett, T.: Data science and its relationship to big data and data-driven decision making. Big Data **1**(1), 51–59 (2013)
40. Romano, Y., Patterson, E., Candes, E.: Conformalized quantile regression. In: NeurIPS, vol. 32, pp. 3543–3553 (2019)
41. Romano, Y., Sesia, M., Candes, E.: Classification with valid and adaptive coverage. NeurIPS **33**, 3581–3591 (2020)
42. Sensoy, M., Kaplan, L., Kandemir, M.: Evidential deep learning to quantify classification uncertainty. NeurIPS **31**, 3183–3193 (2018)
43. Shafer, G., Vovk, V.: A tutorial on conformal prediction. JMLR **9**(3), 371–421 (2008)
44. Smith, R.C.: Uncertainty quantification: theory, implementation, and applications. SIAM (2024)
45. Srivastava, N., Hinton, G., Krizhevsky, A., Sutskever, I., Salakhutdinov, R.: Dropout: a simple way to prevent neural networks from overfitting. JMLR **15**(1), 1929–1958 (2014)
46. Takeuchi, I., Le, Q.V., Sears, T.D., Smola, A.J., Williams, C.: Nonparametric quantile estimation. JMLR **7**(45), 1231–1264 (2006)
47. Umek, L., Zupan, B.: Subgroup discovery in data sets with multi-dimensional responses. Intell. Data Anal. **15**(4), 533–549 (2011)
48. Vovk, V., Gammerman, A., Shafer, G.: Algorithmic learning in a random world. Springer (2005)
49. Wrobel, S.: An algorithm for multi-relational discovery of subgroups. In: Proceedings of the PKDD, pp. 78–87 (1997)

Author Index

A
Abuissa, Maryam 57
Adriaens, Florian 75
Aquino, Yan 283

B
Barbiero, Pietro 478
Behzadi-Khormouji, Hamed 460
Bengali, Vedangi 75
Bento, Pedro 283
Bich, Philippe 478
Bocklandt, Sieben 425
Buzelin, Arthur 283

C
Cai, Zijian 19
Cao, Guiming 369
Cao, Yunyang 443
Cerquitelli, Tania 478
Chakrabarti, Deepayan 193
Chen, Bowen 300
Chen, Guihai 177
Chen, Tong 141
Cheng, Xueqi 228
Ciravegna, Gabriele 478

D
de Boer, Bart 512
De Laet, Jasper 460
De Raedt, Luc 425
De Santis, Francesco 478
Deckers, Lucas 460
Demir, Caglar 495
Denoodt, Fabian 512
Derkinderen, Vincent 425
Du, Xin 528
Du, Yalei 37
Duan, Yijun 92
Duan, Yutai 108
Duivesteijn, Wouter 528
Dutenhefner, Pedro 283

F
Fernandes, Jose 283

G
Gao, Hui 177
Gao, Jinzhen 211
Gao, Xiaofeng 177
Gao, Yucen 177
Giordano, Danilo 478
Guo, Fangda 228
Guo, Peijin 300
Guo, Zikang 300
Gupta, Siddharth 125

H
Hassan, Shayan Ali 387
Hemachandra, Nandyala 160
Hu, Lijie 317
Hu, Shengqing 300
Hu, Shengshan 300
Hua, Yuan 317
Humair, Danish 387
Huo, Huan 369
Huo, Yifan 211

J
Jaspers, Kurt 425
Jiang, Haiyang 141
Jin, Bo 443

K
Kumar, Akash 125
Kumar, Pintu 160
Kumpulainen, Iiro 75

L
Lai, Songning 317
Li, Chen 333
Li, Minghui 300
Li, Wenhao 443

Li, Xinle 177
Li, Yong 141
Li, Zhuoran 177
Lin, Juekai 443
Liu, Jialin 108
Liu, Jie 108
Liu, Kang 211
Liu, Pengwei 3
Liu, Xin 92
Lu, Xiaoling 37
Lu, Xuan 211
Luo, Minnan 19
Lynden, Steven 92

M
Ma, Qiang 92
Mahmood, Yasir 495
Matono, Akiyoshi 92
Meert, Wannes 425
Meira Jr., Wagner 283
Miana, Gabriela 283

N
Nandakumar, Rahul 193
Ngomo, Axel-Cyrille Ngonga 495
Nguyen, Quoc Viet Hung 141
Ni, Dong 3

O
Oramas, Jose 460
Oramas, José 512
Ou, Yuming 369

P
Pan, Hewen 300
Pappa, Gisele L. 283
Pechenizkiy, Mykola 528
Peng, Furong 211
Pijpops, Wouter 425
Porfirio, Luisa G. 283

Q
Qazi, Ihsan Ayyub 387
Qazi, Zafar Ayyub 387
Qiao, Pengpeng 263

R
Ren, Xingyu 3
Rezende, Turi 283

Ribeiro, Antonio 283
Riondato, Matteo 57
Röder, Michael 495

S
Santana, Caio 283
Sarpe, Ilie 244
Shao, Jiangli 228
Shen, Huawei 228
Shen, Jianbing 350
Shi, Boshen 228
Sun, Kaiwei 405

T
Tang, Zixuan 37
Tatti, Nikolaj 75

U
Upfal, Eli 57

V
Vanderstraeten, Koen 425
Vandin, Fabio 244
Veldt, Nate 75
Venturin, Giorgio 244

W
Wang, Chenglin 350
Wang, Di 317
Wang, Guoren 263
Wang, Heng 19
Wang, Hongye 443
Wang, Jin 405
Wang, Luhan 405
Wang, Sheng 211
Wang, Yadong 263
Wang, Yongqing 228
Wang, Zhe 350
Wu, Jianhua 108
Wu, Qinxin 3
Wu, Yang 300
Wu, Zonghan 369

X
Xu, Guandong 369

Y
Yamanishi, Yoshihiro 333
Yang, Shu 317

Yang, Sikun 528
Yekini, Moshood 495
Yin, Hongzhi 141
Yin, Yu 177
Yuan, Ye 263
Yuan, Yuan 141

Z

Zeng, Zinan 19
Zhai, Zijie 350
Zhang, Haokai 19

Zhang, Jingfeng 317
Zhang, Kai 350
Zhang, Leo Yu 300
Zhang, Shengtao 19
Zhang, Wentao 141
Zhang, Yuanyuan 37
Zhang, Zhiwei 263
Zhao, Kaiqi 37
Zhao, Yaya 37
Zhou, Yucheng 350
Zhu, Ruixuan 19

MIX
Papier aus verantwortungsvollen Quellen
Paper from responsible sources
FSC® C105338

If you have any concerns about our products,
you can contact us on
ProductSafety@springernature.com

In case Publisher is established outside the EU,
the EU authorized representative is:
**Springer Nature Customer Service Center GmbH
Europaplatz 3, 69115 Heidelberg, Germany**

Printed by Libri Plureos GmbH
in Hamburg, Germany